SECOND EDITION

TERRORISM
IN PERSPECTIVE

Dedicated to
Aubrey, Ellis, and Ansel Harlan
and
Doug Jr., Katie, Todd, Emily, Margaret, and Catherine Griset

SECOND EDITION

TERRORISM IN PERSPECTIVE

SUE MAHAN • PAMALA L. GRISET

University of Central Florida

SAGE Publications
Los Angeles • London • New Delhi • Singapore

For information:

Sage Publications, Inc.
2455 Teller Road
Thousand Oaks, California 91320
E-mail: order@sagepub.com

Sage Publications Ltd.
1 Oliver's Yard
55 City Road
London EC1Y 1SP
United Kingdom

Sage Publications India Pvt. Ltd.
B 1/I 1 Mohan Cooperative Industrial Area
Mathura Road, New Delhi 110 044
India

Sage Publications Asia-Pacific Pte. Ltd.
33 Pekin Street #02–01
Far East Square
Singapore 048763

Printed in the United States of America

Library of Congress Cataloging-in-Publication Data

Mahan, Sue.
Terrorism in perspective/Sue Mahan, Pamala L. Griset.—2nd ed.
    p. cm.
Griset's name appeared first on previous ed.
Includes bibliographical references and index.
ISBN 978-1-4129-5015-2 (pbk.)
    1. Terrorism. I. Griset, Pamala L., 1946- II. Title.
HV6431.G75 2008

363.325—dc22

2007011268

Printed on acid-free paper

07   08   09   10   11   10 9 8 7 6 5 4 3 2 1

Acquiring Editor:	Jerry Westby
Associate Editor:	Elise Smith
Editorial Assistant:	Melissa Spor
Production Editor:	Sarah Quesenberry
Copy Editor:	Gail Naron Chalew
Typesetter:	C&M Digitals (P) Ltd.
Proofreader:	Colleen Brennan
Indexer:	Sheila Bodell
Cover Designer:	Edgar Abarca
Marketing Manager:	Jennifer Reed

TABLE OF CONTENTS

LIST OF MAPS

ACKNOWLEDGMENTS

Heather Pepe provided invaluable assistance in the revision of this book. Her tireless and insightful work was much appreciated. We also thank Angela Johnson for her support and encouragement. Katie Pomp, Christine Baker, and Misty Martin were stellar in preparing tables and problem-solving computer glitches. A special thanks goes to the reviewers of the first edition. We followed their wise counsel throughout the revision process. They are David N. Baker (University of Toledo); Robert Grubb (Marshall University); Jennifer Kunz (West Texas A&M University); Annamarie Oliverio (Arizona State University); Mitchel P. Roth (Sam Houston State University); William "Jack" Sidoran (Webster University); George S. Yacoubian, Jr. (Nova Southeastern University); and Hani Zubida (New York University). The Sage team deserves our gratitude for their encouragement and hard work in bringing this project to fruition. Jerry Westby, executive editor, was unfailingly positive and helpful. Elise Smith, associate editor, brought her sharp organizational skills to bear on this second edition, and for that we are very grateful.

Today there is no longer a choice between violence and nonviolence. It is either nonviolence or nonexistence. I feel that we've got to look at this total thing anew and recognize that we must live together. That the whole world now it is one—not only geographically but it has to become one in terms of brotherly concern. Whether we live in America or Asia or Africa we are all tied in a single garment of destiny and whatever affects one directly, affects [all] indirectly.

—Dr. Martin Luther King, Jr.

INTRODUCTION

This is not the end. It is not even the beginning of the end. But it is, perhaps, the end of the beginning.

—Winston Churchill

More than five years ago, a series of brazen terrorist attacks against the United States imprinted the word *terrorism* on the nation's collective conscience. September 11, 2001, which began like any ordinary morning, quickly turned into one of unfathomable destruction. In the years since, the United States has launched attacks against the Taliban in Afghanistan for supporting al-Qaeda and its leader, Osama bin Laden. Neither the leader of the Taliban, Mullah Omar, nor bin Laden has been captured by the time this second edition of *Terrorism in Perspective* has gone to print, and al-Qaeda and its offshoots have been very active: London, Madrid, Riyadh, Casablanca, Amman, and Bali are only a few of the places that have witnessed coordinated terrorist attacks, with devastating results. The war in Iraq that deposed Saddam Hussein is ongoing as this book is being finalized, and even with the death of the alleged al-Qaeda leader in charge of resistance to the U.S. occupation of Iraq, Abu Musab Al-Zarqawi, on June 7, 2006, U.S. military and civilian personnel are killed and injured all too frequently, as are Iraqi citizens and government officials.

Several terrorists have been thwarted in their attempts to attack the U.S. homeland in the past five years, including Richard Reid, the so-called shoe bomber, and José Padilla, who was originally accused of planning to set off a dirty bomb in the United States. Although no successful terrorist attempts have been launched in the United States in more than five years, the threat has not diminished. Much has changed in the world since the 9/11 assault on the United States, but the basic premise underlying the first edition of the book remains unaltered.

Like its predecessor, the second edition provides a broad-based conceptual scheme that focuses on acts of terrorism and their relationship to culture, religion, history, politics, economics, and ideology. State-sponsored terrorism, religious terrorism, suicide terrorism, transnational terrorism, and homegrown terrorism are considered, as are the media's role in terrorism reporting and the importance of female terrorists. Terrorist tactics, from the conventional to the unconventional, including digital terrorism, are discussed. Counterterrorism strategies and their impact on terrorists, human rights, and the rule of law are considered. Terrorism is thus viewed comprehensively, and the reader is afforded a panorama of historical, contemporary, and futuristic positions.

Although al-Qaeda and its affiliates are generally the focus of the popular U.S. media, the subject of terrorism is not limited to extremist Islamic fundamentalists, Middle East conflicts, or Osama bin Laden. This book examines terrorism around the globe in all of its various forms. For example, the book highlights many non-Muslim terrorist organizations, including Sri Lankan Tamils, South American revolutionaries, Basque separatists, U.S. ecoterrorists, and far-right antigovernment extremists.

PHOTO 01.1   The Twin Towers on fire.

LOOKING BACK AT 9/11

The most devastating terrorist attack waged to date against the United States began on September 11, 2001, shortly before 8:45 A.M., as hijackers crashed an American Airlines plane into the north tower of the World Trade Center in lower Manhattan. A few minutes later, as smoke billowed from the damaged tower and just as the enormity of the disaster was starting to sink in for stunned observers and television viewers, a United Airlines plane slammed into the south tower. In less than an hour, one of the 110-story towers collapsed, followed shortly by the other. The 25-year-old glass and steel complex, which symbolized New York City's position as the economic center of the world, crumbled into a mountain of debris, ash, and death.

At about 9:30 A.M., another American Airlines plane smashed into the Pentagon, the five-sided headquarters of the American military. One side of the building collapsed as smoke rose over the Potomac River. About a half-hour later, another United Airlines plane crashed outside Pittsburgh, apparently headed for the White House or Capitol Hill.

Comparisons were quickly made to another day that lives in infamy in the American psyche: December 7, 1941. On that day 183 Japanese warplanes bombed U.S. Navy forces in Hawaii's Pearl Harbor. Nearly 2,400 were killed and more than 1,100 wounded in that early morning sneak attack.

The death toll in the 9/11 attack was much higher. The initial estimates were more than 6,000 lives lost, but by September 2002, these estimates were reduced to around 3,000. President George W. Bush compared the attack to one on "freedom itself" and vowed to defend the nation's freedom.

For years, experts had warned government officials that the United States was vulnerable to a terrorist assault with unconventional weapons of mass destruction, especially chemical and biological weapons. But on 9/11, conventional weapons yielded unconventional results, as hijacked airplanes were transformed into weapons of mass destruction.

In the immediate aftermath of the attacks, the United States came to a virtual standstill. Public facilities were evacuated and top government officials were whisked away to undisclosed locations. Guards armed with sophisticated weapons patrolled the nation's capital, and military aircraft secured the skies. The Federal Aviation Administration closed airports nationwide. Bus and railroad service were suspended in the Northeast. Security was tightened at all U.S.-Canada border crossings. Financial markets, including the New York Stock Exchange, the NASDAQ stock market, and the Chicago Board of Trade, shut down. The United Nations was evacuated, General Motors sent Detroit employees home, and Chicago's Sears Tower closed. New York City's mayoral primary election was postponed, as were all Major League baseball games and Broadway shows. In Florida, Walt Disney World closed its theme parks and the Kennedy Space Center shut down.

Federal law enforcement authorities quickly identified Osama bin Laden, a Saudi Arabian millionaire living in Afghanistan, as the terrorists' mastermind and financier. He was already suspected of planning and financing several other attacks, including the 1993 bombing of the World Trade Center, the shooting of U.S. troops in Somalia in the same year, the 1996 bombing of the Khobar military complex in Saudi Arabia, the nearly simultaneous explosion of car bombs outside the U.S. embassies in Kenya and Tanzania in 1998, and the attack on the Navy destroyer USS Cole in Yemen in 2000.

Bin Laden had supported the U.S.-backed Afghan warriors in their war with the Soviet Union in the 1980s, but he turned against the United States after the 1991 Gulf War, when it ousted Iraq from Kuwait. The United States had desecrated sacred Saudi land when it based its soldiers on Saudi soil, bin Laden said, and he called on Muslims worldwide to join in a holy war against the United States. However, the al-Qaeda movement's ultimate goal—toppling the pro-U.S. regimes in Saudi Arabia, Yemen, Pakistan, Egypt, Jordan, and other areas in the Middle East—reaches far beyond the U.S. borders (Doran, 2002). Although bin Laden has not yet achieved his primary goal and terrorism has rarely been a successful tactic in the history of humankind, the suffering brought on by al-Qaeda and other terrorist organizations around the globe is both breath taking and heartbreaking.

9/11: THE AFTERMATH

Terrorism has now entered the daily lexicon of the average citizen. The shock of the attacks and the grief and fear they engendered were a new experience for many Americans. The subsequent and ongoing military and political responses by the United States and its allies to the 9/11 attacks have changed the world in many ways; many of these changes are yet unknown.

Yet, like the color-coded threat-level system adopted by the Department of Homeland Security, which was formed in the aftermath of 9/11, the level of fear to which Americans are exposed is variable. With no successful attack inside our country since 2001, it is natural that many people want to turn their attention away from terrorism and toward other concerns. Still, the threat of another major terrorist attack on U.S. soil has not receded, and the perspectives afforded by this second edition can be helpful in understanding future, perhaps inevitable, terrorist actions within U.S. borders.

Regardless of the number of victories won in the current "war," history teaches that terrorism is endemic to the human condition and cannot be eliminated by diligent application of the "right" strategies. Terrorism is not a disease that can be wiped out, but it can perhaps be managed and confined, at least temporarily (Pillar, 2001).

CHAPTER OUTLINE

Terrorism in Perspective combines original thematic overview essays with the best of the existing literature on terrorism. Each of the nine chapters is divided into two parts. The first part is an overview of the issues, actors, organizations, and actions relevant to the specific topic under discussion. The second part of each chapter presents two previously published articles or book chapters culled from a wide variety of popular, academic, and governmental sources. The selected articles deepen one's understanding of terrorism by focusing more intently on specific themes.

Chapter 1 examines issues surrounding the definition, incidence, and motivations for terrorism. By examining the "what, where, when, and why" of terrorism, this opening chapter lays the foundation for the remainder of the book. The first article selected examines the multifaceted problems of definition. The author stresses the political and ideological problems inherent in defining terrorism. The second article selected analyzes the motives of terrorists. Focusing on the link between motivation and strategic choice, this article also provides a solid basis for comprehending the information and analysis provided in the remaining chapters of the book.

Chapter 2 links contemporary terrorism to the endless conflicts of history that will remain part of the human experience as long as the conditions that breed them—ethnic and class conflicts, religious fanaticism, extreme ideologies, and ancient hatreds—remain. Terrorists have altered the course of history time and again, putting their indelible mark on many of the colossal events of the past. The chapter highlights a few of them, including Guy Fawkes and the religiously motivated Gunpowder Plot, the French Revolution, the growth of anarchism and the philosophy of "propaganda by deed," the Russian Narodnaya Volya, the nationalist movement in India, and the Latin American urban guerrilla movement.

The first article selected for Chapter 2 compares three ancient terrorist organizations: the Jewish Zealots who died defending Masada in the first century A.D.; the Hashashin (Arabic for "hashish-eaters"), known also as the Brotherhood of Assassins and active in Persia from the 11th through 13th centuries, who believed killing was their holy mission, much as some of today's Islam extremists have launched a Jihad with religious blessing (*fatwa*); and the Hindu Thugs of the 13th through 19th centuries. The second article focuses on a few of history's most tyrannical regimes that were also state sponsors of terrorism. It examines the self-destructive relationships that mark the interaction between state sponsors of terrorism and their subjects.

Chapter 3 is devoted to international terrorism in the age of globalization. It illustrates the continuing importance of historical relationships, ideology, religion, and economics in global terrorism; clearly the world's terrorists are animated by a variety of causes. The analysis focuses on state-sponsored terrorism, religious and politically motivated terrorism, long-standing ethnic conflicts, separatist movements, and class struggles. Among the infamous terrorists discussed are Che Guevara, Carlos the Jackal, Osama bin Laden, and Velupillai Prabhakaran (the leader of the Tamil Tigers of Sri Lanka). The interconnectedness of our world often means that a single terrorist incident can reverberate around the globe. The worldwide implications of terrorism are presented through a discussion of the 1988 bombing of Pan Am flight 103 over Lockerbie, Scotland.

The first article selected for Chapter 3 analyzes the synergistic relationship between terrorism and organized crime. The economic allure of the illegal drug and arms trade often blurs the distinction between terrorism and organized crime. The second article discusses the 2004 Madrid bombings that killed nearly 200 people and injured 1,400 more. When it became clear that the attacks were carried out by a radical Islamic network, many Spaniards realized, for the first time, that they were not immune from the al-Qaeda threat.

Chapter 4 discusses terrorist tactics: assassinations, hijackings, kidnappings, and bombings. As the events of September 11, 2001, vividly demonstrated, traditional tactics, which are still the popular first choice of terrorists, can have devastating results. The chapter also discusses the tactic of leaderless resistance as well as the use of children in terrorist campaigns. The first article examines the logic of suicide terrorism. Although the suicide terror campaigns against Israel are the focus of study for this article, the inside look at this country yields international implications. The second article in this chapter discusses conventional terrorist tactics as applied to al-Qaeda. It is an in-depth analysis of a terrorist network that focuses on weapons acquisition, recruitment, and an organizational imperative—sources of funds.

Homegrown terrorism is the topic of Chapter 5. It places our nation's experience with terrorism from within in historical and contemporary perspective. The ideological far left, the socialists and communists of the 1960s and 1970s, including the Weather Underground and the Symbionese Liberation Army, were replaced in the 1980s and 1990s by an untold number of right-wing groups, including antigovernmental extremists, hate groups, and Christian fanatics. In the 21st century ecoterrorists (ELF) and animal rights activists (ALF) are the largest terrorist groups involving U.S. citizens. The first article covers the relationship between religion and racist violence. The author examines the factors that must be present to form a theology of hate. His focus is on eschatology or "end of time" theology and its relationship to political violence. The second article considers the moral constraints against terrorism and applies them to ecoterrorism, which is aimed at corporate and government interests rather than people.

Chapter 6 analyzes the organic relationship between the media and terrorism. Former British Prime Minister Margaret Thatcher called the media the oxygen of terrorism, and this chapter explores the critical issues in the complex, symbiotic relationship between terrorism and the media. The discussion explores various forms of media involvement, from journalism and reporting to participation. The positive and negative consequences of media involvement in terrorist situations are analyzed. The first article reports on a study of television news coverage following September 11. It analyzes whether the additional time allotted to the event led to more in-depth segments and more contextual reporting. The second article is based on the firsthand experiences and insights of Terry Anderson, an American journalist kidnapped in Lebanon in 1985 by a group of Iranian-inspired terrorists.

Women are not represented in decision-making positions in most terrorist organizations, but they have played a vital role in many causes. Chapter 7 discusses the history of female involvement in social conflict and the types of roles assigned to female terrorists. The Black Widows of Chechnya are described as examples of women who are vital to the separatist cause, yet are not in positions of control. In contrast, case studies are presented of women who dominated terrorist groups: Ulrike Meinhof of the German Red Army Faction and Augusta La Torre Guzmán of the Peruvian Shining Path.

The first article selected for Chapter 7 compares the media portrayal of female terrorists and of women in politics. The common framing patterns in the news coverage demonstrate stereotypes about women and power. The second article is a historical study of women in organized racial terrorism in the United States beginning in the post–Civil War period up to the present. It is interesting both for its analysis of women's roles and for its explanation of the development of homegrown racial terrorism.

Technology and terrorism are the subject of Chapter 8. The chapter discusses the history and potential impact of weapons of mass destruction, such as chemical, biological, and nuclear weapons, as well as examining the threats posed by digital terrorism. The anthrax attacks in the United States following 9/11 suggest that traditional constraints against the use of unconventional weapons may be eroding. The chapter discusses the only nonstate terrorist organization known to have tried to use these weapons on a large scale: Aum Shinrikyo, the Japanese apocalyptic and millenarian cult controlled by a messianic and highly eccentric leader who launched a sarin gas attack on Tokyo's subways. The first article examines the lessons to be learned from the sarin gas attacks. Using the 9/11 attacks for comparison, the article analyzes the psychological barriers to interagency communications under disaster conditions. The second article discusses the process used for arriving at an official estimate of the likelihood of nuclear terrorism. It examines the political, as opposed to the purely scientific, nature of that official estimate.

The final chapter discusses counterterrorism from the perspectives of foreign affairs and domestic policy. Terrorist acts against the United States are placed in a global perspective, as are the events and alliances that occurred subsequent to the September 11 attacks. As the only remaining superpower, the United States has evoked hatred and retaliation in many parts of the world. The chapter discusses the so-called clash of civilizations, which some observers believe will define international relations in the future. It also highlights issues concerning the role of the United Nations, as well as other international alliances, in counterterrorism. The chapter is framed in terms of U.S. civil liberties, with a special focus on four issues: antiterrorism legislation, including the USA PATRIOT Act (2001); the detentions of Arabs and Muslims that occurred after September 11; the use of military tribunals to try terrorists; and infamous counterterrorism operations from U.S. history that many consider to have been overly zealous.

The first article selected for Chapter 9 discusses the likely growth in terrorism from the "blowback" of the war in Iraq, which the authors of the article see as "breeding a new generation of terrorists." The second article analyzes the cases of the most infamous names in terrorism since 9/11: Zacarias Moussaoui, John Walker Lindh, Richard Reid, José Padilla, and Yaser Hamdi. The author explains the concepts embodied in extraordinary renditions, enemy combatants, and military tribunals in terms of a model of political justice.

1

WHAT IS TERRORISM?

Any creative encounter with evil requires that we not distance ourselves from it by simply demonizing those who commit evil. . . . [W]hen it comes to coping with evil, ignorance is our worst enemy.

—Kathleen Norris

What is terrorism? How can it be defined, studied, and understood? How many incidents of terrorism occur? What areas in the world experience the most terrorism and which the least? What are the most common terrorist tactics and targets? Why do men and women become terrorists? What motivates people to embrace violence and risk their own lives as well as the lives of others?

This chapter discusses these questions, but it does so with an appreciation that they cannot be answered fully or satisfactorily. Although we can shed light on the what, where, how, and why of terrorism, much will inevitably remain in darkness. Human behavior has always been hard to predict, control, and comprehend. Relatively rare behavior, like terrorism, is even harder to understand.

The adversarial and political postures embedded in the practice of terrorism make it unlikely that a universally accepted definition or a widely shared strategy for controlling it will soon emerge. Nevertheless, putting terrorism in perspective is essential, and thus this book focuses on acts of terrorism and their relationship to culture, religion, history, politics, economics, and ideology.

DEFINITIONS OF TERRORISM

A definition is a precise statement of meaning, and defining the term under discussion is a fundamental principle of philosophy, law, psychology, engineering, and most other realms of human endeavor. Defining terrorism might seem easy, but it is not.

The meaning associated with the word *terrorism* has varied over the years. The word came into the popular lexicon through its association with the French Revolution of 1789 and the ensuing "régime de la terreur." Characterized by brutal repression, "la terreur" centralized political power in the Committee of Public Safety, thus undercutting the democratic goals that inspired the French Revolution.

PHOTO 1.1   Funeral of Chechens killed in an attack by unidentified terrorists.

The word *terrorism* is still often used interchangeably with the word *terror,* causing definitional confusion and blurring the boundaries between other types of violent behavior and terrorism. Many activities, from wars to rampages by youth gangs to writing science fiction, are meant to strike terror into the enemy (or reader). In this context, the scope of potential definitions is limitless.

Definitions of terrorism are not immutable; they change over time. For example, John Brown, the abolitionist whose attack on the federal arsenal at Harpers Ferry further fueled regional animosity and seeded the Civil War, was at one time lionized as a hero. At another time, Brown was condemned as a terrorist; in a still different era, he was seen as a madman (Reynolds, 2005).

A more recent example of the political and ideological nature of the term *terrorism* comes from anti-abortion violence. During the 1980s, the federal government agencies in charge of responding to crime and political violence "were controlled by partisans of the political Right, many of whom sympathized with the goals if not the methods of pro-life extremists" (Jenkins, 1999, p. 112). Thus, anti-abortion violence was labeled simply as a crime. That changed with the 1992 presidential election of William Clinton, after which federal government agencies were more likely to be controlled by partisans of the political left, who had pro-choice ideologies. Anti-abortion violence was then labeled terrorism, thus clearly demonstrating that politics and ideology underscore the definitional process (Jenkins, 1999).

More than a hundred definitions of terrorism exist (Laqueur, 1999, p. 5). Proffered by government officials, scholars, the media, and terrorists themselves, the varying definitions present a bewildering array of approaches to defining terrorism. The difficulty of definition is not new, however. Cooper (2001, p. 881) notes that "there has never been, since the topic began to command serious attention, some golden age in which terrorism was easy to define."

Yet, no matter how difficult the task, defining terrorism is crucial. In some other areas of contemporary life, definitions and conceptualizations may be purely theoretical and of interest primarily to academics. Scholars need to establish specific parameters for their research, but their definitions may have limited real-world consequences. The definition of terrorism, in contrast, has very real consequences. Coordinating international counterterrorism operations, for example, requires accepted standards and rules (Deflem, 2006; Ganor, 2006). Arrests, wiretaps, prosecutions, pretrial detentions, and sentencing under terrorist statutes likewise require precise definitional distinctions.

Similarly, labeling someone or something as terrorist has real-world consequences. People and organizations are degraded when labeled as terrorist, and political or religious movements can lose followers and funding as a result of the label. Citizens, even those in a democracy, may be more apt to accept repressive government actions if they are presented in terms of countering terrorism.

Terrorism is an ideological and political concept. Politics, by its nature, is adversarial, and thus any definition evokes adversarial disagreement. The meaning given to terrorism is part of a person's or nation's philosophy. Thus, the determination of the "right" definition of terrorism is subjective and not likely to be reached by consensus.

Therefore, if you disagree with my position, you are a terrorist; if you agree with my position, you are not a terrorist (Cooper, 2001). Yet, the cliché that "one man's terrorist is another man's freedom fighter" provides little help in achieving definitional precision (Ganor, 2006, p. 1). Repressive regimes call those who struggle against them terrorists, but those who commit violence to topple those same regimes call themselves freedom fighters. Hoffman (2006) notes that terrorists' organizations are most likely to consider themselves as fighters for freedom and liberation, or as armies or other military organizations, or as self-defense movements, and or even as seekers of righteous vengeance. In an ideal world, politics and ideology would be separated from definition, and it would not matter who does what to whom: Terrorism ought to be defined by the nature of the act itself (Cooper, 2001).

Terrorism is also difficult to define because "there is not one but many different terrorisms" (Laqueur, 1999, p. 46). Separating the tactics of terror from the concept of terrorism is necessary but difficult. The distinction among terrorism, guerrilla warfare, conventional warfare, civil wars, riots, and criminal activity is often blurry. Terrorists are not the only ones who use the tactics of terror. Violent and terrifying acts are common to terrorism, but these tactics are also common elements in rapes, murders, and other violent crimes. Yet, despite the definitional difficulties, distinctions must be made among the different forms of violent behavior.

The discussion to follow begins with some of the definitions of international and domestic terrorism offered by the U.S. government. It then turns to the definitions suggested by some of the most eminent scholars of terrorism. Commonalities among definitions are then presented.

U.S. Government Definitions

The Office of the Law Revision Counsel of the U.S. House of Representatives prepares and publishes the United States Code, which codifies by subject matter all of the laws of the United States. The United States Code defines terrorism "*as premeditated, politically motivated violence perpetrated against noncombatant targets by subnational groups or clandestine agents*" (Title 22, Chapter 38, §2656f). It also specifies that international terrorism is "terrorism involving citizens or the territory of more than one country."

The United States Code does not include regulations issued by executive branch agencies, decisions of the federal courts, treaties, or laws enacted by state or local governments. Regulations issued by executive branch agencies are contained in the Code of Federal Regulations, which defines terrorism as "*the unlawful use of force and violence against persons or property to intimidate or coerce a government, the civilian population, or any segment thereof, in furtherance of political or social objectives*" (28, C.F.R. Section 0.85).

That these two definitions issued by different branches of the federal government are not identical is emblematic of the general problem with definition. Although the United States Code's definition includes the concept of political motivation, it does not mention, as does the Code of Federal Regulations, the purpose of the violent act (to coerce the government and its citizens).

It is difficult to craft a single sentence that covers all aspects of the phenomena of terrorism, and thus it is no surprise that some attempts at definition are inelegant, cumbersome, and bereft of the power of precision. For example, the Federal Bureau of Investigation (FBI) defines international terrorism as violent acts that *"appear to be intended to intimidate or coerce a civilian population; influence the policy of a government by intimidation or coercion; or affect the conduct of a government by mass destruction, assassination or kidnapping and occur primarily outside the territorial jurisdiction of the United States or transcend national boundaries in terms of the means by which they are accomplished, the persons they appear intended to intimidate or coerce, or the locale in which their perpetrators operate or seek asylum"* (FBI, 2006). A different definition is offered by the FBI for domestic terrorism: *"activities that involve acts dangerous to human life that are a violation of the criminal laws of the United States or of any state; appear to be intended to intimidate or coerce a civilian population; to influence the policy of a government by mass destruction, assassination, or kidnapping; and occur primarily within the territorial jurisdiction of the United States"* (FBI, 2006).

Scholarly Definitions

Bruce Hoffman notes that terrorism "is fundamentally and inherently political. It is also ineluctably about power: the pursuit of power, the acquisition of power, and the use of power to achieve political change" (Howard & Sawyer, 2004, p. 4). Hoffman defines terrorism as the *"deliberate creation and exploitation of fear through violence or the threat of violence in the pursuit of political change"* (Hoffman, 2006, p. 41; Howard & Sawyer, 2004, p. 23).

Eqbal Ahmed, an outspoken and highly acclaimed Indian anti-colonialism scholar, noted that the "terrorist of yesterday is the hero of today, and the hero of yesterday becomes the terrorist of today. This is a serious matter of the constantly changing world of images in which we have to keep our heads straight to know what terrorism is and what it is not" (Ahmed, 1998, p. 2). Ahmed identified five types of terrorism: state terrorism, religious terrorism, criminal terrorism, political terrorism, and oppositional terrorism, all of which fit his simple definition of terrorism as *"the use of terrorizing methods of governing or resisting a government"* (1998, p. 5).

Ahmed provided many examples of the shifting nature of the label of terrorism. One relates to an Israeli prime minister, the late Menachem Begin, who was a former commander-in-chief of the Irgun Tsval Leumi, a Zionist terrorist organization. Begin once had had a £1,000 reward issued for his capture (Ahmed, 1998, p. 1), yet he later became prime minister.

Another example comes from 1985, when Ronald Reagan was the U.S. president. Reagan had an audience in the White House with several Afghan Mujahiddin, and afterward he said that they were "the moral equivalent of America's Founding Fathers" (Ahmed, 1998, p. 2). Reagan supported the Mujahiddin because they were fighting the Soviet Union and communism in Afghanistan, but among their supporters was the Saudi-born Osama bin Laden. In 1998, then-President William Clinton launched an unsuccessful missile strike intended to kill bin Laden and his troops in Afghanistan. Thus, the shifting political and ideological climate of the times influences the definition of terrorism; it is both an unstable and a subjective concept.

Jessica Stern argues that terrorism can be distinguished from other forms of violence by only two characteristics: It is aimed at noncombatants and it is intended to instill fear in the target audience. Thus, Stern defines terrorism as *"an act or threat of violence against noncombatants with the objective of exacting revenge, intimidating, or otherwise influencing an audience"* (2003, p. xx).

Walter Laqueur has written extensively on the problem of definition. He argues that a comprehensive definition does not now and may never exist. Nevertheless, he defines it as *"the use of covert violence by a group for political ends"* (2001, p. 79).

Military historian Caleb Carr, noting that terrorism is as old as human conflict itself, makes a strong argument that international terrorism is equivalent to war. Carr places terrorism in the discipline of military history, as opposed to the disciplines of political science or sociology. He states that international terrorism *"is simply the contemporary name given to, and the modern permutation of, warfare deliberately waged against civilians with the purpose of destroy-ing their will to support either leaders or policies that the agents of such violence find objection-able"* (2002, p. 6).

Carr argues that world leaders have generally identified international terrorism as a type of crime, rather than as war, "in an effort to rally global indignation against the agents of such mayhem and deny them the more respected status of actual soldiers" (2002, p. 7). According to Carr, denying that terrorism is the same as war has created a problem: It has limited our gov-ernment to reactive, rather than proactive, responses to terrorism.

In Carr's view, "our leaders (and we as their citizens) have in the past been, and in disturbing numbers remain, prepared to treat terrorists as being on a par with smugglers, drug traffickers, or, at most, some kind of political Mafiosi, rather than what they have in fact been for almost half a century: organized, highly trained, hugely destructive paramilitary units that were and are con-ducting offensive campaigns against a variety of nations and social systems" (2002, p. 9).

Commonalities in Definitions

Some definitions specifically include religious motivations; others include hate, millenarian, and apocalyptic groups. Not everyone agrees that people who employ terrorist tactics on behalf of animals or the environment are terrorists. Several definitions refer only to nonstate actors, whereas others include state-sponsored terrorism. Terrorism by groups is an essential part of several definitions, but some definitions include terrorism by individual actors as well.

Most definitions include violence or a threat of violence. Most also include motivations (e.g., political, religious, economic). Distinctions between international and domestic terrorism are part of some definitions, but not others.

In a study of 109 definitions of terrorism, a group of researchers collapsed the definitional elements into 22 categories. The most common elements were violence or force (84% of the definitions), followed by political motivation (65%), engendering fear or terror (51%), using a threat (47%), psychological effects (42%), and victim-target differentiations (38%). The least common definitional elements included demands made on third parties (4%), repetitiveness or serial violence (7%), and clandestine, covert nature (9%; Schmid & Jongman, 1988).

Finally, H. H. A. Cooper, the author of the first reprint selected to accompany this chapter, defines terrorism as "the intentional generation of massive fear by human beings for the pur-pose of securing or maintaining control over other human beings" (Cooper, 2001, p. 883). For the purpose of this book, we use Cooper's definition, although like him, we recognize that no single definition will ever be satisfactory to everyone.

INCIDENTS OF TERRORISM

This section examines incidents of terrorism by looking at the phenomena from multiple angles. Focusing on the where, when, what, and how of terrorism provides an essential background for understanding the dimensions of this type of conflict.

Determining what constitutes terrorism is not easy. The information on the incident may be sketchy, and various interpretations of it may be proffered. Divining the intent of the attackers is not always possible. The overlap between terrorism and other forms of conflict, such as geno-cide, could affect the criteria used in recording incidents.

The way in which terrorism is counted is linked closely to its definition. An example comes from the U.S. government's official source for terrorism data, the National Counterterrorism Center (NCTC). For 2005, the NCTC reported that there were 11,100 terrorist incidents, which resulted in 14,500 noncombatants killed, 25,000 wounded, and 35,000 kidnapped. The numbers reported by NCTC for 2005 were much higher than they were in 2004, in large measure because its definition of international terrorism had changed from "involving citizens or territory of more than one country" to "premeditated, politically motivated violence perpetrated against noncombatant targets" (NCTC, 2006). The later definition is broader than the former one, thus resulting in many more incidents being counted as terrorism. NCTC has chosen to use 2005 as a baseline from which to measure international terrorism in future years. The NCTC has not noted how it will count terrorism incidents if and when the definition of terrorism is again altered.

NCTC recognizes that the "definition of terrorism relative to all other forms of political violence is open to debate" and that any effort to count the incidents of terrorism "involves incomplete and ambiguous information" (NCTC, 2006, p. 2). Not only are the data often distorted but reasonable people can also disagree about some fundamentals of reporting terrorism. NCTC notes that, for example, on August 17, 2005, about 350 small bomb attacks were carried out in Bangladesh; NCTC counted these as one event, but it might be reasonable to argue that 350 separate incidents should be recorded.

Further complicating the link between defining and counting terrorist events is the high level of underreporting bias, which is directly associated with the political process (Drakos & Gofas, 2006). Scholarly research has demonstrated a connection between the reporting of terrorist incidents and political, economic, and social systems (Eubank & Weinberg, 2001; Li & Schaub, 2004). Nondemocratic regimes without a free press account for a great deal of underreporting. As Drakos and Gofas (2006, p. 715) note, "A considerable number of (nondemocratic, we would stress) countries, for a substantial length of time, seemed to have experienced no terrorism at all." Thus, if the media do not report on the terrorist event, it will not be counted in official sources.

Another source of data on the incidence of terrorism comes from the National Memorial Institute for the Prevention of Terrorism (MIPT), which is a nonprofit think tank established after the 1995 bombing of the Alfred P. Murrah Federal Building in Oklahoma City. MIPT is funded by the Department of Homeland Security, and its team of contributors include, among others, the DFI International, a Washington-based knowledge management company, and the RAND Corporation, a non-profit research institute. MIPT gets most of its data from media reports, which leads to underreporting, as discussed in the previous paragraph.

MIPT's definition of terrorism, which determines those incidents that it counts as terrorism, is "*violence, or the threat of violence, calculated to create an atmosphere of fear and alarm.*" MIPT expands on its definition by noting the following:

> These acts are designed to coerce others into actions they would not otherwise undertake, or refrain from actions they desired to take. All terrorist acts are crimes. Many would also be violation of the rules of war if a state of war existed. This violence or threat of violence is generally directed against civilian targets. The motives of all terrorists are political, and terrorist actions are generally carried out in a way that will achieve maximum publicity. Unlike other criminal acts, terrorists often claim credit for their acts. Finally, terrorist acts are intended to produce effects beyond the immediate physical damage of the cause, having long-term psychological repercussions on a particular target audience. The fear created by terrorists may be intended to cause people to exaggerate the strengths of the terrorist and the importance of the cause, to provoke governmental overreaction, to discourage dissent, or simply to intimidate and thereby enforce compliance with their demands.

MIPT's Web site, the Terrorism Knowledge Base at http://www.tkb.org, provides data on domestic and international terrorism, specific terrorist attacks, and targets of terrorism, as well as on all known terrorist groups. The database includes interactive maps and biographies on key terrorists and their organizations. It also has a sophisticated analytical capacity that allows users to manipulate the database and display the results pictorially. Although the MIPT database covers 1968 through the present, unfortunately it has limited utility for long-term analysis because the data from 1968 to 1998 reflect only international terrorism, whereas the data since 1998 capture both international and domestic terrorism. As a result, the discussion to follow focuses only on 1998–2006 to avoid comparing the incomparable.

The MIPT data are examined by geographic region, types of tactics, types of targets, and group classifications. Tables 1.1 to 1.4 should be considered as illustrative only because of the

TABLE 1.1   Incidents by Geographic Region, January 1, 1998–November 21, 2006

	Incidents	Injuries	Fatalities
Africa	400	7859	2319
East & Central Asia	128	393	164
Eastern Europe	1278	4946	1928
Latin America & the Caribbean	1758	2464	1600
Middle East/Persian Gulf	10363	34769	18433
North America	111	2407	2996
South Asia	4939	17264	7094
Southeast Asia & Oceania	516	3528	1010
Western Europe	2980	1750	397
Total	22473	75380	35941

SOURCE: MIPT Terrorism Knowledge Base. (2006). TKB Incidents by Region (1/1/98–11/22/06). Retrieved November 22, 2006, from www.tkb.org.

many different ways of counting terrorism. Although far from definitive, the data are useful in creating a general picture of the incidence of terrorism.

Table 1.1 examines the frequency of terrorist incidents, injuries, and fatalities by geographic region from 1998 to 2006. During this time, the Middle East and Persian Gulf area have had the highest number of incidents, as well as the most injuries and fatalities. The number of fatalities in the Middle East and Persian Gulf is greater than the total of all the other regions combined. North America has experienced the fewest incidents, but the number of injuries and fatalities are higher in North America than in several other regions. It should be noted that the numbers for Africa do not include the genocides that have plagued that continent; again counting terrorist events depends on the definition used.

Table 1.2 examines the frequency of terrorist incidents, injuries, and fatalities by the tactic employed. Bombings are clearly the most favored tactic of terrorists: More than 80,000 people have been injured or killed by terrorist bombs. The second most commonly used tactic is armed attack, with more than 17,000 people killed or injured through this method. Note the categories of "other" and "unknown": Many terrorist events are not easily categorized by tactic.

Table 1.3 examines the frequency of terrorist incidents, injuries, and fatalities by the target of the attack. Private citizens have suffered the most at the hands of terrorists: Almost 30,000 noncombatants have been killed or injured since 1998. Police officers have been the second most favored target of terrorists and government officials the third. Note that, although six incidents of terrorism of food or water supply have been recorded, they have yielded no reported injuries or fatalities.

Table 1.4 examines the frequency of terrorist incidents, injuries, and fatalities by group classification. Terrorist organizations motivated by religion have been responsible for the highest number of deaths and injuries since 1998: Over 37,000 people have been victims of religiously inspired terrorism. Nationalist/separatist groups have claimed the second highest body count, with more than 23,000 dead or injured. Although 71 incidents involving environmental terrorists have been recorded, they have yet to result in the loss of life or injury to humans.

These group classifications are tied closely to motives for violence. The discussion to follow centers on three types of explanations for terrorism: collective, individual, and moral. It concludes by offering a useful explanation for understanding the motives of terrorists.

TABLE 1.2   Incidents by Tactic, January 1, 1998–November 21, 2006

	Incidents	Injuries	Fatalities
Armed Attack	5600	6988	10103
Arson	778	174	293
Assassination	1682	959	2409
Barricade/Hostage	55	1412	604
Bombing	12451	62591	17793
Hijacking	30	5	26
Kidnapping	1320	118	1137
Other	143	418	115
Unconventional Attack	48	2435	3004
Unknown	366	280	456
Total	**22473**	**75380**	**35940**

SOURCE: MIPT Terrorism Knowledge Base. (2006). TKB Incidents by Tactics (1/1/98–11/22/06). Retrieved November 22, 2006, from www.tkb.org.

TABLE 1.3   Incidents by Target, January 1, 1998–November 21, 2006

	Incidents	Injuries	Fatalities
Abortion Related	5	2	2
Airports and Airlines	128	225	98
Business	1828	7851	4529
Diplomatic	393	6505	507
Educational Institutions	542	1339	532
Food or Water Supply	6	0	0
Government	4690	9436	4861
Journalists & Media	439	306	218
Maritime	11	83	32
Military	122	1031	466
NGO	192	178	219
Other	1486	2080	2007
Police	3683	12546	7048
Private Citizens & Property	5030	19667	10041
Religious Figures/Institutions	899	5083	2006
Telecommunication	155	77	63
Terrorist/Former Terrorist	127	75	159
Tourists	96	1180	399
Transportation	1008	6322	2021
Unknown	672	913	348
Total	**21512**	**74899**	**35556**

SOURCE: MIPT Terrorism Knowledge Base. (2006). TKB Incidents by Tactics (1/1/98–11/22/06). Retrieved November 22, 2006, from www.tkb.org.

TABLE 1.4   Incidents by Group Classifications, January 1, 1998–November 21, 2006

	Incidents	Injuries	Fatalities
Anarchist	96	6	0
Antiglobalization	86	15	7
Communist/Socialist	2145	3906	2043
Environmental	71	0	0
Leftist	106	112	28
Nationalist/Separatist	2871	16430	6635
Other	76	194	90
Racist	25	14	1
Religious	1966	25715	11477
Right-Wing Conservative	85	12	248
Right-Wing Reactionary	11	8	14
Total	7538	46412	20543

SOURCE: MIPT Terrorism Knowledge Base. (2006). TKB Incidents by Group Classification (1/1/98–11/22/06). Retrieved November 22, 2006, from www.tkb.org.

MOTIVATION

The "why?" question has preoccupied many scholars from many disciplines for many years. However, two problems plague those who would analyze terrorist behavior (Reich, 1998). On the one hand, analysts often overgeneralize about motivation, ignoring its variety and complexity. Bratkowki (2005, p. 764) has written, for example: "Humankind has always provided a justification for killing and instilling terror in fellow humans." On the other hand, analysis is also likely to be reductionistic, attributing all or much of terrorist behavior to one or another specific cause. Along those lines, Salij (2005) states that the root cause of terrorism is terrorists' mistaken beliefs.

Collective Explanations

General, simplistic explanations have inherent validity, but they lack the specificity that would make them useful for policy or control decisions. Crenshaw (1998b) notes that explanations of terrorist behavior must consider both the individual practitioner and the collective actor, the terrorist group. In turn, both the individual and the group must be seen in relation to society as a whole. Terrorism alters the behavior not only of individuals and collective actors, such as the terrorist organization or the government, but also of the members of entire societies (p. 249).

Some analysts believe that the explanation for when, where, and why people engage in terror is found in the political relationships among groups and the levels of development of those groups. "All this amounts to saying that terror is a strategy, that the strategy involves interactions among political actors, and that to explain the adoption of such a strategy we have no choice but to analyze it as part of a political process" (Tilly, 2005, p. 21). These analysts believe that explanations of terrorism grounded in political relations and group development will serve us far better than systemic explanations that focus on social structures or dispositional explanations that consider individual traits as the starting point for understanding.

In understanding terrorism, we must consider the historical dimension as well. Both the behavior of terrorists and our understanding of their motivation are influenced by historical context (Crenshaw, 1995). The time and place in which terrorism occurs are relevant to the motivations behind terrorism for many reasons. The socialization of members of a society or subgroup with regard to violence and its justification must be considered. When there is a long violent history, as in Ireland for example, generation after generation of youth have been taught values that support the conflict. The violence in a terrorist act may be a response to a particular offense or part of a sustained, long-term effort. The conflict in Palestine, as another example, has given rise to numerous terrorist groups that have come forward only to fall or splinter and then regroup. In some contexts, terrorist behavior may be linked to nonviolent, legitimate political activities. For example, terrorist organizations may enter candidates in state elections and even control the legitimate political process, as is the case with Hamas in Palestine in 2007. The continuity or discontinuity of the terrorists' campaign is also relevant to motivation. Underlying the Zapatistas movement of the 1990s in Mexico, for example, was the public image of the revolutionary movement for land reform led by Emile Zapata in Mexico in the early 1900s. The opportunities for effective, non-terrorist collective action within the political arena must also be taken into consideration. Chechnyan terrorists, for example, are reacting to their perceived isolation and alienation from the larger, Russian political process. Finally, considering the purpose of the terrorist behavior is basic to understanding. Crenshaw (1995, p. 19) points out that terrorism can develop a momentum that diverts it from its original purpose. Terrorism can merge into a cycle of revenge and retaliation that neither side controls.

This cycle of revenge and retaliation has been called "violence as a logic of action" by Wieviorka (1995, p. 602). He makes a distinction between violence as a method of action performed by those who pursue a specific purpose and are able to abandon terrorism when it no longer appears useful for their purposes, and violence as a logic of action on the part of those who neither foresee nor expect an end to it. In the latter case, terrorist behavior comes to satisfy an insatiable inner need; the means become the end. Wieviorka has shown that a shift to violence as a logic of action is generally the outcome of an ideological process. It involves a break with a commonly held doctrine, religious belief, or conception of history. The shift to violence as a logic of action is also part of social or political distancing. The terrorists lose contact with the class, nation, or community in whose name they claimed to speak. The group no longer represents an actual cause or reference group (Wieviorka, 1995, p. 603). Or as Sprinzak (1998, p. 85) described it, "Ideological terrorism is the simulated revolution of the isolated few."

Individual Explanations

Miller (2006) explains terrorist motivation as a three-stage process. Stage one begins with unacceptable conditions: "It's not right." Stage two follows with resentment and a sense of injustice: "It's not fair." In Stage three the cause of the injustice is personified: "It's your fault." Though such patterns are evident, it is also evident that only a few of those affected by oppressive social, economic, and historic contexts are actually motivated to become terrorists.

Crenshaw (2000) points out that a psychology of terrorists must take multiple levels of analysis into account. In addition, political terrorism is not simply a product of psychological forces; its central strategy is psychological. Terrorism is at base a vicious species of psychological warfare.

Post (1998) introduces the term "psycho-logic" to describe processes of reasoning that he believes are particular to terrorists. He asserts, "Political terrorists are driven to commit acts of violence as a consequence of psychological forces. In addition, their special psycho-logic is constructed to rationalize acts they are psychologically compelled to commit. Individuals are drawn to the path of terrorism in order to commit acts of violence" (p. 25).

Although most studies do not find that members of terrorist groups demonstrate serious psychopathology, Post and others use the vocabulary of psychiatry in their explanations for terrorist motivation. Freud's theoretical concepts about the importance of early childhood experiences on personality are borne out in their later observations of the behavior of terrorists. For example, Post finds an extremely high frequency among terrorists of a process of externalization and splitting that is also characteristic of individuals with narcissistic and borderline personality disorders. He believes that externalization and splitting contribute significantly to the uniformity of terrorists' rhetorical style and special psycho-logic (Post, 1998, p. 26).

Externalization refers to projecting onto others one's hatred and devalued weakness from within; in other words, looking outward for the source of difficulties and needing an enemy to blame. Dividing the world into "us" and "them" is the basic manifestation of this process. Seeing a large group of others impersonally as "not like us" enables a worldview that makes violence toward "them" more acceptable.

Splitting is a process that is shaped by a particular type of psychological damage occurring during childhood, which separates good and bad parts of the injured self into "me" and "not me." Splitting shows up in a weakened sense of identity and a need for a cause or group to support one's self-concept (Post, 1998, p. 27). For a person with no identity or sense of self, assuming a role as a terrorist appears valuable and provides purpose to an otherwise meaningless existence.

Kellen (1998) also refers to psychological damage in his explanation of terrorist motivation. He believes that many, but not all, terrorists have experienced a psychological trauma that has two results. First, it makes them see the world in a grossly unrealistic light. Second, it motivates them to extreme violence (p. 43).

Many psychological studies of terrorist behavior focus on a broken family background as the source of trauma (Merari, 1998). Some researchers have shown a high incidence of fragmented families among terrorists, but the field is largely characterized by theoretical speculation based on subjective interpretation of anecdotal observations (Victoroff, 2005).

It is important to understand that any effort to uncover the "terrorist mind" will more likely result in uncovering a spectrum of terrorist minds. Yet mental illness is not commonly found among terrorists. Although terrorist groups are sometimes led by insane individuals and a few terrorist acts might be attributed to unequivocally insane persons, terrorists rarely meet psychiatric criteria for insanity (Victoroff, 2005).

In his review and critique of psychological approaches to explaining the mind of the terrorist, Victoroff (p. 2005, p. 35) concludes that, although terrorists form a heterogeneous group, four traits may possibly be characteristic of "typical" terrorists who lead or follow in substate groups:

1. extreme opinions and emotions regarding a belief system

2. a personal stake—such as strongly perceived oppression, humiliation, or persecution; an extraordinary need for identity, glory, or vengeance; or a drive for expression of innate aggression—that distinguishes them from the vast majority of those who fulfill trait #1

3. low cognitive flexibility—including a low tolerance for ambiguity, distaste for complexity, and disregard for multiple layers of reality—that leads to a very high likelihood of a mistaken sense of causality and a need for blame

4. a capacity to suppress all moral constraints against harming innocents whether due to intrinsic or acquired factors, individual, or group forces—probably influenced by #1, 2, and 3

Moral Explanations

Motivations for "typical" violence have been studied extensively by Albert Bandura (1973), who is best known for developing social learning theories of aggression. According to Bandura in his later work (1998, p. 163), the motivation to slaughter innocent women and children in buses, department stores, and airports requires a powerful psychological mechanism of moral disengagement. Bandura believes that converting socialized people into dedicated combatants is not achieved by altering their personality structures, aggressive drives, or moral standards. Rather it is accomplished by cognitively restructuring the moral value of killing; that is, by changing the way the person thinks about killing so that killing can be done free from self-censuring restraints

(Bandura, 1998, p. 164). Self-censure and self-sanctions are the internal mechanisms that serve to prevent most individuals from acting violently. Bandura explains that self-sanctions can be disengaged in a number of ways. Terrorists may reconstruct their horrific conduct as serving moral purposes. They may obscure their own role in the violence and deny that their acts are the cause of the carnage. They may distort the consequences of the act by focusing on the good that is to come from it and minimizing the evil done. Terrorists may also avoid self-censure by dehumanizing their victims, considering those who are killed as expendable or collateral damage (Bandura, 1998, p. 161).

The moral value of killing has been the ongoing subject of debate not only among warriors, politicians, journalists, and social scientists, but religious figures also have dominated the study of the morality of violence. Thomas Aquinas is one example of a well-known religious writer whose works have been exploited by terrorists to restructure the moral value of terrorism. In 1894, Max Losen explained that Thomas Aquinas's commentary on the Magister Sententiarum in which he noted, "He who kills the tyrant in order to liberate his country is praised and rewarded," has been taken out of context to justify violence against the state. According to Lossen (1894/2004) "Undue weight should not be placed on this single ambiguous passage from a youthful work, at the expense of those others where he declares himself to be firmly opposed to tyrannicide" (p. 27). More recently, Baard's (2004, p. 165) analysis of Aquinas's writings, as applied to the Animal Liberation Front as a form of terrorism, claims, "Anger against a sin is virtuous, whereas anger against the sinner is sinful." Baard interprets this moral observation as legitimizing vengeance against corporations and enterprises. She distinguishes, as did Aquinas, between antecedent anger, which precedes rational judgment and is not good, and consequent anger following judgment, which may be good if it leads to action against injustice. Consequent anger provides energy for action, increasing resolve. Revenge gives us hope and pleasure (Baard, 2004, p. 161).

These examples from the writings of Aquinas show how those who are constructing an image of their terrorist conduct as serving moral purposes have used the writings of familiar religious figures to support an image of their own violence as morally justified. A distorted view of other Christian religious principles has been used to sustain terrorist motivation throughout the world. Meanwhile, Muslim religious figures have played a critical role in Islamist terrorist motivation as well. Following the word of God, as a terrorist sees it, contributes to a sense of ethical superiority. Identifying with religious figures can also provide terrorists with a code of self-sacrifice and support a belief in a higher calling (Martin, 2006, p. 83).

Useful Explanations

There are serious obstacles to the study of terrorist motivation. Terrorists who are available for study are not likely to be typical because interaction with active terrorist groups in order to analyze motivation is highly dangerous and decidedly suspect. Many materials and publications about terrorists are extreme and sensationalistic. In addition, social scientists lack cross-cultural methods of investigation that would take advantage of the experience of history to develop comparisons and developmental studies (Crenshaw, 2000). These are all formidable obstacles. However, the biggest obstacle to developing a useful explanation of terrorist motivation is the lack of understanding of the value of that explanation. Despite the possibility of global data sharing and the international consortiums that study the causes of terrorism, little progress has been made toward developing an explanation of terrorist motivation that effectively informs public policy.

State leaders and those with influence in global politics seldom concede the essentiality of theory in their day-to-day decisions. Yet, beliefs about motivations and causes of terrorism are critical to the policies and courses of action they recommend. As Crenshaw (1998b, p. 287) notes, "Officials may deny that theory is relevant, but they rely on it constantly, at no time more than during a crisis when they think they have escaped its influence." While denying the influence of political theory, policymakers in law enforcement, the military, and government depend on assumptions about causality at no time more than in the heat of an emergency. Thus, useful theories about terrorist motivation are essential.

As Victoroff (2005) and others conclude, meaningful research is likely to be interdisciplinary, empirical, controlled, ethical, conducted across levels of analysis, and directed at root causes and modifiable risk factors along the entire chain of causality from historical forces to childhood influences to the moment of a terrorist act: "For the purposes of long-term security policy formulation an increased emphasis should be placed on the analysis of the interaction between those psychological, cultural, economic, and political factors that influence uncommitted but impressionable young people to turn toward terrorism" (Victoroff, 2005, p. 35).

HIGHLIGHTS OF REPRINTED ARTICLES

The two readings that follow, the first of which is on definitional issues and the second on theoretical ones, were selected because of their in-depth coverage of the issues and the unique insights of their well-respected authors. The first reading, by H. H. A. Cooper, stresses the political and ideological nature of the problems of definition. The second reading, by Margaret Crenshaw, explores a strategic theory for understanding terrorist motivation.

H. H. A. Cooper (2001). Terrorism: The problem of definition revisited. *American Behavioral Scientist, 44*(6), 881–893.

Cooper defines terrorism as "the intentional generation of massive fear by human beings for the purpose of securing or maintaining control over other human beings" (p. 883). Cooper's theme is similar to that of David Rapoport's reprint in Chapter 2: Both argue that terrorists seek to exploit their opponents' weaknesses. In Cooper's view, "terrorism is a naked struggle for power, who shall wield it, and to what ends" (p. 890). It is thus an extreme form of political coercion.

Cooper addresses the phenomenon of the state as terrorist by noting that the "state's power to wage war to maintain its integrity against external foes . . . turns on the ability to secure the desired result through intimidation. Here lies the road to Dresden, Hiroshima, and Nagasaki, but we accord the nation-state considerable latitude in these matters. But, there comes a point when the line is crossed and we would say that the state has begun to rule by terror" (p. 885).

Cooper's article was published a few months before the attacks on September 11, 2001; unfortunately many of his dire prophecies have come true.

Martha Crenshaw (1998). The logic of terrorism: Terrorist behavior as a product of strategic choice. In Walter Reich (Ed.), *Origins of terrorism.* Washington, DC: Woodrow Wilson Center Press.

Crenshaw wrote this chapter long before 9/11, but her perspective has grown more valuable with time. Charles Tilly reiterated Crenshaw's theme in 2005: "When it comes to terror, the beginning of wisdom is to recognize it as a strategy" (p. 27). Terror is not the outflow of a uniform mentality but a strategy employed by a wide array of actors whose motives, means, and organization vary greatly.

This article was chosen as the exemplar of a strategic theory of terrorism, even though it first appeared in a collection of articles that are psychological in theme. According to the editor of that book, Crenshaw's work was included to balance the perspective of the book and to place its main theme within a realistic context. It is because of the realistic nature of the strategic approach that it was selected for inclusion in this chapter on motivation. We chose this classic article because it is succinct, comprehensive, and clear. In it, Crenshaw provides a complete outline of a strategic approach, as well as recommendations for application of the explanations to be derived from an instrumental study of terrorism.

In a later chapter in that same book, *Origins of Terrorism,* Crenshaw suggests that future theoretical inquiry might expand the logic of terrorism to center on causes, conduct, and consequences of terrorism (Crenshaw, 1998b). There is a significant need for more study of the link between motivation and terrorist behavior. As Tilly points out, "Good explanations put us on the path to effective action and counteraction" (2005, p. 22). However, Crenshaw makes it clear that "no single explanation for terrorist acts will ever be satisfactory" (1998b, p. 24). Explanations of motivation must be flexible and contextual. And as Martin (2006, p. 103) reminds us, "The progression of explanations by the social and behavioral sciences in the future will naturally reflect the sociopolitical environments of the times in which they are developed."

EXPLORING THE WHAT OF TERRORISM FURTHER

- Examine the definitions of terrorism offered by different government agencies; for example, the Department of Homeland Security, the Department of Defense, and the Department of State.
- What is the difference between terrorism and guerrilla warfare, struggles for national liberation, genocide, warfare, and violent crime? A good place to start your examination is Boaz Ganor's article titled "Defining Terrorism: Is One Man's Terrorist Another Man's Freedom Fighter?". The article can be found at http://www.ict.org.il/articles/define.htm.
- What is your definition of terrorism? State it in a single sentence. Using your definition, how would you distinguish terrorism from violent crime, war, guerrilla warfare, civil war, genocide, etc?
- Based on your definition of terrorism, explain your answer to the following questions:
  o Were the Sons of Liberty terrorists?
  o During the Civil War, could the acts of either the Union or the Confederacy be deemed terrorism?
  o Does the U.S. treatment of Native Americans under the Removal Act of 1830 constitute state-sponsored terrorism?
  o Was it state-sponsored terrorism when the National Guard fired in 1970 on students at Kent State University who were protesting the Vietnam War?
- Elaborate on the real-world consequences of defining terrorism. Be specific in describing why a precise definition matters in terms of the operation of counterterrorism activities.
- In the first reprint, Cooper discusses the difficulty of defining terrorism. Explain his reasoning and what is meant by the concept of "one man's terrorist is another man's freedom fighter."
- What emphasis does Cooper place on the element of hate? Does he think people should be punished for their hatred of others? What is your feeling on this?
- According to Crenshaw, the author of the second reprint, what is the difference between a dispositional explanation and a strategic explanation of terrorist motivation?
- Based on your reading of Crenshaw, do you think social learning is related to cognitively restructuring the moral value of killing? Why or why not?
- How would suicide bombing be studied and explained from a strategic perspective?
- How could a strategic perspective be applied in developing policy to prevent bus bombings in Miami?

VIDEO NOTES

The film, *Paradise Now* (Warner Brothers, 2005, 91 min.) is recommended as a most insightful and unvarnished look at the motivations of terrorists.

❖

Terrorism

The Problem of Definition Revisited

H. H. A. Cooper

How can terrorism be defined when the process of defining is wholly frustrated by the presence of irreconcilable antagonisms? It is certainly not easy to define, much less comprehend. With respect to terrorism, there is among the many participants to the discussion no agreement on the basic nature of the fruit under consideration. In any case, the definition of terrorism has undergone a number of small refinements as experience has suggested. This article considers how to define terrorism or at least know it when it is seen in the coming decades.

A living language has no existence independent of culture. It is not the loom of culture but its data bank. As such, it serves the needs, past and present, of a given community. As those needs change, language evolves to accommodate them.

—Raymond Cohen (1990, pp. 41–42)[1]

With the advent of the new millennium, whatever one's preference for the mathematics of the event, a certain nostalgia for the past is inevitable. Although it is still difficult for many of us to adjust to no longer living in the 20th century, it seems even harder for others to let go of even the most recent of bygone memories. As the century raced to its anticlimactic close, a wave of recall swept through the media worldwide, made possible by new technologies that have given potent meaning to the yet ill-defined term *globalization*. Amid this feverish search for the most memorable this and the most renowned that, the sensitive observer might discern a hankering for earlier times, a kind of golden age in which everything was simpler, much easier to understand, and, to use appropriate *fin de siècle* terminology, less stressful. No examination of these impressions in general is essayed here. Yet, it is of some importance to notice them in relation to the present topic if for no other reason than to offer a pertinent rejoinder. It can be stated with absolute certainty that there has never been, since the topic began to command serious attention, some golden age in which terrorism was easy to define or, for that matter, to comprehend. And, as we plunge gaily into the brave new world of the 21st century, there is not the slightest reason to suppose that the problem of definition, or as it was once described, the problem of the problem of definition (Cooper, 1978), will come any closer to sensible resolution. With that solemn caveat in place, let us proceed to consider how, variously, we may come to define terrorism or at least know it when we see it in the coming decades.

DEFINITION IS TRULY AN ART

Parenthetically, we must deal here with what is implied in the process of definition itself. Definition is truly an art. The artist seeks to represent,

SOURCE: From "Terrorism: The Problem of Definition Revisited" in *American Behavioral Scientist* by Cooper, H. H. A., 2001: 41: 881. Reprinted with permission from Sage Publications.

in concrete or abstract terms, something he or she has conceptualized or observed so as to give it some meaning of a distinctive character. The resultant work is a vehicle of communication for the thought or revelation that the artist seeks to convey to others. The central problem in the process is that no two human beings ever see the same thing, however simple, in exactly the same light or from the same standpoint. There is rarely, if ever, an exact correspondence of interpretation, and the introduction of but the slightest complexity can alter the meaning intended by the artist. Most ordinary, social communication is imprecise by nature. It simply is not necessary that we define our terms with exactitude; it suffices that we are generally understood. Of course, misunderstandings abound, especially between the genders[2] and persons of differing status, culture, occupation, education, and the like. This is sometimes a source of irritation and occasionally cause for amusement, but it is not often of great consequence. Yet, in serious discourse, especially on matters involving a potential for substantial disagreement or those bearing controversial or emotional overtones, the closest correspondence of understanding as to the meaning of the language employed is imperative. If we are discussing fruit, and I believe you are talking about apples when in fact you are trying to convey to me that you are referring to oranges, we are not going to get very far without timely clarification. With respect to terrorism, there is among the many participants to the discussion no agreement on the basic nature of the fruit under consideration. For some, it will always, unalterably be apples; for others, with equal rigor, it will remain oranges. No amount of sophistry or the introduction of other varietals will be helpful in resolving the issue of meaning. One person's terrorist will ever remain another's freedom fighter. The process of definition is wholly frustrated by the presence of irreconcilable antagonisms.

A DEFINITION OF TERRORISM

Hope springs eternal in the human breast, and perhaps for this reason alone, so many conferences and writings on the subject of terrorism begin with the obligatory, almost ritualistic recitation by the presenter of some preferred definition of terrorism.[3] This is not wholly an exercise in futility; whatever the discrepancies detected by others, the definitions at least provide starting points for debate. The search has always been for one all-embracing statement that could stand at least a chance of gaining a high degree of acceptance by others as well as covering a majority of the bases. It can be reasonably confidently asserted that this procedure will continue unaltered as we transit the 21st century. In a similar spirit, then, the following definition of terrorism is offered here so that we may have a basis for reflection on the problems of terrorism and how it is likely to present itself in the new millennium.

Terrorism is the intentional generation of massive fear by human beings for the purpose of securing or maintaining control over other human beings.

This definition evolved over some 25 years of teaching about the topic of terrorism in a university setting, and during that time, it has undergone a number of small refinements as experience has suggested. Other definitions have similarly been subject to modification as those who propounded them sought to meet criticisms extended by others and to perfect the concepts enshrined in the words employed. In a very real sense, all the earlier definitions had to be subject to this process of refinement if they were to survive at all. Even the most assiduous wordsmiths were humbled by the task of encapsulating such powerful, at their simplest, contradictory ideas in one all-embracing sentence. It is no surprise, then, to encounter definitions that run for paragraphs, even pages, in frantic attempts to capture the elusive meaning embodied in the word *terrorism*. This is dialectic rather than definition, but it is an inescapable part of the process whether it is reduced to writing or articulated only in discussion. The above definition, in the form it is presented here, owes much to classroom discussion and the acuity of the students to whom it was offered as a starting point for an exploration of the subject. Before examining its components in detail, it seems helpful to explain the underlying philosophy orienting its construction. Although it is always dangerous to generalize, it may be observed that university students tend to be an unforgiving bunch. They are quick to seize on any errors or inconsistencies they detect in the formula. And, if they have cause to doubt as a result, their overall confidence in the instruction and the instructor is shaken. In particular, in the matter of defining terrorism, the product offered had necessarily to address succinctly the thorny issue of "one person's terrorist is another's freedom fighter"; hence the formulation offered here.

Again, a further thought has to be inserted at this juncture. However much you may buy into the freedom fighter argument, you are forced, if you are intellectually honest, to the conclusion that whatever label it might bear, terrorism is a bad thing. All you can sensibly say in its defense is that sometimes it may be necessary to do bad things to other people, most usually with the apologetic justification that it is done to prevent or deter them from doing bad or worse things to you. If it is conceded that there is no "good" terrorism, that such an import would be a contradiction in terms, any definition must unambiguously take this into account, for it goes to the fundamental nature of the concept. In practice, the definition of terrorism has been consistently plagued by an ever increasing need to justify the reprehensible. This has proved the biggest obstacle to the production of anything approaching a widely acceptable definition, especially in the international arena. It must be stressed that there is a basic antinomy here: What *I* do, however unpleasant is not terrorism; what *you* do is terrorism. From the point of view of definition, this is not a question of degrees such as dogs, for example, the term *high crimes and misdemeanors* in the impeachment realm (see Posner, 1999, pp. 98–105). What is asserted is a difference in kind; *I* don't commit terrorism; *you* do. You can no more have a little bit of terrorism than you can be a little bit pregnant. From a definitional perspective, it ought not to matter who does what to whom. Terrorism should be defined solely by the nature and quality of what is done. Difficult as this is, definition should strive for impartiality in this field, or the exercise must fail in its purposes.

Is Terrorism a Freestanding Concept?

Is terrorism, then, a freestanding concept? In terms of penal policy or normative configuration, is it something autonomous or simply a constituent element of certain kinds of criminal behavior that are already defined? What is

offered above certainly has to be carefully considered in that light. An examination of any coherent legal system will reveal many crimes where the creation of great fear in the victim (e.g., rape) is a central, defining feature. Many would agree that rape is a terroristic act, especially when it is employed in warfare as an instrument of subjugation or humiliation. In any unbiased analysis, it might reasonably be put forward as terrorism par excellence. Yet, it is not the crime of rape that comes readily or immediately to mind in any discussion of the meaning of terrorism. This is not to deny the terroristic content within what is understood about the crime of rape, at least in its violent manifestation, but rather an unexpressed preference for seeing terrorism as something separate, distinct, and having an existence all its own. For those taking such a position, and no objection is taken to it here, terrorism seems to inhabit a different universe from the ordinary, from even the most heinous of otherwise criminal behavior. That it can or should do so comes as no surprise to the legal positivist. Although norms cannot be simply conjured up out of thin air, the power to create new crimes in response to altered circumstances is an inherent faculty of any legal system. At this point, it must be made clear that what has been offered above as a conceptualization of terrorism is in no way to be regarded as an inchoate norm awaiting the interposition of the legal system's authority to give it independent being. And, herein lies the central dilemma, which cannot be readily overcome by recourse to any legal artifice. It is only possible to construct a freestanding penal figure denominated *terrorism* out of elements borrowed from preexisting crimes already defined as such in their own right. Thus, rape can in this view be seen as a constituent element of an autonomous crime of terrorism, just as terrorism can be seen as a necessary ingredient in a violent rape. Although this does little to advance the process of definition per se, it does serve to expose a critical problem that cannot be evaded.

Even the most cursory examination of the many definitions of terrorism on offer should quickly persuade the critic how many of these rely for any sort of precision on the adjectives employed in their elaboration. These definitions tend to focus on purpose, and that, in each of them, is primarily political. Reduced to its simplest terms, terrorism is seen as extreme political coercion. This, truth to tell, is the *raison d'être* of virtually all these definitional exercises. For it is only in the realm of the political that these definitions have any useful employment; hence their adversarial nature. Yet, assuredly, the abused child knows exactly what terrorism is, even though he or she might be quite unable to enunciate the word. More is revealed in this of the purposes of the definers, or refiners, than of the nature of terrorism itself. All who seek to find a meaning in the term *terrorism* would have to agree on the centrality of the massive fear, or terror,[4] it inspires in those on whom it is inflicted, as well as its coercive nature. What is in dispute is whether there is anything in the nature of a right to inflict such misery on others and, if so, in whom it inheres. Here, we come to another dilemma that cannot escape the notice of anyone seeking to define terrorism. In its nature, terrorism, by reason of its coercive aspects, has a marked similarity to the corrective and deterrent functions vested by common understanding and political theory in the state—and the responsible parent. The distinction is in degree rather than anything else. Consider, for example, the ultimate sanction permitted the nation-state seeking to exercise its authority internally to control crime, namely the death penalty. Those who subscribe to a belief in its efficacy, whether by way of deterrence or social hygiene, can only rely on its intimidatory effect; if it does not frighten others by way of example, its value is very limited. The state's power to wage war to maintain its integrity against external foes can be viewed in much the same way. Clearly, effectiveness turns on the ability to secure the desired result through intimidation. Here lies the road to Dresden, Hiroshima, and Nagasaki, but we accord the nation-state considerable latitude in these matters. But, there comes a point when the line is crossed and we would say that the state has begun to rule by terror. There are issues of proportionality involved of a most delicate kind, but they are the ones that perturb the definitional process in most awkward ways. Terrorism becomes, for those in power, an affront to established authority. Power, when stretched to its limits is, to many, no more than a reign of terror. Any definition that ignores this is open to attack as pure cant. The point here is that the way in which these things are done has always assumed lesser importance from the point of view of their characterization as terrorism than who does them and to whom.[5]

It should be observed that there is a kind of parallel in this regard with what have come to be known in recent times as "hate crimes." Those who oppose the promulgation, altogether, of such a category argue simply that it is otiose; murder is murder is murder. What can be done to increase the gravity with which certain matters seem to clamor for attention? Is any greater protection afforded potential victims by this increment? Nothing is added, for example, to the crime of murder that might serve as a special deterrent to those who would commit it against some class supposedly in need of particular protection. Many behaviorists and mental health professionals would argue, with considerable force on their side, that an individual who kills any victim in a singularly vicious way is exhibiting a hatred of that person regardless of the class to which that person belongs; in fact, so personalized may be the hatred that no issue of a class character enters into the matter (see Gourevich, 2000). None of this would satisfy those who argue for special hate crime legislation. Once more, the focus is plainly on who does what to whom and why. Hatred is an emotion and one that in civilized society is regarded as reprehensible, unhealthy, and socially harmful. It is the "why" of the matter that is troubling to those who see themselves as likely to be victimized by those who bear and exhibit these ugly emotions. The problem resides herein: The feelings we characterize as hatred cannot be punished unless they are exhibited in a way that is criminal in itself or in association with conduct that is already criminalized. If the device of making the element of hate is a way of making this latter punishable in a more severe fashion than would otherwise be the case, the position has something to commend it, but in the case of the most serious crimes, such as murder, they are already punishable to the limit; the rest is merely posturing. As with terrorism, we should define by reference to what is done rather than by shifting our focus to those who are victimized and the reasons they are targeted.

GOOD NEWS/BAD NEWS

Viewed in the formulation set down here, terrorism is a game of fixed quantities. It is cold comfort, but comfort nevertheless, that as we enter the new millennium, no new terrorism is possible. How can this be? Creating massive fear in human beings is based on the same principles that have always informed the process: You can kill them, you can mutilate them or otherwise damage their physical or mental integrity, you can deprive them of their liberty, you can damage or destroy their relationships with people and things, you can adversely alter the quality of their lives by affecting their environment or their economic prospects or by imposing onerous burdens on them, or you can achieve your ends by credibly threatening to do all or any of these things. It is not possible to conceive of anything else that might accomplish the goal of creating the massive fear, or terror, that is at the heart of terrorism. That is the good news. The bad news—and it is very, very bad—is that with each passing moment ever newer and more horrible ways of undertaking these things are being imagined and made possible by the implacable, onward sweep of technology. That is the awful prospect that looms before us as we proceed into the new millennium. The 19th-century terrorist, if he or she were lucky, might have anticipated a body count in the hundreds, although none attained that target. It was probably easier for the terrorist, especially the anarchist, to concentrate on trying to effect change through coercion against selected individual targets, for example, the assassination of key members of the ruling classes. The 20th-century terrorist never truly reached his or her potential, for which we should be devoutly grateful. The ingredients were there, but somehow, the deadly brew was never administered to its deadliest effect. With regard to the concept and the resources available to it, the attack by Aum Shinrikyu on the Tokyo subway, judged on its results, was puny in the extreme; a 19th-century anarchist operating alone with black powder might have accomplished much more. The World Trade Center bombing in New York, similarly from the terrorists' point of view, produced a pathetically small death toll and nothing like the property damage that was possible. Although the horrific attack on the Murrah Building in Oklahoma City stands above them all in terms of execution, magnitude, and a lasting impression on the psyche of the American people, it is not difficult to imagine how much worse it might have been. This is the frightening face of the future, but in the matter of definition, it is no different from what we have struggled with in the past. This is

the fact that is urged here on those who will have to cope with the practical implications of terrorism in the new millennium.

COMPREHENDING TERRORISM

We seek to define terrorism so as to be better able to cope with it. We cannot begin to counter effectively that which we are unable to fully comprehend or agree on as to its nature. Some 50-odd years have been wasted in trying to disentangle the topic of terrorism from the much grander subject of wars of national liberation.[6] A great deal of time and effort has been expended in trying to make the truly reprehensible politically respectable. As the awesome possibilities of the new millennium are translated into ever more frightening realities, we can no longer afford the fiction that one person's terrorist may yet be another's freedom fighter. Fighting for freedom may well be his or her purpose, but if the mission is undertaken through the employment of terroristic means, a terrorist he or she must remain; we ought not to confuse the sophistry of refinement for the process of definition. This assumes considerable importance as the older forms of terrorism give way, as they must, before the newer and more horrible ways of going about this grim business. For the advances of technology have not all aided the terrorist's purposes. As in so many other departments of modern life, the audience has become increasingly difficult to shock. Indeed, the terrorist nowadays has to struggle mightily against a kind of ennui affecting those he or she would seek to impress. The audience, with the ever present assistance of television reporting of the contemporaneous, has become sated on a diet of death and destruction. The misery of others is fast losing its ability to horrify or, at least, to horrify for very long. Terroristic violence on the screen, whether fact or fiction, has become commonplace; much of the mystery has faded. This has made the terrorist's task increasingly difficult: How do you recapture and refocus the jaded attention of such an audience? The possibilities are really quite limited. You can strive to increase the toll in terms of the body count; compared to conventional warfare, deaths resulting from acts of terrorism have been numerically insignificant. To measure the true potential of terrorism, one would have to look to, say, Rwanda. Alternatively, the terrorist has to imagine novel, strikingly horrible means for doing the traditional things; and, significantly, the execution must match the imaginings. Clearly, whichever course is chosen, some of the mystery has to be reintroduced. Fear feeds off the unknown. We must be careful not to allow this development to warp the process of definition.

FROM WEAPONS OF MASS DESTRUCTION TO CYBERTERRORISM

The expression "weapons of mass destruction" has now entered firmly into common currency. The expression conjures up visions of lots and lots of casualties and people dying in horrid ways as a result of the employment of such weapons. Because of its awesome, proved potential, nuclear weaponry is perhaps the first type to come to mind when the expression is used. Credible fears of the terrorist nuclear bomb go back at least to the 1970s; much fiction has been written around the theme of the "basement nuclear bomb." The concept has dominated futuristic theorizing about the direction terroristic escalation might take. Nuclear terrorism has, thankfully, remained in the realm of fiction. But, as we stand on the threshold of the new millennium, we would be most unwise to conclude that it will be ever thus. Indeed, it is little short of a miracle that we have not had to face the realities of nuclear terrorism to date. The knowledge and the materials have long been available to those who might have been tempted to engage in some feat of superterrorism (see Schweitzer, 1998). The point here is that if and when this awful eventuality materializes, it will not require any redefinition of terrorism; it will simply sharpen the terms with which it is drawn. We might remind ourselves at this juncture that it matters little to the instant victims whether they are done to death with a hatpin or consigned to perish in a nuclear conflagration. But, viewed in prospect, which is the more fearful, which the more likely to produce social nightmares? Even serially, you cannot account for a great many victims with hatpins. A simple nuclear device in the possession of a competent terrorist would demolish much property, alter the landscape, and kill and horribly maim a great many human beings. Its employment would alter forever the face of terrorism, and the way we have

come to think about it. It would not, however, require us to alter the way we define it.

Until the late 1980s, many tended to think of terrorism in almost climatological terms, as though it were blown by a cold wind out of the East. It was, for the most part, an indelibly Cold War phenomenon; terrorism was often referred to as a form of surrogate warfare. Unpleasant it undoubtedly was, especially for the instant victims, but there did exist a useful measure of control applied by the patron states. The euphoria of the early 1990s blinded us to the dangers inherent in the collapse of the control factor. Whether or not one subscribed to the mutually assured destruction theory, it was very unlikely that the principal antagonists would encourage their surrogates to use weapons of mass destruction that they would be unwilling themselves to employ. The disintegration of the "evil empire" had another unpleasant consequence for terrorism: It unleashed deadly material and put a lot of disengaged experts on the "free" market. Now, we have to face the real possibility of a revitalized Cold War with old Cold Warriors such as Vladimir Putin in the driver's seat. What is uncertain is whether the old controls will be reimposed, or even whether they can. Although none of this is likely to unleash fresh fears of small-group nuclear terrorism in the West, it is likely to have an impact in other areas of perhaps greater concern. The fearful instruments of chemical and biological warfare, largely eschewed by a majority of civilized nations, have acquired the soubriquet of "the poor man's nuclear bomb." Certainly, as death-dealing implements, the term is well applied. There is a kind of inevitability about the employment of these weapons by terrorists. The amount of publicity they have received over the past decade or so alone would have assured that outcome. It is worthy of note, yet again, that these possibilities encouraged by technological advances and political shifts have no definitional significance. The alterations have been simply adjectival. But, they will change the way we think about terrorism as well as about those whose job it is to undertake countermeasures. Sooner maybe than later, one of those packets or envelopes is going to contain anthrax spores, the real thing, rather than the miscellaneous hoax powders that have turned up so far. There is a kind of fearfulness about handling this stuff that, as much as anything else, has probably protected society until now. The fears are not misplaced. Considering the number of terrorists who have blown themselves up with their own bombs, the very unfamiliarity with the handling of some of these substances, especially the nerve gases, suggests perils of an entirely different order from those previously experienced. The first successful employment of chemical and biological agents by terrorists will doubtlessly overcome any lingering inhibitions.

Now, yet another term has to be employed by those seeking to give precision to their particular definitions of terrorism. Not long after heaving a sigh of relief and congratulating ourselves at having avoided the catastrophes of Y2K predicted by the doomsayers, we have been hit with a wave of what is being called "cyberterrorism." Modern society is becoming more and more computer dependent. Everything from electronic commerce to the supply of energy is vulnerable, and although this may not be the immediate objective of the perpetrators, the potential for the associated loss of human life is not inconsiderable.[7] This cyberterrorism is still very much in its infancy; the methods are primitive and unsophisticated but effective. This is not "virtual" terrorism or Game Boy stuff. Cyberspace is a real place; real operations and real functions take place there, and real interests are at risk. The methods are new, but the principles behind their application are as old as terrorism itself. The technology employed has enabled the terrorists to reintroduce a useful, from their point of view, element of mystery into the process. They can, for a little while at least, operate from a considerable distance, concealing their identities and their purposes. The authorities, for the moment, can only confess to a sense of bafflement and try to reassure the affected public that everything possible is being done to protect the systems at risk and to apprehend the culprits. All this is going to generate a new lexicon, and already familiar terms such as *hackers, computer viruses, trap doors,* and the like will gain greater currency. Yet, we could as easily say these cybersystems were being "kidnapped," "hijacked," or "taken hostage," and when demands are presented to desist, the term *extortion* will come into play. Of greatest interest, perhaps, for the present purposes, a participant in an online discussion opined, "Hackers are freedom fighters for cyberspace" (Weise, 2000, p. 2A). Those who do not learn the lexical lessons of history are obliged to repeat the semester!

Terrorism, by its nature, seeks out and exploits its opponents' weaknesses. Again, a well-known aphorism has it that "terrorism is the weapon of the weak." This was a definitional device intended to characterize those tarnished with the terrorist label as being those who challenged rightful authority rather than those who abused it through practices that smacked of vicious cruelty. The nation-state has always been ultrasensitive to accusations that it is guilty of terrorism, whether against its own lawful residents or others (see, e.g., Herman & O'Sullivan, 1989). Where these cruelties are egregious, as in the case of Nazi Germany, few would cavil at defining what is done as terrorism. Yet, even that awful regime would claim its actions were in the nature of self-defense, a deterrent to behavior that threatened its cohesiveness and purposes.[8] Unhappily, such state terrorism is very far from being a thing of the past. As we proceed into the new millennium, we shall be confronted more and more with terrorism that proceeds from the mighty rather than the weak. A practical consequence of this delicacy in the matter of labeling can be seen by studying in any particular year the nations that find themselves on the U.S. State Department's list of "terrorist states," and those that do not. There is a kind of hypocrisy about this process that no definitional sophistry can hide; it simply highlights the perennial difficulty of describing forthrightly what terrorism is, for fear of upsetting those we might find it inconvenient to criticize. This is unfortunate on much more than a linguistic level. Definition is dictated under such circumstances by the harsh realities of power: None dare call it by its rightful name. This is surely the road to Tiananmen Square, and the consequences of ignoring the route are much more than merely academic.

Terrorism is a naked struggle for power, who shall wield it, and to what ends. The coercive character of what is done is plain enough to require little beyond description. Where the process does not produce the requisite submission, escalation is inevitable; action begets reaction. This is the real challenge to the high-minded. It is here that the state finds it especially needful to characterize what its opponents do as terrorism while seeking to distinguish its own counteraction as something quite different, lacking in reprehensible qualities. While looking at the conduct of those whose political philosophies we do not share, we ought not to disregard too cavalierly the mote in our own eye. No nation-state can relinquish its sovereign authority to an adversary, attempting to seize it by force, and retain its own integrity. Retaliation is an imperative in such cases, but one of the objectives of the adversary is to produce an overreaction. Brutal repression serves the adversary's purposes, so as to give rise to the charge, "See, you are as bad, or worse, than we are. Who is the terrorist now?" The audience is the community of nation-states, which has become increasingly censorious in judging the responses of others, especially when the judges are not directly confronted, for the moment, with terrorism problems of their own. In an ideal world, responses would be measured by much the same criteria as those against which an individual's rights of self-defense at law are evaluated, namely that the response should be necessary, reasonable, and proportionate to the harm suffered or apprehended (Cooper, 1998). We are forced to recognize that the real world in which modern-day terrorism takes place is very far from ideal. It is, rather, a Hobbesian universe in which all life is to be regarded as "nastie, brutish and shorte"—and cheap in the bargain. Terrorism thus becomes a battle for the moral high ground, with those in legitimate power trying to preserve their positions against opponents bent on dragging them into the gutter. The outcome is yet another phenomenological element in the process of defining terrorism that is likely to be of increasing importance in coming decades.

THE PROBLEM OF DEFINITION REMAINS UNALTERED THROUGHOUT

Thus, at the start of the new millennium, we can say with a high degree of certainty that the definition of terrorism is as needful and as illusory as ever. The fine minds that have engaged in the task over the past three decades or so have provided much fuel for the crucible and a great deal of raw material for the process, but a truly pure ingot has eluded all. Once again, the focus here has been on the problem of definition, which remains unaltered throughout. It is realism rather than pessimism that prompts the observation that this is really a problem without a solution, for none can voluntarily yield the high ground to the others. Terrorism is not a struggle for the hearts and minds of the victims nor for their immortal souls. Rather, it is, as Humpty Dumpty would have said, about who is to be master, that is all. Yet, withal, no

one who has experienced terrorism in the flesh has the slightest doubt about what it is or the sensations that it engenders.[9] Ask any concentration camp survivor. Ask those fortunate enough to have returned from the gulag. Ask those who have experienced the more recent examples of ethnic cleansing in the former Yugoslavia or in East Timor. They may not be able to encapsulate the horrors of their respective experiences in a finely turned phrase or two, but what they have undergone is to them and countless others not in the slightest doubt, for it is indelibly engraved on their psyches. Although this cannot suffice for the purposes of the polemic, it does help to focus the debate. As with obscenity, we know terrorism well enough when we see it. For the minds and bodies affected by it, this suffices; definition for these is otiose. This will not and cannot change in the years to come, strive as we may to give precision to the concept. It is diffidently opined here that we would be better employed in refocusing our efforts on what is done, the terrible acts themselves, whether by way of original initiative or retaliation. It might be more admirable to call a spade a spade, in the hands of whoever might be wielding it. These pathetic attempts at making the contemptible respectable will seem as ridiculous to those approaching the end of the present millennium as efforts to rehabilitate Attila the Hun or Genghis Khan would appear in our own times. So we are left, as we began, with our own imperfect formulas and the ever insistent need to explain and expound. As the incomparable Ludwig Wittgenstein (1921/1961) instructed us, "There are, indeed, things that cannot be put into words. *They make themselves manifest. They are what is mystical*" (p. 151). Terrorism is one of those things.

NOTES

1. Cohen's (1990) *Culture and Conflict in Egyptian-Israeli Relations: A Dialogue of the Deaf* is an excellent scholarly work that deserves to be more widely known.

2. See, for example, the excellent scholarly works of Deborah Tannen, especially *You Just Don't Understand: Women and Men in Conversation* (1990).

3. Representative of these worthy efforts is *International Terrorism: National, Regional, and Global Perspectives* (1976), edited by Yonah Alexander.

4. Terror and terrorism tend to be confused, somewhat awkwardly, in Frederick J. Hacker's (1976)

well-known work *Crusaders, Criminals, Crazies: Terror and Terrorism in Our Time.*

5.   See, generally, the thoughtful arguments of Noam Chomsky, especially his chapter "International Terrorism: Image and Reality" in *Western State Terrorism* (1991), edited by Alexander George.

6.   One of the more thoughtful and eclectic symposia on this subject was held in 1976 at Glassboro State College. The splendidly edited proceedings volume, *International Terrorism in the Contemporary World* (Livingston, 1978), contains the following, written by the author, on its first page: "Many nations have recognized the great potential of terrorism; the terrorist is now the spearhead of a developing theory and practice of surrogate warfare."

7.   Such an attack on the air traffic control system, for example, has long been feared.

8.   "Terrorism was the chief instrument of securing the cohesion of the German people in war purposes" (Office of the Chief Counsel for the Prosecution of Axis Criminality, 1946, p. 144).

9.   There is something faintly paradoxical about this that is reminiscent of the renowned cat of Schrödinger, seemingly capable of being alive and dead at the same time.

References

Alexander, Y. (Ed.). (1976). *International terrorism: National, regional, and global perspectives.* New York: Praeger.

Chomsky, N. (1991). International terrorism: Image and reality. In A. George (Ed.), *Western state terrorism* (pp. 12–38). New York: Routledge.

Cohen, R. (1990). *Culture and conflict in Egyptian-Israeli relations: A dialogue of the deaf.* Bloomington: Indiana University Press.

Cooper, H. H. A. (1978). Terrorism: The problem of the problem of definition. *Chitty's Law Journal, 26*(3), 105–108.

Cooper, H. H. A. (1998). Self-defense. In *Encyclopedia Americana* (Vol. 25, pp. 532). Danbury, CT: Grolier.

Gourevich, P. (2000, February 14). A cold case. *The New Yorker,* 42–60.

Hacker, F. J. (1976). *Crusaders, criminals, crazies: Terror and terrorism in our time.* New York: Norton.

Herman, E., & O'Sullivan, G. (1989). The Western model and semantics of terrorism. In *The terrorism industry: The experts and institutions that shape our view of terror.* New York: Pantheon.

Livingston, M. H. (with Kress, L. B., & Wanek, M. G.). (Eds.). (1978). *International terrorism in the contemporary world.* Westport, CT: Greenwood.

Office of the Chief Counsel for the Prosecution of Axis Criminality. (1946). *Nazi conspiracy and aggression.* Washington, DC: Government Printing Office.

Posner, R. A. (1999). *An affair of state: The investigation, impeachment, and trial of President Clinton.* Cambridge, MA: Harvard University Press.

Schweitzer, G. E. (with Dorsch, C. C.). (1998). *Superterrorism: Assassins, mobsters, and weapons of mass destruction.* New York: Plenum.

Tannen, D. (1990). *You just don't understand: Women and men in conversation.* New York: Ballantine.

Weise, E. (2000, February 10). Online talk is of conspiracy, crime and punishment. *USA Today,* p. 2A.

Wittgenstein, L. (1961). *Tractatus logico-philosophicus.* London: Routledge Kegan Paul. (Original work published 1921)

❖

The Logic of Terrorism

Terrorist Behavior as a Product of Strategic Choice

Martha Crenshaw

This chapter examines the ways in which terrorism can be understood as an expression of political strategy. It attempts to show that terrorism may follow logical processes that can be discovered and explained. For the purpose of presenting this source of terrorist behavior, rather than the psychological one, it interprets the resort to violence as a willful choice made by an organization for political and strategic reasons, rather than as the unintended outcome of psychological or social factors.[1]

In the terms of this analytical approach, terrorism is assumed to display a collective rationality. A radical political organization is seen as the central actor in the terrorist drama. The group possesses collective preferences or values and selects terrorism as a course of action from a range of perceived alternatives. Efficacy is the primary standard by which terrorism is compared with other methods of achieving political goals. Reasonably regularized decision-making procedures are employed to make an intentional choice, in conscious anticipation of the consequences of various courses of action or inaction. Organizations arrive at collective judgments about the relative effectiveness of different strategies of opposition on the basis of observation and experience, as much as on the basis of abstract strategic conceptions derived from ideological assumptions. This approach thus allows for the incorporation of theories of social learning.

Conventional rational-choice theories of individual participation in rebellion, extended to include terrorist activities, have usually been considered inappropriate because of the "free rider" problem. That is, the benefits of a successful terrorist campaign would presumably be shared by all individual supporters of the group's goals, regardless of the extent of their active participation. In this case, why should a rational person become a terrorist, given the high costs associated with violent resistance and the expectation that everyone who supports the cause will benefit, whether he or she participates or not? One answer is that the benefits of participation are psychological. Other chapters in this volume explore this possibility.

A different answer, however, supports a strategic analysis. On the basis of surveys conducted in New York and West Germany, political scientists suggest that individuals can be *collectively* rational.[2] People realize that their participation is important because group size and cohesion matter. They ate sensitive to the implications of free-riding and perceive their personal influence on the provision of public goods to be high. The authors argue that "average citizens may adopt a collectivist conception of rationality because they recognize that what is individually rational is collectively irrational."[3] Selective incentives are deemed largely irrelevant.

One of the advantages of approaching terrorism as a collectively rational strategic choice is that it permits the construction of a standard from which deviations can be measured. For example, the central question about the rationality of some terrorist organizations, such as the

SOURCE: From "The Logic of Terrorism: Terrorist Behavior as a Product of Strategic Choice" in *Origins of Terrorism: Psychologies, Ideologies, Theologies, States of Mind* by Reich, Walter (ed.), 1998: 7–24, Woodrow Wilson International Center for Scholars. Reprinted with permissions from The Johns Hopkins University Press.

West German groups of the 1970s or the Weather Underground in the United States, is whether or not they had a sufficient grasp of reality—some approximation, to whatever degree imperfect—to calculate the likely consequences of the courses of action they chose. Perfect knowledge of available alternatives and the consequences of each is not possible, and miscalculations are inevitable. The Popular Front for the Liberation of Palestine (PFLP), for example, planned the hijacking of a TWA flight from Rome in August 1969 to coincide with a scheduled address by President Nixon to a meeting of the Zionist Organization of America, but he sent a letter instead.[4]

Yet not all errors of decision are miscalculations. There are varied degrees of limited rationality. Are some organizations so low on the scale of rationality as to be in a different category from more strategically minded groups? To what degree is strategic reasoning modified by psychological and other constraints? The strategic choice framework provides criteria on which to base these distinctions. It also leads one to ask what conditions promote or discourage rationality in violent underground organizations.

The use of this theoretical approach is also advantageous in that it suggests important questions about the preferences or goals of terrorist organizations. For example, is the decision to seize hostages in order to bargain with governments dictated by strategic considerations or by other, less instrumental motives?

The strategic choice approach is also a useful interpretation of reality. Since the French Revolution, a strategy of terrorism has gradually evolved as a means of bringing about political change opposed by established governments. Analysis of the historical development of terrorism reveals similarities in calculation of ends and means. The strategy has changed over time to adapt to new circumstances that offer different possibilities for dissident action—for example, hostage taking. Yet terrorist activity considered in its entirety shows a fundamental unity of purpose and conception. Although this analysis remains largely on an abstract level, the historical evolution of the strategy of terrorism can be sketched in its terms.[5]

A last argument in support of this approach takes the form of a warning. The wide range of terrorist activity cannot be dismissed as "irrational" and thus pathological, unreasonable, or inexplicable. The resort to terrorism need not be an aberration. It may be a reasonable and calculated response to circumstances. To say that the reasoning that leads to the choice of terrorism may be logical is not an argument about moral justifiability. It does suggest, however, that the belief that terrorism is expedient is one means by which moral inhibitions are overcome.

THE CONDITIONS FOR TERRORISM

The central problem is to determine when extremist organizations find terrorism useful. Extremists seek either a radical change in the status quo, which would confer a new advantage, or the defense of privileges they perceive to be threatened. Their dissatisfaction with the policies of the government is extreme, and their demands usually involve the displacement of existing political elites.[6] Terrorism is not the only method of working toward radical goals, and thus it must be compared to the alternative strategies available to dissidents. Why is terrorism attractive to some opponents of the state, but unattractive to others?

The practitioners of terrorism often claim that they had no choice but terrorism, and it is indeed true that terrorism often follows the failure of other methods. In nineteenth-century Russia, for example, the failure of nonviolent movements contributed to the rise of terrorism. In Ireland, terrorism followed the failure of Parnell's constitutionalism. In the Palestinian-Israeli struggle, terrorism followed the failure of Arab efforts at conventional warfare against Israel. In general, the "nonstate" or "substate" users of terrorism—that is, groups in opposition to the government, as opposed to government itself—are constrained in their options by the lack of active mass support and by the superior power arrayed against them (an imbalance that has grown with the development of the modern centralized and bureaucratic nation-state). But these constraints have not prevented oppositions from considering and rejecting methods other than terrorism. Perhaps because groups are slow to recognize the extent of the limits to action, terrorism is often the last in a sequence of choices. It represents the outcome of a learning process. Experience in opposition provides radicals with information about the potential consequences of their choices. Terrorism is likely to be a reasonably informed choice among available alternatives, some tried unsuccessfully. Terrorists also learn from the experiences of others, usually communicated to them via the news media. Hence the existence of patterns of contagion in terrorist incidents.[7]

Thus the existence of extremism or rebellious potential is necessary to the resort to terrorism but does not in itself explain it, because many revolutionary and nationalist organizations have explicitly disavowed terrorism. The Russian Marxists argued for years against the use of terrorism.[8] Generally, small organizations resort to violence to compensate for what they lack in numbers.[9] The imbalance between the resources terrorists are able to mobilize and the power of the incumbent regime is a decisive consideration in their decision making.

More important than the observation that terrorism is the weapon of the weak, who lack numbers or conventional military power, is the explanation for weakness. Particularly, why does an organization lack the potential to attract enough followers to change government policy or overthrow it?

One possibility is that the majority of the population does not share the ideological views of the resisters, who occupy a political position so extreme that their appeal is inherently limited. This incompatibility of preferences may be purely political, concerning, for example, whether or not one prefers socialism to capitalism. The majority of West Germans found the Red Army Faction's promises for the future not only excessively vague but distasteful. Nor did most Italians support aims of the neofascist groups that initiated the "strategy of tension" in 1969. Other extremist groups, such as the *Euskadi ta Askatasuna* (ETA) in Spain or the Provisional Irish Republican Army (PIRA) in Northern Ireland, may appeal exclusively to ethnic, religious, or other minorities. In such cases, a potential constituency of like-minded and dedicated individuals exists, but its boundaries are fixed and limited. Despite the intensity of the preferences of a minority, its numbers will never be sufficient for success.

A second explanation for the weakness of the type of organization likely to turn to terrorism lies in a failure to mobilize support. Its members may be unwilling or unable to expend the time and effort required for mass organizational work. Activists may not possess the requisite skills or patience, or may not expect returns commensurate with their endeavors. No matter how acute or widespread popular dissatisfaction may be, the masses do not rise spontaneously; mobilization is required.[10] The organization's leaders, recognizing the advantages of numbers, may combine mass organization with conspiratorial activities. But resources are limited and organizational work is difficult and slow even under favorable circumstances. Moreover, rewards are not immediate. These difficulties are compounded in an authoritarian state, where the organization of independent opposition is sure to incur high costs. Combining violent provocation with nonviolent organizing efforts may only work to the detriment of the latter.

For example, the debate over whether to use an exclusively violent underground strategy that is isolated from the masses (as terrorism inevitably is) or to work with the people in propaganda and organizational efforts divided the Italian left-wing groups, with the Red Brigades choosing the clandestine path and Prima Linea preferring to maintain contact with the wider protest movement. In prerevolutionary Russia the Socialist-Revolutionary party combined the activities of a legal political party with the terrorist campaign of the secret Combat Organization. The IRA has a legal counterpart in Sinn Féin.

A third reason for the weakness of dissident organizations is specific to repressive states. It is important to remember that terrorism is by no means restricted to liberal democracies, although some authors refuse to define resistance to authoritarianism as terrorism.[11] People may not support a resistance organization because they are afraid of negative sanctions from the regime or because censorship of the press prevents them from learning of the possibility of rebellion. In this situation a radical organization may believe that supporters exist but cannot reveal themselves. The depth of this latent support cannot be measured or activists mobilized until the state is overthrown.

Such conditions are frustrating, because the likelihood of popular dissatisfaction grows as the likelihood of its active expression is diminished. Frustration may also encourage unrealistic expectations among the regime's challengers, who are not able to test their popularity. Rational expectations may be undermined by fantastic assumptions about the role of the masses. Yet such fantasies can also prevail among radical undergrounds in Western democracies. The misperception of conditions can lead to unrealistic expectations.

In addition to small numbers, time constraints contribute to the decision to use terrorism. Terrorists are impatient for action. This impatience may, of course, be due to external factors, such as psychological or organizational pressures. The personalities of leaders, demands from followers, or competition from rivals often constitute impediments to strategic thinking. But it is not necessary to explain the felt urgency of some radical organizations by citing reasons external to an instrumental frame-work. Impatience and eagerness for action can be rooted in calculations of ends and means. For example, the organization may perceive an immediate opportunity to compensate for its inferiority vis-à-vis the government. A change in the structure of the situation may temporarily alter the balance of resources available to the two sides, thus changing the ratio of strength between government and challenger.

Such a change in the radical organization's outlook—the combination of optimism and urgency—may occur when the regime suddenly appears vulnerable to challenge. This vulnerability may be of two sorts. First, the regime's ability to respond effectively, its capacity for efficient repression of dissent, or its ability to protect its citizens and property may weaken. Its armed forces may be committed elsewhere, for example, as British forces were during World War I when the IRA first rose to challenge British rule, or its coercive resources may be otherwise overextended. Inadequate security at embassies, airports, or military installations may become obvious. The poorly protected U.S. Marine barracks in Beirut were, for example, a tempting target. Government strategy may be ill-adapted for responding to terrorism.

Second, the regime may make itself morally or politically vulnerable by increasing the likelihood that the terrorists will attract popular support. Government repressiveness is thought to have contradictory effects: it both deters dissent and provokes a moral backlash.[12] Perceptions of the regime as unjust motivate opposition. If government actions make average citizens willing to suffer punishment for supporting antigovernment

causes, or lend credence to the claims of radical opponents, the extremist organization may be tempted to exploit this temporary upsurge of popular indignation. A groundswell of popular disapproval may make liberal governments less willing (as opposed to less able) to use coercion against violent dissent.

Political discomfort may also be internationally generated. If the climate of international opinion changes so as to reduce the legitimacy of a targeted regime, rebels may feel encouraged to risk a repression that they hope will be limited by outside disapproval. In such circumstances the regime's brutality may be expected to win supporters to the cause of its challengers. The current situation in South Africa furnishes an example. Thus a heightened sensitivity to injustice may be produced either by government actions or by changing public attitudes.

The other fundamental way in which the situation changes to the advantage of challengers is through acquiring new resources. New means of financial support are an obvious asset, which may accrue through a foreign alliance with a sympathetic government or another, richer revolutionary group, or through criminal means such as bank robberies or kidnapping for ransom. Although terrorism is an extremely economical method of violence, funds are essential for the support of full-time activists, weapons purchases, transportation, and logistics.

Technological advances in weapons, explosives, transportation, and communications also may enhance the disruptive potential of terrorism. The invention of dynamite was thought by nineteenth-century revolutionaries and anarchists to equalize the relationship between government and challenger, for example. In 1885, Johann Most published a pamphlet titled *Revolutionary War Science*, which explicitly advocated terrorism. According to Paul Avrich, the anarchists saw dynamite "as a great equalizing force, enabling ordinary workmen to stand up against armies, militias, and police, to say nothing of the hired gunmen of the employers."[13] In providing such a powerful but easily concealed weapon, science was thought to have given a decisive advantage to revolutionary forces.

Strategic innovation is another important way in which a challenging organization acquires new resources. The organization may borrow or adapt a technique in order to exploit a vulnerability ignored by the government. In August 1972, for example, the Provisional IRA introduced the effective tactic of the one-shot sniper. IRA Chief of Staff Sean MacStiofain claims to have originated the idea: "It seemed to me that prolonged sniping from a static position had no more in common with guerrilla theory than mass confrontations."[14] The best marksmen were trained to fire a single shot and escape before their position could be located. The creation of surprise is naturally one of the key advantages of an offensive strategy. So, too, is the willingness to violate social norms pertaining to restraints on violence. The history of terrorism reveals a series of innovations, as terrorists deliberately selected targets considered taboo and locales where violence was unexpected. These innovations were then rapidly diffused, especially in the modern era of instantaneous and global communications.

It is especially interesting that, in 1968, two of the most important terrorist tactics of the modern era appeared—diplomatic kidnappings in Latin America and hijackings in the Middle East. Both were significant innovations because they involved the use of extortion or blackmail. Although the nineteenth-century Fenians had talked about kidnapping the prince of Wales, the People's Will (Narodnaya Volya) in nineteenth-century Russia had offered to halt its terrorist campaign if a constitution were granted, and American marines were kidnapped by Castro forces in 1959, hostage taking as a systematic and lethal form of coercive bargaining was essentially new. This chapter later takes up the issue in more detail as an illustration of strategic analysis.

Terrorism has so far been presented as the response by an opposition movement to an opportunity. This approach is compatible with the findings of Harvey Waterman, who sees collective political action as determined by the calculations of resources and opportunities.[15] Yet other theorists—James Q. Wilson, for example—argue that political organizations originate in response to a threat to a group's values.[16] Terrorism can certainly be defensive as well as opportunistic. It may be a response to a sudden downturn in a dissident organization's fortunes. The fear of appearing weak may provoke an underground organization into acting in order to show its strength. The PIRA used terrorism to offset an impression of weakness, even at the cost of alienating public opinion: in the 1970s periods of negotiations with the British were punctuated by outbursts of terrorism because the PIRA did want people to think that they were negotiating from strength.[17] Right-wing organizations frequently resort to violence in response to what they see as a threat to the status quo from the left. Beginning in 1969, for example, the right in Italy promoted a "strategy of tension," which involved urban bombings with high numbers of civilian casualties, in order to keep the Italian government and electorate from moving to the left.

CALCULATION OF COST AND BENEFIT

An organization or a faction of an organization may choose terrorism because other methods are not expected to work or are considered too time-consuming, given the urgency of the situation and the government's superior resources. Why would an extremist organization expect that terrorism will be effective? What are the costs and benefits of such a choice, compared with other alternatives? What is the nature of the debate over terrorism? Whether or not to use terrorism is one of the most divisive issues resistance groups confront, and numerous revolutionary movements have split on the question of means even after agreeing on common political ends.[18]

The Costs of Terrorism

The costs of terrorism are high. As a domestic strategy, it invariably invites a punitive government reaction, although the organization may believe that the government reaction will not be efficient enough to pose a serious threat. This cost can be offset by the advance preparation of building a secure underground. *Sendero Luminoso* (Shining Path) in Peru, for example, spent ten years creating a clandestine organizational structure before launching a campaign of violence in 1980. Furthermore, radicals may look to the future and calculate that present sacrifice will not be in vain if it inspires future resistance. Conceptions of interest are thus long term.

Another potential cost of terrorism is loss of popular support. Unless terrorism is carefully controlled and discriminate, it claims innocent victims. In a liberal state, indiscriminate violence may appear excessive and unjustified and alienate a citizenry predisposed to loyalty to the government. If it provokes generalized government repression, fear may diminish enthusiasm for resistance. This potential cost of popular alienation is probably least in ethnically divided societies, where victims can be clearly identified as the enemy and where the government of the majority appears illegal to the minority. Terrorists try to compensate by justifying their actions as the result of the absence of choice or the need to respond to government violence. In addition, they may make their strategy highly discriminate, attacking only unpopular targets.

Terrorism may be unattractive because it is elitist. Although relying only on terrorism may spare the general population from costly involvement in the struggle for freedom, such isolation may violate the ideological beliefs of revolutionaries who insist that the people must participate in their liberation. The few who choose terrorism are willing to forgo or postpone the participation of the many, but revolutionaries who oppose terrorism insist that it prevents the people from taking responsibility for their own destiny. The possibility of vicarious popular identification with "symbolic acts of terrorism may satisfy some revolutionaries, but others will find terrorism a harmful substitute for mass participation.

The Advantages of Terrorism

Terrorism has an extremely useful agenda-setting function. If the reasons behind violence are skillfully articulated, terrorism can put the issue of political change on the public agenda. By attracting attention it makes the claims of the resistance a salient issue in the public mind. The government can reject but not ignore an opposition's demands. In 1974 the Palestinian Black September organization, for example, was willing to sacrifice a base in Khartoum, alienate the Sudanese government, and create ambivalence in the Arab world by seizing the Saudi Arabian embassy and killing American and Belgian diplomats. These costs were apparently weighed against the message to the world "to take us seriously." Mainstream Fatah leader Salah Khalef (Abu Iyad) explained: "We are planting the seed. Others will harvest it. . . . It is enough for us now to learn, for example, in reading the Jerusalem Post, that Mrs. Meir had to make her will before visiting Paris, or that Mr. Abba Eban had to travel with a false passport."[19] George

Habash of the PFLP noted in 1970 that "we force people to ask what is going on."[20] In these statements, contemporary extremists echo the nineteenth-century anarchists, who coined the idea of propaganda of the deed, a term used as early as 1877 to refer to an act of insurrection as "a powerful means of arousing popular conscience" and the materialization of an idea through actions.[21]

Terrorism may be intended to create revolutionary conditions. It can prepare the ground for active mass revolt by undermining the government's authority and demoralizing its administrative cadres—its courts, police, and military. By spreading insecurity—at the extreme, making the country ungovernable—the organization hopes to pressure the regime into concessions or relaxation of coercive controls. With the rule of law disrupted, the people will be free to join the opposition. Spectacular humiliation of the government demonstrates strength and will and maintains the morale and enthusiasm of adherents and sympathizers. The first wave of Russian revolutionaries claimed that the aims of terrorism were to exhaust the enemy, render the government's position untenable, and wound the government's prestige by delivering a moral, not a physical, blow. Terrorists hoped to paralyze the government by their presence merely by showing signs of life from time to time. The hesitation, irresolution, and tension they would produce would undermine the processes of government and make the Czar a prisoner in his own palace.[22] As Brazilian revolutionary Carlos Marighela explained: "Revolutionary terrorism's great weapon is initiative, which guarantees its survival and continued activity. The more committed terrorists and revolutionaries devoted to anti-dictatorship terrorism and sabotage there are, the more military power will be worn down, the more time it will lose following false trails, and the more fear and tension it will suffer through not knowing where the next attack will be launched and what the next target will be."[23]

These statements illustrate a corollary advantage to terrorism in what might be called its excitational function: it inspires resistance by example. As propaganda of the deed, terrorism demonstrates that the regime can be challenged and that illegal opposition is possible. It acts as a catalyst, not a substitute, for mass revolt. All the tedious and time-consuming organizational work of mobilizing the people can be avoided.

Terrorism is a shortcut to revolution. As the Russian revolutionary Vera Figner described its purpose, terrorism was "a means of agitation to draw people from their torpor," not a sign of loss of belief in the people.[24]

A more problematic benefit lies in provoking government repression. Terrorists often think that by provoking indiscriminate repression against the population, terrorism will heighten popular disaffection, demonstrate the justice of terrorist claims, and enhance the attractiveness of the political alternative the terrorists represent. Thus, the West German Red Army Faction sought (in vain) to make fascism "visible" in West Germany.[25] In Brazil, Marighela unsuccessfully aimed to "transform the country's political situation into a military one. Then discontent will spread to all social groups and the military will be held exclusively responsible for failures."[26]

But profiting from government repression depends on the lengths to which the government is willing to go in order to contain disorder, and on the population's tolerance for both insecurity and repression. A liberal state may be limited in its capacity for quelling violence, but at the same time it may be difficult to provoke to excess. However, the government's reaction to terrorism may reinforce the symbolic value of violence even if it avoids repression. Extensive security precautions, for example, may only make the terrorists appear powerful.

Summary

To summarize, the choice of terrorism involves considerations of timing and of the popular contribution to revolt, as well as of the relationship between government and opponents. Radicals choose terrorism when they want immediate action, think that only violence can build organizations and mobilize supporters, and accept the risks of challenging the government in a particularly provocative way. Challengers who think that organizational infrastructure must precede action, that rebellion without the masses is misguided, and that premature conflict with the regime can only lead to disaster favor gradualist strategies. They prefer methods such as rural guerrilla warfare, because terrorism can jeopardize painfully achieved gains or preclude eventual compromise with the government.

The resistance organization has before it a set of alternatives defined by the situation and by the objectives and resources of the group. The reasoning behind terrorism takes into account the balance of power between challengers and authorities, a balance that depends on the amount of popular support the resistance can mobilize. The proponents of terrorism understand this constraint and possess reasonable expectations about the likely results of action or inaction. They may be wrong about the alternatives that are open to them, or miscalculate the consequences of their actions, but their decisions are based on logical processes. Furthermore, organizations learn from their mistakes and from those of others, resulting in strategic continuity and progress toward the development of more efficient and sophisticated tactics. Future choices are modified by the consequences of present actions.

HOSTAGE TAKING AS BARGAINING

Hostage taking can be analyzed as a form of coercive bargaining. More than twenty years ago, Thomas Schelling wrote that "hostages represent the power to hurt in its purest form."[27] From this perspective, terrorists choose to take hostages because in bargaining situations the government's greater strength and resources are not an advantage. The extensive resort to this form of terrorism after 1968, a year that marks the major advent of diplomatic kidnappings and airline hijackings, was a predictable response to the growth of state power. Kidnappings, hijackings, and barricade-type seizures of embassies or public buildings are attempts to manipulate a government's political decisions.

Strategic analysis of bargaining terrorism is based on the assumption that hostage takers genuinely seek the concessions they demand. It assumes that they prefer government compliance to resistance. This analysis does not allow for deception or for the possibility that seizing hostages may be an end in itself because it yields the benefit of publicity. Because these limiting assumptions may reduce the utility of the theory, it is important to recognize them.

Terrorist bargaining is essentially a form of blackmail or extortion.[28] Terrorists seize hostages in order to affect a government's choices, which are controlled both by expectations of outcome (what the terrorists are likely to do, given the government reaction) and preferences (such as humanitarian values). The outcome threatened by the terrorist—the death of the hostages—must be worse for the government than compliance with terrorist demands. The terrorist has two options, neither of which necessarily excludes the other: to make the threat both more horrible and more credible or to reward compliance, a factor that strategic theorists often ignore.[29] That is, the cost to the government of complying with the terrorists' demands may be lowered or the cost of resisting raised.

The threat to kill the hostages must be believable and painful to the government. Here hostage takers are faced with a paradox. How can the credibility of this threat be assured when hostage takers recognize that governments know that the terrorists' control over the situation depends on live hostages? One way of establishing credibility is to divide the threat, making it sequential by killing one hostage at a time. Such tactics also aid terrorists in demonstrating a commitment to carrying out their threat. Once the terrorists have murdered, though, their incentive to surrender voluntarily is substantially reduced. The terrorists have increased their own costs of yielding in order to persuade the government that their intention to kill all the hostages is real.

Another important way of binding oneself in a terrorist strategy is to undertake a barricade rather than a kidnapping operation. Terrorists who are trapped with the hostages find it more difficult to back down (because the government controls the escape routes) and, by virtue of this commitment, influence the government's choices. When terrorists join the hostages in a barricade situation, they create the visible and irrevocable commitment that Schelling sees as a necessary bond in bargaining. The government must expect desperate behavior, because the terrorists have increased their potential loss in order to demonstrate the firmness of their intentions. Furthermore, barricades are technically easier than kidnappings.

The terrorists also attempt to force the "last dear chance" of avoiding disaster onto the government, which must accept the responsibility for noncompliance that leads to the deaths of hostages. The seizure of hostages is the first move in the game, leaving the next move—which determines the fate of the hostages—completely up to the government. Uncertain communications may facilitate this strategy.[30] The terrorists can pretend not to receive government messages that might affect their demonstrated commitment. Hostage takers can also bind themselves by insisting that they are merely agents, empowered to ask only for the most extreme demands. Terrorists may deliberately appear irrational, either through inconsistent and erratic behavior or unrealistic expectations and preferences, in order to convince the government that they will carry out a threat that entails self-destruction.

Hostage seizures are a type of iterated game, which explains some aspects of terrorist behavior that otherwise seem to violate strategic principles. In terms of a single episode, terrorists can be expected to find killing hostages painful, because they will not achieve their demands and the government's desire to punish will be intensified. However, from a long-range perspective, killing hostages reinforces the credibility of the threat in the next terrorist incident, even if the killers then cannot escape. Each terrorist episode is actually a round in a series of games between government and terrorists.

Hostage takers may influence the government's decision by promising rewards for compliance. Recalling that terrorism represents an iterative game, the release of hostages unharmed when ransom is paid underwrites a promise in the future. Sequential release of selected hostages makes promises credible. Maintaining secrecy about a government's concessions is an additional reward for compliance. France, for example, can if necessary deny making concessions to Lebanese kidnappers because the details of arrangements have not been publicized.

Terrorists may try to make their demands appear legitimate so that governments may seem to satisfy popular grievances rather than the whims of terrorists. Thus, terrorists may ask that food be distributed to the poor. Such demands were a favored tactic of the *Ejercito Revolucionario del Pueblo* (ERP) in Argentina in the 1970s.

A problem for hostage takers is that rewarding compliance is not easy to reconcile with making threats credible. For example, if terrorists use publicity to emphasize their threat to kill hostages (which they frequently do), they may also increase the costs of compliance for the government because of the attention drawn to the incident.

In any calculation of the payoffs for each side, the costs associated with the bargaining process must be taken into account.[31] Prolonging the hostage crisis increases the costs to both sides. The question is who loses most and thus is more likely to concede. Each party presumably wishes to make the delay more costly to the other. Seizing multiple hostages appears to be advantageous to terrorists, who are thus in a position to make threats credible by killing hostages individually. Conversely, the greater the number of hostages, the greater the cost of holding them. In hijacking or barricade situations, stress and fatigue for the captors increase waiting costs for them as well. Kidnapping poses fewer such costs. Yet the terrorists can reasonably expect that the costs to governments in terms of public or international pressures may be higher when developments are visible. Furthermore, kidnappers can maintain suspense and interest by publishing communications from their victims.

Identifying the obstacles to effective bargaining in hostage seizures is critical. Most important, bargaining depends on the existence of a common interest between two parties. It is unclear whether the lives of hostages are a sufficient common interest to ensure a compromise outcome that is preferable to no agreement for both sides. Furthermore, most theories of bargaining assume that the preferences of each side remain stable during negotiations. In reality, the nature and intensity of preferences may change during a hostage-taking episode. For example, embarrassment over the Iran-*contra* scandal may have reduced the American interest in securing the release of hostages in Lebanon.

Bargaining theory is also predicated on the assumption that the game is two-party. When terrorists seize the nationals of one government in order to influence the choices of a third, the situation is seriously complicated. The hostages themselves may sometimes become intermediaries and participants. In Lebanon, Terry Waite, formerly an intermediary and negotiator, became a hostage. Such developments are not anticipated by bargaining theories based on normal political relationships. Furthermore, bargaining is not possible if a government is willing to accept the maximum cost the terrorists can bring to bear rather than concede. And the government's options are not restricted to resistance or compliance; armed rescue attempts represent an attempt to break the bargaining stalemate. In attempting to make their threats credible—for example, by sequential killing of hostages—terrorists may provoke military intervention. There may be limits, then, to the pain terrorists can inflict and still remain in the game.

CONCLUSIONS

This essay has attempted to demonstrate that even the most extreme and unusual forms of political behavior can follow an internal, strategic logic. If there are consistent patterns in terrorist behavior, rather than random idiosyncrasies, a strategic analysis may reveal them. Prediction of future terrorism can only be based on theories that explain past patterns.

Terrorism can be considered a reasonable way of pursuing extreme interests in the political arena. It is one among the many alternatives that radical organizations can choose. Strategic conceptions, based on ideas of how best to take advantage of the possibilities of a given situation, are an important determinant of oppositional terrorism, as they are of the government response. However, no single explanation for terrorist behavior is satisfactory. Strategic calculation is only one factor in the decision-making process leading to terrorism. But it is critical to include strategic reasoning as a possible motivation, at a minimum as an antidote to stereotypes of "terrorists" as irrational fanatics. Such stereotypes are a dangerous underestimation of the capabilities of extremist groups. Nor does stereotyping serve to educate the public—or, indeed, specialists—about the complexities of terrorist motivations and behaviors.

NOTES

1. For a similar perspective (based on a different methodology) *see* James DeNardo, *Power in Numbers: The Political Strategy of Protest and Rebellion* (Princeton, N.J.: Princeton University Press, 1985). See also Harvey Waterman, "Insecure 'Ins' and Opportune 'Outs': Sources of Collective Political Activity," *Journal of Political and Military Sociology* 8 (1980): 107–12, and "Reasons and Reason: Collective Political Activity in Comparative and Historical Perspective," *World Politics* 33 (1981): 554–89. A useful review of rational choice theories is found in James G. March, "Theories of Choice and Making Decisions," *Society* 20 (1982): 29–39.

2. Edward N. Muller and Karl-Dieter Opp, "Rational Choice and Rebellious Collective Action," *American Political Science Review* 80 (1986): 471–87.

3. Ibid., 484. The authors also present another puzzling question that may be answered in terms of either psychology or collective rationality. People who expected their rebellious behavior to be punished were more likely to be potential rebels. This propensity could be explained either by a martyr syndrome (or an expectation of hostility from authority figures) or intensity of preference—the calculation that the regime was highly repressive and thus deserved all the more to be destroyed. See pp. 432 and 485.

4. Leila Khaled, My *People Shall Live: The Autobiography of a Revolutionary* (London: Hoddar and Stoughton, 1973), 128–31.

5. See Martha Crenshaw, "The Strategic Development of Terrorism," paper presented to the 1985 Annual Meeting of the American Political Science Association, New Orleans.

6. William A. Gamson, *The Strategy of Social Protest* (Homewood, Illinois: Dorsey Press, 1975).

7. Manus L. Midlarsky, Martha Crenshaw, and Fumihiko Yoshida, "Why Violence Spreads: The Contagion of International Terrorism," *International Studies Quarterly* 24 (1980): 262–98.

8. See the study by David A. Newell. *The Russian Marxist Response to Terrorism: 1878–1917* (Ph.D. dissertation, Stanford University, University Microfilms, 1981).

9. The tension between violence and numbers is a fundamental proposition in DeNardo's analysis; see *Power in Numbers,* chapters 9–11.

10. The work of Charles Tilly emphasizes the political basis of collective violence. See Charles Tilly, Louise Tilly, and Richard Tilly, *The Rebellious Century 1830–1930* (Cambridge: Harvard University Press, 1975), and Charles Tilly, *From Mobilization to Revolution* (Reading, Mass.: Addison-Wesley, 1978).

11. See Conor Cruise O'Brien, "Terrorism under Democratic Conditions: The Case of the IRA," in *Terrorism, Legitimacy, and Power: The Consequences of Political Violence,* edited by Martha Crenshaw (Middletown, Conn.: Wesleyan University Press, 1983).

12. For example, DeNardo, in *Power in Numbers,* argues that "the movement derives moral sympathy from the government's excesses" (p. 207).

13. Paul Avrich, *The Haymarket Tragedy* (Princeton: Princeton University Press, 1984), 166.

14. Sean MacStiofain, *Memoirs of a Revolutionary* (N.p.: Gordon Cremonisi, 1975), 301.

15. Waterman, "Insecure 'Ins' and Opportune 'Outs'" and "Reasons and Reason."

16. *Political Organizations* (New York: Basic Books, 1973).

17. Maria McGuire, *To Take Arms: My Year with the IRA Provisionals* (New York: Viking, 1973), 110–11, 118, 129–31, 115, and 161–62.

18. DeNardo concurs; see *Power in Numbers,* chapter 11.

19. See Jim Hoagland, "A Community of Terror," *Washington Post,* 15 March 1973, pp. 1 and 13; also *New York Times,* 4 March 1973, p. 28. Black September is widely regarded as a subsidiary of Fatah, the major Palestinian organization headed by Yasir Arafat.

20. John Amos, *Palestinian Resistance: Organization of a Nationalist Movement* (New York: Pergamon, 1980), 193; quoting George Habash, interviewed in *Life Magazine,* 12 June 1970, 33.

21. Jean Maitron, *Histoire du movement anarchiste en France (1880–1914),* 2d ed. (Paris: Société universitaire d'éditions et de librairie, 1955), 74–5.

22. "Stepniak" (pseud. for Sergei Kravshinsky), *Underground Russia: Revolutionary Profiles and Sketches from Life* (London: Smith, Elder, 1883), 278–80.

23. Carlos Marighela, *For the Liberation of Brazil* (Harmondsworth: Penguin, 1971), 113.

24. Vera Figner, *Mémoires d'une révolutionnaire* (Paris: Gallimard, 1930), 206.

25. *Textes des prisonniers de la "fraction armée rouge" et dernières lettres d'Ulrike Meinhof* (Paris: Maspéro, 1977), 64.

26. Marighela, *For the Liberation of Brazil,* 46.

27. Schelling, *Arms and Influence* (New Haven, Conn.: Yale University Press, 1966), 6.

28. Daniel Ellsbuig, *The Theory and Practice of Blackmail* (Santa Monica: Rand Corporation, 1963).

29. David A. Baldwin, "Bargaining with Airline Hijackers," in *The 50% Solution,* edited by William 1. Zartman, 404–29 (Garden City, N.Y.: Doubleday, 1976), argues that promises have not been sufficiently stressed. Analysts tend to emphasize threats instead, surely because of the latent violence implicit in hostage taking regardless of outcome.

30. See Roberta Wohlstetter's case study of Castro's seizure of American marines in Cuba: "Kidnapping to Win Friends and Influence People," *Survey* 20 (1974): 1–40.

31. Scott E. Atkinson, Todd Sandier, and John Tschirhart, "Terrorism in a Bargaining Framework," *Journal of Law and Economics* 30 (1987): 1–21.

2

HISTORY OF TERRORISM

History is a relentless master. It has no present, only the past rushing into the future.
To try to hold fast is to be swept aside.

—John Fitzgerald Kennedy

To study the history of terrorism is to study the history of human civilization. From the murder of Julius Caesar in 44 B.C. to the atrocious airplane attacks of September 11, 2001, to the battle between Israel and Lebanon's Hizbollah in 2006, terrorists have been the cause of many of the monumental events of human experience. Terrorism has been part of the history of virtually every country in the world, and its causes have varied widely over time and place.

This chapter links the terrorist act with the terrorist philosophy by highlighting a few of the major moments and people in the history of terrorism. The discussion analyzes how social, economic, political, and religious conditions have fueled terrorism over the centuries.

By dagger or dynamite, by bullet or bomb, terrorists have sought to achieve their goals through whatever technologies were available to them. The technology of mass destruction is now potentially part of the terrorists' arsenal. Yet, despite changes in its manifestations, modern terrorism is similar in many ways to terrorism of earlier eras. Many of the concerns that motivate today's terrorists have existed over the entire span of human history. Many of the terrorist organizations of the 21st century are inspired by events that occurred hundreds, even thousands, of years ago. Contemporary terrorist groups often justify their actions in terms of theoretical arguments that were popular in much earlier eras. It is this connection between past and present that makes understanding the history of terrorism so fundamental to understanding modern terrorism.

EARLY JUSTIFICATIONS FOR TERRORISM

The concept of terrorism is closely linked to the great theoretical debates of history. Since antiquity, philosophers have asked whether, and under what conditions, it is permissible to kill a political opponent. Some early Greeks, for example, glorified the killing of a tyrant (tyrannicide).

To many of history's great thinkers, violent resistance to a despotic ruler was not a crime: It was a civic duty. The Greek philosopher Aristotle (384–322 B.C.) presented several examples of assassinated tyrants who deserved their fate.

Aristotle argued that there

are two chief motives which induce men to attack tyrannies—hatred and contempt. Hatred of tyrants is inevitable, and contempt is also a frequent cause of their destruction. Thus we see that most of those who have acquired, have retained their power, but those who have inherited, have lost it, almost at once; for living in luxurious ease, they have become contemptible, and offer many opportunities to their assailants. Anger, too, must be included under hatred, and produces the same effects. It is oftentimes even more ready to strike—the angry are more impetuous in making an attack, for they do not listen to reason. And men are very apt to give way to their passions when they are insulted. (*Politics,* Book V, as quoted in Laqueur, 1978, pp. 12–13)

Those who killed tyrants were often seen as heroes, as was Brutus, the assassin of the Roman emperor Julius Caesar. Cicero, although not part of the assassination plot, justified the killing when he wrote that

there can be no such thing as fellowship with tyrants, nothing but bitter feud is possible. . . . For, as we amputate a limb in which the blood and the vital spirit have ceased to circulate, because it injures the rest of the body, so monsters, who, under human guise, conceal the cruelty and ferocity of a wild beast, should be severed from the common body of humanity. (*De Officiis,* as quoted in Laqueur, 1978, p. 16)

The terrorist attack on Julius Caesar has remained a potent symbol spanning the centuries. Political leaders always been the targets of terrorists. When, in 1865, John Wilkes Booth jumped onto the stage at the Ford Theatre shouting in Latin, "sic semper tyrannis" ("thus always to tyrants"), the despot he felt justified in killing was Abraham Lincoln, president of the United States (Poland, 1988, p. 180).

The Jewish Zealots of the first century, also known as the Sicarii, constituted one of the earliest large-scale terrorist organizations. Their goal was to prevent Roman rule over Judaea (now Israel). They died for their efforts in a mass suicide at Masada in 20 A.D., but not before they had incited an insurrection of the populace against the Roman occupation of Judaea. This ancient terrorism organization is analyzed more fully at the end of this chapter in the reprinted article by David Rapoport (1984).

RELIGIOUS TERRORISM: GUY FAWKES AND THE GUNPOWDER PLOT

Another religiously inspired terrorist group, whose best-known member was Guy Fawkes, was much less successful than the Zealots in attracting popular support. Many people have heard of Guy Fawkes—in Great Britain, there is a holiday named for him—but most people don't know that he was caught red-handed in 1605 trying to blow up London's Houses of Parliament (see, e.g., Fraser, 1996; Haynes, 1994; Nicholls, 1991).

Fawkes and about a dozen other conspirators hoped to kill King James I of England and all the government officials who would be attending the opening day of Parliament. The plot (known as the Gunpowder or Papacy Plot) was foiled after the king was shown an anonymous letter warning a brother-in-law of one of the co-conspirators to stay away from Parliament on opening day. On November 5, 1605, the king's officials captured Fawkes, who was guarding the gunpowder. The others fled, but they were soon tracked down. The terrorists were dragged through the streets of London and then brutally drawn and quartered by galloping horses before the crowds at Westminster.

Like many terrorists throughout history, Fawkes and his colleagues justified their actions in terms of religion. Like other instances of "holy terror," the Gunpowder Plot was deeply rooted in events that had occurred long before. In 1529, King Henry VIII was obsessed with producing a male heir and maintaining his dynasty. He asked Pope Clement VII for an annulment from his marriage to Catherine of Aragon to marry Anne Boleyn in hopes of having a son, but the pope

Photo 2.1   An effigy of Guy Fawkes is paraded during Bonfire Night celebrations in England. The festivities include the burning of an effigy representing Guy Fawkes' unsuccessful attempt in 1605 to blow up the Houses of Parliament.

refused. The king retaliated by separating from the Roman Catholic Church and forming the Church of England, with himself as its head. The king accomplished the break from Rome with the help of Parliament, which passed a variety of laws giving the king power over religious affairs.

The king's chancellor, Thomas Cromwell, confiscated Catholic Church property and closed the monasteries. When Elizabeth I came to power in 1558, Catholics were driven underground. After 1563, all of the Queen's subjects were required to swear an oath attesting that Elizabeth was the Supreme Governor of the Church. Catholics who refused to submit to the Church of England were known as recusants.

Guy Fawkes, who used the alias John Johnson, was among those recusants. Many of the recusants were aristocrats, who wanted to instigate a counter-reformation and install the Roman pope as head of England. Fawkes and his co-conspirators incorrectly believed that Catholics in England would rise up against the government after the bombing of Parliament. Like many other terrorists throughout history, Fawkes grossly misjudged the mood of others of his religion, most of whom were content to keep their religious practices secret while publicly swearing obedience to the monarch. Today, Guy Fawkes Day is celebrated each November 5 with bonfires, fireworks, and burning of effigies of Fawkes, all commemorating the failure of the conspirators to blow Parliament and James I sky high.

Religious motives are often cited as a justification for much of contemporary terrorism. Yet, the desire for political power may be an equally strong motive for many so-called religious terrorists. For example, Doran (2002) argues that Osama bin Laden's primary motive on 9/11 was to overthrow the pro-U.S. governments of some Arab and Muslim nations, including Saudi Arabia, Egypt, and Pakistan. Religious and political motivations are often difficult to separate.

STATE-SPONSORED TERRORISM: THE FRENCH REVOLUTION

Religious impulses have not been the only driving force behind terrorism. The Enlightenment and other intellectual movements of the 18th century challenged the divine right of kings, arguing against a society of privilege and in favor of a political system that recognized the equality of men. The squalid conditions that defined the lives of most people stood in stark contrast to the extravagant wealth of the aristocrats. Terrorists of the 18th and 19th centuries fought against the system that conferred amazing riches on a few and subjected all others to hard work and deprivation.

Not only have hereditary rulers and their representatives been targeted for assassination by terrorists who reject the existing government but in addition revolutionary governments have themselves turned on their citizens, launching terrorist attacks of breath-taking cruelty and slaughtering untold numbers of civilians.

It was through such state-sponsored evil that the word *terrorism* entered our lexicon. On July 14, 1789, a French mob attacked the Bastille prison in Paris, massacring the soldiers stationed there. The rioters later walked through the streets carrying the heads of the prison commandant and several of the guards on pikes. The mob was supported by a group of radical revolutionaries, who soon gained control of the government. In October of the same year, the radicals forced King Louis XVI and the royal family to move from Versailles to Paris; later, the king unsuccessfully tried to flee. He ultimately was tried by the revolutionary court and, on January 21, 1793, was executed.

Immediately after the execution of the king, the Committee of Public Safety and the Revolutionary Tribunal were established under the leadership of Maximilien Robespierre, and the *régime de la terreur* began. From May 1793 to July 1794, the new government engaged in widespread surveillance of all strata of society, searching for possible enemies of the revolution (see, e.g., Blanning, 1998; Hunt, 1998; Lefebvre, 1962).

Robespierre and his followers depicted themselves as saviors of the people and portrayed terrorism as the solution to internal anarchy and external invasion by other European monarchs. Arrests were made on the flimsiest evidence, and people were expelled from the country, imprisoned, and executed, all in the name of the revolutionary cause.

Scholars disagree about how many people fell victim to state-sponsored terrorism in France. Estimates of the number of executions range from 17,000 (Anderson & Sloan, 1995, p. xxiii) to 40,000 (Hoffman, 1998, p. 16). Between 300,000 and 500,000 people were arrested, and up to 200,000 may have died in prison as the result of either starvation or brutal treatment (Crenshaw & Pimlott, 1997, p. 48). In Lyon, 700 people were sentenced to death by the revolutionaries and gunned down by cannons in the village square. In Nantes, boats holding thousands of prisoners were sunk in the Loire River (Crenshaw & Pimlott, 1997, pp. 46, 48).

Like modern terrorists, the French revolutionaries took advantage of technological advances. Dr. Joseph Guillotine, the inventor of a new execution technology, saw himself as a humanitarian. His machine was intended to make capital punishment less painful to the victim. Dr. Guillotine's idea for a "merciful killing machine" was the perfect fit for France's ruthless state-sponsored terrorism.

The end came for Robespierre when he announced in the summer of 1794 that he had a new list of enemies of the state. Fearing that their names might be on the list, a group of deputies

PHOTO 2.2   The storming of the Bastille, July 14, 1789. Painting by Jean-Pierre Louis Laurent Houel.

staged a coup d'état, and Robespierre was assassinated. The so-called White Terror followed, with victims of the reign of terror attacking the former terrorists. Not until Napoleon Bonaparte came to power 1799 was the counter-revolution crushed.

In his youth, Robespierre was opposed to violence and cast himself as a humanitarian, yet he is remembered in history as a prototype for such brutal dictators as Adolf Hitler of Germany, Benito Mussolini of Italy, Joseph Stalin of Russia, and Pol Pot of Cambodia. The second reprint at the end of this chapter by Kets de Vries (2006) provides an in-depth examination of some of history's most vicious state sponsors of terrorism.

POLITICAL TERRORISM: ANARCHISTS AND PROPAGANDA BY DEED

Hereditary rulers and their representatives all over the world have often been the targets of anarchists, who rejected all ruling authority. Most anarchists simply gave speeches and handed out leaflets, a few published newspapers, and some became terrorists. As was true for other revolutionaries, their acts of terrorism had philosophical justifications.

In 1849, a German radical, Karl Heinzen, published *Der Mord* (Murder), which has been called "the most important ideological statement of early terrorism" (Laqueur, 1978, p. 47). Heinzen justified political murder in terms of its positive impact on history:

> We must call a spade a spade. The truth must out, whether it seems amiable or terrible, whether it is dressed in the white of peace or the red of war. Let us then be frank and honest, let us tear away the veil and spell out in plain speech what the lesson is which is now being illustrated every day before our eyes in the form of actions and threats, blood and torture, cannons and gallows by both princes and freedom-fighters . . . ; to wit, that murder is the principal agent of historical progress. (Heinzen, 1849, quoted in Laqueur, 1978, p. 53)

In a chilling prelude to Hitler's Nazi era, Heinzen justified terrorism on a massive scale: "If you have to blow up half a continent and pour out a sea of blood in order to destroy the party of the barbarians, have no scruples or conscience" (quoted in Laqueur, 1987, p. 28). Heinzen foresaw the importance of technology to terrorism, and he even suggested that prizes be given to researchers who developed more powerful explosives and poisons (Laqueur, 1977).

John Most, whose newspaper *Freiheit* was published in London, was a strident supporter of terrorism. The September 13, 1884, issue of his newspaper contained his "Advice for Terrorists," in which he asked, "What is the purpose of the anarchists' threats—an eye for an eye, a tooth for a tooth—if they are not followed up by action?" He advised fellow anarchists to get money for their operations any way they could, and he chastised anyone who complained about ruthless methods:

> No one who considers the deed itself to be right can take offense at the manner in which the funds for it are acquired. . . . So let us hear no more of this idiotic talk of "moral indignation" as "robbery" and "theft" from the mouths of socialists, this sort of blathering is really the most stupid nonsense possible. (Most, 1884, as quoted in Laqueur, 1978, p. 101)

Later, Most published a book with the following subtitle: *A Handbook of Instruction Regarding the Use and Manufacture of Nitroglycerine, Dynamite, Gun Cotton, Fulminating Mercury, Bombs, Arson, Poisons, etc.* (Vetter & Perlstein, 1991, p. 32). Again, terrorists made use of technological and scientific advances. Today's cyberterrorism is no exception to this historical pattern.

Carlo Pisacane, an Italian anarchist, is credited with developing the concept that would become known as "propaganda by the deed" (Hoffman, 1998; Laqueur, 1977). Pisacane argued that the masses were too exhausted at the end of their long working day to read leaflets and listen to speeches and that only violent actions could catch their attention: "The propaganda of the idea is a chimera. Ideas result from deeds, not the latter from the former, and the people will not be free when they are educated, but educated when they are free" (as quoted in Hoffman, 1998, p. 16). The phrase "propaganda by deed" was coined around 1886 by Paul Brousse, a French anarchist (Stafford, 1971).

Political Terrorism of the Russian Narodnaya Volya

One of the early anarchistic theorists, the Russian Michael Bakunin, published a manifesto in 1848 calling on the Russian people to revolt against the tsar and attack state officials (Vetter & Perlstein, 1991). His advice was taken by one of the most successful, if short-lived, terrorist groups in history: the Narodnaya Volya.

A secret society of about 500 members, the Narodnaya Volya existed from 1878 to 1881. It is credited as being the first group to put into practice Pisacane's "propaganda by deed." Unlike the state-sponsored terrorists in the French Revolution, who jailed and killed thousands of their countrymen, the Russian terrorists targeted only high-level officials. The Narodnaya Volya counted on toppling the tsar's regime as a result of their assassinations: "If ten or fifteen pillars of the establishment were killed at one and the same time, the government would panic and would lose its freedom of action. At the same time, the masses would wake up" (Laqueur, 1977, p. 34).

Land distribution was at the heart of the struggle in Russia. In 1861, Tsar Alexander II abolished serfdom and lifted strict government controls over freedom of speech and assembly. These progressive actions were influenced by the ideas of the European Enlightenment, but they would prove to be the tsar's undoing and lead eventually to his assassination.

The newly freed serfs expected to be given the land that they had always tended, plus additional land, but the rich landowners had other ideas. Former serfs were forced to pay high prices for small parcels of land. Some of the Russian aristocracy rebelled against their own class and made quick use of the new freedoms of expression to criticize the tsar for the continued enslavement of the lower classes.

The Narodnaya Volya terrorist group was guided by the ideas contained in the famous booklet from 1869 called the *Catechism of the Revolutionist* by Sergey Nechaev (quoted in Laqueur, 2004, pp. 71–76), which taught that the true revolutionary must always be prepared to face torture or death and must give up love, friendship, and gratitude in the single-minded pursuit of his mission. The *Catechism* discusses the principles guiding the true revolutionary. The revolutionary has

> only one science, the science of destruction. To this end, and this end alone, he will study mechanics, physics, chemistry, and perhaps medicine. To this end he will study day and night the living science: people, their characters and circumstances and all the features of the present social order at all possible levels. His sole and constant object is the immediate destruction of this vile order. . . . For him, everything is moral which assists the triumph of revolution. Immoral and criminal is everything which stands in its way. (quoted in Laqueur, 1978, pp. 68–69)

Believing that the tsar's regime was evil and that society could not advance until it was overthrown, the Narodnaya Volya assassinated prominent officials in the tsar's government, including police chiefs, government agency heads, members of the royal family, and the tsar himself. More than a quarter of the Narodnaya Volya members were women (Vetter & Perlstein, 1991). One female terrorist, Vera Zasulich, committed the group's first terrorist act when she tried to assassinate the governor-general of St. Petersburg in July 1877. Another, Vera Figne, was part of the group's last terrorist attack—the murder of the tsar.

Hoffman (1998) tells the story of the tsar's end:

> Four volunteers were given four bombs each and employed along the alternate routes followed by the Tsar's cortege. As two of the bomber assassins stood in wait on the same street, the sleighs carrying the Tsar and his Cossack escort approached the first terrorist, who hurled his bomb at the passing sleigh, missing it by inches. The whole entourage came to a halt as soldiers seized the hapless culprit and the Tsar descended from his sleigh to check on a bystander wounded by the explosion. "Thank God, I am safe," the Tsar reportedly declared—just as the second bomber emerged from the crowd and detonated his weapon, killing both himself and his target. (pp. 18–19)

The end of the Narodnaya Volya came quickly, as its members were caught and hanged. Yet, the seeds planted by this group ultimately sprouted in the Bolshevik Revolution of 1917, which ushered in the communist era. In London, at the first meeting of the International Congress of Anarchists, shortly after the tsar's murder, the activities of the Narodnaya Volya were warmly endorsed (Laqueur, 1977, p. 51).

TERRORISM AND COLONIALISM: THE PHILOSOPHY OF THE BOMB

The Russian terrorists pioneered the systematic use of bombs to destroy their enemies, but it was not until a half-century later that Indian terrorist Bhagwati Charan illegally distributed a manifesto titled *The Philosophy of the Bomb* (Laqueur, 1978, p. 137).

Colonialism and Indian Terrorism

Nationalism and the desire for independence from colonial rulers were at the heart of the social, economic, political, and religious struggle in India. British rule over India began in 1857, and isolated instances of terrorism occurred from the beginning of British colonialism (Laqueur, 1977). In 1947, massive nonviolent resistance to colonial rule led the British to withdraw, and India became independent (see, e.g., Chandra, 1989; Farwell, 1991; French, 1998; Ramarkrishnan, 1994).

Indians opposed to British rule split over tactics. On one side, Mahatma Gandhi and his followers advocated nonviolent resistance to colonial rule. Noncooperation and peaceful civil disobedience were their favored tactics; Gandhi explicitly rejected terrorism. Gandhi wanted Hindus and Muslims to unite against the British, and he wanted the religious strife that had long characterized the subcontinent of Asia to cease.

Bhagwati Charan and his colleagues in the Hindustan Socialist Republican Association (HSRA) took the opposite tack. Their manifesto reasoned that terrorism

> instills fear in the hearts of the oppressors, it brings hope of revenge and redemption to the oppressed masses. It gives courage and self confidence to the wavering, it shatters the spell of the subject race in the eyes of the world, because it is the most convincing proof of a nation's hunger for freedom. . . . It is a pity that Gandhi does not understand and will not understand revolutionary psychology. . . . To think a revolutionary will give up his ideals if public support and appreciation are withdrawn from him is the highest folly. . . . A revolutionary is the last person on the earth to submit to bullying. . . . There is not a crime that Britain has not committed in India. Deliberate misrule has reduced us to paupers, has bled us white. As a race and as a people we stand dishonored and outraged. . . . We shall have our revenge, a people's righteous revenge on the tyrant. (Charan, 1930, excerpted in Laqueur, 1978, pp. 137–140)

Bhagwati Charan not only preached violence but also practiced it. He died when a bomb exploded in his hands (Charan, 2000).

Although the HSRA tried to blow up a train, shot a police officer, and threw bombs from the public gallery in the Legislative Assembly, Gandhi's nonviolent resistance movement was much more effective than terrorist attacks in convincing the British to leave India (Laqueur, 1977). Gandhi's dream for fellowship between Hindus and Muslims was shattered, however, when independence in 1947 was followed by terrible violence between the two sects and the partition of the country into Muslim Pakistan and Hindu India.

Colonialism, Racism, and Algerian Terrorism

France invaded Algeria, in Northern Africa, in 1830. Thereafter, tens of thousands of Western European settlers flocked to Algeria, where they were given land that had been confiscated from the local people. *Pieds-noirs,* the name used for people of European descent, were given full French citizenship, whereas most of the Muslim Algerians received neither citizenship nor the right to vote. The division of society into White (*pieds-noirs*) and Black (Muslim Algerians) tore asunder the fabric of social and cultural life in Algeria.

In 1954, the National Liberation Front (FLN) began a struggle for independence from French colonial rule by attacking military installations, police stations, and public utilities. The French refused to negotiate with the FLN, and over the next eight years, terrorism against civilians on both sides of the conflict resulted in at least 30,000 war-related deaths and probably more. France finally relinquished its hold on Algeria in 1962, after which more than one million *pieds-noirs* fled for France. The leader of the FLN, Ahmed Ben Bella, became Algeria's first president.

The FLN was inspired in large part by the writings and activism of its fellow member and leading political theorist, Frantz Fanon, who was born in 1925 in the French colony of Martinique and who was educated in psychiatry in France. Fanon's *Black Skin, White Mask* (1952/1962) and his *Wretched of the Earth* (1959/1963) became seminal writings in what would come to be known as "postcolonial studies." Fanon's personal experiences as a Black man raised in a White society shaped his psychological theories about culture and revolution. His works inspired anticolonial liberation movements for the remainder of the 20th century, making him one of the preeminent scholars on the psychopathology of colonization.

Fanon argued that the mixture of racism and colonialism blinded the Black man to his subjugation to a White norm and alienated him from his own consciousness. Adopting the language of the conqueror meant implicit acceptance of the collective consciousness of Frenchness, which associated Black with evil and White with good. Thus, the Black man dons a White mask and in the process robs himself of psychological health.

The only viable way to end colonialism and to overcome racism, Fanon said, was through violence and revolution. Violence acts as a cleansing force, according to Fanon, freeing the oppressed from their inferiority complexes and restoring their self-respect. The revolution must start with the peasants, or *fellaheen,* Fanon argued. Not surprisingly, the FLN based its operations in the countryside (see, e.g., Gibson, 1999; Gordon, 1995; Macey, 2000).

Colonialism Makes Latin America a Hotbed of Terrorism

In Latin America, as well as in India and Algeria, terrorism was tied to colonial rule and the desire for self-determination; resistance to the Spanish conquistadors dates from the 16th century. The linkage among terrorism, guerrilla warfare, conventional warfare, and criminal activity is particularly murky in Latin America, where state-sponsored terrorism and brutal military repression have been widespread. During the Cold War with Russia, Latin American dictators were tolerated, even feted, by the United States in the name of anticommunism, providing further justifications for those seeking to use terrorist tactics to depose dictatorial rule (see, e.g., Halperin, 1976; Rosenberg, 1991; Tarazona-Sevillano, 1990).

Both Western and Eastern philosophers heavily influenced the growth of terrorist thought in Latin America. Germany's Karl Marx, Russia's Vladimir Lenin, and China's Mao Zedong were studied carefully by Fidel Castro and Che Guevara, who launched the Cuban Revolution of 1959; by Abimael Guzmán, the founder of Peru's Shining Path, which has been called one of the world's "most elusive, secretive, and brutal guerrilla organizations" (Tarazona-Sevillano, 1990, p. xv); and by Carlos Marighella, the author of the *Manual of the Urban Guerrilla* (1969/1985) and the leader of the Brazilian terrorist organization Action for National Liberation (ALN).

The Urban Guerrilla

Mao Zedong began his revolution in the Chinese countryside, as did the Algerian FLN, but Carlos Marighella thought that urban terrorism should be the first stage of the revolution. From March 1968 through November 1969, the ALN robbed more than 100 banks, blew up military installations, attacked prisons and freed inmates, bombed the buildings of U.S. companies, and kidnapped important people, including an American ambassador (Marighella, 1969/1985, p. 25).

The *Manual of the Urban Guerrilla* may be the most widely read terrorist manual in modern history (Hanrahan, 1985). It has been the official guidebook of many terrorist organizations, including the Italian Red Brigade, the German Red Army Faction, and the Irish Republican Army.

The *Manual of the Urban Guerrilla* lays out the fundamentals of terrorism. It states that terrorists should be in good physical shape so they can withstand the rigors of their chosen craft. They must study chemistry and mechanics, and

> dynamite must be well understood. The use of incendiary bombs, of smoke bombs, and other types is indispensable prior knowledge. To know how to make and repair arms, prepare Molotov cocktails, grenades, mines, homemade destructive devices, how to blow up bridges, tear up and put out of service rails and sleepers, these are requisites in the technical preparation of the urban guerrilla that can never be considered unimportant. (Marighella, 1969/1985, as excerpted in Laqueur, 1978, p. 163)

Marighella advocated "a scorched-earth strategy, the sabotage of transport and oil pipelines, and the destruction of food supplies" (Laqueur, 1977, p. 185). Urban terrorism would create a crisis atmosphere, Marighella argued, causing the government to overreact and repress ordinary people, who would then join the revolution and overthrow the government. Like Guy Fawkes and other terrorists throughout the centuries, Marighella overestimated the will of the people to join in the struggle to topple the government. After he was lured into a trap and killed in a police ambush in 1969, the ALN was crushed.

LESSONS LEARNED FROM HISTORY

Walter Laqueur observes that terrorism has taken so many forms that "[a]ny explanation that attempts to account for all its many manifestations is bound to be either exceedingly vague or altogether wrong" (1977, p. 133). No theory has emerged from political science, criminal justice, economics, philosophy, or any other discipline to satisfactorily explain terrorism.

From all corners of the earth, terrorism has been carried out by ideologues on the left and the right, by wealthy aristocrats and poverty-stricken farmers, and by men and women, although men significantly outnumber women. Similarly, the ends sought by terrorist have varied enormously. Some terrorists hoped to overthrow the government so they could assume power, and autocratic and democratic regimes alike have served as terrorists' targets. Liberating their country from colonial rule has motivated some terrorists, and nationalist and separatist movements have flourished in many places. Religion has been a driving force for some terrorist organizations, whereas others have been decidedly secular. Terrorism often has been directed against governments, but it also has been used by governments to frighten the populace, eliminate perceived enemies, and quell dissent. Terrorist organizations have ranged in size from just a handful of members to many thousands, and many of history's most memorable terrorist acts have been committed by lone individuals without the help of any organization.

Thus, terrorism is a complex phenomenon that varies from country to country and from one era to another. The best way to understand terrorism is to examine the social, economic, political, and religious conditions and philosophies existing at a particular time and place.

Has terrorism been a successful strategy for change? Military historian Caleb Carr (2002), who equates international terrorism with war, argues,

> Perhaps the most significant thing that the terrorists of today share with those who practiced warfare against civilians in earlier times is an abiding inability to see that the strategy of terror is a spectacularly failed one . . . this is a form that has never succeeded. (p. 11)

Carr further notes,

> Warfare against civilians, whether inspired by hatred, revenge, greed, or political and psychological insecurity, has been one of the most ultimately self-defeating tactics in all of military history. . . . And yet those same imperatives—hatred, revenge, greed, and insecurity—have driven nations and factions both great and small to the strategy of terror and the tactic of waging war on civilians time and time again. Some parts of the world, in fact, have become so locked into the cycle of outrages and reprisals against civilians that their histories comprise little else. (p. 12)

Carr insists that "warfare against civilians must never be answered in kind" (p. 13). Yet, he acknowledges that, throughout history, most leaders

> have been unable to resist the temptation to make war against civilians, no matter how threatening to their own interests that indulgence may ultimately have proved to have been—for terror's lure as a seemingly quick and gratifying solution is a powerful one . . . whenever and wherever such tactics have been indulged, they have been and are still destined to ultimately fail. (p. 12)

HIGHLIGHTS OF REPRINTED ARTICLES

The two readings that follow concerning the history of terrorism were selected to provide two different types of comparative analysis. The first article, by David Rapoport, focuses on three manifestations of religious terrorism in different time periods and geographic regions. The second reprinted article, by Manfred F. R. Kets de Vries, examines the development of state-sponsored terrorism and the unusual relationship that has developed over the centuries between despotic leaders and their subjects.

David C. Rapoport (1984). Fear and trembling: Terrorism in three religious traditions. *American Political Science Review, 78*(3), 658–677.

Rapoport's article focuses on the Jewish Zealots-Sicarii of the 1st century, the Islamic Assassins of the 11th through 13th centuries, and the Hindu Thugs of the 13th through 19th centuries. Longer lasting and, in that sense, more successful than modern terrorist groups, these three early versions of groups advocating "holy terror" are revealing for what they teach us about contemporary terrorism.

Rapoport disputes the myth that terrorism has increased as technology has advanced. Terrorists have always had weapons, transportation, and communication—no matter how rudimentary. From the sword of the Zealots-Sicarii to the dagger of the Assassins to the silk scarf noose of the Thugs, terrorists have used whatever technology was available to them. Rapoport concludes that "the critical variable cannot be technology; rather, the purpose and organizations of particular groups and the vulnerabilities of particular societies to them are decisive factors" (1984, p. 659) in understanding terrorism. Rapoport thus echoes the theme emphasized throughout this book: Understanding the culture, religion, politics, economics, and ideology of a country and its people is the best way to comprehend the phenomena of terrorism.

Table 2.1 compares key features of these three ancient terrorist organizations. Their objectives were in many ways similar to those of contemporary terrorists. The parallels between past and present are revisited in subsequent chapters.

TABLE 2.1   "Holy Terror": Comparisons of Three Terrorist Organizations

	Thugs	*Assassins*	*Zealots-Sicarii*
Religion	Hinduism	Islam	Judaism
Country of origin	India	Persia (Middle East)	Judaea (Israel)
Years of duration	600+ (13th–19th centuries)	200+ (11th–13th centuries)	25+ (1st century)
Method of attack	Noose	Dagger	Sword
Primary victims	Travelers on remote roads	Political elites in public places	Prominent Jews, especially priests, in public places; Greek citizens and Roman rulers
Intended audience	Kali, God of Terror—avoided publicity	God and Islamic world—sought publicity	God and Jews in Judaea and Roman occupiers—sought publicity
Objective	Human sacrifices to the god Kali (victims' suffering pleases Kali)	Purify/spread Islam (political conquest for religious purposes)	Mass insurrection against Roman rulers (national liberation)
Contemporary parallels	Religious fanatics and cults that shun publicity	Middle Eastern martyrs (*fidayeen*) for Islam	Movements to overthrow colonial rulers in South America and Asia

Manfred F. R. Kets de Vries (2006). The spirit of despotism: Understanding the tyrant within. *Human Relations, 59*(2), 195–220.

The second reading explores the dynamics underlying some of history's most tyrannical regimes. Despots from the earliest eras—such as Caligula, Nero, Vlad the Impaler, and Ivan the Terrible—were replaced in later eras by the likes of Joseph Stalin, Adolf Hitler, Mao Zedong, Pol Pot, and Idi Amin. More recently, state sponsors of terrorism have included Kim Jong Il of North Korea, Saddam Hussein of Iraq, Robert Mugabe of Zimbabwe, and the late Slobodan Milošević of Yugoslavia.

The article provides insights on the self-destructive relationships that despots and their subjects, leading to the disintegration of the moral fiber of society. State sponsors of terrorism, whether perpetuated against their own subjects, citizens of other countries, or both, have been a hallmark of tyrannical regimes throughout history.

EXPLORING THE HISTORY OF TERRORISM FURTHER

- Several chronologies of terrorism are available on the Internet. One Web site, maintained by the Office of the Historian for the U.S. Department of State, briefly discusses the major terrorist events between 1961 and 2003. Its Web address is http://www.state.gov/r/pa/ho/pubs/fs/5902.htm. Find as many other Internet sites containing chronologies as you can.
- The history of anarchism, along with pictures of some of the world's most remembered anarchists, including Michael Bakunin, Peter Kropotkin, and Emma Goldman, can be found at http:// dwardmac.pitzer.edu/anarchist_archives/index.html. Can you think of any contemporary parallels to the anarchists of earlier eras?
- Some people consider the United States to be among the worst state sponsors of terrorism in the world. Examples that are used to support this claim include the "American genocide" of the Native people of America in the 1600s, the U.S. intervention in the Philippines from 1945 to 1953, and the U.S. involvement in China from 1945 to 1953. Examine these and other events from U.S. history and discuss why you believe that the United States was (or was not) a state sponsor of terrorism. What examples from contemporary U.S. interventions might qualify as state-sponsored terrorism?
- Briefly describe the three ancient terrorist organizations discussed by David Rapoport (reprint #1). Focus on the ways in which these three groups were alike and the ways in which they were not alike. Then, discuss any ways in which these groups are similar or dissimilar to contemporary terrorist organizations.
- What is David Rapoport's thesis in regards to technology and terrorism? What does Rapoport believe causes terrorism?
- The Rapoport reprint was published in 1984. Would Rapoport likely change his thesis if he were writing the article today? Why or why not?
- Kets de Vries, the author of the second reprint for this chapter, discusses the concept of "inner rot." Clarify this theory, describe its characteristics, and explain why it can result in ruin for despotic regimes.
- According to Kets de Vries, what are the differences between totalitarianism and authoritarianism? What are the similarities?
- What part does religion play in totalitarianism regimes? How important a role does it play?
- What does Kets de Vries think about wars of insurrection to topple despots? What circumstances would justifiy the assassination of an abusive leader? What other options are available?

VIDEO NOTES

Many historical films about regional and class conflicts might be useful for envisioning the present global situation. For example, the history of the Irish Republican Army is portrayed in *Michael Collins* (Warner Bros., 1996, 132 min.).

Another classic video is *Battle of Algiers* (Criterion Collection, 1966, 125 min.). Portraying the French Foreign Legion using the tactic of torture and the Algerians using homemade bombs, this gripping film presents an unbiased account of one of the bloodiest revolutions in modern history.

Fear and Trembling

Terrorism in Three Religious Traditions

David C. Rapoport

As the first comparative study of religious terror groups, this article provides detailed analyses of the different doctrines and methods of the three best-known groups: the Thugs, Assassins, and Zealots-Sicarii. Despite using primitive technology, each developed much more durable and destructive organizations than has any modern secular group.

The differences among the groups reflect the distinguishing characteristics of their respective originating religious communities: Hinduism, Islam, and Judaism. The distinctive characteristics of religious terror are discussed, and relationships between religious and secular forms of terror are suggested.

In 1933 *The Encyclopaedia of the Social Sciences* published fascinating, useful articles on assassination (Lerner) and terrorism (Hardman), which ended on a strange note, namely that the phenomena, which had reached an exceptionally high point at the turn of the century, were declining so much that the subjects would remain interesting only to antiquarians. Future events would be determined by classes and masses, because modern technology had made our world so complex that we had become increasingly *invulnerable* to determined actions by individuals or small groups. Terrorist activity became extensive again after World War II, not in Europe and America, as was the case earlier, but in western colonial territories, particularly in the Palestine Mandate, Cyprus, Malaya, Kenya, Vietnam, and Algeria. But the second edition of the *Encyclopaedia*, which was published in 1968, ignored both subjects; perhaps the editors believed the prophecies in the earlier edition!

Academics returned to the subject when terrorist activity revived again in the center of the Western world. The flow of articles and books began in the 1970s, and that flow continues to increase every year. A journal entitled *Terrorism* has been established, and many universities offer courses on the subject. As they did 50 years ago, political scientists dominate the field, and in some respects the conventional wisdom governing terrorist studies has not changed: the technological, not the political, environment is normally seen as the decisive determining condition for terrorist activity. Many contemporary studies begin, for example, by stating that although terrorism has always been a feature of social existence, it became "significant" for the first time in the 1960s when it "increased in frequency" and took on "novel dimensions" as an international or transnational activity, creating in the process a new "mode of conflict." The most common explanation for this "new mode of conflict" is that now we are experiencing the cumulative impacts of specific developments in modern technology. Individuals and tiny groups have capacities that they previously lacked. Weapons are cheaper, more destructive, easier to obtain and to conceal. "The technological quantum jumps from the arrow to the revolver and from the gun to the Molotov Cocktail" (Hacker, 1976, p. ix). Modern communications and transport allow hitherto insignificant persons to coordinate activity quickly over vast spaces. Finally, by giving unusual events extensive coverage, the mass media complete the picture. "You can't be a revolutionary without a color TV: it's as necessary as a gun" (Rubin, 1970, p. 108).

Although one can never be sure of what is meant by the term "modern terrorism," the characterizations normally focus on increases in the number of incidents or amounts of damage and on the fact that assaults transcend state borders. Because early experiences are insignificant in these respects, they are deemed irrelevant. One purpose of this article is to show that this view is simply wrong and that the past can provide materials for useful comparisons.

I shall do this by a detailed analysis of three groups: the Thugs, the Assassins, and the Zealots-Sicarii.[2] I have chosen them for several reasons. They are the examples most often cited to illustrate the ancient lineage of terrorism, but they are not discussed in our literature. We cite them because they are so well known elsewhere; no other early terror group has received as much attention. Ironically, although the words thug, assassin, and zealot have even become part of our vocabulary (often to describe terrorists), and most educated persons can identify the groups, they have never been compared.

The cases are inherently interesting and peculiarly instructive. Each group was much more durable and much more destructive than any modern one has been; operating on an international stage, they had great social effects too. Yet the noose, the dagger, and the sword were the principal weapons they employed, travel was by horse or foot, and the most effective means of communication was by word of mouth. Although a relatively simple and common technology prevailed, each example displayed strikingly different characteristics. The critical variable, therefore, cannot be technology: rather, the purpose and organization of particular groups and the vulnerabilities of particular societies to them are decisive factors. Although the point may be more easily seen in these cases, it must be relevant, I shall argue, in our world too.

Furthermore, the three cases illustrate a kind of terror nowhere adequately analyzed in our theoretical literature, terror designated here as holy or sacred (cf. Laqueur, 1977; Price, 1977; Rapoport, 1971, 1977, 1982a; Thornton, 1964; Walter, 1969). Before the nineteenth century, religion provided the only acceptable justifications for terror, and the differences between sacred and modern expressions (differences of nature, not scale) raise questions about the appropriateness of contemporary definitions. The holy terrorist believes that only a transcendent purpose which fulfills the meaning of the universe can justify terror, and that the deity reveals at some early moment in time both the end and means and may even participate in the process as well. We see terrorists as free to seek different political ends in this world by whatever means of terror they consider most appropriate. This trait characterizes modern terrorism since its inception in the activities of Russian anarchists more than a century ago, and it is found also in many modern terrorist organizations in our century that have had important religious dimensions, i.e., the IRA, EOKA (Cyprus), the FLN (Algeria), and the Irgun (Israel). Sacred terror, on the other hand, never disappeared altogether, and there are signs that it is reviving in new and unusual forms.

As instances of sacred terror, the Thugs, the Assassins, and the Zealots-Sicarii seem remarkably different from each other, and hence they provide some orientation to the range of possibilities associated with the concept. On the other hand, each closely resembles other deviant groups within the same parent religion, Hinduism, Islam, and Judaism, and the three kinds of deviant groups reflect or distort themes distinctive to their particular major religion. In the last respect, what seems to be distinctive about modern terrorists, their belief that terror can be organized rationally, represents or distorts a major theme peculiar to our own culture: a disposition to believe that any activity can be made rational.

I shall begin with a detailed analysis of the cases and in an extended conclusion draw out some implications and comparisons. My concern is largely with methods and doctrines, not the social basis of group activity. The order of the presentation (Thugs, Assassins, and Zealots-Sicarii) is designed to carry the reader from situations where only religious ends are served to one where the political purpose seems, but in fact is not, altogether dominant. The order also illustrates an irony, namely that there can be an inverse relationship between proximity in time and distance from us in spirit. Although extinguished in the nineteenth century, the Thugs seem wholly bizarre because they lacked a political purpose, and we invariably treat terror as though it could only serve one. The Assassins, who gave up terror in the thirteenth century, are comprehensible because their ends and methods remind us of nineteenth-century anarchists who originated modern rebel terror and were themselves conscious of affinities. But it is the Zealots-Sicarii, destroyed in the first century, who appear almost as our true contemporaries because they seem to have purposes and methods that we can fully understand. By means of provocation they were successful in generating a mass insurrection, an aim of most modern terrorists, but one that has probably never been achieved. The purpose of the Zealots-Sicarii, it seems, was to secure national liberation inter alia. The striking resemblances between their activities and those of terrorists with whom we are familiar will put us in a better position to conclude by elaborating the differences already suggested between holy and modern terror.

THUGS

"Terror," Kropotkin wrote, is "propaganda by the deed." We are inclined to think of it as a crime for the sake of publicity. When a bomb explodes, people take notice; the event attracts more attention than a thousand speeches or pictures. If the terror is sustained, more and more people will become interested, wondering why the atrocities occurred and whether the cause seems plausible. Hence virtually all modern conceptions of terrorism assume that the perpetrators only mean to harm their victims incidentally. The principal object is the public, whose consciousness will be aroused by the outrage.

For the holy terrorist, the primary audience is the deity, and depending upon his particular religious conception, it is even conceivable that he does not need or want to have the public witness his deed. The Thugs are our most interesting and instructive case in this respect. They intend their victims to experience terror and to express it visibly for the pleasure of Kali, the Hindu goddess of terror and destruction. Thugs strove to avoid publicity, and although fear of Thugs was widespread, that was the unintended

result of their acts. Having no cause that they wanted others to appreciate, they did things that seem incongruous with our conception of how "good" terrorists should behave.

Indeed, one may ask, were the Thugs really terrorists? They are normally identified as such in the academic literature (DeQuincey, 1877; Freedman, 1982; Gupta, 1959; Laqueur, 1977; Lewis, 1967). As persons consciously committing atrocities, acts that go beyond the accepted norms and immunities that regulate violence, they were, according to one established definition, clearly terrorists. Their deceit, unusual weapon (a noose), and practice of dismembering corpses (thereby preventing cremation or proper burial) made Thug violence outrageous by Hindu standards, or, for that matter, by those of any other culture. Cults of this sort may not exist anymore, but as the case of the Zebra Killers or the Fruit of Islam in San Francisco in 1975 demonstrates, the religious purposes of a group may prescribe murders that the public is not meant to notice. A city was terrorized for months, but no one claimed responsibility. It is doubtful whether any American terrorist group produced as much panic as this one did, although terror may not have been its purpose.

No one knows exactly when the Thugs (often called Phansigars or stranglers) first appeared. Few now believe that the ancient Sagartians, whom Herodotus (VII, 85) describes as stranglers serving in the Persian army, are the people whom the British encountered in India some 2,500 years later. [2] But there is evidence that Thugs existed in the seventh century, and almost all scholars agree that they were vigorous in the thirteenth, which means that the group persisted for at least six hundred years. By our standards, the durability of the Thugs is enormous; the IRA, now in its sixth decade, is by far the oldest modern terrorist group.

There are few estimates of the number of people killed by the Thugs. Sleeman (1933) offers a conservative figure of one million for the last three centuries of their history. [10] This figure seems too large, but half that number may be warranted, and that, indeed, is an astonishing figure, especially when one remembers that during the life of modern terrorist organizations, the deaths they cause rarely exceed several hundred, and it would be difficult to find one group that is directly responsible for more than ten thousand deaths. The Thugs murdered more than any known terrorist group, partly because they lasted so much longer. Their impact on Indian economic life must have been enormous, although there is no way to calculate it. If the significance of a terrorist group is to be understood by these measures, the Thugs should be reckoned the most important ever known. The paradox is that, unlike most terrorist groups, they did not or could not threaten society for the simple reason that their doctrine made them attack individuals rather than institutions.

The reinterpretation of a cardinal Hindu myth and theme provided the Thugs with their peculiar purpose and method. Orthodox Hindus believed that in early times a gigantic monster devoured humans as soon as they were created. Kali (also known as Bhavani, Devi, and Durga) killed the monster with her sword, but from each drop of its blood another demon sprang up, and as she killed each one, the spilled blood continued to generate new demons. The orthodox maintained that Kali solved the problem of the multiplying demons by licking the blood from their wounds. But the Thugs believed that Kali sought assistance by making two men from her sweat who were given handkerchiefs from her garment in order to strangle the demons, that is, kill them without shedding a drop of blood. Upon completing their mission, they were commanded to keep the handkerchiefs for their descendants.

In Hindu mythology Kali has many dimensions. She represents the energy of the universe, which means, as the legend suggests, that she both sustains and destroys life. She is also the goddess of time, who presides over endless cycles in which both essential aspects of the life process are carried out. The Thug understood that he was obliged to supply the blood that Kali, his creator, required to keep the world in equilibrium. His responsibility was to keep himself alive as long as possible so that he could keep killing, and it has been estimated that each Thug participated in three murders annually: one claimed to have helped strangle 931 persons.[12] No one retired until he was physically unable to participate in expeditions. The logic of the cycle or balance required the brotherhood to keep its numbers relatively constant. New recruits came largely from the children of Thugs, and the deficiencies were made up by outsiders. The children were initiated into the tradition early by a carefully calculated gradual process—a circumstance that contributed to their resoluteness. Adult Thugs never seemed to experience revulsion, but sometimes the young did; invariably the cases involved those who witnessed events before they were supposed to. Drugs were used rarely, and then only among the young.

For obscure religious reasons Thugs attacked only travellers, and although they confiscated the property of their victims, material gain was not their principal concern, as indicated by their custom of "distinguish(ing) their most important exploits" not by the property gained but "by the number who were killed, the Sixty Soul Affair . . . the Sacrifice of Forty" (Russell & Hira, 1916, vol. 4, p. 567). The legend of their origin also shows murder to be the Thugs' main business, murder in which the death agony was deliberately prolonged to give Kali ample time to enjoy the terror expressed by the victims. It was forbidden to take property without killing and burying its owner first. The Thugs judged the ordinary thief as morally unfit.[13] When religious omens were favorable, many without property were murdered. Similarly, unfavorable omens protected rich travellers.

Although murder was the Thugs' main object, they needed loot—enormous quantities of it—to pay princes who provided their expeditions with international sanctuaries. Without those sanctuaries the brotherhood would not have persisted for such a long time. As we have learned again and again in the contemporary world, when international sanctuaries are provided, relations between states are exacerbated constantly. After numerous frustrating experiences, British authorities decided that appropriate cooperation from neighboring native states was not forthcoming. Nor did recourse to doctrines of hot pursuit prove adequate (Sleeman, 1836, p. 48).[14] Ultimately, the international law governing piracy was utilized, enabling British officials to seize and punish Thugs wherever they were found. The cost was a more massive violation of the rights of independent states, culminating in a direct expansion of imperial jurisdictions, the result that critics of the policy feared most.

A striking feature of Thug operations was that virtually all activity was hemmed in by self-imposed restraints. From the moment he joined an annual sacred expedition until it was disbanded, a Thug was governed by innumerable rules, laid down by Kali, that specified victims, methods of attack, divisions of labor, disposal of corpses, distribution of booty, and training of new members. In a sense, there were no choices to be made because in dubious circumstances Kali manifested her views through omens.

British observers were impressed with the extraordinary "rationality" of the rules established. "Whatever the true source may be, (the system) is beyond all doubt the work of a man of genius, no ordinary man could have fenced and regulated it with so elaborate a code of rules—rules which the Thugs seem to believe are of divine origin, but in each of which we can trace a shrewd practical purpose" (Sleeman, 1839, p. 31). "Ridiculous as their superstitions must appear . . . they serve the most important purposes of cementing the union of the gang, of kindling courage, and confidence; and by an appeal to religious texts deemed infallible of imparting to their atrocities the semblance of divine sanction" (A religion of murder, 1901, p. 512). "The precautions they take, the artifices they practice, the mode of destroying their victims, calculated at once to preclude any possibility of rescue or escape—of witnesses of the deed—of noises or cries for help—of effusion of blood and, in general of trades of murder. These circumstances conspire to throw a veil of darkness over their atrocities" (Sherwood, 1820, p. 263).

The list of persons immune from attack—women, vagabonds, lepers, the blind, the mutilated, and members of certain artisan crafts (all considered descendants of Kali, like the Thugs themselves)—suggests, perhaps, that the cult may once have had a political purpose. Nonetheless, there can be no politics without publicity.

Whatever purpose these rules were designed to serve, they could not be altered even when the life of the brotherhood was at stake, because they were perceived to be divine ordinances. Europeans, for example, were immune from attack—a prohibition that virtually enabled Thugs to escape attention. When the Thugs were discovered, the same rule kept them from retaliating directly against the small, relatively unprotected group of British administrators who ultimately exterminated them. Their commitment to rules produced another unanticipated consequence: in the nineteenth century when some of its members became increasingly concerned with loot, the brotherhood became lax. This gave the British a unique opportunity to persuade older, more tradition-bound members that the ancient Thug belief that Kali would destroy the order when its members no longer

served her required them now to help their goddess by becoming informers.

To us, a Thug is a brute, ruffian, or cutthroat, but the word originally signified deceiver, and the abilities of Thugs to deceive distinguish them radically from other related Hindu criminal associations, which also worshipped Kali but "exercised their (criminal) profession *without* disguise." Thugs literally lived two very different sorts of lives, which continually amazed the British. For the greater portion of the year (sometimes 11 out of 12 months), Thugs were models of propriety, known for their industry, temperance, generosity, kindliness, and trustworthiness. British officers who unwittingly had employed them as guardians for their children lavishly praised the reliability of Thugs who had strangled hundreds of victims. An extraordinary capacity for deception was a cardinal feature of Thug tactics too. Long journeys in India always involved great hazards, requiring parties large enough to repel attacks by marauders. Groups of Thugs disguised as travellers, sometimes numbering as many as 60 persons, were often successful in persuading legitimate travellers to join forces, thereby increasing the security of all. In some cases, the intimate congenial associations would last months before the opportunity to strike occurred. (Strangling is a difficult art and requires exceptional conditions.) Usually, close contacts of this sort create bonds between people which make cold-blooded murder difficult. In fact, the striking way in which intimacy can transform relationships between potential murderers and their victims in our own day has stimulated academics to invent a new concept—the Stockholm syndrome (Lang, 1974). But the Thugs seemed indifferent to the emotions that make such transformations possible, testifying that pity or remorse never prevented them from acting. Nonetheless, their victims were never abused. The early judicial records and interviews do not provide a single case of wanton cruelty: the victims were sacrifices, the property of Kali, and, as in all religions, the best sacrifices are those offered without blemish.[18] "A Thug considers the persons murdered precisely in the light of victims offered up to the Goddess, and he remembers them, as a Priest of Jupiter remembered the oxen and as a Priest of Saturn the children sacrificed upon the altars" (Sleeman, 1836, p. 8).

Thugs believed that death actually benefited the victim, who would surely enter paradise, whereas Thugs who failed to comply with Kali's commands would become impotent, and their families would become either extinct or experience many misfortunes. British observers admired the cheerfulness of convicted Thugs about to be hanged, sublimely confident that they would be admitted to paradise.[19] Thugs spoke also of the personal pleasure that their particular methods generated. "Do you ever feel remorse for murdering in cold blood, and after the pretense of friendship, those whom you have beguiled into a false sense of security?" a British interrogator asked. "Certainly not. Are you yourself not a hunter of big game, and do you not enjoy the thrill of the stalk, the pitting of your cunning against that of an animal, and are you not pleased at seeing it dead at your feet? So it is with the Thug, who indeed regards the stalking of men as a higher form of sport. For you *sahib* have but the instincts of wild beasts to overcome, whereas the Thug has to subdue the suspicions and fear of intelligent men . . . often heavily guarded, and familiar with the knowledge that the roads are dangerous. Game for our hunting is defended from all points save those of flattering and cunning. Cannot you imagine the pleasure of overcoming such protection during days of travel in their company, the joy in seeing suspicion change to friendship until that wonderful moment arrives. . . . Remorse, *sahib*? Never! Joy and elation often" (Sleeman, 1839, pp. 3–4).

ASSASSINS

The Assassins (known also as Ismailis-Nizari) survived two centuries (1090–1275). Unlike the Thugs they had political objectives; their purpose was to fulfill or purify Islam, a community whose political and religious institutions were inseparable. Although by Thug standards they inflicted few casualties and wrought negligible economic damage, the Assassins seriously threatened the governments of several states, especially those of the Turkish Seljuk Empire in Persia and Syria.

As Weber (1955, p. 2) pointed out, Islam has always been preeminently dedicated to delivering a moral message aimed at transforming social existence in *this* world. Terror in Islam, therefore, has an extra dimension not present in Hinduism. The Thugs were concerned with three parties (the assailant, his victim, and a deity), but the Assassins reached out to a fourth one as well, a public or a moral community whose sympathies could be aroused by deeds that evoked attention. They did not need mass media to reach interested audiences, because their prominent victims were murdered in venerated sites and royal courts, usually on holy days when many witnesses would be present.

To be noticed is one thing, to be understood is another, and when the object of a situation is to arouse a public, those threatened will try to place their own interpretations on the terrorist's message. Their opportunities to do so will be maximized if the assailant breaks down, or even if he tries to evade arrest. The doctrine of the Assassins seems constructed to prevent both possibilities. One who intends his act to be a public spectacle is unlikely to escape in any case. The Assassins prepared the assailant for this circumstance by preventing him from even entertaining the idea that he might survive. His weapon, which "was always a dagger, never poison, never a missile," seems designed to make certain that he would be captured or killed. He usually made no attempt to escape; there is even a suggestion that to survive a mission was shameful. The words of a twelfth-century Western author are revealing: "When, therefore, any of them have chosen to *die* in this way . . . he himself [i.e., the Chief] hands them knives which are, so to speak, 'consecrated'" (Lewis, 1967, p. 127).

Martyrdom, the voluntary acceptance of death in order to "demonstrate the . . . truth" to man, is a central, perhaps critical, method of message-giving religions, used both to dispel the doubts of believers and to aid proselytizing efforts. One cannot understand the Assassins without emphasizing the deeply embedded Muslim admiration for martyrs, particularly for those who die attempting to kill Islam's enemies. Assassin education clearly prepared assailants to seek martyrdom. The word used to designate the assailants—*fidayeen* (consecrated or dedicated ones)—indicates that they (like the victims of the Thugs) were considered religious sacrifices who freed themselves from the guilt of all sins and thereby gained "entry into paradise" (Kohlberg, 1976, p. 72).

The Hindu image of history as an endless series of cycles makes Thuggee conceivable. Message-oriented religions are inclined to assume a unilinear view of history that may be fulfilled when all humans hear and accept the message. Because this aspiration is frustrated, these religions periodically produce millenarian movements predicated on the belief that an existing hypocritical religious establishment has so corrupted their original message that only extraordinary action can renew the community's faith.

Islamic millenarian movements are largely associated with the Shia (the minority), who believe that eventually a *Mahdi* (Messiah or Rightly Guided One) would emerge to lead a holy war (*Jihad*) against the orthodox establishment to cleanse Islam. In the various Jewish and Christian messianic images violence may or may not appear, but "an *essential* part of the Mahdist theory regards the *Jihad* in the sense of an armed revolutionary struggle, as the method whereby a perfected social order *must* be brought into being" (Hodgkin, 1977, p. 307; see also Kohlberg, 1976; MacEoin, 1982; Tyan, 1960). The believer's obligation is to keep his faith intact until the *Mahdi* summons him. To protect a believer among hostile Muslims until the moment arrives, the Shia permit pious dissimulation, *taqiyya*. The pure are allowed to conceal their beliefs for much the same reason that we condone deception during war. Should an opportunity materialize, the Shia must "use their tongues," or preach their faith openly; but not until the *Mahdi* arrives are they allowed to "draw the sword" (MacEoin, 1982, p. 121).

The Assassins apparently interpreted the injunction prohibiting swords against other Muslims to mean that the true believer could use other weapons, or perhaps even that he should do so in order to expedite the arrival of the *Mahdi*. In this respect, they resemble earlier Islamic millenarian groups, which always attached a ritual significance to particular weapons. Some eighth-century cults strangled their victims, and one clubbed them to death with wooden cudgels (Friedlaender, 1907, 1909; Watt, 1973, p. 48). In each case the weapon chosen precluded escape and invited martyrdom.

The Assassins originated from the more active Shia elements who "used their tongues," organizing missionaries or summoners to persuade fellow Muslims with respect to the true meaning of their faith. Although their roots were in Persia, many were educated in Egyptian missionary schools. When the capabilities of the Shia (Ismaili) state in Egypt to promote millenarian doctrines waned, the founder of the Assassins declared his independence, seized several impregnable mountain fortresses, and made them hospitable to all sorts of refugees. Here the Assassins developed a distinctive systematic Gnostic theology which promised a messianic fulfillment of history in a harmonious anarchic condition in which law would be abolished and human nature perfected.

Like the Thugs, the Assassins moved across state lines constantly. But the differences are important. The Thugs found it easy to make arrangements for princes who would protect them for profit and upon condition that they operate abroad. But the Assassins, aiming to reconstitute Islam into a single community again, were compelled by their doctrine to organize an international conspiracy that could not be planted in an existing Islamic state. Therefore, they had to establish their own state: a league of scattered mountain fortresses or city-states (Hodgson, 1955, p. 99).

For the first time in history, perhaps, a state found its principal raison d'être in organizing international terror. The state provided means for the creation of an efficient enduring organization that could and did recover from numerous setbacks. The earlier millenarian sodalities were too scattered, their bases were too accessible, and their consequent insignificance often made them unable to achieve even the acknowledgment of historians, which alone could make them known to us. Isolation gave the Assassins both the space and the time required to create a quasi-monastic form of life and to train leaders, missionaries, and *fidayeen*. When their popular support in urban centers evaporated after 50 years, the Assassins survived for still another century and a half and would have persisted much longer had not Mongol and Arab armies destroyed their state (Hodgson, 1955, p. 115).

To facilitate their work they organized an extensive network of supporting cells in sympathetic urban centers. Often key persons in the establishment provided internal access, support the Assassins gained through conversion, bribery, and intimidation. Since orthodox Muslims understood the importance of internal support, the Assassins manipulated apprehensions by implicating enemies as accomplices—a maneuver that multiplied suspicions and confusion.

A successful assassination policy depended upon establishing the purpose of a murder as a measure necessary to protect missionaries.

Thus, one professional soldier likens the *fidayeen* to armed naval escorts, which never engage the enemy unless the convoy itself is attacked (Tugwell, 1979, p. 62). Victims were orthodox religious or political leaders who refused to heed warnings, and therefore provoked an attack by being scornful of the New Preaching, by attempting to prevent it from being heard, and by acting in ways that demonstrated complicity in Islam's corruption.

Assassin legends, like those of any millenarian group, are revealing. A most remarkable one concerned the victim-*fidayeen* relationship. Normally the movement placed a youthful member in the service of a high official. Through devotion and skill over the years he would gain his master's trust and then at the appropriate time the faithful servant would plunge a dagger into his master's back. So preternatural did this immunity from personal or ordinary feelings seem to orthodox Muslims that they described the group as "hashish eaters" (*hashashin*), the source of our term assassin. (Although there is no evidence that drugs were used, the ability to use the doctrine of *taqiyya* and the fact that training began in childhood may help explain *fidayeen* behavior.) The legend is significant, too, for what it demonstrates about public responses. Everywhere Assassins inspired awe. Those favorably disposed to their cause would find such dedication admirable, whereas opponents would see it as hateful, repulsive, and inhuman fanaticism. Less obvious but much more interesting, perhaps, as a clue to responses of neutrals, is the transformation that the meaning of the term "assassin" underwent in medieval Europe, where initially it signified devotion and later meant one who killed by treachery (Lewis, 1967, p. 3).

The potential utility of an assassination policy is obvious. Dramatically staged assassinations draw immense attention to a cause. In the Muslim context too, the basis of power was manifestly personal. "When a Sultan died his troops were automatically dispersed. When an Amir died his lands were in disorder" (Hodgson, 1955, p. 84). When conceived as an alternative to war, assassinations can seem moral too. The assassin may be discriminating; he can strike the great and guilty, leaving the masses who are largely innocent untouched.

The problems created by an assassination policy become clear only in time. A series of assassinations must provoke immense social antagonism in the normal course of events; popular identification with some leaders will exist and assassinations themselves entail treachery. "There can be good faith even in war but not in unannounced murder. Though Muslims... commonly... used an assassination as an expedient, the adoption of... a regular and admitted (assassination) policy horrified them and has horrified men ever since" (Hodgson, 1955, p. 84). A similar logic moved Immanuel Kant (1948, p. 6) to describe belligerents who employ assassins as criminals; such a breach of faith intensifies hatred and diminishes the possibility of achieving a peace settlement before one party exterminates the other.

As one might expect, the orthodox often responded by indiscriminately slaughtering those deemed sympathetic to the *fidayeen* (Hodgson, 1955, pp. 76–77, 111–113). The Assassins, however, reacted with remarkable restraint, eschewing numerous opportunities to reply in kind. Acts of urban terrorism occurred, the quarters of the orthodox were firebombed, but so infrequent were these incidents that one can only conclude that the rebels believed that another assassination was the only legitimate response to atrocities provoked by assassination. The political consequence of this restraint was clear; after forty years, support for the Assassins among urban elements disappeared, and the massacres ceased (Hodgson, 1955, p. 115).

The commitment to a single, stylized form of attack is puzzling. Most of the Assassins' early millenarian predecessors found assassination attractive too, but other forms of terror were known. More than any other millenarian group, the Assassins had resources to use other tactics and much to lose by failing to do so. Still, Assassin armies only protected their bases and raided caravans for booty, for it seems that Assassin doctrine made assassination and war mutually exclusive alternatives. The pattern is quite conspicuous during one of those strange periods in the movement's history when, for tactical reasons, it decided to become an orthodox community. "Instead of dispatching murderers to kill officers and divines, Hasan III sent armies to conquer provinces and cities; and by building mosques and bathhouses in the villages completed the transformation of his domain from a lair of assassins to a respectable kingdom, linked by ties of matrimonial alliance to his neighbors" (Hodgson, 1955, pp. 217–239; Lewis, 1967, p. 80). Assassin encounters with Christians also reflected the view that the dagger was reserved for those who betrayed the faith and the sword for persons who had never accepted it. When the Assassins first met invading Crusaders in Syria during the early twelfth century, they used their armies, not their *fidayeen* (Lewis, 1967, p. 108).

The peculiar reluctance to modify their tactics or to use their resources more efficiently probably had its origins, as the doctrines of all millenarian groups do, in reinterpretations of major precedents in the parent religion. To the millenarian, those precedents explain the religion's original success, and the abandonment of those precedents explains why there has been a failure to realize its promise. The life of Mohammed probably prescribed the model for Assassin strategy. The group began, for example, by withdrawing to primitive places of refuge (*dar al-hijra*), a decision that "was a deliberate imitation of that archetype from Mohammed's own career," who fled to remote but more receptive Medina when he failed to convert his own people in Mecca. "Medina was the first *dar al-hijra* of Islam, the first place of refuge—whence to return in triumph to the unbelieving lands from which one had to flee persecuted" (Hodgson, 1955, pp. 79–80). Islam's calendar dates from this event, and the pattern of withdrawing in order to begin again became one that millenarian elements in Islam normally followed and in fact do still, as recent studies of Muslim terrorist groups in Egypt show (Hodgkin, 1977; Ibrahim, 1980).

Mohammed's unusual employment of military forces and assassins while in Medina seems particularly instructive. Initially, the army had only two tasks, to defend the community against attacks and to raid caravans for booty. Simultaneously, he permitted (authorized?) assassinations of prominent persons within or on the fringes of Islam, "hypocrites" (*munafikun*) who had "provoked" attacks by displaying contempt for some aspect of Mohammed's teachings. Their deaths released hitherto latent sympathies for Islam among their followers. The process of purifying, or consolidating the original nucleus of the faith, seemed to be the precondition of expansion. When Mohammed decided the community was ready to become universal, the army was given its first offensive role and assassinations ceased!

Other aspects of the assassination pattern may have seemed suggestive too. The assassins' deeds were means to compensate or atone for deficiencies in ardor. The ability to overcome normal inhibitions or personal attachments to the victim was a significant measure of commitment. In every case, for example, assassin and victim were kinsmen, and no stronger bond was known then. The victims were not likely to defend themselves (e.g., they might be asleep or be women or old men), and they were often engaged in activities likely to evoke the assailant's compassion (e.g., they were playing with children or making love). As known associates of Mohammed, the assassins could only gain access to their victims by denying their faith or denouncing the Messenger of Allah.

A major difference between the earlier assassins and the later *fidayeen* is that one group returned to Mohammed for judgment, whereas the other actively sought martyrdom. In explaining this difference, remember that the origin of the *fidayeen* is in the Shia and Ismaili sects. Those groups link themselves to Ali and Husain, whom they consider Mohammed's true heirs. Ali and Husain were themselves both martyred after authorizing assassinations, and their martyrdoms became as central to their followers as Christ's passion is to Christians.

We do not have the primary sources to determine how the Assassins actually justified their tactics, but we know they saw themselves as engaged in a struggle to purify Islam and made extraordinary efforts to demonstrate that they acted defensively. The *fidayeen* put themselves in situations in which intimate bonds or personal feelings would be violated in order to demonstrate conviction. Assassin armies had one purpose in the *hijra;* later, they were likely to have another. The precedents were well known to anyone familiar with Mohammed's life and with the lives of figures most central to the Shia. Can there be justifications more compelling for believers than those that derive directly from the founders of their faith?

Zealots-Sicarii

There are resemblances between the Assassins and the Zealots-Sicarii. Both were inspired by messianic hopes to seek maximum publicity. Both interpreted important events in the founding period of their religion as precedents for their tactics and to mean also that those who died in this struggle secured their places in paradise. Like the Assassins, the Sicarii (dagger-men) were identified with a particular weapon, and both rebellions had an international character. Nonetheless, the differences between the two, which derive from variations in the content of their respective messianic and founding myths, are even more striking.

The Zealots-Sicarii survived for approximately 25 years, a brief existence by the standards of the Assassins, but their immediate and long-run influence was enormous. Holy terrorists are normally concerned with members of their own religious culture, but the Jews were also interested in generating a mass uprising against the large Greek population that lived in Judea and against the Romans who governed them both. The revolt proved disastrous and led to the destruction of the Temple, the desolation of the land, and the mass suicide at Masada. Moreover, Zealot-Sicarii activities inspired two more popular uprisings against Rome in successive generations, which resulted in the extermination of the large Jewish centers in Egypt and Cyprus, the virtual depopulation of Judea, and the final tragedy—the Exile itself, which exercised a traumatic impact on Jewish consciousness and became the central feature of Jewish experience for the next two thousand years, altering virtually every institution in Jewish life. It would be difficult to find terrorist activity in any historical period which influenced the life of a community more decisively.

The impact of the Jewish terrorists obviously stems from their ability to generate popular insurrections, an unusual capacity among religious terrorists which makes them particularly interesting to us because ever since the Russian Anarchists first created the doctrine of modern terror, the development of a *levee-en-masse* by means of provocation tactics has been the principal aim of most groups. Very few have succeeded, and none has had as much success as the Zealots-Sicarii did. Why were they so peculiar?

The nature of their messianic doctrines simultaneously suggested the object of terror and permitted methods necessary to achieve it. Jewish apocalyptic prophecies visualize the signs of the imminence of the messiah as a series of massive catastrophes involving whole populations, "the upsetting of all moral order to the point of dissolving the laws of nature" (Scholem, 1971, p. 12). This vision saturated Judaism for a generation preceding the genesis of Zealot-Sicarii activity,

creating a state of feverish expectancy. "Almost every event was seized upon ... to discover how and in what way it represented a Sign of the Times and threw light on the approach of the End of the Days. The whole condition of the Jewish people was psychologically abnormal. The strongest tales and imaginings could find ready credence" (Schonfield, 1965, p. 19). New messianic pretenders flourished everywhere, because so many people believed that the signs indicating a messianic intervention were quite conspicuous: Judea was occupied by an alien military power, and prominent Jews were acquiescing in "the desecration of God's name" or accepting the culture of the conqueror.

In all apocalyptic visions God determines the date of the redemption. Still, these visions often contain some conception that humans can speed the process. Prayer, repentance, and martyrdom are the most common methods. When these do not produce results and a period of unimaginable woe is perceived as the precondition of paradise, it will only be a matter of time before believers will act to force history, or bring about that precondition. Jewish terrorist activity appeared to have two purposes: to make oppression so intolerable that insurrection was inevitable, and, subsequently, to frustrate every attempt to reconcile the respective parties.

The names Zealot and Sicarii both derive from a much earlier model in Jewish history, Phineas, a high priest in the days of Moses. His zeal or righteous indignation averted a plague that afflicted Israel when the community tolerated acts of apostasy and "whoring with Moabite women." Taking the law into his own hands, he killed a tribal chief and his concubine who flaunted their contempt for God in a sacred site. Phineas is the only Biblical hero to receive a reward directly from God (*Numbers* 25:11). In purifying the community, his action prepared the way for the Holy War (*herem*) which God commanded Israel to wage against the Canaanites for the possession of the Promised Land. The Bible repeatedly refers to the terror that the *herem* was supposed to produce and to Israel's obligation to destroy all persons with their property who remain in the land, lest they become snares or corrupting influences. The word *herem*, it should be noted, designates a sacred sphere where ordinary standards do not apply, and in a military context, a *herem* is war without limits.

The name Sicarii comes from the daggers (*sica*) used when the group first made its appearance. Rabbinic commentary indicates that Phineas used the head of his spear as a dagger, and the Sicarii normally assassinated prominent Jews, especially priests, who in their opinion had succumbed to Hellenistic culture. As in Phineas's case, these acts were also efforts to create a state of war readiness, and, more specifically, to intimidate priests who were anxious to avoid war with Rome and whose opposition could prevent it from materializing.

> The Sicarii committed murders in broad daylight in the heart of Jerusalem. The holy days were their special seasons when they would mingle with the crowd carrying short daggers concealed under their clothing with which they stabbed
> their enemies. Thus, when they fell, the murderers joined in cries of indignation, and through this plausible behavior, were never discovered. The first assassinated was Jonathan, the High Priest. After his death there were numerous daily murders. The panic created was more alarming than the calamity itself; everyone, as on the battlefield, hourly expected death. Men kept watch at a distance on their enemies and would not trust even their friends when they approached (Josephus, 1926a, vol. 2, pp. 254–257).

Although their name reminds us of Phineas's weapon, his spirit and purpose were more decisive influences. Unlike the *fidayeen,* the Sicarii did not limit themselves to assassinations. They engaged military forces openly, often slaughtering their prisoners. They took hostages to pressure the priests and terrorized wealthy Jewish landowners in the hopes of compelling a land redistribution according to Biblical traditions. The Zealots illustrate the point even more clearly. Their Hebrew name signified the righteous indignation that Phineas personified, but they rarely plotted assassinations, and their principal antagonists were non-Jews who dwelled in the land. Phineas was also known for his audacity, which Zealot-Sicarii assaults often reflect. (It is not without interest that rage and audacity are qualities most admired and cultivated by modern terrorists.) Their atrocities occurred on the most holy days to exploit the potential for publicity therein, and, more important, to demonstrate that not even the most sacred occasions could provide immunity. Note, for example, Josephus's description of how the Sicarii massacred a Roman garrison, after it had secured a covenant (the most inviolable pledge Jews could make) that guaranteed the troops safe passage.

> When they had laid down their arms, the rebels massacred them; the Romans neither resisting, nor suing for mercy, but merely appealing with loud cries to the covenant! . . . The whole city was a scene of dejection, and among the moderates there was not one who was not racked with the thought that he should personally have to suffer for the rebels' crime. For to add to its heinousness the massacre took place on the Sabbath, a day on which from religious scruples Jews abstain from even the most innocent acts. (Josephus, 1926a, vol. 2, p. 451)

The massacre electrified the Greeks, who constituted a significant portion of the population in Judea and were the local source of Roman recruitment. Jews in numerous cities were massacred, and everywhere the Greeks were repaid in kind. The action and the response illustrate vividly some salient differences between Muslim and Jewish terrorists. *Fidayeen* terror was an auxiliary weapon designed to protect their missions where the main work of the movement was done, converting the population to a particular messianic doctrine. Patient and deliberate, the Assassins acted as though they expected to absorb the Muslim world piecemeal. The Zealots and the Sicarii saw themselves not as the propagators of a doctrine but as revolutionary catalysts who moved men by force of their audacious action, exploiting mass expectations that a cataclysmic messianic deliverance was imminent.

To generate a mass uprising quickly and to sustain constantly increasing polarizing pressures, the Zealots-Sicarii developed an array of tactics unusual by Thug and Assassin standards. Participants (despite their contrary intentions) were pulled into an ever-escalating struggle by shock tactics which manipulated their fear, outrage, sympathy, and guilt. Sometimes these emotional effects were provoked by terrorist atrocities which went beyond the consensual norms governing violence; at other times they were produced by provoking the enemy into committing atrocities against his will.

Thugs and Assassin tactics always remained the same, but in the different phases of the Jewish uprising, striking changes occurred which seemed designed for specific contexts. The rebellion began with passive resistance in the cities. This tactic, of which the Jewish example may be the earliest recorded by historians, merits comment, for in our world (e.g., Cyprus and Northern Ireland), passive resistance has often appeared as an initial step in conflicts which later matured into full-scale terrorist campaigns. Our experience has been that many who would have shrunk from violence, let alone terror, often embrace passive resistance as a legitimate method to rectify grievances, without understanding how the ensuing drama may intensify and broaden commitments by simultaneously exciting hopes and fanning smoldering hostilities.

In the Jewish case, before antagonisms had been sufficiently developed and when Roman military strength still seemed irresistible, passive resistance might have been the only illegal form of action that many Jews would willingly undertake. Initially, the confrontations involved Jewish claims, sometimes never before made, for respect due to their sacred symbols, and governments learned that, willy-nilly, they had backed, or been backed, into situations in which they either had to tolerate flagrant contempt for the law or commit actions that seemed to threaten the Jewish religion, the only concern that could unite all Jews. More often than one might expect, the Romans retreated in the face of this novel form of resistance. They admired the Jews' displays of courage, restraint, and intensity, and they learned how difficult and dangerous it was to break up demonstrations that included women and children (Josephus, 1926a, vol. 2, pp. 169, 195; 1926b, vol. 18, pp. 55, 269). They feared a rebellion that could engulf the eastern portion of the Empire, which was at least one-fifth Jewish and contained a significant class of Jewish sympathizers (*sebomenoi*, God-fearers) whose influence seemed to reach members of Rome's ruling circles.

The possibility that the conflict could become an international one troubled Rome. Judea was on the frontier next to Parthia, the last remaining major power in the ancient world. Parthia had intervened in earlier conflicts. Even if Parthia wanted to avoid involvement, she might find it difficult to do so because her Jewish population was large, and one Parthian client state had a Jewish dynasty that bore a special hatred for Rome. Parthian Jews were important figures in the early stage of the rebellion. The great annual pilgrimages of Parthian Jews to Jerusalem and the massive flow of wealth they contributed to maintain the Temple gave evidence of the strength of their tie to Judea, a bond that a modern historian compares to that which knitted American Jews to those in Palestine during the uprising against Britain.

For some time before the rebellion, Rome kept expanding the unusual exemptions given Jews, and the uprising was fueled partly by rising expectations. But Rome's anxiety to avoid a serious conflict simply made her more vulnerable to tactics calculated to produce outrage. Her restraint encouraged reckless behavior and weakened the case of Jewish moderates who argued that although Rome might be conciliatory, she was wholly determined to remain in Judea.

Large passive demonstrations against authority tend to produce violence unless both sides have discipline and foresight. When some on either side prefer violence, or when passive resistance is viewed not as an end in itself, but as a tactic that can be discarded when other tactics seem more productive, explosions will occur. Whatever the particular reason in this case, demonstrators soon became abusive, and bands of rock-throwing youths broke off from the crowds. When Roman troops (trying to be inconspicuous by discarding military dress and exchanging swords for wooden staves) were attacked, Roman discipline dissolved. The crowds panicked, and hundreds of innocent bystanders were trampled to death in Jerusalem's narrow streets. This pattern kept repeating itself, and the atrocities seemed especially horrifying because they normally occurred on holy days when Jerusalem was crowded with pilgrims, many of whom were killed while attending religious services. The massive outrage generated by Roman atrocities and the assassination campaign against the moderates finally intimidated reluctant priests into refusing to allow Roman sacrifices at the Temple. Rome viewed that act as a rejection of her sovereignty or as a declaration of war, and this gave the militants a plausible case that the war was indeed a *herem*.

When the war finally occurred, many on both sides hoped to conclude it quickly with a political settlement. These hopes were given a severe jolt early after the first military engagement. When the tiny Roman garrison in Jerusalem, which had laid down its arms for a covenant of safe passage, was massacred, a pattern of reprisal and counter-reprisal spread throughout the eastern portion of the Empire. Roman troops ran amuck. Yet when military discipline was finally restored, the Roman campaign quite unexpectedly was restrained. Military advantages were not pressed, as hope persisted that the olive branch offered would be peace. Rome believed that the atrocities of Jew against Jew would eventually destroy the popular tolerance requisite for all terrorist movements. A significant Jewish desertion rate, including many important personalities, kept Roman hopes alive for negotiating a peace without strenuous military efforts. But various Jewish atrocities, which culminated in the cold-blooded murder of Roman peace envoys, led to the conclusion that only total war was feasible (Josephus, 1926a, vol. 2, p. 526).

Zealot-Sicarii strategy seemed admirably designed to provoke a massive uprising. Consecutive atrocities continually narrowed prospects for a political, or mutually agreeable, solution, serving to destroy the credibility of moderates on both sides while steadily expanding the conflict, which enlisted new participants. But no master hand can be detected in this process, and one can see it as an irrational process. Jewish terrorists reflect a bewildering assortment of forces. Several Zealot and at least two Sicarii organizations existed, and many other groups participated, but only a few can be identified. Then, as now, the effect of multiplicity was to encourage each element toward even more heinous atrocities, in order to prove the superiority of its commitments, and in time the groups decimated each other. As these extraordinary actions unfolded, the participating groups, like so many of their modern counterparts, found it necessary to make even more fantastic claims about their enemies and even more radical promises about the social reconstruction that would result from their victory. Ferrero's comment on the dynamics of the French Reign of Terror seems quite pertinent. "The Jacobins did not spill all that blood because they believed in popular sovereignty as a religious truth; rather they tried to believe in popular sovereignty as a religious truth because their fear made them spill all that blood" (1972, p. 100; cf. Josephus, 1926b, vol. 18, p. 269).

To focus on popular insurrection as the principal object, however, is to misconstrue the Zealot-Sicarii view. Insurrection was only a sign of messianic intervention, and because they were concerned with a divine audience, they did things that no one preoccupied with a human audience alone would dream of doing. The decision of Zealot leaders to burn the food supply of their *own* forces during Jerusalem's long siege becomes intelligible only if one believes that He might see it as proof that the faithful had placed all their trust in Him. God, therefore, would

have no choice; was He not bound by His promise to rescue the righteous remnant? Because many thought God would be moved by their sufferings, the most profound disaster often created new hopes. When the Temple was burning (and the war irretrievably lost), a messianic imposter persuaded six thousand new recruits that the fire signified that the time for deliverance had finally arrived. Compared to the Thugs and Assassins, the Zealots-Sicarii seem free to choose their tactics, but how can one be free to follow an impossible goal?

CONCLUSION

These cases provide materials to broaden the study of comparative terrorism. Each contains parallels worth pondering, and the three together illustrate the uniqueness of sacred terror and thus provide a perspective for viewing modern terror and a glimpse of the latter's special properties.

Our obliviousness to holy terror rests on a misconception that the distinction between it and the modern form is one of scale, not of nature or kind. A most conspicuous expression of this misconception is the conventional wisdom that terrorist operations require modern technology to be significant. There are relationships between changes in technology and changes in terrorist activity, but they have not been seriously studied. More important, every society has weapon, transport and communication facilities, and the clear meaning of our cases is that the decisive variables for understanding differences among the forms terror may take are a group's purpose, organization, methods, and above all the public's response to that group's activities.

This conclusion should shape our treatment of the dynamics of modern terrorism. There is no authoritative history of modern terrorism that traces its development from its inception more than a century ago. When that history is written, the cyclical character of modern terror will be conspicuous, and those cycles will be related not so much to technological changes as to significant political watersheds which excited the hopes of potential terrorists and increased the vulnerability of society to their claims. The upsurge in the 1960s, for example, would be related to Vietnam just as the activities immediately after World War II would appear as an aspect of the decline in the legitimacy of Western colonial empires. Since doctrine, rather than technology, is the ultimate source of terror, the analysis of modern forms must begin with the French, rather than the Industrial Revolution.

When the assumption concerning technology is abandoned, early cases seem more valuable as a source for appropriate parallels. We have already suggested a number of potentially instructive instances. For example, the Zealot-Sicarii case may be the only instance of a successful strategy that actually produced a mass insurrection—the announced objective of modern revolutionary terror. It illuminates predicaments inherent in this strategy while exposing aspects of societies especially vulnerable to it. It is worth noting that the problems illustrated by this particular experience concerned Menachem Begin greatly, because his strategy as the leader of the Irgun in the uprising against Britain was in part conceived to avoid "mistakes" made by the Zealots-Sicarii (Rapoport, 1982b, pp. 31–33).

The international context provides another parallel. It played a crucial role in sustaining the terror. The Thugs and Assassins had valuable foreign sanctuaries. Favorable, albeit different, international climates of opinion helped all three groups. In each case there was cooperation among terrorists from different countries; in one instance a state was actually directing an international terrorist organization, and in another there existed the threat of potential military intervention by an outside power. The problems posed and the constraints involved provide useful points of comparison with modern experiences. The difficulties in dealing with terrorists who have foreign sanctuaries and the ways in which those difficulties may exacerbate international relations are familiar. Rome's vulnerability to terror tactics reminds one of Western colonial empires after World War II, but the ultimate reason for the different outcomes was that Rome never doubted her right to rule. Britain's ability to exterminate the Thugs quickly in the nineteenth century was to a large extent the consequence of a favorable British and an indifferent international opinion. Perhaps the doubt expressed in the 1930s by a student of the Thugs that Britain could not have acted as decisively to deal with the same problem a century later was unwarranted, but the concern reflected a very different political environment, one that is even more deeply rooted today.

How should we characterize sacred terror? Obviously there are enormous variations in its expressions which extend to purposes, methods, responses, and differences that derive from the ingenuity of the individual terror cult which in turn is limited by boundaries established by the original religion. In an odd, interesting way, the terrorist as a deviant highlights unique features of the parent religion that distinguish it from other religions, e.g., concepts of the relation of the divine to history and to social structure.

Because Hinduism provides no grounds for believing that the world can be transformed, the Thugs could neither perceive themselves nor could they be perceived as rebels. In imagining themselves obligated to keep the world in balance, they were part of the established order, though obviously not in it. In Islam and Judaism, the potentialities for radical attacks on institutions are inherent in the ambiguity of unfulfilled divine promises, which no existing establishment can reconcile fully with its own dominance. Because the promises are known to every member of the religious community, the Islamic or Jewish terrorist has a human audience not present in Hinduism. To reach this audience Islamic and Jewish terrorists must become visible and must either conquer all or be extinguished. There can be no such imperative with respect to the Thugs, as the extra-ordinarily long life of the order suggests. Initially the British were very reluctant to suppress the Thugs because they believed that it would be dangerous to disturb the local and foreign interests embedded in Thug activity. The decisive impetus was a rekindling of evangelical feeling in Victorian England which struck out at the world slave trade and was outraged by accounts of three ancient Hindu practices: infanticide, immolation of widows, and Thuggee. Under Hindu administration, Thuggee would have survived much longer.

If a particular religion creates boundaries for its terrorists, it follows that similarities within traditions will be as striking as differences among traditions. In the Hindu world, an ancient species of criminal tribes, all of which worshipped Kali, persisted. Each performed a particular criminal vocation, was committed to a special way of achieving it, and believed that its actions were legitimate by Hindu standards. The Thugs were unique among those tribes in not professing their practices openly; perhaps they could not have been able to survive the outrage and horror provoked by them. The Assassins' situation is more straightforward; they were the latest and most successful Muslim millenarian assassination cult and the only one that established a state, the mechanism required for thorough organization. The Assassins consummated a millenarian tradition of terror, but the Zealots-Sicarii appeared to have initiated one, which ended after three disastrous massive revolts in as many generations. Holy terrorists normally victimize members of the parent religion, but the Jews attacked non-Jews too, those who resided in the land. The concern with the land as the site of the messianic experience may be a distinguishing feature of Jewish terror. The conception of a war without limits in which large military forces are engaged probably had its roots in the extraordinary Holy War (*herent*), which, according to the Bible, God Himself authorized in the original conquest of Canaan. The belief that assimilation impeded messianic deliverance and that all members of the community were culpable gave Jewish terror a character that seemed indiscriminate, certainly by the standards of the Assassins, who held leaders responsible.

Sacred terrorists find their rationale in the past, either in divine instructions transmitted long ago or in interpretations of precedents from founding periods of the parent religions. Their struggles are sanctified with respect to purpose and with respect to means; this is why their violence must have unique characteristics. The very idea of the holy entails contrast with the profane, the normal, or the natural. The noose of the Thug and the dagger of the Assassin illustrate the point. It is difficult, in fact, to avoid feeling that the act of terror is holy just because one is acting against his natural impulses. The immunities of Assassins and Thugs to natural feelings (i.e., the Stockholm syndrome) astonished observers. But, unlike terrorists we are familiar with, they began training for their tasks as children. Our sources provide no information on the personal stress that the methods of the Jewish terrorists might have created for them, but perhaps it is relevant that the Bible relates instance after instance of individuals, including King Saul himself, who violate commands for indiscriminate destruction in the original *herem* to conquer Canaan.

Religion normally embodies ritual, and it does seem natural that rules prescribe every detail of Hindu and Islamic terror. As observers of the Thugs pointed out, those rules may have been rationally designed to resolve perennial practical problems, thus helping the groups to endure and become more effective. Still, divinely authorized rules cannot be altered even when they become destructive. So conspicuous were the Assassins' political concerns that an eminent historian has described them as the first to use "political terror" in a "planned systematic fashion" (Lewis, 1967, p. 269); but their religious mandate kept them committed to the same tactics even when they proved politically counterproductive. Jewish terror appears unique, being thoroughly antinomian and embracing a large variety of activities. The success in provoking insurrection and the freedom regarding means suggest that political considerations were paramount. But since their ultimate concern was to create *the* catastrophe that would compel God to redeem the righteous remnant, in the end they, like the Thugs and Assassins, continued to act in manifestly self-destructive ways.

The transcendent source of holy terror is its most critical distinguishing characteristic; the deity is perceived as being directly involved in the determination of ends and means. Holy terror never disappeared, and it seems to be reviving in new forms especially in, but not exclusive to, the Middle East. Still, modern terror, which began initially in the activities of *Narodnaya Volya,* a nineteenth-century Russian organization, now is much more common. The modern terrorist serves political ends to be achieved by human efforts alone, and he, not God, chooses the most appropriate ends and means. It is also true that modern terrorist organizations (especially the most durable and effective ones) are often associated with religious groups, for religion can be a major factor of ethnic identity. Although the IRA attracts Catholics and repels Protestants, its object is political, and no member believes that God participates in the struggle. The FLN in Algeria stressed its Muslim character, and EOKA in Cyprus was affiliated with the Greek Orthodox church, but the tactics in both cases were designed to appeal to various domestic and international audiences.

When the members of *Narodnaya Volya,* the first modern rebel terrorists, began their activities, they seemed to be engaged in a kind of sacred ritual. More specifically, they remind one of the Assassins. Highly ranked officials who symbolized the system and bore some responsibilities for its injustices were the victims, and the assailant hoped to attract moral sympathy through his own suffering, specifically by his willingness to accept death in a public trial where he could indict the system. Even his weapon—a hand-thrown bomb—suggests the *fidayeen's* dagger because it forced face-to-face encounters virtually precluding escape, which persuaded many observers that his will to die was more compelling than his desire to kill (Ivianski, 1982). But, unlike the Assassins, the possibility of other terror tactics was visualized early by their contemporaries, and their initial patterns were soon discarded.

Modern terrorism has two unique, dominant features. Organizations and tactics are constantly modified, presumably to enhance effectiveness, and terror is used for very different ends, ranging from those of anarchists with millenarian visions to anti-colonialists, to individuals who simply want to call attention to a particular situation that they find offensive. The early forms of sacred terror cannot be characterized this way. The ends are predetermined, and no real evidence exists that the participants learn to alter their behavior from others within their own tradition, let alone from those outside it. Modern terrorists take their lessons from anyone, and in an important sense they constitute a single tradition which reflects and caricatures a much-observed tendency in our world to subject all activities to efficiency tests. Over the decades the tendency has been to choose methods that minimize the terrorist's risks; the targets, accordingly, are, increasingly, defenseless victims who have less and less value as symbols or less and less responsibility for any condition that the terrorists say they want to alter. The question is whether one can place a premium on reducing the assailant's risk without undermining his potential impact. The problem did not exist for the sacred terrorist, which may be one reason why he was so effective.

The desire to make terror "rational" dominated the first modern terrorist text, Nechaev's *Revolutionary Catechism,* produced before the birth of *Narodnaya Volya.* "The revolutionary (terrorist) . . . knows only one science: the science of destruction. For this reason, and only for this reason, he will study mechanics, chemistry, and perhaps medicine. But all day and night he studies the living science of peoples, their characteristics and circumstances, and all the phenomena of the present social order. The object is the same. The prompt destruction of this filthy order" (1971, p. 71). Nechaev's work is simply an exercise in technique, suggesting devices for provoking governments to savage their peoples until the latter can bear it no longer.

It has had numerous successors, the latest and most notorious being Marighella's *Minimanual of the Urban Guerrilla.*

Although the disposition to apply standards of expediency distinguishes modern from holy terror, the presence of this disposition itself cannot mean that modern terrorists are rational. Some ends in principle may be impossible to achieve, like those of the anarchist; others may be so ill-considered that no means can be made rational—the situation, it seems, of the Baader Meinhoff group and the Italian Red Brigades. Sometimes, under the guise of expediency, the safety of the terrorist might become the prime concern. More fundamentally, the very idea of a rational or expedient terror may be contradictory, since by definition terror entails extranormal violence, and as such, is almost guaranteed to evoke wild and uncontrollable emotions. Indeed, the people attracted to it may be so intrigued by the experience of perpetrating terror that everything else is incidental.

REFERENCES

A religion of murder. *Quarterly Review,* 1901, *194,* 506–513.

Applebaum, S. The Zealots: the case for revaluation. *Journal of Roman Studies,* 1971, *61,* 155–170.

Betz, O., Haacker, K., & Hengel, M. *Josephus-Studien.* Gottingen: Vanderhoeck and Ruprecht, 1974.

Bilde, P. The causes of the Jewish War according to Josephus. *Journal for the Study of Judaism,* 1979, *10,* 179–202.

Borg, M. The currency of the term "Zealot." *Journal of Theological Studies,* 1971, *22,* 504–513.

Bruce, C. *The Stranglers.* London: Longmans, 1968.

Buhl, Fr Munafikun. *Encyclopedia of Islam.* London: Luzac, 1913.

Clark, H. *Zebra.* New York: Merek, 1979.

Cohen, S. J. D. *Josephus in Galilee and Rome.* Leiden: Brill, 1979.

Cohn, N. *The pursuit of the millennium: revolutionary messianism in medieval and reformation Europe and its bearing on modern totalitarian movements.* New York: Harper Torchbooks, 1961.

Collins, W. *The moonstone.* London: Tinsley, 1868.

DeQuincey, T. Supplementary paper on murder considered as one of the fine arts. In *Works.* Boston: Houghton Mifflin, 1877.

Dugard, J. International terrorism and the Just War. In D. C. Rapoport & Y. Alexander (Eds.). *The morality of terrorism: religions and secular justifications.* New York: Pergamon, 1982.

Farmer, W. R. *Maccabees, Zealots, and Josephus.* New York: Columbia University Press, 1956.

Ferrero, G. *The principles of power.* New York: Arno, 1972.

Freedman, L. Z. Why does terrorism terrorize? In D.C. Rapoport & Y. Alexander (Eds.). *The rationalization of terrorism.* Frederick, Md.: University Publications of America, 1982.

Friedlaender, I. The heterodoxies of the Shi-ites in the presentation of Ibh Hazm. *Journal of the American Oriental Society,* 1907, *28,* 1–80, *29,* 1–183.

Gillie, D. R. Justice and Thugs. *The Spectator.* 1944, *172,* 567–568.

Gordon, S. N. Scarf and sword: Thugs, marauders and state formation in 18th century Malwa. *Indian Journal of Economic and Social History,* 1969, *6,* 403–429.

Grant J. *The Jews in the Roman world.* London: Wiedenfeld, 1973.

Gupta, H. A critical study of the Thugs and their activities. *Journal of Indian History,* 1959, *38,* 167–176.

Gurr, T. Some characteristics of terrorism. In M. Stohl (Ed.). *The politics of terrorism.* New York: Dekker, 1979.

Hacker, F. *Crusaders, criminals, and crazies.* New York: Norton, 1976.

Hardman, J. Terrorism. *Encyclopedia of the Social Sciences.* New York: Macmillan, 1933.

Hengel, M. *Die Zeloten.* Leiden: Brill, 1961.

Herodotus. *Persian Wars.*

Hervey, J. *Some records of crime.* London: Sampson Low, 1892.

Hodgkin, T. Mahdism, Messianism and Marxism in the African setting. In P. Gurkind & P. Waterman (Eds.). *African social studies: A radical reader.* New York: 1977.

Hodgson, M. G. S. The Ismaili state. In W. B. Fisher (Ed.), *The Cambridge history of Iran.* Cambridge: Cambridge University Press, 1968.

Hodgson, M. G. S. *The order of Assassins.* The Hague: Mouton, 1955.

Horsley, R. A. Josephus and the bandits. *Journal for the Study of Judaism,* 1979, *10,* 38–63.(b)

Horsley, R. A. The *Sicarii;* ancient Jewish "terrorists." *Journal of Religion,* 1979, *59,* 435–458.(a).

Hutton, J. *A popular account of the Thugs and Dakoits.* London: W. H. Allen, 1857.

Hutton, J. H. *Caste in India.* Oxford: Clarendon Press, 1961.

Ibrahim, S. Anatomy of Egypt's militant Islamic groups. *International Journal of Middle Eastern Studies,* 1980, *12,* 423–453.

Ivianski, Z. The moral issue: some aspects of individual terror. In D. C. Rapoport & Y. Alexander (Eds.), *The morality of terrorism: religious and secular justifications.* New York: Pergamon, 1982.

Jenkins, B. *International terrorism: a new mode of conflict.* Los Angeles: Crescent, 1975.

Josephus. The Jewish War. In *Works.* Loeb Classical Library. London: Heinemann, 1926(a).

Josephus. Antiquities of the Jews. In *Works.* Loeb Classical Library. London: Heinemann, 1926 (b).

Kant, I. *Perpetual peace.* M. Smith (Trans.). New York: Liberal Arts, 1948.

Kingdom, H. Origin of the Zealots. *New Testament Studies,* 1971, *79,* 74–61.

Kingdom, H. Who were the Zealots? *New Testament Studies,* 1970, *71,* 68–72.

Kohlberg, R. The development of the Imami Shii doctrine of *Jihad. Deutschen Morgenlandischen Gesellschaft Zeitschrift,* 1976, *126,* 64–82.

Kohler, K. Zealots. *The Jewish Encyclopedia.* New York: Funk & Wagnalls, 1905.

Lang, D. A reporter at large: the bank drama (Swedish hostages). *The New Yorker,* 1974, *50*(40), 56–126.

Laqueur, W. *Terrorism.* Boston: Little Brown, 1977.

Lerner, M. Assassination. *Encyclopedia of the Social Sciences.* New York: Macmillan, 1933.

Lewis, B. *The Assassins: a radical sect in Islam.* London: Nicholson and Weidenfeld, 1967.

Lewis, B. *Origins of Islamism.* Cambridge: Cambridge University Press, 1940.

MacEoin, D. The Babi concept of the Holy War. *Religion,* 1982, *12,* 93–129.

Malcolm, J., Sir. *A memoir of Central India.* London: Kingsbury, Parbury and Allen, 1823.

Marighella, C. *For the liberation of Brazil.* Harmondsworth: Penguin, 1972.

Margoliouth, D. S. *Mohammed and the rise of Islam.* London: G. P. Putnam, 1923.

Masters, J. *The deceivers.* New York: Viking, 1952.

Mickolus, E. F. *Transnational terrorism: a chronology of events.* Westport, Conn.: Greenwood, 1980.

Nechaev, S. The revolutionary catechism. In D. C. Rapoport, *Assassination and terrorism.* Toronto: Canadian Broadcasting Corp., 1972.

Pal, B. *Memoirs of my life and times.* Calcutta: Modern Book Agency, 1932.

Pfirrmann, G. *Religioser character und organisatin der Thag-Bruederschaften.* Tuebingen: Ph.D. dissertation, 1970.

Poonawala, K. *Bibliography of Ismaili literature.* Malibu, Calif.: Undena, 1977.

Price, H., Jr. The strategy and tactics of revolutionary terrorism. *Comparative Studies in Society and History,* 1977, *19,* 52–65.

Rapoport, D. C. Introduction. Religious terror. In D. Canadian Broadcasting Corp. 1971.

Rapoport, D. C. The politics of atrocity. In Y. Alexander & S. Finger (Eds.), *Terrorism: Interdisciplinary perspectives.* New York: John Jay, 1977.

Rapoport, D. C. Introduction. Religious terror. In D. C. Rapoport & Y. Alexander (Eds.), *The morality of terrorism: religious and secular justifications.* New York: Pergamon, 1982(a).

Rapoport, D. C. Terror and the messiah; an ancient experience and modern parallels. In D. C. Rapoport & Y. Alexander (Eds.), *The morality of terrorism: Religious and secular justifications.* New York: Pergamon, 1982(b).

Rapoport, D. C. & Alexander, Y. (Eds.). *The morality of terrorism: Religious and secular justifications.* New York: Pergamon Press, 1982.

Rodinson, M. *Mohammed.* London: Penguin, 1971.

Roth, C. The Zealots and the war of 66–70. *Journal of Semitic Studies,* 1959, *4,* 332–334.

Rubin, J. *Do it.* New York: Simon and Schuster, 1970.

Russell, C. A., Banker, L. J., & Miller, B. H. Out-inventing the terrorist. In Y. Alexander, D. Carlton, & P. Wilkinson (Eds.), *Terrorism: theory and practice.* Boulder, Colo.: Westview, 1979.

Russell, R. V., & Hira, L. *The tribes and castes of the Central Provinces of India.* London: Macmillan, 1916.

Sandler, T., Tshirhart, J. T., & Cauley, J. A theoretical analysis of transnational terrorism. *American Political Science Review,* 1983, *77,* 36–54.

Scholem, G. *The messianic idea in Judaism.* New York: Schocken, 1971.

Schonfeld, J. *The Passover plot.* New York: Geis, 1965.

Sherwood, R. On the murderers called P'hansigars *Asiatic Researchers,* 1820, *13,* 250–281.

Shutt, R. J. H. *Studies in Josephus.* London: S.P.C.K. 1961.

Sleeman, J. L. *Thugs; or a million murders.* London: S. Low and Marston, 1933.

Sleeman, W. H. *Ramaseeana.* Calcutta: Huttman, 1836.

Sleeman, W. H. *The Thugs or Phansigars of India.* Philadelphia: Carey and Hart, 1839.

Sleeman, W. H. *A journey through the kingdom of Oudh in 1849–50.* London: Bentley, 1858.

Sleeman, W. H. *Rambles and recollections of an Indian official.* V. A. Smith (Ed.). Westminster: Constable, 1893.

Sleeman, W. H. *Report on the depredations committed by the Thug gangs of Upper and Central India.* Calcutta: Huttman, 1940.

Smallwood, E. J. *The Jews under Roman rule.* Leiden: Brill, 1976.

Smith, M. Zealots and *Sicarii:* their origins and relations. *Harvard Theological Review,* 1971, *64,* 1–19.

Spry, H. *Modern India.* London: Whitaker, 1837.

Stern, J. Zealots. *Encyclopedia Judaica Yearbook.* New York: Macmillan, 1973.

Taylor, M. *Confessions of a Thug.* London: R. Bentley, 1839.

Taylor, M. *The story of my life.* London: Oxford University Press, 1920.

Thackeray, H. St. J. *Josephus, the man and the historian.* New York repr. Ktva, 1967.

Thornton, E. *Illustrations and practices of the Thugs.* London: W. H. Allen, 1837.

Thornton, T. P. Terror as a weapon of political agitation. In H. Eckstein (Ed.), *Internal War.* New York: Free Press, 1964.

Tugwell, M. *Revolutionary propaganda and possible counter-measures.* Kings College, University of London: Ph.D. dissertation, 1979.

Tyan, E. Djihad, *Encyclopedia of Islam.* Leiden: Brill, 1960.

Vattel, E. *The law of nations.* London: Newbery, 1760.

de Vaux, R. *Ancient Israel.* New York: McGraw-Hill, 1972.

Walter, E. V. *Terror and resistance: a study of political violence.* New York: Oxford University Press, 1969.

Watt, M. W. *The formative period of Islamic thought.* Edinburgh: University Press, 1973.

Watt, M. W. *Mohammed at Medina.* Oxford: Clarendon Press, 1956.

Weber, M. *The Sociology of religion.* E. Fischoff (Ed.). London: Methuen, 1955.

Zeitlin, S. The Sicarii and the Zealots. *Jewish Quarterly Review,* 1967, *57,* 251–270.

NOTES

1. "Terrorism is an activity that has probably characterized modern civilization from its inception. In the past decade, however, terrorist activity has increased in frequency and has taken on novel dimensions. For example, incidents are being employed more as a means of political expression and are becoming characterized by a transnational element" (Sandler, Tshirhart, & Cauley, 1983, p. 36). The phrase "new mode of conflict" was coined by Jenkins (1975). See also Mickolus (1980, Introduction) and Hacker (1976, Preface). As is often the case with conventional wisdom, the view is expressed without elaboration in the first paragraph or preface. To Gurr (1979, p. 23), the "conventional wisdom (concerning terrorism) is a fantasy accepted as an onimous political reality by (virtually) everyone." Cf. Rapoport (1982a, Introduction).

2. I do not distinguish Zealots from Sicarii, although they are distinctly different groups, as Smith (1971) demonstrates. The Sicarii terrorized mostly Jews, whereas the Zealots were more concerned with Romans and Greeks. But for our purposes this is not a critical distinction. A more extensive discussion of the Jewish uprising appears in Rapoport (1982b). Horsley (1979a) is the only other essay I know which discusses the Jewish activity as terrorist activity.

3. The cases are so well known and interesting that Thomas DeQuincey (1877), a nineteenth-century

Romantic writer and the first student of comparative terrorism, pointed out the importance of comparing them. DeQuincey himself concentrates on the Sicarii in various essays. Lewis (1967, chap. 6) compares the three briefly.

4. It would be useful to extend the analysis by treating Christian terror, but the materials are not as conveniently available. No single Christian terror group has caught the public imagination in a way that is comparable to those I have chosen. Unlike those groups discussed here, the numerous millenarian sects using terror in the late medieval period did not rely on hit-and-disappear tactics. Their terror was a sort of state terror; the sects organized their communities openly, taking full control of a territory, instituting gruesome purges to obliterate all traces of the old order, and organizing large armies, which waged holy wars periodically sweeping over the countryside and devastating, burning, and massacring everything and everyone in their paths. The military pattern reminds one of the Crusades, an unlimited or total war launched by the Papacy (Cohn, 1961; cf. Rapoport & Alexander, 1982), in which seven essays discuss relationships between sacred and modern justifications, focusing largely on Christian traditions.

5. Although the Thugs may do what they do because they know that ordinary Hindus regard such actions as terrifying and horrible, they want victims only to experience terror. The earliest contemporary discussions of terrorism emphasized the extranormal character of its violence as the distinguishing feature, but the importance of that distinction has been largely lost. Compare Thornton (1964), Walter (1969), Rapoport (1977), and Price (1977). Since terror is extranormal violence, it is likely to flow initially from a doctrine, and it tends to be a historical rather than a universal phenomenon. In recent years our definitions generally treat terror and violence as synonyms. (See, for example, Russell, 1979, p. 4.) Since violence is a universal phenomenon, it is not surprising that there is a tendency for those who do not distinguish between violence and terror to treat differences in the latter as largely differences in scale. Hostile sources compiled the materials for all three groups, which poses important questions of reliability. Specific footnotes for each case treat these problems, although obviously only historians of each period can assess the documents adequately. The pictures drawn for each group differ so dramatically that at the very least they represent archetypes of specific religious traditions.

6. When early twentieth-century Hindu terrorist groups used Kali to justify their activities, secrecy was shunned because they had a political purpose, the independence of India (Pal, 1932). Because terror can give the perpetrator joy, it can be undertaken for its own sake. An example might be the Tylenol killer in the fall of 1982, who laced capsules with arsenic, terrorizing the American public and drug industry in the process. Publicity would be important in this case of terror for terror's sake only if the terrorist desired an audience too.

7. The experience is described in a reasonably accurate, overly gruesome bestseller (Clark, 1979). The group apparently believed that a race war would develop from its efforts, and perhaps at this point it would become visible.

8. Primary sources on the Thugs are extensive. Numerous archival and published government materials exist for virtually every year from 1826 to 1904, the latter being the termination date of the special Indian institution created to deal with Thuggee and related problems, the Thag and Dakaiti Department. By 1850 Thug activity itself ceased almost entirely. Pfirrmann (1970) is the only person who has examined all the primary source materials. His conclusions are substantially those offered by W. H. Sleeman, the remarkable officer who made the Thugs an issue in British politics, contrived the specials methods used to destroy them, and proved to be a perceptive sociologist of religion. Sleeman's six published books (1836, 1839, 1940, 1893, 1858, and 1849) are listed in order of their pertinence. Two useful nineteenth-century secondary accounts based on Sleeman are Hutton (1847) and Thornton (1837). The best twentieth-century books published before Pfirrmann are Sleeman (1933) and Bruce (1968).

The Thugs have captured literary imaginations. Meadows Taylor, a British officer with Sleeman, wrote a bestselling novel (1839) which was reprinted several times. Wilkie Collins's novel, *The Moonstone,* has gone through eleven editions at least, and John Masters (1952) has provided the latest fictional account.

9. The thirteenth-century writings of Jalalu-d din Firoz Khilji, Sultan of Delhi, refer to the banishment of a thousand persons generally identified as Thugs. But before their demise, not much was known about them. Afterward, the thoroughness of British officials, trial records, and police informants provided much material. Although the information was compiled by British police administrators and the Thugs were denied public trials, legal counsel, and the right to question witnesses, the picture developed from this information was accepted completely for more than a century. Recently, it was challenged by Gupta (1959) and Gordon (1969), who believe that the group developed only when the British arrived. Gupta provides no evidence for this view, and Pfirrmann is justified in simply brushing it aside as a polemic. Gordon's thesis seems more substantial and depends on allegations of inconsistencies in the primary sources. His essay was published too late for Pfirrmann to evaluate, but I found that the inconsistencies cited come largely from Gordon's tendency to take quotations out of context, which may explain why he did not develop this thesis in subsequent writings and why it has been ignored by others.

10. The estimate is incorporated in J. L. Sleeman's title (1933). Every estimate flounders because we don't know the age of the organization or its size in various periods. It is generally assumed that the number remained constant because the group was largely hereditary. In my view, the administrative chaos that prevailed in the wake of the Moghul Empire's collapse when the British arrived gave the brotherhood unusual opportunities for new victims and swelled its ranks, which suggests that Sleeman's "conservative estimate" represents a maximum, not a minimum, one.

11. When terrorist activities are part of a larger military struggle (i.e., Vietnam and Algeria), we have no reliable statistics on the terror alone. In situations when terror alone prevails (e.g., Cyprus, Aden, Northern Ireland) the casualties terrorists inflict rarely exceed three figures.

12. "Bhowanee is happy and most so in proportion to the blood that is shed. . . . Blood is her food. . . . She thirsts for blood!" (Sleeman, 1836, p. 36). The estimates made by various British officials are compiled in a review article which also provides a list of 20 leading Thugs who murdered 5120 persons, an average of 256 each (A religion of murder, 1901)!

13. "There are many thieves in my village but I would not go with them. My father Assa used to counsel me against the thieves saying—do not join them, they take money without thugging. Go with Thugs. If I had a (farthing) by Thuggee, I would take it, but never by theft" (Pfirrmann, 1970, p. 70). Another on-the-spot observer, Sir John Malcolm (1823, vol. 2, p. 187), suggested that robbery was the prime concern, "their victims . . . are always selected for having property. . . ." But the evidence seems to be clearly against him.

14. To allay Hindu anxieties concerning Thug reprisals, the British waived many rights of the defendants. Individuals could be convicted simply for being members of the group and then would be interned for the rest of their lives on grounds that they perceived Thuggee as a religious obligation and would always continue to do so. Thomas Macauley probably drew up the legislation. The rationale is explained by Hervey (1892, vol. 2, pp. 443–45 and Appendixes E and F). In World War II Gillie (1944) contended that the principles should be revived to dispose of Nazi leaders, and to some extent they were embodied at Nuremberg.

15. No serious argument has been made that the Thugs ever had a political purpose. Russell and Hira (1916) conclude that the immunities were probably linked with Hindu concepts of luck and impurities, although the immunities may have represented tribes from which Thugs originated or disguises Thugs often assumed.

16. Thirty to forty Europeans normally participated in these operations against some 10,000 Thugs. A few assassination attempts against officials occurred, but the assailants lost their nerve, so pervasive must have been the taboo. As far as we know, the Thugs murdered only one or two European travellers.

17. "So far from shrinking at the appellation, when one of them is asked who he is, he will coolly answer that he is a robber" (Hutton, 1961, p. 127).

18. The prolongation of the death agony (the only exception?) was required by Thug doctrine.

19. Apparently the major anxiety of Thugs was that they might be hung by a person of a lower caste (Spry, 1837, vol. 2, chap. 5).

20. For the convenience of readers unfamiliar with Islamic references, I shall refer to the Nazari by their more familiar name, Assassins. When I refer to sympathetic elements, I have in mind the Shia and especially the Ismaili, the groups from which the Assassins originated. Orthodox Muslims are Sunni.

Few Assassin documents have survived, and our picture of the sect is reconstructed mostly from bitterly hostile orthodox chroniclers who obviously could not pierce the veil of secrecy, even if they had wanted to do so. Poonawala (1977) provides the most recent bibliography of sources and secondary works. Many items are annotated. The difficulties of the contemporary historian are aptly described in Hodgson (1955, pp. 22–32). Universally recognized as the best source, Hodgson's work was later sharpened (1968). My analysis is based largely on these accounts and on Lewis (1940, 1967).

21. The reference is to Shia doctrine, but it applies equally to the Assassins.

22. "A state ought not during war to countenance such hostilities as would make mutual confidence in a subsequent peace impossible such as employing assassins, poisoners, breaches of capitulation, secret instigations to treachery and rebellion in the hostile state . . . (for there must be) some kind of confidence in the disposition of the enemy even in the midst of war, or otherwise . . . the hostilities will pass into a war of extermination. . . . Such a war and . . . all means which lead to it, must be absolutely forbidden" (Cf. Vattel, I, 19, 233).

23. The sect, of course, was the subject of many allegations, but it was never charged with instigating counter-atrocities against groups or individuals. The sober Sunni view was that the Nizari wanted "to destroy Islam but not necessarily any . . . Muslims" (Hodgson, 1955, p. 123).

24. The Azraqites apparently practiced indiscriminate slaughter, arguing that every member of a family of unbelievers was an unbeliever (Watt, 1973, p. 22).

25. The initial assassination, that of Asma bent Marwan, was occasioned by Mohammed's question, "Will no one rid me of (her)?" Henry II encouraged

his knights in the same way when he grumbled about Becket. But how different the results were! Becket was martyred, the knights were punished, and the English king did penance. For a discussion of Greco-Roman and Christian attitudes toward assassination, see Rapoport (1971, chap. 1).

26. In the Koran, the term hypocrite (munafikun) refers to those whose fidelity and zeal Mohammed could not rely upon, persons "in whose hearts there is sickness, weakness, and doubt . . . who had joined Islam perhaps reluctantly . . . usually members of the aristocracy" (Buhl, 1913). Most of those assassinated were Jews, but Mohammed's "Constitution of Medina" clearly indicates that his original community included Jews, and initially he intended to bring Islam as close as possible to Judaism. When that policy failed, the assassinations were an essential aspect of the struggle to separate the two religious bodies and to gain converts out of the Jewish tribes. The process is illustrated in the aftermath of the first assassination, that of a Jewish poetess by 'Umayr, her kinsman: "'Umayr returned to his own clan, which was in a great uproar. Decide what is to be done with me, but do not keep me waiting! No one moved. . . . That was the day when Islam first showed its power over the Banu Katma. 'Umayr had been the first among them to become a Muslim. On the day the daughter of Marwan was killed, the men of the Banu Khatma were converted because of what they saw of the power of Islam" (Ibn Hisham quoted by Rodinson, 1971, p. 171).

27. Margoliouth (1923, p. 116) notes that Muslim initially meant "traitor, one who handed over his kinsmen or friends to their enemies," and that "Mohammed . . . displayed great ingenuity" in transforming its meaning into "one who handed over his own person to God." The new religion, he believes, could not survive without challenging the kin bond; and "Islam, as appears from the most authorized traditions, had the effect of making men anxious . . . to signalize their faith by parricide or fratricide" (p. 265). The traditional or orthodox interpretations of these incidents is that the assailants, shamed by their kinsmen's behavior, acted on their own initiative.

28. No terrorist campaign before the nineteenth century is better known, and virtually all our information comes from Josephus Flavius, a Jewish commander who later became a Roman supporter and portrays the Zealots and Sicarii as provoking the popular uprising when no irreconcilable issues divided Roman and Jew. How reliable is Josephus?

Historians have always disagreed. He has been seen as a "mere Roman apologist," and the accounts he challenges have vanished. His description, like those of all ancient historians, wildly exaggerates statistics and contains inconsistencies which serve explicit didactic purposes. Still, moderns increasingly find him credible, except on particular matters where good reason to mistrust him exists. When his sources can be checked, he "remains fairly close to the original. Even when he modifies the source to suit a certain aim, he still reproduces the essence of the story. More important, he does not engage in the free invention of episodes . . . like other (ancient) authors . . ." (Cohen, 1979, p. 233). All other extant sources, Roman and Jewish materials alike, are more hostile to the rebels than Josephus himself was. Although some say "that Josephus' good faith as a historian cannot be seriously questioned" (Shutt, 1961, p. 123), most agree that despite other concerns he truly had "an interest as a historian in the course of events themselves" (Bide, 1979, p. 201).

The second issue is which of Josephus' different and contradictory assessments or motives is most credible? I have followed the modern tendency in playing down the criminal and personal motives Josephus gives to the rebels in order to emphasize their religious and political concerns. And I have taken seriously his frequently repeated contention, which some scholars question, that the terrorists forced their will on reluctant parties. The process of polarizing a society by exploiting latent hostilities through shock tactics was not understood well by the nineteenth- and early twentieth-century commentators on Josephus who knew of no terror campaigns with which to compare the revolt. More recent scolars display less skepticism on this point. My earlier study (1982b) is a step-by-step analysis of the dynamic presupposed by Josephus' account, and the description above is based upon that essay.

The literature on the revolt is quite extensive. The following articles (in addition to those cited above) were particularly helpful: Applebaum (1971), Betz et al. (1974), Borg (1971), Farmer (1956), Grant (1973), Hengel (1961), Horsley (1979b), Kingdom (1970, 1971), Kohler (1905), Roth (1959), Smallwood (1976), Stern (1973), Thackeray (1967), and Zeitlin (1967).

29. For a convenient discussion of the herem and its revival by the Zealots-Sicarii as reflected in the Dead Sea Scrolls, see de Vaux (1972, pp. 258–267). The later conception had new elements: the war would be a war to end all wars, it would involve all men, and the enemy was under Satan's influence.

30. Rapoport (1982b, pp. 36–37) discusses relationships between the process described here and modern campaign experiences. For a general discussion of passive resistance and terrorism, see Thornton (1946, p. 75.)

31.   A third reason for studying sacred terror is that there are direct links between some of its concepts and those that animate modern forms (Dugard, 1982).

32.   In 1933, J. L. Sleeman wrote, "it is of interest to speculate as to what the procedure would be today were such an organization of murder to be discovered in India, and imagination runs riot at the long vista of Royal Commissions, Blue, Red, and White Books, Geneva Conferences and the political capital which would be made of it, the procrastination and the delay, tying the hands of those on the spot, and the world propaganda which would ensue. . . . Thuggee could shelter behind disunited party government" (p. 103).

33.   The Crusades are the major exception, for they were inspired by the herem and undertaken to regain the Holy Land in order to initiate a messianic era.

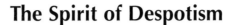

The Spirit of Despotism

Understanding the Tyrant Within

Manfred F. R. Kets de Vries

The objective of this article is to better understand the developmental history of despotic regimes and the existence of leadership by terror. To gain greater insight into this phenomenon, it explores the unusual relationship between leaders and followers in despotic regimes and examines the self-destructive cycle that characterizes such regimes. The article highlights the price paid in the form of human suffering and the breakdown of the moral fabric of a society. In this article, particular attention is paid to highly intrusive totalitarian regimes. It discusses in detail the levers used by such regimes to consolidate their power base. The role of ideology, the enforcement of mind control, the impact of the media, the inception of the illusion of solidarity, and the search for scapegoats are part of the review. Finally, the article makes suggestions on how to prevent despotic leaders from gaining a hold on power. Observations are made about the newly founded International Criminal Court, a permanent international judicial body that has been specially set up to try despotic rulers for genocide, crimes against humanity, and war crimes.

The people have always some champion whom they set over them and nurse into greatness . . . This and no other is the root from which a tyrant springs; when he first appears he is a protector.

—Plato, *The Republic*

The possession of unlimited power will make a despot of almost any man. There is a possible Nero in the gentlest human creature that walks.

—Thomas Bailey, *Leaves From a Notebook*

INTRODUCTION

Whether we talk about autocrats, tyrants, despots, totalitarian regimes, or violent rule, the subject of terror is a contemporary problem, although this generation did not invent it. Indeed, throughout the ages, autocratic governments have been more the rule than the exception; in fact, democratic forms of government have been relatively rare. In the recent past, despots, such as Joseph Stalin,

Adolf Hitler, Mao Zedong, Pol Pot, Idi Amin, Nicolae Ceausescu, Joseph Désiré Mobutu, Kim Il-Sung, and Slobodan Milošević, replaced Caligula, Nero, Tamerlane, Vlad the Impaler, Shaka Zulu, and Ivan the Terrible; and these leaders have, themselves, been followed by the likes of Saddam Hussein, Fidel Castro, Kim Jong Il, Muammar Qaddafi, and Robert Mugabe. Although some of these leaders have been lionized as nation-builders, despite the atrocities they have committed, they stand out as examples of the kinds of horror

SOURCE: From "The Spirit of Despotism: Understanding the Tyrant Within" in *Human Relations* 59(2) by Kets de Vries, Manfred F. R. © 2006, pp. 195–220. Reprinted with permissions from Sage, Ltd.

humans can inflict on other humans, many having murdered millions. They stand as dramatic examples of how to inflict human misery and suffering. Hitler, Stalin, Mao Zedong, and Pol Pot in the previous century were grandmasters of bloodshed, leaving tens of millions of dead in their wake.

What makes the existence of such violent leaders particularly disturbing is that it seems so inevitable: the history of absolute, totalitarian regimes is a long one, with no apparent beginning and no end in sight. We like to think that the world is growing more civilized, and yet the crop of potential new despotic leaders is burgeoning. The explanation is disturbing: studies of human behavior indicate that the disposition to violence exists in *all* of us; *everyone* may have a despot in his or her basement (Asch, 1956; Lifton, 1961; Schein, 1961; Haney et al., 1973; Milgram, 1975; Kets de Vries, 2004). Lord Acton's dictum, 'All power tends to corrupt, and absolute power corrupts absolutely,' is truer now than ever. Humankind appears to be the only member of the animal kingdom that has the potential for mass murder, and we realize that potential with disturbing frequency. Given the psychological makeup of the human animal, we must assume that there are untold numbers of tyrants in the making among us, who will be revealed if and when the opportunity for power arises. The human tendency to lionize leaders and excuse their excesses encourages an endless line-up of new candidates for fame and glory.

The objective of this article is to better understand the developmental history of despotic regimes. Because prevention requires knowledge, and change requires insight, an understanding of the mechanics of terror can be seen as a modest step toward preventing despotic leaders and totalitarian regimes from coming to the fore. Such an understanding will help us find our way through what remains a largely unexplored domain. It will, for example, give us an insight into the unusual relationship between leaders and followers in totalitarian regimes, help us deal more effectively with potential and existing tyrants, and give us tools of prevention.

Leadership by terror can be seen as a form of leadership that achieves its ends and gains compliance through the deliberate use of violence and fear. It is the use of arbitrary power beyond the scope permitted by law, custom, and tradition. The lust for power pushes true despots beyond the boundaries of their mandate to rule,

causing them to abandon respect for human rights and individual freedom, and to behave in ways that prevent others from living their lives with dignity and self-respect. In a nutshell, tyrannical leadership is the arbitrary rule by a single person who, by inducing a psychological state of extreme fear in a population, monopolizes power to his or her own advantage (unchecked by law or other restraining influences), exercising that power without restraint and, in most cases, contrary to the general good. Despots hamper justice, the right to fair process, excellence, and the development of the human potential of a population.

CLARIFYING CONFUSING TERMINOLOGY

In contrast to many other writers dealing with the subject, in this article the terms *dictatorship, despotism, tyranny, authoritarianism,* and *totalitarianism* will be used somewhat interchangeably. The polemics of the various nuances of these terms is not the objective of this article; classification is a topic unto itself. I will simply mention briefly that some writers have made an effort to classify non-democratic forms of government, putting at one extreme traditional, relatively benevolent authoritarian regimes, and at the other extreme, totalitarian governments of the Nazi and Soviet variety (Walter, 1969; Arendt, 1973; Reich, 1990; Chirot, 1994; Herschman & Lieb, 1994; Glass, 1995; Boesche, 1996; Robins & Post, 1997).

Totalitarianism

At the most dangerous extreme of the control spectrum, the term *totalitarianism* is used by these writers to refer to regimes under which a population is completely subjugated to a political system that aspires to total domination of the collective over the individual. Totalitarian regimes strive to invade and control their citizenry's social, economic, political, and personal life. Such forms of government are typically permeated by a secular or theocratic ideology that professes a set of supreme, absolute values that are propagated by the leadership. Repression of individual rights and loyalty to that ideology are their salient characteristics. The overriding importance of ideology means that every aspect of every individual's life is subordinate to the state. Because totalitarian governments want to transform human nature, they exercise thought-control and control moral education. In other words, repression is carried out not only against people's *actions* but also against their *thoughts*.

Such regimes retain control only so long as the terror of totalitarianism does not ease up. Thus any objection to governmental control is viewed as a danger to the regime, a threat to its delicate equilibrium. As a result, such regimes are more likely than others to 'eat their own'—that is, to do away with (by exile, imprisonment, or death) government supporters tainted by the merest suspicion of rebellion. These regimes need the sacrifice of an endless stream of new enemies to retain their focus (Friedrich, 1954; Friedrich & Brezezinsky, 1965; Arendt, 1969, 1973; Boesche, 1996).

Authoritarianism

Authoritarian regimes, on the other hand, are perceived by those who make this distinction, as being less invasive. Although repression of the populace takes place, there is no intrusive ideology. Such regimes do not profess the benefits of a future utopian state; they do not seek to transform human nature. The goal of authoritarian leadership is much more mundane: retaining power. Authoritarian rulers strive to keep the riches and privileges that come with holding on to power, and they exert whatever level of repression that it takes (Boesche, 1996).

Although both types of regime can be extremely brutal to political opponents, in an authoritarian state, the government's efforts are directed primarily at those who are considered political opponents. The government lacks the desire (and often the means) to control every aspect of each individual's life, and thus intervention in the day-to-day life of the citizenry is limited. Grounded in greed rather than ideology, authoritarian leadership does not claim to represent a specific historical destiny or possess the absolute truth; it is not in the business of creating a new type of social life or a new kind of human being. Under the guise of promising social reform, authoritarian leaders seize power only to enrich themselves and their friends, ruling with brutal terror and arbitrary force for personal gains only. The amassing of wealth, the betrayal of social reforms, the development of a

military power base, and rampant paranoia are characteristics associated with authoritarianism.

In a way, totalitarianism and authoritarianism can be viewed as specific positions on a spectrum, according to the degree of mind-control enforced. Although many of the observations made in this article will refer to both positions, special attention will be given to the extreme, most intrusive position: totalitarianism.

RIDING THE WAVES WITH DESPOTS

Whenever people gather in groups, there is the potential for the abuse of power. Would-be despots are everywhere, although they thrive best in the fertile ground of tribal or nation formation. The turbulence of the formative period makes people anxious, and anxiety prompts them to look for some forms of 'containment' and search for strong leadership (Bion, 1959; Kets de Vries, 2001a, 2006). The prevalence of human anxiety explains why totalitarianism and authoritarianism have been with us since the dawn of time. The early civilizations that grew up along great rivers such as the Nile, the Tigris, the Euphrates, the Yangtze, the Yellow, and the Ganges, clamored for leaders to give their public waterworks a modicum of centralized direction. A brief look at history tells us, however, that centralized leadership can easily become perverted. We see, for instance, how ancient Egypt, Mesopotamia, China, India, and the pre-Columbian Central and South American cultures positioned an absolute, often despotic ruler at the center of the ruling bureaucracy. We also observe the rise and inevitable fall of such regimes.

Much has been said and written about absolute rulers. Philosophers, in particular, have tackled this subject. Plato, for example, was one of the earliest recorded observers of tyranny. Tyranny evoked, for him, associations of disharmony and disease, and he viewed tyrants as individuals governed by out-of-control desires. According to Plato, 'drunkenness, lust, and madness' differentiate the tyrant from other people. A tyrant

> becomes, in reality, what he was once only occasionally in his dreams, and there's nothing, no taboo, no murder, however terrible, from which he will shirk. His passion tyrannizes over him, a despot will be without restraint or law . . . (Plato, 1955: 348)

In other words, tyrants act out in the light of day what most of us only dare to dream about at night. Plato concluded that to act on such dreams—to satisfy one's darkest desires—leads the tyrant into an unending, spiraling cycle of desire, gratification, and more desire.

Most students of despotic regimes acknowledge the application of violence of such entities. As Niccolò Machiavelli (1966: 132) advised, cynically, half a millennium ago, 'Men must either be caressed or else annihilated.' Machiavelli, who was one of the first statesmen to build a political science based on the study of humankind, saw no alternative to love and violence as motivators. But tyranny goes beyond the 'simple' violence of, say, execution; it evokes images of madness and sadistic desires run amok.

The terror and violence that characterize despotic regimes take two forms: outwardly directed and inwardly directed. Both forms often lead to mass murder and genocide. Outwardly directed terror is used to intimidate or even exterminate enemies outside one's borders. Typically, enemies are viewed by despots as forces of darkness that need to be destroyed by a force of light. They are described in derogatory terms and depicted by tyrannical leadership as less than human. This dehumanization makes the administration of violence more palatable to members of the enforcement arm of the government. After all, it is only the enemy—no more than a lower subspecies—upon whom violence is inflicted (Volcan, 1988).

Leadership by terror is particularly devastating when it is directed—as it often is—not only outwardly but also inwardly. Inwardly directed terror heightens considerably the fear and anxiety of living under despotic regimes. Using violent acts directed against the despot's own population, inwardly directed terror results in subjugation of the citizenry, classification as a subspecies of one part (or multiple parts) of the population, loss of various freedoms, and ultimately the suffocation of the mind. A reign of terror is superimposed on the conventional systems of power and authority.

The ability to enact terror—whether against an external enemy or against one's own people—is viewed by many tyrannical leaders as a sign of privilege. It is seen as a special prerogative. To despots, boundaries of acceptable behavior apply only to others. Living in a narcissistic 'soup,' having little concern for the needs of others, despots perceive few restraints on their actions. They believe that 'divine providence' (however they construe divinity) has given them power over life and death. In other words, they believe that they have the *right* to act as they do. This sense of entitlement is especially frightening when it spreads: the specific psychology or psychopathology of a leader can become institutionalized (as with Hitler, Stalin, Pol Pot, and Bin Laden), so that the common people come to support the distorted and dangerous ideology articulated by the leadership (Kets de Vries, 1989).

Leadership by terror succeeds only in the hands of a despot skilled at the fine art of boundary management. If, on the one hand, terror is taken to its extreme and executed too forcefully, there is soon nothing left to terrorize; the 'objects' of terror are destroyed. If, on the other hand, terror is applied too lightly, it does not result in the desired compliance. Maintaining the devilish bond between the terrorized and the tyrant requires a delicate balancing act: traditional mechanisms in society need to be modified but cannot be destroyed.

SORCERERS' APPRENTICES

Why is it that some societies can pass through an initial despotic phase into freedom while others become mired in despotism? What creates fertile ground for the cultivation of despotism? How does the process of despotic rule evolve?

In general, despots are leaders who take personal advantage of a chaotic situation. They tend to flourish in societies in transition. If we review historical processes, we see that the greatest despots have emerged in situations of war or class war. Consider Germany after the First World War, dealing with a sense of national humiliation and a class struggle verging on civil war. Consider China, still haunted by the affront of Western powers intruding in their sovereignty, a process that started in the 19th century. The lingering presence of the memory of such indignities is typical of the world's breeding grounds for tyranny. Societies in which democratic traditions and institutions are still lacking or are poorly developed, societies with weak political systems and/or an ineffective judiciary, and societies in severe economic distress seem to be particularly vulnerable. These social conditions, especially occurring together, facilitate a power grab by a power-hungry despot. They allow such a leader, generally with the help of a gangster-like regime, to exploit the lack of organization, alienation, and bewilderment of the citizenry.

Notwithstanding the 20th century's much-vaunted progress in the scientific and economic realms, that period witnessed the rise of some of the most brutal and oppressive regimes in the history of humankind. Nations just emerging from colonial or communist rule seemed to be particularly vulnerable. Such nations have had institutions imposed on them—institutions not rooted in their original culture—making them susceptible to despotism. Many such examples can be seen in the history of Africa, Asia, and the Middle East. The proliferation of recent, new dictatorships in countries formerly belonging to the Soviet Union also illustrates this vulnerability.

When formerly colonial or communist countries become independent, people generally have sky-high expectations about the future. These expectations are followed by deep disappointment once the gap is seen between hope and harsh reality. Deep contrasts between wealth and haunting poverty, both within nations and between nations, and the prevalence of corruption that is made more visible through the media add to this state of discontent.

All the above social conditions create alienation within a society, and that alienation paves the way for tyranny. When social institutions disintegrate, and when there is little to hold on to, people are more willing to subject themselves to despotic regimes. They are more inclined to search for messiahs who promise economic and political salvation from the hardships the population is experiencing. Those individuals who are insecure and lonely are looking for a safe harbor, searching for the 'containment' that they hope a strong leader offers; they are looking for a 'holding environment' that will contain their existential anxiety and deal with their sense of alienation, dislocation, and aloneness (Winnicott, 1975). They can find all these things in one mass movement or another. Mass movements, whatever their ideology, typically offer solidarity, an end to loneliness and anxiety, and hope for a better future.

IN PRAISE OF TYRANNY

Niccolò Machiavelli viewed the adoption of the despot's role as a natural phase in nation-building—one that would, of necessity, last until the nation-builder had achieved his or her primary goals (Machiavelli, 1966). Many leaders take on the role of tyrant without hesitation, but fail to temper their violence or modify their rule after they have consolidated their power base. Because of that intemperance, such countries never become societies based on the rule of law, and the populace will never have a say in how that rule of law should be applied. Unable to make the transition that Machiavelli believed possible, many of these rulers unleashed powers that they could not ultimately control.

Many political scientists share Machiavelli's outlook that dictatorship is a transitional phase that many countries have to go through on their way to democracy (Friedrich & Brezezinsky, 1965; Boesche, 1996). Those who support this view argue that non-democratic political configurations do not deserve the harsh condemnation they receive from democratic idealists. Like it or not, they remonstrate, simplistic Western political formulas do not suit certain societies at an early stage of development. Given the mindset of the people in these developing societies, democratic structures would turn out to be highly ineffective—worse, in the end, than a transitional tyranny. The people in these societies are simply not ready to deal with the freedom that democracy not only offers but also demands. While acknowledging the darker side of dictatorship, these proponents are quick to point out the advantages of being ruled by an autocratic government. Although despots repress their citizens, they may also protect the population from outside dangers, re-knit a society torn apart by violent upheaval, put an end to internal strife, introduce law and order, and eradicate certain forms of corruption. Some despots even create a new prosperity (or at least the illusion of prosperity) by embarking on great public works and by providing such services as schools, housing, hospitals, and roads.

What these Machiavellian proponents fail to acknowledge is the likelihood—the all-but-certainty—that autocratic leadership will turn into all-out tyranny. Positive contributions notwithstanding, the shadow side of power-based leadership almost inevitably comes to the fore. As time passes, most leaders with despotic tendencies increasingly feel entitled to do whatever they want, however inappropriate their behavior may be. As excessive narcissism raises its ugly head, feelings of entitlement sway behavior (Kets de Vries, 2001b, 2006). Gradually, the perks and privileges, appropriated by the ruling elite, become increasingly glaring. The leader and his henchmen engage in regressive activities, the arbitrary use of power, the grabbing of scarce resources, the repression of free will, and the violation of human rights, all of which mean misery for the populace and decline for the economy.

While dictatorships are one-way streets, democracies are two-way streets: in the latter, the people have a voice. That does not mean that democracy is perfect. Life in freedom is not always easy. After all, having choices implies having responsibilities. Moreover, democratic decision-making can be cumbersome and slow. Democratic leaders are often unwilling to bite the bullet and make unpopular but necessary decisions, because they are concerned more about being re-elected than about the good of the country. Furthermore, compromise and coalition politics do not always lead to the best outcome. The latter, for example, sometimes results in a paradox of voting whereby the least attractive candidate wins the election.

And yet the alternative to democracy is not really an option. While benevolent autocracy is a theoretical possibility, rule by a solitary leader typically ends in servile obedience to authority and abuse of human rights. In contrast, democracy (though flawed) safeguards human dignity, protects individual freedoms, assures free choice, and gives people a voice in decisions that affect their destiny, allowing them to work for a better future for their children. Humankind's desire for *justice* and fair play makes democracy possible. Humankind's capacity for *injustice* makes democracy necessary. Given the shadow side of human behavior, we need democracy, with its many checks and balances on power, such as the judiciary, varied political parties, independent administrative bodies, a free press, and a comprehensive legal system. These elements help prevent leadership and followers alike from falling into a regressive abyss; they serve as boundaries against humankind's excesses.

But a political system that grants fairness to all should never be taken for granted. Given the ever-present potential for individual and societal regression, democratic practices must be continuously defended. All human beings have a darker side, a violent streak ready to erupt as circumstances dictate. Every leader, every individual, has this potential. Modern tyrants hang on to ideologies whose dogma they interpret according to their own needs, not the needs of their people. They will resort to repressive measures. By engaging in demagoguery, they will oppress their people, depriving them of freedom and hope. They will prevent them from developing their capabilities to their fullest potential. They will taint their rule with fear, misery, degradation, and poverty, and create an outwardly passive, subjugated populace, dead to critical inquiry. And, not to mention, they will eventually eat their own.

THE DESPOT'S TOOL BOX

Beyond the obvious tool of violence, what do tyrants use to remain in power? What levers of action do they pull? What kind of 'instrumentation' do they possess to stay in power? How are they able to subject a population? The answer varies, depending on the society and its circumstances, but the strongest weapon of the more despotic regime is ideology. As suggested, the resort to an intrusive ideology is what differentiates authoritarianism from its more extreme manifestation: totalitarianism.

The Enchantment of Ideology

To Hannah Arendt, a major aspect of the totalitarian despot's tool box is the introduction of an ideology with supreme values—a political religion that replaces traditional religion (Arendt, 1969). That ideology claims to have the answer to all-important social and historical dilemmas. To use the words of the sociologist, Robert Jay Lifton:

> Behind ideological totalism lies the ever-present human quest for the omnipotent guide—for the supernatural force, political party, philosophical ideas, great leader, or precise science—that will bring ultimate solidarity to all men and eliminate the terror of death and nothingness. (Lifton, 1961: 436)

We observe how, particularly in totalitarian states, virtue and evil—the forces of light and of darkness—become bound in the state ideology, which presents the pursuit of virtue as a universally accepted ideal. Frequently, the promise is a laudable, utopian-like solution to the human condition, but the ideological goals of totalitarian systems vary. While the Soviet Union under Stalin and the People's Republic of China under Mao Zedong sought the universal fulfillment of humankind through the establishment of a classless society, Germany under Hitler's National

Socialism attempted to establish a Thousand Year Reich based on the superiority of the so-called Aryan race. Ironically, in the process of universalizing that pursuit, despotism destroys the moral fabric of a society. Frequently, the leaders of such totalitarian entities create huge bureaucratic machines to institutionalize their allegedly virtue-based worldview. The existence of such institutions goes a long way toward creating a submissive, obedient populace that reiterates the party's propaganda.

As has been noted, the urge to surrender to some form of idealistic belief system is most prominent in fragmented, divided societies plagued by stress and uncertainty. Although what the outside world sees of despotism is the merciless leader, the belief system that supports him is often in place before he steps up to take the reins. Alienated and frustrated intellectuals and/or theocrats in such a society are often the ones who first develop and speak of a particular vision of utopian society. They typically establish a pseudo-scientific or extremist religious base for their theories, thereby undergirding their 'formula' for the perfect society. Through their convoluted ideology, they offer a form of 'salvation' to a select group of true believers—those who are chosen to attain the 'promised land.'

Thus, ideology is everything in totalitarian states. It serves the leader's narcissistic fantasies, and it creates a 'fusion' of leader and led. By facilitating conscious and unconscious dreams of togetherness, of shared purpose, it creates a false sense of group solidarity. Maintaining this delicate mental equilibrium implies the abdication of autonomous functioning. Thus, any attempt at individuation, at independent thinking, is seen as high treason, an attack on the state. Because individuation starts early, the family is important as a training ground, a forum for building patterns of obedience to authority. Someone who knew no freedom in childhood is less likely to protest a lack of freedom later on.

And given the importance of early indoctrination, many totalitarian governments use preschool and later schooling to eliminate undesirable attitudes that the parents may have passed on. Some totalitarian regimes have even taken children away from their parents and raised them in communal houses. The Soviet Union, for example, experimented with communal houses in the 1920s and the 1950s. Likewise, during the war with Afghanistan during the 1980s, the Soviet government forcibly took tens of thousands of young Afghan children to the USSR to be raised away from their families. The *Hitlerjugend*, the Pioneers, the Komsomols, the Red Guards, and the Khmer Rouge can all be seen as tools to brainwash young people, gain their support for the prevailing ideology, and even make them spy and inform on their parents.

These ideologists paint a stark world of good and evil, truth and falsehood, and stake an absolute claim on the former. As a test that will determine their entry into the 'promised land,' followers are challenged to overcome a number of obstacles posed by 'nonbelievers.' These opponents are depicted, at best, as evildoers, at worst, as 'sub-humans' (Erikson, 1963; Des Pres, 1976). The ideologists encourage their followers to fight these 'evil' adversaries with whatever force is necessary. As time evolves and the group of followers grows, a political party (either established or new) embraces the ideology, with believers unquestioningly parroting its tenets. And out of that party emerges the leader, the 'high priest,' who will turn vision into tyranny.

Leaders of ideology-based totalitarian states will do anything to win new converts. They want to spread their creed—but only to people 'worthy' of conversion, of course. They are convinced that sharing their ideology, whether secular or theocratic, will bring enlightenment to the masses. There is a sect-like intensity to this need to convert others: the fragility of the ideology demands constant validation from others, to bolster faith in the worldview, create solidarity, and reinforce the righteousness of the cause. In contrast, people who resist conversion threaten the ideology and make the converted uncomfortable. They remind true believers of the shakiness of their belief system, often triggering anger and violence.

Whichever party adopts the totalitarian ideology, it generally attempts to give the appearance of propriety. For example, it typically makes participation in politics, especially voting, compulsory. As we all know, though, in totalitarianism, the right to vote does not mean the right to choose. The only real choice is the party and the party's leader. The lack of choice is enforced through political repression. The ruling party and its leader restrict the rights of citizens to criticize the government, the rights of opposition parties to campaign against the government, and the rights of certain groups, associations, and political parties to convene (or even exist). They try to shape the thoughts of their subjects through control of educational institutions and the media. In fact, they seek to dominate all economic and political matters, including the attitudes, values, and beliefs of the population, thereby erasing the distinction between state and society. The citizen's duty to the state is thus the primary concern of the community, and the goal of the state is the replacement of the existing society with the utopian society depicted by the favored ideology.

Because divine authority is a particular threat, totalitarian regimes typically combine spiritual and secular guidance, gaining a monopoly on correct interpretation of both secular and religious thought. The totalitarian state's ideology then becomes the nation's religion, as it did in Nazi Germany, Stalin's Russia, and Mao Zedong's China, often claiming to represent the 'general good' or the liberation of some oppressed group. Totalitarian regimes also deprive individuals of the sense of community that lateral relationships bring, severing those ties in favor of stronger ties to the state. The resulting loss of personal identity is compensated for by shared identification with the powerful leader, who has all the answers as proclaimed through his ideology.

In totalitarian-like societies, individual rights get lost. Every aspect of human activity is dominated by the prevailing ideology; all spheres of life are under the control of the state and its leadership. To make such total control truly effective, all legally recognized buffers between the leader and his subjects need to be eliminated. No reliable, independent, authoritative body can stand between the leader and the masses. This means that tyrants need to subvert existing institutions, particularly the judiciary, to make their control absolute. Traditional groups such as labor unions, political parties, an independent press, and other associations of any kind, need to be destroyed. Meaningful participation in a vibrant political community cannot be tolerated, though participation (or better, *imprisonment!*) in ideologically 'correct' institutions and in front organizations is allowed, encouraged, or even mandated.

Enforcing Mind-Control

Under such despotic systems, ordinary people are nothing more than cogs in a merciless political machine. The leader uses the police, the military, and other specially designated henchmen to spread fear in the general population and to impose the extreme sanctions of imprisonment, internment in hospitals and camps, torture, and execution on those who oppose the government. Such is the imprimatur of a dictatorship. In the case of truly despotic regimes, the secret police often becomes like a state within a state, suppressing freedom in the name of law and order but holding its own actions above the law, free from accountability. As despots use a segment of the population to keep the other people under their oppression, terror gradually becomes not only a means to an end but an end in itself. In this vicious circle, those who carry out purges one day may be purged the next. The consequence is a totally cowed, subdued population.

Despotism's total control over the armed forces and the police helps ensure survival of the regime's ideology. Typically, a terrorist-type police force and omnipresent informers monitor and enforce the despotic leader's monopolistic control over the economy and the media. These military institutions are used to terrify the populace, ensuring that the people toe the party line—whatever the prevailing theological or ideological belief systems that define themselves as the embodiment of goodness and light. We have all heard how the Gestapo and the SS in Hitler's Germany, the NKVD in Stalin's Soviet Russia, and the Khmer Rouge in Pol Pot's Cambodia used terror to paralyze the populace. People who protested against the limits to freedom imposed by these regimes were threatened, tortured, interned in concentration camps, and/or executed. The Ministry of Intelligence and Security, the Ministry of Interior, and the Revolutionary Guards in Iran have used similar tactics to shore up an unpopular theocratic regime; and during Saddam Hussein's regime, his Special Republican Guards maintained an iron grip on the population.

The Role of the Media

Distorted mass communication is a hallmark of any despotic, totalitarian regime, propagating the prevailing utopian goals and official ideologies through thought-control. Ideological propaganda and morality-education permeate such regimes. While in ancient societies the indoctrination by despots was rather crude, contemporary totalitarian leaders use modern propaganda techniques to brainwash their subjects into the 'right' way of thinking, forcing a mendacious ideology down their subjects' throats. In today's totalitarian states, information flowing from the party is severely censored, with distorted discourse and 'news-speak' sanitizing corruption and abhorrent acts. Absolutely no honest, open debate is permitted; any moral or spiritual authority, independent of the leader or contrary to party doctrine, is prohibited. Rote memorization of the party line is encouraged, and people who engage in critical inquiry or speak out against the party line are arrested, or worse. Ideological jargon and magical celebrations replace open discussion as the party and its leader engage in verbal acrobatics to hide the reality of the situation.

The Illusion of Solidarity

Another important element that fosters the continuation of tyranny is the isolation that despots enforce. The very idea of totalitarianism implies the breaking of lateral relationships between individuals—the original sense of community—in favor of strong ties to the state. This dissolution of the original ties between people creates helplessness, dependency, and loneliness. There are those familiar words again—the very traits that encourage people to look for a savior and to hope for salvation. It is a vicious circle: helplessness breeds a need for strong leadership, and excessive leadership breeds helplessness.

Despots understand the psychological vulnerability of humans. They are aware that people are more easily manipulated when they feel isolated and powerless. Lacking reference points, lacking other people to exchange opinions with, isolated individuals gradually lose their common sense and their ability to think independently. Regressing to a state of passivity, they become increasingly helpless. And in that helpless state, they are open to a salvific ideology and a leader apparently endowed with superhuman, omniscient, omnipotent qualities—qualities touted by the state propaganda department. In the person of the leader, the power of the state, the people, and the ideological movement become unified.

Thus, tyrants look for ways of keeping their subjects isolated. They go to great lengths to break up traditional relationship patterns. Further, they prohibit all associations between citizenry that could lead to free debate, knowing that the loss of 'voice,' the inability to speak one's mind and talk with others who cherish similar 'apostate' ideas, enhances feelings of isolation. To ensure that the populace cannot coordinate any form of political opposition, tyrants suppress or destroy all organizations and individuals that espouse views diverging from the main secular or theocratic ideology. To that end, they rely on an elaborate network of spies and informers (many of whom are happy to turn in friends and associates in the hope of saving themselves), and they use police terror to prevent lateral communication.

Having destroyed existing relationship patterns, tyrants can then transform their fragmented society so that it better achieves their purpose. They do so by replacing connectedness with magical thinking, and human intimacy with the pursuit of an illusion—that same illusion that lies at the heart of the regime's ideology. Propped up by their propaganda machine, these leaders encourage their subjects in the fantasy that they are wise, noble, kind, and understanding. They offer evidence that they are doing whatever they can to create a perfect society—one in which, according to the propaganda machine, there will be justice for all, everyone's needs will be met, there will be meaningful work for everyone, and hunger and poverty will be eradicated. The result, they promise persuasively, will be a just, humane society, a society in which children can grow up safely.

The Search for Scapegoats

Rarely do things work out that way, however. In the process of striving for their utopia, despots create injustice and misery. And whose fault is that? Well, not the tyrants,' certainly. They can always find someone else to blame. The typical tyrant might, when 'learning' of an incident of cruelty or injustice, announce that he did not know of the problem; if he had, of course, he would have handled things differently. It was some key person or group that was actually responsible for people's privations. This is a nice fairy tale, but it lacks even the smallest kernel of truth. Of *course* the despot is responsible. He knew exactly what was going on (or if he did not, it was because he *chose* not to know). The very definition of a totalitarian state is that nothing can be done without the leader's knowledge and say-so. If the inner circle or the military behaves cruelly, it is because he tells them to. He selects his henchmen; he dispenses orders and permission; he rewards obedient behavior. And the henchmen oblige. They follow his wishes, sometimes even exceeding his demands to show their loyalty (especially if they 'identify with the aggressor').

Because the leader sets the tone for the whole society, his unwillingness to take responsibility creates an entire culture of blame. Each henchman passes on blame to his or her underlings, who, in turn, do the same to theirs. But somewhere in that cascading blame, the responsibility has to finally come to rest. Thus, scapegoating comes into play in every tyranny, the inevitable result of dichotomous thinking. The 'nonbelievers' described earlier—forces of evil (so designated by those in power)—are seen as posing a great threat to the purity of society and the well-being of 'believers,' and are thus deserving of 'elimination.' The Jews in Nazi Germany, the kulaks and capitalists under the Soviet regime, the educated elite in Pol Pot's Cambodia, the non-Arab Christians and animists in southern Sudan, and the Muslims in Kosovo were all victims of scapegoating. *They* were the source of all the problems their countries were experiencing.

Enemies—real or imagined—are essential to tyrannical regimes (Volcan, 1988). With the help of propaganda, despots inspire intense hatred for their chosen scapegoats, creating a primitive level of commitment to the cause. In the process, they create a sense of belonging in their followers, give them a sense of purpose, and distract them from the real issues of the day. Indoctrinated by a constant stream of virulent propaganda, people become willing to inform on neighbors, friends, and family members. But there is an even uglier side to scapegoating: it has a genuine attraction to people. Violence repels most people, yes; but it also intrigues and draws them. In addition, as with participating in violent spectator sports, engaging in scapegoating is a way of overcoming one's own fears. Violent participation is, for many, a way of dealing with their own anxiety and feelings of doubt about the regime. It is a form of insurance as well: people hope that, by showing commitment to the regime and its policies of violence, they can save themselves. Even those who only stand at the sidelines are affected. Those who watch this macabre 'spectator sport' are bound together by shared guilt over not putting an end to the violence.

THE ULTIMATE COST OF TERROR WITHIN

While that may be a cultural bias, history shows irrefutably that enduring great societies are built on freedom of spirit and freedom of expression. Such freedoms cannot flourish in the absence of basic standards of morality, civic virtue, and justice for *all,* fairly administered. Far-reaching restrictions on freedom inevitably result in economic decline. Freedom in the economic sphere makes for individual initiative and entrepreneurship, creates employment, and helps eradicate poverty. In this way, it supports all the other freedoms. Someone with a job and three square meals a day feels freer to express his/her opinion than someone dependent on others for survival.

Totalitarian-like governments, on the other hand, with their gigantic bureaucracies, are not conducive to the spirit of entrepreneurship. Bureaucracy, corruption, and uncertainty, combined with the lack of individual freedom and human rights, sap the energy and rend the moral fabric of a country. Creating special rights for some people, as despotic regimes do, undermines individual freedom and civil rights, and thus undermines civilization itself. A government that does not hold itself accountable cannot create a foundation for economic growth. As totalitarian states mature, their practices are greater and greater obstacles to economic development. Unemployment, poverty, and hunger typically result, as in the regimes of Mengistu Haile Mariam of Ethiopia, Joseph Désiré Mobutu of the Democratic Republic of Congo, and Robert Mugabe of Zimbabwe. Despots, then, although they may enjoy a temporary honeymoon period, bring on economic decline.

They also destroy a country's cultural institutions and sense of national pride. The discontent that grows in a populace around inequities and lack of freedom eventually turns even an environment of creativity and free thought into a breeding ground for the disenfranchised. In their anger and desperation, seeing enemies and conspiracies everywhere, citizens begin to commit desperate terrorist acts. Unable to touch the leader, they strike out wherever they can, destroying their own society in the process.

Once people embrace a theological or secular belief system that has no room for compassion, goodness, and hope, it is only a matter of time before violence sets in. And once violence takes hold, civilization itself is condemned. Dictatorships and totalitarian governments kill civil society, Iraq being a very good example. Thus, people have to combat despots *before* totalitarian states are established. They need to be able to dream, to envisage a better society for their children and for future generations, and to incorporate their dreams into positive goals, both individual and collective. Without meaningful work, close ties to family and friends, and reasonable hope of a positive future, people quickly become alienated. That alienation becomes universal when totalitarianism deprives people of these essential rewards, and an entire population loses its sense of humanity and compassion.

Homo Homini Lupus

All leaders are susceptible to the darker side of power (Latey, 1969; Zaleznik & Kets de Vries, 1975; Kets de Vries, 1989, 2004; Applebaum, 2003). No single individual should ever be in control of an organization, community, or society. That human susceptibility to cruelty and violence turns people in high positions into villains with alarming frequency. The statement *Homo homini lupus* ('Every man is a wolf to every other man') is all too painfully true. However admirable leaders may be when they first take the scepter, however enlightened they may be, however much they may resemble Plato's philosopher-king, they are not exempt from the pull of psychological regression.

Perhaps the best test of a person's character is to put him or her in a position of power. That's the *hardest* test, certainly. Unfortunately, most leaders fail the test miserably. Even the most 'normal' human being can become cruel and callous when given too much power. Power is so intoxicating, so addictive, that only the hardiest individuals can survive it without psychopathology. Even those on the receiving end of power feel its psychopathological effects: they often become dangerously overdependent.

Power and reason cannot coexist peacefully, and reason is always the loser. Excessive power blurs the senses, triggers delusional paranoia, and corrupts reality testing. And paranoiacs do not take their delusions lightly. Many a reign has been steeped in the blood of enemies more *perceived* than *real;* many a ruler, from Roman emperors to modern despots, has been more *executioner* than *diplomat.* And in every case, those who are carried away by power eventually self-destruct—but not before sacrificing countless victims on the altar of their ambitions.

The history of many despotic regimes is a string of cautionary tales, reminding us that every culture needs to build and maintain strong checks and balances against the abuse of power.

Without these safeguards, any regime, no matter how benign, can give way to despotic rule. Thus power retained should always be a check to power conferred.

The Need for Countervailing Powers

Democracy requires well-entrenched social systems of checks and balances that protect against the destructive potential that lies dormant in humankind. Only political diversity, a well-established legal code, and freedom of expression and economy can ensure democratic rule. But these things alone are not sufficient. In addition, individuals must have a civilized personal code of conduct and endorse a civic mindset that supports democratic social structures. In other words, the populace has to internalize a civic culture that protects against the abuse of power. That internalization comes from learning the fundamentals of democratic government at home and in school, seeing democratic government at work in daily life, witnessing open and honest elections, and hearing respected adults support human rights (and question authority when it restricts those rights). Only through the combination of supportive social structures and an internalized civic culture can the relinquishing of power follow the assumption of power.

It is bad enough when a regular guy becomes intoxicated by power (as victims of child abuse can attest). But when that intoxication strikes a national leader—someone reading his or her lines on a world stage—the consequences can be devastating. The paranoia that such intoxication spawns makes despots trigger-happy: fearing that others are seeking to overthrow them, they resort to what psychologists call 'protective reaction'— that is, they take the aggressive initiative, attacking before they can be attacked. If their protective reaction gains a base in reality (if, for example, dissidents from their own regime form an alliance with external forces), it is as if oil has been thrown on their paranoid fire. Even when paranoia does not argue for war, despots are motivated into combat by the sense of purpose and solidarity it gives the people, and the distraction it offers from the despot's own misdeeds.

What makes despots so dangerous for the world community is not so much their tendency toward violence as the ease with which that tendency can be indulged. Starting a war—engaging in *any* form of violence, for that matter—is so much easier for despots than for democratic leaders. Despots do not need to ask permission from various executive and legislative bodies. Despots do not have to convince the populace. The most they have to do—if that—is to get an official-sounding agency to rubber-stamp their war effort. They have the power to do pretty much as they wish.

It goes without saying that wars come at an incredible price in human suffering for the citizens involved. But the visible costs of war—death of soldiers and civilians, homelessness, privation, economic disaster—are only the tip of the iceberg. There are hidden effects of war that can take generations to rebuild—for example, the loss of self-respect and national pride, and the obliteration of culture and creativity. These desolating consequences are a persuasive argument for humankind to rid the world of dictatorships—even if, paradoxically, it takes war to do so. If the cause is just, it is much better to have a short, preventive war than years of stretched-out agony. Certain regimes are so corrupt and destructive that they have to be restrained, no matter what. Beneficial as such a war may be, if no steps are taken to create a civil society, such a war can become the foundation for the next dictatorship.

Just as despots are the instigators of war, so can they be its victims. After a career of villainy and deception, many despots are brought down, regime in tow, by victors in battle. Others survive losing a war only to be brought down by segments of their own population who, seeing the devastation that accompanied defeat, decide that enough is enough and mount a successful insurrection.

Sometimes, what brings a despot to ruin is rot within the regime. The idealism that flourished when the regime was first put in place gradually becomes cynicism as the ideals lose their meaning. Those true believers who once fought for an ideal now fight only for the perks that loyalty brings. The lure of those perks is strong: in a society built on favoritism, corruption is inevitable. And with the onset of corruption, the regime loses two of its most powerful sources of control: moral authority and political legitimacy. Furthermore, corruption breeds dissension among the exploited masses, who nurture thoughts of revolution as the only answer to their disenfranchisement.

A good illustration of a regime brought down by inner rot is the decades-long reign of the despot Nicolae Ceausescu of Romania. His secret police, known as the *Securitate,* maintained rigid controls over free speech and the media, tolerating no internal opposition. He encouraged an extensive personality cult and appointed his wife, Elena, and some members of his family to high posts in the government. His regime, despite the glowing promises of the early years, was marked by disastrous economic schemes that led to great suffering for the populace. Over time, his regime became increasingly repressive and corrupt. After years of agony, that regime finally collapsed. The catalyst was his order, given to his security forces, to fire on antigovernment demonstrators. A December 1989 uprising of the people, in which the army participated, led to his arrest, his trial and sentencing (by a hastily assembled military tribunal), and his execution. His wife and other key figures were also put to death.

DETERRING TERROR

The execution of Nicolae Ceausescu is a rare exception; many despots are never held accountable for their evil acts. The tragic paradox of history is that those individuals who murder *one* person are more likely to be brought to justice than those who plot the genocide of *millions.* Despots who commit crimes against humanity far too often go into quiet retirement rather than being brought to justice. A small sampling of the many examples available:

- More than 9,000 people disappeared during the 'Dirty War' in Argentina that started at the end of the 1970s, to end at the beginning of the 1980s. The perpetrators are living happily ever after.
- Syria's late dictator, Hafez al-Assad, also had a happy ending to his life, although he ordered the death of at least 10,000 people in the city of Hama after an insurrection, and then bulldozed the city.
- The late North Korean dictator, Kim Il-Sung, who kept a tight rein on his totalitarian state, advocated what he called a self-reliance policy. The net effect? He caused the starvation of millions of his people. He also lived happily ever after, and died peacefully in his bed.
- Few people recall the holocaust inflicted by the Ottoman Empire on Armenians in 1915,

although more than a million people died. Nobody was ever held accountable for this 'troublesome' mass murder. In fact, the Turks never even acknowledged that it happened.

This pattern of denial is changing, however. Since the milestone International Military Tribunal at Nuremberg in 1946, where war crimes and crimes against humanity were prosecuted, the world has been taking increasing notice of despots. That tribunal, and the subsequent tribunal in Tokyo (which reviewed war crimes committed by the command of the Japanese Imperial Army), established a precedent for holding the leader of a country accountable for crimes committed by that country. Unfortunately, these trials did not lead to the establishment of a permanent international court that would be specially empowered to deal with crimes against humanity. In the decades just after these two large tribunals, the prosecution of war criminals lessened significantly again—most likely due to the effects of the Cold War—and power politics froze meaningful decision-making. During (and because of) this passivity, Pol Pot, a criminal responsible for the deaths of over two million Cambodians, was never brought to justice.

Since the fall of the Berlin Wall and the end of the Cold War, however, the United Nations has been taking a more active position against despots. Shamed into action by the tragic events in the former Yugoslavia and Rwanda, the Security Council established two specialized ad hoc tribunals. The first, the International Criminal Tribunal, set up in The Hague, began by bringing to justice the instigators of various crimes against humanity in Yugoslavia, convicting a number of the key players, the most important one being Slobodan Milošević. Similar steps were then taken to bring to justice the people responsible for the genocide in Rwanda. The second International Criminal Tribunal, convened in Arusha, sentenced Jean Kambanda, former prime minister of Rwanda, to life imprisonment (the harshest penalty available) for supporting and promoting the massacre of some 800,000 Tutsis, when the Hutus briefly held power. Though these results have been encouraging, even more needs to be done. This means that the serious political, practical, linguistic, and financial difficulties presented by the international tribunals need to be overcome, and without delay.

Difficulties notwithstanding, these tribunal convictions—further milestones in the effort to bring high-level perpetrators of crimes against humanity to justice—are a warning to dictators everywhere that the world is changing and that they can no longer expect to escape consequences. Another positive step is the willingness of many national courts to bring charges against dictators. The court in Chile, for example, acted against Augusto Pinochet, former president of that country, for human rights abuses that occurred during a period when many members of the political opposition disappeared. The same is now happening in Iraq, where his fellow citizens judged Saddam Hussein. Such indictments are a signal by and to the world community that nobody stands above the law.

These changing attitudes toward instigators of crimes against humanity, including mass murder and the repression of various freedoms, have led to open discussion on what more could be done to prevent a despot's genocide. The United Nations, accused by many of doing too little too late in both the former Yugoslavia and Rwanda, entered that discussion with serious soul-searching concerning its proper role in the 21st century. One of the primary objectives of the United Nations is securing universal respect for human rights and fundamental freedoms of individuals throughout the world. Its reluctance to intervene against war crimes and other crimes against humanity—to halt them immediately, rather than condemn them later—has come to haunt the institution. Many politicians and military strategists believe that if the UN had taken preventive action in hot spots around the world, considerable violence could have been avoided, millions of lives could have been saved, and many countries could have avoided political and economic ruin.

Such discussions have contributed to a greater preparedness on the part of the UN and the world community generally to deal with situations of tyranny. The world community today is reluctant to turn a blind eye to leaders and regimes that engage in civil war, mass murder, ideological intolerance, and murderous repression. The mass media have played a huge role in that shift, awakening the conscience of the world. In this day and age, atrocities are difficult to conceal. The work done by a despot's henchmen today may be broadcast tomorrow on CNN or BBC World News. That visual awareness of human atrocities, projected by television into billions of homes, has helped many of the world's key decision-makers—always attuned to the pressure of their citizens—to recognize the exponential costs in human suffering of standing by as spectators. These leaders have seen that preventive action would be a bargain, in cost–benefit terms, compared to an after-the-fact salvage operation.

The lessons learned from the events in the former Yugoslavia and Rwanda have made the United Nations increasingly prepared to engage in military intervention. The disastrous attacks of 9/11 were another wake-up call to the world. Those attacks, which announced that acts of terror do not honor national boundaries, succeeded in weakening the isolationist position of the United States. It is now clear to the world—and to the United States in particular—that certain regimes consider terrorism as one of their finest export products. Although we have long known that despots will not hesitate to alienate whole segments of their society, destroying their civil, civic culture in the process, it is now clear that those alienated citizens—unable to find a level playing field in their own society—will readily look for scapegoats outside. We now see that if we want to prevent further 9/11s, we have to get to the root of the problem: alienation and brutalization of any population must be stopped at all costs.

The activities of the Taliban, Al-Qaeda, and Iraq's ruling elite have made it clear that sometimes the only way to get rid of despots and totalitarianism is through outside intervention. Like it or not, force is often the only way to change such regimes. In the past, the world community has been reluctant to violate any nation's territorial integrity, believing that war should be instigated only for defensive purposes. The questions of territorial integrity and defensive war become less significant, however, if the price of inaction is the terrorization and impoverishment of an entire population, or the imprisonment or murder of opposition groups. Territorial integrity is even less an issue when a despotic regime itself ignores borders, exporting terror by threat or action.

Having just ended the bloodiest century in human history, the international community is now more prepared than before to send UN troops, or troops from specific countries, to prevent or stop civil war or mass murder fostered by despotic regimes—in other words, to take preemptive military action. The international community is also eager to build on the successes of its ad hoc tribunals by establishing, under the auspices of the United Nations, an independent International Criminal Court (ICC), a permanent international judicial body, specially set up to try individuals for genocide, crimes against humanity, and war crimes. This body became official in 2002, when the so-called Rome Statute received adequate ratification and was 'entered into force.'

Unfortunately, the United States has not been willing to ratify the treaty, fearing that U.S. service members and officials could be brought before the court in politically motivated cases. This fear is unwarranted: the treaty stipulates that the ICC will take on only cases that national courts are demonstrably unable or unwilling to prosecute, and it includes numerous safeguards to protect against frivolous or unwarranted prosecutions.

The ICC will have a much wider jurisdiction than the earlier tribunals. This international court will complement existing national judicial systems, however, stepping in only if national courts are unwilling or unable to investigate or prosecute crimes falling under the mandate of the ICC. The ICC will also help defend the rights of groups that have often had little recourse to justice, such as women and children. The establishment of such a court is more than just a symbolic move; it promises to end the impunity long enjoyed by gangster-like world leaders. It is a much-needed step in the direction of universal, global criminal justice.

The ICC will make international standards of conduct more specific, provide an important mechanism for implementation of these standards, and ensure that potential violators are brought to justice. In addition to determining the criminal responsibility of today's despots, it is expected to serve as a strong deterrent for possible future despots. Because it will be able to investigate and begin prosecutions at an early stage, it is also expected to shorten the span of violence and hasten expedient resolution of conflict. Furthermore, it may have a positive impact on national laws around the world, because ratifying nations will want to ensure that crimes covered by the ICC can be tried within their own borders. It is the hope of the international community that the ICC will ensure that future Hitlers, Pinochets, Pol Pots, Mengistus, Amins, Savimbis, and Mobutus will not escape justice.

With the help of this new council, all despots will face a day of reckoning. Budding despots the world over had best beware.

That is the hope. Is it realistic? Will the existence of such a criminal court affect the behavior of potential despots? Will it make them less violent—or at least less determined to act out their violent disposition? Will it lead to more humanitarian nation-building? Or is it true, as many people believe, that personality is destiny? We will always have despots among us!

Winston Churchill is reputed to have said that democracy is the worst form of government, except all the other forms that have been tried. While acknowledging the imperfections of democracy, our choices seem to be limited. We need to make the best of an imperfect thing. From what we know about our own struggles with our inner demons, we need to constantly remind ourselves that the death of democracy is not likely to be a sudden implosion. More likely, it will be a slow extinction from apathy, indifference, and lack of care. To save the next generation from human misery that would accompany such extinction, we should do everything in our power to prevent such a situation from coming to the fore!

REFERENCES

Applebaum, A. *Gulag: A history of the Soviet camps.* New York: Random House, 2003.

Arendt, H. *On violence.* New York: Harcourt, Brace & World, 1969.

Arendt, H. *The origins of totalitarianism.* New York: Harcourt Brace Jovanovitch, 1973.

Asch, S. E. Studies of independence and conformity. A minority of one against a unanimous majority. *Psychological Monographs,* 1956, *70* (Whole No. 416).

Bion, W. R. *Experiences in groups.* London: Tavistock, 1959.

Boesche, R. *Theories of tyranny: From Plato to Arendt.* University Park: The Pennsylvania State University Press, 1996.

Chirot, D. *Modern tyrants.* Princeton, NJ: Princeton University Press, 1994.

Des Pres, T. *The survivor: An anatomy of life in the death camps.* New York: Oxford University Press, 1976.

Erikson, E. H. *Childhood and society.* New York: W.W. Norton, 1963.

Friedrich, C. *Totalitarianism.* Cambridge, MA: Harvard University Press, 1954.

Friedrich, C. & Brezezinsky, Z. *Totalitarian dictatorship and autocracy.* Cambridge, MA: Harvard University Press, 1965.

Glass, J. M. *Psychosis and power: Threats to democracy in the self and the group.* Ithaca, NY: Cornell University Press, 1995.

Haney, C., Banks, W. C. et al. The interpersonal dynamics of a simulated prison. *International Journal of Criminology and Penology,* 1973, *1,* 69–97.

Herschman, J. & Lieb, J. *Brotherhood of tyrants: Manic depression and absolute power.* Amherst, NY: Prometheus Books, 1994.

Kets de Vries, M. F. R. *Prisoners of leadership.* New York: Wiley, 1989.

Kets de Vries, M. F. R. *The leadership mystique.* London: Financial Times/Prentice Hall, 2001a.

Kets de Vries, M. F. R. *Struggling with the demon: Essays in individual and organizational irrationality.* Madison, CT: Psychosocial Press, 2001b.

Kets de Vries, M. F. R. *Lessons on leadership by terror: Finding Shaka Zulu in the attic.* Cheltenham: Edward Elgar, 2004.

Kets de Vries, M. F. R. *The leadership mystique.* London: Prentice-Hall/Financial Times, 2006.

Latey, M. *Tyranny.* New York: Atheneum, 1969.

Lifton, R. J. *Thought reform and the psychology of totalism.* New York: W.W. Norton, 1961.

Machiavelli, N. *The prince.* New York: Bantam, 1966.

Milgram, S. *Obedience to authority.* New York: Harper & Row, 1975.

Plato. *The republic.* Harmondsworth: Penguin, 1955.

Reich, W. (Ed.) *Origins of terrorism: Psychologies, ideologies, theologies, states of mind.* Washington, DC: Woodrow Wilson Center Press, 1990.

Robins, R. S. & Post, J. M. *Political paranoia: The psychopolitics of hatred.* New Haven, CT: Yale University Press, 1997.

Schein, E. *Coercive persuasion.* New York: W.W. Norton, 1961.

Volcan, V. *The need to have enemies and allies.* Northvale, NJ: Jason Aronson, 1988.

Walter, E. V. *Terror and resistance: A study of political violence.* New York: Oxford University Press, 1969.

Winnicott, D. W. *Through paediatrics to psychoanalysis.* New York: Basic Books, 1975.

Zaleznik, A. & Kets de Vries, M. F. R. *Power and the corporate mind.* Boston: Houghton Mifflin, 1975.

3

INTERNATIONAL TERRORISM

An eye for an eye only leads to more blindness.

—Margaret Atwood

The attacks of September 11, 2001, were among the most horrific acts of transnational terrorism in history. Yet, as is true for other terrorist strikes throughout the ages, understanding the atrocities of 9/11 requires knowledge of the social, economic, political, and religious conditions from which terrorism arises.

As in earlier eras, advances in communication, transportation, and weaponry are exploited by today's terrorists. Contemporary terrorists have a vast and terrifying array of choices, but they also face a new enemy: the forces of globalization.

Our world has become more unified, and evidence of interconnections is everywhere. Commerce and technology have brought the people of our planet together in ways previously unimaginable. The Internet has penetrated into remote corners of the planet, and new discoveries in digital and optical technologies are likely to drive human beings even closer together. McDonald's sells hamburgers in Beijing, and American music and videos can be heard and seen in remote corners of the world. Free-trade agreements make national borders more porous; someday, they may make them obsolete. Falling stock markets in Tokyo devastate investors in Chicago. The International Monetary Fund intervenes in the economies of many underdeveloped countries because of global interdependence and the push for prosperity. International peace and stability are invaluable in this new world order. Problems and their solutions are no longer isolated geographically.

Terrorism is at odds with civilization's march toward globalization. Terrorists often focus on separatism and pitting one religious, ethnic, or social group against another. Terrorism generally is not about coming together as a unified whole; it is about breaking apart into smaller, autonomous units. Some terrorists would like to impose their religion or political ideology on the whole world, but their tactics are brute force, not the international collaboration that is the hallmark of globalization.

Barber (1992) captures this phenomenon when he notes that the "planet is falling precipitantly apart *and* coming reluctantly together at the very same moment" (p. 53). He labels this division as "Jihad" versus "McWorld." *Jihad,* which means "struggle" in Arabic, can be applied to either the internal struggle against evil or the external struggle against the perceived enemies of Islam. It is the latter meaning of Jihad that has been invoked by many contemporary terrorists, placing them on a collision course with the forces of globalization.

The effects of globalization were quickly evident after 9/11. The day after the attacks, the North Atlantic Treaty Organization (NATO), founded in 1949 and at that time comprising 19 member states, invoked, for the first time, Article 5 of the Washington Treaty, which declares that an armed attack on one member was an attack against all of them. Other nations around the world joined in condemning the terrorists and demonstrating solidarity with the United States. Many Muslim leaders in Africa and Asia expressed sympathy with the United States, noting that the Koran and Islamic teachings prohibit the slaughter of innocents.

The international display of unity in the immediate aftermath of the attacks does not diminish the reality that, in many spots around the globe, the United States and Western nations are despised. Anti-American sentiment is particularly virulent in portions of southwestern Asia and northern Africa, an area known as the Middle East, although negative feelings toward the United States also exist elsewhere. Poverty, authoritarian governments, and U.S. intervention around the globe have provided fertile ground for the growth of religious extremists and denunciations of the United States as the "Great Satan."

TERRORISM AROUND THE WORLD

Although the outcome of the clash between "Jihad" and "McWorld" is unknown, it is clear that terrorism continues to exist in virtually every region of the globe. No one knows the true number of foreign terrorist groups. U.S. law requires the Secretary of State to provide Congress a report on terrorism, entitled *Country Reports on Terrorism*. This report has replaced the previously published *Patterns of Global Terrorism.*

The *Country Reports* (2005) document divides groups into two categories: Foreign Terrorist Groups (FTOs), which meet the criteria of 8 USC Section 1189, and Other Terrorist Groups (OTGs), which do not meet the criteria. The difference between the two designations is that FTOs are seen as threatening the security of U.S. nationals or the national security of the United States; OTGs are not seen as presenting this type of threat to our country. The 2005 *Country Reports* names 42 FTOs and 41 OTGs.

A list published by the Terrorism Research Center (2006), an independent institute dedicated to research on terrorism, includes 423 active foreign and domestic terrorist groups. The Terrorist Knowledge Base (www.tkb.org), maintained by the Memorial Institute for the Prevention of Terrorism (MIPT), lists more than 200 foreign and domestic terrorist organizations. Precise counts are difficult, in part, because terrorist organizations are dynamic; change is therefore inherent to the phenomenon. Some terrorist organizations splinter into subgroups, and others disband and reassemble with new names. Equally important, as discussed in previous chapters, the ways in which terrorist events are counted depend on the definition applied to the counting.

Being labeled as a terrorist organization carries political repercussions. The legal and fiscal consequences of being designated an FTO are severe. It is a crime to donate money or otherwise assist an FTO, even if the funds are to be used for charitable purposes. Some FTOs have used charitable donations to provide sorely needed basic social services, such as hospitals and schools. Nevertheless, U.S. citizens are prohibited from contributing to these organizations on the premise that receiving charitable donations makes it easier for the groups to recruit supporters. In addition, members of FTOs are denied visas and barred from the United States. Financial institutions are required to block any funds intended for FTOs.

A few highlights of terrorist organizations, both FTOs and OTGs, from the U.S. Secretary of State's list (*Country Reports,* 2005) follow:

1. Europe
   - The Basque Fatherland and Liberty (ETA) group, founded in 1959, aims to create an independent homeland based on Marxist principles in the Basque regions of northern Spain and southwestern France. Immediately following a series of horrendous train bombings in

Madrid in March 2004, which were conducted by Islamic extremists, Spanish police began cracking down harder on the ETA. The group has killed more than 850 people and injured hundreds.

- Issued during the Easter Rising of 1916, the *Proclamation of the Republic*, which declared Ireland independent from England, is considered to be the founding document of the Irish Republican Army (IRA). The Easter Rising was crushed and its leaders were executed, but the struggle for Irish independence continued. Since its formation in 1969, the IRA has been the terrorist wing of Sinn Féin, the Northern Ireland political organization trying to unite Ireland and expel British forces. In 1999, for the first time, the IRA was identified as an OTG, not an FTO, because of its willingness to enforce a ceasefire and participate in the peace process in Northern Ireland. Those opposed to the peace process formed at least two new radical splinter groups, the Real IRA (RIRA) and the Continuity IRA (CIRA).
- Established in 1974, Kongra-Gel (formally called the Kurdistan Worker's Party or PKK) is made up primarily of Turkish Kurds. The goal of this group is to create an independent Kurdish state in southeastern Turkey, northern Iraq, and parts of Iran and Syria. It is responsible for more than 30,000 casualties. Its leader, Chairman Abdullah Ocalan, was captured in 1999 and sentenced to death; the sentence was later commuted to life imprisonment when Turkey abolished the death penalty. Although Ocalan ordered his members to lay down their arms and stop their terrorist activity, attacks have continued against targets in the Turkish government and ordinary citizens.

2. South America
   - The Revolutionary Armed Forces of Colombia (FARC), established in 1964 as the military wing of the Colombian Communist Party, is responsible for atrocities claiming untold numbers of innocent victims. Targeting political, military, and economic targets, FARC is believed to have about 12,000 members and thousands of supporters, primarily in the rural regions of the country. Its ties to narcotics trafficking are well documented.
   - Begun in 1965 by Jesuit priests influenced by the Marxist ideals of Fidel Castro and Che Guevara, the National Liberation Army (ELN) of Colombia is, like FARC, primarily based in rural areas. It engages in widespread kidnapping for ransom, often targeting foreign companies, especially in the petroleum industry. In waging an insurgent war against the Colombian government, ELN has damaged oil pipelines, electrical networks, and other vital parts of Colombia's infrastructure.
   - Peru's Túpac Amaru Revolutionary Movement (MRTA), founded in 1983 as a Marxist-inspired organization, is known for its infamous 1996 assault on the Japanese ambassador's residence in Lima, where 72 hostages were held for more than 4 months. No new terrorist activities have been attributed to MRTA since Peruvian armed forces rescued all but one of the hostages and killed the group's leaders. MRTA is now classified by the State Department as an OTG.
   - *Sendero Luminoso* (Shining Path), founded in the late 1960s by Abimael Guzmán, a university professor, is, like many other Latin American terrorist groups, based on a Marxist ideology. One of the most ruthless terrorist organizations in the Western hemisphere, the Shining Path is believed to be responsible for roughly 30,000 deaths. Leaders of the group were the focus of massive counterterrorism operations by the Peruvian government during the 1990s, but the group has apparently resumed its attacks in recent years.

3. East Asia and Pacific Islands
   - Aum Shinrikyo (Aum), founded in 1987 by Shoko Asahara, was granted official recognition as a religious organization in 1989. Over time, Aum evolved into a doomsday cult intent on bringing about Armageddon. It released sarin nerve gas on several Tokyo subway trains in 1995, killing 12 and injuring thousands. Asahara was convicted of masterminding the nerve gas attack and sentenced to death. The group subsequently reassembled under the name Aleph. Although still labeled an FTO by the U.S. government, it is unclear whether Aleph currently presents a serious threat to Japan or any other country.
   - The Abu Sayyaf Group (ASG) operates in the southern Philippines. It is a radical Islamic terrorist organization, and many of its leaders allegedly fought in Afghanistan during the Soviet invasion in the 1980s. The goal of the group is to form an independent Islamic state in the southern Philippines. It received considerable notoriety for kidnapping and murdering Western tourists.

- Jemaah Islamiya (JI) is based in Indonesia and seeks to form an Islamic republic spanning Indonesia, Malaysia, southern Thailand, Singapore, Brunei, and the southern Philippines. The group is believed to be responsible for the 2002 bombing in the Indonesian island of Bali, which killed more than 200 people, many of whom were foreign tourists. Abu Bakar Bashir, the group's alleged spiritual leader, was sentenced to prison for his role in the Bali bombing; he was released in 2005. The group was also implicated in another series of coordinated terrorist attacks in Bali in 2005.
- The Liberation Tigers of Tamil Eelam (LTTE), founded in 1976, engages in assassinations and bombings to promote its goal of creating an independent Tamil state in Sri Lanka. LTTE is known outside Sri Lanka for the suicide bomb attack that killed India's Prime Minister Rajiv Gandhi in 1991. Although peace negotiations have been conducted during the past several years, the Tigers are still considered a powerful secessionist group.

4. Middle East and North Africa
   - For the first time, the 1999 report listed al-Qaeda, meaning the "Base," the organization led by Saudi millionaire Osama bin Laden, as an FTO. The organization's goal is to unite Muslims throughout the world to overthrow pro-U.S. regimes and destroy Israel. Allegedly, al-Qaeda's overarching goal is to establish a pan-Islamic republic throughout the world.
   - Abu Nidal Organization (ANO) split from the Palestine Liberation Organization (PLO) in 1974 and launched an international campaign of terrorism, carrying out attacks in 20 countries against the United States, Britain, Israel, and various Arab countries. Sabri al-Banna (a.k.a. Abu Nidal), the group's leader, died in Baghdad in 2002; it is rumored that he was killed on the orders of Saddam Hussein.
   - Hamas (Islamic Resistance Movement) was formed in 1987 by Shaikh Ahmed Yassin of the Muslim Brotherhood at the beginning of the first *Intifada,* or uprising, between the Israelis and the Palestinians. Like other radical Islamic groups in the region, Hamas is dedicated to expelling Israel from the Middle East. Hamas has widespread support among Palestinians, and in 2006 it won a surprise victory in parliamentary elections, capturing more than half of the seats.
   - Hizbollah (Party of God; also called Islamic Jihad) was formed in 1982 in response to the Israel invasion of Lebanon. Inspired by the Iranian revolution, Hizbollah is believed to be responsible for the bombings of the U.S. embassy and U.S. Marine barracks in Beirut in 1983, as well as for the kidnapping of Western hostages in Lebanon in the 1980s. More recently, with the withdrawal of Syrian troops from Lebanon in 2005, Hizbollah has increased its participation in the Lebanese government. It launched a war against Israel in the summer of 2006 that resulted in fierce counter-attacks.

STATE-SPONSORED TERRORISM

A traditional view of terrorism is that it pits an individual or an organization against a sovereign state. Another type of terrorism, however, presents perhaps an even greater threat: the secret use of terrorism by a sovereign state. As was discussed in Chapters 1 and 2, state-sponsored terrorism is deeply rooted in the story of human civilization; it is as old as the history of military conflict.

States may opt to use terrorism instead of conventional armies for many reasons. Modern warfare is extraordinarily expensive and is likely to provoke counter-attacks. A state can sponsor terrorism covertly, allowing it to deny its role as an aggressor and avoid retaliation. The relationship between the patron state and the terrorist organization can be mutually beneficial: terrorists obtain the sponsorship necessary to maintain and expand their struggle, and the state obtains a potent weapon against its enemies.

State-sponsored terrorism takes many forms. At one extreme, a government can establish its own brutal death squads, whose sole purpose is to advance the interest of the state. At the other extreme, a state can simply provide a safe haven for terrorists, allowing them to operate without restrictions. Some states that sponsor terrorism take a middle path by assisting terrorists financially and refusing to extradite them to face criminal charges in another state. Government funds can be channeled to terrorists directly or indirectly through social, cultural, or charitable associations, many of which "serve as front organizations for groups that engage in terrorism" (Paz, 2000, p. 4).

The U.S. Secretary of State is authorized to identify state sponsors of terrorism. The primary threat to the United States and its allies is reported to come from South Asia and the Middle East. Six states were designated as state sponsors of terrorism in 2005: Iran, Syria, North Korea, Cuba, Sudan, and Libya. Prior to the U.S. invasion, Iraq had also been designated as a state sponsor of terrorism. In 2006, Libya was removed from the list.

Economic and political sanctions accompany the designation of a state as a sponsor of terrorism. The sanctions are intended to force state sponsors of terrorism to renounce the use of terrorism and cooperate with the United States in extraditing terrorists to stand trial for their past crimes. The sanctions include bans on arms-related exports and sales, controls on other types of exports, and prohibitions on economic assistance. The effects of the sanctions experienced by the people living in countries designated as state sponsors of terrorism are significant, and they have contributed to famine, economic stagnation, and other deprivations.

The designated state sponsors of terrorism are believed to have engaged in a variety of activities. For example, Iran supports numerous terrorist groups, including Lebanon's Hizballah, in its effort to undermine the process of procuring peace in the Middle East between the Palestinians and Israel. Further, Iran's effort to develop nuclear weapons has seemingly guaranteed its continued presence on the State Department's list.

Syria has long been considered a safe haven for radical Islamic terrorists, including Hizballah, Hamas, Palestinian Islamic Jihad, the Popular Front for the Liberation of Palestine, and other terrorist organizations that share a desire to destroy Israel. Not only does Syria provide money, arms, and training for terrorists but it also allows other countries, including Iran, to use its land to ship aid to terrorists fighting against Israel.

North Korea (the Democratic People's Republic of Korea; DPRK) harbors members of the Japanese Red Army who hijacked a Japanese airliner in the 1970s. DPRK is believed to have sponsored the bombing of a Korean Airlines flight in 1987.

Cuba harbors U.S. fugitives from justice. Maintaining what appears to be close contact with Iran and North Korea, Cuba is believed to be a safe haven for fugitives from justice from other countries. In Sudan, the Lord's Resistance Army (LRA) is a threat to Uganda, Congo, and southern Sudan. The Sudanese appear to have contributed to the continued fighting in Iraq, and Sudan is considered to be a meeting place and training hub for several terrorist groups.

Libya was considered a state sponsor of terrorism, in part, because of its refusal to pay compensation for the 1988 bombing of Pan Am Flight 103 over Lockerbie, Scotland. Eventually, in a movement toward detente, in 1999 Libya surrendered for trial the two Libyans accused of the bombing. Later, the Libyan leader, Colonel Muammar al-Qaddafi, agreed to pay compensatory damages; Libya was removed from the list of state sponsors in 2006.

The list of state sponsors of terrorism breathes life into the concept that the meaning of terrorism is in the eyes of the beholder. The countries on the U.S. list no doubt have their own list of terrorist states, and the United States is likely at the top of many of them.

For example, Chileans would be justified in considering the U.S. intervention in their country in the 1970s as state-sponsored terrorism. According to documents declassified in 2000 and released by the National Security Archives, the United States tried to overthrow the government of Chile and its democratically elected Marxist president, Dr. Salvador Allende, in the early 1970s (National Security Archive, 2000). President Richard M. Nixon ordered the Central Intelligence Agency (CIA) to mount a covert terrorist operation to keep Allende from taking office. When that failed, the CIA tried to undermine Allende's rule. It eventually succeeded when the Chilean military seized power under General Augusto Pinochet, who ruled until 1990. Pinochet's death squads murdered more than 3,000 people, and government forces jailed and tortured thousands more. The definition of terrorism thus depends on the experience of the definer.

RELIGIOUS FANATICISM: AN OLD TREND AND A NEW THREAT

"Holy Terror" was practiced in earlier centuries by such groups as the Jewish Zealots, the Assassins, and the Thugs, and contemporary observers are particularly concerned about the growth of religious fanaticism. According to Laqueur (1999), the new terrorism is different from the old,

> aiming not at clearly defined political demands but at the destruction of society and the elimination of large sections of the population. In its most extreme form, this new terrorism intends to liquidate all of what it deems to be "satanic forces," which may include the majority of a country or of mankind, as a precondition for the growth of another, better, and in any case different breed of human. In its maddest, most extreme form it may aim at the destruction of all life on earth, as the ultimate punishment for mankind's crimes. (p. 81)

FTO activity in the Middle East and North Africa continues to be of major concern to the U.S government. Most of these groups are dedicated to replacing secular society with strict Islamic law and rejecting all Western influences. Of particular concern is the spread of Islamist terrorist activity to Eastern Europe and central and southern Asia. Terrorism in Kosovo, Chechnya, Uzbekistan, Afghanistan, Kashmir, Indonesia, and the Philippines has been associated with radical interpretations of Islam that elevate terrorism to a religious duty (Paz, 2000). More recently, mass transportation attacks in Madrid and London have demonstrated that Western Europe is not immune to the reach of Islamic radical terrorists.

Many Americans and Europeans equate Islam with terrorism, but this is incorrect and unfortunate. Most Muslims, even most fundamentalists, are not terrorists. Instead, they have overwhelmingly been the victims of violent conflicts. Hundreds of thousands of Muslims were killed in the war between Iran and Iraq during the 1980s, and the civil wars in Afghanistan and Algeria led to similarly horrific numbers of casualties. Noncombatant Muslims have suffered untold losses in the war between Chechnya and Russia, in the turmoil in Indonesia, and throughout much of Africa and the Middle East. Terrorism has destroyed the lives of many Muslims and non-Muslims throughout the world.

How can people who profess to be very religious become terrorists? How can an ideology of hate be part of a religious belief (White, 2001)? Yet, violence based on religious zealotry has been common to every age, and violence based on faith is not the exclusive province of radical Islamists. Krakauer (2003) explains this phenomenon:

> There is a dark side to religious devotion that is too often ignored or denied. As a means of inciting evil, to borrow from the vocabulary of the devout—there may be no more potent force than religion. When the subject of religiously inspired bloodshed comes up, many Americans immediately think of Islamic fundamentalism, which is to be expected in the wake of the September 11 attacks on New York and Washington. But human beings have been committing heinous acts in the name of God ever since mankind began believing in deities, and extremists exist within all religions. Muhammad is not the only prophet whose words have been used to sanction barbarism; history has not lacked for Christians, Jews, Hindus, Sikhs, and even Buddhists who have been motivated by scripture to butcher innocents. Plenty of these religious extremists have been homegrown, corn-fed Americans. (pp. xxi-xxii)

A FEW INFAMOUS TERRORISTS

The above discussion focused on terrorist groups and their sponsors. The discussion now shifts to the terrorists themselves and the causes for which they fought. Hundreds of thousands of human beings have filled this terrorist role, but a few names stand out in history. The following discussion highlights the careers of three terrorists with worldwide name recognition: Che Guevara, Carlos the Jackal, and Osama bin Laden. It then describes the causes and careers of two less well-known terrorist leaders who have long reigned at the helm of their organizations:

PHOTO 3.1   Crowds celebrating the 26th of July Revolution gathered in front of a huge sign with an image of Ernesto Che Guevara and a quote from his writings: CREATE TWO, THREE, MANY VIETNAMS.

Velupillai Prabhakaran of the Tamil Tigers and Subcomandante Marcos of Mexico's Zapatista National Liberation Army.

Che Guevara

Che Guevara is a pop-political legend whose romantic photograph, taken in 1960 at a funeral for dead seamen in Cuba, today adorns murals and posters, T-shirts, Internet Web sites, and CD covers all over the world. Although he died in 1967, Guevara remains a potent symbol for the disaffected everywhere. His image represents freedom and is the epitome of youthful rebellion against authority. A Marxist revolutionary, a philosopher, a poet, and a warrior, Guevara is remembered not as a terrorist but for his deep convictions, for living his dream and dying for his ideals. Philosopher Jean-Paul Sartre called Guevara "the most complete human being of our age" (Che Guevara Information Archive, 2001).

Guevara influenced the structure of violent revolution throughout Latin America. Revolution, he maintained, should begin in the countryside, and indiscriminate urban terrorism should serve as a supplementary form of revolt (Laqueur, 1977, p. 180). He authored three books—*Guerrilla Warfare* (1961), *Man and Socialism in Cuba* (1967), and *Reminiscences of the Cuban Revolutionary War* (1968)—read by left-wing radicals around the world.

Ernesto "Che" Guevara was born in 1928 into a middle-class family in Rosario, Argentina. He earned a medical degree from the University of Buenos Aires in 1953, but his interests turned from medicine to helping the poor and challenging authority through revolution. He participated in riots against the Argentine dictator Juan Perón. He worked in a leper colony and joined the pro-communist regime of Jacobo Arbenz Guzmán in Guatemala. When Arbenz was overthrown in 1954, Guevara fled to Mexico, where he met Fidel Castro and other Cuban rebels (White, 1998, p. 56). He later fought in Castro's guerrilla war against Cuban dictator Fulgencio

Batista, becoming a chief strategist and respected guerrilla fighter. When Castro assumed power, Guevara served as president of the national bank and later as minister of industry, traveled widely to communist countries, and even addressed the United Nations on behalf of Cuba.

Guevara wanted to export the Cuban experience to other countries. Convinced that peasant-based revolution was the only remedy for Latin America's poverty and social inequities, Guevara, who may have fallen out of favor with Castro, left Cuba and became a revolutionary leader in Bolivia. He believed that acts of terrorism would create an environment of fear that would be ripe for revolution. According to Vetter and Perlstein (1991), Guevara "resorted to terrorizing Bolivian village leaders and elders in a deliberate program of mutilation and assassination when he found himself unable to influence the peasants to support his revolution" (p. 45). Guevara was captured and executed by the Bolivian army in 1967. Today, the circumstances of his activities in Bolivia and his capture, killing, and burial are still the subject of intense public interest around the world, and some have suggested that the U.S. CIA was involved in his death. (For more on Guevara, see, e.g., Anderson, 1998; Camejo, 1972; Castaneda, 1997; Harris, 1970; Hodges, 1977.)

Carlos the Jackal

Che Guevara is remembered as a romantic figure, but Carlos the Jackal's legend is shrouded in mystery (Follain, 2000). Frequently blamed for crimes he did not commit, including the killing of 11 Israeli athletes at the 1972 Olympics in Munich, Carlos collaborated with terrorists in Japan, Germany, Spain, and Italy. He was particularly well known for his activities on behalf of Arab terrorists seeking to drive Israel out of Palestine. He lived freely under the protection of communist-bloc countries (Laqueur, 1999, p. 164) and is believed to have worked for Libya's Colonel Muammar al-Qaddafi, Iraq's Saddam Hussein, and Cuba's Fidel Castro. When finally arrested in Sudan in 1994, Carlos the Jackal was 44 years old and until shortly before that time had been living in Syria with his wife, Magdalena Kopp, a former member of the German Baader-Meinhof terrorist group.

Separating the myth from the reality of Carlos is not easy, in part because he spread false stories about himself, used multiple disguises, and changed his name and passport frequently. He was dubbed "the Jackal" after the sinister assassin in a Frederick Forsyth novel. A wanted poster showing his wide, unemotional face in dark glasses became a symbol for left-leaning terrorist movements around the globe.

A Venezuelan whose real name is Ilich Ramirez Sanchez, Carlos was born in 1949 and named by his Marxist father after the Russian leader, Vladimir Ilich Ulyanov, or Lenin, as he was better known. His brothers were named Lenin and Vladimir. As a youth, Carlos joined the Venezuelan Communist Youth in their violent demonstrations against the ruling government. Later, he attended Moscow's Lumumba University, a training center for future leaders of the Soviet Union's expansion into underdeveloped countries. There he met Palestinian students and came to admire the teachings of George Habash, the leader of the Popular Front for the Liberation of Palestine (PFLP). After the PFLP hijacked several airlines, Carlos left Russia for the Middle East and began his terrorist career in earnest (Bellamy, 2000).

Carlos's most notorious terrorist act was the kidnapping of 11 oil ministers at an Organization of Petroleum Exporting Countries (OPEC) meeting in Vienna in December 1975. Three people died in the takeover, and Carlos and his fellow terrorists, along with several hostages, were flown to Algeria and released, reportedly with a big payoff from an undisclosed Arab state. Carlos was also a suspect in several bombings and grenade attacks, and he publicly admitted to a 1973 assassination attempt on British millionaire Edward Sieff, a Jewish businessman and owner of the Marks & Spencer stores in London. He was convicted in absentia in France in 1992 and was sentenced to life imprisonment for the 1975 murder of two French intelligence agents who wanted to question him about attacks on Israeli El Al planes at Orly Airport in Paris. In the shootout with the police, Carlos also killed a fellow terrorist and PFLP member whom he suspected of being an informer.

Carlos seemed to drop out of sight during the late 1980s, and reports circulated of his death, although other reports had him living in Mexico, Colombia, and Syria. The collapse of the Soviet Union may have left him with few sponsors, and he was eventually betrayed by the Sudanese police. After being arrested in 1994 and flown to France, he was convicted in 1997 and sentenced to life imprisonment.

At his trial, Carlos said he was a "professional revolutionary." After hearing the guilty verdict against him, he raised his fist and shouted, "Viva la revolución." In prison, Carlos went on a hunger strike to protest being held in solitary confinement, but ended it at the request of his father. In 2006, he filed a lawsuit against the head of French intelligence for illegally capturing him while he was sedated in a liposuction clinic in Khartoum, Sudan (Bell, 2006). Several excellent biographies of this "superterrorist" have been written (see, e.g., Dobson, 1977; Follain, 2000; Smith, 1977; Yallop, 1993).

Osama bin Laden

Osama bin Laden is the best-known contemporary terrorist. Born in Saudi Arabia around 1957 to a father of Yemeni origin and a Syrian mother, bin Laden grew up fabulously wealthy. His father, Mohammed bin Laden, had many wives and more than 50 children. Having been favored with royal patronage and awarded the contract to rebuild, among other buildings, the mosques in the holy cities of Mecca and Medina, Mohammed bin Laden became a billionaire.

At Abdul Aziz University in Jedda, Saudi Arabia, the young Osama was introduced to the wider world of Islamic politics. The 1979 Soviet invasion of Afghanistan was a turning point for him. He began to use his wealth and organizational skills to help train thousands of young Arabs and Muslims to fight in the Afghan resistance, which was supported by the United States.

After the Soviet Union withdrew from Afghanistan, bin Laden returned to Saudi Arabia and founded an organization to assist veterans of the Afghan war. In 1990, when Iraqi forces invaded Kuwait, the United States was allowed to station its troops in Saudi Arabia. This action outraged bin Laden, who saw it as a sacrilege that nonbelievers should occupy the birthplace of Islam. When bin Laden turned against the Saudi government, it expelled him from the country. He moved to Sudan, where he continued training recruits in terrorist tactics.

Bin Laden subsequently returned to Afghanistan, where he was given sanctuary under the protection of the Taliban, the fundamentalist Islamic movement that came to power in 1996. The Taliban arose out of the chaos produced at the end of the Cold War. When the Soviets withdrew from Afghanistan in the late 1980s, the United States also left, leaving Afghanistan devastated. Into this vacuum marched the Taliban (Rashid, 2001).

Bin Laden, with the help of the Taliban, jeopardized the stability of south and central Asia and Africa by training radical Arabs and Muslims in the tools of terrorism. Students from all over the region have studied in Afghanistan, and thousands are determined to carry out Taliban-style Islamic revolutions in their homelands.

Bin Laden is a hero to radical Muslim youth throughout the world (Bodansky, 1999), and his organization oversees a loosely tied network of local cells that operate independently of each another.

A glimpse into bin Laden's mind was provided by a 1998 interview with an ABC news correspondent:

> It is hard for one to understand if the person does not understand Islam. . . . Allah is the one who created us and blessed us with this religion, and orders us to carry out the holy struggle "Jihad" to raise the word of Allah above the words of the unbelievers. . . . It does not worry us what the Americans think. What worries us is pleasing Allah. The Americans impose themselves on everyone who believes in his religion and his right. They accuse our children in Palestine of being terrorists. Those children that have no weapons and have not even reached maturity. At the same time they defend a country with its airplanes and tanks, and the state of the Jews, that has a policy to destroy the future of these children. . . . Each action will solicit a similar reaction. We must use such punishment to keep your evil away from Muslims, Muslim children and women. American history

does not distinguish between civilians and military, and not even women and children. They are the ones who used the bombs against Nagasaki. Can these bombs distinguish between infants and military? America does not have a religion that will prevent it from destroying all people. (Miller, 1998)

In addition to the attacks on September 11, 2001, bin Laden's al-Qaeda organization has been held responsible for the bombings at the Khobar Towers housing complex in Saudi Arabia that killed 19 U.S. servicemen; the nearly simultaneous blasts on the U.S. embassies in Nairobi and Tanzania, which left more than 300 people dead; and the 1993 truck bomb attack on the World Trade Center in New York.

Bin Laden is also suspected of being involved in the bombing of the destroyer *USS Cole*, which was attacked as it refueled in the Yemen port of Aden on October 12, 2000. The attack killed 17 Navy sailors and wounded dozens more. A motorized skiff, carrying explosives and two suicide bombers, tore a ragged hole in the *USS Cole*, which is the length of a football field and equipped with long-range cruise missiles.

More recently, al-Qaeda has been linked directly or indirectly to, among other attacks, the 2002 car bombing explosions in the tourist area of Bali, which killed more than 200 and injured hundreds of others; the series of explosions in 2004 on Madrid commuter trains, which killed nearly 200 people and injured almost 2,000; and the 2005 attacks on underground trains in London, which killed more than 50 people and injured hundreds more. Bin Laden and his organization are also tied, again directly or indirectly, to the insurgency group known as al-Qaeda in Iraq.

In 2001, a Federal District Court in Manhattan began hearing testimony in the case of the bombing of the U.S. embassy in Kenya. A key witness in the trial was a top deputy to bin Laden, Jama Ahmed Al-Fadl, who was caught stealing money from al-Qaeda. Fearing retaliation from bin Laden, he became an informer for the United States and entered the witness protection program. Al-Fadl testified against the four defendants at the embassy bombing trial and provided details of bin Laden's terrorist organization. He described a thoroughly modern organization that used international companies and social relief agencies as fronts; communicated by fax, coded letters, and satellite phones; and trained recruits in the use of sophisticated weapons.

PHOTO 3.2   Osama bin Laden, the Saudi Arabian leader of al-Qaeda, as shown on the FBI's Most Wanted Terrorist poster.

Al-Fadl testified that the American embassies were chosen for terrorist attacks because bin Laden was angry about U.S. intervention in the civil war in Somalia. Regardless of the truthfulness of the informer's claim, the embassy bombings did not go unpunished. Shortly after the bombings, the United States launched missile attacks on what was believed to be bin Laden's camp in Afghanistan. Again, attack and counter-attack are the familiar pattern. (For more on bin Laden, see Bodansky, 1999; Engelberg, 2001; Huband, 1999; Reeve, 1999).

The lives of Che Guevara, Carlos the Jackal, and Osama bin Laden illustrate some of the variations in the experiences of a few terrorists who have gained worldwide attention. The next illustrations concern less well-known, but very important, contemporary terrorists named Velupillai Prabhakaran and Subcomandante Marcos.

Velupillai Prabhakaran

The island of Sri Lanka (formerly named Ceylon) is situated about 50 miles to the southeast of India, in the Indian Ocean. The vast majority of Sri Lankans are members of the Sinhalese ethnic group, most of whom are Buddhists. The Tamil people predominate in the northern and eastern parts of the country, and they have their own culture, traditions, and language. Most Tamils are Hindu.

Velupillai Prabhakaran was born in 1954; when he was only 18 years of age, he founded the Tamil New Tigers, which changed its name in 1976 to the Tigers of Tamil Eelam (LTTE). Prabhakaran began by organizing student protests against restrictions on the admittance of Tamils to universities, and he soon developed into the leader of what many countries, including the U.S., India, and Sri Lanka, consider a terrorist organization.

Seeking an independent Tamil state called Eelam, LTTE is categorized as a nationalist/separatist terrorist group. Its formidable fighting force is estimated to have about 8,000 members (Terrorist Knowledge Base, 2006). It has its own navy, the Sea Tigers; its own elite troop of suicide bombers, the Black Tigers; and an air force of ultra-light planes. It also operates a police force, a television network, hospitals, and schools. It runs humanitarian organizations to assist the Tamil victims of the fighting. It adeptly uses the Internet to spread its message (Enteen, 2006).

Like many other contemporary conflicts, the movement for Tamil self-rule in northeastern Sri Lanka is rooted in history. Ceylon first came into being in 1833 under British rule. The minority Tamils took advantage of educational opportunities and assumed positions of power in government. Many in the Sinhalese majority felt threatened by colonialism and the rise of the Tamils to power.

Concerned that their unique language and culture would be lost, the Sinhalese promoted the idea that the island existed to protect a purely Buddhist society. In 1948, D.S. Senanayake, a Sinhalese, was elected the first prime minister of an independent Ceylon, setting the stage for the domination of the island by the majority Sinhalese and the subjugation of the Tamil minority.

Tamil power was undermined by a series of measures that provided more educational opportunities for Sinhalese, increased the proportion of Sinhalese in the government bureaucracy, and deprived Tamil schools of funding. In 1956, a "Sinhala Only" Act was passed that replaced English with Sinhala as the language of official government business. For many Tamils, this law meant that they either had to learn Sinhala or hire an interpreter to fill out government forms. In the 1970s, the Sinhalese began enforcing ethnic quotas for university entrance, leading to the exclusion of many Tamil students.

Prabhakaran and his organization have directed their violence against a wide range of targets, including government officials, police, and private citizens. Nearly 3,000 injuries and more than 600 fatalities have been reported since the conflict began (Terrorist Knowledge Base, 2006).

Several efforts have been made to find a peaceful solution to the ethnic conflict, most recently with Norway acting as a mediator. A ceasefire was negotiated in 2002, but after the 2004 tsunami disaster intense disputes over the distribution of international aid again pitted the Sinhalese against the Tamils. Another ceasefire was agreed to in 2006, but hostilities have again resumed.

Prabhakaran is wanted for murder, organized crime, and terrorism by Interpol, the world's largest international police information organization, with 186 member countries. Arrest warrants have also been issued against him in Sri Lanka and India for the assassination of Indian Prime Minister Rajiv Gandhi.

Seen as a terrorist by much of the world community, Prabhakaran is seen by the Tamils as a combatant against the racial oppression in Sri Lanka. (For more on the Tamil Tigers, see, e.g., Hoffman & McCormick, 2004; Laqueur, 2004; Roberts, 2005; Zwier, 1998).

Subcomandante Marcos

The last terrorist to be discussed in this section is perhaps the most enigmatic of all: Subcomandante Marcos of Mexico's EZLN (Ejército Zapitista de Liberación Nacional), the Zapatista National Liberation Front. Although this group is not listed by the United States as either an FTO or an OTG, it is seen as a terrorist group by many Mexicans. The Terrorist Knowledge Base (2006) categorizes it as a nationalist/separatist, communist/socialist, antiglobalization terrorist organization.

EZLN was formed in 1983 as a communist-inspired organization dedicated to forcing the Mexican government to give more rights to indigenous Mexicans in the poor southern provinces. Focusing on the grievances of the rural peasants in the Mexican state of Chiapas, Subcomandante Marcos and the EZLN are said to have the support of thousands of impoverished indigenous Mexicans.

In 1994, the EZLN launched a violent campaign to coincide with the initiation of the North American Free Trade Agreement (NAFTA), which has been opposed by antiglobalization groups around the world. Nearly 150 people were killed before a truce was agreed on between the EZLN and Mexico (Martin, 2006). Although there has been no major violence since 1994, the group remains heavily armed and active in organizing marches and political rallies, making public appeals to voters, opposing globalization and free trade, and more recently entering the political process in Mexico.

Subcomandante Marcos is a mysterious figure, and his true identity has been concealed behind a black ski mask that he wears for all public appearances. He also goes by the name Delegate Zero; the Mexican government says his real name is Rafael Guillen, a former philosophy teacher, but Marcos denies this. Marcos had said that the real leader of the group was a woman named Comandante Ramona, who died in 2006. In 2005, Marcos came out of hiding and began touring Mexico on a motorcycle while advocating for the rights of indigenous peoples. For more on Subcomandante Marcos and the EZLN see, for example, Subcomandante Marcos and Juana Ponce de Leon, 2002; Subcomandante Marcos and Paco Ignacio Taibo II, 2006 (a novel); and Henck, 2002.

Perhaps the best way to appreciate the motivation of Subcomandante Marcos is to examine his own words. In a 1997 interview with Kerry Appel, Marcos said (as translated):

> Since the independence of 1810 and until our time, there has been a sector of the population of Mexico that is more than 10% of the population, that is 10–12 million indigenous people, that have never been recognized within the nation as citizens. It is pretended that the indigenous are equal to any other citizen of the town or the countryside and it is forgotten that they have their own culture and history and that they arrived here, or have been here, a long time before the conquest and the colonies and before Mexico's independence and Mexico's revolution. . . . [W]e think that the demands of the EZLN in particular and the Indian peoples of Mexico in general put in first place the problem that's appearing in this time of globalization. It's neo-liberalism. At the same time that it tries to erase borders and globalize economies it begins to exclude social groups that aren't economically productive. And paradoxically, those social groups are the oldest and have the most historical tradition. . . . It is not possible that in the modern world the only way to value a person is by their purchasing power or credit capacity. It is necessary to refer to history as to what makes a human being, or their dignity as we say in the EZLN, without converting them into nothing more than a consumer or producer or another number in profit indexes or the statistics of multinational corporations.

PHOTO 3.3   Zapatista rebel leader, Subcommander Marcos, right, attends a student rally in Mexico City in 2001.

The discussion now turns from specific terrorist organizations and their leaders to a single terrorist event that had worldwide implications: the bombing of Pan Am Flight 103.

AN INFAMOUS TERRORIST ATTACK: PAN AM FLIGHT 103

On December 21, 1988, liquid fire and twisted metal fell from the skies over the tiny village of Lockerbie, Scotland, after the explosion of Pan Am Flight 103. All 259 passengers and crew were killed, including 189 Americans, along with 11 people on the ground. The explosion of Pan Am Flight 103, en route from London to New York, exemplified the political nature of international terrorism (see, e.g., Emerson & Duffy, 1990; U.S. Congress, 1991; Wallace, 2001).

In 1991, two Libyan intelligence agents were charged with the bombing, and the government of Colonel Muammar al-Qaddafi was widely believed to have been involved. When al-Qaddafi refused to surrender the suspects for trial, the United Nations Security Council imposed sanctions on Libya in 1992. The UN resolution banned all airline flights to and from Libya, prohibited sales of weapons and aircraft to Libya, forced drastic reductions in oil sales, and limited Libyan diplomatic presence in foreign capitals. The economic and political sanctions were designed to pressure al-Qaddafi to turn over the two suspects. In 1999, 11 years after the downing of Flight 103, he complied, and the suspects were handed over to a special Scottish court in the Netherlands. The United Nations suspended the sanctions against Libya, but the United States did not.

On January 31, 2001, Abdelbaset Ali Mohmed al-Megrahi was found guilty of arranging for the bomb, hidden in a Toshiba radio-cassette player inside a brown Samsonite suitcase, to be loaded onto the flight. No witnesses saw the suitcase placed on board the plane, but the Lockerbie prosecutors were able to link al-Megrahi to the bomb-making materials. He was sentenced to life imprisonment and must serve a minimum 20 years before he is eligible for parole.

His co-defendant, Al Amin Khalifa Fhimah, the station manager for Libyan airlines in Malta, was acquitted because the court found no convincing evidence that he knowingly helped put the suitcase in the international baggage system. He returned to a hero's welcome in Libya. In an internationally broadcast ceremony, Colonel al-Qaddafi railed against the guilty verdict and objected to the way the entire case had been handled, with particularly vitriolic comments reserved for the United States.

Libya was considered by the West to be one of the most vigorous state sponsors of international terrorism during the 1970s and 1980s. Colonel al-Qaddafi, who came to power in a coup d'état in 1969, wanted "to spearhead an Arab-Islamic revolution in which he saw himself not only as the chief ideologist (by virtue of his little 'Green Book') but also as a chief strategist" (Laqueur, 1999, p. 168). Thousands of foreign terrorists were trained in Libya, including Carlos the Jackal, who was believed to be on al-Qaddafi's payroll.

Attack and counter-attack were building blocks of the Pan Am terrorist attack. The Libyan government was believed by the United States to have arranged terrorist attacks in airports in Vienna and Rome, as well as the 1986 bombing of the La Belle Discothèque in West Berlin, in which two American servicemen were killed. In retaliation, the United States launched an air strike, dubbed El Dorado Canyon, against the Libyan capital, Tripoli. Among the casualties was the daughter of Colonel al-Qaddafi.

President George H. W. Bush responded to the Lockerbie verdict by vowing to continue the U.S. sanctions and calling for the Libyan government to pay compensation to the families of the victims. At the welcome home ceremony for the Libyan acquitted of the bombing, al-Qaddafi likewise demanded compensation. He wanted the United States to pay for the bombings on Tripoli.

Finally, the Libyan leader agreed to pay compensation to the victims' families. Libya was then removed from the U.S. list of state sponsors of terrorism.

The events surrounding the bombing of Pan Am Flight 103 illustrate how one terrorist event had repercussions around the globe. The September 11, 2001, attacks on the United States were consistent with this pattern of transnational terrorism with worldwide ramifications.

HIGHLIGHTS OF REPRINTED ARTICLES

The two readings that follow were selected to illustrate two aspects of international terrorism not discussed above. The first discusses the interconnections between terrorism and narcotics trafficking and other crimes. The second focuses on the strategies and motivations underlying the simultaneous attacks in 2004 on four commuter trains in Madrid, Spain.

Svante E. Cornell (2005). The interaction of narcotics and conflict. *Journal of Peace Research*, 42(6), 751–760.

Svante E. Cornell discusses the connection between narcotics trafficking and terrorism. Specifically, the article addresses the use of narcotics as an economic means of support for violent, radical groups seeking to redress grievances and for criminal enterprises in search of illicit profits. The author points out that areas of the world engaged in civil unrest, so-called conflict zones, are increasingly becoming targets for large-scale and lucrative drug operations. Cornell argues that not enough research has been conducted to determine why the presence of narcotics in these conflict zones prolongs the duration of the conflict.

Cornell suggests that, by combining the knowledge from studies done on the crime-terror nexus with research on the profitability of armed conflict, researchers may be able to clarify the apparent connection between conflict and drugs. The author points out that the current trend of many terrorist organizations is to themselves engage in illegal activities for profit. This is a change from the previous pattern in which terrorist groups would associate with organized criminal elements to help fund their operations.

Javier Jordan and Nicola Horsburgh (2005). Mapping Jihadist terrorism in Spain. *Studies in Conflict and Terrorism, 28*, 169–191.

On March 11, 2004, explosions on four trains in Madrid killed nearly 200 people and injured over 1,400 more. At first, the attacks were attributed to the long-standing Basque terrorist group, ETA. Quickly thereafter, however, it became clear that they were carried out by a radical Islamic network linked to Al-Qaeda. This was a shock to most Spaniards, who viewed themselves as relatively immune to the al-Qaeda threat.

Jordan and Horsburgh examine the ways in which Islamic terrorist networks emerged over the past two decades in Spain, how they are organized, and the likelihood of future attacks. They analyze four separate networks: the Algerian Jihadist, the Syrian Jihadists, the Madrid attack network, and the minority group network.

The article examines the attack from multiple perspectives, including the use of profits from the sale of illegal drugs grown in Morocco, the manner in which false documents were obtained, the use of mosques to recruit young Muslims to infiltrate Iraq, and the use of radical Web sites to advance the global Jihad discourse.

EXPLORING GLOBAL TERRORISM FURTHER

- Many FTOs and OTGs have their own Internet sites, although they are unlikely to identify themselves as terrorists. The Web site of the Liberation Tigers of Tamil Eelam (LTTE; http://www.eelam.com) declares that the "Tamil people of the island of Ceylon (now called Sri Lanka) constitute a distinct nation. They form a social entity, with their own history, traditions, culture, language and traditional homeland. The Tamil people call their nation Tamil Eelam."
- The Palestine Information Center, at http://www.palestine-info.com, has a strong pro-Hamas slant and an even stronger anti-Israel position. This Web site presents an interesting array of news stories from Palestine and other countries in the region.
- Sinn Féin, the political wing of the IRA, has been a key participant in the peace process, yet it remains committed to a united Ireland free from British rule. Its Web site is http://www.sinnfein.ie.
- What other terrorist organizations can you find that have Internet sites? What types of justifications for violence are offered by the terrorist organizations on the Web?
- A variety of bibliographies on international terrorism are available online. The Dudley Knox Library at the Naval Post Graduate School in Monterey, California, has one divided by subject and region at http://www.nps.edu/library. This Web site is full of interesting information on terrorism.
- Define the term *globalization*. What are some of the pros and cons of globalization? Try to gather empirical information on both sides of the issue. Your answer should include a discussion of the likely consequences of the international movement toward globalization.
- In what ways does globalization threaten the values and operations of terrorists? What do you think of the metaphors of McWorld vs. Jihad? Can you provide a different, even better metaphor for this situation?
- In his article, "The Interaction of Narcotics and Conflict," Svante E. Cornell claims that the "conditions of armed conflict boost, exacerbate, transform and occasionally shift preexisting patterns of narcotics production." What are the reasons he gives for these effects, and how do they relate to the "Grey Area of Cooperation" he also discusses?
- Cornell contends that a large volume of the global cultivation of cocaine/heroin crops, which used to be found in Turkey, Iran, and Bolivia, is now taking place in "conflict zones" located in Southwest and Southeast Asia and in Latin America. How does this influence terrorist organizations?
- What does Cornell claim that research suggests about the effect of narcotics trafficking on the duration of the conflict?
- Do you agree with Cornell that civil war is caused more frequently by economic than by sociopolitical factors? What are some economic factors that could lead to conflict?
- Jordan and Horsburgh, the authors of the second reprint in this chapter, note that Spanish society was shocked to find out the train bombings were conducted by groups inspired by al-Qaeda. Why had the Spanish viewed themselves as relatively immune to the threat of Islamic extremists?
- What is the significance of the four separate networks (Algerian Jihadist, Syrian Jihadists, Madrid attack, and minority group) discussed by Jordan and Horsburgh?

- According to Jordan and Horsburgh, what impact did the sale of illegal drugs, the procurement of false documents, and the use of mosques for recruiting young Jihadists have on the Madrid attacks?
- According to Jordan and Horsburgh, how did the terrorists use videos and Web sites to promote the view that the United States, with all of its military superiority, imposed unspeakable suffering on Muslim women and children?

VIDEO NOTES

The background of international terrorism is explained often in documentaries about the Central Intelligence Agency. One noted exploration of the U.S. role in the "blowback" of transnational terrorism is titled *C.I.A.: America's Secret Warriors* (Discovery Channel, 1997, 2 vols., 50 min. each).

With its focus on big money, the movie *Syriana* (Warner Brothers, 2005, 128 min.) covers the deadly web of corruption and deceit stretching from Houston, to Washington, and on to the Middle East, which ensnares industrialists, princes, spies, politicos, oilfield laborers, and terrorists.

The Interaction of Narcotics and Conflict

Svante E. Cornell

The link between armed conflict and the production and trafficking of illicit drugs has been frequently noted in the popular literature. Recent academic research on the matter has taken place mainly within the framework of studies of the role of natural resources in civil wars. These have tended to lump drugs together with other 'lootable' resources such as diamonds. The results have been mixed, with the main contribution so far being to show that drugs are not linked to the onset of conflict but appear to be linked to the duration of conflict. Yet, the specific dynamics and, in particular, the causal mechanisms of the linkage between narcotics and conflict remain poorly understood. Nevertheless, recent literature on terrorism and its link with organized crime provides important insights that are applicable to the relationship between narcotics and conflict. This review essay combines the economics and conflict literature with the crime-terror nexus, which provides useful insights as to the causal mechanism linking narcotics and conflict. Empirical cases indicate that where a pre-existing drug production exists, the conditions of armed conflict boost narcotics production and enable insurgents to become involved in the drug trade to finance their struggle, thereby increasing their capabilities and the challenge they pose to states. In some cases, involvement in the drug trade also seems to affect the motivational structures of insurgent groups, creating an economic function of war and vested interests in the continuation of armed conflict.

The link between armed conflict and the production and trafficking of illicit drugs has been frequently noted in the popular literature. Recent academic research on the matter has taken place mainly within the framework of studies of the role of natural resources in civil wars. These have tended to lump drugs together with other 'lootable' resources such as diamonds. The results have been mixed, with the main contribution so far being to show that drugs are not linked to the onset of conflict but appear to be linked to the duration of conflict. Yet, the specific dynamics and, in particular, the causal mechanisms of the linkage between narcotics and conflict remain poorly understood. Nevertheless, recent literature on terrorism and its link with organized crime provides important insights that are applicable to the relationship between narcotics and conflict. This review essay combines the economics and conflict literature with the crime–terror nexus, which provides useful insights as to the causal mechanism linking narcotics and conflict. Empirical cases indicate that where a pre-existing drug production exists, the conditions of armed conflict boost narcotics production and enable insurgents to become involved in the drug trade to finance their struggle, thereby increasing their capabilities and the

SOURCE: From "The Interaction of Narcotics and Conflict" in *Journal of Peace Research* by Cornell, Svante E. © 2005 pp. 751. Reprinted with permissions from Sage, Ltd.

AUTHOR'S NOTE: Research for this article was made possible by grants from the Swedish National Drug Policy Coordinator's Office and the Swedish Emergency Management Agency. Contact: info@silkroadstudies.org.

challenge they pose to states. In some cases, involvement in the drug trade also seems to affect the motivational structures of insurgent groups, creating an economic function of war and vested interests in the continuation of armed conflict.

Introduction

The interaction between civil war and the cultivation of narcotics has become increasingly observable in areas of the world as varied as Latin America, Southwest Asia and Southeast Asia. This is particularly the case regarding coca and opium, the crops from which cocaine and heroin, the most potent and profit-bringing psychotropic substances are derived. The bulk of the global cultivation of these crops is presently taking place in conflict zones. Yet, in the 1960s, countries such as Turkey, Iran and Bolivia produced much of the world's opium and coca, without experiencing armed conflict. Afghanistan, Burma, Colombia and Peru form the chief cultivation areas of opium poppy and coca and have been areas of prolonged armed conflict.

A link between narcotics and conflict, much noted in popular literature and in case studies, has also been borne out by recent comparative research suggesting that narcotics extend the duration of conflict (Ross, 2003, 2004a, b; Fearon, 2004). These findings raise a number of important questions regarding the dynamics whereby narcotics and conflict interact, which are presently not well understood. The question of why narcotics are linked to conflict duration has not been convincingly addressed. Indeed, the link could be spurious; the same conditions, for example state weakness, could be the cause of both armed conflict and the production of narcotics. Even should this be the case, however, the possible interaction between them in conditions of state weakness and its consequences deserves study.

This article reviews research on economic incentives in armed conflict and, specifically, the link between natural resources and intrastate conflict, seeking to complement it by a second emerging body of research, the so-called 'crime–terror nexus' theory concerning the interaction between violent nonstate actors and transnational organized crime. The article suggests the advantages of combining the lessons of these two bodies of literature. Adapted to the study of civil war, the crime–rebellion nexus provides a useful explanatory framework for the study of the link between conflict and narcotics.

Economic Factors in Civil War

Literature on economic incentives in civil war has challenged established notions of the driving forces in intrastate conflict (Keen, 1998; Collier & Hoeffler, 2004; Berdal & Malone, 2000a; Ballentine & Sherman, 2003). Berdal & Malone (2000: 1) note that 'comparatively little *systematic* attention has been given [in . . . the recent literature on conflict] to the precise role of economically motivated actions and processes in generating and sustaining contemporary civil conflicts.' Indeed, a tendency has existed to portray war as a result of an irrational decision due to, for example, 'information failure,' reflecting an underlying assumption that war benefits no one and must, therefore, be an outcome that actors seek to avoid.

Greed and Grievance

Collier & Hoeffler (2004), Grossman (1999) and others have argued that more civil wars are caused by economic than sociopolitical factors and that loot-seeking (greed) is more important than justice-seeking (grievance). The economic approach to understanding civil war differs from political science approaches by focusing on a different motivation for violence (greed), as well as a different explanation for the outbreak of war (atypical opportunities). As Keen (2000: 22) has observed, war is not simply the breakdown of order, economy and social organization, but 'the emergence of an alternative system of profit, power, and even protection.' Insecurity and unpredictability, coupled with the weakening of law and order, imply the turn to a more opportunistic society; an increase in criminality; the disruption of markets; and opportunities for what Collier (2000: 102) calls 'rent-seeking predation.' While this is immensely detrimental for society at large, it provides opportunities for armed groups to benefit economically. Collier & Hoeffler (2004: 587–588) argue that 'a model [of initiation of civil war] that focuses on the opportunities for rebellion performs well, whereas objective indicators of grievance add little explanatory power.'

Yet, the greed theory has been criticized as simplistic, corresponding poorly with reality. Empirical studies have found that incentives for self-enrichment were neither the primary nor the sole cause of numerous conflicts (Ballentine & Nitzschke, 2003: 1). Ross (2004a: 337–338) concludes that 'there appears to be little agreement on the validity of the resources–civil war correlation.' Largely because of differing methodologies and differing data, there is strong disagreement on whether natural resources at all increase the risk of war or extend the duration of war.

Natural Resources

Dividing resources into smaller categories, especially lootable and non-lootable resources (Le Billon, 2001), generates more interesting results. Ross (2003) argues that the degree to which a commodity is linked to conflict depends on its lootability, obstructability and legality. Drugs, like alluvial diamonds, are easy for a limited number of individuals to appropriate and transport to markets, as opposed to oil, gas, timber or minerals. Given their high value-to-size ratio, they are not easily obstructable, unlike oil, minerals and timber, which require much more time and complicated enterprises to be looted. Finally, the illegality of drugs makes them benefit insurgents, who are less susceptible to influence by international prohibition regimes, unless governments are willing to endure international sanctions.

Ross (2004a: 344–345) indicates that 'most evidence thus far suggests that gemstones and narcotics are linked to the duration of conflict, but surprisingly not to the initiation of conflict.' Diamonds, however, are different in their effect, depending on their lootability. Primary diamonds are generally not lootable and seem unrelated to conflict onset, whereas alluvial, or secondary, diamonds have been statistically linked with the onset of civil war in the post-Cold War period (Lujala, Gleditsch & Gilmore, 2005). No such finding has been made for drugs. Fearon notes a link between 'valuable contraband,' including drugs, and conflict duration. Moreover, conflicts where rebels relied extensively on contraband financing had a mean duration of 48.2 years, compared to just 8.8 years for other conflicts (Fearon, 2004: 283–284).

These studies indicate that the presence of narcotics is unlikely to play a role in the initiation of conflict, but that conflict duration is increased by the presence of narcotics. It does not, however, explain convincingly why this would be the case. It does suggest that the capabilities of insurgents are increased by the presence of narcotics. But is this the entire story? If increased capabilities mean a balance between belligerents, this could imply a greater possibility for a negotiated solution (Zartman, 2000).

THE CRIME–REBELLION NEXUS

An emerging body of literature on the modes of interactions between nonstate violent actors and organized crime has important implications for understanding the causal mechanism of the interaction of narcotics and conflict.

The End of the Cold War and Insurgency Financing

The increasing linkage between violent nonstate actors and organized crime has been noted since the end of the Cold War (Makarenko, 2003). This linkage was counter-intuitive, as the ideal-type violent movement strives for a self-defined higher cause and is disinterested in (or opposed to) the pursuit of profit through crime. Conversely, the ideal-type organized criminal network is motivated simply by the pursuit of monetary profit, power and status (Williams, 1994: 96). As Hoffman (1998: 43) notes, 'the terrorist is fundamentally an altruist: he believes he is serving a "good" cause designed to achieve a greater good for a wider constituency [whereas] the criminal serves no cause at all, just his own personal aggrandizement and material satiation.' Crime is perceived as a domestic problem, and 'law enforcement and national security are based on very different philosophies, organizational structures and legal frameworks' (Williams, 1994: 96). As a result, transnational organized crime has not been viewed as a national, let alone international, security issue. Yet, this depiction no longer holds up to closer scrutiny, as 'many of today's terrorist groups have not only lost some of their more comprehensible ideals, but are increasingly turning to smuggling and other criminal activities to fund their operations' (Thachuk, 2001: 51).

The end of the Cold War drastically reduced the availability of state financing for terrorist and insurgent movements (Labrousse, 2004a: 72).

With the bipolar confrontation gone, simply being in opposition to a communist or non-communist regime no longer translated into financial support from one of the superpowers or their proxies (Makarenko, 2005). The need for alternative funding made organized crime attractive to many groups. The international efforts to combat terrorism financing after 11 September 2001 are further pushing nonstate violent actors toward organized criminal financing (Sanderson, 2004). This move is facilitated by the rapidly developing processes of globalization, simplifying transportation and communications (Harriss-White, 2002; Williams, 2000; Levitsky, 2003; Cornell, 2004)

Operational Involvement and Motivational Change

The construct of a security continuum placing organized crime and pure ideological groups at opposite ends of a spectrum clarifies the blurring picture between criminal and political groups (Makarenko, 2002). Between these extremes lies a 'grey area' with different variations and combinations of the two: cooperation between a criminal and an ideological group; involvement of an ideological group in crime; and involvement of a criminal group in political violence. Research has shown that cooperation between groups at opposing ends of the spectrum tends to give way to self-involvement; that is, ideological groups tend to engage directly in criminal operations (Dishman, 2001). The growth of a narcotics industry in a conflict zone is likely to disproportionally benefit the nonstate actor (typically the weaker actor) in financial terms. This enables it to pay fighters, acquire weapons and, potentially, even buy legitimacy with the local population. Such increased capabilities make insurgent groups more dangerous adversaries to governments. Crime and drugs are, hence, instrumental in enabling a group to threaten the state's monopoly of the use of force and control over territory, as well as the security of individuals (Ballentine, 2003: 262).

Criminal involvement implies, at first, the operational use of crime to raise capabilities to further original goals but, potentially, affects the motivational structures of groups. Occasionally, it is difficult to assert whether a violent group's actions are motivated by ideological or criminal aims; that is, 'organized crime and terrorism are indistinguishable from one another' (Makarenko, 2002; see also Brown, 1999; Cornell, 2005a).

Criminal involvement seems to affect the motivational structures of some originally ideologically motivated groups. Such insurgent or terrorist groups have either adopted a predominantly criminal nature or acquired a criminal purpose at the side of their ideological purpose (Makarenko, 2004; Schweitzer, 2002: 287–289).

Implications

The idea of a crime–rebellion nexus complements the literature on economics and conflict. In particular, it furthers understanding of the mechanisms whereby narcotics and conflict have become linked. As state financing declined, nonstate violent actors gradually overcame their aversion to financing from organized crime. Some discovered the enormous potential arising from involvement in narcotics production and smuggling. This provided a financial base to strengthen the organization, resist government onslaught and, indeed, to deny governments control of significant parts of their territories for extended periods of time. This helps to explain why narcotics seem linked to conflict duration but not to onset.

Further, most research on economic incentives in civil war takes a 'snapshot,' implicitly assuming that motivational structures are static: rebels are fully motivated by either greed or grievance from the beginning and engage in crime only for operational purposes. The crime–rebellion nexus model suggests that the opportunity of economic profit may mutate the motivations of originally ideologically motivated insurgents. Indeed, the possibility that rebel motivational structures may change over time has substantial implications for understanding the evolution of a conflict.

If this is empirically corroborated, it would have profound implications for conflict resolution. The narcotics industry inherently makes conflicts harder to resolve, as it reduces rebel incentives for a negotiated solution. International mediation seeking to find a compromise on the publicly stated incompatibility of a conflict may simply be missing the point. If rebels have become less interested in justice than in money, offering them justice is unlikely to end a war. As the drug trade is inherently illicit in the present international system, it is infeasible to offer rebels a negotiated solution whereby they would be allowed to retain control over the drug trade. Herein lies a main difference between drugs and other natural resources. Theoretically, understanding the change in motivations could be used by negotiators to offer the insurgents an 'exit' option, for instance by keeping their money. But, precisely because this aspect of conflicts is as yet poorly understood, there is little empirical experience to indicate whether this is a workable proposition.

NARCOTICS AND CONFLICT: EMPIRICAL EXPERIENCE

Few of the world's conflict zones experience drug production. But drug cultivation is increasingly likely to occur in a conflict zone. The 9 states out of 190 (4.7%) that produced opium or coca in significant quantities accounted for 15 of the 109 intrastate armed conflicts (13.7%) recorded by the Uppsala Conflict Data Project (UCDP) in the period 1990–2003.[1] Among the nine drug producers (Afghanistan, Bolivia, Burma, Colombia, Laos, Mexico, Pakistan, Peru and Thailand), only Bolivia and Thailand did not experience armed conflict.

In Afghanistan, Burma, Colombia and Peru, the four major drug-producing countries in the past 15 years, traditional and minor production of opium or coca existed long before the conflicts.[2] However, the large-scale industrial production of drugs developed *after* the initiation of conflict. Among mid-level and minor producers of drugs, there is no clear pattern. Bolivia and Thailand experienced no armed conflict; Mexico and Pakistan experienced minor conflicts unrelated geographically to the drug industry; and Laos had a low-intensity conflict involving an opium-producing ethnic minority. Large-scale drug production seems closely related to armed conflict, while minor production is not.

Insurgent Involvement

The empirical experience indicates a strong link between insurgent groups and drug production. Only one insurgent group in the drug-producing countries, Mexico's Ejército Zapatista de Liberación Nacional, decidedly avoided involvement in the drug trade. The EZLN received significant external funding in the form of donations etc. and may have anticipated that involvement in the drug trade would jeopardize its significant international goodwill and lead to increased counter-insurgency assistance from the USA to the Mexican government (Dishman, 2001: 47). In Pakistan, the Mohajir nationalist Mohajir Quami movement was active in Karachi and had no specific link to opium production, though parts of the group engaged in various urban criminal activities. Laos's Hmong minority, inhabiting the country's opium-producing hill areas, has been waging a low-intensity conflict against the communist government since it took power in 1975 (Johnson, 1993; McCoy, 1991). Opium production in Laos peaked in 1989–90, coinciding with the peak of the insurgency, the only two years that it was actually registered in the UCDP data (U.S. Department of State, 1998).

In the four major drug-producing countries, all major nonstate actors have been strongly involved in the drug trade. In Afghanistan, this includes Gulbuddin Hekmatyar's Hezbe-Islami (HI) since the 1980s (McCoy, 1991; Cooley, 2002; Griffin, 2001). After the Soviet withdrawal and U.S. disengagement, HI increasingly relied on the drug trade (Rupert & Coll, 1990; Haq, 1996; Ahmad, 2004: 41). Today, HI is again a leading actor in the insurgency and remains deeply involved in the opium trade (Ghafour, 2004a,b; IRIN, 2004; Ahmed, 2004). The Shura-i-Nazar and Jumbush-i-Millli factions of the Northern Alliance have also benefited from taxing or supervising opium production and trade (Goodhand, 2000; U.S. Department of State, 2002). The Taliban movement taxed the opium trade while in opposition and in government, before banning it in 2001 (Cornell, 2005b). Foreign organizations, such as Al-Qaeda and the Islamic Movement of Uzbekistan, have also been connected with the drug trade in Afghanistan (Makarenko, 2002; Cornell, 2005a).

Tribal independence movements among the hill tribes of eastern Burma after the end of the Second World War increasingly came to be financed through heroin, enabling otherwise impoverished tribal areas to finance armed struggles against the Burmese state (DEA, 2002: 2; Chouvy, 2002: 78–84; Dupont, 1999: 442). From the 1970s onwards, the heroin industry grew heavily under the control of various warlords, including Luo Xinghan's Kokang Self-Defense Forces and Khun Sa's Shan United Army (Chouvy, 2002: 118; Dupont, 1999: 442; Brown, 1999). After the 1989 splintering of the Burmese Communist Party (BCP) and Khun Sa's surrender in 1996, the drug trade was fragmented as splinter groups took on a greater role, especially the United Wa State Army (UWSA) and splinter Shan nationalist groups (DEA, 2002: 5; Chouvy, 2002: 120).

In Colombia, the Revolutionary Armed Forces of Colombia (FARC) and the Army of National Liberation (ELN), as well as right-wing paramilitary forces (AUC), have become heavily involved in the drug trade through alliance and self-involvement (Chalk & Rabasa, 2001). Colombia was first a transit and processing area for Bolivian and Peruvian coca (Craig, 1989: 44). By the early 1980s, coca cultivation spread to Colombia, mainly to FARC-controlled areas, where 80% of Colombia's coca was grown (Labrousse, 2004b: 32–39; Chalk & Rabasa, 2001; Lee, 1988: 99). A recent study found that 47% of coca-growing communities had FARC activity, whereas a control group had only 28%. Likewise, municipalities with coca cultivation experienced an average of 4.2 incidents involving FARC, while the control group had only 1.3 (Díaz & Sánchez, 2004: 53). The ELN long refrained from large-scale involvement in the drug industry, but this restrained policy changed with a succession of leadership in the organization (Chalk & Rabasa, 2001: 33). As for the AUC, its leader Castaño admitted in 2000 that 70% of AUC funding was drug-related (*Economist*, 2000). Colombia provides a clear example of the way in which nonstate violent actors have exploited the narcotics industry through protection, taxation and direct involvement to increase their capabilities and extend the territories under their control.

In Peru, the Maoist guerrilla Sendero Luminoso (SL) launched its insurgency immediately following a process of democratization, largely owing to fear of electoral marginalization (Ron, 2001). The drug trade provided SL with growing military capabilities, enabling it to pose a formidable challenge to the state for a decade. SL moved into the coca-cultivating Upper Huallaga valley area by 1984, established itself as a middleman, charging landing fees for aircraft transporting drugs to Colombia for processing and trafficking northward (Kay, 1999: 102; Tarazona-Sevillano & Reuter, 1990; Palmer, 1992: 70). The normally highly dogmatic Sendero adopted a more flexible and moderate course in its relations with the local population in coca-producing areas (Kay, 1999: 104). As the conflict receded in the 1990s, coca production declined concomitantly. By 1999, it stood at under 40,000 ha, compared to over 100,000 ha in 1992–95.

Motivational Changes: An Unclear Picture

Particularly in Afghanistan and Burma, many nonstate violent groups have repeatedly switched allegiances, siding with or against government forces and other nonstate actors. Maintenance of organizational autonomy, finances and control over territory seem to have become the major motivational factors for such groups, including those in Colombia. By contrast, Peru's Sendero Luminoso stands out as a continuously ideologically motivated group.

The literature does not allow any straightforward conclusion regarding the drug industry's effect on insurgent motivational structures. Burma is the clearest case of ideological movements losing much of their original purpose (Brown, 1999). The leaderships of many Burmese groups appear to have been increasingly motivated by profit. On the other hand, no such motivation change can be observed in Peru's SL. Afghanistan's HI, SN and the Taliban, among others, taxed opium production and supervised heroin processing. Changing alliances and allegiances among factions indicate motivations increasingly focused on the pursuit of power rather than ideology, with the possible exception of the Taliban. But no single faction can readily be classified as mainly greedy. The FARC, ELN and AUC in Colombia are closer to the convergence scenario, having entered into alliances with drug cartels, protected and taxed coca cultivation and, over time, increasingly involved themselves in the trade. FARC's involvement with drugs and in abducting people for ransom tends to indicate a gradual change of motivation. That said, parts of the organization may very well remain motivated by ideology.

CONCLUSIONS

The link between narcotics and conflict is treated in two separate strains of the theoretical literature: economics and conflict, and the 'crime–terror nexus.' The former has helped establish the existence of a link between conflict and narcotics (as well as other lootable resources); the latter provides important insights into the complex causal mechanisms linking the two. The overwhelming conclusion in the literature is that conditions of armed conflict boost, exacerbate, transform and occasionally shift preexisting patterns of narcotics production. Where narcotics production exists, armed conflict is likely to fundamentally alter its dynamics—and to be fundamentally altered itself. Where the opportunity of involvement in narcotics arises, most insurgent groupings in prolonged armed conflict seem to seize that opportunity. This expands their capabilities and compounds the challenge they pose to states.

Perhaps the most dangerous impact of the link between narcotics and conflict is the potential for changing motivational structures within insurgent groups arising from involvement in the drug trade. Increasing drug production in situations of civil war creates economic functions of violence for actors on both sides of the conflict and, hence, incentives for the continuation of conflict. Motivational changes do not occur in all cases but have important implications, as they fundamentally change the dynamics of conflict. The interaction between narcotics and armed conflict is more complex than it seems at first glance, but it has important implications for strategies of conflict resolution as well as for counter-narcotics efforts.

NOTES

1. Data on drug production are unavailable for many countries prior to this period, making a larger historical sample difficult.

2. Major producers are understood to be producing over one-third of the global supply of the drug over several years.

REFERENCES

Ahmad, Ishtiaq, 2004. *Gulbuddin Hekmatyar: An Afghan Trail from Jihad to Terrorism.* Islamabad: Society for Tolerance and Education Pakistan.

Ballentine, Karen, 2003. 'Beyond Greed and Grievance: Reconsidering the Economic Dynamics of Armed Conflict,' in Ballentine & Sherman (259–283).

Ballentine, Karen & Heiko Nitzschke, 2003. *Beyond Greed and Grievance: Policy Lessons from Studies in the Political Economy of Armed Conflict.* New York: International Peace Academy Policy Report.

Ballentine, Karen & Jake Sherman, eds, 2003. *The Political Economy of Armed Conflict.* Boulder, CO: Lynne Rienner.

Berdal, Mats & David M. Malone, eds, 2000. *Greed and Grievance: Economic Agendas in Civil Wars.* Boulder, CO: Lynne Rienner.

Brown, Catherine, 1999. 'Burma: The Political Economy of Violence,' *Disasters* 23(3): 234–256.

Chalk, Peter & Angel Rabasa, 2001. *The Colombian Labyrinth: The Synergy of Drugs and Insurgency and Its Implications for Regional Stability.* Santa Monica, CA: RAND.

Chouvy, Pierre-Arnaud, 2002. *Les Territoires de l'Opium: Conflits et Trafics du Triangle d'Or et du Croissant d'Or* [The Territories of Opium: Conflict and Trafficking in the Golden Triangle and Golden Crescent]. Geneva: Olizane.

Collier, Paul, 2000. 'Doing Well Out of War: An Economic Perspective,' in Berdal & Malone (91–111).

Collier, Paul & Anke Hoeffler, 2004. 'Greed and Grievance in Civil War,' *Oxford Economic Papers* 56(4): 563–595.

Cooley, John K., 2002. *Unholy Wars: Afghanistan, America and International Terrorism.* London: Pluto.

Cornell, Svante, 2004. 'Crime Without Borders,' *Axess Magazine* 6: 18–21 (http://www.silkroadstudies .org/pub/0408Axess_EN.htm).

Cornell, Svante, 2005a. 'Narcotics, Radicalism and Armed Conflict in Central Asia: The Islamic Movement of Uzbekistan,' *Terrorism and Political Violence* 17(3): 577–597.

Cornell, Svante, 2005b. 'Taliban Afghanistan: Case Study of an Ideological State?,' in Brenda Shaffer, ed., *The Limits of Culture: Foreign Policy, Islam, and the Caspian.* Cambridge, MA: MIT Press.

Craig, Richard B., 1989. 'U.S. Narcotics Policy Towards Mexico: Consequences for the Bilateral Relationship,' in Guadalupe Gonzalez & Marta Tienda, eds, *The Drug Connection in U.S.–Mexican Relations.* San Diego, CA: University of California Center for U.S.–Mexican Studies (37–47).

Díaz, Ana María & Fabio Sánchez, 2004. *Geography of Illicit Crops (Coca Leaf) and Armed Conflict in Colombia.* Working Paper. London: Crisis State Program, London School of Economics.

Dishman, Chris, 2001. 'Terrorism, Crime and Transformation,' *Studies in Conflict and Terrorism* 24(1): 43–58.

DEA (Drug Enforcement Administration), 2002. 'Burma: Country Brief,' *Drug Intelligence Brief,* May (http://www.dea.gov/pubs/intel/ 02021/02021.html).

Dupont, Alan, 1999. 'Transnational Crime, Drugs and Security in East Asia,' *Asian Survey* 39(3): 433–455.

The Economist, 2000. 'The Andean Coca Wars: The Crop that Refuses to Die,' 4 March.

Fearon, James D., 2004. 'Why Do Some Civil Wars Last So Much Longer Than Others?,' *Journal of Peace Research* 41(3): 275–301.

Ghafour, Hamida, 2004a. 'Spicy Solution to the Afghan Poppy Problem,' *Los Angeles Times,* 5 April: A3.

Ghafour, Hamida, 2004b. 'Poverty and Terrorism Fuel Booming Drug Trade in Afghanistan,' *Daily Telegraph,* 24 August.

Goodhand, Jonathan, 2000. 'From Holy War to Opium War? A Case Study of the Opium Economy in North Eastern Afghanistan,' *Central Asian Survey* 19(2): 265–280.

Griffin, Michael, 2001. *Reaping the Whirlwind: The Taliban Movement in Afghanistan.* London: Pluto.

Grossman, Herschel I., 1999. 'Kleptocracy and Revolutions,' *Oxford Economic Papers* 51(2): 267–283.

Haq, Ikramul, 1996. 'Pak-Afghan Drug Trade in Historical Perspective,' *Asian Survey* 36(10): 945–963.

Harriss-White, Barbara, 2002. 'Globalisation, Insecurities and Responses: An Introductory Essay,' in Barbara Harriss-White, ed., *Globalisation and Insecurity: Political, Economic and Physical Challenges.* New York: Palgrave (1–43).

Hoffman, Bruce, 1998. *Inside Terrorism.* New York: Columbia University Press.

IRIN (Integrated Regional Information Network), 2004. 'Afghanistan: Donor-Supported Approaches to Eradication,' 24 August.

Johnson, Stephen T., 1993. 'Laos in 1992: Succession and Consolidation,' *Asian Survey* 33(1): 75–82.

Kay, Bruce H., 1999. 'Violent Opportunities: The Rise and Fall of "King Coca" and Shining Path,' *Journal of Interamerican Studies and World Affairs* 41(3): 97–127.

Keen, David, 1998. *The Economic Functions of Violence in Civil Wars.* Adelphi Paper 320. London: International Institute for Strategic Studies.

Keen, David, 2000. 'Incentives and Disincentives for Violence,' in Berdal & Malone (19–42).

Labrousse, Alain, 2004a. *Géopolitique des Drogues* [The Geopolitics of Drugs]. Paris: Presses Universitaires de France.

Labrousse, Alain, 2004b. 'Colombie: Le role de la drogue dans l'extension territoriale des FARCEP (1978–2002)' [Colombia: The Role of Drugs in the Territorial Expansion of the FARC-EP (1978–2002)], *Géopolitique des Drogues Illicites.* Hérodote (112). Paris: La Découverte.

Le Billon, Philippe, 2001. 'The Political Ecology of War: Natural Resources and Armed Conflicts,' *Political Georgraphy* 20(5): 561–584.

Lee, Rensselaer III, 1988. 'Dimensions of the South American Cocaine Industry,' *Journal of Interamerican Studies and World Affairs* 30(2/3): 87–103.

Levitzky, Melvin, 2003. 'Transnational Criminal Networks and International Security,' *Syracuse Journal of International Law and Commerce* 30: 227–240.

Lujala, Päivi; Nils Petter Gleditsch & Elisabeth Gilmore, 2005. 'A Diamond Curse? Civil War and a Lootable Resource,' *Journal of Conflict Resolution* 49(4): 538–562.

McCoy, Alfred, 1991. *The Politics of Heroin: CIA Complicity in the Global Drug Trade.* New York: Lawrence Hill.

Makarenko, Tamara, 2002. 'Crime, Terror, and the Central Asian Drug Trade,' *Harvard Asia Quarterly* 6(3) (fas.harvard.edu/~asiactr/haq/200203/0203a004.htm).

Makarenko, Tamara, 2003. 'A Model of Terrorist–Criminal Relationships,' *Jane's Intelligence Review,* 1 August (http://www.janes.com/jir).

Makarenko, Tamara, 2004. 'The Crime–Terror Continuum: Tracing the Interplay Between Transnational Crime and Terrorism,' *Global Crime* 1(1): 129–145.

Makarenko, Tamara, 2005. 'Terrorism and Transnational Organized Crime: Tracing the Crime–Terror Nexus in Southeast Asia,' in Paul Smith, ed., *Terrorism and Violence in Southeast Asia: Transnational Challenges to States and Regional Stability.* New York: Sharpe (in press).

Palmer, David Scott, 1992. 'Peru, the Drug Business and Shining Path: Between Scylla and Charybdis?,' *Journal of Interamerican Studies and World Affairs* 34(3): 65–88.

Ron, James, 2001. 'Ideology in Context: Explaining Sendero Luminoso's Tactical Escalation,' *Journal of Peace Research* 38(5): 569–592.

Ross, Michael L., 2003. 'Oil, Drugs and Diamonds: The Varying Roles of Natural Resources in Civil Wars,' in Ballentine & Sherman (47–70).

Ross, Michael L., 2004a. 'What Do We Know About Natural Resources and Civil War?,' *Journal of Peace Research* 41(3): 337–356.

Ross, Michael L., 2004b. 'How Do Natural Resources Influence Civil War? Evidence from Thirteen Cases,' *International Organization* 58(1): 35–67.

Rupert, James & Steve Coll, 1990. 'U.S. Declines to Probe Afghan Drug Trade,' *Washington Post,* 13 May.

Sanderson, Thomas M., 2004. 'Transnational Terror and Organized Crime: Blurring the Lines,' *SAIS Review* 24(1): 49–61.

Schweitzer, Glenn E., 2002. *A Faceless Enemy: The Origins of Modern Terrorism.* Cambridge, MA: Perseus (287–289).

Tarazona-Sevillano, Gabriela & John Reuter, 1990. *Sendero Luminoso and the Threat of Narcoterrorism*. Washington Papers Series. New York: Praeger & Center for Strategic and International Studies.

Thachuk, Kimberley, 2001. 'Transnational Threats: Falling Through the Cracks?,' *Low Intensity Conflict & Law Enforcement* 10(1): 47–67.

U.S. Department of State, 1998. *International Narcotics Control Strategy Report 1997*. Washington, DC: Bureau for International Narcotics and Law Enforcement.

U.S. Department of State, 2002. *International Narcotics Control Strategy Report 2001*. Washington, DC: Bureau for International Narcotics and Law Enforcement.

Williams, Phil, 1994. 'Transnational Criminal Organizations and International Security,' *Survival* 36(1): 96–113.

Williams, Phil, 2000. 'Transnational Criminal Networks,' in John Arquilla & David Ronfeldt, eds, *Networks and Netwars: The Future of Terror, Crime and Militancy*. Santa Monica, CA: RAND (61–97).

Zartman, I. William, 2000. 'Ripeness: The Hurting Stalemate and Beyond,' in Paul C. Stern & Daniel Druckman, *International Conflict Resolution: After the Cold War*. Washington, DC: National Academic Press (225–250).

❖

Mapping Jihadist Terrorism in Spain

Javier Jordan and Nicola Horsburgh

The presence of radical Islamic networks in Spain can be traced back a decade prior to the attacks on Madrid in March 2004. This article intends to offer a panoramic view of the different groups that compose the Jihadist map in Spain. The activities, general profile of the members, and major structural characteristics of these networks are described. Ultimately, factors that could influence the future evolution of this phenomenon are outlined.

Early in the morning on 11 March 2004, several explosions on four *Cercanias* trains in Madrid claimed the lives of 191 people and injured over 1,400 others. Initially, most Spanish analysts attributed the attack to a change in strategy from the terrorist organization ETA. However, it did not take long before it became known that the attack was the work of a radical Islamic network linked to Al Qaeda. The news shook not only Spanish society but also all other European societies. Until then, most Europeans considered Al Qaeda a distant threat that only directly concerned the United States and countries of Muslim majority. As in New York and Washington on 11 September 2001, the attacks on Madrid brought to the fore horror and death in a territory previously untouched and relatively safe from the Al Qaeda threat. Once past the initial shock, several questions emerged: When and how did Islamic terrorist networks emerge in Spain? How are they organized? Will new attacks occur? This article endeavors to answer these questions, providing the most up-to-date picture of radical Islamic networks in Spain. It should be noted at the outset that the lack of open sources on personal data of those arrested prevents the conducting of an empirical study into the motivations and causes behind this terrorism. The data on detainees provided by security agencies that has not appeared in the press is protected under Spanish law, shielding personal information. However, this article has benefited from personal interviews with members of the Spanish security services that fight terrorism. These sources permit better understanding of the context surrounding the tragic events in Madrid and what could be the future evolution of the radical networks in Spain. In sum, with the available information a generalized "map" of the different groups, the attacks they have conducted, the general profile of the members and the structural organization adopted will be assessed.[1]

HISTORY BEHIND THE JIHADIST NETWORKS IN SPAIN

In Spain, the history of terrorism inspired by Islamism can be traced back over two decades. On 24 July 1984, the Spanish police arrested an Iranian command belonging to the "Martyrs of

---

the Islamic Revolution," who sought to attack a Saudi plane in Madrid. A month later, a group known as the "Islamic Jihad" (possibly related to the Egyptian group of the same name) attacked the owner of a Kuwaiti newspaper in Marbella, southern Spain. Months later, the same group assassinated a Saudi engineer. In 1985, the Islamic Jihad was also suspected of bombing a restaurant near the U.S. military base in Torrejón, killing 18 and wounding 82. In 1989, the police arrested eight individuals in Valencia supposedly linked to Hizbollah, together with 258 detonators and 220 kg of explosives in tin cans, from Lebanon on route to France.[2] In 1991, the Spanish security agencies were alerted by Arab intelligence services of a plan to hijack a plane and crash it into the Orient Palace during the celebration of a Middle East peace summit in Madrid. The cell that planned said attacks was arrested in an unnamed Arab state. This information was made public ten years later in an interview between Julián García Vargas and Rafael Vera, two figures that in 1991 fulfilled the roles of Defence Minister and Secretary of State for Security in Spain.[3]

The common denominator of all the activity just outlined is that these actions were carried out by non-residents, individuals that were not living on a permanent basis in Spain. It was therefore an external form of terrorism. Spain was merely the scene for action. This is in sharp contrast to the 1990s, when resident and permanent Jihadist networks emerged in Spain. In order to aid discussion in this article, the networks will be examined in terms of four groups: the Algerian, the network of Syrian origin, the Madrid attack network, and the minority groups. A map illustrating these four groups can be found in Figure 1.

Algerian Jihadist Networks

The Algerian Jihadist network was probably the first to embed itself in Spain, shortly after civil violence broke out in Algeria in 1992. Initially, the network was composed of members of the Armed Islamic Group (GIA). The GIA's origins can be traced back to the early years of Al Qaeda. Many GIA members were Afghan Algerians that had fought against the Soviet Union and had later return to Algeria to continue the Jihad.[4] The organization maintained links to bin Laden and received aid and training from Al Qaeda camps in Sudan until 1996.

The GIA then transferred its strategy to Western Europe where a considerable Algerian community in France favoured the implantation of support networks and recruitment.[5] Similar networks emerged in Italy, Germany, the Netherlands, U.K., and Spain. In Spain, the GIA networks settled in the east. It is in this region that the Algerian immigrant community is concentrated (around 38,000). From this region, access to Algeria is facilitated by ports linking Alicante and Valencia with Oran and Algiers.

The first arrests of Algerian network members were carried out in March 1995. The police arrested Ghebrid Messaoud in Barcelona. In March 1996, 12 residents were arrested in Cataluna for belonging to the GIA. In June 1996, the police arrested Farid Rezgui in Madrid. Rezgui provided false passports to GIA members. In April 1997, 15 Algerians were arrested in Valencia and Barcelona for links to the GIA. Two weeks later, the police detained four Algerians in Barcelona, three of which were released the following day.[6]

In June 2001, the police arrested in Alicante Mohamed Benshakria, an important member of the Salafist Group for the Predication and Combat (GSPC), an Algerian network linked to Al Qaeda. Benshakria passed as an economic migrant and sought refuge in Spain after a GSPC group was disbanded in Frankfurt by German police in December 2000. This was the "Meliani cell," which was preparing a massive attack on a cathedral in Strasburg and the market in that city.[7] Benshakria was extradited to France on 12 July 2001. Two months later, on 26 September 2001, the police arrested six members of the GSPC in Germany and in diverse localities in Spain: Navarra, Huelva and Murcia.[8] These individuals were in contact with a Tunisian, Nizar Trabelsi (who visited Spain in August 2001). In the personal diary of one of the GSPC members, Mohamed Belaziz, the desire to become a martyr together with Trabelsi in a suicide attack on a North American embassy in Paris was revealed. This cell also maintained contact with the Tunisian Essid Sami Ben Khemais, one of those responsible for the Jihadist networks in Italy composed largely of Moroccans and Tunisians. This network planned an attack on the U.S. embassy in Rome. The network was disbanded by Italian police in April 2001. Prior to his arrest, Ben Khemais stayed for four days in Spain, meeting with members of the GSPC disbanded

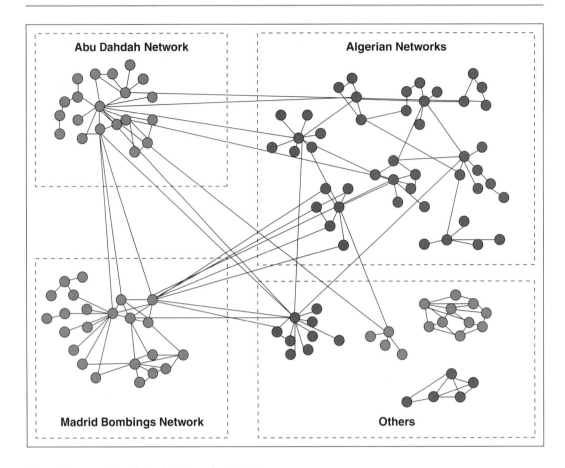

FIGURE 1   Map of Jihadist Networks in Spain

NOTE: This figure performs only an illustrative function and does not represent the real structure of inter-personal relations (or relations between individuals) within Jihadist networks in Spain.

in Pamplona and Valencia.[9] More recently, in December 2002, the Algerian Abdelkrim Hammad, alias "Aldelnassa," was arrested in La Rioja. A month later, on 24 January 2003, the police conducted arrests in Barcelona and Girona of 16 suspected members of the GSPC.[10] Early 2004, new arrests were carried out. In February, two suspected members of the GSPC in Torrevieja and Murcia were arrested. In March, four suspected members of the GIA were arrested in Valencia.[11]

More recently, in October 2004, the Spanish police detained 35 individuals linked to a network composed mostly of Algerians and Moroccans. The leader of the network was an Algerian, Mohamed Achraf, who had been arrested in Spain for belonging to the GIA. Between late 2001 and early 2002 he formed a new network, recruiting members in prison.[12] Following his

release he recruited old members of the Algerian networks in Valencia.[13] The objective was to execute a terrorist attack as soon as possible using a lorry packed with 500 kg of explosives to bomb the National Audience (the Court specialized in terrorism) in Madrid. It appears that they also intended to carry out a second phase of attacks in other locations in the capital, targeting Atocha train station and the Real Madrid football stadium.[14]

Network of Syrian Origin (or Abu Dahdah Network)

The presence of Jihadist networks of Syrian origin in Spain (also known as the Abu Dahdah network or Al Qaeda in Spain) dates back to 1994. Many members came from Syria, but most have acquired Spanish nationality. This network was less homogenized than the Algerian one as other nationalities, like Moroccans, were part of the group.

In 1994, the information services of the Spanish police were monitoring a radical group in Madrid led by the Palestinian Anwar Adnan Mohamed Salah, known as the "Chej Salah" and most members were of Syrian origin. Several had been part of the *Talia al-Mukatila* group (The Fighting Vanguard), military arm of the Muslim Brotherhood in Syria.[15] In 1982, the Hafez el-Assad regime harshly reprimanded Islamists and many members sought refuge in Jordan, Afghanistan, and Saudi Arabia. Others relocated to Europe, and several settled in Spain. Some married, secured employment, and began a new life. Nevertheless, radical ideas and links to other "brothers" in the United States, Europe and the Middle East remained. Chej Salah played a crucial role in grouping together those that lived in Madrid to carry out activities related to the global Jihad. The Syrian Mustafa Setmarian is also suspected of performing a crucial role in the formation of the group. Setmarian lived in Granada and in 1995 abandoned Spain to settle in London and work for "Al-Ansar," the official magazine of the GIA. Previously, Setmarian went to Afghanistan and was in charge of a training camp there.[16] Currently, his whereabouts are unknown. There are suspicions that he could be implicated in the attacks on Madrid, if only as ideological inspiration.[17] Chej Salah also attempted, without much success, to take control of the Madrid mosque Abu Bakr, controlled by the moderate Syrian *Muslim Brothers*. In November 1995, Chej Salah informed his group that he would make a short visit to Granada, southern Spain. That was not his real plan and shortly afterward he resurfaced in Pakistan.[18] Since then, Chej Salah became a gateway for voluntary recruits later sent to training camps in Afghanistan. In Pakistan, he worked with Abu Zubaydah, a senior member of Al Qaeda, arrested in April 2002.

Since 1995, a Syrian (nationalized Spanish) known as Imad Eddin Baraliast Yarkas, alias "Abu Dahdah," became head of the Syrian origin network in Spain. In 1996, Abdullah Khayata Catan, alias "Abu Ibrahim," a former Mujahaddin from Bosnia, challenged the leadership and the group experienced temporary division. However, Abu Ibrahim lacked leadership skills and was accused of collaborating with the Syrian intelligence services. In 1996, Ibrahim fled Spain and the network was reunited.[19] In November 2001, Abu Dahdah was arrested together with ten other members of his group, in Madrid and Granada. Months prior, over a dozen individuals were accused of belonging to that network. The last arrests were made in Granada in September 2003. Please see Figure 2 for more information on arrests carried out on the networks. One was a journalist for Al-Jazeera, Taysir Allouny, and several others linked to him accused of forming a group of young Mujahaddin in Granada.[20] Currently, Abu Dahdah and other collaborators are on bail, awaiting trail. They deny all charges against them.

Networks With Minority Presence

In Spain, there is a presence of minority elements from other networks and radical groups, in particular Ennahda, Hamas, Ansar Al Islam, Salafía Yihadia, and Hizbollah. The Abu Dahdah network cooperated in a restricted manner with these elements, like the Tunisian Ennahda, to obtain false documentation,[21] funds, and distribute propaganda.[22] Abu Dahdah also maintained relations with members of the Moroccan Jihadist groups (known generically as Salafia Yihadia) that resided in Spain. Among them, Mustafa El Mauymouni, one of the leaders of the networks in Spain, was arrested during a visit to Morocco and sentenced there for involvement in the Casablanca attack in 2003.[23] Several detainees in relation to the attacks on Madrid have links to Salafia Yihadia, like the Moroccan Jamal Zougam, who was also in contact with Abu Dahdah.[24] Some of these are in Spain undertaking university studies; others are immigrants with employment of no relation to the Jihad. They maintain ideological links with respective groups but scarce operative relation. In some cases, commitment to the Jihad cause is greater. In May 2004, police detained four individuals for their presumed role in the financial and falsification racket led by Ansar Al Islam. They were also recruiting young Muslims to infiltrate Iraq.[25] In September 2004, ten Pakistanis were arrested in Barcelona for links to Jihadist networks. In house raids, police found false passports and credit cards, along with drugs, extremist literature, and numerous videotapes. In one video, over an hour of footage was dedicated to two high-rise buildings in Barcelona, paying attention to structural details.[26]

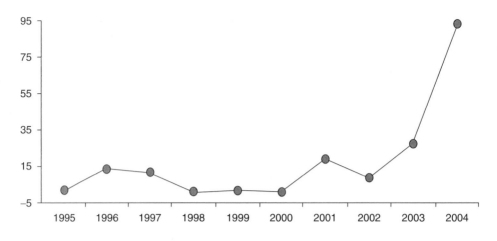

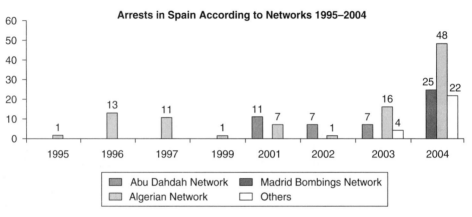

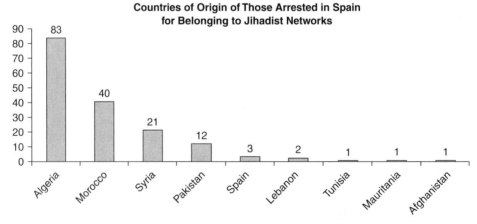

Figure 2   Number of Arrests for Links to Jihadist Networks in Spain, 1995–2004. In the elaboration of these graphs, non-Jihadist common delinquents, accused of collaborating with the networks, have not been included. In some instances, the arrest of an individual has been accounted for more than once when that person has later re-integrated into the network. For this reason, the graph on nationalities (numbers of total detainees) offers a smaller number than the sum of detentions. Both graphs account for those that committed collective suicide in Leganés (5 Moroccans, 1 Tunisian, and 1 Algerian).

SOURCE: Office of Information and Social Relations, Spanish Home Office; and press summaries facilitated by the Police Studies Institute in Spain.

Network That
Carried Out the Madrid Attack

The attack on Madrid constitutes an unprecedented act both in Spain and Europe. The simultaneous explosion of 10 bombs placed on 4 trains in the early hours of 11 March 2004 caused 191 deaths and 1,400 injuries.[27] Had the trains not been delayed, the explosion would have taken place inside Atocha train station, provoking possibly the collapse of its structure and a much higher number of victims.

Two days later, the police carried out the first arrests. However, the principal nucleus of the network continued operations and three weeks later placed a bomb on the railway line of the fast train between Madrid and Sevilla. Fortunately, the bomb was discovered by a railworker and did not explode.[28] The following day, the police located the integral members of the network in an apartment in Leganés, a town near Madrid. After a shoot out and hours under siege, the terrorists ignited an explosive charge, taking the lives of them all and the life of a special operations police agent.[29] Following the collective suicide, more explosives and planning details of massive attacks against a commercial center in Leganés and a Jewish establishment in Madrid were discovered.[30] In the two videos threatening new attacks recorded by the network, the individuals that appeared in the videos were dressed as death, a sign interpreted by the Spanish intelligence services that the terrorists would continue with their campaign until death.[31] Several days following the collective suicide, unidentified individuals desecrated the tomb of the dead special operations police agent. According to police sources from the Home Office, this could have been an act of revenge on behalf of radical Islamists.[32]

Many details, which could prove relevant, remain classified. However, present open sources provide some detail on the principal characteristics of this network. Judicial and police sources currently consider the essential nucleus of the investigation clear.[33] The Madrid bombing investigations attribute the planning and execution of the attacks to an ad hoc group created in Spain. The current investigations on the Madrid attack point to the Algerian Allekema Lamari as a leading figure in the event. Lamari was a member of the Algerian network detained in Valencia in 1997. He was released in 2002, re-settled in

Tudela (Navarra), and then moved to Valencia and Madrid. Since July 2003, Lamari was under a warrant for capture and arrest, for violating bail (failing to appear before court to fulfill his sentence as dictated by the Supreme Court).[34] Both the National Police and the National Centre of Intelligence consider him as possibly the emir (leader) of the group.[35] Apparently, following his release, he established contact with a radical group in Madrid with links to the Abu Dahdah network and members of the Moroccan Salafia Yihadia. Among them, key figures like Serhane ben Abdelmajid, alias "the Tunisian"; Rabei Osman El Sayed Ahmed, alias "Mohamed the Egyptian"; and the Moroccan Amer Azizi, stand out. In turn, these entered into contact with new individuals to prepare the terrorist campaign in Spain.[36] In total, the Spanish police have arrested 56 individuals in connection to the attacks (although several are not Jihadist, simply delinquents that collaborate with the network). Of that figure, 14 remain in prison. It is known that the terrorists acquired explosives from a group of Spanish delinquents that traffic stolen dynamite from a mine in Asturias.[37] It has also been established that the attacks were financed largely by money from drugs trafficking in North Morocco.[38]

Lamari and Serhane "the Tunisian" died together with five members in the suicide at Leganés. Rabei alias "Mohamed the Egyptian" was arrested by the Italian police in Milan in June 2004. Although in a conversation recorded by the police Rabei considers himself the intellectual author behind the attacks, it is doubtful that he fulfilled this role because he abandoned Spain in January 2003.[39] Amer Azizi and five other members of the network managed to escape and their whereabouts are currently unknown. The Spanish police suspect that they are in a European country (possibly Belgium, Holland, France or Italy). It is feared that they are preparing a new attack, as a form of vengeance for the death of their compatriots in Leganés. Within radical circles, these seven suicides have become the "martyrs of Europe."[40]

It is not clear what the intentions of the attacks were, beyond that of the general motivations that Spain was part of the Christian and Western "axis." On the one hand, the attack could be interpreted as an act of vengeance for past arrests of Jihad militants. Even Lamari had passed five years in Spanish prison and it is possible that he developed these desires during his imprisonment. On the other hand, Aznar's government support for the U.S.-led war on Iraq could have reinforced terrorist motivations. Already the wider global Jihad had made public its animosity toward Spain in this regard. In November 2003, Osama bin Laden directly threatened Spain for its military presence in Iraq. In a document published on the internet in December 2003, he urged followers to attack Spanish troops stationed in Iraq. One also has to consider that Spanish public opposition to the government's foreign policy in Iraq made Spain a weak link in the Western alliance.[41] Possibly the network that carried out the attacks in Madrid came to the same conclusion, thus deliberately timing the attacks just three days before the general elections. Moreover, on the eve of the elections the network made public a video threatening more killings and attacks because of the support Spain had given to the United States on the War on Terror, manifested in its military presence in Afghanistan and Iraq.[42]

ROLES AND FUNCTIONS

Propaganda

Until 11 March 2004, radical group influence in Spain was limited to support roles for the global Jihad. Accordingly, the first activities were propaganda related. Jihadists attempted to extend the circle of sympathizers to obtain candidates for the holy war and secure financial and material support. They obtained videos and documents from the decentralized global Jihad propaganda machine. Posters, magazines, pamphlets, and photocopies of communiqués by bin Laden were distributed in several mosques around Madrid, without the consent of the imam. Projections of videos on the Jihad were also shown in small prayer rooms or in homes.[43] A key figure in the propaganda endeavor was Abu Omar, alias "Abu Qatada," a Jordanian of Palestinian origin. He is one of the principal visionaries of the global Jihad in Europe. He settled in London in 1993 as a political refugee and like Omar Bakri and Abu Hamza, preached the Jihad to hundreds of young people in nearby mosques. Most of these became followers and later went to Afghanistan.[44] In 2002, the British police arrested Abu Qatada. Abu Qatada has maintained a distant relationship with bin Laden and was one of the editors of Al-Ansar. He is also author of the infamous *Articles between*

two Doctrines, a recompilation of 98 articles in which his vision of the world is outlined. In it, Abu Qatada offers one of the clearest explanations of the global Jihad. He criticizes moderate Islamists for accepting the rules of the political game that the apostates impose and establishes as a key goal the elimination of these regimes. In a second phase, he calls for the re-instatement, via armed struggle, of Islam throughout the world.[45] The collection was available online until recently but the website is now closed.

Abu Dahdah also maintained a distant relationship with Abu Qatada. It is contended that over a period of five years he went seventeen times to London to meet with him.[46] Abu Qatada would deliver propaganda previously distributed in Spanish networks. Abu Dahdah also took money collected by his network for Jihadis in other countries, principally Jordan.[47] Occasionally, publications were posted online until money was obtained to edit them.[48]

There is also an internal consumption of propaganda to maintain cohesion and group motivation. Via radical webpages, Jihadists maintain informed of the status of the global Jihad, of the casualties and victories abroad.[49] This was a frequent topic of conversation in meetings.[50] It is thus thanks to the information revolution that it is possible to belong to global communities like the Jihad, despite the fact that its values might be contrary to the host society in which they are physically immersed.[51] Propaganda distributed by the networks in Spain transmits the classic contents of the global Jihad discourse: the existence of a Western and Jewish conspiracy to exterminate Muslims and the need to join the struggle against the enemies of Islam.[52] It is through this prism that Jihadis interpret current events. In house raids, the police have found news clippings documenting the fear of new attacks from Al Qaeda in Spain and news reports on communiqués by bin Laden.[53] Thus, there existed awareness within these networks of the host society's reaction to Al Qaeda.

In propaganda-related videos, arguments are strengthened by images demonstrating the military superiority of the United States and its allies in contrast to the suffering of Muslim women and children in scenes of combat filmed by the Mujahaddin. Frequently, these videos contain harsh images, in which prisoners are murdered in front of the camera. Despite the crudeness of these images, they attract sympathy and new members. In a phone conversation intercepted by the police between members of the Abu Dahdah network, it is told how, after the showing of one of these videos to a group of young people, one commented that it was worth more than a thousand sermons.[54] Several other networks in Spain have used Jihad videos as a key propaganda instrument. The GSPC cell arrested in Valencia in September 2001 had several similar videos[55] and some of the members that executed the attacks on Madrid used to meet to watch these videos.[56]

Together with internal consumption of propaganda via videos or online, the Jihadist networks used to support each other through interpersonal relations, to attract new recruits and maintain old ones. The role of interpersonal relations or the group dynamic in motivation has been stressed by Marc Sageman in his recent study of Jihadist networks[57] and by Donatella Della Porta in relation to the Red Brigades and the Red Army Faction.[58] Police surveillance of the Abu Dahdah network over a period of five years, which is reflected in the judicial summary, highlights that the majority of the network limited the circle of friends to those with similar ideas and moderate Muslims (although often they were considered weak and renegades[59]). The relationship to neighbors and work colleagues was polite but minimal. Within the network, meetings in mosques and daily telephone conversations were very common. On the weekends, families usually got together. The members of the network that had fought in Bosnia organized excursions, trips and weekend breaks outside Madrid to which Arab sympathizers would often join.[60] Apart from friendships, sometimes parentage links existed and marriages to Muslim girls were arranged.[61]

Logistics and Finance

The logistics of the Al Qaeda networks in Spain have consisted in material support to the Jihad abroad. In this way, Jihadis feel like active members of the "resistance community." Support comes in various guises: finance, passport/visa falsification, refuge, dual use equipment for use in Chechnya and Algeria, links to Jihadist networks outside Spain and locations for new training camps.

The attainment of funds is usually via illicit means. Abu Dahdah's network was engaged in robbery in shopping centers and credit card fraud. To carry out these activities, a small network of common delinquents of Moroccan origin was necessary. They also preyed on airports, using the extra few hours before the victim could denounce the robbery to the police and cancel the card.[62] Two members of Abu Dahdah's network owned a shop selling goods of little value; this was used as a front, selling false goods with stolen credit cards.[63] Sometimes, identification papers were obtained. Mobile phones were also stolen to be used for free calls without police interception.[64] The GSPC cells arrested in Valencia and Cataluña were also funded by petty crime. The Madrid attacks network achieved part of the money to carry out the attack via the sale of drugs cultivated in the north of Morocco.[65] For the members of the networks, these illicit activities are admissible on a religious level if they promote the Jihad cause.[66]

Although the funds acquired by the aforementioned means are habitually scarce, it is enough to sustain the activities of a network. This is possible because the Jihadist lifestyle is very austere. It is normal to share accommodation, and when travelling to stay with other "brothers."[67] There are thus little personal costs. Moreover, most members have work in Spain and therefore do not depend financially on their networks.

The Abu Dahdah network also laundered money and made bank transactions to other countries using front construction companies in Madrid. From 1996 to 2001, Mohammed Galeb Kalaje, alias "Abu Talha," sent close to 700,000 Euros to different accounts related to Al Qaeda throughout Europe, the United States, Asia, and the Middle East.[68] Of these transfers, 231,664 Euros sent as "donations" to Nabil Sayadi, alias "Abu Zeinab," linked to bin Laden in Belgium, and senior responsible of the Islamic Foundation *Secours Mundial* in Europe (linked to Al Qaeda), stand out.[69] According to documentation obtained from "Abu Talha" in both his home and his office, he had transferred 17.094 Euros to two other presumed members of Al Qaeda: one resident in Hamburg, Germany and another close to Mohamed Atta.[70]

Auxiliary Support

Auxiliary support to Jihadist networks abroad was another essential activity carried out by

Jihadist networks in Spain. The Abu Dahdah network obtained visas for persecuted activists in other countries. The network also obtained residence permits for former Mujahaddin thanks to the construction company owned by "Abu Talha." This company offered work contracts to the former paramilitaries, an essential prerequisite for a residence permit under Spanish law. It is important to note that Abu Dahdah kept well informed on immigration legislation in Europe so as to effectively funnel in those that needed refuge.[71] In other cases, support consisted in the provision of temporary accommodation to a group of combatants in country homes. Occasionally, GSPC cells sheltered Algerian commandos, providing rest and relaxation away from the conflict zone. Abu Dahdah also financed an eye operation for a Mujahaddin injured in Chechnya. Dahdah even personally accompanied him to a hospital in Madrid.[72] Other forms of support consisted of collaboration with Human Rights NGOs to appeal the imprisonment of Islamic activists in the Middle East.[73]

The linkage of information, via frequent visits abroad to other members of the grand network, was another activity carried out by Jihadists. According to the police, these visits were used to maintain contact with various points of the network and to interchange experiences and instructions. As already highlighted, Abu Dahdah regularly visited the United Kingdom, but also Turkey, Belgium, Denmark, Sweden, Indonesia, Malaysia, and Jordan, for meetings with senior Al Qaeda members.[74] Ghasoub Al-Abrash, a member of the Abu Dahdah network, travelled to the United States in 1997. There he recorded a video of the World Trade Center in New York, the Golden Gate Bridge in San Francisco (paying particular attention to suspension pillars), the Brooklyn Bridge, the Statue of Liberty, the Sears Tower in Chicago, and Disneyland and Universal Studios in California.[75]

Spain was used in the preparations for the 11 September 2001 attacks, but the extent of involvement is unclear. Four of the terrorists that planned or directly participated in the operation, among them Mohamed Atta and Ramzi binalshib, visited Spain in July 2001.[76] There is no evidence that during their stay they were in contact with members of the Abu Dahdah network. It is also unlikely because, at the time, Abu Dahdah was conscious that he was under police surveillance. Even so, a relationship between those that prepared the attacks on the United States in 2001 and Abu Dahdah is suspected following a cryptic telephone conversation in which reference to an "imminent operation" and a "aviation field"[77] is made; and because Abu Dahdah's telephone number was discovered following a police search of Ramzi binalshib's home in Germany.[78] The conclusion is that the Abu Dahdah network could have provided logistic support (money and false passports) to the cell in Hamburg.

Recruitment

The recruitment of volunteers to receive training in Afghanistan or fight on Jihad fronts in Bosnia, Chechnya, Algeria, and Indonesia is another crucial activity carried out by Jihadis.[79] Spain has witnessed in recent years the largest growth of immigrants in both relative and absolute terms in the European Union. A considerable proportion of the immigrants come from Morocco (over half a million) and this number is expected to rise due to Morocco's economic decline and its overwhelming young population. Al Qaeda has a great interest in recruiting Muslim immigrants because of the operational potential these offer: they are usually well educated, they know how to move around in the West, and in some cases already have European passports.[80] As a result of propaganda and the personal "hands on" approach employed by networks in Spain, several have managed to recruit a considerable number of new members. During the 1990s, the Abu Dahdah network managed to recruit 20 new members; these were later sent to training camps in Afghanistan.[81] Some returned to Spain and other Jihad fronts. One such member was Hamed Abderramán, the only Spanish citizen of Moroccan origin to pass through Guantanamo Bay.[82]

The Madrid attack network and the Algerian network, disbanded in October 2004, were formed by recruiting tens of new members in Spain. The ultimate objective was not to send these recruits abroad to fight for the Jihad but to carry out a terrorist campaign on Spanish soil.

The presence of Islamic communities in Spain is thus instrumental to recruitment. In Islam, the mosque is not only a space for worship but also a meeting place.[83] Police recordings of conversations between members of the Abu Dahdah network reveal how meetings were arranged with individuals interested in the Jihadist cause in mosques. In this process of captivation, security measures were adopted and background checks were carried out; sometimes even character references were necessary.[84] The recruitment of "converts" (non Muslims) is practically non-existent. The Spaniard José Luis Galán, alias "Yusuf Galán," is the most well-known exception. However, Galán has a history of anti-systemic militancy. After conversion, he was president of an Islamic culture association, known as "Ibn Taymiyyah," linked to pacifist movements, anti-globalization, and pro-Palestine and pro-Chechnya causes. Yusuf Galán shared a flat in Madrid with Jihadis and even passed through a Mujahaddin training camp in Indonesia. However, he has not performed any function of responsibility for Spanish networks.[85] In general, Jihadis are reluctant to trust converts.

Apart from specific cases, no members have preached on a regular basis in Spanish mosques. The only cases are: Bouchaib Maghder, a Moroccan who resided legally in Spain and is currently under arrest in Morocco for links to the 2003 Casablanca attacks. Maghder was a part-time imam of a mosque in Burgos.[86] The other one is the Algerian, Abdelkrim Hammad, alias "Aldelnassa," arrested in La Rioja in December 2002.[87] Hicham Tensamani, a Moroccan and imam of a mosque in Toledo, had links to members of the network that executed the attacks on Madrid. Tensamani was arrested in June 2003 by the Spanish police for his suspected involvement in the Casablanca attacks. In October 2004, Abu Javer was arrested. Javer is an imam in Almeria, where an important number of immigrants, working the land, are concentrated.[88] Despite preaching in places of worship, there is no evidence that his public discourses promoted the use of violence. In other words, Spain has not yet witnessed a phenomenon similar to Abu Qatada or Abu Hamza in London, where both promoted explicit Jihadist propaganda. Leaders of principal Islamic communities in Spain have continuously condemned the terrorist activities of Al Qaeda and are seriously concerned that society at large will equate Islam with terrorism. They reiterate that the message Islam offers the majority of these communities in Spain is moderation and represents no danger to society at large.

PROFILE OF MEMBERS

Any profile analysis of network members encounters a grave obstacle in the lack of relevant open sources. Information that appears in the declassified portions of the summary, in the informative notes of the Home Office, and the media is fragmented, preventing a systematic study of the personal characteristics of Jihadis in Spain. Nevertheless, information presently available does permit the highlighting of general characteristics of members of the different Jihadist networks in Spain. These general characteristics are:

1. *First Generation Immigrants.* Most were born outside Spain and have settled in Spain. Many had been in contact and established relationships with radical Islam prior to settlement in Spain. This is true of the Algerian network, the Syrians linked to the Abu Dahdah network and some of the Moroccans from the Madrid attack network. Others radicalized once in Spain, when developing ties with Jihadist networks.

2. *Scarce Educational Qualifications.* Most of the members did not possess a high level of academic achievement or enjoy highly paid employment. There are some exceptions however; Serhane "the Tunisian" undertook a Ph.D. in economics at a university in Madrid. The Indonesian Parlin Siregar, linked to the Abu Dahdah network and whose whereabouts are currently unknown, studied aeronautical engineering in Madrid. The Syrian Basel Ghayoun, member of the Madrid bombings network, studied IT, although he worked as a builder to sustain himself financially. Within the same network, it is presumed that the Moroccan Abderrahim Zbak graduated in Chemistry. The Syrian Mohammed Galeb Kalaje, of the Abu Dahdah network, was the owner of a small construction company. Taysir Alouny, arrested in Granada and currently released on bail on health grounds, was a star journalist for Al-Jazeera. The other cases (around 90% of those arrested in Spain) earned a living through jobs that did not require prior qualifications: working for small businesses, mechanics, carpenters, and builders. In the Algerian networks, some of the members had no jobs and earned money through common

delinquency.[89] This was also the case for members of the Madrid attack network, like Jamal Ahmidan, who although working in a clothes shop (owned by his parents), also sold drugs and for this reason is currently imprisoned in Morocco.[90]

3. *Part-Time Dedication to the Jihad.* Apart from the Algerian network, which was sustained largely via illicit means, other Jihadis in Spain were employed. Dedication to the Jihad was on a part-time basis, and therefore these individuals were not clandestine; many led apparently normal lives.

4. *Age.* Present data prevents one from establishing an average age of the Jihadist in Spain. Of the 151 individuals arrested in Spain, there is only access to the birth details of 53. Of the 53, only 14 are under the age of 30 and only 2 under the age of 25. The rest are around 30–39 years of age. This level of maturity can be explained by the fact that most had already led militant lives prior to arriving in Spain, becoming immigrants at a later age. In other cases, individuals have experimented with the process of radicalization after settling in Spain. Lack of information prevents access to supporting evidence for this hypothesis; but it is possible that once in unemployment, living in marginal surroundings or not having a family in Spain, the attractive quality of being part of the Jihadist micro-society becomes pivotal in decision making.

5. *Gender.* As is common among Islamic terrorism, there is no significant presence of women. The only exception is Naima Oulad Akcha, sister of Mohamed and Rachid Oulad Akcha (both suicides in Leganés). The judge that presided over her case has imputed her for collaborating with a terrorist organization.[91]

6. *Family Situation.* Like the age characteristics, present information prevents cross-network comparisons. However, it should be highlighted that those that fulfilled special or senior roles in networks, with a greater dedication to the Jihad both in terms of time and exposure to personal risk, like Abu Dahdah, Rabei Osman, Serhane, Amer Azizi, and Mustafa El Mauymouni, were married. Some of the wives were Spanish who had converted to Islam, facilitating the obtaining of Spanish citizenship.[92]

ORGANIZATIONAL MODEL OF JIHADIST NETWORKS IN SPAIN

The organizational structure of Jihadist networks in Spain presents interesting characteristics for a comparative study of structures adopted by networks in the West and countries with a Muslim majority.

Internal Hierarchy

Although the global Jihad is a decentralized phenomenon, at the network level elements of hierarchy, crucial to internal security and group efficiency, do exist. The image of concentric circles (see Figure 3) aids understanding, dictated by levels of authority or personal commitment.[93]

In the *first concentric circle,* senior members can be found. These individuals have an almost exclusive dedication to the Jihadist cause. The average age of these participants is superior to that of lower level members. They also have a higher level of religious instruction and are usually better educated

In the *second circle,* individuals engaged in the cause but with a lower level of operational involvement can be found. Members at this level represent the confidants of those in the first circle. In the case of cells led by Abu Dahdah, members are of different nationalities and they recruit people of the same nationality to the third level. Many share old relations with other members and some have passed together through foreign training camps or were Mujahaddin in Bosnia and Chechnya.[94] These experiences instill a sense of trust into the network. In Spain, these individuals have professions (generally non-academic) providing sufficient financial means for themselves and their families. Sometimes, these jobs are of benefit to the network. For example, a commercial establishment can be used to carry out fraud on stolen credit cards; a photocopy shop can print propaganda; and a construction company could launder money, transfer money to radical groups abroad, or employ former Mujahaddin. On other occasions, the profession is of no use to the network. Most members in this second circle are married to Spanish women and thanks to them have become Spanish citizens. In the network of Syrian origins, second-level members lead normal lives and their arrest

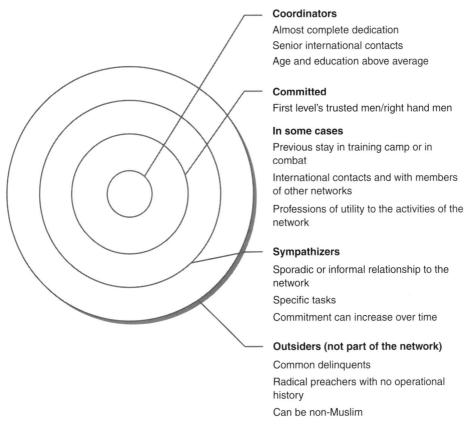

Coordinators

Almost complete dedication

Senior international contacts

Age and education above average

Committed

First level's trusted men/right hand men

In some cases

Previous stay in training camp or in combat

International contacts and with members of other networks

Professions of utility to the activities of the network

Sympathizers

Sporadic or informal relationship to the network

Specific tasks

Commitment can increase over time

Outsiders (not part of the network)

Common delinquents

Radical preachers with no operational history

Can be non-Muslim

FIGURE 3   Levels of Member Participation in a Jihadist Network

usually comes as a surprise to neighbors. In the Algerian networks, there are those that lead normal lives and others that survive through common delinquency in the name of the Jihad.

In the *third concentric circle,* members on the periphery of the network can be located. These are individuals that sympathize with the Jihad but maintain an informal relationship with members more immersed in the network. They lead normal lives and carry out very specific tasks: the provision of temporary accommodation, information and residence papers, and the delivery of propaganda or money. Eventually, some are sent abroad to receive religious and combat training or fight in the Jihad. It is through this passage that third-level members jump to the second level. Others carry out tasks of little overall importance. They know people in the network and on occasion have some vague idea of the activities these are involved in. Sometimes, the only accusation that can be levied at these third-level members is that of sharing "dangerous friendships." The level

of education varies; some are graduates but some fill the typical immigrant profile, working in the construction industry. Third-level members usually maintain relationships with the second concentric circle (the confidants of the coordinators) to avoid compromising the first level.

Beyond and *exterior to the network,* but still linked to it, are individuals that carry out activities of interest to a network: the subtraction of credit cards, the falsification of identification papers, illegal recharge of pay-as-you-go mobile phones, and the sale of explosives. For ordinary tasks, the network generally relies on Maghreb delinquents. If this is not possible, non-Muslim delinquents will be used. Dynamite and grapeshot, materials used in the attack on Madrid, were brought by a network of delinquents dedicated to the illegal sale of explosives used in mines in the Asturias region of Spain. The network of Algerian origins arrested in October 2004 entered into contact with a Gypsy explosives trafficker, with the aim of purchasing stolen dynamite in Portugal.

Primacy of Personal Relations and Permeable Frontiers Between Networks

As Marc Sageman highlights in his study of Egyptian Jihadist networks, in order to understand these groups it is easier to discuss networks linked to concrete leaders.[95] The same is true in Spain. Loyalty ties exist among individuals with a common reference: the global Jihad. Evidence suggests that these individuals do not have an abstract idea of the organization that transcends loyalty and interpersonal ties. Two main arguments in support of this theory can be found.

The first is the absence or the secondary importance of organization names. In the network of Syrian origin, it seems that its first name was *Alianza Islámica* (Islamic Alliance) and then *Los Soldados de Alá (Soldiers of Ala).*[96] Documentation collected by the police and via intercepted telephone conversations suggests that members paid little attention to the name of the group. In contrast, interpersonal relations were of key importance. In the case of the network that carried out the attacks on Madrid, the group name used in the film found by the police in Leganés was "Al Mufti and Ansar Al Qaeda Brigades." However, in a note written by Serhane and sent by fax to a Spanish newspaper a few days before the collective suicide, the terrorists called themselves "the Death Battalion."[97] The name of the group was temporal because they had decided on death in the forthcoming attacks. Similarly, the Algerian network detained in October 2004 called itself "Martyrs for Morocco" but in a communiqué sent by members of that group to a newspaper in Almeria, they called themselves "Suicide Brigades of Andalucia."[98] Naming is thus of little importance to members; the wider organization of Al Qaeda is really just an abstract entity. Despite the hierarchical structure and different roles discussed earlier, the Jihadist networks in Spain do not appreciate a bureaucratic structure, where, as Weber has posited, role distribution is impersonal. In Spain, network structures are personalized and informal relations are key.

Secondly, simultaneous allegiance and membership of various networks suggest that personal relations and the commitment to the Jihad are more significant characteristics than loyalty to an abstract organization. For example, Abu Dahdah was a member of the "Fighting Vanguard" and leader of a network in Spain; Allekema Lamari was a member of the GIA and possibly played a senior role in the Madrid attacks network; Rabei Osman started out as a militant in the Egyptian group Jihad, linked to several Moroccan based networks in Europe and with links to the network that executed the attacks on Madrid; the Moroccans Amer Azizi and Said Berraj were members of the Abu Dahdah network, playing a crucial role in the Madrid attacks network and are presently under a warrant for arrest, possibly in relation to other Jihadist networks in Europe.[99] The Moroccan Salah Eddin Benyaich, alias Abu Mughen, participated in the Abu Dahda network, fighting alongside the Mujahaddin in Bosnia and Chechnya, and is currently imprisoned in Morocco accused of belonging to the Salafia Yihadia movement and implicated in the Casablanca attacks in May 2003.[100]

This primacy of personal relations within the networks has both advantages and disadvantages. John Arquilla and David Ronfeldt have highlighted this in their works on the netwar.[101] Decentralized networks are more resistant to decapitation in contrast to strong hierarchical structures, and although the destruction of several interconnected links and points can reduce the efficiency of the network, with time it can repair itself, developing new interconnections between elements that have survived. This is true of the Abu Dahdah network, which was left severely disbanded following the arrest of its leader and over 20 of its members. Approximately two years later, a new network emerged (that of the Madrid attacks) composed partly of former Abu Dahdah network members that had not been arrested and members of other networks to which it had connections. The same can be said of the Algerian network, arrested in October 2004, which drew largely on former members of the GIA networks arrested in Spain.

Interconnection Between Networks

Interconnection between networks is a particular aspect of global Jihadism, explaining its high level of decentralization. The networks present in Spain are interconnected both nationally and internationally. As is well known, Jihadism extends beyond national and ethnic borders, uniting followers in a virtual space of believers. The establishment of multiple inter-relations between groups was a key success of the Al Qaeda founders.[102]

The network of Syrian origin had connections with members of minority groups in Spain. Abu Dahdah was in contact with one of the leaders of the Algerian networks, Mohamed Boualem Khouni, who delivered a machine used to obtain fraudulent money from stolen credit cards.[103] Moreover, the Abu Dahdah and Algerian networks co-operated in the attainment of falsified identification papers. Indeed, for this purpose they established contact with a few members of the radical Tunisian group Ennahda in Spain.[104] The relationships between Abu Dahdah and members of the global Jihad abroad were also plentiful. It has already been mentioned that he was in frequent contact with Abu Qatada in London. He also visited other influential Jihadis in Europe and the Middle East, like Tarek Maroufi in Belgium and Mamoun Darkazanli, alias "Abu Ilyas" in Germany. Both men are related to bin Laden networks in Europe. Abu Dahdah denies the charges against him but in an interview granted recently in prison, he stated that: "those of us that left Syria over 20 years ago [from persecution by Hafez el Assad against the Muslim Brotherhood] knew each other. We could say that we were right wing and were much persecuted. For this reason we now help each other: hospitality is a Koranic rule. This allows me to travel with little cost to Muslim homes, this does not mean that I had contact with terrorists" [translated].[105] This inter-connectivity constitutes a good example of the decentralized dynamic of Al Qaeda. The Jihadist network led by Abu Dahdah distributed propaganda that was delivered by other networks of Al Qaeda outside Spain. Funds were secured and sent abroad to similar groups. Young Maghrebians were recruited in Spain and sent to training camps in Bosnia and particularly to Afghanistan (they were infiltrated via Pakistan by a representative of the Spanish network). The network also helped initiate a training camp in the Indonesian region of Poso, through which between 2,000 and 3,000 Mujahaddin passed.[106] Abu Dahdah's network moved into the general directives of the global Jihad but acted in an autonomous style thanks to the initiative and personal contacts of the members of the first and second level.

In relation to the network that carried out the attacks on Madrid, international connections have yet to be ascertained. Although it is likely that the attacks were thought out and organized within Spain, the terrorists, in particular, Rabei Osman and Amer Azizi, had contacts abroad.[107] Serhane also had connections with a radical imam resident in the UK, known as "Ben Salawi" and he apparently phoned him prior to the collective suicide in Leganés.[108]

Networks Open to the Exterior

The concentric circle model presents both advantages and disadvantages to the Jihadist cause. An advantage is the enormous difficulty security agencies face in infiltrating the center to obtain quality preventive intelligence and the contents of the international relations of the network. The disadvantage consists in that exterior circles are vulnerable to infiltration and detection. From these circles, it is possible to ascertain who inhabits the inner circles, and these could be arrested. This explains the relative ease with which the Jihadist networks in Spain have been disabled. Once the police operation is underway, a large number of members have been arrested.

The vulnerability of these networks manifests itself in that they are obliged to be open to the exterior and count with a wide periphery outer circle. They are obliged as a consequence of the tasks they fulfill: propaganda, recruitment, logistical support or terrorist activity preparation. In this way the concentric circle structure, which is open to the outside, has a robust defense to the obtaining of quality preventive intelligence but a great weakness against police persecution for the obtaining of a minimum level of intelligence.

CONCLUSION: FUTURE PERSPECTIVES

Following the attacks on Madrid, the government has adopted a wide package of measures directed at combating terrorism, tripling resources of antiterrorist units, improving coordination among security services, legal amendments, and improving diplomatic relations between Spain and Islamic communities in the country.[109] Despite recent arrests, and particularly since the Madrid bombings, the Jihadist grand network has yet to be eradicated from Spain. In May 2004, police information services recognize that there still resided around 300 radicals, of different nationalities, in Spain.[110] The dismantlement in October this year of the network composed of over 50 individuals that sought to attack Madrid demonstrates that fears for continued Jihadist terrorism in Spain are well founded.

There are three main reasons to believe that Spain will continue to remain a target. First, Spain continues to represent the enemy infidel and old Islamic territory. Although historical references to "Al Andalus" are rhetorical in nature, it is true that the network that executed the attacks on Madrid referred to Spain as the land of Tarek Ben Ziyad (the Arab leader that launched the Spanish conquest in 711). The video planted after the attacks also makes reference to the crusades on the Iberian Peninsula against the Muslims, and the Inquisition.[111] Thus, historical arguments, although not the primary motivation, are part of the process rationalizing violence. Second, a major motivator could be the desire for revenge following the arrests of members and the suicide of seven members in Leganés. From intercepted Jihadist e-mail, it is clear that they consider themselves heroes. It is also possible that with time, wanted network members will seek revenge for their fallen brothers.[112] Third, although the socialist government has distanced itself from Washington over Iraq, Spain has continued to contribute to the War on Terror, increasing its military commitment to Afghanistan since the attacks on Madrid. For the elections in Afghanistan in October 2004, the number of Spanish troops totalled over 1,100.[113] In the latest Jihadist video, they threaten to continue the campaign because of the socialist government's decision to not withdraw troops from Afghanistan.[114]

Beyond these three reasons, which explain Jihadist motivation to attack Spain, there exist a crucial set of variables, which should be monitored because their evolution will determine the apparition and proliferation of new radical networks in Spain. These variables are related to the increase in Maghreb immigration in Spain; the integration of this immigration community and the Spanish attitude toward this; and Jihadist proselytizing in certain places of worship and prisons.

(a) The increase in immigration represents a key issue that will affect Spanish society profoundly in the future. Currently, there are over half a million Moroccans in Spain. It is very likely that this number will increase dramatically in the next two decades. According to statistics in 2003, the population in Morocco exceeds 30 million. Of this figure, 30% are below the age of 15. It is very likely that the Moroccan labor market will be incapable of accommodating and incorporating over nine million young people into the workforce, and thus many are likely to opt for immigration. In Morocco, grave socioeconomic problems already exist (13% of the population live below the level of national poverty) and in this context, unemployment of the young (affecting 34%) is a major destabilizing factor. Spain is separated from Morocco by a considerably higher level of living (the income per capita in Morocco is about 4,000 dollars compared to 22,000 in Spain). In these circumstances, such a gap in earning will see increased human transfer from Morocco to Spain.[115] It is argued here that the increase of Moroccan immigrants and the success or failure of their integration constitute two elements of great transcendence. Presently, the Moroccan immigrant community in Spain suffers from a meager labor and economic situation.[116] In the end, this could lead to pockets of marginalization, giving way to unfavorable positions for second generations and generating frustration within wide sections of the immigrant community. The experience of other countries demonstrates that this kind of situation can be exploited by the promoters of the global Jihad when attempting to extend their network. In numerous Western countries, the Jihad has emerged from within Muslim immigrant communities. Indeed, nearly all those arrested in Europe and the United States for connections to the Jihad were immigrants.[117]

(b) The integration of this immigration is also a key factor. The creation of marginal and isolated immigrant communities favors frustration and antisocial conduct, attitudes that can be exploited by radical groups. The French case is illustrative. During the 1990s, various Islamic organizations related to the Jihad grand network captivated young second-generation immigrants on the dole or immersed in a world of crime, taking advantage of the solidarity in marginal neighborhoods of Paris and other French cities.[118] In Spain, the integral members of the Jihadist grand work are first-generation immigrants, of middle class, which does not correspond to the profile of French radicals. Although there are areas with high concentrations of

Moroccan immigrants corresponding to a dire socioeconomic situation there are few second-generation immigrants.[119] Thus, via a wide array of integration politics and preventive measures, Spain is still in time to avoid the attacks on Madrid becoming a sign of worse to come.

(c) A factor related to integration is the social attitude of the host country toward immigrants. Spanish attitude is generally positive (only 5% demonstrate rejection in surveys), cases of xenophobia are limited and it is difficult to imagine the emergence of a political party like the *Front Nationale* led by Jean-Marie Le Pen in France. However, in the survey carried out, prejudice toward Maghreb immigration is highlighted.[120] In the countries listed, Moroccans are among the least valued. At the same time, the survey results reveal that Moroccan immigrants believe they are undervalued by Spaniards[121] and resent this discrimination.[122] Therefore, increased pockets of marginalization, composed of Moroccan immigrants, delinquency associated with this community, and the arrest of new Jihadist networks with members from the Maghreb, can lead to further distrust among Spaniards toward Moroccan and Algerian immigration. Recruitment to the Jihad is clearly facilitated under these conditions. Rejection both socially and in the labor market generates resentment among the victims of xenophobia. The French experience offers important lessons in this regard, where resentment is a factor for integration into a Jihadist network.[123] In sum, the continuation of this trend could frustrate the proper integration of immigrants and aid recruitment to the Jihad in Spain.

(d) Finally, it is likely that the networks present today or that could appear in the near future will try to continue to mobilize resident Muslims in Spain. Recruitment via radical places of worship and in prisons will be crucial to the success of this task. First, as highlighted earlier, in Spain there does not exist a phenomenon similar to the mosque in Finsbury Park, London or the Cultural Islamic Centre in Milan, where the Jihad was openly preached and radicals would often meet. In the past two years, the police information services have detected the presence of Wahhabi preachers of Moroccan origin assuming control of mosques frequented by immigrants of a similar nationality. In Cataluña, 15 prayer rooms have been identified

as having this orientation.[124] Without actually preaching the Jihad, the radical imam motivates followers to isolate themselves in the community, immerse themselves in religion, and condemn any form of integration into Spanish society. Furthermore, it is expected that due to increased pressure on Wahhabies in Morocco since the Casablanca attack in May 2003, many will transfer to Spain to preach in immigrant communities. Indeed, indicators exist that this is already underway. According to the Association of Moroccan Immigrant Workers (called *Asociación de Trabajadores Inmigrantes Marroquíes*) in Spain, a reputable representative of Moroccans, most preachers are Wahhabies.[125] Professor Mohamed Darif, the main academic expert in Morocco on Islamic terrorism, also shares this opinion.[126]

Second, prisons can become recruitment ground for Jihadis. This is the experience of other European states, like France.[127] In some Spanish prisons, a concentration of Maghrebians has emerged and there are indications that Islamists in some prisons oblige Moroccans to practice religion and unite.[128] If the socioeconomic integration of the immigrants cannot be accommodated, pockets of marginalization and delinquency can emerge, increasing the reclusive Muslim population. Indeed, this process is already underway as a consequence of the high number of Moroccans in Spanish prisons. In 2003, there were 4,600 Moroccans and 1,182 Algerians, of a total of 52,000 detainees.[129] The experience of Allekema Lamari, who before joining the Madrid attacks network spent time in prison for his links to the GIA, called attention in this regard. The Algerian network arrested in October 2004, which attempted to carry out another attack in Madrid, had also formed in a Spanish prison. After March 2004, during which the attacks on Madrid took place, the Spanish government has dispersed and transferred 60 radical Islamists to avoid the creation of Jihadist groups in prison. However, trade unions and prisons reject this measure as limited because Jihadists can still create new radical nucleus elsewhere.[130]

To conclude, this article has described the current situation and past events within a ten-year period. It has also considered future challenges. As has been determined, Jihadist terrorism will continue to threaten Spanish society, and as a consequence, the rest of the European Union.

NOTES

1. Among the open sources, the most important are 600 pages made public of the 35/01 summary against the Spanish Al Qaeda cell (which the authors term as the network of Syrian origin or Abu Dahdah network in this article). Another noted source is the informative notes by the Information and Social Relations Office, of the Spanish Home Office. The news and reports of certain newspapers are also of interest, particularly those in *El País*. The latest summary, concerned with the attacks on Madrid, remains classified.

Most literature on terrorism in Spain is focused on ETA. There are few publications concerned with Jihadist networks in Spain prior to the attacks in Madrid and of those that do exist most are only available in Spanish. An interesting book, of journalistic nature, is Javier Valenzuela, *España en el punto de mira. La amenaza del integrismo islámico (Spain in the spotlight. The threat of integrated Islamism)* (Madrid: Temas de Hoy, 2002). Prior to the 11 March 2004 attacks, one the major Spanish think tanks, the Real Instituto Elcano (http://www.realinstitutoelcano.org) had published some analysis in this area: Juan Aviles "¿Es Al-Qaeda una amenaza para Europa?" (Is Al Qaeda a threat to Europe?) 16 July 2002 and Javier Jordán "Las redes de terrorismo islamista en España. Balance y Perspectivas de futuro" (Islamic terrorist networks in Spain. Balance and Perspectives for the future) 13 October 2003. Another think tank, the Grupo de Estudios Estratégicos (http://www.gees.org) also published some analysis in the area, almost one year prior to the attacks: Juan Avilés, "La amenaza del terrorismo islamista en España" (the Islamic terrorist threat in Spain), 3 March 2003.

The topic has been tangentially touched on in more general publications on terrorism: Carlos Echeverría "La nebulosa terrorista Al Qaida, ¿mito o realidad?" (the nebulous terrorist Al Qaida, myth or reality?), *Cuadernos de la Guardia Civil*, Nu.º 25, 2001, pp. 9–17; Fernando Reinares, *Terrorismo global (Global Terrorism)* (Madrid: Taurus, 2003); Javier Jordán *Profetas del miedo. Aproximación al terrorismo islamista (Prophets of fear. Introduction to the Islamist terrorism)* (Pamplona: EUNSA, 2004); Javier Jordán and Luisa Boix. *"Al-Qaeda and Western Islam,"* *Terrorism & Political Violence*, 16(1), 2004, pp. 1–17; Carlos Echevarría, "Radical Islam in the Maghreb," *Orbis*, 48(2), Spring 2004, pp. 351–364; and the Spanish edition of Rohan Gunaratna, *Inside Al Qaeda. Global Network of Terror* (New York: Columbia University Press, 2002), which includes a special appendix on the presence of Al Qaeda in Spain.

2. These figures appear in a report elaborated via press news, facilitated by the Spanish Police Studies Institute.

3. *El Mundo*, 14 September 2001.

4. Shaul Shay and Yoram Schweitzer, "The 'Afghan Alumni' Terrorism. Islamic Militants against the Rest of the World," International Policy Institute for Counter-Terrorism, 6 November 2000.

5. Gunaratna, *Inside Al Qaeda*, p. 124.

6. Press report by the Police Studies Institute, Spain.

7. Information and Social Relations Office (hereafter referred to as summary 35/01 or ORIS), Home Office, Spain, 22 June 2001.

8. Ibid., 26 September 2001.

9. *El País*, 5 October 2001.

10. ORIS, 24 January 2003.

11. Ibid., 22 March 2004.

12. ORIS, 18–19 October 2004.

13. Ibid., 3 November 2004.

14. *El País*, 7 November 2004.

15. Indictment of Al-Qaida Cells in Spain, Summary 35/01, Central Court of Instruction, Number Five, National Audience, Madrid, 2003, p. 43 (hereafter referred to as summary 35/01).

16. *El País*, 12 September 2004.

17. Ibid., 12 October 2004.

18. Interview with members of the Exterior Information Unit of the National Police, Madrid, January 2004.

19. Summary 35/01, p. 228.

20. ORIS, 18 September 2003.

21. Ibid., p. 451.

22. Ibid., p. 118.

23. *El País*, 8 May 2004.

24. Ibid., 18 September 2004.

25. ORIS, 13 May 2004.

26. *El País*, 21 September 2004.

27. ORIS, 11 March 2004.

28. *El País*, 3 April 2004.

29. ORIS, 3 April 2004.

30. *El Mundo*, 13 April 2004.

31. Appearance of Mr. Jorge Dezcallar, ex-Director of the Centre National for Intelligence in the Parliamentary Commission investigating Madrid bombings, 19 July 2004.

32. *El Mundo*, 20 April 2004.

33. *El País*, 10 September 2004.

34. Ibid., 20 October 2004.

35. Ibid., 16 October 2004.

36. ORIS 13 March—20 August 2004.

37. *El País*, 12 October 2004.

38. Ibid., 31 March 2004.

39. Appearance of the Chief of the Brigade of the Central Unit for Exterior Information of the National Police, Rafael Gomez-Menor, in the Parliamentary Commission investigating Madrid bombings, 25 October 2004 Available at (http://www.congreso.es).

40. *El País*, 9 November 2004.

41. In "The information institution in support for the Iraqi people—the center of services for the

Mujahidin" the Jihad situation in Iraq is evaluated and the withdrawal of Spanish troops is discussed. Following a detailed appreciation of the Spanish political situation, the authors conclude that, as a result of a series of attacks on Spanish troops and the widespread social unrest towards the war, the Aznar government will be pressured and a withdrawal of troops is likely. The entire report can be found in The Project for the Study of Islamist Movements, Global Research in International Affairs (GLORIA) Center (http://www.e-prism.org).

42. *El Mundo,* 14 March 2004.

43. Summary 35/01, pp. 59–60, 447.

44. Omar Guendouz, *Les soldats perdus de l'Islam: les reseaux français de Ben Laden* (Paris: Éditions Ramsay, 2002) , pp. 112–113.

45. Reuven Paz, "Middle East Islamism in the European Arena," *Middle East Review of International Affairs,* (10)3, 2002, pp. 65–76.

46. Summary 35/01, p. 26.

47. Ibid., p. 375.

48. Ibid., p. 421.

49. Ibid., pp. 429–431, 589.

50. Ibid., p. 361.

51. Manuel Castells, *The power of identity,* (Malden: Blackwell, 2004), p. 8.

52. Summary 35/01, pp. 180–181, 229–230, 306–310, 439–444.

53. Ibid., pp. 358–359.

54. Ibid., p. 585.

55. *El País,* 5 October 2001.

56. Ibid., 12 September 2004.

57. Marc Sageman, *Understanding Terror Networks* (Philadelpia: University of Pennsylvania Press, 2004), pp. 110–120.

58. Donatella Della Porta, Social Movements, Political Violence and the State. A Comparative Analysis of Italy and Germany (Cambridge: Cambridge University Press, 1995), pp. 136–185.

59. Summary 35/01, p. 679.

60. Ibid., p. 460.

61. Ibid., p. 469.

62. Ibid., p. 511.

63. Ibid., p. 209.

64. Ibid., p. 148.

65. *El País,* 12 September 2004.

66. Summary 35/01, p. 491.

67. Ibid., p. 160.

68. Ibid., pp. 114–142.

69. Ibid., p. 55–56.

70. Ibid., pp. 114–117.

71. Ibid., pp. 189–191.

72. Ibid., p. 274.

73. Ibid., p. 121.

74. Ibid., p. 57–58.

75. Ibid., pp. 160–163.

76. Summary 35/01, pp. 317–321.

77. Ibid., p. 88.

78. Ibid., p. 320.

79. ORIS, 13 November 2001.

80. Rohan Gunaratna, "The Post-Madrid Face of Al Qaeda," *The Washington Quarterly,* 27(3), 2004, p. 95.

81. Summary 35/01, p. 595.

82. *El Mundo,* 13 February 2004.

83. Joan Lacomba, *El Islam inmigrado. Transformaciones y adaptaciones de las prácticas culturales y religiosas* (Madrid: Ministerio de Educación, Cultura y Deporte, 2001), p. 82.

84. Summary 35/01, p. 365.

85. Summary 35/01, p. 257.

86. *Crónica El Mundo,* No 405, 20 July 2003.

87. ORIS, 26 December 2002.

88. *El País,* 20 October 2004.

89. ORIS, 26 September 2001; *El País,* 20 October 2004.

90. *El País,* 2 August 2004.

91. ORIS 13 March–20 August 2004.

92. Ibid., 13 November 2001.

93. This image was used by the Exterior Information Units of the Spanish Police with one of the authors in January 2004.

94. ORIS, 13 November 2001; Summary 35/01, pp. 63–64.

95. Sageman, *Understanding Terror Networks,* p. 26.

96. ORIS, 13 November 2001.

97. *El País,* 10 October 2004.

98. *Ideal,* 20 October 2004

99. *El País,* 12 September 2004

100. *El Mundo,* 21 March 2004

101. John Arquilla and David Ronfeldt "The Advent of Netwar (Revisited)," in John Arquilla & David Ronfeldt (Eds.), *Networks and Netwars: The Future of Terror, Crime, and Militancy* (Santa Monica: RAND, 2001), pp. 1–25.

102. Gunaratna, *Inside Al Qaeda,* p. 13.

103. Summary 35/01, p. 59.

104. Ibid., p. 451.

105. Interview in the *Diario de León,* 13 May 2004.

106. Summary 35/01, pp. 68–70.

107. Appearance of Mr. Jorge Dezcallar, ex-Director of the Centre National for Intelligence in the Parliamentary Commission investigating Madrid bombings, 19 July 2004.

108. *El País,* 13 April 2004; *The Observer* 18 April 2004.

109. A relation to preventive measures can be found in the intervention of the Home Office Minister, Mr. Jose Antonio Alonso, in the Parliamentary Commission of Interior, 24 May 2004. Available at (http://www.congreso.es).

110. *El País,* 17 May 2004.

111. *La Vanguardia,* 10 April 2004.

112. *El País,* 3 October 2004.

113. *Revista Española de Defensa*, nº 124, October 2004, pp. 3–7.

114. *La Vanguardia*, 10 April 2004.

115. Data obtained from the Internacional Monetary Fund (http://www.imf.org) and Statistics Division of the United Nations (http://unstats.un.org).

116. Víctor Pérez-Díaz, Berta Álvarez-Miranda, and Elisa Chuliá, *La inmigración musulmana en Europa. Turcos en Alemania, argelinos en Francia y marroquíes en España* (Barcelona: Fundación La Caixa, 2003), pp. 229–234.

117. Robert S. Leiken, *Bearers of Global Jihad? Immigration and National Security after 9/11* (Washington, DC: The Nixon Center, 2004), pp. 14

118. Omar Guendouz, *Les soldats perdus de l'Islam: les reseaux français de Ben Laden*, pp. 57–58.

119. Alfonso de Esteban, Javier Curiel Díaz, Salvador Perelló, "Inmigración y segregación urbana," *Papeles de Economía Española*, No. 98, 2003, pp. 262–289.

120. Juan Díez Nicolas, *Actitudes hacia los inmigrantes* (Madrid: Dirección General del Instituto de Migraciones y Servicios Sociales, 1999).

121. Salustiano Del Campo and Juan Manuel Camacho, *La opinión pública española y la política exterior* (Madrid: INCIPE, 2003), pp. 70–71; Juan Diez Nicolás, *Actitudes hacia los inmigrantes* (Madrid: Dirección General del Instituto de Migraciones y Servicios Sociales, 1999).

122. Rosa Aparicio, *Estrategias y dificultades características en la integración social de los distintos colectivos de inmigrantes llegados a España* (Madrid: Instituto de Migraciones y Servicios sociales, 2001), p. 116.

123. Mohamed Sifaui, *La France, malade de l'islamisme: menaces terroristes sur l'Hexagone* (Paris: Cherche Midi, 2002); Abd Samad Moussaoui and Florence Bouquillat, *Zacarias Moussaoui. The Making of a Terrorist* (London: Serpent's Tail, 2003); Omar Guendouz, *Les soldats perdus de l'Islam: les reseaux français de Ben Laden*, pp. 57–58.

124. *El Periódico*, 2 April 2004.

125. *El País*, 7 April 2004.

126. Interview in *El País*, 15 March 2004.

127. Omar Guendouz, *Les soldats perdus de l'Islam: Les reseaux français de Ben Laden*, Éditions Ramsay, Paris, 2002, pp. 46–47.

128. *El Mundo*, 9 September 2004.

129. *El País*, 31 October 2004.

130. Ibid., 21 October 2004.

4

TERRORIST TACTICS
AROUND THE GLOBE

Fighting terrorism is like being a goalkeeper. You can make a hundred brilliant saves but the only shot that people remember is the one that gets past you.

—Paul Wilkinson

"A collusive dance of reciprocal suicide" is Albrecht's (2001, p. 1) description of conventional terrorism, which conveys an image of the treachery and destruction involved. This chapter details present-day deadly tactics of terrorists, but many of the strategies are ages old. Despite the basic repetitive patterns in the terrorist dance macabre, a consensus exists among analysts that the face of terrorism is changing, as are its methods. A new breed of terrorists is said to be seeking out and using weapons of extreme deadliness that create ever greater numbers of victims spread over larger areas (Cilluffo & Tomarchio, 1998).

According to Bruce Hoffman (1999), terrorism is where politics and violence intersect in the hopes of producing power. Violence (or the threat of violence) is thus the essential tactic of terrorism. Terrorists strongly maintain that only through violence can their cause triumph and their long-term political aims be attained. A violent act may be designed to achieve attention, acknowledgment, or even sympathy and support for the terrorists' cause. A goal of terrorist violence might also be to achieve recognition of their rights and of their organization. Their intention may even be to take complete control of the national government, their separate homeland, and/or their people by force (Hoffman, 1997).

All terrorists have one trait in common: They live in the future (Hoffman, 1998a). Every terrorist is driven by burning impatience coupled with an unswerving belief in the potency of violence. Terrorist attacks are generally as carefully planned as they are premeditated. A terrorist campaign must keep moving forward, no matter how slowly, or it will die (Hoffman, 1998a).

The *Final Report of the National Commission on Terrorist Attacks upon the U. S.*, known as the 9/11 Commission Report, provides a list of requirements needed to organize and conduct a complex international terrorist operation (Kean & Hamilton, 2004). For a successful attack, a terrorist organization needs able leaders, sufficient communications, a personnel system to recruit and train members, an intelligence effort to gather required information, the ability to move people, and the ability to raise and move the necessary money.

PHOTO 4.1   A member of the International Olympic Committee (bottom right) speaks with a masked member of Black September (top photo and bottom left), the PLO faction that invaded the Olympic Village in 1972, killing 11 members of the Israeli Olympic team.

Some categories of terrorist groups have better chances of survival than others. Historically, religious movements have persisted for centuries, but in more modern times ethnonationalist/ separatist terrorist groups typically have lasted longest and been the most successful (Hoffman, 1998a). As one example, armed Muslim separatist rebellions have persisted in Southeast Asia since the 1940s. Although the amount of violence they perpetrated has varied over time, the Muslim separatists have raised credible challenges to the authority of their central governments for more than half a century. For example, the Abu Sayyaf, which split from the Moro National Liberation Front in 1991, has its roots in colonial history in the southern Philippines. The Aceh rebellion in Indonesia is also based on long-standing demands for a distinct Islamic state (Tan, 2000).

CHILDREN AT WAR

Often forgotten in analyses of terrorist tactics is the most horrific element of terrorism. At the beginning of the 21st century, an estimated 300,000 children, some as young as 7 years old, are being used as combatants, sometimes after being kidnapped. They are exploited by both established governments and rebel movements in scores of armed conflicts around the world. Whether or not the conflicts are defined as terroristic, the children are trained in violent tactics (Hansen, 2001; Human Rights Watch, 2006).

TABLE 4.1   Child Soldiers Fighting in Recent and Ongoing Conflicts

Afghanistan	(A)
Angola	(G)
Australia	(G)
Austria	(G)
Bahrain	(G)
Bangladesh	(G)
Burundi	(G, A)
Canada	(G)
Chad	(G, A)
Colombia	(A)
Congo, Democratic Republic of	(G, A)
Congo, Republic of	(A, possible G)
Côte d'Ivoire	(G, A)
Cuba	(G)
Eritrea	(G)
Germany	(G)
Guinea	(A, possible G)
Iran, Islamic Republic of	(G, A)
Ireland	(G)
Liberia	(G, A)
Luxembourg	(G)
Myanmar	(G, A)
Nepal	(A)
Netherlands	(G)
New Zealand	(G)
Occupied Palestinian Territories	(A
Pakistan	(A)
Paraguay	(G)
Philippines	(A)
Rwanda	(G, A)
Somalia	(G, A)
Sudan	(G, A)
Tanzania, United Republic of	(A)
Uganda	(G, A)
United Kingdom	(G)
United States of America	(G)
Zambia	(G)
Zimbabwe	(G)

SOURCE: Data retrieved January 19, 2007, from Child Soldiers Report 2004.

NOTE: A = Armed political groups; G = Government forces

Young combatants participate in all aspects of contemporary political strife. They wield AK-47s and M-16s on the front lines of combat, serve as human mine detectors, participate in suicide missions, carry supplies, and act as spies, messengers, or lookouts. Physically vulnerable and easily intimidated, children typically make obedient soldiers. In Sierra Leone, at present, children forced to take part in atrocities are often given drugs to overcome their fear or reluctance to fight. Most of the child soldiers have no voice, but Ishmael Baeh, who was a child in the army of Sierra Leone in 1994, is an exception. He was released from the army and rehabilitated

PHOTO 4.2   Samboo, a 12-year-old soldier in the Karen rebel army fighting against Myanmar's military, poses in 2000 with his rifle in a jungle camp on the border with Thailand. UNICEF has called for the demobilization of child soldiers.

by a UNICEF-supported organization and has become an articulate and outspoken opponent of children being used as soldiers (Swango, 2006).

Beah's first battle took place when he was 13. He was indoctrinated with Rambo films and speeches about honor and soon learned the ideology of hate. His anger over the loss of his home, family, and friends to the rebels was maintained and fueled with intoxicants given him by the army: "We walked for long hours and stopped only to eat sardines and corned beef, sniff brown-brown (cocaine mixed with gunpowder) and take more white capsules. The combination of these drugs made us fierce. The idea of death didn't cross my mind, and killing had become as easy as drinking water"(Beah, 2007, p. 3). Restoring Beah to civilian life was difficult. His squad was his family. He remembers, "I would stand holding my gun and feeling special because I was part of something that took me seriously and I was not running from anyone anymore (p. 4)." Now, Beah can look back on his life as a child soldier and realize, "My childhood had gone by without my knowing, and it seemed as if my heart had frozen" (p. 4).

In 2007, Caryl reports that children in Iraq who have lost parents and homes, and watched as their communities were torn apart, have come to believe in the principles of violence. Instead of being trained to rebuild their country they are being trained to use weapons of destruction.

Kids will set bombs for as little as $20, and sectarian warfare is creating the next generation of Jihadists. Caryl observes, "We're far closer to the beginning of this cycle of violence than to its end" (p. 24).

Girls are also participants in terrorist acts, both willingly and unwillingly. Like boys, girls may play a part both in killing enemies and destroying infrastructure. In addition to combat duties, girls are subjected to sexual abuse and may be taken as "wives" by rebel leaders. Girl soldiers are exposed to depravity, drug use, physical deprivation, and psychological degradation (McKay, 2005).

Because of their immaturity and lack of experience, child soldiers suffer higher casualties than adults. Schooled only in war, even after a conflict is over, former child soldiers are often drawn into crime or become easy prey for future recruitment by terrorists (Human Rights Watch, 2006).

In India, the Inter-Parliamentary Union issued a statement following a conference on cross-border terrorism. The chairperson noted, "In their most impressionable age these terrorist groups are inculcating racial and sectarian hatred among children. Religious and cultural bigots are misleading future citizens of the world into cults of hatred and intolerance" ("Najma's Call," 2001, p. 1). According to Israelis, a sermon by Sheik Mohammed Ibrahim as-Madhi, broadcast on state-controlled TV in Palestine, admonished: "We must educate our children on the love of holy war for the sake of God and the love of fighting for the sake of God" ("Palestinian Women and Children," 2001).

Many young children recruited by terrorists have parents who were terrorists. Some have grown up in terrorist camps and among a cult of extremists. Many of them are nobody's children now. They may have seen their fathers or mothers brutally killed. Some may even have been born moments after their mothers had died, many more were delivered underground, and a few had their umbilical cords cut inside jail. Most of the children remember the gruesome scenes they experienced, but few know what their parents fought for or why they were gunned down. The widows and widowers of militants may be forced to abandon their children out of sheer desperation. These children commonly experience isolation and hopelessness. Efforts to restore the families of terrorists to the mainstream are rare (Pushkarna, 1998).

FINANCING TERRORIST NETWORKS

Terrorist groups raise money in four ways as reported by Stern (2003) in the article reprinted at the end of this chapter. Various criminal activities from smuggling to the sex trade provide funds. Businesses, including construction companies, banking and securities institutions, and other apparently legitimate enterprises, are also part of the terror financing network. Assistance from states or state agents has also supported terrorism. For example, Iran has provided Hizballah with hundreds of millions of dollars each year, which is why it has been said that Iran is the central banker of terror (Levey, 2006). Finally charitable donations from both legitimate and bogus social service groups are fundamental to the finances of terrorist organizations.

Two ancient Islamic traditions are basic to funding of extremist Muslim terrorists. The Arabic word for "charitable giving" is *zakat*, which is a pillar of the Islamic faith and is required of all observant Muslims. *Zakat* reflects the Islamic belief that civic and religious life are not separate; therefore, it includes not only humanitarian aid but also functions as a form of income tax, educational assistance, foreign policy, and political expression. Many terrorist financing organizations posing as charities have exploited this religious duty to convince Muslims to give money to causes from which they then embezzle the money (TerroristFinancing.com, 2006).

The second tradition is that of *hawala* (Arabic for "transfer" or "trust"), which is a centuries-old practice of transferring money across the country or around the globe through an intermediary (known as a *Hawalar*) without formal paperwork or costly money-changing services. Having no formal paper trail, this transferred money is very hard to trace. The system relies on trust rather than professional or legal institutions, which may make it possible for disloyal *Hawalars* to skim off funds, but is also immensely useful to terrorist networks (TerroristFinancing.com, 2006). *Hawala* may be used not only for money transfers but also for money laundering. Yet, banning the networks of *hawala* would suppress a long-established Muslim tradition of alternative remittance.

In the aftermath of 9/11, the White House (2001) issued an Executive Order on Terrorist Financing, which called for additional legal tools to enable U.S. and foreign financial institutions to combat the financing of terrorism. In 2006, the guiding principle of the U. S. Treasury Department was to marshal policy, enforcement, regulatory, and intelligence functions to sever the lines of financial support to international terrorists and other threats to our national security. Combating terrorism had become a new role and a top priority for the Treasury Department (Levey, 2006). Yet, despite this focus at the highest levels of government, terrorist groups continue to find new and more lucrative money-making methods. Efforts to destroy terrorist funding networks have not had a significant impact on worldwide terrorist activity.

Money laundering is one example of a basic element of terrorist financing that has been difficult for officials to control. Policies and interagency cooperation used to combat money laundering by criminal syndicates may not be as effective when used against terrorist networks. In criminal activities the illegal activity begins the process, and the question is, "Where do assets come from?"(Lauber, 2004). For terrorists the illegal activity is located at the end of the process. In reverse money laundering the question becomes, "Where do assets go?"

The Financial Action Task Force (FATF) is an intergovernmental body that was given the responsibility of examining international money laundering techniques and trends and recommending measures that still need to be taken to control them. In 1990 the FATF issued a comprehensive plan with 40 action recommendations to fight money laundering. In 2004 the FATF reiterated those suggestions and focused on a set of nine special recommendations on terrorist financing:

1. mutual support of UN resolutions and conventions

2. criminalizing the financing of terrorism

3. freezing and confiscating terrorist assets

4. encouraging reporting of suspicious transactions

5. providing mutual legal assistance, information exchange, and investigations

6. controlling informal systems of remittance

7. monitoring wire transfers and documenting the links in the payment chain

8. ensuring that nonprofit organizations are not misused

9. detecting cross-border transportation of currency and bearer-negotiable instruments

Any efforts directed at stopping funding for terrorist networks must be international. Yet at the same time policies must consider differences in practices and priorities among individual nations. Despite the long-term and increasing attention to this issue, the necessary political will to bring about the required legislative and regulatory reforms on the national and global level is lacking (FATF-GAFI, 2004).

CONVENTIONAL TACTICS BECOMING MORE DEADLY

Terrorist tactics have not grown increasingly complex, nor are terrorists' weapons likely to be technologically more demanding today. Instead, conventional terrorist weapons have been used in successive incidents with increasing sophistication. Three events in the transnational terrorist campaign against the United States provide examples of the ways in which rising levels of lethality have been achieved without using more complex munitions. The most deadly terrorism has resulted from using conventional weapons with intense planning and some innovation.

The chain of events linking the United States directly with transnational terror began with the first World Trade Center bombing in 1993, moved to the continent of Africa, and returned to the World Trade Center in 2001, with a vengeance. In 1993, the weapon was an explosive device of 1,200 pounds of combustible material left in a rented van in a basement parking garage. In that bombing, 6 people died and 1,042 were injured. Before that first World Trade Center bombing, most U.S. citizens considered international terrorism to be somebody else's problem; they were reluctant to believe that New York had joined the roster of international cities where terrorism is expected (Greenberg, 1994; Kelly, 1998; Reeve, 1999).

The perpetrators of the 1993 bombing were captured, and the damage to New York from the incident was limited. However, although the plot may have been flawed technically, it was shrewd psychologically in making the point that the very heart of the U.S. economy, located in a major population center, was vulnerable to the crippling blows of a dedicated group of believers (Kelly, 1998). Islamic extremists were charged with the 1993 bombing, and the investigation uncovered their connections to Afghanistan and training in terrorist tactics. The terrorists were said to be furious over the U.S. support of Israel and the treatment of Palestinians. They were outraged by the presence of Western control in sacred Muslim sites in Saudi Arabia (Reeve, 1999).

After the attack, Ramsi Yousef, who was eventually charged as the leader of the operation, returned to his wife and children living in Pakistan just across the border from the Afghan town of Kandahar. Investigators believe he may have received support and funding from Osama bin Laden via his relatives and associates (Reeve, 1999). After his capture in Pakistan, Yousef was returned to the United States, where he was sentenced to 240 years in prison for the bombing ("World Trade Center Bombing," 2001).

Five years later, terrorists demonstrated how this same tactic of truck bombing could be used with increasing deadliness. On the morning of August 7, 1998, in Dar es Salaam, Tanzania, an attack on the U.S. embassy killed 12 people and injured another 85. Most of the victims were Africans. The bomb vehicle was blocked by an embassy water truck at the closed embassy gates and did not succeed in penetrating the embassy's outer perimeter. Five local guards in the vicinity of the bomb vehicle were killed (Accountability Board Report, Dar es Salaam, 1998).

At approximately the same time, on the same morning of August 7, 1998, terrorists driving another truck detonated a large bomb in the rear parking area of the U.S. embassy in Nairobi. A total of 213 people were killed. An estimated 4,000 in the vicinity of the embassy were injured by the blast (Accountability Board Report, Nairobi, 1998).

The incidents in Dar es Salaam and Nairobi gave notice that, although transnational terrorism would be an unparalleled threat to U.S. security in the 21st century, tactics would remain conventional. The embassy bombings also show the increased deadliness of the tactics, because suicide bombers proclaimed their message with their lives. The East African bombings occurred in a region of the world that had been considered outside the maelstrom of international terrorism. The embassies presented excellent targets both because security was lax and because they were centrally located. They were symbols of the vulnerability of U.S. power, even though most of the victims were not Americans (Simonsen & Spindlove, 2000).

The massive attacks involved ad hoc amalgamations of like-minded individuals who seemed to have been brought together for a specific mission (Hoffman, 1998b). Terrorist cells had been built carefully and patiently in Africa, and the simultaneous detonation of the bombs demonstrated a high level of operational skill (Harmon, 2000). Although no one took credit for or gave a reason for the violence, evidence shows that the embassy strikes were financed by Osama bin Laden as part of his worldwide declaration of war against the United States. The bombings were outgrowths of an ideology that encouraged violence as retribution for the desecration of Muslim holy places in Mecca and Medina, Saudi Arabia. The terrorists promised to pursue U.S. forces and strike at U.S. interests everywhere.

Immediately after the embassy bombings, security measures were strengthened at embassies and military facilities throughout the region and around the world. A reward of $2 million was offered for information about the East African bombings. However, increased security after these and further attacks did not prevent the attacks with airliners against the World Trade Center on September 11, 2001, or numerous other terrorist incidents since 1998. Use of security technologies can enable more "hardened targets," but terrorists will seek out overlooked weaknesses. Even when terrorists have no specialized skills and few technical resources, their level of lethality may continue to escalate because conventional tactics remain a significant threat.

LEADERLESS RESISTANCE

Fundamentalist Islamic terrorists are not the only extremists who have threatened the United States. Serious threats have been made by self-styled defenders of righteousness from within as well. Transnational and homegrown terrorists have striking similarities. Both promote urban guerrilla warfare conducted by subversives who use the cellular model of organization. Both Islamic and homegrown ad hoc groups may be well funded and have support networks that provide them with freedom of movement and opportunities to attack U.S. interests on a global basis. These groups are more dangerous than traditional hierarchical organizations because they decentralize and compartmentalize their actions (DoCeuPinto, 1999). They advocate the use of the same violent methods and the same goal of destruction of the U.S. government. According to the public voice of neo-Nazis in the United States, William Pierce, "When people are pushed as far as they are willing to go and when they have nothing to lose, then they resort to terrorism. There will be more and more such people in the future" (Grigg, 1996, p. 5).

The tactic of leaderless resistance is commonly linked with Louis Beam in the late 20th century (Harmon, 2000), but this type of organization is identical to the methods used by the Committees of Correspondence during the U.S. Revolutionary War. Using this tactic, all individuals and groups operate independently of each other and do not report to a central headquarters or single leader for direction or instruction. According to Beam, this is not as impractical as it appears, because in any movement, all involved persons usually have the same general outlook, are acquainted with the same philosophy, and react to given situations in similar ways. Beam proposed, "America is quickly moving into a long dark night of police state tyranny . . . let the coming night be filled with a thousand points of resistance. Like the fog which forms when conditions are right and disappears when they are not, so must the resistance to tyranny be" (Beam, 1992, p. 6).

The bombing of the Murrah Federal Building in Oklahoma City is almost a textbook case of what Beam termed leaderless resistance. To a lesser degree and on a smaller scale, factions within the direct action anti-abortion movement have systematically applied the doctrine for a number of years (Burghardt, 1995). The Aryan Republican Army, charged with 22 bank robberies in eight U.S. states, openly promoted leaderless resistance in a video. Members use the Bible to justify their actions. "Study your Scriptures," they say. "Then you'll understand why you have to go out and kill" (Pattillo, 1998).

Leaderless resistance is a tactic, not an ideology, and as such it can be applied by anyone opposing an overwhelming force. Leaderless resistance allowed the Unabomber to elude the FBI for 18 years. It is the tool of the disenfranchised, the poor, and the weak, who have neither the status, the power, nor the resources to confront those they wish to fight on even terms. Its greatest strength is that, although it is easy for the state to infiltrate a large, anonymous organization, it's much harder to slip undercover agents into small cells where everybody knows everybody else (Kaplan, 1997).

GUIDEBOOKS OF TERROR TACTICS

Some people believed that Mao Zedong's *Little Red Book* is the world's most widely read manual on the strategy and tactics of terror. Carlos Marighella's *Manual of the Urban Guerrilla* (1969/1985) and William Pierce's *The Turner Diaries* (1996) are also well-known guidebooks for terrorists. Those interested in directions for staging a terrorist incident can find them in many places. Not only can readers find philosophical and strategic directions but detailed plans and instructions are also published. Some guerrillas develop tactics from studying counterterrorist strategy manuals prepared by police or military forces to direct their own proactive strikes.

Technical details and up-to-date intelligence about strategic targets are also available in public policy manuals and on Internet sites (SANS Institute, 2001). The intelligence community is hard at work with researchers from other disciplines creating sophisticated detection programs capable of identifying incidents of online steganography. Derived from the Greek words meaning "covered writing," steganography refers to hiding information or communications inside something so unremarkable that no one would suspect it is there. Steganography is a good way for terrorist cells to communicate. The sender can transmit a message without ever communicating directly with the receiver. It's an old concept described by Herodotus. According to Greek history, a secret message was tattooed on the scalp of a slave. When his hair grew back, he was dispatched to the Greeks, who shaved the slave's head and recovered the message (L. Hoffman, 2001).

Among Islamic extremists, the members of "God's Brigade" are reported to have an 11-volume Arabic-language encyclopedia of *Jihad* that serves as a guidebook. It has 6,000 pages detailing practices of terror and urban-guerrilla warfare (Jacquard, 2001). Many other documents recovered in Afghanistan after the fall of the Taliban documented the tactics planned and carried out by warriors for *Jihad*. Guidebooks for terrorists were available in written, electronic, and video formats.

Following the September 11 bombings of the World Trade Center, three identical letters, handwritten in Arabic, surfaced. They linked 3 of the 19 hijackers who crashed into the World Trade Center and the Pentagon and who were forced into a crash landing in western Pennsylvania. According to Attorney General John Ashcroft, "It is a disturbing and shocking view into the mind set of these terrorists. The letter provides instructions to the terrorists to be carried out both prior to and during their terrorist attacks" (as quoted in Ross, 2001). It is illustrative that the instructions for this deadly incident were handwritten as letters, the most conventional of all forms of communication.

THE BASICS

As fanatical or irrational as the terrorists of today may seem, their operations have remained remarkably conventional. Terrorists continue to rely on the same basic weapons that they have used successfully for more than a century (B. Hoffman, 2001). Terrorists of the 21st century adhere to the familiar and narrow tactical patterns because they have mastered them. Equally important, they are likely to believe that conventional tactics optimize their likelihood of success (B. Hoffman, 2001). The four basic tactics that singly or jointly make up most terrorist incidents continue to be (1) assassinations of public figures, murder of civilians, and genocide; (2) hijackings; (3) kidnapping, hostage taking, and barricade incidents; and (4) bombings and armed assaults.

Terrorists in the 21st century have demonstrated the ease with which modifications and combinations of basic tactics can be made across the technological spectrum. They have shown their willingness to adapt technology as opportunities present themselves (Hoffman, 1997). Death and destruction from multifarious attacks with conventional high explosives have been far higher than in cases involving unconventional weapons (B. Hoffman, 2001).

Assassinations

Assassinations have always been a basic tactic of terrorists. One of the most noted examples was the death of Israeli Prime Minister Yitzhak Rabin on November 4, 1995. Rabin had become noteworthy because of his involvement in peace negotiations with the Palestinians. His progress toward a settlement was celebrated by many, but it aroused the ire of extremists. Rabin was a target because he was perceived as a significant leader whose removal would change the course of global relations. Shortly before his murder, there were documented threats against Rabin's life, and he was advised not to make public appearances. He refused to avoid crowds and was not willing to wear a bullet-proof vest to the peace rally in Malchei Yisrael square in Tel Aviv where he was shot.

His assassin, Yigal Amir, had been arrested twice before at demonstrations in opposition to Rabin's policies of negotiation. Amir was a 25-year-old Israeli student who belonged to a loosely organized group of dissidents opposed to making any concessions toward Palestine. He disguised himself as a driver and waited with other chauffeurs near Rabin's limo. His Beretta pistol was loaded with hollow-point bullets. Amir hit Rabin in the thorax and abdomen with two bullets, and Rabin was dead within hours. Amir was apprehended at the scene of the crime, arrested by security officers (Praesidia-Defence, 1996), and charged with conspiracy to kill the prime minister. A huge arms cache was found in his home (Israeli Ministry of Foreign Affairs, 1995).

Analysts debate the impact of Rabin's death on the Israeli-Palestinian peace process. For a time, some believed that his death blazed a path toward unity between the two nations. Critics asserted that his assassination was part of a larger plot and pointed out attempts to cover up complicity in the murder by the Israeli secret service (Shuman, 2001).

The amount of social change and upheaval that has resulted from assassinations is immeasurable. As a tactic of war, a single strategic fatality can have an impact that makes an assassination a compelling choice for a strike against an enemy.

The United States has witnessed many attempts and several successful assassinations of public figures by individuals considered to be mentally unstable, rather than terrorists. The prevailing explanations for their actions included personal conflicts and religious delusions. Despite conspiracy theories that question whether the assassins of political and public figures, including John F. Kennedy and Dr. Martin Luther King, Jr., really acted alone, links between assassins in the United States and recognized group interests remain in question. Members of one celebrated terrorist group, however, were convicted for carrying out a well-planned, although inept, assassination attempt on an American president.

Various factions of the Puerto Rican terrorist group known as the FALN (Fuerzas Armadas Liberación Nacional) were active in the United States for more than four decades (Tooley, 1999). In addition to pulling a high-profile armored car robbery, the group conducted bombings, assassinations, and even a rocket attack against FBI headquarters in San Juan (McLaughlin, 1999). Two Puerto Rican extremists attempted to assassinate President Harry Truman on November 1, 1950. One of the terrorists died in the attempt, along with a police officer, while Truman watched from an upstairs window. Two other security guards and the surviving assassin were wounded. He was later convicted of first-degree murder and sentenced to die; however, his sentence was commuted by President Truman, without explanation, to life in prison. On December 10, 1979, President Jimmy Carter, also without explanation, commuted his sentence, and he was released at age 64. An estimated crowd of 5,000 supporters greeted him when he returned to San Juan, Puerto Rico, 29 years after the attempt, refusing to denounce the use of violence and vowing to continue his struggle for Puerto Rican independence (Poland, 1988, p. 183).

An alternative form of assassination is focused on unknown victims whose deaths are meant to harm a notorious or corporate target. Product tampering and poisoning are variations on the ancient tactic of assassination that may appeal to those whose adversary can be through a product (Dietz, 1988). Product tampering is included here as a conventional tactic because it is likely to be based on low-end technology and usually targets a limited number of victims.

Another variant on assassination is genocide. Extremists intent on removing all of their enemy, rather than a symbolic few, have resorted to mass murder. In the worst massacres, entire kinship groups and subcultures have been destroyed. In many of the cases of genocide and attempted genocide, the members of a targeted group were assassinated by state-sponsored terrorist organizations (Simonsen & Spindlove, 2000).

Hijacking

Hijacking gained increased attention in 2001, but it was a conventional terrorist weapon long before that. In a hijacking, a vehicle on the public thoroughfare is taken over and turned into a

PHOTO 4.3   Gaza City, Gaza: Mohammed Abbas, the organizer of the 1985 hijacking of the Italian cruise
liner *Achille Lauro*, in which Leon Klinghoffer, a U.S. citizen died, talks to reporters in 1996
in Gaza City. Abbas said that the incident had been a mistake and was now "in the past."

terrorist weapon. Terrorists may target autos, buses, trains, ships, military vehicles, aircraft, or
even spacecraft depending on their technical resources and development. Car theft at knife-
point or gunpoint has become one of the most serious threats to motoring overseas. Statistics
are lacking, but there are many reports that seizing vehicles is a common terrorist tactic (Bush
Telegraph, 1997). There is no way to determine how many international hijackings of autos are
politically motivated acts of terrorists or to separate them from acts of criminally motivated
perpetrators.

One of the most dramatic hijackings in history occurred on October 7, 1985, when the *Achille
Lauro,* a luxury cruise ship flying the Italian flag, was seized while sailing from Alexandria to Port
Said, Egypt. The hijackers were members of the Palestine Liberation Front (PLF), a faction of the
Palestine Liberation Organization (PLO), who had boarded the ship in Genoa, posing as tourists.
They held the ship's crew and passengers hostage, and they threatened to kill the passengers unless
Israel released 50 Palestinian prisoners. They also threatened to blow up the ship if a rescue mis-
sion was attempted. When their demands had not been met by the following afternoon, the
hijackers shot Leon Klinghoffer, an American Jew who was partly paralyzed and in a wheelchair.
They threw his body and wheelchair overboard (Halberstam, 1988). The perpetrators surrendered
in exchange for a pledge of safe passage, but the Egyptian jet that was to fly the hijackers to freedom was intercepted by U.S. Navy F-14 fighters. The terrorists were forced to land in Sicily and
were taken into the custody of Italian authorities. At least two of the most notorious of the convicted terrorists escaped from Italian jurisdiction. In 2000, the mastermind of the *Achille Lauro*
hijacking, Mohammed Zaidan, better known as Abu Abbas, was a public figure in Palestine, a
notorious supporter of the peace process, and a close associate of Yasser Arafat who was then
chairman of the PLO (Goldenberg, 2000; Simonsen & Spindlove, 2000). More than 15 years after
the hijacking he was living comfortably under Saddam Hussein's protection in Baghdad in 2003

when he was captured and taken into U.S. custody. Abu Abbas died of unspecified natural causes in 2004 after being in detention for 11 months in Iraq (Mannes, 2004).

Terrorism at sea is a menace that has been traditionally overlooked, yet which could be the world's next great threat (Stankiewicz, 2005). Criminals and terrorists can commandeer lucrative cargoes and also hijack lethal shipments of chemicals, gas, arms, and specialized dual equipment, which may be converted from a legitimate or corporate use to use as a weapon. Another nightmare scenario would be the hijacking and sinking of one or more ships in one of the world's most important shipping lanes or checkpoints. The 5,000,000-ton vessels that traverse the world's waterways carry a crew of about 30 and have no armed guards. A scuttled supertanker in the midst of maritime traffic could create major economic disruption (TerroristFinancing.com, 2006).

Kidnapping and Hostage Taking

Kidnapping and hostage taking involve seizing, detaining, or threatening to kill, injure, or continue to detain someone. The victim is held to compel a third party to act or abstain from acting as a condition for the release of the seized person (Simonsen & Spindlove, 2000, p. 24). The tactic of seizing captives has been used to terrorists' advantage and disadvantage throughout the ages. Although kidnapping and hostage taking share common elements, it is possible to distinguish between them. Kidnappers confine their victims in secret locations and make ransom demands, threatening to kill the victim if these demands are not met. Hostage takers openly confront the police or military, in known locations, with the objective often being to make demands with full media coverage (Poland, 1988). Wilson analyzed the demands made by hostage takers in 100 incidents and found that four primary demands occurred with the greatest frequency: the release of a specific prisoner or a general group of unnamed prisoners, travel, publicity, and money (2000, p. 417).

Hostage taking has a long relationship with rebellion and warfare. A well-publicized incident that involved barricading and hostage taking began on December 17, 1996, and ended when Peruvian armed forces stormed the residence of the Japanese ambassador in Lima on April 22, 1997. An armed group of approximately 20 members of the Túpac Amaru Revolutionary Movement (MRTA) held 400 people hostage, including a government minister, several ambassadors, and members of the Peruvian congress. The guerrillas, disguised as waiters and carrying champagne and canapes, sneaked into a celebration on the birthday of Japan's emperor. The terrorists demanded the release of their leaders and some 300 other members of their group who were in state custody. Their long-term goal entailed reconstructing Peru's economic model to benefit the masses. To ensure their escape, they also asked for transport of the rebel commandos to a jungle location, with a number of dignitaries as hostages. The siege of the Japanese embassy lasted for 126 days. Some of the hostages were released in the early hours of the takeover, and some reportedly were sent out of the embassy because of health problems. Others were traded for concessions during the negotiations. Seventy-two hostages were held through the entire 18-week siege. When Peruvian counterterrorist forces stormed the embassy, at least 14 of the terrorists were alive. Reports followed of extra-judicial executions of the MRTA rebels after they had been captured. All the terrorists were reportedly shot in the head by the Peruvian military (Derechos Human Rights, 1997). A hostage and two Peruvian soldiers also lost their lives. This attack led to the defeat of the MRTA as an organization. The absorbing novel, *Bel Canto,* by Ann Patchett (2002) parallels this long-term hostage taking incident from the fictionalized point of view of those who were held captive and those who held them

In general, hostage taking is costly, with little positive return for terrorists. On the other hand, kidnapping victims for ransom has provided significant financial resources to perpetrators. Groups, such as the ELN in Columbia and the Abu Sayyaf Group in the southern Philippines, periodically kidnap foreign employees of large corporations and hold them for huge ransom payments (Federation of American Scientists, 1998). Although kidnapping may be undertaken more from economic expediency than as a strategy for political advance, targets are often among those considered enemies to the terrorists. The kidnapping of important business people, corporate executives, and members of their families has provided terrorist groups with a lucrative, low-risk source of revenue for a very long time (Poland, 1988).

U.S. citizens may be favorite targets of kidnappers because it is not U.S. government policy to intercede. Terrorists as well as professional kidnappers also may believe that many U.S. firms carry vast sums in kidnapping and ransom insurance protection (Clancy, 2001). In the late 1990s, Latin America was the region where kidnapping was most prevalent and where ransom demands were highest. More incidents took place in Colombia than in any other country (Shepherd, 1997), but kidnapping is also a threat outside Latin America. The BBC reported in 1999 that kidnapping was "almost a national sport among terrorists in Yemen" (Fryer, 1999).

Bombing

Bombing is another essential tactic for terrorists. With the increase in information about different types of explosives, the types of bombs available continue to proliferate. Explosives are considered in this section as conventional tools of warfare. Yet, bombs are also unconventional weapons as technology and innovation combine to create explosive weapons of mass destruction.

The history of terrorist bombing begins with dynamite, black powder, and Molotov cocktails and carries on with Semtec and daisy cutters. The real hazard of conventional explosives persists despite concerns about the threat of nuclear bombs. The objectives of bombing remain essentially the same regardless of the technology employed: to blow up a notable target and gain attention for a cause, slow down the opposition, get rid of political adversaries, and destroy property. Some bombings intend to achieve all these goals, whereas others are meant simply to gain attention.

Between 1998 and July 2006 there were at least 74 separate terrorist attacks on railways worldwide, including heavy rail, metro subway systems, and light rail systems. There were even more credible threats against trains and rail infrastructure (Hinds, 2006). Railway systems offer easy access and escape if necessary. There is anonymity in a collection of strangers; being in a confined environment makes a maximum impact possible. Railway systems pass through some of the most densely populated urban landscapes in the world, which provide even greater potential for death and destruction (Hinds, 2006).

Car bombs have also been widely used by terrorists, such as the Real Irish Republican Army. Dingley (2001) documents the car bombing in Omaugh, Northern Ireland, of 1998 that killed 29 people and injured more than 200 others. It is noteworthy that in spite of intensive planning, this car bomb was parked in a market district, rather than in front of the courthouse as intended. The plan had been to call in a warning to clear the area, and the goal was destruction of property, rather than the loss of life. Instead, courthouse evacuees were led into the market street precisely where the car bomb was parked. The horrific results led to a change in the public image of the Real IRA and a concentration of anti-terrorist forces against them (Dingley, 2001). The bombing of Omaugh demonstrates both the lethality and unpredictability of bombing as a strategy of conflict.

Bombing remains the most commonly used tactic in the terrorist arsenal. With more than a century of deployment, with countless examples of death and destruction, with numerous types and combinations of explosives, terrorists continue to use bombing more than any other action.

SUICIDE TERRORISM

The suicide bombings at the embassies in Tanzania and Kenya brought U.S. attention to a terrorist tactic that other nations had learned to fear long ago. The suicide bombing of the USS Cole in October of 2000 was another in the series of incidents directed against the United States (Daly, 2001). On September 11, 2001, the use of suicide bombs became an even more salient threat to U.S. interests. After that event, analysts determined that suicide terrorists were the last link of a long organizational chain that involved numerous actors (Sprinzak, 2000, p. 66).

Suicide bombing has become a serious tactical concern in transnational terror. One explanation of the notable increase in the resort to martyrdom in different conflicts is based on the internationalization of terrorist groups, including increased interpersonal contact among members. A perception of similarity of causes is likely to lead to sharing and modeling strategies across groups (Zedalis, 2004, p. 11). Reporting on the First International Conference on Countering Suicide Terrorism, held in Israel in 2000, Gunaratna provided background information on the tactic of suicide bombing and documented that suicide attacks by terrorists were known as early as the 1st century (Gunaratna, 2000). There are similarities among diverse instances of public-spirited suicide in which the perpetrators intend to take numbers of other victims with them in death. Some examples include the Islamic martyrs of yesterday and today, the Anarchists, the Japanese kamikaze of World War II, and the Tamil Tigers of Sri Lanka (Ferrero, 2006).

Suicide terrorism is virtually always a response to foreign occupation, but only some occupations lead to this result. Pape (2005) notes that a conflict across a religious divide increases fears that the enemy will transform the occupied society; demonization and killing of enemy civilians are thus made easier. Using religious ideology, suicide—rather than a taboo—is seen as a form of martyrdom (2005, p. 22). In most religious traditions, martyrdom is regarded not only as a testimony to the degree of one's commitment but also as a performance of a religious act, specifically an act of self-sacrifice (Juergensmeyer, 2003, p. 170). However, suicide bombing has its roots in secular ideologies as well.

Charu Lata Joshi's article about Sri Lankan suicide bombers titled "Ultimate Sacrifice" (2000) describes the 17-year war for independence fought by the Liberation Tigers of Tamil Eelam (LTTE). That war created a pantheon of martyrs. Each one's picture is framed, garlanded, and hung on the wall of his or her training camp to be revered by hundreds of other teenagers willing to sign their lives away for the cause. They will receive the title *mahaveera* (brave one), and their mothers will be called *veeravati*, or brave mother.

In rural areas of Sri Lanka, farming is no longer a reliable source of employment and income. For young Tamils who make it to secondary school, jobs are scarce and movement within the country is restricted. The lack of opportunity and work in an area that has exhibited no visible signs of development for a decade is often cited to explain wide support for the LTTE. The war that has consumed more than 70,000 lives and drained the economy of Sri Lanka continues to find human ammunition (Joshi, 2000).

An 18-year-old volunteer explained: "This is the most supreme sacrifice I can make. The only way we can get our homeland is through arms. That is the only way anybody will listen to us. Even if we die." Another volunteer, age 19, asked "I lost two brothers in the war, why should I stay behind?" (Joshi, 2000, p. 3)

Nothing symbolizes the Tamil Tigers and their culture of death and martyrdom quite so succinctly as a small glass vial no longer than a cigarette worn with a little black string as a pendant. Rebels wear them when on duty, believing that death is better than capture. According to myth, a Tiger dies smiling. It is not called a "suicide" but "donating yourself to the cause." Rebels are not buried in what most would call a cemetery but in what is called a sleeping arena. There are no bodies, only seeds, according to the myth. Once the dream of Tamil Eelam is achieved, the story goes, they will rise up as trees (Luthra, 2006).

There are two levels of analyzing suicide bombing—the individual bombers who blow themselves up and the organizations that send them. It is unlikely that suicide bombers share personality traits (Lester, Yang, & Lindsay, 2004). However, all analysts agree that suicide bombers are primarily young people (Zedaris, 2004). All of the bombers are first and foremost members of organizations that train them, select their targets, buy their explosives, issue orders, and try to convince the larger population that their cause is just (Bloom, 2005).

It is possible to see three different levels of logic operating when a suicide bombing takes place. On the wider level, it is important to consider suicide terror as a form of coercive power. What is the situation in which this type of action appears to advance political goals? On a social level, terrorism has received mass support in some events. Why do suicide attacks receive collective support in some societies? On a personal level, suicide bombing appeals to altruistic motives and the desire for martyrdom. Why is there a ready supply of willing attackers in some places and times? (Pape, 2005).

Following the suicide attacks on the systems of mass transportation in London in 2005, Dalrymple (2005) expressed growing concerns about the recruitment of suicide bombers from among British Muslims. His analysis points out that the motivation for young Islamic men to join extremist groups in the United Kingdom exists on the three levels of logic: politics, mass society, and personal experiences. Recruitment of suicide terrorists was fueled, in his words by

> the hurtful experience of disdain or rejection from the surrounding society; the bitter disappointment of a frustrated materialism and a seemingly perpetual inferior status in the economic hierarchy; the extreme insufficiency and unattractiveness of modern popular culture that is without value; the readiness to hand of an ideological and religious solution that is flattering to self esteem and allegedly all-sufficient, . . . an oscillation between feelings of inferiority and superiority, between humiliation about that which is Western and that which is non-Western in the self; and the grotesque inflation of the importance of personal existential problems typical of modern individualism—all ensure fertile ground for the recruitment of further "martyrs" for years to come. (p. 3)

Female Suicide Bombers

Female suicide terrorists are said to be the ultimate asymmetrical weapon (Zedalis, 2004). There is often more shock value if the suicide bomber is a woman (p. 7). By both attracting attention and precipitating widespread fear, women provide a tactical advantage (Cunningham, 2002, p. 171). Using females also significantly increases the number of combatants available to a terrorist group.

The image of a female suicide bomber is different in different conflicts. The Chechen women bombers and those in Sri Lanka have been characterized as lacking alternatives, desperate, and devastated by war (Handwerk, 2004). In contrast the image of Palestinian female suicide bombers is that of educated and professional women, economically well off and adjusted within their families (Atran, 2004). There is not likely to be any one single overriding motivation for female suicide bombers, but rather a number of motivations working in concert. These motivations interact with emotional predispositions, creating an explosive mixture. A traumatic event can release all its destructive energy (Fighel, 2003).

In the words of Wafa al-Bas, one attempted suicide bomber,

> I love Allah, I love the land of Palestine and I am a member of Al-Aksa Brigades . . . my dream was to be a martyr. I believe in death. . . . Since I was a little girl I wanted to carry out an attack. (HonestReporting, 2005)

HIGHLIGHTS OF REPRINTED ARTICLES

Bruce Hoffman (2003, June). The logic of suicide terrorism. *Atlantic Monthly*. Retrieved May 25, 2007, from www.theatlantic.com/doc/200306/hoffman

Written about the scene in Israel, where suicide terror attacks are an ongoing threat, the first article by Bruce Hoffman explores the topic of suicide terrorism in depth and from a pragmatic as well as strategic perspective. Hoffman has not only described the situation from the perspective of the Israeli authorities, but he has also related the situation in Israel to the international context in which suicide bombing has developed a logic all its own.

Following his analysis, Hoffman offers six precautions based on Israel's experience. From the positive and negative experiences of other countries where suicide terrorist campaigns have been waged for decades can be derived sensible, effective, and valid policy responses to this deadly weapon of asymmetrical warfare. In addition these responses will increase the public's confidence that the threat of suicide terrorism will be substantially reduced. Yet, Hoffman ends this article with the warning: "There are thousands more young followers who look forward to death like Americans look forward to living."

Jessica Stern (2004). The ultimate organization: Networks, franchises and freelancers, in *Terror in the name of God*. New York: Harper-Collins.

The tactics of al-Qaeda are covered in a way that is both careful and fascinating in the second article included with Chapter 4. Jessica Stern has studied al-Qaeda as "The Ultimate Organization," which operates with many of the characteristics of other multinational enterprises. Stern has studied the networks that support al-Qaeda and their vast business holdings, detailed planning of operations, placement of sleeper cells, and acquisition of weapons.

Recruitment is one of the significant aspects of terrorist operations that is painstakingly covered in the article by Stern. The ability to attract loyal and willing cadres of followers is essential, and al-Qaeda has been honing this ability for decades. In addition, the mission of al-Qaeda is explained thoroughly in this article. Understanding the evolution and distortion of their mission is essential to confronting these adversaries or any other.

EXPLORING CONVENTIONAL TERRORIST TACTICS FURTHER

- The journals *Terrorism and Political Violence* and *Studies in Conflict and Terrorism* provide valuable research articles about assassination, hijacking, kidnapping, and bombing.
- The PBS series for *Frontline*, "The IRA & Sinn Fein," is available on the Web. It includes interviews and historical and cultural information as well as maps and other links.
- The global intelligence organization Interpol presents information about terrorist tactics on the Internet.
- In Israel, a heavy police presence in occupied territories was described by Hoffman as the response to suicide terrorism that law enforcement agencies consider to be most effective. Compare this to the perspective explored in Jimmy Carter's 2006 book, *Palestine: Peace Not Apartheid*.
- What are the common elements in suicide terror campaigns against Israel, Sri Lanka, and Russia?
- According to Stern what are the most useful and practical ways in which al-Qaeda acquires weapons?
- What could cause al-Qaeda's mission to destroy the New World Order to lose its appeal to people made vulnerable by humiliation, human rights violations, poverty, confused identities, and poor governance?
- The 9/11 Commission Report, which is the final report of the *National Commission on Terrorist Attacks Upon the U. S.*, was published in 2004. It includes a detailed background description of al-Qaeda. It adds depth to some of the issues that are introduced in the chapter by Stern.

VIDEO NOTES

A documentary produced by a former CIA agent titled *The Cult of the Suicide Bomber* (Disinformation, 2005, 96 min.) untangles the history, background, and nations behind suicide bombing.

A fascinating drama about conventional terrorism enfolds in *Four Days in September* (Miramax, 1998, 110 min.). The film relates both the political and the personal demands inflicted when an ambassador is kidnapped by terrorists.

The television series, *Sleeper Cell*, which began airing on the Showtime Channel in 2006, is an intriguing look at a group of Jihadists who come from various parts of the world to Los Angeles to plot acts of destruction. The threat may be exaggerated in the series, but there are enough accurate details in the programs to make them interesting.

The award winning film, *God Grew Tired of Us* is scheduled for release in 2007 by New Market Films (89 min.). This true story of child soldiers in Sudan was originally released by Lost Boys Productions and also by National Geographic films.

The Logic of Suicide Terrorism

Bruce Hoffman

First you feel nervous about riding the bus. Then you wonder about going to a mall. Then you think twice about sitting for long at your favorite café. Then nowhere seems safe. Terrorist groups have a strategy—to shrink to nothing the areas in which people move freely—and suicide bombers, inexpensive and reliably lethal, are their latest weapons. Israel has learned to recognize and disrupt the steps on the path to suicide attacks. We must learn too.

Nearly everywhere in the world it is taken for granted that one can simply push open the door to a restaurant, café, or bar, sit down, and order a meal or a drink. In Israel the process of entering such a place is more complicated. One often encounters an armed guard who, in addition to asking prospective patrons whether they themselves are armed, may quickly pat them down, feeling for the telltale bulge of a belt or a vest containing explosives. Establishments that cannot afford a guard or are unwilling to pass on the cost of one to customers simply keep their doors locked, responding to knocks with a quick glance through the glass and an instant judgment as to whether this or that person can safely be admitted. What would have been unimaginable a year ago is now not only routine but reassuring. It has become the price of a redefined normality.

In the United States in the twenty months since 9/11 we, too, have had to become accustomed to an array of new, often previously inconceivable security measures—in airports and other transportation hubs, hotels and office buildings, sports stadiums and concert halls. Although some are more noticeable and perhaps more inconvenient than others, the fact remains that they have redefined our own sense of normality. They are accepted because we feel more vulnerable than before. With every new threat to international security we become more willing to live with stringent precautions and reflexive, almost unconscious wariness. With every new threat, that is, our everyday life becomes more like Israel's.

The situation in Israel, where last year's intensified suicide-bombing campaign changed the national mood and people's personal politics, is not analogous to that in the United States today. But the organization and the operations of the suicide bombers are neither limited to Israel and its conflict with the Palestinians nor unique to its geostrategic position. The fundamental characteristics of suicide bombing, and its strong attraction for the terrorist organizations behind it, are universal: Suicide bombings are inexpensive and effective. They are less complicated and compromising than other kinds of terrorist operations. They guarantee media coverage. The suicide terrorist is the ultimate smart bomb. Perhaps most important, coldly efficient bombings tear at the fabric of trust that holds societies together. All these reasons doubtless account for the spread of suicide terrorism from the Middle East to Sri Lanka and Turkey, Argentina and Chechnya, Russia and Algeria—and to the United States.

To understand the power that suicide terrorism can have over a populace—and what a populace can do to counter it—one naturally goes to the society that has been most deeply affected. As a researcher who has studied the strategies of terrorism for more than twenty-five years,

I recently visited Israel to review the steps the military, the police, and the intelligence and security services have taken against a threat more pervasive and personal than ever before.

I was looking at x-rays with Dr. Shmuel Shapira in his office at Jerusalem's Hadassah Hospital. "This is not a place to have a wristwatch," he said as he described the injuries of a young girl who'd been on her way to school one morning last November when a suicide terrorist detonated a bomb on her bus. Eleven of her fellow passengers were killed, and more than fifty others wounded. The blast was so powerful that the hands and case of the bomber's wristwatch had turned into lethal projectiles, lodging in the girl's neck and ripping a major artery. The presence of such foreign objects in the bodies of his patients no longer surprises Shapira. "We have cases with a nail in the neck, or nuts and bolts in the thigh . . . a ball bearing in the skull," he said.

Such are the weapons of war in Israel today: nuts and bolts, screws and ball bearings, any metal shards or odd bits of broken machinery that can be packed together with homemade explosive and then strapped to the body of a terrorist dispatched to any place where people gather—bus, train, restaurant, café, supermarket, shopping mall, street corner, promenade. These attacks probably cost no more than $150 to mount, and they need no escape plan—often the most difficult aspect of a terrorist operation. And they are reliably deadly. According to data from the Rand Corporation's chronology of international terrorism incidents, suicide attacks on average kill four times as many people as other terrorist acts. Perhaps it is not surprising, then, that this means of terror has become increasingly popular. The tactic first emerged in Lebanon, in 1983; a decade later it came to Israel, and it has been a regular security problem ever since. Fully two thirds of all such incidents in Israel have occurred in the past two and a half years—that is, since the start of the second intifada, in September of 2000. Indeed, suicide bombers are responsible for almost half of the approximately 750 deaths in terrorist attacks since then.

Last December, I walked through Jerusalem with two police officers, one of them a senior operational commander, who were showing me the sites of suicide bombings in recent years. They described the first major suicide-terrorist attack in the city, which occurred in February of 1996, early on a Sunday morning—the beginning of the Israeli work week. The driver of the No. 18 Egged bus was hurrying across a busy intersection at Sarei Yisrael Street as a yellow light turned red. The bus was about halfway through when an explosion transformed it into an inferno of twisted metal, pulverized glass, and burning flesh. A traffic camera designed to catch drivers running stop lights captured the scene on film. Twenty-five people were killed, including two U.S. citizens, and eighty were wounded.

The early years of suicide terrorism were a simpler time, the officers explained. Suicide bombers were—at least in theory—easier to spot then. They tended to carry their bombs in nylon backpacks or duffel bags rather than in belts or vests concealed beneath their clothing, as they do now. They were also typically male, aged seventeen to twenty-three, and unmarried. Armed with these data, the authorities could simply deny work permits to Palestinians most likely to be suicide bombers, thus restricting their ability to cross the Green Line (Israel's pre-1967 border) into Israel proper from the West Bank or the Gaza Strip.

Today, though, suicide bombers are middle-aged and young, married and unmarried, and some of them have children. Some of them, too, are women, and word has it that even children are being trained for martyrdom. "There is no clear profile anymore—not for terrorists and especially not for suicide bombers," an exasperated senior officer in the Israel Defense Forces told me last year. Sometimes the bombers disguise themselves: male *shaheed* (Arabic for "martyrs") have worn green IDF fatigues; have dressed as *haredim* (ultra-Orthodox Jews), complete with yarmulkes and tzitzit, the fringes that devout Jews display as part of their everyday clothing; or have donned long-haired wigs in an effort to look like hip Israelis rather than threatening Arabs. A few women have tried to camouflage bombs by strapping them to their stomachs to fake pregnancy. And contrary to popular belief, the bombers are not drawn exclusively from the ranks of the poor but have included two sons of millionaires. (Most of the September 11 terrorists came from comfortable middle- to upper-middle-class families and were well educated.) The Israeli journalist Ronni Shaked, an expert on the Palestinian terrorist group Hamas, who writes for *Yedioth Ahronoth*, an Israeli daily, has debunked the myth that it is only people with no means of improving their lot in life who turn to suicide terrorism. "All leaders of Hamas," he told me, "are university graduates, some with master's degrees. This is a movement not of poor, miserable people but of highly educated people who are using [the image of] poverty to make the movement more powerful."

Buses remain among the bombers' preferred targets. Winter and summer are the better seasons for bombing buses in Jerusalem, because the closed windows (for heat or air-conditioning) intensify the force of the blast, maximizing the bombs' killing potential. As a hail of shrapnel pierces flesh and breaks bones, the shock wave tears lungs and crushes other internal organs. When the bus's fuel tank explodes, a fireball causes burns, and smoke inhalation causes respiratory damage. All this is a significant return on a relatively modest investment. Two or three kilograms of explosive on a bus can kill as many people as twenty to thirty kilograms left on a street or in a mall or a restaurant. But as security on buses has improved, and passengers have become more alert, the bombers have been forced to seek other targets.

The terrorists are lethally flexible and inventive. A person wearing a bomb is far more dangerous and far more difficult to defend against than a timed device left to explode in a marketplace. This human weapons system can effect last-minute changes based on the ease of approach, the paucity or density of people, and the security measures in evidence. On a Thursday afternoon in March of last year a reportedly smiling, self-satisfied bomber strolled down King George Street, in the heart of Jerusalem, looking for just the right target. He found it in a crowd of shoppers gathered in front of the trendy Aroma Café, near the corner of Agrippas Street. In a fusillade of nails and other bits of metal two victims were killed and fifty-six wounded. Similarly, in April of last year a female suicide bomber tried to enter the Mahane Yehuda open-air market—the fourth woman to make such an attempt in four months—but was deterred by a strong police presence. So she simply walked up to a bus stop packed with shoppers hurrying home before the Sabbath and detonated her explosives, killing six and wounding seventy-three.

Suicide bombing initially seemed the desperate act of lone individuals, but it is not undertaken alone. Invariably, a terrorist organization such as Hamas (the Islamic Resistance Movement), the Palestine Islamic Jihad (PIJ), or the al Aqsa Martyrs Brigade has recruited the bomber, conducted reconnaissance, prepared the explosive device, and identified a target—explaining that if it turns out to be guarded or protected, any crowded place nearby will do. "We hardly ever find that the suicide bomber came by himself," a police officer explained to me. "There is always a handler." In fact, in some cases a handler has used a cell phone or other device to trigger the blast from a distance. A policeman told me, "There was one event where a suicide bomber had been told all he had to do was to carry the bomb and plant explosives in a certain place. But the bomb was remote-control detonated."

The organizations behind the Palestinians' suicide terrorism have numerous components. Quartermasters obtain the explosives and the other materials (nuts, bolts, nails, and the like) that are combined to make a bomb. Now that bomb-making methods have been so widely disseminated throughout the West Bank and Gaza, a merely competent technician, rather than the skilled engineer once required, can build a bomb. Explosive material is packed into pockets sewn into a canvas or denim belt or vest and hooked up to a detonator—usually involving a simple hand-operated plunger.

Before the operation is to be launched, "minders" sequester the bomber in a safe house, isolating him or her from family and friends—from all contact with the outside world—during the final preparations for martyrdom. A film crew makes a martyrdom video, as much to help ensure that the bomber can't back out as for propaganda and recruitment purposes. Reconnaissance teams have already either scouted the target or received detailed information about it, which they pass on to the bomber's handlers. The job of the handlers, who are highly skilled at avoiding Israeli army checkpoints or police patrols, is to deliver the bomber as close to the target as possible.

I talked to a senior police-operations commander in his office at the Russian Compound, the nerve center of law enforcement for Jerusalem since the time when first the Turks and then the British ruled this part of the world. It was easy to imagine, amid the graceful arches and the traditional Jerusalem stone, an era when Jerusalem's law-enforcement officers wore tarbooshes and pressed blue tunics with Sam Browne belts rather than the bland polyester uniforms and blue baseball-style caps of today. Although policing this multi-faith, historically beleaguered city has doubtless always involved difficult challenges, none can compare with the current situation. "This year there were very many events," my host explained, using the bland generic noun that signifies terrorist attacks or attempted attacks. "In previous years we considered ten events as normal; now we are already at forty-three." He sighed. There were still three weeks to go before the end of the year. Nineteen of these events had been suicide bombings. In the calculus of terrorism, it doesn't get much better. "How easy it has become for a person to wake up in the morning and go off and commit suicide," he observed. Once there were only "bags on buses, not vests or belts" to contend with, the policeman said. "Everything is open now. The purpose is to prove that the police can do whatever they want but it won't help."

This, of course, is the age-old strategy of terrorists everywhere—to undermine public confidence in the ability of the authorities to protect and defend citizens, thereby creating a climate of fear and intimidation amenable to terrorist exploitation. In Jerusalem, and in Israel as a whole, this strategy has not succeeded. But it has fundamentally changed daily behavior patterns—the first step toward crushing morale and breaking the will to resist.

The terrorists appear to be deliberately homing in on the few remaining places where Israelis thought they could socialize in peace. An unprecedented string of attacks in the first four months of last year illustrated this careful strategy, beginning at bus stops and malls and moving into more private realms, such as corner supermarkets and local coffee bars. In March, for example, no one paid much attention to a young man dressed like an ultra-Orthodox Jew who was standing near some parked cars as guests left a bar mitzvah celebration at a social hall in the ultra-Orthodox Jerusalem neighborhood of Beit Yisrael. Then he blew himself up, killing nine people, eight of them children, and wounding fifty-nine. The tight-knit religious community had felt that it was protected by God, pointing to the miraculous lack of injury a year before when a booby-trapped car blew up in front of the same hall. Using a strategy al Qaeda has made familiar, the terrorists revisited the site.

Less than a month after the Beit Yisrael attack the suicide bombers and their leaders drove home the point that Israelis cannot feel safe anywhere by going to the one large Israeli city that had felt immune from the suspicion and antipathy prevalent elsewhere—Haifa, with its successful mixture of Jews, Christian and Muslim Arabs, and followers of the Bahai faith. The University of Haifa has long had the highest proportion of Arab students of any Israeli university. The nearby Matza restaurant, owned by Jews but run by an Israeli Arab family from Galilee, seemed to embody the unusually cordial relations that exist among the city's diverse communities. Matza was popular with Jews and Arabs alike, and the presence of its Arab staff and patrons provided a feeling of safety from attack. That feeling was shattered at two-thirty on a quiet Sunday afternoon, when a suicide bomber killed fifteen people and wounded nearly fifty.

As we had tea late one afternoon in the regal though almost preternaturally quiet surroundings of Jerusalem's King David Hotel, Benny Morris, a professor of history at Ben Gurion University, explained, "The Palestinians say they have found a strategic weapon, and suicide bombing is it. This hotel is empty. The streets are empty. They have effectively terrorized Israeli society. My wife won't use a bus anymore, only a taxi." It is undeniable that daily life in Jerusalem, and throughout Israel, has changed as a result of last year's wave of suicide bombings. Even the police have been affected. "I'm worried," one officer told me in an aside—whether in confidence or in embarrassment, I couldn't tell—as we walked past Zion Square, near where some bombs had exploded. "I tell you this as a police officer. I don't come to Jerusalem with my children anymore. I'd give back the settlements. I'd give over my bank account to live in peace."

By any measure 2002 was an astonishing year for Israel in terms of suicide bombings. An average of five attacks a month were made, nearly double the number during the first fifteen months of the second intifada—and that number was itself more than ten times the monthly average since 1993. Indeed, according to a database maintained by the National Security Studies Center, at Haifa University, there were nearly as many suicide attacks in Israel last year (fifty-nine) as there had been in the previous eight years combined (sixty-two). In Jerusalem alone there were nine suicide attacks during the first four months of 2002, killing thirty-three and injuring 464. "It was horrendous," a young professional woman living in the city told me. "No one went out for coffee. No one went out to restaurants. We went as a group of people to one another's houses only."

Again, terrorism is meant to produce psychological effects that reach far beyond the immediate victims of the attack. "The Scuds of Saddam [in 1991] never caused as much psychological damage as the suicide bombers have," says Ami Pedahzur, a professor of political science at Haifa University and an expert on political extremism and violence who manages the National Security Studies Center's terrorism database. As the French philosopher Gaston Bouthoul argued three decades ago in a theoretical treatise on the subject, the "anonymous, unidentifiable threat creates huge anxiety, and the terrorist tries to spread fear by contagion, to immobilise and subjugate those living under this threat." This is precisely what the Palestinian terrorist groups are trying to achieve. "The Israelis . . . will fall to their knees," Sheikh Ahmad Yassin, the spiritual leader of Hamas, said in 2001. "You can sense the fear in Israel already; they are worried about where and when the next attacks will come. Ultimately, Hamas will win." The strategy of suicide terrorists is to make people paranoid and xenophobic, fearful of venturing beyond their homes even to a convenience store. Terrorists hope to compel the enemy society's acquiescence, if not outright surrender, to their demands. This is what al Qaeda hoped to achieve on 9/11 in one stunning blow—and what the Palestinians seek as well, on a more sustained, if piecemeal, basis.

After decades of struggle the Palestinians are convinced that they have finally discovered Israel's Achilles' heel. Ismail Haniya, another Hamas leader, was quoted in March of last year in *The Washington Post* as saying that Jews "love life more than any other people, and they prefer not to die." In contrast, suicide terrorists are often said to have gone to their deaths smiling. An Israeli policeman told me, "A suicide bomber goes on a bus and finds himself face-to-face with victims and he smiles and he activates the bomb—but we learned that only by asking people afterwards who survived." This is what is known in the Shia Islamic tradition as the *bassamat al-farah*, or "smile of joy"—prompted by one's impending martyrdom. It is just as prevalent among Sunni terrorists. (Indeed, the last will and testament of Mohammed Atta, the ringleader of the September 11 hijackers, and his

"primer" for martyrs, *The Sky Smiles, My Young Son*, clearly evidence a belief in the joy of death.)

This perceived weakness of an ostensibly powerful society has given rise to what is known in the Middle East as the "spider-web theory," which originated within Hizbollah, the Lebanese Shia organization, following a struggle that ultimately compelled the Israel Defense Forces to withdraw from southern Lebanon in May of 2000. The term is said to have been coined by Hizbollah's secretary general, Sheikh Hassan Nasrallah, who described Israel as a still formidable military power whose civil society had become materialistic and lazy, its citizens self-satisfied, comfortable, and pampered to the point where they had gone soft. IDF Chief of Staff Moshe "Boogie" Ya'alon paraphrased Nasrallah for the Israeli public in an interview published in the newspaper *Ha'aretz* last August.

"The Israeli army is strong, Israel has technological superiority and is said to have strategic capabilities, but its citizens are unwilling any longer to sacrifice lives in order to defend their national interests and national goals. Therefore, Israel is a spider-web society: it looks strong from the outside, but touch it and it will fall apart."

Al Qaeda, of course, has made a similar assessment of America's vulnerability.

A society facing such a determined foe can respond. Israel, with its necessarily advanced military and intelligence capacities, was able in the first four months of last year to meet the most concerted effort to date by Palestinian terrorists to test the resolve of its government and the mettle of its citizens. Twelve Israelis were killed in terrorist attacks in January, twenty-six in February, 108 in March, and forty-one in April. The population of the United States is roughly forty-seven times that of Israel, meaning that the American equivalent of the March figure would have exceeded 5,000—another 9/11, but with more than 2,000 additional deaths. After April of 2002, however, a period of relative quiet settled over Israel. The number of suicide attacks, according to the National Security Studies Center, declined from sixteen in March to six in April, six in May, five in June, and six in July before falling still further to two in August and similarly small numbers for the remainder of the year. "We wouldn't want it to be perceived [by the Israeli population] that we have no military answers," a senior IDF planner told me. The military answer was Operation Defensive Shield, which began in March and involved both the IDF's huge deployment of personnel to the West Bank and its continuing presence in all the major Palestinian population centers that Israel regards as wellsprings of the suicide campaign. This presence has involved aggressive military operations to preempt suicide bombing, along with curfews and other restrictions on the movement of residents.

The success of the IDF's strategy is utterly dependent on regularly acquiring intelligence and rapidly disseminating it to operational units that can take appropriate action. Thus the IDF must continue to occupy the West Bank's major population centers, so that Israeli intelligence agents can stay in close—and relatively safe—proximity to their information sources, and troops can act immediately either to round up suspects or to rescue the agent should an operation go awry. "Military pressure facilitates arrests, because you're there," one knowledgeable observer explained to me. "Not only do you know the area, but you have [covert] spotters deployed, and the whole area is under curfew anyway, so it is difficult for terrorists to move about and hide without being noticed, and more difficult for them to get out. The IDF presence facilitates intelligence gathering, and the troops can also conduct massive sweeps, house to house and block to block, pick up people, and interrogate them."

The IDF units in West Bank cities and towns can amass detailed knowledge of a community, identifying terrorists and their sympathizers, tracking their movements and daily routines, and observing the people with whom they associate. Agents from Shabak, Israel's General Security Service (also known as the Shin Bet), work alongside these units, participating in operations and often assigning missions. "The moment someone from Shabak comes with us, everything changes," a young soldier in an elite reconnaissance unit told me over coffee and cake in his mother's apartment. "The Shabak guy talks in Arabic to [the suspect] without an accent, or appears as an Arab guy himself. Shabak already knows everything about them, and that is such a shock to them. So they are afraid, and they will tell Shabak everything." The success of Defensive Shield and the subsequent Operation Determined Way depends on this synchronization of intelligence and operations. A junior officer well acquainted with this environment says, "Whoever has better intelligence is the winner."

The strategy—at least in the short run—is working. The dramatic decline in the number of suicide operations since last spring is proof enough. "Tactically, we are doing everything we can," a senior officer involved in the framing of this policy told me, "and we have managed to prevent eighty percent of all attempts." Another officer said, "We are now bringing the war to them. We do it so that we fight the war in *their* homes rather than in *our* homes. We try to make certain that we fight on their ground, where we can have the maximum advantage." The goal of the IDF, though, is not simply to fight in a manner that plays to its strength; the goal is to actively shrink the time and space in which the suicide bombers and their operational commanders, logisticians, and handlers function—to stop them before they can cross the Green Line, by threatening their personal safety and putting them on the defensive.

Citizens in Israel, as in America, have a fundamental expectation that their government and its military and security forces will protect and defend them. Soldiers are expected to die, if necessary, in order to discharge this responsibility. As one senior IDF commander put it, "It is better for the IDF to bear the brunt of these attacks than Israeli civilians. The IDF is better prepared, protected, educated." Thus security in Israel means to the IDF an almost indefinite deployment in the West Bank—a state of ongoing low-level war. For Palestinian civilians it means no respite from roadblocks and identity checks, cordon-and-search operations, lightning snatch-and-grabs, bombing raids, helicopter strikes, ground attacks, and other countermeasures that have turned densely populated civilian areas into war zones.

Many Israelis do not relish involvement in this protracted war of attrition, but even more of them accept that there is no alternative. "Israel's ability to stand fast indefinitely is a tremendous advantage," says Dan Schueftan, an Israeli strategist and military thinker who teaches at Haifa University, "since the suicide bombers believe that time is on their side. It imposes a strain on the army, yes, but this is what the army is for." Indeed, no Israeli with whom I spoke on this visit doubted that the IDF's continued heavy presence in the West Bank was directly responsible for the drop in the number of suicide bombings. And I encountered very few who favored withdrawing the IDF from the West Bank. This view cut across ideological and demographic lines. As we dined one evening at Matza, which has been rebuilt, a centrist graduate student at Haifa University named Uzi Nisim told me that Palestinian terrorists "will have the power to hit us, to hurt us, once [the IDF] withdraws from Jenin and elsewhere on the West Bank." Ami Pedahzur, of Haifa University, who is a leftist, agreed. He said, "There is widespread recognition in Israel that this is the only way to stop terrorism." I later heard the same thing from a South African couple, relatively new immigrants to Israel who are active in a variety of human-rights endeavors. "Just the other day," the husband told me, "even my wife said, 'Thank God we have Sharon. Otherwise I wouldn't feel safe going out.'"

Nevertheless, few Israelis believe that the current situation will lead to any improvement in Israeli-Palestinian relations over the long run. Dennis Zinn, the defense correspondent for Israel's Channel 1, told me, "Yes, there is a drop-off [in suicide bombings]. When you have bombs coming down on your heads, you can't carry out planning and suicide attacks. But that doesn't take away their motivation. It only increases it."

Given the relative ease and the strategic and tactical attraction of suicide bombing, it is perhaps no wonder that after a five-day visit to Israel last fall, Louis Anemone, the security chief of the New York Metropolitan Transit Authority, concluded that New Yorkers—and, by implication, other Americans—face the same threat. "This stuff is going to be imported over here," he declared—a prediction that Vice President Dick Cheney and FBI Director Robert Mueller had already made. In March, Secretary of Homeland Security Tom Ridge also referred to the threat, saying in an interview with Fox News that we have to "prepare for the inevitability" of suicide bombings in the United States. Anemone even argued that "today's terrorists appear to be using Israel as a testing ground to prepare for a sustained attack against the U.S." In fact, Palestinians had tried a suicide attack in New York four years before 9/11; their plans to bomb a Brooklyn subway station were foiled only because an informant told the police. When they were arrested, the terrorists were probably less than a day away from attacking: according to law-enforcement authorities, five bombs had been primed. "I wouldn't call them sophisticated," Howard Safir, the commissioner of police at the time, commented, "but they certainly were very dangerous." That suicide bombers don't need to be sophisticated is precisely what makes them so dangerous. All that's required is a willingness to kill and a willingness to die.

According to the Rand Corporation's chronology of worldwide terrorism, which begins in 1968 (the year acknowledged as marking the advent of modern international terrorism, whereby terrorists attack other countries or foreign targets in their own country), nearly two thirds of the 144 suicide bombings recorded have occurred in the past two years. No society, least of all the United States, can regard itself as immune from this threat. Israeli Foreign Minister Benjamin Netanyahu emphasized this point when he addressed the U.S. Congress nine days after 9/11. So did Dan Schueftan, the Israeli strategist, when I asked him if he thought suicide terrorism would come to America in a form similar to that seen in Israel this past year. He said, "It is an interesting comment that the terrorists make: we will finish defeating the Jews because they love life so much. Their goal is to bring misery and grief to people who have an arrogance of power. Who has this? The United States and Israel. Europe will suffer too. I don't think that it will happen in the U.S. on the magnitude we have seen it here, but I have no doubt that it will occur. We had the same discussion back in 1968, when El Al aircraft were hijacked and people said this is your problem, not ours."

The United States, of course, is not Israel. However much we may want to harden our hearts and our targets, the challenge goes far beyond fortifying a single national airline or corralling the enemy into a territory ringed by walls and barbed-wire fences that can be intensively monitored by our armed forces. But we can take precautions based on Israel's experience, and be confident that we are substantially reducing the threat of suicide terrorism here.

The police, the military, and intelligence agencies can take steps that work from the outside in, beginning far in time and distance from a potential attack and ending at the moment and the site of an actual attack. Although the importance of these steps is widely recognized, they have been implemented only unevenly across the United States.

• Understand the terrorists' operational environment. Know their *modus operandi* and targeting patterns. Suicide bombers are rarely lone outlaws; they are preceded by long logistical trails. Focus not just on suspected bombers but on the infrastructure required to launch and sustain suicide-bombing campaigns. This is the essential spadework. It will be for naught, however, if concerted efforts are not made to circulate this information quickly and systematically among federal, state, and local authorities.

• Develop strong, confidence-building ties with the communities from which terrorists are most likely to come, and mount communications campaigns to eradicate support from these communities. The most effective and useful intelligence comes from places where terrorists conceal themselves and seek to establish and hide their infrastructure. Law-enforcement officers should actively encourage and cultivate cooperation in a nonthreatening way.

• Encourage businesses from which terrorists can obtain bomb-making components to alert authorities if they notice large purchases of, for example, ammonium nitrate fertilizer; pipes, batteries, and wires; or chemicals commonly used to fabricate explosives. Information about customers who simply inquire about any of these materials can also be extremely useful to the police.

• Force terrorists to pay more attention to their own organizational security than to planning and carrying out attacks. The greatest benefit is in disrupting pre-attack operations. Given the highly fluid, international threat the United States faces, counterterrorism units, dedicated to identifying and targeting the intelligence-gathering and reconnaissance activities of terrorist organizations, should be established here within existing law-enforcement agencies. These units should be especially aware of places where organizations frequently recruit new members and the bombers themselves, such as community centers, social clubs, schools, and religious institutions.

• Make sure ordinary materials don't become shrapnel. Some steps to build up physical defenses were taken after 9/11—reinforcing park benches, erecting Jersey barriers around vulnerable buildings, and the like. More are needed, such as ensuring that windows on buses and subway cars are shatterproof, and that seats and other accoutrements are not easily dislodged or splintered. Israel has had to learn to examine every element of its public infrastructure. Israeli buses and bus shelters are austere for a reason.

• Teach law-enforcement personnel what to do at the moment of an attack or an attempt. Prevention comes first from the cop on the beat, who will be forced to make instant life-and-death decisions affecting those nearby. Rigorous training is needed for identifying a potential suicide bomber, confronting a suspect, and responding and securing the area around the attack site in the event of an explosion. Is the officer authorized to take action on sighting a suspected bomber, or must a supervisor or special unit be called first? Policies and procedures must be established. In the aftermath of a blast the police must determine whether emergency medical crews and firefighters may enter the site; concerns about a follow-up attack can dictate that first responders be held back until the area is secured. The ability to make such lightning determinations requires training—and, tragically, experience. We can learn from foreign countries with long experience of suicide bombings, such as Israel and Sri Lanka, and also from our own responses in the past to other types of terrorist attacks.

America's enemies are marshaling their resources to continue the struggle that crystallized on 9/11. Exactly what shape that struggle will take remains to be seen. But a recruitment video reportedly circulated by al Qaeda as recently as spring of last year may provide some important clues. The seven-minute tape, seized from an al Qaeda member by U.S. authorities, extols the virtues of martyrdom and solicits recruits to Osama bin Laden's cause. It depicts scenes of *Jihad*ists in combat, followed by the successive images of twenty-seven martyrs with their names, where they were from, and where they died. Twelve of the martyrs are featured in a concluding segment with voice-over that says, "They rejoice in the bounty provided by Allah. And with regard to those left behind who have not yet joined them in their bliss, the martyrs glory in the fact that on them is no fear, nor have they cause to grieve." The video closes with a message of greeting from the Black Banner Center for Islamic Information.

The greatest military onslaught in history against a terrorist group crushed the infrastructure of al Qaeda in Afghanistan, depriving it of training camps, operational bases, and command-and-control headquarters; killing and wounding many of its leaders and fighters; and dispersing the survivors. Yet this group still actively seeks to rally its forces and attract recruits. Ayman Zawahiri, bin Laden's chief lieutenant, laid out a list of terrorist principles in his book, *Knights Under the Prophet's Banner* (2001), prominent among them the need for al Qaeda to "move the battle to the enemy's ground to burn the hands of those who ignite fire in our countries." He also mentioned "the need to concentrate on the method of martyrdom operations as the most successful way of inflicting damage against the opponent and the least costly to the mujahideen in terms of casualties." That martyrdom is highlighted in the recruitment video strongly suggests that suicide attacks will continue to be a primary instrument in al Qaeda's war against—and perhaps in—the United States. Suleiman Abu Gheith, al Qaeda's chief spokesman, has said as much. In rhetoric disturbingly reminiscent of the way that Palestinian terrorists describe their inevitable triumph over Israel, Abu Gheith declared, "Those youths that destroyed Americans with their planes, they did a good deed. There are thousands more young followers who look forward to death like Americans look forward to living."

The Ultimate Organization

Networks, Franchises, and Freelancers

Jessica Stern

One of the surprises of September 11 was that some of the suicide bombers had been living and studying in the West for years. We like to think that our way of life and the freedoms we enjoy are so attractive that anyone who lives among us will inevitably become pro-Western. The globalization of Al Qaeda—its recruitment of locals to participate in attacks—and its careful grooming of operatives, were discussed by the terrorists themselves in a New York City courtroom, where four of the 1998 African-embassy bombers were tried a year and a half before September 11. It is too bad that the terrorists' revelations, including about the organization's vast business holdings, its detailed planning of operations, its emplacement of sleepers, and its attempts to acquire weapons of mass destruction, didn't receive more attention. If they had, perhaps we would not have been so astonished by Al Qaeda's ability to operate inside America.

This chapter begins with a discussion of a terrorist who participated in the bombing of the U.S. embassy in Dar es Salaam, Tanzania, in August 1998. His story is important for two reasons. First, he was a sleeper. A "talent scout" noticed that he attended a radical mosque regularly, and that he was increasingly agitated about the plight of Muslims around the world. Told that he would have to be trained at a camp to earn the trust of his new Islamist friends, he spent his own money to travel to Afghanistan. The real purpose of his training was to assess his potential. He was found to be barely educated, with few skills. But he had something else critically important to Al Qaeda at the time: language skills and Tanzanian citizenship. This is

exactly the kind of operative that Americans are beginning to fear—a confused young man who thinks he is helping Muslims by serving as a sleeper for a terrorist group, whose principal value to the terrorists is his country of residence. Now we fear that the terrorist sleepers may be our next-door neighbors.

The second reason this operative's story is important is that he comes from Africa, an area of the world that may well become an enclave of Islamist extremism and anti-American sentiment in the future. Americans tend to fixate on enemies that can be fought with military might. We have a much harder time seeing failing states, where terrorists thrive, as a source of danger. We need to assess why bin Laden's and other extremists ideas spread. And we need to look for clues globally, not just in the Middle East.

America has had the luxury of ignoring countries at far geographic remove throughout most of its history. This is no longer possible. Nor is it sufficient to concentrate exclusively on one or two villains in a given decade. We have to be alert to the possibility that the villain may be a seductive, hateful idea about Us versus Them, rather than an individual; and that the hateful idea may be taking hold—in seemingly obscure or remote locations. The growing availability of powerful weapons, porous borders, and the communications revolution make it possible for smaller and smaller groups to wreak havoc almost anywhere on the globe.

In the spring of 2000 two American defense attorneys contacted me to ask whether I would be willing to serve as an expert witness in the trial of Khalfan Khamis Mohamed, an Al Qaeda operative who was involved in the bombing of the U.S. embassy in Dar es Salaam, Tanzania, in August 1998. That attack, and the simultaneous bombing of the American embassy in Nairobi, Kenya, killed 224 people, most of them Africans, and injured thousands.

Mohamed had already admitted his guilt at the time his lawyers called me. He had told the FBI that he had rented the house where the bomb was built, bought the truck used to transport components, bought a grinder for grinding the explosive, and ground some of the TNT himself. After the bombing, he fled to South Africa with a new identity, a new passport, and $1,000 in cash, this last procured for him by Al Qaeda.

After a worldwide manhunt lasting longer than a year, South African authorities found Mohamed in Cape Town, working at an Indian fast-food restaurant called Burger World. The South African government extradited him to the United States. The U.S. government wanted him executed for his crimes. Mohamed's lawyers wanted my help in arguing that his punishment should be to spend the rest of his life behind bars in a maximum-security federal prison, but that he should not be put to death.

Khalfan Khamis Mohamed was born in 1973 on the island of Pemba and grew up in the village of Kidimni on Zanzibar Island. His twin sister, Fatuma, was born in the evening, but he didn't arrive until morning, giving his mother a lot of trouble, she recalls. But from that point on, she says, "He was just an ordinary child who went to school. . . . After school he performed the normal domestic chores and liked playing football, like all youth. He didn't indulge in any antisocial behavior."[1]

The family was poor. They lived in a mud hut with a thatched roof. His father died when Mohamed was six or seven years old. People on Zanzibar don't pay close attention to dates, and Mohamed's mother doesn't recall exactly when her husband died. After the death of his father, Mohamed helped his mother support the family by working on the farm, harvesting fruits that grow wild in the forest, and taking care of a neighboring farmer's cows.

Mohamed comes from a very different sort of place than many of the terrorists—a place that, ironically, benefited from globalization long before the term become popular. Zanzibar consists of two islands: Zanzibar (known locally as Unguja) and Pemba. The islands are in the Indian Ocean, twenty-five miles off the coast of

Tanzania, six degrees south of the equator. Clove, jackfruit, mango, and breadfruit grow in the valleys of Pemba Island. Coconut trees, brought by Indian traders centuries ago, now grow wild. Monkeys, civets, bushpigs, and mongooses thrive in the forests. Some one hundred species of birds live in Tanzania, and thirteen species of bats have been identified on Pemba. The islands are also famous for their butterflies and the great variety of game fish found in the waters between them. Fishing and agriculture are Zanzibar's main industries.

Today, Pemba and Zanzibar are largely isolated from the rest of the world. Foreign visitors tend to be adventurers attracted by the lush, undisturbed reefs or the profusion of game fish found in Pemba Channel. Visitors describe an extraordinarily friendly people who seem utterly mesmerized by their foreign looks and ways. They write of the remarkable melee of cultures—African, Arab, Persian, and Indian—magnificent Arabic architecture, abundant fruits and fishes, but also poverty and squalor, with the scent of spices rising above the stench of sewage and rotting fish.

Although it is relatively isolated today, Zanzibar was once the trading center for all of Africa, with trade links to Arabia, China, India, Persia, and Southeast Asia. The nineteenth-century English explorer Richard Burton described Pemba as an "emerald isle" in a "sea of purest sapphire." The scent of cloves, he said, was enticing even from the sea. The people were a mixed race who had retained, despite their conversion to Islam, the skills of divination and other "curious practices palpably derived from their wild ancestry."[2] The traditional dhow, a single-masted ship with a lateen sail, used by Arab merchants for two millennia to sail on the monsoon winds, is still in use today and is still built in the same way—with a hull of mangrove or teak, and ribs of acacia—with no nails.

A succession of invading powers left remnants of their cultures and languages. Shirazi Persians, who settled on the coast of East Africa in the tenth century, intermarried with the locals, giving rise to an Afro-Persian race.[3] Omani Arabs, who settled on Zanzibar some six centuries later, have had the largest influence on the culture and language. The name Zanzibar is the Arabic expression for "land of blacks." Kiswahili, Tanzania's official language, contains a substantial fraction of Arabic, Farsi, and Hindi words, as well as some Portuguese and English ones.

Tanzania was formed as a sovereign state in 1964 through the union of Tanganyika, on the African mainland, and Zanzibar. Zanzibar and Pemba Islands have a separate government administration from the rest of Tanzania. Zanzibaris are seeking greater autonomy for their archipelago. They would like to reap more of the profits of the export of cloves, which the central government taxes heavily, and to control more of the tourist trade.

Tanzania's ruling party, and Tanganyika itself, are predominantly Christian. The ruling party refers to any threat to its rule as motivated by Islamism, which, ironically, may incite precisely the kind of extremism the ruling party fears. During the last decade, elections have been declared fraudulent by multiple international observers, and protests have been met with violence perpetrated by the police, who are predominantly Christian, against Zanzibaris, who are predominantly Muslim. To the extent that Islamism is indigenous in the region, it is found more on the mainland than on the islands, as well as in neighboring Kenya, although this could change. Zanzibaris are deeply disappointed that the United States did not protest Tanzania's tampering with the election results of 1995 and 2000 or the violence that ensued, although the government's crimes were published widely.[4] Although the region is remarkably tolerant historically, stimulated by its long-time exposure to multiple cultures, anti-Western Islamist sentiment could easily take root here if democracy fails and state repression continues.[5]

Muslims represent 97 percent of the population of Zanzibar, most of them Sunni. Shia represent 12 percent of the population. As in Indonesia, Islam coexists with Zanzibar's traditional religions, including animism. Zanzibar is famous for its sorcerers, seers, and witch doctors. Spells often involve Arabic texts, and witches often dress in traditional Arab garb. Evelyn Waugh wrote that novices came to Pemba from as far away as Haiti to study magic and voodoo. A cult of witches "still flourishes below the surface," he wrote, expressing his frustration that "everything is kept hidden from the Europeans."[6] Zanzibar is the home of a secret sect known as the Wachawi, who practice their arts even today. They are said to be able to take on the shapes of animals and birds. Haitian voodooists learned to animate corpses for labor in the fields by studying with the Wachawi, who reportedly developed the technique to escape their masters' notice when they fled bondage. The Wachawi are said to be able to bring the recently deceased back to life, with personality and memory intact. Locals describe their neighbors returning from midnight meetings in the bush, pale and speechless, having seen their recently deceased loved ones restored to life. Early-twentieth-century visitors said that natives told them of powerful witch guilds, which required prospective members to offer up a near relation—a spouse or a child—to be eaten by other initiates.[8]

As a child, Mohamed attended a *madrassah* in the afternoons. The family described him as serious and quiet—more observant than his siblings, but also a better student. When he was in the middle of tenth grade, his older brother, Mohamed Khalfan Mohamed, asked Mohamed to come to live with him and his family in Dar es Salaam on the mainland to help out in the family dry-goods store. Mohamed intended to complete his schooling in Tanzania, but his time was taken up with his work at the shop and attending mosque. He had always been somewhat of a loner, his siblings recounted, but he became even more isolated after dropping out of high school, spending time only with his family and people he met at the mosque.[9]

The mosques in Dar es Salaam were more political than the one Mohamed attended in Zanzibar. There was a great deal of discussion about the plight of Muslims in Chechnya and especially in Bosnia. Worshipers were told that it was their duty to help fellow Muslims around the world in any way they could.[10] One of Mohamed's new friends was a man named Sulieman. Sulieman was from Zanzibar, but he worked on a fishing boat based in Mombasa, Kenya, owned by a man whom Mohamed knew only as "Mohamed the Fisherman." Mohamed the Fisherman turned out to be Mohamed Sadiq Odeh, a Saudi of Palestinian origin who was a member of Al Qaeda. Odeh would play an important role in the embassy-bombing conspiracy.[11]

Sulieman introduced Mohamed to Fahid, who would also participate in the bombing, who visited Dar es Salaam only occasionally. Mohamed started spending much of his free time with Fahid and Fahid's friends, who were very religious. Sometimes they met in Dar es Salaam, and sometimes in Mombasa, Kenya. Mohamed says that they mainly talked about how to help Muslims around the world. Often, he said, they would meet in cars.[12]

By 1994, Mohamed began to despair at his own life, family members said. He spent more and more time at the mosque. He was radicalized in that mosque, his sister-in-law recalled.

Mohamed told Fahid he wanted to go to Bosnia to fight against the Serbs. Fahid told him that you cannot become a soldier for Islam without training. Fahid also told Mohamed that he did not trust him, and that he could earn Fahid's trust only if he went to Afghanistan to be trained. Mohamed saved his earnings from the dry-goods shop and in 1994 traveled with Sulieman to Pakistan. Fahid had given them a contact in Karachi, who arranged for their trip to the camp. Fahid had been at the camp for around a month when Mohamed and Sulieman arrived. Mohamed told FBI investigators that the camp was called Markaz Fath, and that it was run by a Pakistani Jihadi group called Harkar-ul-Ansar. He said his teacher was a Pakistani named Abu Omar. Mohamed said that he met a lot of people at the camp, one of whom was an American known as Sulieman America. The people he met were interested in helping Muslims around the world, Mohamed said, and in waging a Jihad against America and against conservative Muslim states. He said he had never heard the name Al Qaeda.[13]

During the first two months at the camp, the group was trained to use light weapons (handguns and rifles), launchers, and surface-to-air missiles. Mohamed and his friends Sulieman and Fahid were selected for advanced training, which included learning how to manufacture explosives and how to join detonators and wires. Mohamed was not trained in the use of chemical weapons, although he said that other members of his group were. Afternoons were taken up with Islamic studies—including films of atrocities perpetrated against Muslims in Chechnya and Bosnia—and sports. Mohamed stayed at the camp for nine or ten months, he says.[14] At the end of his training, Mohamed wanted to go to Bosnia, but he was not selected. He was told to leave a number in case he was needed at a later date. Mohamed went back to Dar es Salaam, bitterly disappointed that he had not been allowed to join the fight against the Serbs.[15]

Mohamed continued to spend time with the "brothers" he had met in the mosque or had gotten to know at the camp. He went to Somalia twice in 1997—once to teach Somali fighters what he had learned in Afghanistan, and once for a meeting with the men who would ultimately bomb the American embassy.[16] Just before his first trip to Somalia, Fahid introduced him to a man named Hussein, who would later lead the group that bombed the U.S. embassy in Dar es Salaam. Fahid told Mohamed that Hussein is our brother, that he is a good man who had been trained to be a *mujaheed*. Odeh, explaining how Mohamed fell under Hussein's influence, described Hussein as "persuasive, authoritarian," and "a very strong leader, a man of compelling personality." Mohamed was impressed by Hussein's knowledge of Islam. Some time after this meeting, Hussein moved to Dar es Salaam with his family. They stayed with Mohamed in a small flat.[17]

Three years after he returned from Afghanistan, Hussein approached Mohamed to invite him to participate in a "Jihad job." Mohamed said that he would like to participate, although he was not informed about what the "Jihad job" would entail. Eventually Hussein asked Mohamed to take certain actions. He instructed him to buy a truck, which Mohamed did in his own name. He paid for the truck, a white Suzuki, with cash that Hussein gave him. Fahid accompanied him and drove the truck because Mohamed did not know how to drive. The group used the truck to transport equipment needed for the bomb, including cylinder tanks, detonators, fertilizer, and TNT. Hussein also asked him to rent a house, large and private enough to conceal the group's activities. Mohamed remembered Hussein telling him that he wanted the house to be hidden from the street, but that it should also be "nice." Mohamed found a house with a high wall, which he rented in his own name. The owner insisted that Mohamed pay a year's rent in advance, which he did, with money Hussein gave him.[18]

Mohamed, Hussein, and Hussein's family moved into the house in the Ilala district of Dar es Salaam. Other team members came to the house, but no one ever discussed his role in the plot. Hussein instructed Mohamed to remain in the house most of the time, so that if any neighbors came by, there would be someone who could speak to them in Swahili. Other team members arrived soon before the bombing: an engineer named Abdul Rahman, whom Mohamed described as working with "all confidence"; and "Ahmed the driver," whom Mohamed thought was Egyptian. Ahmed was the suicide bomber who would drive the truck into the embassy. Some five days before the attack, Hussein told Mohamed that the target of the bombing would be the American embassy. Mohamed helped load the tanks, boxes of TNT, and sandbags into the back of the truck. When the truck got stuck in the sand behind the house, Mohamed helped the driver dig it out.[19]

Hussein and the rest of the team left several days before the bombing. Most of them said they were going to Mombasa, without specifying their final destination. In fact, they had been instructed to return to Afghanistan before the bombing took place. Hussein asked Mohamed to remain in Dar es Salaam, to help the driver with any last-minute details, and to remove incriminating evidence from the house. Mohamed did as he was told, with one exception. He did not like the idea of throwing away the food grinder he had used to grind the TNT, since it was still usable. So he gave it to his sister Zuhura, asking her to clean it well and to pass it on to his mother.[20]

When he was captured by the FBI in October 1999, Mohamed told investigators he was not sorry that Tanzanians were killed, which he said was part of the business. He said he had bombed the embassy because it was his responsibility, according to his study of Islam. He said he thought the operation was successful because the bomb worked, it sent a message to America, and because it kept American officials busy investigating it. He also said that if he had not been caught, he would continue participating in the Jihad against America or possibly against Egypt, and that if the U.S. government were to release him from custody, he would bomb Americans again. He told his investigators that he thought about Jihad all the time. He told them he wants Americans to understand that he and his fellow warriors are not crazy, gun-wielding people, but are fighting for a cause.[21]

I travel to New York to watch Mohamed's trial. Security is tight. The taxi drops me several blocks from the entrance to the courthouse because the street is blocked to traffic. You must pass through several layers of security before you get to the room where the trial is being held. There are metal detectors and guards on the first floor, and you have to show identification and sign in outside the courtroom. A guard is suspicious about why I am here. I explain that I am a defense-team visitor, and an agent instructs me

to sit in the third wooden bench on the right. I can see from the back of the room that the bench is already full. When she sees that I mean to sit there, a woman pulls a child onto her lap and slides closer in toward her neighbor on the hard wooden bench. This is Mohamed's family, I realize. The women wear bright Zanzibar cottons. The boys and men wear prayer caps. The little boy immediately to my right is wearing pressed white cotton. He stares at me with velvety eyes, not at all shy, seemingly delighted with the opportunity to examine such a strange foreign creature, whom good fortune has brought conveniently near at hand. His mother is too distracted to notice his staring and he is free to inspect every inch of me, which he does with obvious pleasure. It is a hot day. I notice the smell of anxiety in my benchmates' sweat, but also the pleasant scent of spices. I see Mohamed's mother at the far end of the bench. She sits tall, with dignity, but she looks modest and kind. She appears surprisingly calm, at least for now. There are brothers, sisters, children, and spouses also sharing the bench, as well as the family with whom Mohamed lived when he fled to South Africa.

A social worker has been called up to the witness stand to provide Mohamed's social history. She has traveled to Zanzibar twice and shows the court pictures of Mohamed's school, the neighborhood where he grew up, and the take-out restaurant where Mohamed worked as chef in Cape Town. When she is done, various members of Mohamed's family are called up to the stand. Each is asked what they remember about Mohamed. An older brother remembers him as good in school and good at soccer. Mohamed was kind and peaceable, he said, and would always try to break up fights. A younger sister recalls him helping her with her schoolwork. Another says that Mohamed played games with her children, his nieces and nephews. The mother of the family for whom he worked in Cape Town recalled how patient and kind Mohamed had been with her children and her elderly parents. He even taught her elderly mother to read the Koran. She said that she would gladly have given up her daughter in marriage to Mohamed. All but one of Mohamed's family members said it was their first time traveling by airplane or traveling abroad.

The last witness was Mohamed's mother, whose name is Hidaya Rubeya juma. There was a hush in the room as a large lady dressed in bright cottons and a turban took the stand. I saw

Mohamed looking down as his mother took her seat. It seemed to me that Mohamed had a harder time facing his mother than he did facing his victims or accusers. There was jolt of pain in the room, as though the air had been ionized with terror—his and ours. Not a fear of death, but the recognition of evil. The recognition that this person who had killed so many has a mother who loves him, despite his crimes, and that he is afraid to look her in the eye. That despite his evil actions, he is human, just like us. It is one thing to understand this intellectually. It is another to see a mother face her killer son, with his many victims looking on, seeing her fear, her agony, and her loss. The loss of her son—first to evil, and maybe to death.

Mohamed's attorney, Mr. David Ruhnke, asked Mohamed's mother, "After you leave and return to Africa next week, do you know whether you will ever see your son again?"

"I don't even know," she answered quietly.[22]

"Do you know what this is about, and that the people here have to decide whether your son is to be executed or put in prison for life? And I want to ask you a very difficult question, which is, if your son were executed, what would that do to you?"

"It will hurt me. He is my son."[23]

Soon after this, the court was adjourned. Hidaya Rubeya Juma was the last witness to appear in the penalty phase of Mohamed's trial. Closing arguments began at the next session.

In his closing arguments, the prosecutor, Mr. Fitzgerald, emphasized what he referred to as Mohamed's two-sided personality. "I submit to sit before you and tell you that Khalfan Mohamed's personal characteristics as an individual human being include the following: one, Khalfan Mohamed has exhibited responsible conduct in other areas of his life; two, Khalfen Mohamed has shown himself to be a person capable of kindness, friendship, and generosity; and three, Khalfan Mohamed lost his father at an early age and worked to help his family, which struggled financially after the death of the major breadwinner." Mohamed can be very kind, Fitzgerald adds. "You want him to marry your daughter. You wouldn't think he would hurt an ant. The next day he is in custody, saying 'Yeah, I bombed people and I'll do it again.' That's what he is. He's got two faces. . . . He fooled his family. . . . He is capable of savagery."[24]

Jury members concluded that, if executed, Mohamed would be seen as a martyr and that his death could be "exploited by others to justify future terrorist acts." He received a life sentence without parole.

When authorities interrogated Mohamed Sadiq Odeh in Pakistan, where he had flown on the day of the bombing, he admitted that he was a member of Al Qaeda and gave his interrogators the names of some of the Al Qaeda members involved in the plots. He also referred to "two or three locals," whose names he appeared not to know, who had been left behind in Dar es Salaam and Nairobi to finish the job. One of those expendable locals was Mohamed.

According to several Al Qaeda members who testified at the trial, Al Qaeda is highly "tiered," and for the most part, Africans were not admitted to the upper ranks. Mohamed was recruited as a sleeper because he had a passport, language skills, and would not stand out as a foreigner in Dar es Salaam. Odeh explained to the FBI that there are several types of Al Qaeda operatives: sophisticated operatives who are involved in intelligence collection, choosing targets, surveillance, and making the bombs. But another category of operatives includes "good Muslims" who "are not experts in anything that would have a long-term benefit to the rest of the group."[25] The main thing they have to offer is their knowledge of the local languages and customs.

These dispensable young men, recruited to act only in the implementation phase of an attack, are unlikely to join Al Qaeda in a formal sense. They are often identified in the mosque, Odeh said. Atrocities against Muslims—anywhere in the world—help to create a climate that is ripe for recruiting young men to become soldiers for Allah. It is not even necessary to mention the name Al Qaeda to recruit them, Odeh told Jerry Post, a psychiatrist who interviewed him.[26] It is possible that many of the American, British, and Southeast Asian sleepers that law-enforcement authorities continue to discover all over the world were recruited to play a similar role. Like Mohamed, the group of Yemeni Americans taken into custody in September 2002 apparently went to Afghanistan for a relatively short course of training. In the camp, potential recruits' skills and commitment can be closely observed so that trainers can funnel them into the appropriate tier of the organization. Because of Al Qaeda's strict policy of sharing information only on a need-to-know basis, sleepers—who serve as a kind of reserve army in the targeted country—are unlikely to know precisely for what they have been recruited until immediately before an attack.

Some of the most important revelations of the trial were contained in an Al Qaeda instruction manual called the "Declaration of Jihad against the Country's Tyrants," which was entered into evidence. The manual makes clear that intelligence and counterintelligence (avoiding detection by the enemy intelligence agencies) are a priority for Al Qaeda. It instructs sleepers in the art of disappearing in enemy territory by shaving their beards, avoiding typical Muslim dress or expressions, not chatting too much (especially with taxi drivers, who may work for the enemy government), and wearing cologne. Sleepers are urged to find residences in new apartment buildings, where neighbors are less likely to know one another. Found by the Manchester (England) Metropolitan Police during a search of an Al Qaeda member's home, the manual was located in a computer file described as "the military series" and was subsequently translated into English.[27] In the "first lesson," the manual describes the "main mission for which the Military Organization is responsible" as "the overthrow of the godless regimes and their replacement with an Islamic regime."[28] The second lesson spells out the "necessary qualifications and characteristics" of the organization's members, which include a commitment to Islam and to the organization's ideology, maturity, sacrifice, listening and obedience, keeping secrets, health, patience, "tranquillity and unflappability," intelligence and insights, caution and prudence, truthfulness and counsel, ability to observe and analyze, and the "ability to act,"[29] Subsequent "lessons" teach the trainee how to forge documents, establish safe houses and hiding places, establish safe communications, procure weapons, and gather intelligence. A large number of training manuals have been discovered in Afghanistan and elsewhere.[30]

Witnesses at the trial explained the structure of the organization in some detail. Bin Laden was known as the "emir," or leader. Directly under him was the Shura Council, which consisted of a dozen or so members.[3] The Shura oversaw the committees. The Military Committee was responsible for training camps and for procurement of weapons. The Islamic Study Committee issued fatwas and other religious rulings. The Media Committee published the newspapers. The Travel Committee was responsible for the procurement of both tickets and false-identity papers and came under the purview of the Finance Committee. The Finance Committee oversaw bin Laden's businesses.[32] Al Qaeda had extensive dealings with charitable organizations. First, it used them to provide cover and for money laundering. Second, money donated to charitable organizations to provide humanitarian relief often ended up in Al Qaeda's coffers. Finally, and perhaps most importantly, Al Qaeda provided an important social-welfare function. It was simultaneously a recipient of "charitable funds" and a provider of humanitarian relief, a kind of terrorist United Way.

In this sense, Al Qaeda is similar to Pakistani and Indonesian Jihadi groups. Al Qaeda has a clear hierarchy. There are commanders, managers, and cadres; and cadres consist of both skilled and unskilled labor. Foot soldiers are likely to be found in schools or mosques, and only the best and brightest make it to the top. Some midlevel operatives are paid enough inside the organization that they may find it difficult to leave, while for others—generally those who come from wealthier families—the spiritual and psychological attractions of Jihad are sufficient. Information is shared on a need-to-know basis, as in an intelligence agency.

Several Al Qaeda functions are worth discussing in somewhat more detail: planning operations, relations with states, recruitment, training, developing the mission, and weapons acquisition.

PLANNING OPERATIONS

Some Al Qaeda operations take years to plan and implement, and sometimes the group reattempts attacks that failed the first time around. The idea to attack the World Trade Center appears to have originated well before the 1993 attack. Ramzi Yousef, who spent three years in a safe house provided by bin Laden prior to his arrest,[33] made clear to the FBI that he intended to knock the two buildings down, but that lack of funds had prevented him from achieving his ambitious goals. He had also plotted, together with his right-hand man, Abdul Hakim Murad, as well as Khalid Sheikh Mohammed, his uncle, to destroy eleven American airplanes midair, a plot that was successfully tested on a Philippine airliner in December 1994, killing one passenger and injuring at least six others.[34] The plot became known as the Bojinka Plot, which is Serbo-Croat for "the explosion."[35] Numerous reports have emerged that Al Qaeda had considered using airplanes as weapons before, including the widely reported plot to attack the CIA headquarters. Bin Laden admitted on videotape that he had not expected the Trade Center buildings to collapse, but that he had rejoiced in the surprising effectiveness of the attack.

For some operations, leaders are involved in detailed planning. Ali Muhammad, an Egyptian-born naturalized U.S. citizen who admitted conducting photographic surveillance of the U.S. embassy in Nairobi, told American investigators that bin Laden himself had looked at surveillance photographs and selected the spot where the suicide truck should explode in the 1998 attack.[36] But not all plots receive this level of oversight. Members of Al Qaeda in Jordan, for instance, who were arrested while preparing for attacks to be carried out during the millennium, were providing for themselves, rather than receiving lavish sums. Ahmed Ressam testified that he had been given what amounted to seed money for his planned attack in Los Angeles during the millennium. During the trial of Mokhtar Haouari, a coconspirator in the "millennium plot," Ressam testified that he had had to raise most of the funds on his own, which he did by making use of his long-standing expertise in credit-card, immigration, and welfare fraud; as well as other criminal activities such as theft and robbery.[37]

The attack on the USS Cole was originally planned on another U.S. destroyer, The Sullivans. The suggested target date for the attack on The Sullivans had been January 3, 2000, at the height of Ramadan. This first attempt to sink a U.S. warship failed when the explosives-laden boat sank.[38]

Al Qaeda is patient. A senior counterterrorism official of the FBI observes, "They plan their operations well in advance and have the patience to wait to conduct the attack at the right time. Prior to carrying out the operation, Al Qaeda conducts surveillance of the target, sometimes on multiple occasions, often using nationals of the target they are surveying to enter the location without suspicion. The results of the surveillance are forwarded to Al Qaeda HQ as elaborate 'ops plans' or 'targeting packages' prepared using photographs, CAD-CAM (computer-aided design/computer-aided mapping) software, and the operative's notes."[39] This sophistication, coupled with a wealth of financial and material resources, allows bin Laden's terrorist network to stage spectacular attacks.

RELATIONS WITH STATES

Jihadi groups build up strong relationships with individual politicians, intelligence agencies, or various factions of divided governments. The Pakistani Jihadis were long sustained by Pakistan's ISI and are still assisted by former ISI agents, who serve as trainers at terrorist-training camps. It is likely that some current ISI agents still support the Jihadi groups, even after President Musharraf's post-September 11 promise to force pro-Jihadi elements out.[40] Active-duty military personnel helped to train Laskar Jihad mujahideen in Indonesia and have had a long-standing relationship with the leader of Jamaah Islamiyah, now closely associated with Al Qaeda.[41] Saddam Hussein offered cash payments to the families of Palestinian suicide bombers, and Saudi charities, purportedly unconnected to the government, do the same. Iran provides funding to a variety of Jihadi groups around the world including Sunni ones, as well as safe haven. Ali Mohamed, a witness for the U.S. government in the African-embassies bombing trial held in 2001, testified that Al Qaeda maintained close ties to Iranian security forces. The security forces provided Al Qaeda with bombs "disguised to took like rocks," he said, and arranged for the group to receive training in explosives at Hezbollah-run camps in Lebanon.[42]

But bin Laden went beyond cooperating with states and state agents. He made himself so indispensable to leaders willing to provide him sanctuary that the assets of the state became his to use. He built a major highway in Sudan. Bin Laden's businesses became major employers of Sudanese citizens. For example, Al-Damazine Farms, which manufactured sesame oil and grew peanuts and corn, employed some four thousand people.[43]

Bin Laden established a close personal relationship with Hassan al-Turabi, leader of the National Islamic Front in Sudan and a leading Islamist intellectual who was educated in the West. Al-Turabi was trying to establish an Islamic state in Sudan based on a strict interpretation of lslamic law. Bin Laden also worked closely with Sudan's intelligence agency and military. As a result of these relationships—and Sudan's financial dependence on bin Laden—he was able to build training camps, establish safe houses, and plan terrorist operations from Sudanese territory. The National Islamic Front supplied bin Laden with communications equipment, radios, rifles, and fake passports for his personnel.

Bin Laden made important foreign contacts while living in Sudan. During an Islamic People's Congress in Sudan in 1995, he met leaders of other radical Islamist groups, including Hamas and PIJ (Palestinian Islamic Jihad), as well as extremist organizations from Algeria, Pakistan, and Tunisia. Al Qaeda further extended its worldwide network of contacts through training, arms smuggling, or providing financial support to groups based in the Philippines, Jordan, Eritrea, Egypt, Yemen, and elsewhere.

After the U.S. government pressured Sudan to expel bin Laden in mid-May 1996, he moved his operation to Jalalabad, Afghanistan. He reportedly lost $300 million in investments that he was forced to leave behind. Despite these losses, soon after his arrival in Afghanistan, bin Laden began buying the services of the Taliban. He offered up members of his elite unit, the 055 Brigade, to assist the Taliban in its efforts to destroy the Northern Alliance.[44] Over five years, he gave the Taliban regime some $100 million, according to U.S. officials.[45] In return, he received the Taliban's hospitality and loyalty. According to Mohammed Khaksar, who served as the Taliban's chief of intelligence, then as deputy minister of the interior prior to his defection to the Northern Alliance in 2001, "Al Qaeda was very important for the Taliban because they had so much money. . . . They gave a lot of money. And the Taliban trusted them."[46]

Does Al Qaeda need the services of a state to continue to function as it did prior to September 11? I think the answer is that it probably does. But there is no reason to think that Al Qaeda and the International Islamic Front (IIF)[47] can't change their way of functioning so that the services of a state are no longer as critical. The IIF is a learning organization. The movement is encouraging resisters, virtual networks, and lone-wolf avengers. The IIF is also increasingly relying on what I will call franchises—groups that have their own regional agendas, but are willing to contribute (including financially) to Al Qaeda's global, anti-American project when invited; and groups or individuals who may not be formal members but were trained at Al Qaeda's camps and are willing to work as freelancers.

WEAPONS ACQUISITION

Conventional

The Al Qaeda body responsible for the procurement of weapons is the Military Committee—one of four committees that are subordinate to the *Shura Majlis,* the consultative council of the network. Apart from being responsible for the development and acquisition of both conventional and unconventional weapons, the Military Committee is also in charge of recruitment and training, as well as the planning and execution phase of Al Qaeda's military operations.[48]

Al Qaeda acquires weapons and explosives from a variety of sources, depending on the type of operation and its location. The 055 Brigade, for instance—Al Qaeda's guerrilla organization that fought alongside the Taliban against the Northern Alliance—used weapons left behind by the Red Army. It also received weapons from the Taliban and the Pakistani intelligence service, the ISI.

During the 1990s, many of Al Qaeda's procurement officers obtained weapons in Western countries. During bin Laden's stay in Sudan, from 1991 to 1996, the establishment of businesses in the East African country provided much of the cover for the network's procurement of weapons.[49] Al Qaeda's global reach has enabled it to establish a worldwide network of procurement officers. One of them, according to terrorism expert Rohan Gunaratna, was bin Laden's personal pilot, Essam al-Ridi, a U.S. citizen who obtained communication equipment from Japan; scuba gear and range finders from Britain; satellite phones from Germany; night-vision goggles, .50-caliber sniping rifles, and a T-389 plane from America.[50] Al Qaeda has also procured weapons from Russian and Ukrainian organized criminal rings. Al Qaeda's and the IIF's links with organized criminal groups are likely to grow stronger in the aftermath of September 11, as many Western states are stepping up the pressure against Al Qaeda cells operating in some of these countries.

Unconventional Weapons

Bin Laden has repeatedly made clear his desire to acquire unconventional weapons. In January 1999 he told a reporter, "Acquiring weapons for the defense of Muslims is a religious duty. If I have indeed acquired these weapons, then I thank God for enabling me to do so. And if I seek to acquire these weapons, I am carrying out a duty. It would be a sin for Muslims not to try to possess the weapons that would prevent the infidels from inflicting harm on Muslims."[51] After September 11, he pronounced that he already possessed chemical and nuclear weapons.[52] Bin Laden's deputy Ayman Zawahiri wrote in his memoirs that "the targets and the type of weapons must be selected carefully to cause damage to the enemy's structure and deter it enough to make it stop its brutality," probably in reference to unconventional weapons.[53]

Chemical and Biological Weapons. Iraqi chemical-weapons experts shifted some of their operations to Sudan after the Gulf War, according to CIA assessments released to the press. Bin Laden moved to Sudan at about the same time. Beginning in 1995, the CIA began receiving reports that Sudanese leaders had approved bin Laden's request to begin production of chemical weapons to use against U.S. troops stationed in Saudi Arabia.[54] Khidhir Hamza, the director of the Iraqi nuclear weapons program from 1987 to 1990, claimed that bin Laden's agents had contacted Iraq agents with the aim of purchasing weapons components from Iraq. Saddam Hussein reportedly sent Ansar al-Islam, the terrorist group that attempted to assassinate the prime minister of the Kurdistan Regional Government, Barham Salih, to train in Al Qaeda camps.

Ahmed Ressam, one of the Al Qaeda operatives apprehended in the millennium plots, described crude chemical-weapons training at camps in Afghanistan, including experiments on animals.[55] In December 2000, special units of the Italian and German police arrested several Al Qaeda agents based in Milan, Italy, and Frankfurt, Germany, who had plotted to bomb the European Parliament building in Strasbourg, France, using sarin, a nerve agent.[56] Other evidence of the group's interest in chemical and biological weapons includes a manual that provides instructions for using chemical weapons;[57] a manual that provides recipes for producing chemical and biological agents from readily available ingredients;[58] and intercepted phone conversations between Al Qaeda operatives who were discussing unconventional agents.[59]

In August 2002, CNN bought a cache of Al Qaeda videotapes in Afghanistan that showed Al Qaeda's gruesome chemical-weapons experiments, substantiating earlier reports about experiments on animals. On one of these videotapes, several men are seen rushing from an enclosed room, shouting at each other to hurry; they leave behind a dog. After the men leave, a white liquid on the floor forms a noxious gas. The dog is seen convulsing and eventually dies.

A large cache of documents and other materials was found during the raid that led to the capture of Al Qaeda's operational planner, Khalid Shaikh Mohammed, in March 2003. The seized documents revealed that Al Qaeda had acquired the necessary materials for producing botulinum and salmonella toxin and the chemical agent cyanide—and was close to developing a workable plan for producing anthrax, a far more lethal agent. Mohammed had been staying at the home of Abdul Quoddoos Khan, a member of Jamaat-i-Islami. Khan is reportedly a bacteriologist with access to production materials and facilities.[60]

The greatest worry, however, is that the International Islamic Front, possibly working together with Hezbollah or other terrorist groups, will acquire assistance from persons who have access to a sophisticated biological-weapons program, possibly, but not necessarily, one that is state run.

Nuclear Weapons. The U.S. government has been concerned about Al Qaeda's interest in acquiring nuclear weapons since the mid-1990s. In early February 2001, Jamal Ahmad al-Fadl admitted that one of bin Laden's top lieutenants ordered him to try to buy uranium from a former Sudanese military officer named Salah Abdel Mobtuk. The uranium was offered for $1.5 million. Documents described the material as originating in South Africa. Al-Fadl received a $10,000 bonus for arranging the deal. He testified that he does not know the outcome.[61]

U.S. government officials reportedly believe that Al Qaeda successfully purchased uranium from South Africa.[62] Mamdouh Mahmud Salim, a senior deputy to bin Laden, was extradited from Germany to the United States in 1998. The U.S. government accuses Salim of attempting to obtain material that could be used to develop nuclear weapons.[63]

Numerous reports have emerged that bin Laden has forged links with organized criminal groups based in the former Soviet Union, Central Asia, and the Caucasus in his attempts to acquire nuclear weapons.[64] Russian authorities suspect the August 2002 murder of a nuclear chemist may have been linked to a clandestine effort to steal the country's nuclear technology.[65] They also report that they had observed terrorists staking out a secret nuclear-weapons storage facility on two occasions, and that they had thwarted an organized criminal group's attempt to steal 18.5 kilograms of highly enriched uranium.[66] This last claim is unusual and alarming, in part because of the quantity—enough to make several nuclear weapons—and in part because the material was actually weapons-usable. Most press reporting about nuclear thefts turn out, after investigation, to refer to caches of low-enriched uranium or radioactive but not nuclear-weapons-usable materials.

American officials are suspicious about the activities of two Pakistani nuclear scientists, Sultan Bashiruddin Mahmood and Abdul Majid, who reportedly met with bin Laden, Ayman Zawahiri, and two other Al Qaeda officials several times during August 2001. Pakistani officials insist that despite Mahmood's experience in uranium enrichment and plutonium production, the two scientists had "neither the knowledge nor the experience to assist in the construction of any type of nuclear weapon."[67] The two scientists, who were eventually released, reported that during one meeting. Osama bin Laden declared he possessed "some type of radiological material" and was interested in learning how he could use it in a weapon.[68]

If Al Qaeda builds a nuclear weapon or already has one, it is probably a relatively crude device. An extensive study conducted by the Institute for Science and International Security in Washington found "no credible evidence that either bin Laden or Al Qaeda possesses nuclear weapons or sufficient fissile material to make them," but that if Al Qaeda obtained sufficient nuclear-weapons-usable material, it would be capable of building a crude nuclear explosive.[69]

RECRUITMENT

In the years following the Soviet invasion of Afghanistan, Al Qaeda's recruitment was conducted by the Maktab al-Khidamat (MAK—Services office). Osama bin Laden and his spiritual mentor, the Palestinian head of the Muslim Brotherhood, Abdullah Azzam, established the MAK in 1984. The MAK recruited young Muslims to come to Afghanistan to fight the Soviet infidels. With branches in over thirty countries, including Europe and the United States, and a sizable budget, the MAK was responsible for propaganda, fund-raising, and coordinating recruitment. While bin Laden covered the costs for transporting the new recruits, the Afghan government provided the land, and training camps were soon established.[70]

Most Al Qaeda operatives appear to have been recruited by Islamist organizations in their home countries. A Spanish investigation in November 2001, for example, concluded that a group known in Spain as Soldiers of Allah gradually assumed control over the Abu Bakr mosque in 1994. It had financial ties with Al Qaeda and regularly sent volunteers for training in Bosnia, Pakistan, and the Philippines.[71] Surveillance of a key recruitment officer based in Italy, Abu Hamza, revealed a tightly linked network of Al Qaeda recruitment officers in Europe, which included Abu Hamza and Sami Ben Khemais in Italy, Tarek Maaroufi in Belgium, and Abu Dahdah in Spain.[72] In Germany, in addition to recruitment through mainstream Islamic associations and charitable agencies, Al Qaeda recruiting officers used amateur videos of fighting in Chechnya to attract recruits.[73] One two-hour-long recruiting video that was probably produced in the summer of 2001 showed a mock assassination of former president Clinton, along with footage of training bases in Afghanistan. Methodically, the film moves from picture frames of Palestinian children killed or wounded by Israeli soldiers and Muslim women being beaten, to pictures of "great Muslim victories" in Chechnya, Somalia, and against the USS Cole. The video concludes with a call for Muslims to embark on the hegira, or migration, to Afghanistan.[74]

In Pakistan, Indonesia, and Malaysia, seminaries are often fertile ground for recruitment. Many of them promote the excitement of joining the Jihad as much as they do the horror stories of atrocities against Muslims. In Malaysia, a school associated with Al Qaeda issued brochures exhorting young radicals to forgo Palestine for Afghanistan, where they were promised three thousand kilometers of open borders and the friendship of many like-minded colleagues, who had made Afghanistan the international center of Islamic militancy. Abu Bakar Ba'asyir, the spiritual leader of Jamaah Islamiyah, a Southeast Asian terrorist group closely affiliated with Al Qaeda, championed bin Laden and exhorted students in Indonesia and Malaysia to carry on a "personal Jihad" following bin Laden's lead.[75]

The way Khalfan Khamis Mohamed was recruited is typical for foot soldiers. Recruiters locate raw talent in a seminary or a mosque. The raw talent is then sent to a camp, where it is assessed on various dimensions: commitment to Islam, psychological reliability, intelligence, and physical prowess. Identifying reliable recruits is considered the most difficult job. Among Al Qaeda's most well-known and successful recruiters of elite operatives are Muhammad Atef, who was reportedly killed by U.S. bombs in November 2002, and Abu Zubaydah, a Palestinian born in Saudi Arabia, now in U.S. custody.

TRAINING

Osama bin Laden provided training camps and guesthouses in Afghanistan for the use of Al Qaeda and its affiliated groups beginning in 1989. Western intelligence agencies estimate that by September 11, 2001, between 70,000 and 110,000 radical Muslims had graduated from Al Qaeda training camps such as Khalden, Derunta, Khost, Siddiq, or Jihad Wal.[76] Of those, only a few thousand graduates—who distinguished themselves spiritually, physically, or psychologically—were invited to join Al Qaeda. The difficulty of making the cut as a full-fledged recruit meant that Islamists from all over the world regarded joining Al Qaeda as the highest possible honor, Gunaratna explains.[77]

The exact number of training camps in Afghanistan that are associated with Osama bin Laden is unknown, and estimates range from one dozen to over fifty such camps.[78] In the mid-1990s, Al Qaeda shifted its headquarters to Khartoum and established or assisted in the establishment of an estimated twenty training camps in Sudan. Other training camps have been identified in lawless corners of Somalia, Yemen, Indonesia, Chechnya, and other countries. The camps serve a variety of purposes in addition to training members and reserves. They create social ties, so that operatives feel committed to the cause on both ideological and solidarity grounds. Specialists then funnel recruits into the right level of the organization and into the right job: public-relations officer, regional manager, trainer, sleeper, or other.

John Walker Lindh told investigators that the camp he attended near Kandahar offered both basic and advanced training. After the basic training course, trainees can select different tracks to follow, one involving battlefield training and the other "civilian warfare training." The battlefield course includes "advanced topography, ambushes, tactics, battlefield formations, trench warfare . . . practicing assassinations with pistols and rifles, and shooting from motorcycles and cars." The civilian warfare course includes "terrorism, forgery of passports and documents, poisons, mine explosions, and an intelligence course which teaches trainees how to avoid detection by police." Most of the trainees were Saudi, he said. He also said that the leader of the camp approached all foreign trainees to recruit them for "foreign operations." The foreign recruits were instructed not to discuss the conversation about foreign operations with their fellow trainees, and they were not given any details about what the foreign terrorist operations might entail.[79] Trainees were also asked whether they were willing to work in their own country. Lindh said that the leader of the camp, Al Musri, interviewed him personally.

Tapes reportedly captured by the U.S. army in Afghanistan show Al Qaeda members training to carry out operations in the West. The tapes show a level of professionalism that suggests that Al Qaeda had received significant assistance from a professional military, according to an analyst who read the army's assessment and viewed the tapes himself. On one tape, operatives are trained to carry out an ambush near a six-lane high-way similar to those that are found in the United States and Europe. Hostage scenarios include raids of large buildings with many occupants. Trainees playing the role of terrorists dictate commands to the hostages in English, and the trainees playing the hostages respond in English. Operatives are trained to determine whether soldiers or other armed personnel are among the hostages so that those with weapons can be segregated from the rest. The armed hostages are then executed in front of television cameras. Another scenario prepares operatives for assassinating dignitaries—possibly national leaders—on a golf course. It is clear from the tapes that Al Qaeda is training its operatives to maximize media coverage, according to the army's assessment.[80]

The most important aspect of training, however, is mental training and religious indoctrination. Religious indoctrination includes Islamic law and history and how to wage a holy war. The story that recruits must learn is about identity— it is about who *we are* as distinct from *them,* to whom Zawahiri, bin Laden's deputy, refers to as the "new Crusaders."[81]

Most importantly, camps are used to inculcate "the story" into young men's heads. The story is about an evil enemy who, in the words of Zawahiri, is waging a "new Crusade" against the lands of Islam. This enemy must be fought militarily, Zawahiri explains, because that is the only language the West understands. The enemy is easily frightened by small groups of fighters, and trainees learn how to function in small cells.[82]

THE MISSION OF TERRORIST ORGANIZATIONS: THE TERRORIST "PRODUCT"

A professional terrorist chooses his mission carefully. He is able to read popular opinion and is likely to change his mission over time. Astute leaders may find new missions—or emphasize new aspects of the mission—when they realize they can no longer "sell" the old one to sponsors and potential recruits, either because the original mission was achieved or, more commonly, because the impossibility of achieving the mission has become obvious.

Terrorism grows out of seductive solutions to grievances. When revolutions succeed, which happens occasionally, the imperative to address the problems of the aggrieved group comes to be accepted by a wider population. But the

techniques of terror—the deliberate murder of innocent civilians—are counter to every mainstream religious tradition. This is why the mission—the articulation of the grievance—is so important. It must be so compellingly described that recruits are willing to violate normal moral rules in its name.

The people on whose behalf the terrorists aim to fight must be portrayed as worthy of heroic acts of martyrdom. In his memoir, Zawahiri says that an alliance of Jihadi groups and "liberated states" is anxious to seek retribution for the blood of the martyrs, the grief of the mothers, the deprivation of the orphans, the suffering of the detainees, and the sores of the tortured people throughout the land of Islam. He says that this age is witnessing a new phenomenon of *mujaheed* youths who have abandoned their families, countries, wealth, studies, and jobs in search of Jihad arenas for the sake of God.[83]

The enemy must be portrayed as a monstrous threat, Zawahiri warns his followers that the new Crusaders respect no moral boundaries and understand only the language of violence. The enemy is characterized by "brutality, arrogance, and disregard for all taboos and customs." He urges Jihadis to choose weapons and tactics capable of inflicting maximum casualties on the enemy at minimal cost to the mujahideen. He warns followers that the enemy makes use of a variety of tools and proxies, including the United Nations, friendly rulers of the Muslim peoples, multinational corporations, international communications and data exchange systems, international news agencies and satellite media channels. The enemy also uses international relief agencies as a cover for espionage, proselytizing, coup planning, and the transfer of weapons.[84] John Walker Lindh told interrogators that he had decided to "join the fight of the Pakistani people in Kashmir" when he was in a *madrassah* in Pakistan, where he heard reports of "torture, rape, and massacre of the Pakistani people by India." He said that he was overwhelmed by the "guilt of sitting idle while these atrocities were committed," and he volunteered for training, first in Pakistan, then in Afghanistan, ultimately ending up fighting with the Taliban.[85] A trainer for HUM who was interviewed for this book said that he decided to join the Jihad when he was in eleventh grade, after hearing about two Muslim women who were raped by Indian forces.[86] Ironically, the enemy's existence—and even his atrocities—help terrorist groups prove the importance of their mission. The Lashkar e Taiba public-affairs director told me he felt "happy" about the growth of the Hindu extremist group Bajrang Dal, the archnemesis of the Pakistani militant groups. It provides a raison d'etre for Islamic fundamentalism in Pakistan, he said. "What is the logic for stopping the Jihadi groups' activities if the Indian government supports groups like Bajrang Dal?" he asked.[87]

Peter Verkhovensky, a character in Dostoyevsky's 1871 novel *The Demons*, claims to be a socialist but is ultimately exposed as a cheat and a fraud. But the real villains in the novel are the bad ideas that seduced young men to join revolutionary movements. Leaders, who may have been true believers in their youth, cynically take advantage of their zealous recruits, manipulating them with an enticing mission, ultimately using these true believers as their weapons. Joseph Conrad described terrorists as "fools victimized by ideas they cannot possibly believe. . . . While they mouth slogans or even practice anarchist beliefs, their motives are the result of self-display, power plays, class confusion, acting out roles."[88]

Both Dostoyevsky and Conrad understood that the prospect of playing a seemingly heroic role can persuade young men to become ruthless killers in the service of bad ideas, but the bad ideas must be seductively packaged. Terrorist groups have to raise money by "selling" their mission to supporters—including donors, personnel (both managers and followers), and the broader public. Selecting and advertising a mission that will attract donations—of time, talent, money, and for suicide operations, lives—is thus critically important to the group's survival.

Zawahiri observes that the New World Order is a source of humiliation for Muslims. It is better for the youth of Islam to carry arms and defend their religion with pride and dignity than to submit to this humiliation, he says.

Violence, in other words, restores the dignity of humiliated youth. This idea is similar to Franz Fanon's notion that violence is a "cleansing force," which frees the oppressed youth from his "inferiority complex," "despair," and "inaction," making him fearless and restoring his self-respect.[89] Fanon also warned of the dangers of globalization for the underdeveloped world, where youth, who are especially susceptible to the seductive pastimes offered by the West, comprise a large proportion of the population.[90]

Part of the mission of Jihad is thus to restore Muslims' pride in the face of a humiliating New World Order. The purpose of violence, according to this way of thinking, is to restore dignity and to help ward off dangerous temptations. Its target audience is not necessarily the victims and their sympathizers, but the perpetrators and their sympathizers. Violence is a way to strengthen support for the organization and the movement it represents. It is a marketing device and a method for rousing the troops.

In this regard, Zawahiri is conforming also with the views of Sayyid Qutb, whom Zawahiri describes as "the most prominent theoretician of the fundamentalist movements" and Islam's most influential contemporary "martyr." Qutb's outlook on the West changed dramatically after his first visit to America, where he was repulsed by Americans' materialism, racism, promiscuity, and feminism. Americans behave like animals, he said. They justify their vulgarity under the banner of emancipation of women and "free mixing of the sexes." They love freedom, but eschew responsibility for their families.[91] He saw the West as the historical enemy of Islam, citing the Crusades, European colonialism, and the Cold War as evidence. Qutb emphasized the need to cleanse Islam from impurities resulting from its exposure to Western and capitalist influence.

Western values have infiltrated the Muslim elites, who rule according to corrupt Western principles. The enemy's weapons are political, economic, and religio-cultural. They must be fought at every level, Qutb warned.[92] The twin purposes of Jihad are to cleanse Islam of the impurifying influence of the West, and to fight the West using political, economic, and religio-cultural weapons—the same weapons the West allegedly uses against Islam.

ADVERTISING THE MISSION

Like more traditional humanitarian relief organizations, terrorists have to advertise their mission to potential donors and volunteers, and they tend to use similar techniques. As we have seen, they hold auctions, fund-raising dinners, and press conferences. They put up posters and put out newspapers. They cultivate journalists hoping for favorable press coverage. They openly solicit donations in houses of worship, at least where the state allows it. They send leaders on fund-raising missions abroad and arrange for private meetings between leaders and major donors. They make heavy use of the mail, the telephone, and the Internet, often providing their bank account numbers and the bank's address. They demonstrate their effectiveness with sophisticated Web sites, often including photographs or streaming-video recordings of successful operations and of the atrocities perpetrated against the group they aim to help. All of these techniques are practiced by humanitarian organizations. Terrorist groups also advertise the kind of weapons that recruits will learn to use, in some cases including cyberwar. Person-to-person contacts, however, remain a critical component of fund-raising and recruitment drives.[93]

CHANGING THE MISSION

Astute terrorist leaders often realize that to attract additional funding, they may need to give up their original mission. The original mission of Egyptian Islamic Jihad, for example, was to turn Egypt into an Islamic state. By the late 1990s, the group had fallen on hard times. Sheik Omi Abdel Rahman was imprisoned in the United States for his involvement in a plot to bomb New York City landmarks in 1993. Other leaders had been killed or forced to move abroad. Zawahiri reportedly considered moving the group to Chechnya, but when he traveled there to check out the situation, he was arrested and imprisoned for traveling without an entry permit.[94] After his release in May 1997, Zawahiri decided that it would be practical to shift his sights away from the "near enemy," the secular rulers of Egypt, toward the "far enemy," the West and the United States. Switching goals in this way would mean a large inflow of cash from bin Laden, which the group desperately needed. Islamists see Egyptian president Hosni Mubarak, who is supported by the United States, as a traitor to Islam on numerous grounds. He has continued his (assassinated) predecessor's controversial policy of appeasing Israel at the expense of the Palestinians. His administration is widely viewed as corrupt and

repressive. He has expelled or imprisoned most members of the Islamic resistance to his rule. Egyptian human rights organizations estimate that some sixteen thousand people with suspected links to Islamic organizations remain jailed in Egypt.[95]

The alliance between Zawahiri and bin Laden was a "marriage of convenience," according to Lawrence Wright. One of Zawahiri's chief assistants testified in Cairo that Zawahiri had confided in him that "joining with bin Laden [was] the only solution to keeping the Jihad organization alive."[96] "These men were not mercenaries, they were highly motivated idealists, many of whom had turned their backs on middle-class careers. . . . They faced a difficult choice: whether to maintain their allegiance to a bootstrap organization that was always struggling financially or to join forces with a wealthy Saudi who had long-standing ties to the oil billionaires in the Persian Gulf," Wright explains.

After Zawahiri shifted his focus away from Egypt, some of his followers left in protest, forming a splinter faction named Vanguards of Conquest (Talaa' al-Fateh), which was weakened as a result of the Egyptian government's clampdown on Islamists. In return for bin Laden's assistance, Zawahiri provided him some two hundred loyal, disciplined and well-trained followers, who became the core of Al Qaeda's leadership. Zawahiri describes the new mission as a "global battle" against the "disbelievers," who have "united against the mujahideen." He adds, "The battle today cannot be fought on a regional level without taking into account the global hostility towards us."

Another example of a group that changed its mission over time to secure a more reliable source of funding is the Islamic Movement of Uzbekistan. Its original mission was to fight the post-Soviet ruler of Uzbekistan, Islam Katimov, whose authoritarian rule is characterized by corruption and repression.[97] When Juma Namangani, leader of the Islamic Movement of Uzbekistan, was forced underground, together with his followers, they eventually made their way to Afghanistan, where they made contacts with Al Qaeda. Abdujabar Abduvakhitov, an Uzbek scholar who has studied the group since its inception, explains that the group found that by adopting Islamist slogans it could "make more money and get weapons."[98] The IMU shifted its mission from fighting injustice in Uzbekistan to inciting

Islamic extremism and global Jihad, thereby gaining access to financial supporters in Turkey, Saudi Arabia, Pakistan, and Iran, Abduvakhitov explains. The group's new literature promoted the Taliban's agenda, reviling America and the West, but also music, cigarettes, sex, and drink. Its new slogans made the movement repulsive to its original supporters in Uzbekistan, however.[99]

When the IMU terrorists returned to Uzbekistan in 2000, they had medical kits, tactical radios, and night-vision goggles. "All of this speaks to better funding, it speaks to better contacts," an unnamed intelligence officer told the *New York Times*. "They made an impression on bin Laden."[100]

In the spring of 2001 the group entered into an agreement with Mullah Omar, the leader of the Taliban, to delay its Central Asian campaign and to fight the Northern Alliance. Namangani became commander of the 055 Brigade, bin Laden's group of foreign fighters. After September 11, Namangani found himself at war with America. He had alienated his original supporters in his country, and the financial backers he attracted with his turn toward Islamism were no longer able to fund him because they were dispersed and largely broke. He was killed during the war in Afghanistan in November 2001.[101]

Changing the mission can cause a variety of problems. Volunteers may be wedded to the original mission and may resent the need to kowtow to donors, rather than focusing on the needs of the beneficiaries, as happened with the part of Egyptian Islamic Jihad that refused to join forces with bin Laden. Managers are vulnerable to the charge of mission creep. From the viewpoint of the original stakeholders in the organization, there is a principal-agent problem if the group's mission shifts. An important example of this is when a state (or agencies within in a divided state) fund insurgent groups in the belief that they will have total control over the groups' activities. But if a group diversifies its revenue stream, the state may find itself losing control. This is the case with regard to the militant and sectarian groups in Pakistan, which were largely created by the ISI. Now that a significant fraction of these groups' income comes from other entities, the groups are increasingly engaging in activities that are counter to the state's interests. Similarly, Indonesian Jihadi groups that raise money from sources in the Gulf are slipping out of the control of their original backers in the

Indonesian military. (In both these cases, it is important to point out again that the state is not a monolithic entity and that individual agents, or even agencies, may be acting in violation of state policy.)

Osama bin Laden himself has changed his mission over time. He inherited an organization devoted to fighting Soviet forces and turned that organization into a flexible group of ruthless warriors ready to fight on behalf of multiple causes. His first call to holy war, issued in 1992, urged believers to kill American soldiers in Saudi Arabia, the Horn of Africa, and Somalia. There was virtually no mention of Palestine. His second, in 1996, was a forty-page document listing atrocities and injustices committed against Muslims, mainly by Western powers. His third, in February 1998, for the first time urged followers deliberately to target American civilians, rather than soldiers. Although that fatwa mentioned the Palestinian struggle, it was only one of a litany of Muslim grievances. America's "crimes" against Saudi Arabia (by stationing troops near Islam's holiest sites), Iraq, and the other Islamic states of the region constituted a clear declaration of war by the Americans against God, his Prophet, and the Muslims . . . By God's leave, we call on every Muslim who believes in God and hopes for reward to obey God's command to kill the Americans and plunder their possessions wherever he finds them and wherever he can," bin he wrote.[102] On October 7, 2001, in a message released on Al Jazeera television immediately after U.S. forces began bombing in Afghanistan, bin Laden issued his fourth call for Jihad. This time he emphasized Israel's occupation of Palestinian lands and the suffering of Iraqi children under UN sanctions, concerns broadly shared in the Islamic world. While most Muslims reject bin Laden's interpretation of their religion, he felt the moment was ripe to win many over to his anti-Western cause. Bin Laden was competing for the hearts and minds of ordinary Muslims. He said that the September 11 "events" had split the world into two "camps," the Islamic world and "infidels"—and that the time had come for "every Muslim to defend his religion" (echoing President Bush's argument that from now on "either you are with us, or you are with the terrorists"[103]).

Bin Laden's aim was to turn America's response to the September 11 attack into a war between Islam and the West. With this new fatwa, bin Laden was striking at the "very core of the grievances that the common Arab man in the street has toward his respective government, especially in Saudi Arabia," Nawaf Obaid, a Saudi analyst, explained.[104] John Walker "Lindh told U.S. investigators that Al Qaeda had come to believe that it, was more effective to "attack the head of the snake" than to attack secular rulers in the Islamic world.

EXPANDING THE NETWORK

Al Qaeda and the IIF are not only changing their mission over time in response to new situations and new needs, but also their organizational style. With its corporate headquarters in shatters, Al Qaeda and the alliance are now relying on an ever shifting network of sympathetic groups and individuals, including the Southwest Asian Jihadi groups that signed bin Laden's February 1998 fatwa; franchise outfits in Southeast Asia; sleeper cells trained in Afghanistan and dispersed abroad; and freelancers such as Richard Reid, the convicted "shoe bomber," who attempted to blow up a plane. Lone wolves are also beginning to take action on their own, without having been formally recruited or trained by Al Qaeda.

The Al Qaeda organization is learning that to evade law-enforcement detection in the West, it will need to adopt some of the qualities of the virtual network style. Coordination of major attacks in the post-September 11 world, in which law-enforcement and intelligence agencies have formed their own networks in response, will be difficult. Al Qaeda is adapting by communicating over the Internet and by issuing messages intended to frighten Americans and boost the morale of followers. The leadership of Al Qaeda appears to be functioning less as a group of commanders and more as inspirational leaders. A Web site that appeared after September 11 (but is no longer available) offered a special on-line training course that teaches the reader how to make time bombs and detonate enemy command centers. The site invited visitors to read a chapter on the production of explosives, saying, "We want deeds, not words. What counts is implementation." Other sites made reference to the Encyclopedia of Jihad, which provides instructions for creating a "clandestine activity cell," including intelligence, supply, planning and

preparation, and implementation.[105] In an article on the "culture of Jihad," a Saudi Islamist urges bin Laden's sympathizers to take action on their own. "I do not need to meet the Sheikh and ask his permission to carry out some operation, the same as I do not need permission to pray, or to think about killing the Jews and the Crusaders that gather on our lands." He accuses the enemies of Islam of attempting to alter the Saudi education system to describe Jihad as a way of thinking rather than as mode of action. Nor does it make any difference whether bin Laden is alive or dead. "If Osama bin Laden is alive or God forbid he is killed, there are thousand Bin Ladens in this nation. We should not abandon our way, which the Sheikh has paved for you, regardless of the existence of the Sheikh or his absence."[106]

An anonymous article in another Islamist forum, "The lovers of Jihad," argues, "The Islamist view of the confrontation with the United States is settled. Furthermore, it is going to be the new ideology of the second generation of the Jihadi movements around the world. They do not need the existence of bin Laden, after he fulfilled his role in the call and agitation for this project."[107]

As with any network, the challenge for the Al Qaeda network of groups is to balance the needs for resilience and for capacity. Resilience refers to the ability of a network to withstand the loss of a node or nodes. To maximize resilience, the network has to maximize redundancy. Functions are not centralized. (This decreases the efficiency of the organization, but terrorist networks are unlikely to optimize efficiency as they do not have to answer to shareholders and they tend to view the "muscle" as expendable.) Capacity— the ability to optimize the scale of the attack— requires coordination, which makes the group less resilient because communication is required. Effectiveness is a function of both capacity and resilience.

Network theorists suggest that a network of networks is a resilient organization. Within each cluster, every node is connected to every other node in what is known as an "all channel" network. But only certain members of the cluster communicate with other clusters, and the ties between clusters are weak, to minimize the risk of penetration.

The strength of ties is not static, however; it varies over time. Training together in camps establishes trust, the glue that holds a network together. (Recall Fahid's claim that he would not be able to trust Mohamed unless he trained in Afghanistan.) But *task ties,* the term network theorists use for relationships needed to accomplish particular tasks, are likely to be weak or even nonexistent until a leader brings a group together to carry out an operation.

In a law-enforcement-rich environment, the most effective terrorist organization probably consists of many clusters of varying size and complexity held together by trust and a shared mission rather than a hierarchical superstructure. Individual clusters may find their own funding through licit or illicit businesses, donations from wealthy industrialists, wealthy diasporas, or the relationships they develop with states or state agents. Individual groups may even compete for funds in what is known as a chaordic network.[108] They may recruit and arm their groups separately. Innovation—such as attempts to acquire or use unconventional weapons—is promoted at all levels. Some of the clusters will remain dormant until a concrete operation is being planned. Those that are active in failing states where the state either supports them or cannot fight them will be able to remain active full-time. The only thing the sub-networks must have in common is a shared mission and goals.

In this network of networks, leadership style will vary. Complex tasks require hierarchies—the commander cadre-type organization. For very small operations, of the kind that are carried out by the Army of God, little coordination or leadership is required: small cells or lone wolves inspired by the movement can act on their own. Individual operatives can have a powerful effect, as the sniper in suburban Washington in the fall of 2002 made clear. As more powerful weapons become available to smaller groups, virtual networks will become more dangerous.

The use of sleepers can make an organization significantly more resilient. Sleepers are informed of their tasks immediately before the operation. They are likely to be told only what they need to know: information is strictly compartmentalized.[109]

Technology has greatly increased the capacity of networks. Networks can now be decentralized but also highly focused. Members can travel nearly anywhere and communicate with one another anywhere. Money is also easily shipped.[110] This is especially true for organizations like Al

Qaeda, which utilize informal financial transactions and convert their cash into gems or gold.

Since September 11 and the war in Afghanistan, Al Qaeda and the IIF have been forming the kind of network of networks connected by weak ties that network theorists argue is the most effective style of organization, and making use of sleepers and freelancers, which increases the resilience of the alliance.

SOURCES OF FUNDS

As is the case for many terrorist groups, Al Qaeda raises money in four ways: criminal activities, businesses, financial or in-kind assistance from states or state agents, and charitable donations.

Businesses

Al-Fadl testified that bin Laden set up a large number of companies in Sudan, including Wadi-al-Aqiq, a corporate shell that he referred to as the "mother" of all the other companies: Al Hijra Construction, a company that built roads and bridges; Taba Investment, Ltd., a currency trading group; Themar al-Mubaraka, an agriculture company; Quadarat, a transport company; Laden International, an import-export business. Al-Fadl said the group controlled the Islamic bank al-Shamal and held accounts at Barclays Bank in London as well as unnamed banks in Sudan, Malaysia, Hong Kong, Cyprus, the United States, and Dubai.[111] According to the U.S. indictment, "These companies were operated to provide income and to support Al Qaeda, and to provide cover for the procurement of explosives, weapons, and chemicals, and for the travel of Al Qaeda operatives."[112]

Like many terrorist groups, Al Qaeda is involved in both licit and illicit enterprises. Bin Laden attempted to develop a more potent strain of heroin to export to the United States and Western Europe, in retaliation for the 1998 air strikes in Sudan and Afghanistan. He provided protection to processing plants and transport for the Taliban's drug businesses, which financed training camps and supported extremists in neighboring countries, according to the United Nations.[113] Al Qaeda used informal financial transactions known as *hawala,* which are based largely on trust and extensive use of family or regional connections,[114] and a network of honey shops, to transfer funds around the world.[115] It is now converting cash into diamonds and gold.

Charitable Donations

Charities, purportedly unaffiliated with the terrorist groups, seek funding for humanitarian relief operations, some of which is used for that purpose, and some of which is used to fund terrorist operations. Many Jihadi groups use charities for fund-raising abroad or as a front for terrorist activities. Al Qaeda members testified that they received ID cards issued by a humanitarian relief organization based in Nairobi called Mercy International Relief Agency. The organization was involved in humanitarian relief efforts, as its name suggests, but it also served as a front organization for operatives during the period they were planning the Africa embassy bombings.[116]

By soliciting charitable donations abroad, groups draw attention to the cause among diaspora populations. The Gulf States, North America, the United Kingdom, and European countries are important sources of funding for terrorist groups. The U.S. government looked the other way when the IRA engaged in fund-raising dinners in the United States, but began to see the downside to such a policy when the groups being funded began killing American citizens.

But perhaps even more importantly, by soliciting money from the people, a terrorist organization (or terrorist-affiliated organization) can establish its bona fides as a group devoted to the interests of "the people." While much of the group's money may actually come from criminal activities, business operations, or government assistance, charitable donations are important as a "defining source of revenue," a point made in regard to more traditional NGOs by Mark Moore, a specialist in non-profits at Harvard University. In my interviews, leaders tend to emphasize charitable donations as the most important source of revenue for their groups; while operatives, presumably less attuned to the public-relations implications of their words, admit that smuggling, government funding or large-scale donations by wealthy industrialists are the main sources of funding.[117] Money flows into Jihadi groups through charities; but money also flows out to the needy. Sophisticated Jihadi organizations function very much like the United Way.

LEADERLESS RESISTERS, FREELANCERS, AND FRANCHISES

The New World Order and its instruments—Al Qaeda's new foes—are attractive targets to a surprising array of groups. By emphasizing the New World Order as its enemy, Al Qaeda will be able to attract a variety of groups that oppose Western hegemony and international institutions.

White supremacists and Identity Christians are applauding Al Qaeda's goals and actions and may eventually take action on the Al Qaeda network's behalf as freelancers or lone-wolf avengers. A Swiss neo-Nazi named Huber, who is popular with both Aryan youth and radical Muslims, is calling for neo-Nazis and Islamists to join forces. Huber was on the board of directors of the Al-Taqwa Foundation, which the U.S. government says was a major donor to Al Qaeda.[118] The late William Pierce, who wrote *The Turner Diaries*, the book that inspired the Oklahoma City bombing, applauded the September 11 bombers. Pierce's organization, the Alliance Nahad, urged its followers to celebrate the one-year anniversary of September 11 by printing out and disseminating flyers from its Web site. One of the flyers included a photograph of bin Laden and the World Trade Center and the caption, "Let's stop being human shields for Israel."[119] Matt Hale, leader of the World Church of the Creator, a white supremacist organization one of whose members killed a number of blacks and Jews, is disseminating a book that exposes the "sinister machinations" that led to September 11, including the involvement of Jews and Israelis, in particular, the Mossad.[120]

Horst Mahler, a founder of the radical leftist German group the Red Army Faction, has moved from the extreme left to radical right. He too rejoiced at the news of the September 11 attacks, saying that they presage "the end of the American Century, the end of Global Capitalism, and thus the end of the secular Yahweh cult, of Mammonism." He accuses the "one-World strategists" of trying to create a smoke screen to prevent ordinary people from understanding the real cause of September 11, which America brought on itself through its arrogance. "This is war," he says, "with invisible fronts at present, and worldwide." September 11 was just the first blow against the Globalists, whose true aim is to exterminate national cultures, he says. "It is not a war of material powers," he says. "It is a spiritual struggle the war of Western civilization, which is barbarism, against the cultures of the national peoples. . . . The oncoming crisis in the World Economy—independent of the air attacks of 11 September 2001—is now taking the enchantment from 'The American Way of Life.' The absolute merchandisability of human existence—long felt as a sickness—is lost, along with the loss of external objects, in which human beings seek recognition and validation—but cannot find them."[121]

The racist right is also applauding the efforts of other "antiglobalists" in addition to bin Laden. Louis Beam, author of a leaderless-resistance essay, is urging all antiglobalists, from all political persuasions, to join forces against the New World Order (NWO). He applauds the participants of the Battle of Seattle, who, he says, faced, "real invasion of black booted, black suited" thugs, while the racist right continued talking endlessly about the impending invasion of foreign troops in United Nations submarines.

"Mark my words," Beam says, "this is but the first confrontation, there will be many more such confrontations as intelligent, caring people begin to face off the Waco thugs of the New World Order here in the United States. The New American Patriot will be neither left nor right, just a freeman fighting for liberty. New alliances will form between those who have in the past thought of themselves as 'right-wingers,' conservatives, and patriots with many people who have thought of themselves as 'left-wingers,' progressives, or just 'liberal.' "[122]

Perhaps the most articulate proponent of forming an anti-NWO coalition is Keith Preston, a self-described veteran of numerous libertarian, anarchist, leftist, labor, and patriot organizations and an active anarchist. He argues that the war between the "U.S. and the Muslim world" is one front in a larger war, "namely, the emerging global conflict between those interests wishing to subordinate the entire world to the so-called 'New World Order' of global governance by elite financial interests in the advanced countries on one side and all those various national, regional, ethnic, cultural, religious, linguistic, and economic groups who wish to remain independent of such a global order." He believes that the rapid drive to create this NWO must be reversed or it will likely produce a system of totalitarian oppression similar to that of the Nazi and Soviet regimes of the twentieth century only with infinitely greater amounts of economic, technological, and military resources. All forces throughout the world seeking to resist this development must join together, regardless of their other differences, and provide mutual support to one another in the common struggle. The current U.S.-led 'coalition' against so-called 'terrorism' is simply a cover for continuing the process of global consolidation of power and crushing all efforts at resistance. Islamic fundamentalists, he says, are fighting the same global interests seeking to impose "global government, international currency systems, firearms confiscation, international police forces, NAFTA, and other regressive economic policies on the American people." He proposes joining forces even with Jewish fundamentalist sects, "such as the Neturei Karta, who have condemned Israeli imperialism and expansionism." He urges the "bandits and anarchists" to join together with the "tribes, sects, warlords, and criminals" to assert themselves forcefully.[123]

While the threat these groups pose is nowhere near as significant as that of current members of the Al Qaeda alliance, some of their members may decide to support Al Qaeda's goals, as lone wolves or leaderless resisters, giving it a new source of Western recruits.

The tri-border area where Argentina, Brazil, and Paraguay meet is becoming the new Libya: The place where terrorists with widely disparate ideologies—the Marxist groups FARC and ELN, American white supremacists, Hamas, Hezbollah, and members of bin Laden's International Islamic Front—meet to swap tradecraft. Authorities worry that the more sophisticated groups could make use of the Americans as participants in their plots, possibly to bring in materials.

Perhaps the best example of a freelancer—an individual trained by Al Qaeda who takes action largely on his own—is Richard Reid. In October 2002, Richard Reid pled guilty to the charge that he tried to blow up a plane with a bomb hidden in his shoe in December 2001. He also admitted that he was trained at an Al Qaeda camp and said that he was a member of Al Qaeda, a statement that some experts suspect is not literally true. Reid gave in to his interrogators almost immediately, suggesting that he had not undergone the kind of rigorous psychological training that is typical for Al Qaeda members. Magnus Ranstorp, a terrorism expert who has studied the Islamist community in London, from which Reid was apparently recruited, argues that Reid is most likely a fringe amateur inspired by what he saw in Afghanistan and by the movement in general. Others point out that Reid was in contact with Al Qaeda members by e-mail.[124]

Jamaah Islamiyah—The Franchise

The group known as Jamaah Islamiyah grew out of Islamic opposition to Soeharto's regime. Its goal was to establish an Islamic community, *jamaah Islamiyah*, throughout Southeast Asia. Its spiritual leader, Abu Bakar Ba'asyir, founded and runs a *pesantren* (seminary) called Ngruki near Solo, Java, close to the *pesantren* we discussed in chapter 3. Ba'asyir and his closest followers fled to Malaysia in 1985 to escape Soeharto's suppression of the group. Some members returned after Soeharto's resignation in 1998, and some remained in Malaysia. Although some members of Jamaah Islamiyah (JI) have clear links to Al Qaeda, JI is the violent wing of a broader movement that supports Ba'asyir. The movement, known as the Ngruki network, named after Ba'asyir's school, includes a broad range of prominent individuals, some of whom are active in the Indonesian government. Many Indonesians are deeply concerned that the war on terrorism, and the U.S. push to arrest suspects without clear evidence, could radicalize the Muslim community.[125]

THE POST-INDUSTRIAL-AGE TERRORIST ORGANIZATION

Mobilizing terrorist recruits and supporters requires an effective organization. Effectiveness requires resources, recruits, hierarchies, and logistics. It requires adopting the mission to appeal to the maximum number of recruits and financial backers.[126] As we have seen, contestants often choose to call competition for natural resources or political power a religious conflict when they believe it will make their grievances more attractive to a broader set of potential fighters or financial backers. (Governments may do the same by labeling opposition groups religious extremists to win international support for crushing them.)

Money—used to buy goods and services—is a critical component of what distinguishes groups that are effective from those that disappear or fail to have an impact. The terrorists discussed in these pages raise money in a variety of ways. They run licit and illicit businesses. They auction off "relics." They run their own informal banks, which take a "charitable donation" in lieu of interest. They solicit donations on the Internet, on the streets, and in houses of worship. They appeal to wealthy industrialists, sympathetic diasporas, and to governments or their agents. By functioning as a foundation that provides social services, the groups spread their ideas to donors as well as the recipients of their largesse. Recipients of charitable assistance may be more willing to donate their sons to the group's cause.

But terrorist organizations need to balance the requirements for optimizing capacity with those of resilience. Resilience (the ability to withstand the loss of personnel) requires redundancy and minimal or impenetrable communication, making coordination difficult absent cutting-edge encryption technologies. The most resilient group discussed in this book is the save-the-babies group Army of God, a virtual network whose members meet only to discuss the mission, not concrete plans. The drawback from the terrorists' perspective to this maximally resilient style organization is that it requires individuals or small groups to act on their own, making large-scale operations difficult.[127]

The best way to balance these competing objectives is to form a network of networks, which includes hierarchical structures (commanders and cadres); leaderless resisters who are inspired through virtual contacts; and franchises, which may donate money in return for the privilege of participating.[128] The networks are held together mainly by their common mission (although some may be pursuing multiple missions, including local agendas of little interest to the rest of the network). By expanding his mission statement, bin Laden was able to expand his network to include most of the Islamist groups. Groups that are not Islamist but oppose globalization may be willing to donate money or operatives to the anti-New World Order cause.

The Al Qaeda network of networks is at the cutting edge of organizations today. Law-enforcement authorities will continue to discover new cells or clusters, but they will not be able to shut down the movement until bin Laden, his successors, and his sympathizers' call to destroy the New World Order loses its appeal among populations made vulnerable by perceived humiliation and violations of human rights, perceived economic deprivation, confused identities, and poor governance.

There is a trade-off for policy makers between the need to destroy the adversary that is about to strike and the need to fight the movement over the long term. Our military action becomes the evidence our enemies need to prove the dangers of the New World Order they aim to fight. It creates a sense of urgency for the terrorists seeking to purify the world through murder.

It is part of the human condition to lack certainty about our identities; the desire to see ourselves in opposition to some Other is appealing to all of us. That is part—but only part—of what religion is all about. One of our goals must be to make the terrorists' purification project seem *less* urgent: to demonstrate the humanity that binds us, rather than allow our adversaries to emphasize and exploit our differences to provide a seemingly clear (but false) identity, at the expense of peace.

NOTES

1. Hidaya Rubea Juma, mother of Khalfan Khamis Mohamed. Quoted in "Special Assignment," SABC Africa News, date unavailable.

2. R. F. Burton, *Zanzibar: City, Island, and Coast* (London: Tinsley Brothers, 1872), 117. The monsoon between December and February blows north, northeast from the Arabian peninsula and the west coast of India, then reverses direction in April. This remarkable pattern of winds made oceangoing trade possible before overland commerce was possible. Michael F. Lofchie, *Zanzibar: Background to Revolution* (Princeton, N.J.: Princeton University Press, 1965), 21.

3. Lofchie, *Zanzibar*, 24. Lofchie explains the Persians mingled completely with the Africans and were no longer detectable as a separate group. Arabs, who arrived later, became the upper classes in Zanzibar, while immigrants from the Indian subcontinent were traders, and the Africans became the lowest class.

4. Nathalie Arnold, telephone conversation with the author, 14 October 2002. Bruce McKim, telephone conversation with the author, 16 October 2002; Human Rights Watch, "Tanzania: 'The Bullets Were Raining'—The January 2001 Attack on Peaceful Demonstrators in Zanzibar." *Human Rights Watch Report*, 14, no. 3 (A) (April 2002), last accessed 16 October 2002, www.hrw.org/reports/2002/tanzania/ zanz0402.pdf.

5. Arnold, telephone conversation. McKim, telephone conversation.

6. Quoted in "Pemba Island," All About Zanzibar Web site, last accessed 16 October 2002, www.allaboutzanzibar.com/indepth/guidebook/pb00–01–11.htm.

7. Alice Werner, *Myths and Legends of the Bantu* (London: Cass, 1968). See chapter 16, "Doctors, Prophets, and Witches," available in the book's on-line version at the Najaco Web site, last accessed 16 October 2002, www.najaco.com/books/myths/bantu/16.htm.

8. Werner, *Myths and Legends*. See also John, E. E. Craster, *Pemba: The Splee Island of Zanzibar* (London: T. F. Unwin, 1913). Werner believes that some of these stories reflect the prejudices of white Christians.

9. *United States of America v. Usama bin Laden, et al.*, S(7) 98 Cr. 1023 (27 June 2001), 8321.

10. Ibid., 8324–25.

11. This material summarizes Federal Bureau of Investigation, FD-302a, of Khalfan Khamis Mohamed, 10/5–7/99 at Cape Town, South Africa. Marked "particularly sensitive." This document was entered into evidence at Mohamed's trial.

12. Ibid.

13. Ibid.

14. Ibid.

15. *United States of America v. Usama bin Laden* (27 June 2001), 8327–28.

16. Ibid., 8329.

17. Ibid., 8328.

18. This material summarizes Federal Bureau of Investigation, FD-302a.

19. *United States of America v. Usama bin Laden*, (2 May 2001), 5437.

20. This material summarizes Federal Bureau of Investigation, FD-302a.

21. Ibid.

22. *United States of America v. Usama bin Laden*, (28 June 2001), 8431.

23. Ibid., 8431–32.

24. Ibid., (3 July 2001), 8740.

25. Quoted in Benjamin Weiser and Tim Golden, "Al Qaeda: Sprawling, Hard-to-Spot Web of Terrorists-in-Waiting," *New York Times*, 30 September 2001, 1B4.

26. Testimony of Jerrold Post, *United States of America v. Usama bin Laden* (27 June 2001), 8311–62.

27. Excerpts of the Al Qaeda training manual are available at the Web site of the U.S. Department of Justice, last accessed 14 January 2003, www.usdoj.gov/ag /trainingmanual.htm.

28. See the Web site of the U.S. Department of Justice, last accessed 11 October 2002, www.usdoj.gov/ag/manualpart1_1.pdf, "Declaration of Jihad (Holy War) against the Country's Tyrants—Military Series," First Lesson, p. 13 (translated version).

29. Ibid., Second Lesson, pp. 15–20 (translated version).

30. Copies of the more extensive *Encyclopedia of the Afghan Jihad* were found from Al Qaeda members arrested in Asia, the Middle East, and Europe. The *Encyclopedia* covers tactics, security, intelligence, handguns, first aid, explosives, topography, land surveys and weapons, and has been compiled since Soviet troops withdrew from Afghanistan in 1989. Originally designed as a record of the Afghan fighters' knowledge and experience in guerrilla warfare, it gradually came to include terrorist tactics, as Al Qaeda developed into a terrorist organization. A work of several thousand pages written and translated over five years, the *Encyclopedia* also appeared in CD-ROM in 1996. For more information on the *Encyclopedia of the Afghan Jihad,* see Rohan Gunaratna, *Inside Al Qaeda: Global Network of Terror* (New York: Columbia University Press, 2002), 70.

31. Well-known members of the Shura Council include Muhammed Atef, an Egyptian who served as military commander and was reportedly killed in Afghanistan in late 2001 and Ayman al-Zawzhiri, a surgeon who runs the Egyptian Islamic Jihad, responsible for the 1981 assassination of President Anwar el-Sadat of Egypt. For other members of the council, see testimony of Jamal Ahmad al-Fadl, *United States of America v. Usama bin Laden* (6 February 2001), 204–07.

32. Ibid., 204–214.

33. Bruce R. Auster et al., "The Recruiter for Hate," *U.S. News & World Report,* 31 August 1998, 48.

34. The explosion blew a hole in the fuselage, and only an extraordinary flight performance by the pilot enabled an emergency landing at Naha airport in Okinawa. Gunaratna, *Inside Al Qaeda,* 175.

35. For more on the Bojinka Plot—also known as Oplan Bojinka—see Simon Reeye, *The New Jackals: Ramzi Yousef, Osama bin Laden and the Future of Terrorism* (Boston, Mass.: Northeastern University Press, 1999), 71–93; and Gunaratna, *Inside Al Qaeda,* 175–77.

36. Judy Aita, "U.S. Completes Presentation of Evidence in Embassy Bombing Trial: Defense Expected to Begin Its Case April 16," The Washington File, Office of International Information Programs, U.S, Department of State, April 2002, last accessed 2 October 2002, www.usinfo.state.gov/regional/af/security/a1040558.htm.

37. See, for example, *United States of America v. Mokhtar Haouari,* S(4) 00 Cr. 15 (3 July 2001), 630–35 (www.news.findlaw.com/cnn/docs/haouari/ushaouari70301rassamtt.pdf).

38. Peter L. Bergen, *Holy War, Inc.: Inside the Secret World of Osama bin Laden* (New York: Free Press, 2001), 185.

39. Statement for the Record of J. T. Caruso, Acting Assistant Director, Counter-Terrorism Division, Federal Bureau of Investigation (FBI), on Al-Qaeda International Before the Subcommittee on International Operations and Terrorism Committee on Foreign Relations, United States Senate, Washington, D.C., 18 December 2001. Available on the Web site of the FBI, last accessed 2 October 2002, www.fbi.gov/congress/congress01/carus0121801.htm.

40. For a summary of President Musharraf's 12 January 2002 speech, see "Musharraf Declares War on Extremism," BBC News Online, 12 January 2002, last accessed 18 October 2002, www.news.bbc.co.uk/1/hi/world/south_asia/1756965.stm. See also "Pakistan's Leader Comes Down Hard on Extremists," CNN.com, 12 January 2002, last accessed 18 October 2002, www.cnn.com/2002/WORLD/asiapef/south/01/12/pakistan.india/.

41. See, for example, "Confessions of an Al-Qaeda Terrorist," *Time,* 23 September 2002, 34.

42. Kit R. Roanet, David E. Kaplan, Chitra Ragavan, "Putting Terror Inc. on Trial in New York," *U.S. News & World Report,* 8 January 2001, 25.

43. See, for example, Bergen, *Holy War, Inc.,* 80.

44. Gunaratna, *Inside Al Qaeda,* 58–59.

45. Peter Baker, "Defector Says bin Laden Had Cash, Taliban in His Pocket," *Washington Post,* 30 November 2001, Al. See also Molly Moore and Peter Baker, "Inside Al Qaeda's Secret World; bin Laden Bought Precious Autonomy," *Washington Post,* 23 December 2001, A1.

46. Baker, "Defector Says bin Laden Had Cash," Al.

47. Osama bin Laden established the International Islamic Front in a statement calling for a Jihad against the Jews and Crusaders on 23 February 1998. Signatories other than Osama bin Laden were Ayman al-Zawahri, leader of Egypt's Jihad group, Rifai Taha, head of Egypt's Gama's al-Islamiya, Mir Hamza, secretary general of Pakistan's Ulema Society, and Fazlul Rahman, head of the Jihad Movement in Bangladesh. Other organizations whose membership in the IIF has been publicized include the Partisans Movement in Kashmir (Harkat ul-Ansar), Jihad Movement in Bangladesh, and the Afghan military wing of the "Advice and Reform" commission led by Osama bin Laden, last accessed 21 March 2003, http://ww.satp.org/satporgtp/usa/IIF.htm.

48. Gunaratna, *Inside Al Qaeda,* 57–58.

49. *United States of America v. Usama bin Laden* (4 June 2001), 7007.

50. Gunaratna, *Inside Al Qaeda,* 60.

51. "Exclusive Interview: Conversation with Terror," *Time,* 11 January 1999, available on-line at *Time Asia last accessed* 8 October 2002, www.time.com/time/asia/news/interview/0,9754,174550–1,00.html.

52. Pamela Constable, "Bin Laden Tells Interviewer He Has Nuclear Weapons," *Washington Post,* 11 November 2001, A32.

53. Ayman al-Zawahirl, *Knights under the Prophet's Banner,* chap. 11. Excerpts of the book were translated by FBIS. See "*Al-Sharq al-Awsat* Publishes Extracts from Al-Jihad Leader Al-Zawahiri's New

Book," *Al-Sharq al-Awsat* (London), 2 December 2001, in FBIS-NES-2002–0108, Document ID GMP20020108000197.

54. James Risen, "Question of Evidence: A Special Report: To Bomb Sudan Plant, or Not: A Year Later, Debates Rankle," *New York Times,* 26 October 1999, A1.

55. Testimony by Ahmed Ressam, *United States of America v. Mokhlar Haouari* (5 July 2001), 620–22.

56. See, for example, Peter Finn, "Five Linked to Al Qaeda Face Trial in Germany; Prosecutors Focus on Alleged Bombing Plans," *Washington Post,* 15 April 2002, A13.

57. This manual was found in the house of a Libyan Al Qaeda member who lived in Manchester, England. Benjamin Weiser, "A Nation Challenged: The Jihad, Captured, Terrorist Manual Suggests Hijackers Did a Lot by the Book," *New York Times,* 28 October 2001, A8.

58. The manual was part of the so-called *Encyclopedia of the Afghan Jihad,* a seven-thousand-pages-long collection, which used to consist of ten volumes, of guidelines for terrorist attacks against targets worldwide. See Gunaratna, *Inside Al Qaeda,* 70. See also Mark Boettcher, "Evidence Suggests Al Qaeda Pursuit of Biological, Chemical Weapons," CNN.com, 14 November 2001, last accessed 8 October 2002, www.cnn.com/2001/WORLD/asiapcf/central/11/14/chemical.bio/.

59. On 13 March 2001, Italian authorities bugged a conversation in which a Milan-based Al Qaeda cell led by a Tunisian, Essid Sami Ben Khomais, spoke of "an extremely efficient liquid that suffocates people" and that was to be "tried out" in France. The liquids, one cell member was overheard saying, could secretly be placed in tomato cans and would be dispersed when the cans were opened. See Peter Finn and Sarah Delaney, "Al Qaeda's Tracks Deepen in Europe; Surveillance Reveals More Plots, Links," *Washington Post,* 22 October 2001, A1. See also "Disturbing Scenes of Death Show Capability with Chemical Gas," CNN.com, 19 August 2002, last accessed 8 October 2002, www.cnn.com/2002/US/08/19/terror.tape.chemical/index.html.

60. Barton Gellman, "Al Qaeda Near Biological, Chemical Arms Production," *Washington Post,* 23 March 2003, A1.

61. *United States of America v. Usama bin Laden,* (7 February 2001), 357–365.

62. Gunaratna, *Inside Al Qaeda,* 36.

63. *United States of America v. Usama bin Laden* (19 June 2001), 7464.

64. "Report Links bin Laden, Nuclear Weapons," *Al-Watan al-Arabi,* 13 November 1998; available from FBIS, Document ID FTS19981113001081. Quoted in Kimberly McCloud and Matthew Osborne, "CNS Reports: WMD Terrorism and Usama bin Laden," Web site of the Center for Nonproliferation Studies, Monterey Institute of International Studies, last accessed 8 October 2002, www.cns.miis.edu/pubs/reports/binladen.htm. The November report in *Al-Watan* followed that in another Arabic newspaper, the London-based *Al-Hayat,* which declared that bin Laden had already acquired nuclear weapons. "An Aide to the Taliban Leader Renews His Refusal to Give Information on Nuclear Weapons to bin Laden from Central Asia," *Al-Hayat,* 6 October 1998, quoted in McCloud and Oshorne, "CNS Reports." See also Joseph, "Chemical Labs Show Al Qaeda Still Active."

65. Joseph, "Chemical Labs Show Al Qaeda Still Active."

66. Steven Erlanger, "Lax Nuclear Security in Russia Is Cited as Way for bin Laden to Get Arms," *New York Times,* November 12, 2001.

67. Kamran Khan and Molly Moore, "2 Nuclear Experts Briefed bin Laden, Pakistanis Say," *Washington Post,* 12 December 2001, A1. See also Peter Baker and Kamran Khan, "Pakistan to Forgo Charges Against 2 Nuclear Scientists; Ties to Bin Laden Suspected," *Washington Post,* 30 January 2002, A1.

68. Ibid.

69. David Albright, Kathryn Buchler, and Holly Higgins, "Bin Laden and the Bomb," *Bulletin of the Atomic Scientists,* January/February 2002, 23.

70. ICT, "Al-Qa'ida (The Base)," International Policy Institute for Counter-Terrorism (ICT), Herzliyya, Israel, last accessed 9 October 2002, www.icr.org.il/inter_ter/orgdet.cfm?orgid=74.

71. "Bin Laden's Martyrs for the Cause: Thousands of Terrorists. Dozens of Cells, One Mission," *Financial Times,* 28 November 2001, 17.

72. The information about the European recruiters is taken from *The Recruiters,* produced by Alex Shprintsen, edited by Annie Chartrand, June 2002, CBC News, Canada. A summary of the documentary is available on the Web site of the Canadian Broadcasting Corporation, last accessed 10 October 2002, www.cbc.ca/national/news/recruiters/network.html/.

73. "Bin Laden's Martyrs for the Cause," 17.

74. Michael Powell, "Bin Laden Recruits with Graphic Video," *Washington Post,* 27 September 2001, A19.

75. "Alliance Says It Has Found a School Run by a Tiran of Terrorism," *New York Times,* 1 December 2001: Jane Perlez, "School in Indonesia Urges 'Personal Jihad' in Steps of Bin Laden," *New York Times,* 3 February 2002.

76. The German Bundeskriminalamt, the Federal Criminal Agency, estimates the number of militant Islamic trainees at Al Qaeda training camps at 70,000. See "Bin Laden's Martyrs for the Cause," 17. The CIA estimates the number at 110,000. Quoted in Gunaratna, *Inside Al Qaeda,* 8. Of the 6–7 million Al Qaeda supporters, some 120,000 are willing to take up

arms. Estimates of the Central Intelligence Agency, quoted in Gunaratna, *Inside Al Qaeda*, 95.

77. Gunaratna, *Inside Al Qaeda*, 8.

78. Walter Pincus and Vernon Locb, "Former Recruits Provide Best Knowledge of Camps; Intelligence on Targeted bin Laden Training Sites Sketchy," *Washington Post*, 8 October 2001, A16.

79. Department of Defense, Interrogation Report of John Walker Lindh, JPWL-000389–000407, 402–03. Declassified 5 March 2002.

80. Bryan Preston, "Inside Al Qaeda's Training Camps," *National Review*, 1 October 2002. Available at the Web site of National Review Online, last accessed 19 October 2002, www .nationalreview .com/comment/ comment-preston100102.asp.

81. "*Al-Sharq al-Awsat* Publishes Extracts." Parts one through eleven of serialized excerpts from Egyptian Al-Jihad Organization leader Ayman al-Zawahiri's book, "Knights under the Prophet's Banner" (FBIS translated text, henceforth: Ayman al-Zawahiri, "Knights under the Prophet's Banner Part: 1).

82. Ibid. Part I

83. Ibid. Part XI

84. Ibid. Part XI

85. Department of Defense, Interrogation Report of John Walker Lindh.

86. Interview with HM-1, Pakistan, 2002. Interviewer: Muzamal Suherwardy.

87. Lashkar e Taiba public affairs officer, interview with the author, 3 August 2001. This interview was attended by a Pakistani journalist who writes under a pseudonym for tehelka.com, an electronic newspaper published in India. He wrote an article that highlighted this surprising admission.

88. Frederick R. Karl, Introduction to Joseph Conrad, *The Secret Agent* (New York and London: Penguin, 1983 edition).

89. Franz Fanon, *The Wretched of the Earth* (New York: Grove Press, 1963), 94.

90. Ibid., 195–97.

91. See John Esposito, *Unholy War: Terror in the Name of Islam* (New York: Oxford University Press, 2002), 43.

92. Ibid.

93. Based on interviews in the United States, Lebanon, Gaza, Israel, Pakistan, and Indonesia, 1998–2001.

94. Andrew Higgins and Allan Cullison, "Saga of Dr. Zawahiri Sheds Light on the Roots of Al Qaeda Terror: How a Secret, Failed Trip to Chechnya Turned Key Plotter's Focus to America and bin Laden," *Wall Street Journal*, 2 July 2002.

95. Neil MacFarquhar, "Islamic Jihad, Forged in Egypt, Is Seen as bin Laden's Backbone," *New York Times*, 4 October 2001, B4.

96. Lawrence Wright, "The Man behind bin-Laden," *New Yorker*, 16 September 2002, 77.

97. See, for example, Ahmed Rashid, "The Taliban: Exporting Extremism," *Foreign Affairs*, November/December 1999; Ahmed Rashid, *Jihad: The Rise of Militant Islam in Central Asia* (New Haven, Conn.: Yale University Press, 2002); and Gunaratna, *Inside Al Qaeda*, 168–72.

98. C. J. Chlvers, "Uzbek Militants Decline Provides Clues to U.S.," *New York Times*, 8 October 2002, A15.

99. Ibid.

100. Ibid.

101. Ibid.

102. Bernard Lewis, "License to Kill," *Foreign Affairs*, November/December 1998, 15.

103. John F. Burns, "Bin Laden Taunts U.S. and Praises Hijackers," *New York Times*, 8 October 2001, A1. A transcript of President Bush's 20 September 2002 speech is available at the Web site of the White House. "Address to a Joint Session of Congress and the American People," United States Capital, Washington, D.C., 20 September 2002, Last accessed 19 October 2002, www.whitehouse.gov/news/releases/2001/09/20010920–8.html.

104. Judith Miller, "Bin Laden's Media Savvy: Expert Timing of Threats," *New York Times*, 9 October 2001, B6.

105. "UK-Based Paper Notes Al-Qa'ida Military Training on internet Site, Encyclopedia in *Al-Sharq al-Awsat* (London), 16 February 2002. Available in FBIS-NES-2002–0216, Article ID GMP20020216000057.

106. *Thaqafat al-Jihad*, placed by "OBL2003." http://members.lycos.co.uk/himmame/vb/printthread.php?threadid=1881. Printed (in translation) in Reuven Paz, editor. The Project for the Research of Islamist Movements (PRISM), Occasional Papers, Volume 1 (2003), Number 3 (March 2003).

107. *Bayan U-Taliban yu'akid an bin Laden taliq walam yu'takjal* (A statement by Taliban confirms that Bin Laden is free and has not been arrested). See on-line In: http://www .o-alshahada.nct/vb/printhead .phb?s=& threadid=82. Printed (in translation) in Reuven Paz, editor. The Project for the Research of Islamist Movements (PRISM), Occasional Papers, Volume 1 (2003), Number 3 (March 2003).

108. Dec Hock, *Birth of the Chsordic Age* (San Francisco: Barrott Koehler Publishers, 1999).

109. Virtual networks of leaderless resisters make sense for groups that will be satisfied with the kind of attacks that can be carried out by small groups or individuals acting on their own. The mission is openly communicated, but detailed plans are not discussed with the leadership of the movement or among groups. The need for secrecy and the need for inspirational leaders to be able to plausibly deny their knowledge of past or present plots distort the communication flow.

110. Manuel Castells, *The Rise of the Network Society* (Cambridge, Mass.: Blackwell Publishers, 1996). Quoted in Joel Garreau, "Disconnect the Dots," *Washington Post,* 17 September 2001, C1.

111. Richard Wolfe, Carola Hoyos, and Harvey Morris, "Bin Laden's Wealth Put in Doubt by Saudi Dissidents," *Financial Times,* 24 September 2001, 5.

112. Paul McKay, "The Cost of Fanatical Loyalty," *Ottauid Citizen,* 23 September 2001, A8.

113. Barry Meler, " 'Super' Heroin Was Planned by bin Laden, Reports Say," *New York Times,* 4 October 2001, B3.

114. For more information on the remittance system of *hawala,* see the Web site of Interpol, last accessed 7 January 2003, www.interpol.inr/Public/FinancialCrime/MoneyLaundering/hawala/default.asp#2.

115. Douglas Frantz, "Ancient Secret System Moves Money Globally," *New York Times,* 3 October 2001, B5. See also Judith Miller and Jeff Gerth, "Business Fronts: Honey Trade Said to Provide Funds and Cover to bin Laden," *New York Times,* 11 October 2001, A1.

116. *United States of America v. Usama bin Laden* (26 February 2001), 1415.

117. Interviews with Laskar Jihad, Jakarta, 9 August 2001, and Yogyakarra, 11 August 2001; questionnaires administered in Pakistan.

118. Mark Hosenball, "Terror's Cash Flow," *Newsweek,* 25 March 2002, 28.

119. See for example, "Hate Literature Blitz Planned by Neo-Nazi Groups to Coincide with Jewish Holidays and 9/11," Anti-Defamation League (ADL) press release, 27 August 2002. Available at the ADL Web site, last accessed 13 January 2003, www.adl.org/ PresRele/ASUS_12/4148_12.asp. The flyer can be viewed at the National Alliance Chicago Web site, last accessed 13 January 2003, www.natallchicago.com/ Human-Shields2.pdf.

120. See the Web site of the World Church of the Creator, last accessed 13 January 2003, www.creator.org/.

121. The article can be found in German at www.cleutsches-reich.de, last accessed 17 March 2003.

122. Louis Beam, "Battle in Seattle: Americans Face Off the Police State," last accessed 14 January 2003, www.louisbeam.com/seattle.htm.

123. See Web site of the American Revolutionary Vanguard, last accessed 14 January 2003, www.attackthesystem.com/islam.html.

124. Thanassis Cambanis and Charles M. Sennott, quoting Magnus Rarustorp et al., "Fighting Terror: Going After the Network Cells; Qaeda Seen Still Dangerous," *Boston Globe,* 6 October 2002, A17.

125. In December 2001, Singapore authorities arrested fifteen Islamist militants who had plotted to bomb U.S. targets, including naval vessels in Singapore. The commander of the group was an Indonesian based in Malaysia named Ruduan Lamuddin (known as Hambali), whom Senior Minister Lee Kuan Yew referred to as Bashir's "right-hand man." The same group was accused of planning to bomb U.S. embassies in Southeast Asia on the anniversary of September 11. Details of the plot, and the relationship of Jamaah Islamiyah to Al Qaeda, were revealed to U.S. investigators by Al Qaeda's regional manager in Southeast Asia, Omar al Faruq.

Jamaah Islamiyah has been involved in a series of failed attempts to attack Western targets in Singapore, and information about its planned attacks led the Untied States to shut embassies in Southeast Asia on several occasions. The group has also attempted several times to assassinate Megawati. Singaporean investigators have learned about how JI functions from the operatives they took into custody in December 2001 and August 2002. Several JI members had been trained in Al Qaeda camps in Afghanistan. Others were trained in Mindanao by the Moro Islamic Liberation Front. JI leaders were instructed by Al Qaeda to stay away from mainstream Muslim life in Singapore to avoid drawing attention to themselves. They were not active in *madrassaht.*

126. A good example of a broad mission statement is the one that was used to mobilize participants in the Battle of Seattle. Groups opposed the World Trade Organization (WTO) for multiple reasons. American unions, supporters of Ralph Nader, and environmentalists were on the same side for completely different reasons. They demanded that WTO members adopt mandatory standards regarding pollution and protecting workers—in the case of the unions, because it would help them compete with their third-world rivals, and in the case of the environmentalists and "Naderites" because it would reduce worldwide emissions and promote workers' health. Developing countries opposed the WTO because they feared it would impose precisely those standards, which would help rich companies in the West at the expense of the poor in the third world.

127. The Battle of Seattle is perhaps the best example of an operation that succeeded despite the inherent difficulties of surmounting this problem. Individuals came to Seattle for their own reasons.

128. Ronfeldt and Arquilla argue, in contrast, that swarming is the ideal approach for networked terrorist organizations. But I argue that the requirement for secrecy will make large-scale swarming difficult for terrorist organizations, absent impenetrable communication systems. For their argument, see David Ronfeldt and John Arquilla, "Networks, Netwars, and the Fight for the Future," last accessed 15 August 2002, www.firstmonday.dk/issues.issue6_10/ronfeldt/.

5

HOMEGROWN TERRORISM
IN THE UNITED STATES

Resistance to tyrants is obedience to God.

—Thomas Jefferson

Terrorism is part of U. S. history, although the image of terrorists may have changed over time. Stories have been written and songs have been passed down about the 19th-century American terrorist John Brown. His army was made up of 18 men, including several of his sons. They took prominent citizens hostage and captured the federal arsenal in Harpers Ferry, Virginia, in 1859. Brown's intention was to liberate slaves from the region, form them into an army, and free all the slaves in the South. His group was surrounded and overcome by local militia and later captured by federal troops. The raid itself was a fiasco. Many in the group were killed during the battle; the rest were hanged later (Oates, 1979). Brown was seen as a fanatic and murderer by slaveholders against whom his uprising was aimed, but in contrast, abolitionists who agreed with his philosophy saw Brown as the embodiment of all that was noble and courageous (Chowder, 2000). The attack on Harpers Ferry polarized the nation and helped propel it into the Civil War.

The United States has a long history of political violence, but until recently, few scholars characterized those actions as terrorism (White, 1998). This limited perspective has resulted in a lack of systematic knowledge and research about terrorism throughout the history of this country. The Uniform Crime Report, since its inception in the 1930s, has continually improved the reporting of other types of criminal behavior, but there is no similar source for domestic terrorism, and official data remain sketchy (Hamm, 1998). The full extent of death and injury that has resulted from homegrown terror will never be known because hate crimes in the United States may be recorded as arsons, homicides, and assaults rather than as terrorism (American Psychological Association, 1998). The Intelligence Report from the Southern Poverty Law Center counted 803 active hate groups in the U.S. in 2005. Although crimes committed by hate groups may not be counted as terrorist events, the groups can be classified into six basic categories, which demonstrate that they have six common belief systems and agree on six political agendas, which may include violence. The six categories are Black Separatist, Ku Klux Klan, Neo-Nazi, Racist Skinhead, Christian Identity, and Neo-Confederate.

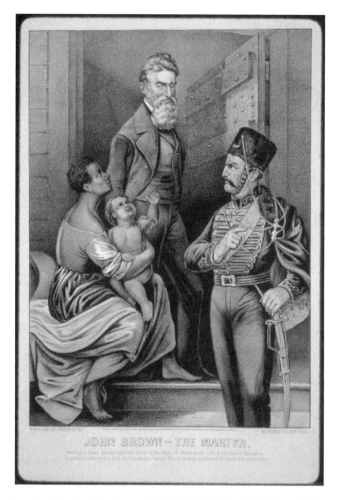

PHOTO 5.1   American abolitionist John Brown (1800–1859). He led the ill-fated raid on Harpers Ferry, West Virginia, in which two of his sons were killed and he was wounded. He was executed on charges of treason and murder. Printed by Currier & Ives, circa 1859.

There are other hate groups that do not fit within these six categories and whose activities have been described by some as terrorism. For example, the anti-immigration forces of the Minuteman Project display weapons on their Internet site in photos of members patrolling the U. S. border. This group of volunteer vigilantes considers the threat of violence to be a meaningful strategy for protecting the U.S. border from illegal immigrants. They have been blamed for ambushes and attacks on illegal immigrants, but their activities are rarely defined as terrorism.

For analytical purposes, in this chapter homegrown terrorist campaigns waged in the United States are divided into five categories, based on their ideologies. The discussion of homegrown terror begins with state-sponsored terror conducted by government authorities. Next, left-wing class struggles including those of communists and socialists are covered. The third category includes anarchists, whose ecoterrorism may be in aid of animals or the Earth itself. The last two categories may both be considered right-wing, but a distinction is made between them based on their aims. The two right-wing categories are White supremacists and religious extremists. These two categories often overlap, but they have also developed separately—White supremacists without religion, and religious extremists without racism (Harmon, 2000; White, 1998; Zulaika & Douglas, 2000).

Photo 5.2   A Ku Klux Klan meeting in Denver, Colorado.

Some striking similarities exist among all terrorist ideologies, regardless of the terrorists' political affiliation, from self-styled defenders of liberty in the United States to Islamic extremists in Iran (McGuckin, 1997). Religious fanatics are emphasized here because they do not appear to recognize any of the political, moral, or practical considerations that constrain other terrorist groups from causing mass death and destruction (Hoffman, 1998). As the following analysis makes clear, these are not discrete categories, however. Of more concern than analytical categories are the actual connections between groups from across the spectrum in the United States, connections based on hatred and an antiglobalization ideology.

STATE-SPONSORED TERRORISM

Terror from above relies on the manufacture and *wholesale* spread of fear by authorities, Congress, and the president (Herman, 1982). U.S. citizens are likely to think that *wholesale* terror is sponsored by tyrannical governments in the Middle East or Latin America, but U.S. authorities have also taken violent military actions against U.S. citizens. Indigenous Americans were attacked and their culture all but eradicated by official government policy throughout the 19th century. For example, the Removal Act of 1830 caused the forced march of the five great Indian tribes (Cherokee, Choctaw, Chickasaw, Creek, and Seminole) from their farms and businesses along the eastern seaboard to the badlands of Oklahoma. Many died from the harsh conditions along the way, known as the Trail of Tears. Those who survived found the way of life on the reservations under government control to be treacherous and bleak. Domination and genocide characterized many of the policies carried out by U.S. government agencies against Native Americans (Cherokee Nation, n.d.; Golden Ink, n.d.).

Labor organizers were also systematically besieged by government forces during their struggle to form unions throughout the early decades of the 20th century. The Ludlow massacre in

Colorado in 1914 is one example of the use of government agents as terrorists. National Guardsmen attacked a tent colony during a strike against the Colorado Fuel and Iron Co. Wives and children of workers were set aflame, adding another chapter to the bloody history of the labor movement in the United States (Millies, 1995).

In both of these examples, and in many others, formal policies were developed to carry out a campaign of terror. Official U.S. forces were used by authorities to threaten or deliver violence, as a means of furthering political agendas. It is essential to understand the impact of *wholesale* (state-sponsored) terrorism in order to understand *retail* terrorism (Herman, 1982). Retail terrorists are isolated individuals and small groups. A substantial proportion of them arise as a response to official failures and wholesale injustices. Terrorism prevention thus begins with dealing intelligently and humanely with local and regional grievances, abandoning *wholesale* (state-sponsored) violence. A government perceived as menacing or predatory provokes extremists who feel threatened and forced to withdraw into heavily armed, seething compounds or to engage in preemptive acts of violence (Hoffman, 1998).

LEFTIST CLASS STRUGGLES

Most of the insurgent movements in the United States that were well known during the 1960s and 1970s, such as the Weather Underground, the Black Panthers, and the Puerto Rican Nationalists (FALN), have been inactive since the 1980s. The Puerto Rican FALN was the last leftist group to continue a terrorist campaign within the United States. Beginning in the 1950s, it conducted bombings, armored car robberies, and assassinations; it even launched a rocket attack against FBI headquarters in San Juan (White, 1998).

In the late 1960s, radicals in the United States calling themselves the "New Left" focused on conflicts over racial disparities and economic inequality. They agreed that their enemies resided in the corporate imperialist system. Their cause was to wage revolutionary war against the United States from within. Attempts were made to forge links among leftist groups, including the Black Panthers, Students for a Democratic Society, and the Weather Underground; however, the radical left was fragmented and worked at cross-purposes. The united front that would have been necessary to pursue common radical political aims in the United States never materialized. A large number of arrests added to the disorder of the organizations.

Leftist terrorists of the 1970s identified with class struggles and Marxist or Maoist communist ideologies. Many of them were involved with universities and were brought together because of anti-war and civil rights issues that were highly politicized during the decade. They turned to underground guerrilla combat when their street demonstrations had no effect on government policy. During their campaigns, leftist insurgent groups planted countless bombs in banks and public areas, in military and police stations, and twice on successive days in the U.S. Capitol. They were responsible for highly publicized kidnappings, prison breaks, and other events designed to get the attention of mainstream U.S. society. Typical of the rhetoric of the time was the *Weather Report*, published by the Weather Underground. In a *Weather Report* issue sent to the Associated Press, a communiqué signed only "weatherman" claimed responsibility for bombing the New York City Police headquarters. It read, in part, "The time is now. Political power grows out of a gun, a Molotov, a riot, a commune and from the soul of the people" (as cited in Jacobs, 1997, p. 111). With the conservative turn of culture in the United States immediately following the 1970s, leftist guerrilla groups like the Weather Underground died out (Jacobs, 1997).

However, the Black Panthers re-emerged at the end of the 20th century. The new Black Panthers group has the same name and appearance as the earlier group, but its ideology has evolved into a rhetoric of hate and Black separatism. The modern Black Panthers are heavily armed. Their mission is to provide protection to African Americans who are being victimized in hate crimes by White supremacists. They have become a group of vigilantes, not followers of the leftist ideology that was the original organizing principle for the Black Panthers (Southern Poverty Law Center, 2000a).

The Symbionese Liberation Army (SLA) are leftist terrorists from the 1970s who returned to the news in the 21st century. The SLA was formed in the fall of 1973 by a group of Berkeley student radicals led by an escaped convict, Donald De Freeze. They grabbed headlines in 1974 by kidnapping newspaper heiress Patricia Hearst. She was found by the police in 1975, but rather than being seen as a victim, Hearst was arrested for her involvement with the terrorists. She was convicted and sentenced to a 7-year prison term for her participation in a bank robbery. In 1979, President Jimmy Carter commuted her sentence, and in 2001 she was pardoned by President Bill Clinton (Staples, 2002).

The other members of the SLA had either died or were fugitives in 1999 when the television show, *America's Most Wanted,* aired a picture of Kathleen Soliah on the 25th anniversary of the SLA's most notorious crimes. The former terrorist was sought for planting bombs and robbing banks. Police in St. Paul, Minnesota, were able to identify Sara Jane Olson, a suburban housewife, from the photo. In 2002, two other members of the SLA were brought to justice for shooting a bank customer with a sawed-off shotgun during a robbery that netted the SLA $15,000. Kathleen Soliah was indicted in this robbery, although Emily Harris was accused of the shooting. Also indicted were William Harris and Michael Bortin. The arrests were based on corroborating forensic evidence using 21st-century technology to prove a case that had been languishing before Kathleen Soliah's arrest. The prosecution granted immunity to another former gang member and to Kathleen Soliah's brother for their testimony against the four defendants (Sterngold, 2002; Wasserman, 2002).

The most notorious evidence in the case came from a book written by Patricia Hearst and published by Doubleday in 1982. In *Every Secret Thing,* Hearst described the bank robbery in detail, admitting that she drove a getaway car, but she was granted immunity for her testimony against the SLA. Her case is still considered newsworthy despite the changing environment of terrorism in the 21st century.

ANARCHISTS/ECOTERRORISTS

The "ecoterror" movement in the United States began with a biocentric ideology that put humans in a position of equality with all forms of life. Those in the movement abhorred the notion of human dominance implied by constant development and encroachment on nature. Their concerns involved preserving wilderness and thwarting expansion of industrialism and materialism. Their actions followed the "monkey-wrenching" dogma, which concentrated on sabotage of equipment and machinery and destruction of property. Ecoterrorism exploded in the anti-industrialism of the Unabomber, Ted Kaczynski, who made its purpose clear: "The people we are out to get are the scientists and engineers, especially in critical fields like computers and genetics" (as quoted in Sadler & Winters, 1996, p. 76).

The Luddites in Nottingham, England, were an ecoterror group that originated two centuries ago. They were thought of as the "antimachine" people because they wanted to stop the Industrial Revolution that began in the late 18th century. The Luddites didn't want a life where they were forced into factories to work with machines they couldn't control and driven from village self-sufficiency into urban dependence and servitude (Sale, 1995).

Ecoterror groups today are concerned with the technological revolution that began late in the 20th century. "Technophobes" and "technoresisters" believe that an inevitable eco-catastrophe will strike the world in the coming decades. The catastrophe in the near future will be caused by a combination of rising sea levels, a decrease in the ozone layer, and the social decay that goes along with disastrous corporate global practices (Kupfer, 2001).

The Earth Liberation Front (ELF) targeted urban sprawl in Long Island, New York, at the end of 2000 and the early months of 2001 with nine acts of economic sabotage against luxury homes under construction. The slogan, "If you build it, we will burn it," was scrawled on one of the homes. Windows were smashed, sites were vandalized, and bulldozers were decommissioned

PHOTO 5.3   Forensic sketch of the Unabomber, commissioned by the FBI, drawn by Jeanne Boylan in 1987.

(Kupfer, 2001). Its campaign focused not only on land use and development but also on the destruction of biogenetic research centers.

According to ABC News (2001), ELF carried out more than 100 acts of destruction beginning in 1997, causing $37 million in damage. The group claimed responsibility for $2.2 million worth of damage in the year 2000. In 2006 two members of the ELF pled guilty to setting a fire in Vail, Colorado, in 1998 that caused $12 million in damages and focused national attention on radical environmentalists. The Vail fire was one of 20 set in Oregon, Washington, California, and Colorado that federal investigators blamed on the ELF, which they characterized as the nation's top domestic terrorism threat (Barnard, 2006).

At the end of the 20th century, ecological terrorists focused their movement in two directions: land-use issues, attacking developers and loggers, and protests against the abuse of animals (White, 1998). The growing membership of the Animal Liberation Front (ALF) targets farmers for their supposed mistreatment of animals. Scientists and researchers are attacked for their use of animals in research. Different businesses, among them lumber companies, meat markets, and restaurants, are victims for different reasons (Miller & Miller, 2000).

According to ALF guidelines, "The ALF carries out non-violent direct action against animal abuse by rescuing animals and causing financial loss, usually through the damage and destruction of property, to animal abusers. ALF actions are illegal and therefore activists work anonymously, either individually or in groups, and do not have any centralized organization or address" ("Guidelines," 2000, p. 25). Connected to the ALF is the Animal Rights Militia (ARM), a group of extremist animal rights activists who are prepared to engage in direct action that might endanger human life (ALFront, 2006).

Ecoterrorists use the "secret cell" structure that has been found in other terrorist organizations. A member of the ALF reported, "You get a call from someone you trust, about an activity which needs to be undertaken. If you trust them, you go out and do it and don't ask many questions. It's much more effective run on a cell-based structure like that" (Arnold, 1997, p. 242).

RACIAL SUPREMACY

The ideology of White supremacists arose from the ashes of the Civil War. For example, the Ku Klux Klan (KKK), which continued carrying out deliberate acts of racist terrorism for more than a century, was spawned by the era of Reconstruction. Some of the KKK groups of the 21st century still reenact ceremonies first conducted before the Civil War and revere the Confederate flag. For many White supremacists, though, the swastika now symbolizes their agenda for a pure Aryan race. During the 1960s, when cultural changes in race relations were a source of conflict and controversy, White ethnic nationalists from many different groups carried out a systematic campaign of terror against Black community leaders and gathering places, especially churches.

There are also Black separatist groups in the United States. Those calling themselves the "Nation of Islam," consider themselves to be the followers of the Messenger Elijah Muhammad. His objective was clear: "I am doing all I can to make the so-called Negroes see that the white race and their religion (Christianity) are their open enemies, and to prove to them that they will never be anything but the devils' slaves and finally go to hell with them for believing and following them and their kind" (Muhammad, 1999). Notable organized separatist efforts took place during the late 1950s and early 1960s in the form of acts of arson and assassinations. The movement went underground after many of the leaders were kept under surveillance and jailed. There were sizable rifts in the black militant organizations, and public support waned after the 1960s. In the 1990s, a black separatist movement came to public notice again, under the guidance of Minister Louis Farrakhan. Thousands of African Americans were involved in marches and demonstrations. Despite the Black racist oratory of the latest movement in the United States, there have been no reported connections to terrorist activities (Anti-Defamation League, 1999).

White supremacists often focus on the illegitimacy of the U.S. Constitution, and therefore of the entire U.S. government. An obsessive suspicion of the government is common, along with beliefs in various conspiracy theories (Snow, 1999). Such issues as gun control, United Nations involvement in international affairs, and clashes between dissidents and law enforcement have provided the momentum for rightist groups at the beginning of the 21st century (Simonsen & Spindlove, 2000). Many right-wing groups purport to rely on a "common law" system rather than the U.S. system of justice. Even though such a system does not exist, common law adherents involve themselves and government agencies in bogus legal manipulations that are both costly and time-consuming. Their idea is to sabotage U.S. government courts and offices by inundating them with writs, suits, and court orders until officialdom collapses under mountains of paper. In recent years, the rightists in the United States have diversified. A list of types of rightist rebels includes militant right-wing gun advocates, antitax protesters, survivalists, far-right libertarians, traditional racists, anti-Semitic Nazi or neo-Nazi movements, and separatist advocates of sovereign citizenship, along with various other groups having negative, hateful attitudes toward the federal government (Abanes, 1996).

Since 1996, the number of known armed militias in the United States has declined, but the militia movement has managed to survive despite disorganization, infighting, and a number of highly publicized arrests (Snow, 1999). Core leaders have developed a communications system using the Internet, radio, and clandestine meetings that has allowed the surviving militia groups to develop consensus around key issues having to do with firearms (Pitcavage, 2001). Other indications suggest that the American right-wing, White supremacist movement is still alive. An alarming connection has been made among the forces of hate in the United States. In 2000, William Pierce, arguably the most influential White supremacist in the world, bought an underground "black metal" hate music company called Resistance. Black metal is a kind of White racist rock music that has been popularized in Europe as well as in the United States by young neo-Nazis. The late William Pierce, founder of the National Alliance, wrote *The Turner Diaries* (1996), a novel that provided the blueprint for many right-wing terrorist attacks (Blythe, 2000).

A connection between the well-established White supremacists, whose active arm was the militias in the 1990s, and racist skinheads, who are the agents of terror most like them to emerge in the new century, is a chilling possibility. This connection is significant for both strategic and analytical reasons. Racist skinheads can best be characterized as a terrorist youth subculture (Hamm, 1998). They provide an avenue for propagating the ideology of hate into the future and translating it into more modern cultural terms.

Racist skinhead groups generally accept Nazi, White supremacist, homophobic, and anti-Semitic themes, but these younger neo-Nazis may not espouse the Christian religious messages included with most radical right music and literature in the United States. Their viewpoints may be purely secular, or racist skinheads may adhere to pagan religions older than Christianity and even more shrouded in legend and mythology (Southern Poverty Law Center, 2000b).

RELIGIOUS EXTREMISTS

The growth of religious terrorism worldwide appears to account for the increased severity of terrorist attacks since 1991 (Enders & Sandler, 2000). For zealots, violence is the only means to overthrow a reviled secular government and attain religious redemption (Hoffman, 1998). Messianic concepts of deliverance, legitimized by theological imperative and achieved through personal action that entails mass indiscriminate murder, are of increasing concern.

Religious extremists prepared for a major crisis at the millennium because they believed that the year 2000 signaled the beginning of the world's end. They foresaw political and personal repression enforced by the United Nations and carried out with the support of the U.S. government. This belief is commonly known as the New World Order Conspiracy. It has survived into the 21st century. Both White supremacists and Christian Identity followers in the United States detest the idea of a "One World Government" that they expect will arise in the face of chaos. They look forward to an upcoming catastrophe as a step toward God's government (Hoffman, 1998).

Rubenstein (1987) asserts that there is no unified domestic terrorist threat but rather a context for social protest arising from a moral and social crisis in the United States. Though lacking unity in its nature and scope, religious terrorism is anything but disorganized or random. It is driven by an inner logic common among diverse groups and faiths that use political violence to further their sacred causes (Ranstorp, 2000).

THE NEW CENTURY

Acts of terrorist violence are inversions of the ideals under which the movements began, according to Wieviorka (1993). The organized practice of indiscriminate and irredeemable violence is not a faltering movement's last best hope and final act of desperation, but rather a substitute for a movement that has either become illusory or has fallen out of sync with its followers and the context in which it developed, along with the hopes pinned on it. Wieviorka (1993) shows that extreme violence is an ideological and pragmatic attempt to recover a meaning that has been lost.

Democratically run governments such as that of the United States promise empowerment, but the vote does not give the individual much power. Democracies often produce groups that feel marginalized and are willing to attack those deemed responsible for their condition. Majority rule works well only when minorities consider themselves part of the political body (Rapoport, 2000). The United States has a history of disgruntled minorities that turn to violent political action, so it is not likely that we have seen the end of terrorism from within. What is most disturbing is the tendency for the various types of terrorists to work collectively as their ideologies increasingly come together. The separate types of terrorists described above are seldom seen in isolation. Increasingly, radical groups on all sides have come to agree on an antigovernment, anti-military, anticorporate worldview. Common action by groups coming from different ideological positions has been demonstrated in resistance to global economics and the opening of international markets. Violent extremists from the left and the right have adopted the secret cell form of organization of leaderless resistance (Arnold, 1997).

The outcome of the battle against the forces of economic globalism, or McWorld, waged by the forces of Jihad, or religious extremism by whatever name, remains unresolved. This essential conflict between universalism and separation continues to fuel domestic and international terrorism into the 21st century (Barber, 1992).

HIGHLIGHTS OF REPRINTED ARTICLES

The two readings selected for this chapter are particularly relevant to the right-wing radical terrorism that was of concern in the United States at the end of the 20th century, but their significance also carries forward into the future. The concerns expressed by the authors are relevant whether terrorism is transnational or homegrown in the United States.

Jonathan White (2001). Political Eschatology: A theology of antigovernment extremism. *American Behavioral Scientist, 44*(6), 937–956.

Jonathan White considers the connections between racist and religious violence in the United States. The term *eschatology* derives from the Greek and is usually interpreted as "the final judgment." White finds that an eschatological philosophy is tailor-made for terrorists who have rejected the material world and believe that the norms of social behavior no longer matter. He describes the extremist right and its objective of restating religious mythology as a call to violence. As the extremist movements intertwined racism with religion, common elements appeared. According to White, one of the most prominent features is the rejection of modernity. Another factor is the belief in a conspiracy of evil forces. Still another common theme running through the extremist right is anti-Semitism. What is of most concern is their utter endorsement of firearm ownership and belief in guns as the mainstays of U.S. society.

Steve Vanderheiden (2005). Eco-terrorism or justified resistance? Radical environmentalism and the 'War on Terror.' *Politics & Society, 33*(3), 425–447.

Ecoterrorism is the focus of Steve Vanderheiden's article about radical environmentalism. Vanderheiden uses the term "ecotage" to signify "economic sabotage of inanimate objects thought to be complicit in environmental destruction." His focus is on the contrast between civil disobedience and terrorism. Included are the ideas of Dr. Martin Luther King, Jr., and a serious discussion of the meaning of sabotage as a tactic of resistance. The goal of the article is to describe ecotage and its relationship to civil disobedience, including similarities and differences. It is the author's position that ecotage must not only be categorically distinguished from terrorism but also that its use might, in some cases, be justified. Because the USA PATRIOT Act has been significantly broadened to include many attacks against inanimate objects as terrorism, the author questions the trivialization of the most serious moral transgressions by their association with far less serious offenses (p. 430).

EXPLORING HOMEGROWN TERRORISM FURTHER

- Two organizations provide in-depth and up-to-date information about hate crimes and hate groups: the Southern Poverty Law Center and the Anti-Defamation League. Search the Southern Poverty Law Center Web site for an interactive map that describes the activities of hate groups in the United States. Which groups are active in your state?
- The Court TV Web site provides extensive information about the Symbionese Liberation Army (SLA), including a chronology of its terrorist actions. What was the common theme in the ideology of the "New Left" in the 1970s?

- In his history of the relationship between religion and racist violence, White in the first article describes characteristics of right-wing extremists in the United States. What are the parallels between the U.S. patterns and militant religious extremist patterns in other countries?
- White's article discusses "end-of-time" theology, or eschatology. He asserts, "In the case of right-wing eschatology, all deities are exceedingly violent." What does this mean? What are some examples?
- To go beyond the operations and ideology of terrorists described by Vanderheiden in his article about justified resistance, it is useful to search for recent events involving the Animal Liberation Front (ALF) and Earth Firsters or Earth Liberation Front (ELF). A good source of information is the Terrorist Research Center, but stories about these organizations pop up in many places.
- From your perspective, what is the difference between justified resistance and terrorism? What are some examples of actions you would be willing to take as justified resistance?
- For more analysis and suggestions for strategies to reduce the violence of neo-Nazi skinheads, see Blazak (2001).

VIDEO NOTES

Many excellent movies have portrayed KKK-inspired attacks and assassinations. *Mississippi Burning* (Orion, 1988, 128 min.) is a film dramatization of a case that has been well researched in many other sources.

An insightful documentary, *Theodore J. Kaczynski: The Unabomber* (Biography: A&E, 1996, 50 min.), provides a developmental look at the life of this terrorist; a good deal of the information came from his family. Several fine documentaries available from the History Channel and A&E Television are relevant and illustrate many aspects of terrorism.

Political Eschatology

A Theology of Antigovernment Extremism

Jonathan R. White

This article explores apocalyptic theology in four American extremist religions: Christian Identity; Nordic Christianity and Odinism; violent, "freewheeling" fundamentalism; and Creatorism. It is argued that violent eschatology interacts with criminology in the sense that politicized religions produce criminal behavior and, at times, terrorism. A brief history of the relationship between religion and racist violence is presented as well as an analysis of the social factors that produce political eschatology. The article concludes with an examination of religious terrorism and technological weapons. Mass destruction is the greatest threat of religiously motivated terrorism.

Religious violence in the name of a holy cause is nothing new in the history of conflict, and terrorism in the new millennium will be influenced by resurgent fundamentalism and religious doctrines of violent intolerance. This will be especially true when religious dogmas embrace eschatological or "end-of-time" theology. The purpose of this article is to explore criminological aspects of eschatology as it is expressed in domestic, right-wing, racist violence and extremism. Two methodologies are employed: historical-descriptive analysis and theological explication. After defining some basic parameters, the article begins by placing right-wing extremism in the context of American history. This is followed by a description of recent events that have spurred the growth of the radical right. A theological discussion follows the historical segment. It is composed of an analysis of commonalities among right-wing religions, an examination of factors that must be present to form a theology of hate, and a critique of the mythology of hate.

It is legitimate to ask if a theological analysis of terrorism is criminologically valid. After all, criminology deals with the science of human behavior, whereas theology deals with an investigation of a divine realm outside objective experience. On the surface, it would appear that theology and criminology cannot be satisfactorily combined. Yet, beneath the surface lies a conjunction that invites a combination of methods. Religious behavior is a factor that shapes social constructs, and it may be positive or negative, social or antisocial. Theological constructs interact with criminology when they are the bases for negative human behavior and when they influence moral, conforming actions. The theological analysis in this article focuses on racist religion as a motivation for violent behavior. In essence, it is an attempt to explain the ideology of hate in religious terms. As such, it presents a valid topic for criminological analysis.

DEFINITIONS

Before beginning the historical and theological analyses of right-wing extremism, it is necessary to define basic terms and parameters. The term *eschatology* derives from the Greek word εσχα τος, a concept dealing with the end of all material

SOURCE: From "Political Eschatology: A Theology of Antigovernmental Extremism," in *American Behavioral Scientist* 44(6) by Jonathan R. White, © 2001, pp. 937–956. Reprinted with permission from Sage Publications, Inc.

and purpose in time and space. In the hellenized version of the Hebrew Bible, eschatology is usually interpreted as the "day of Yahweh"; that is, a final judgment and the realization of God's purpose for creation. This Jewish idea influenced early Christian writers, but the meaning of God's final presence fluctuated in early Christian dogma (Kittel, 1964, p. 697). Christians have expected God's final judgment for 2,000 years, yet they have not agreed on the form it will take. Crossan (1999, pp. 257–287) describes four commonly held eschatological frameworks: ascetic, apocalyptic, ethical, and political. Ascetic eschatology refers to the process of self-denial, whereas the apocalyptic version envisions God's destruction of the existing order. Ethical eschatology, according to Crossan, is quite different. It calls for followers to embrace radically moral behavior in recognition of God's imminent reign. Crossan says that political eschatology is frequently ignored today because it combines expectations of religious judgment with political action. People fear political eschatology. Lewy (1974, p. 40) agrees, arguing that linking political beliefs with an end-of-time theology is a prescription for violence. Given the variety of meanings attached to eschatological expectations, it is not surprising to find that American right-wing extremists have developed their own philosophy of the "end of the age" in various apocalyptic theologies. As Lewy implies, some of these theologies are indeed quite dangerous.

As the new millennium conjures prophecies of doom in some circles, it also brings the threat of increased terrorist violence. There are people who would like to violently usher in the new *eschaton*, and religious terrorism has increased over the past decade (Hoffman, 1995). An eschatological philosophy is tailor made for individual terrorists who have rejected both the material world and the norms of social behavior. It provides a cosmic battlefield where forces for good are called to fight some unspeakable evil. The consequences are dramatic; indeed, they are cosmic in proportion. All deterrents to violence have been rendered meaningless by the promise of the new *eschaton*. When violent eschatology is politicized on a cosmic battlefield, Armageddon's warriors need no further justification to bear arms. They fight for a holy cause, and all actions are justified.

The term *right-wing religion,* as used in this article, refers to belief systems that incorporate some form of hatred or racism in their basic doctrines. There are four prominent forms of these theologies in America today: Christian Identity, Nordic Christianity or Odinism, freewheeling fundamentalism, and Creatorism. These theologies are extremist religions based on the demonization of other racial, religious, or national groups. This article neither refers to mainstream conservative American religious movements nor attempts to critique Christian fundamentalism. Fundamentalists and conservative Christians differ from their racialist counterparts in that the conservatives base their value system on universal love, they believe that God's actions in history have yet to take place, and they feel they will be raptured into heaven prior to a general tribulation (Barkun, 1997, pp. 105–119; White, 1986). The militant extremists examined in this article believe they must fight to create conditions conducive for the *eschaton.*

Christian Identity is a theology that grew from a 19th-century concept known as Anglo-Israelism. Its basic tenet is that the ancient tribes of Israel were Caucasians who migrated to Europe shortly after the death of Jesus. Whites are actually the descendants of the chosen tribes of Israel, and Whites are asked to identify with the Israelites of old. Christian Identity is strongly anti-Semitic, claiming that humans originated from "two seed lines." Whites are directly descended from God, whereas Jews originated from an illicit sexual union between the devil and the first White woman. Non-White races evolved from animals and are categorized as subhumans. Identity Christians believe that biblical covenants apply only to the White race and that Jesus of Nazareth was not a Jew but the White Israelite son of God. Christian Identity views are championed by Aryan Nations, a variety of prominent Identity pastors, Posse Comitatus, and the American Institute of Theology.

Nordic Christianity or Odinism is a hybrid form of Christianity and old Norse religion. It exists in two forms. On the one hand, Nordic Christianity combines a pantheon of Nordic gods under the triune deity of Christianity. Odin, Thor, and other Nordic gods serve Christ by militantly protecting the White Norse race. Pure Odinism, on the other hand, ignores Christian concepts. It simply involves the resurrection of old Nordic mythology and the acceptance of the Nordic pantheon. After enjoying a rebirth in 19th-century Germany, Odinism migrated to the United States through the neo-Nazi movement.

Both forms of Nordic religion call for the militant defense of race, bloodlines, and homeland.

Another form of militant, right-wing Christianity can simply be called freewheeling fundamentalism. This form of religion rejects both the blatant racism of Christian Identity and the hybrid nature of Nordic religions. The freewheelers are fiercely patriotic and use religion to reinforce social beliefs, values, and behavior. They tend to believe that the federal government is not mystically evil but that it is opposed to the reign of God. They also believe that agents of the government are in conspiracy to destroy America's monetary system and national sovereignty. Many of these groups oppose racism, and some claim that they are not anti-Semitic. Freewheeling fundamentalism is the religion of the patriot movement and the gun-show circuit.

The last form of religion discussed in this article is called Creatorism, a religion originating with the World Church of the Creator (WCOTC). Founded by Ben Klassen, the WCOTC is secular, deistic, and racist. Klassen's purpose was to divorce White people from weak, theistic religions, claiming that such religions were ridiculous expressions of utopian ideals. The Creator, Klassen said, placed things in motion and left people on their own. Klassen's slogan was "Our race is our religion." Creating his own mythology in tracts on naturalistic health and in *The White Man's Bible* (Klassen, 1986), he called on White people to fight Jews, non-White races, and Whites who disagreed with racist philosophy. His successor, Matt Hale, who has taken the secular title Pontifex Maximus from Julius Caesar, endorses conflict to protect the White race. The cry of Creatorists is "RAHOWA," an acronym for "racial holy war."

A HISTORY OF RIGHT-WING RELIGIOUS HATE

In 1995, when reports of the bombing of the federal building in Oklahoma City began to flow from the media, many Americans were surprised to hear of a twisted religion called Christian Identity. Some of them asked about its origins and questioned the belief system of its strange ideology. Was it a new racist religion? Did it have a theological base? Were Christian Identity churches included in mainstream Protestantism? The answer to these and many other questions can be found in the history of ethnocentrically based right-wing religions.

When the first Congregationalists landed at Plymouth in 1620, they brought a feeling of Protestant determinism to the shores of the new world. Hudson (1981, pp. 36–41) states that the Congregationalists hoped to create a new city set on a hill to shine a religious light for the entire world. Albeit unintentionally, the light soon refracted into a multiplicity of scattered divisions. Such continual divisions characterized early American religion.

Marty (1984) states that America has been a land of many religions despite the dominant influence of Protestantism on the popular culture. Native Americans had their own forms of religion, and each group of immigrants came to America with its unique mores, culture, and religious values. Every religious congregation became, in Marty's words, a Pilgrim in its own land, but this did not sit well with the established original Protestant settlers. Beginning in the 19th century, groups of "native" Americans, primarily Protestant, began to form protective associations to dispel the influence of immigrant groups and "foreign" religions (White, 1986). The emergence of the Know Nothings just before the Civil War serves as an appropriate example. An urban, Protestant movement, the Know Nothings formed a secret anti-Catholic society to discourage emigration from Ireland.

The Know Nothings could not compete with the hate-filled religions that emerged after 1865. The most notorious group in the immediate post-Civil War period was the Ku Klux Klan (KKK). The Klan has undergone three distinct phases in its history, starting with an organizational period after the Civil War (Chalmers, 1987). The 1920s brought a conservative attempt to gain mainstream political power, and the Klan entered its current phase after World War II, emphasizing rhetoric, political violence, and fragmentation. The Klan's initial ideology did not lay the foundation for a unified movement, but one factor has remained constant in KKK history: It is a religious organization, and Klansmen base their hatred on the rhetoric of American Protestantism. As a result, the ideology of the Klan and the theology of Christian Identity go hand in hand (Sargent, 1995, pp. 139–143).

Other extremist, right-wing movements also embraced religious rhetoric. The radical grangers of the far West and other agrarian movements of the 19th century laced their political positions with religious phrases. Xenophobic religious zealots began appearing in the 1930s, calling for an uncompromising ethnocentric adoration of the United States and a blind acceptance of religious doctrine. The Depression witnessed the continued blossoming of militant Protestantism, and elements of the Roman Catholic church joined the fray. Marty (1984, pp. 373–389) argues that the clash between modern and traditional theology provided an environment conducive to linking conservative Protestants and Catholics.

At issue, Marty (1984) states, was the clash between the modern world and the traditional one. Traditional values were challenged by modernity, and all forms of American Christianity had to meet the modern world in one way or another. World War I created a momentary illusion of religious unity in America, but the Jazz Age and the Roaring Twenties brought an end to the superficial unification. A dividing line formed, Marty argues, between traditional values and emerging morality. In separate works, Berger (1980, pp. 56–60) and Berlet (1998) arrive at similar conclusions. The traditional dividing lines between Protestants and Catholics began to fade in the Great Depression as Christians began to argue over the fundamental concepts of religion. Both Catholics and Protestants produced champions who defended traditional fundamentals, while each side also produced those who embraced modernization. As the Catholic and Protestant conservatives moved closer together, the extremists in each camp were not far behind.

Father Charles E. Coughlin rose to fame in the 1930s through the medium of radio. His message was one of xenophobia, anti-Semitism, and blind patriotism. Although Catholic, his words resonated with fundamental American Protestants. Dr. Theodore Stoddard, for example, joined the fray with a rash of racially motivated, anticommunist rhetoric. He called for selective Nordic breeding to eliminate both racial impurity and communism. Other Protestants turned their concerns to Judaism, blaming the Jews for not only being "Christ killers" but for ushering in the age of modernity (Marty 1984, pp. 390–400). Right-wing extremism was ripe for a champion.

Such a figure emerged in the person of Wesley Swift (Holden, 1986). A California radio preacher, Swift uncovered a 19th-century British doctrine called Anglo-Israelism. In a nutshell, Anglo-Israelism claimed that White people in the British Isles were descended from the tribes of ancient Israel (Barkun, 1997, pp. 1–14). The house of David was, in fact, the ruling house of Scotland. According to this doctrine, the other White nations of northern Europe were the true Israelites and the actual heirs to God's promises to the Hebrew patriarchs. Barkun (1997, p. 60) says that Swift modified the doctrine of Anglo-Israelism to fit the United States so that American Whites could lay claim to being Israelites. He encouraged Whites to identify with the ancient Israelites, giving rise to the notion of Identity or Christian Identity. Two of the people influenced by Swift's message were William Potter Gale and a young engineer named Richard Butler. Gale went on to create a militant antitax group known as Posse Comitatus, while Butler left a corporate job to found the most influential Christian Identity church in America, Aryan Nations.

Conspiracy theories also emerged in the 20th century. The American extremist right held that Christianity was under attack by a secret group of secular scientists known as The Order of the Illuminati. Berlet (1998) argues that Adam Weishaupt, an 18th-century Bavarian professor of canon law, was frustrated by the lack of intellectual activity in the priesthood. As a result, he formed a secret society called the Illuminati in 1775. The purpose of his secret society was to promote knowledge and rational discourse within the church, and branches of the Illuminati spread throughout Western Europe. Skeptical of any society that criticized religion and the social order, the Bavarian government banned the Illuminati in 1786. The Illuminati, however, were too entrenched to be eliminated by the actions of a single German state. Branches appeared in several European cities, and the organization spread.

Holden (1999) points out that the extremist right resurrected fear of the Illuminati after World War II, claiming that it was a secret group of intellectual elitists who systematically attacked Christianity. Today, many members of the patriot movement and other extremist groups believe that the Illuminati operate against White American Christians. They cite the pyramid on the back on the dollar bill as evidence that the Illuminati operate secretly in the American government.

Many sources of conspiracy exist in extremist minds. Berlet (1998) points to the Freemasons as one such source. Masonry had been at odds with the established church in Europe since the 1700s, and some members of the church charged the Masons with devil worship. Such a charge was too tempting for the radical right, and fear of the Masons began to spread in the mid-20th century. Fear of socialism, communism, and economic control also provided Protestant and Catholic extremists with "evidence" that groups of conspirators were plotting to destroy American rights. Berlet also points to the demonization of Judaism as a prime source for conspiracy theories.

Animosity between Judaism and Christianity originated in early Christian apologetics, and the history of Christianity is darkened with anti-Semitic strains. Yet, the American extremist right gave anti-Semitism a new twist. As Anglo-Israelism gained ground in the religious right, new "proof" of a global conspiracy emerged with the publication of *The Protocols of the Learned Elders of Zion*. Originally published as a French satire, Czarist police used *The Protocols* as an attempt to trump up evidence against Russian Jews. American industrialist Henry Ford's agent, a fierce anti-Semite named William Cameron, published *The Protocols* in English and distributed it to Ford workers (Barkun, 1997, p. 34). It is still cited by radical religious leaders as proof of a Jewish conspiracy against Christianity. Such conspiracy theories provided for the ideological underpinnings of right-wing religion following World War II (White, 1997).

RECENT HISTORY OF ANTIGOVERNMENT EXTREMISM

American right-wing extremism fell out of vogue when left-wing violence grew in the 1960s and 1970s, but it experienced a rebirth around 1981. The rejuvenation came as shifting economic conditions threatened the social status of working-class Whites. Sapp (1985) describes the resurrection in terms of three distinct trends: White supremacy, religious extremism, and survivalism. The racial aspect of the movement solidified with the ideological unification of White supremacy under the banner of the Aryan Nations. Richard Butler, a disciple of Wesley Swift, formed a compound in Hayden Lake, Idaho, and his Aryan fortress provided the ideological soil to unite various Klan, Nazi, and other White supremacy groups. Butler became the most important actor in the American racist camp.

Sapp (1985) believes that religion played an important role in the right-wing resurgence, and, once again, he points to Butler. The Identity pastor Butler founded the Church of Jesus Christ, Christian in his White supremacy compound. As his power spread among the racists, his church became a beacon to unite Identity ministers throughout the country. Robert Miles of Cohoctah, Michigan, joined Butler with his own Mountain Church of Jesus. James Wickstrom preached an Identity message from the Sheriff's Posse Comitatus. Even William Pierce, the agnostic author of *The Turner Diaries*, joined the trend by sending his fictional protagonist Earl Turner through a religious experience when he encountered *The Book*. Christian Identity was the dominant force in the contemporary period of right-wing extremism.

Sapp (1985) cites survivalism as the third aspect of the rebirth of the extremist right. Spawned by fears of an impending race war and the collapse of government, survivalists retreated to heavily fortified compounds to ready themselves for Armageddon. Sapp also notes that extremists practiced a type of "dualism"; that is, participants in one type of group tended to share membership in another kind of group. For example, members of White supremacy groups could be found in survivalist camps or in Identity churches. Survivalism gave the extremist right its most militant potential.

Despite regeneration in the 1980s, right-wing extremism was in trouble by 1989. Smith (1994), in one of the best examinations of domestic terrorism available to the public, explains why right-wingers were simply not effective. The two groups that practiced the most violence, The Order and Posse Comitatus, actually turned other extremists away from the movement because they were appalled by actual murder. Like most potential terrorists, the majority of right-wingers were happier when practicing right-wing rhetoric. Ideology was safe, but violence was another matter. From a religious view, the hate-filled theology of Christian Identity had the same impact (White, 1998, pp. 217–224). Identity preachers called on their congregations to despise non-Whites and Jews. The call for hatred confused many potential followers, even though they believed in their own ethnic superiority. As a result, some Christian extremists evolved into freewheelers, and they broke from Identity congregations to form independent fundamentalist groups. By 1991, it seemed that right-wing extremism would become a thing of the past. Unfortunately, three issues reanimated the extremists (Stern, 1996, pp. 58–60).

After James Brady, President Ronald Reagan's press secretary, suffered a crippling brain injury in the assassination attempt on Reagan, Brady and his family became champions of gun control legislation. A bill named in his honor and subsequent federal gun control legislation sent an alarm throughout the extremist right. Guns, from the extremist perspective the one thing that could save the country, were under attack. As racists, millennialists, Identity theologians, and other extremists closed ranks, they found that they were on the fringe of a mainstream political issue. By 1991, they were taking theology to the gun-show circuit to seek converts.

Two other sources of rejuvenation came in the form of armed confrontations with the federal government. In 1992, Randy Weaver failed to appear in court on a federal weapons violation charge. During the attempt to serve Weaver with a bench warrant, Weaver's son and a U.S. marshal were killed. Weaver barricaded his family in a mountain cabin in Ruby Ridge, Idaho, and challenged the government to come and get him. The situation was exacerbated when a Federal Bureau of Investigation (FBI) sniper killed Weaver's wife. Former Green Beret Lieutenant Colonel James "Bo" Gritz came to the scene to negotiate with Weaver, but the attention he drew helped turn Weaver's standoff at Ruby Ridge into a rallying point for the extremist right.

Closely related to the Weaver incident, at least in the minds of the extremist right, was a Bureau of Alcohol, Tobacco, and Firearms (ATF) raid on the Branch Davidian compound at Waco, Texas, in 1993. Armed with probable cause and a search warrant, ATF agents attempted to raid a religious cult compound to seize illegal firearms. They were met with overwhelming firepower and driven back after suffering more than a dozen casualties, including four agents who were killed. Although ATF agents successfully negotiated a cease-fire and managed to retrieve their wounded officers, FBI agents quickly came to the scene and assumed control. Three months later, the FBI assaulted the compound, only to find that the cult leader, Vernon Howell (a.k.a. David Koresh), had soaked the building with gasoline. More than 70 people were killed in the ensuing blaze, including all the children in the compound.

The Branch Davidian compound had little to do with the racist right, but it had all the elements the extremists loved: guns, a compound standing in the face of federal agents, and religion. Shortly after the failed FBI attack, John Trochmann revealed a new creation: the Militia of Montana. It was an organization, he claimed, designed to protect constitutional rights. Within months, militias popped up all over the United States, each with its own commander. The survivalists of the 1980s reemerged in the form of paramilitary groups, and survivalism has become the dominant theme of extremism at the turn of the millennium.

COMMON THEOLOGICAL ELEMENTS OF RIGHT-WING EXTREMISM

As the extremist movement intertwined racism with religion, common elements appeared in the message. One of the most prominent features of the extremist right is its rejection of modernity. It favors biblical literalism over modernism, and it remains centered in Protestantism despite the influence of some Catholic extremists. By the same token, it should not be described as fundamentalism or confused with conservative Christianity. The xenophobic religion of the extremist right does not accept the Christian call for universal love only; it accepts the idea of love for one's own kind. As a result, right-wing extremism is defined by hate. One does not simply love; one loves in conjunction with hate. For example, one loves Christians because one hates everyone who is not a Christian. One loves Whites because one hates everyone who is not White. Religion is defined by exclusivity.

Barkun (1997, pp. 104–108) also notes that racial extremists in the movement have another profound theological difference with American Christian fundamentalists. Both fundamentalists and extremists tend to be premillenialists; that is, they believe that Jesus of Nazareth will return prior to a 1,000-year reign of peace described in Revelation. Most fundamentalists contend that the Second Coming of Christ will unfold according to biblical prophecies, and believers will experience a rapture prior to Christ's return. Extremists, especially in the Christian Identity movement, believe that prophecies have already been fulfilled and that no rapture will take place. As a result, believers will be forced to endure a

7-year tribulation before the Second Coming. Extremists believe that they must be prepared for the tribulation, and survivalism is a common theme in extremist theology. They are called to prepare militantly for Christ's return.

Another factor emerging from the history of the extremist right is the belief in a conspiracy of evil forces. Each group of extremists endorses some concept of conspiracy, and although the source of conspiracy changes, the belief in conspiracy has remained historically constant. In the 1930s, Father Coughlin preached about an antireligious conspiracy of satanic origin, and after World War II, Wesley Swift and others endorsed this view. Reflecting the mainstream culture, preachers pointed to a conspiracy of communism. As conspiracy theories emerged in the second half of the 20th century, right-wing extremists began to develop a list of potential conspirators that included local governments that fluoridated water supplies, U.S. industrial leaders, international economic groups, the U.S. government, and, eventually, the United Nations. Christian Identity ministers could not make peace with either the Roman Catholic church or with conservative Protestants. They added televangelists and the Vatican to groups of conspiracy theories. In such a world, anything that is not in the extremist camp is potentially involved in a conspiracy of evil.

The most common theme running through the extremist right is anti-Semitism. Regardless of who is blamed for the conspiracy against American values, all right-wingers seem to agree on one point: They find Judaism at the base of the problem. Christian Identity sees Judaism as the result of a cosmic battle between God and the Devil. Even extremists who walked away from religion, such as William Pierce, found Jews to be contemptible. Many claimed that Judaism was behind the periodic economic crises of capitalism because they believed that Jewish bankers controlled the money supply. Christian Identity ministers even claimed that Jewish bankers and the Pope worked in collusion.

It is legitimate to ask how such an extreme, almost nonsensical philosophy of hatred could become popular. The answer can be found in the social structure of extremist groups. In many instances, they tend to be lower-working-class Whites with little formal education. They tend to follow the precepts of traditional, literalized religion, and conspiracies of bankers, Jews, communists, and the United Nations seem to make sense. Similar to members of the old Know Nothing movement of the 19th century, they believe that immigrants and racial minorities are at the base of their decreasing economic status. Blood hatred is endemic to right-wing theology.

A final commonality can be found in the utter endorsement of firearms. The only ultimate protection for White, working-class men, in extremist ideology, is the gun. It will stop a variety of social ills and protect true Americans even as the United Nations attempts to trample constitutional rights. Guns are the mainstays of American society. Finch (1983) sums it up well by describing the right-wing movement as "God, guts, and guns." Gibson (1994) describes it as a displaced desire to fulfill the role of the warrior male. Regardless, the extremist right is a full participant in America's love affair with guns.

Theological commonalties in the extremist right separate the realm of God from the realm of evil. Berlet (1998) says that the right wing sees dichotomies between Christ and the Antichrist, between spirituality and materiality, and between fundamentalism and modernism. The nature of such separations gives rise to religious conflict. God is wholly in partnership with Christ, spirituality, and fundamentalism against the Devil and the dark forces of the cosmos. This is a dualistic, Manichaean struggle between right and wrong. In this atmosphere, Christianity must take a stand against Judaism for the sake of creation, and Christians must stand for the Constitution in the face of socialism, economic conspiracies, or the New World Order. This process does not simply separate one camp from the other; it calls the chosen into a holy war with drastic consequences. If the holy warrior loses, God's creation is lost.

A THEOLOGY OF TERRORISM

Theology creates neither violence nor terrorist behavior, but it can provide an atmosphere that justifies an attack on social structures. Three circumstances must be present to motivate believers to move from thought to violent action: (a) believers must perceive a terminal threat to their religious values and attitudes; (b) a theology embracing cosmic salvation, universal love, or worldly peace must be transformed into a dogma of nationalistic, racial, or some other ethnocentrically based protectionism; and (c) the true believers among the faithful must embrace violence as a means for preserving the faith. When these three circumstances are present, terrorism becomes part of a theological process.

Perceived Terminal Threat to Religious Values and Attitudes

Walter Laqueur (1996) argues that the structure of terrorism has evolved throughout the 20th century, and the new millennium will witness yet another metamorphosis as religion becomes one of the dominant factors in terrorist violence. Eschatological religious movements are sweeping the globe and affecting violent fringe elements. Referring to this process as "apocalypse soon," Laqueur points to the presence of eschatological references in mainstream politics, and he believes that religion will become the primary influence on terrorist behavior. The danger in the process, Laqueur argues, is that eschatological terrorists want to "give history a push."

Although Lacqueur's (1996) primary unit of analysis is international terrorism, his conclusions are applicable to right-wing domestic extremism. Economic changes and global politics have created conditions that threaten the status of White, working-class men. Despite the economic boom of the 1990s, uneducated White men have not prospered in the global economy, and they lack the educational tools to do so (Hamm, 1994, pp. 105–149). Economic displacement is a real threat, and their anxiety has been exacerbated by heated debates in mainstream American Christianity over such issues as the authority of the Bible, the nature of Christ, and the role of culture in religion. The extremists feel that their world is falling apart, and they are looking for a place to stand. Yet, not every threatened group embraces an extremist theology. Why is the right wing so prone to idiosyncratic theologies? Why do some people embrace ethnocentric religion as a means of social salvation? Martin Marty and Peter Berger have separate but complementary answers.

Marty and Appleby (1991, 1993) argue that the movement toward intolerant fundamentalism is part of an international trend. In a lengthy project that resulted in a five-volume series on fundamentalist religions, Marty and Appleby (1991, pp. vi-xii) find that the retreat to traditional, militant religion is a global phenomenon. They argue that fundamentalism is a defense against forces of change and that people will defend themselves by grabbing the traditions of the past. Militant fundamentalists fight for God, and they fight under God's leadership. Religion becomes the glue that provides group identity and cohesion. It copes with a confusing social situation by rejecting all threats. Only the fundamentals are safe; everything else is relegated to the realm of the unholy.

Berger (1980, pp. 3–29) makes the same argument from a slightly different vantage point. He argues that the modern world is in collision with traditional values. People cope with this situation in one of three differing ways: rejecting change, coping with change, or seeking new ideologies that preserve tradition within change. Those who reject change may turn to militant protectionism. The logical extension of Berger's argument is that violence can become a method for protecting the traditional world. By applying Berger's thesis to the theology of the extremist right, the logic of intolerance becomes apparent. Right-wing extremism is trying to recapture some idealized element of America's past. Extremists long for the days of White American Protestantism, and some of them will fight for it.

The extremist right looks at change through the spectacles of political eschatology. In other words, there are cosmic consequences if they fail to restore White America. Change does not simply represent social evolution; it is a direct confrontation with evil. In right-wing theology, an incarnate evil force is struggling with a creating deity for control of the world, and the Devil has the same power as God. When threatened with modernity, change, multiculturalism, taxes, or any number of other concepts, extremists cannot compromise. Fanatics who cannot compromise are willing, as Laqueur (1996) says, to give history a push.

Carl D. Haggard, commander of the United States Special Field Forces Militia, provides an example of this logic (Bushart, Craig, & Barnes 1998, p. 219). Haggard believes that the U.S. government has declared war on Christian men and women. He claims that he has no concern with racism or multiculturalism but that he fears the government is out of control. Haggard fears centralized government power, and his faith tells him to expect individual freedom. There are hundreds of Identity Christians, freewheelers, and others who espouse the same beliefs with a few twists. Most of their actions are rhetorical, and most of them retreat from actual violence.

Other extremists, such as Timothy McVeigh, feel they must take action. Former Identity pastor Kerry Noble (1998) says the primary motivation for action is religious faith.

Transforming Universality to Ethnocentrism

For religion to play a dominant role in violence, it is necessary to transform a transcendent message of universality into ethnocentric protectionism. In the case of American Protestantism, there is a tension between two poles. On one hand, Christians are told to embrace everyone. The apostle Paul (Gal. 3:28–29, New Revised Standard Version), for example, states that there is neither Gentile nor Jew, slave nor free, nor woman nor man; all are one in Christ. He argues (Rom. 8) that the Christ event provided cosmic unification. Some theologians (Fox, 1988, pp. 129–154; Kung, 1995, pp. 782–789; Rowe, 1994, pp. 127–152) argue that this call varies little from many of the world's religions, and it has roots in secular, Western philosophy. Kung even argues that such logic is the basis for unification and understanding among three sister religions: Judaism, Christianity, and Islam. On the other hand, Christian communities have not historically embraced everyone. It is harrowing in some circles—indeed, it is frequently blasphemous—to include those who do not believe, behave, or worship in a particular way. American Protestantism, and most other religions, exist somewhere in the tension between these two poles.

The growth of violent Christian extremism in the United States involves a willingness of some groups to embrace the pole defining orthodox behavior and to subjugate it to ethnocentric rather than transcendent norms. Universalism is out of the question from this perspective. God's love is only applicable to those who believe, look, think, and act like members of the ethnic group. Right-wing love is reserved only for its own kind. This is the logic behind the extremist right's "Christian patriotism." Right-wing theologians have called for the death of lower-case *c* Christians, and White, militant patriots argue that patriotism is reserved only for those with the proper Christian beliefs (White, 1986, 1997).

The WCOTC serves as a perfect example of ethnocentric transformation. The creed of the church is "our religion is our race," and even a cursory review of WCOTC writings reveals the emphasis on love of one's own kind. On the church's Web site, Hale (1999) writes that the Creator makes a distinction between his loved ones and his enemies. In addition, the Creator expects followers to use love and hate in a constructive manner. Whites are to be loved; all other people are to be hated. Hale goes even further in the "Sixteen Commandments":

> Remember that the inferior mud races are our deadly enemies, and the most dangerous of all is the Jewish race. . . . The guiding principle of all your actions shall be: What is best for the White Race? . . . Do not employ niggers or other coloreds. . . . Destroy and banish all Jewish thought and influence from society. . . . Throughout your life you shall faithfully uphold our pivotal creed of Blood, Soil, and Honor. (Hale, 1999)

Ben Klassen (1986) states that Christianity is a suicidal religion indulging in a world of fantasy and make-believe. Nature's religion, on the other hand, calls believers to life by telling them to fight for their survival. A passage from his *The White Man's Bible* is quoted on the WCOTC Web site: "When I say 'our' survival, I am talking about the White Race, since I am not a bird, or an alligator, or a nigger, or an Indian." Such attitudes clearly indicate the nature of right-wing extremism. In a process of ethnocentric transformation, a potential call for universal love is transformed into ethnocentric love. The by-product is hatred for anyone outside the group.

Bruce (1993, pp. 50–67), writing in the Marty-Appleby project, provides a description of the process of ethnocentric transformation. Examining the conflict in Northern Ireland and comparing it to the rise of the mainstream religious right in the United States, Bruce finds two differing trends in fundamentalism. In Ireland, for example, the struggle focuses on ethnic identity and fighting associated with the birth of a political entity. If one is labeled *Catholic*, it does not necessary imply that one's life is subjugated to Catholic theology. Being Catholic can mean that one is fighting for ethnic identity against Protestants. The same principle is applicable to Protestantism in Ireland. Ethnicity takes precedence over religious affinity, and religious identification becomes part of ethnic identity. A religious label in Ireland is synonymous with ethnic identification. Bruce finds the opposite situation in America's Christian right. Mainstream fundamentalism in the United States is not related to ethnic identification because of the American tradition of religious pluralism.

American extremism, however, is not in the same position as mainstream Christian conservatism. Right-wing extremists violently advocate the protection of their ethnic identity, making them more akin to Bruce's (1993) concept of emerging nationalism in Ireland. Ethnicity and political perspectives dominate the right-wing call to religion. Any transcendent experience designed to unite theological expressions is out of the question for right-wing extremists. Their purpose is not to seek compromise or even find their own enclave in a pluralistic environment. The purpose of the extremist right is to destroy the opposition. This becomes the basis for a call to arms.

True Believers and the Doctrine of Necessity

The perception of a threat and ethnocentric protectionism do not necessarily produce religious violence. Extremists need not turn to their weapons. They might, for example, withdraw from society or practice nonviolent forms of confrontation. Indeed, most extremists follow these paths. Violence is an extreme action that is embraced only by a few hard-core believers. The central question is, Why do some extremists cross the line from rhetoric to violence? H. H. A. Cooper (1977) provides the best answer in one of the early works on modern terrorism.

All terrorists must feel justified in their actions, and religious zealots are no different. Cooper (1977) believes that terrorists are motivated by the same factors that influence everyone else, and they look for similar rewards for their behavior. Like most individuals, terrorists want neither to engage in violence nor to harm innocent victims. Terrorists, however, have a problem. They cannot accept the world as it is. Even though they know they will kill people by engaging in violence, terrorists reluctantly accept this burden because they cannot tolerate the status quo. Terrorists justify violence by convincing themselves that the injustices of society outweigh the amount of harm caused by their actions. Violence becomes necessary to save society from cosmic evil. Cooper refers to this as the "doctrine of necessity."

Cooper's (1977) theory applies to the religious warrior. Most of America's extremists are rhetorical. They call for violence, they go to Identity

meetings and KKK rallies, they carry guns with various militias, and they declare "war" on the federal government. Smith (1994) points out that these "militants" quickly retreat from organizations whenever real violence takes place. Yet, there are those who differ from the extremists described by Smith. A violent few have planted bombs, driven through the streets killing minorities, ambushed police officers, attacked homosexuals, and entered day care centers to shoot children. These terrorists act from necessity. To them, maintaining the status quo does more damage than murdering innocent people. In an age when weapons of mass destruction are available to many disenfranchised groups, this becomes a frightening scenario.

RESTATING A MYTH

The theological danger of right-wing political eschatology is profound, perhaps even more profound than its adherents comprehend, and it is laced with potential violence. The reason is simple. In rejecting the dominant mythology of the age, they are restating the basis of human existence in terms of exclusivity and hate. In other words, they are restating mythology.

Eliade (1968) defines mythology as the sacred stories that bind a group together. The truth of the story is not in question, Eliade says; rather, the myth contains the social truths that a group accepts as normative. Campbell (1990) defines this in terms of common elements. All myths have certain isomorphic properties. The same types of characters, images, and actions manifest themselves in the stories of various religions. A central question for Campbell (1985) focuses on religions based on love and those based on conflict. Mythology and violence can combine in ethnocentric religions.

To be sure, the history of religion is replete with examples of violent mythology used to justify ethnocentrism. Gottwald (1979), for example, traces the social development of ancient Israel in terms of its settlement of Canaan. According to his thesis, two groups of monotheistic Israelites, a group in the north worshipping El and a migrant group from the south loyal to Yahweh, joined forces for the political domination of Canaan. They cast their political struggle in religious terms, while sometimes conquering and sometimes coexisting with the Canaanites. Bright (1981, pp. 144–146) reinforces this view, claiming that the Israelites looked back on their struggle for Canaan and wrote its history through theological eyes. The result was an ethnocentric myth based on conquest.

The structure of modern mythology provides an atmosphere conducive to the birth and growth of new myths. Campbell (1988) states that our age has lost touch with the myths of the past and that we are searching for a grounding of our existence. Spong (1999) says it another way: Christianity (and by implication, Judaism and Islam) is based on mythological concepts that predate the Scientific Revolution, the Enlightenment, Darwin, and Freud. From Spong's perspective, the West is in a state of religious anomie. The myth must be restated, or it will die. This need not be a frightening or destructive process. Borg (1991) believes that it is possible to shape a new myth from the old structure in a very gentle fashion. Unfortunately, this is not the only alternative. Just as monotheistic Israelites pitted a militant God against the baals of the Canaanites, an emerging combative mythology can claim the hearts and minds of its people. In the case of right-wing eschatology, all deities are exceedingly violent.

It is beyond the scope of this article to critique completely the mythology of the extremist right, but it is worthwhile to present examples. Each of the four theologies discussed in this paper attempts to restate the mythological foundations of Christianity in violent terms. Christian Identity attempts to accomplish this by adopting Hebrew arguments of Jewish exclusivity and by embracing militant texts of the Hebrew Bible. For example, the Phinehas Priesthood, a nebulous, "leaderless" organization, justifies its existence by pointing to Numbers 25:1–16. In this text, a Hebrew priest kills an Israelite man and a Midianite woman for intermarrying. Phinehas priests cite this passage as God's call to purify the White race. Identity Christians use this passage to restate the Christian myth with a militant passion. Ironically, it is worth noting that Moses married a Midianite woman (Exod. 2:21). Extremists are not shy about removing biblical passages from their historical and social contexts.

The freewheelers of the patriot movement have also tried to create a mythology of violence by quoting passages out of context. A favorite quotation comes from Luke 22:35–38. In this passage, Jesus tells his followers to sell their cloaks to buy a sword as a symbolic act of spiritual struggle. This passage repeatedly appears at gun shows and was even quoted in The Covenant, the Sword, and the Arm of the Lord's *Defense Manual* (Covenant, the Sword, and the Arm of the Lord, 1982). When the disciples tell Jesus that they already have two swords, Jesus lets them know that they missed the point. Jesus' admonishment, however, is not cited on the gun-show circuit. Other partial passages from Joshua, Judges, Daniel, Matthew, and Revelation are used to transform Christianity into a militant religion. John and Matthew are also frequently cited for their anti-Jewish rhetoric. As the Christian myth is restated in terms of hate, many followers believe that this is simply basic Christianity (Bushart et al., 1998, p. 107). They have no idea that by removing concepts from their social, historical, and theological foundations, they are proclaiming a new religion.

Klassen (1986) takes up similar lines in *The White Man's Bible.* In a tract entitled, *Never Again Through the Serpent's Eyes,* Klassen asks readers to imagine a pioneer woman in a cabin with her young children. A rattlesnake has entered the cabin and threatens to strike one of the children. Klassen poses a debate over the issue. From the liberal humanitarian view, he says, the woman should consider the situation from the snake's point of view. He has just as much right to strike the children as the children have to exist. Of course, Klassen concludes, this is foolish. The only sensible answer is to kill the snake. Theologically, the snake and the mother are in natural, eternal conflict. Nature tells her to destroy any species threatening her children. In his final point, Klassen argues that other races and religions are representative of other species.

Of course, Klassen knew that he was replacing mythology in the WCOTC. The same can be said of Nordic Christianity and Odinism. When Thor strikes the sky with his mighty hammer or Odin calls warriors to Valhalla, Odinists are blatantly substituting an ideological call to violence for a religious call to love. Warrior gods replace Christian archetypes, and the race is called to defend itself. A theology of peace will never serve the extremist right, and they seek to restate mythology in a call to violence.

THEOLOGICAL DANGERS

It is difficult to describe the feeling of grace to those who have not had a religious experience of peaceful revelation. Indeed, to many modern skeptics, the nature of religion seems to be bound in social conflict. The results can be seen in Ireland, where Protestants and Catholics still wage war on each other. It is also apparent in the Balkan Peninsula as ethnic hatred and ethnocentric religion result in the modern massacres. Media commentators speak about violent Islamic fundamentalists from the Middle East, and few Americans can forget the devastating scene in Oklahoma City where Identity extremists killed more than 200 people. In the wake of the new millennium, religious zealots seem to be peddling social conflict as they anxiously await the final struggle of Armageddon. To those who have not experienced peaceful transcendence, religion may seem to be a dark force written in a theology of blood.

This essay has examined the dark side of religious behavior. Religious conflict will dominate the early stages of the new millennium, and it will continue to appear in domestic extremism. Religious violence, especially in the form of terrorism, is a result of politicized eschatological expectations. Yet, religious conflict has swirled around the periphery of human experience in struggles ranging from dirty little wars to cataclysmic, long-term massacres. Why should it merit continued review today, especially with respect to right-wing extremism? Chip Berlet (1998) provides one of the best answers.

In an examination of the apocalyptic paradigm, Berlet (1998) argues that the extremist right's capacity to restate mythology in terms of a cosmic struggle between good and evil is a prescription for violence. Evil is conspiratorial in nature. Extremists believe that secret groups of elites or parasites from lower classes have plotted together to secretly control history. Right-wingers make illogical leaps from evidence to "prove" conspiratorial links, and they simplify social conflicts by blaming problems on a demonized group. They construct theological worlds that are impervious to outside criticism. Such groups have histories of violence.

Walter Laqueur (1999, p. 78) points to the potential for increased violence. The world of terrorism has been limited in the past by the technology available to terrorists and the reluctance of terrorists to use massively destructive force. The world has changed, Laqueur believes, and terrorism is increasingly dominated by religious fanatics. They have access to nuclear devices, chemical and biological weapons, and

terminals for computer attacks. Religion gives terrorists the motivation to use such weapons.

Religious doctrines serve as the cement holding right-wing extremism in place. Among its four theological orientations (Christian Identity, Nordic Christianity or Odinism, freewheeling fundamentalism, and Creatorism), beliefs differ, but religion is the basis for claiming ethnic, racial, and national superiority. Other religions are demonized, and the ethnocentric proclamation of theology becomes the basis for violence and terrorism. Extremists have divided the world into the City of God and the City of Satan, and the fundamentalists are God's warriors. With access to weapons of mass destruction, Armageddon beckons warriors who have developed a mythology of hate. Political eschatology is not an abstract theological concept; it is a dangerous reality of the new century.

REFERENCES

Barkun, M. (1997). *Religion and the racist right: The origins of the Christian Identity movement* (2nd ed.). Chapel Hill: University of North Carolina Press.

Berger, P. L. (1980). *The heretical imperative: Contemporary possibilities of religious affirmation.* Garden City, NY: Anchor.

Berlet, C. (1998). *Dances with devils: How apocalyptic and millennialist themes influence right wings scapegoating and conspiracism* [Online]. Available: http://www.publiceye.org/ Apocalyptic/Dances_with_Devils_TOC.htm

Borg, M. J. (1991). *Jesus: A new vision: Spirit, culture, and the life of discipleship.* San Francisco: Harper.

Bright, J. (1981). *A history of Israel.* Philadelphia: Westminster.

Bruce, S. (1993). Fundamentalism, ethnicity, and enclave. In M. E. Marty & R. S. Appleby (Eds.), *Fundamentalisms and the state* (pp. 28–49). Chicago: University of Chicago Press.

Bushart, H. L., Craig, J. R., & Barnes, M. (1998). *Soldiers of God: White supremacists and their holy war for America.* New York: Kensington.

Campbell, J. (1985). *The inner reaches of outer space: Metaphor as myth and religion.* New York: A. van der Marck.

Campbell, J. (1988). *The power of myth.* New York: Doubleday.

Campbell, J. (1990). *The hero with a thousand faces.* Princeton, NJ: Princeton University Press.

Chalmers, D. M. (1987). *Hooded Americanism: The history of the Ku Klux Klan.* Durham, NC: Duke University Press.

Cooper, H. H. A. (1977). What is a terrorist? A psychological perspective. *Legal Medical Quarterly, 1,* 8–18.

The Covenant, the Sword, and the Arm of the Lord. (1982). *Defense manual.* Zorapath-Horeb, MO: Author.

Crossan, J. D. (1999). *The birth of Christianity: Discovering what happened in the years immediately after the execution of Jesus.* San Francisco: Harper.

Eliade, M. (1968). *The sacred and the profane: The nature of religion.* New York: Harcourt Brace.

Finch, P. (1983). *God, guts, and guns.* New York: Seaview Putnam.

Fox, M. (1988). *The coming of the cosmic Christ: The healing of mother earth and the birth of a global renaissance.* San Francisco: Harper.

Gibson, J. W. (1994). *Warrior dreams: Paramilitary culture in post-Vietnam America.* New York: Hill and Wang.

Gottwald, N. K. (1979). *The tribes of Yahweh: A sociology of the religion of liberated Israel, 1250–1050 B.C.E.* Maryknoll, NY: Orbis.

Hale, M. (1999). *WCOTC membership manual* [Online]. Available: http://www.rahowa.com/manual.htm.

Hamm, M. S. (1994). A modified social control theory of terrorism: An empirical and ethnographic assessment of American neo-Nazi skinheads. In M. S. Hamm (Ed.), *Hate crime: International perspectives on causes and control* (pp. 105–149). Cincinnati, OH: Anderson.

Hoffman, B. (1995). Holy terror: The implications of terrorism motivated by a religious imperative. *Studies in Conflict and Terrorism, 18,* 271–284.

Holden, R. N. (1986). *Postmillenialism as a justification for right-wing violence.* Gaithersburg, MD: International Association of Chiefs of Police.

Holden, R. N. (1999, March). *Illuminati, Bilderbergers, and the Trilateral Commission: The new world order and global conspiracies.* Paper presented at the Academy of Criminal Justice Sciences Annual Meeting, Orlando, FL.

Hudson, W. S. (1981). *Religion in America: An historical account of the development of American religious life.* New York: Scribner.

Kittel, G. (1964). *Theological dictionary of the New Testament,* Vol. II: *Delta-eta.* Grand Rapids, MI: Eerdmans.

Klassen, B. (1986). *The White man's Bible.* Costa Mesa, CA: Noontide.

Kung, H. (1995). *Christianity: Essence, history, and future.* New York: Continuum.

Laqueur, W. (1996, September/October). Postmodern terrorism: New rules for an old game. *Foreign Affairs,* 24–36.

Laqueur, W. (1999). *The new terrorism: Fanaticism and the arms of mass destruction.* New York: Oxford University Press.

Lewy, G. (1974). *Religion and revolution.* New York: Oxford University Press.

Marty, M. E. (1984). *Pilgrims in their own land: 500 years of religion in America.* Boston: Little Brown.

Marty, M. E. & Appleby, R. S. (1991). *Fundamentalisms observed.* Chicago: University of Chicago Press.

Marty, M. E., & Appleby, R. S. (1993). *Fundamentalisms and the state: Remaking policies, economies, and militance.* Chicago: University of Chicago Press.

Noble, K. (1998). *Tabernacle of hate: Why they bombed Oklahoma City.* Ontario, Canada: Voyageur.

Rowe, S. C. (1994). *Rediscovering the West: An inquiry into nothingness and relatedness.* Albany: State University of New York Press.

Sapp, A. D. (1985, March). *Basic ideologies of right-wing extremist groups in America.* Paper presented at the Academy of Criminal Justice Sciences Annual Meeting, Las Vegas, NV.

Sargent, L. T. (1995). *Extremism in America.* New York: New York University Press.

Smith, B. L. (1994). *Terrorism in America: Pipe bombs and pipe dreams.* Albany: State University of New York Press.

Spong, J. S. (1999). *Why Christianity must change or die: A bishop speaks to believers in exile.* San Francisco: Harper.

Stern, K. S. (1996). *A force on the plain: The American militia movement and the politics of hate.* New York: Simon & Schuster.

White, J. R. (1986). *Holy war: Terrorism as a theological construct.* Gaithersburg, MD: International Association of Chiefs of Police.

White, J. R. (1997). Militia madness: Extremist interpretations of Christian doctrine. *Perspectives: A Journal of Reformed Thought, 12,* 8–12.

White, J. R. (1998). *Terrorism: An introduction.* Belmont, CA: Wadsworth.

❖

Eco-Terrorism or Justified Resistance?

Radical Environmentalism and the "War on Terror"

Steve Vanderheiden

Radical environmental groups engaged in ecotage—or economic sabotage of inanimate objects thought to be complicit in environmental destruction—have been identified as the leading domestic terrorist threat in the post-9/11 "war on terror." This article examines the case for extending the conventional definition of terrorism to include attacks not only against noncombatants, but also against inanimate objects, and surveys proposed moral limits suggested by proponents of ecotage. Rejecting the mistaken association between genuine acts of terrorism and ecotage, it considers the proper moral constraints upon ecotage through an examination of just war theory and nonviolent civil disobedience.

In the atmosphere of political opportunism that has characterized the current "war on terror," the language and rhetoric of terrorism have been used against persons and groups that oppose entrenched political and economic powers, including not only genuine terrorists but also legitimate anti-war, anti-globalization, and environmental groups.[1] Describing someone as a "terrorist" serves an explicitly rhetorical purpose in contemporary discourse, though the very language and imagery the term conjures obscure its rational analysis: it implies a moral claim for their aggressive pursuit and prosecution unconstrained by the conventional limits set upon military or law enforcement action. A "terrorist" refuses to observe any moral or legal limits against harming others, and thus a "war on terror" ought likewise to be freed from any such limits (or so the argument goes). Recent U.S. anti-terrorism laws have significantly eroded civil liberties such that mere suspicion of terrorism has become sufficient cause for invasive surveillance and even indefinite detention,

creating powerful and potentially abusive tools for suppressing dissent. Included in the current loosely defined dragnet against "terrorism" has been (along with the pursuit of real terrorists) a politically charged smear campaign by regimes in power against various enemies, both foreign and domestic.

Lost in the recent public discourse surrounding the concept are several crucial distinctions that might restore some measure of credibility to a campaign against a serious moral offense by dissociating it from other actions with which it has been mistakenly (and sometimes disingenuously) associated. Some process of sorting out true from false accusations of terrorism is desperately needed if the current "war on terror" is to deploy its considerable resources appropriately, and if the concept is to be used in a coherent sense to identify a specific kind of moral offense. An exemplary case highlights the need for conceptual clarification and illustrates the contrasts between genuine terrorism and less objectionable political tactics with which it has been unfairly

SOURCE: From "Eco-terrorism or Justified Resistance? Radical Environmentalism and the 'War on Terror'" in *Politics & Society* 33(3) by Steve Vanderheiden, © 2005, pp. 425–447. Reprinted with permission from Sage Publications, Inc.

AUTHOR'S NOTE: The author thanks James Sheppard, Dale Murray, and the participants in the Virginia Commonwealth University Philosophy Colloquium series, as well as members of the Editorial Board of *Politics & Society,* for their helpful comments on earlier versions of this article.

conflated: despite the recent appearance of several homicidal social movements that present genuine cases of domestic terrorism, the FBI in 2001 named the Earth Liberation Front (ELF)—an organization that destroys property but directs no violence toward persons—as the nation's leading domestic terrorist threat.

What has the ELF done to earn such notoriety? The group formed in 1992 as an offshoot of Earth First! when some members became convinced that the original radical environmental group was moving too mainstream. Perhaps its most publicized action was the 1998 torching of a ski lodge under construction at Vail in which arsonists caused $12–26 million in damage to a ski resort expansion which the group claims encroached upon critical habitat of the Canadian lynx. Over the past five years, the group has claimed responsibility for attacks against property associated with urban sprawl, air pollution, animal testing, genetic engineering, and public lands logging, and has caused an estimated $100 million in damage.

While the property damage caused by ELF actions is considerable, the FAQ on the group's website notes that "in the history of the ELF internationally no one has been injured from the group's actions and that is not a coincidence."[2] Guidelines stress that all necessary precautions must be taken in order to protect life during group actions, and that the goal of property attacks is to cause targeted economic harm to anti-environmental offenders in order "to remove the profit motive from killing the earth and all life on it." Rejecting the label *eco-terrorist* (preferring *economic sabotage* or *ecotage*) as a descriptive label for the group's tactics, they suggest that the FBI's aggressive campaign against the ELF, combined with a spate of recent state and municipal "eco-terrorism" laws, "are a definite sign that the authorities are considering the ELF a viable threat to the westernized way of life and to the idea of profits and commerce at any price."[3]

Though the ELF has been painted by these authorities with the brush of terrorism (triggering the legal powers to pursue activists free from the constraints of conventional civil liberties), can the charges stick? Should radical environmentalists who commit acts of ecotage—sabotage of inanimate objects (machinery, buildings, fences) that contribute to ecological destruction—be equated (by inclusion within a common definition of terrorism) with sociopaths like Timothy McVeigh who regard the slaughter of innocents

as "collateral damage" in an ideological war? According to the tenets of just war theory, the primary moral transgression of terrorism lies in its failure to respect the distinction between combatants and noncombatants (known as the principle of discrimination in *jus in bello*), and the so-called eco-terrorists in the ELF commit crimes against property but adhere staunchly to a similar principle (though one that admits of no legitimate human targets, distinguishing instead between persons and the inanimate objects they use to degrade the environment). Does this distinction make a difference? Moreover, might ecotage (insofar as it is to be conceptually distinguished from actual terrorism) ever be justifiably employed? On what grounds might such a defense rest?

This article shall consider two primary questions in an examination of the ethical issues surrounding ecotage. First, is it accurate to classify acts of ecotage as either a variety of or the equivalent to acts of terrorism? Is violence against inanimate objects categorically similar to that against persons such that both might legitimately be described as intending to "terrorize" some population for political ends? Insofar as some might fear for the integrity of their property as well as their persons in the face of perceived threats, is the secondary harm of ecotage (in which the primary harm is to property and not life) morally equivalent to the secondary harm caused by attacks against persons? Second, insofar as ecotage might be treated as an intermediate case between terrorism (which is always wrong) and nonviolent civil disobedience (which is sometimes justified), might ecotage ever be defensible as a tactic of justified political resistance? If one person's terrorist is another's freedom fighter (as is often claimed), might ecotage be defended as not only morally permissible but also (in some cases, at least) morally required?

EXPANDING THE DEFINITION OF TERRORISM TO INCLUDE INANIMATE OBJECTS

Does ecotage (that is, violence against inanimate objects rather than persons) constitute a genuine instance of terrorism? Insofar as it does not, what is the nature of its moral offense, and how might it be compared with other tactics for social change? To attempt an answer to these questions (and thus to define the term), one must first identify the specific offense inherent in terrorist acts. Terrorism is conventionally defined as "the calculated use of violence or threat of violence to attain goals that are political, religious, or ideological in nature . . . through intimidation, coercion, or instilling fear."[4] Within just war theory, Michael Walzer identifies its specific offense as the refusal to adhere to the conventional limits of *jus in bello*, especially that of noncombatant immunity.[5] Accordingly, merely threatened violence may constitute terrorism, so long as the threat is sufficiently palpable and directed toward these public ends (as opposed to merely private gain, about which persons may be similarly terrorized but with different moral effect). Whether or not actual or threatened violence toward property should be considered as the equivalent to violence or threats of violence against persons is a question that shall be addressed presently, but the relevant point here is that terrorism's unique offense lies not in its actual violence (which is straightforwardly wrong on obvious grounds, at least when directed against persons) but in its threatened future violence, which may not necessarily require some initial act of violence in order to produce that characteristic terror (though a successful terrorist attack surely makes the threat of future violence more palpable to a targeted population).

Furthermore, acts of terrorism have both a primary target (those on whom violence is actually inflicted) and a secondary one (the larger population against whom further violence is threatened, producing the characteristic terror), and the unique wrong of terrorism concerns not the primary target but the secondary one. Absent the threat of further violence (should some set of demands not be met), a terrorist act is identical with mass murder (or whatever else comprises the initial strike against the primary target). Again, the relevant question in this inquiry shall be whether or not the secondary target may be adequately terrorized when the primary target includes property but not persons and the threatened future attack promises adherence to the same distinction, and shall be discussed below.

Finally, terrorism is conventionally understood such that those targeted must not only be randomly selected (in the sense of targeting a specific *people* but not specific *persons*) but also be innocents. Otherwise similar acts against non-innocents (for example, attacking armies or colonial oppressors) present categorically distinct (and less objectionable) cases and warrant their exclusion from the conventional definition. Absent the random selection condition (as in targeted assassinations of persons based on some criteria that exclude larger populations, such as membership in a government), a larger population cannot be suitably terrorized by the prospect of becoming the next victim of a terrorist campaign. While the *wrongness* of terrorist acts depends upon the fact that its victims don't deserve the harm they receive (or are threatened with), its *efficacy* in intimidating a larger population turns on the randomness condition. Insofar as ecotage targets only the property of specific offenders (and, moreover, the very inanimate objects used in ecological destruction), it lacks the randomness of genuine terrorism. Not only are persons themselves not targeted, but also (at least in those cases where ecotage targets only the property of extraordinary offenders) ordinary persons need not fear for their property.

Conventionally, then, the moral offense of terrorism is captured in the injunction against intentionally harming (or threatening to harm) innocent persons found in a standard principle of nonmaleficence, and is most clearly instantiated in the principle of noncombatant immunity in *jus in bello* (the person-affecting component of the more general principle of discrimination, which binds agents to respect the distinction between military and civilian targets) and its manifestation in international law (most notably, the Geneva Conventions), which both define and provide the legal means for addressing acts of terrorism. Terrorist acts are, in short, conventionally regarded as acts or threats of illegitimate killing (where acts contain implicit threats to further such acts), and therefore (conventionally, at least) treat differently acts of violence against mere property from that against persons. As vandalism is a lesser offense than murder, threatened further vandalism must also be a lesser offense than threatened future murder, even if persons can be made to fear (and thereby be illegitimately coerced by) either.

At issue in the labeling of ELF acts of ecotage as instances of "terrorism" is whether or not actual persons need to be either the primary or secondary targets of terrorist attacks, or whether the term ought to incorporate all manner of inducements that may illegitimately coerce some targeted population into accepting some set of public demands. Even if the conventional definition draws the line between violence (or threats thereof) against persons and that against inanimate objects (as it does), this distinction requires further critical scrutiny. Suppose the definition of terrorism were expanded to include acts of violence against property in which persons were not physically harmed as primary targets or threatened with future harm as secondary targets, but their economic interests were the actual or intended targets of attack.

In fact, the legal definition of terrorism under U.S. law (generally, an act that "is calculated to influence or affect the conduct of government by intimidation or coercion, or to retaliate against government conduct")[6] has, as part of the 2001 USA PATRIOT Act, been significantly broadened to include many such attacks against inanimate objects. This legislation added an extensive list of specific offenses to the federal crime of terrorism, including "arson within special maritime and territorial jurisdiction" and the "destruction of communication lines, stations, or systems." But perhaps the most expansive category of offense upgraded from an ordinary felony to the status of terrorism (with its concomitant heightened penalties and diminished rights of the accused) includes any act which maliciously damages or destroys, or attempts to damage or destroy, by means of fire or an explosive, any building, vehicle, or other real or personal property used in interstate or foreign commerce or in any activity affecting interstate or foreign commerce.[7]

This addendum to the federal criminal law specifically and intentionally includes ecotage within the legal and rhetorical arsenal of the "war on terror" by criminalizing acts of sabotage, thereby sharply curtailing the civil liberties of suspected saboteurs and their associates.

The question, then, is not whether the law recognizes violence against inanimate objects as acts of terrorism, but whether or not it is proper to do so. By the expansive definition given above, the ELF would appear to deserve the reproach given it by the FBI, for its history of property destruction is both significant and calculated to produce a political or ideological result. Likewise, as several U.S. administrations have argued, the sabotage of Occidental Petroleum's Colombian pipeline seems to be a fitting candidate for the "war on terror," as does the Taliban for its destruction of centuries-old Buddhist statues in Afghanistan. More controversially, perhaps, but clearly falling under the above definition, the participants in the Boston Tea Party willfully destroyed property in order "to retaliate against government conduct" and so must be guilty of exactly the kind of terrorism now proscribed under the USA PATRIOT Act. Once harm to property interests is allowed to count as the equivalent to harm to persons in the moral assessment of terrorism, one begins on a perilous slope down which this initial expansion leads inevitably to a trivialization of what ought to be among the most serious moral transgressions by association with far less serious offenses. At the bottom of the slope, those illegally downloading music from the Internet likewise may become enemies in an all-consuming "war on terror" that knows no principled boundaries.

In order to avoid this absurd conclusion, the temptation (manifest in the conventional definition of terrorism as the violation of the principle of discrimination) has been to circumscribe the definition of terrorism so as to include only harm (or threatened harm) to persons, relegating attacks (or threatened attacks) against inanimate objects to a distinct and less objectionable (though not necessarily benign) category of offense. Such a restrictive view, however, may be unjustified, as consideration of some kinds of attacks against property appears to contain the requisite ingredients of terrorist acts. If a person or people can be "terrorized"—that is, illegitimately intimidated by the calculated use of force and implication of further violence—by random killing, then surely they can also be similarly terrorized by the significant destruction of certain kinds or quantities of property. The burning of civilian areas has long been a psychological weapon of war designed to intimidate and demoralize a population that deserves the name *terrorism* for its violation of the principle of discrimination. Such wanton destruction produces the secondary fear characteristic of terrorism (that is, such attacks make persons fear for their lives and not only for their property) and so seems a fitting candidate for inclusion within the definition. Similarly, the targeting of critical infrastructure (power plants, water treatment facilities) during wartime likewise serves as a psychological weapon designed to coerce civilian populations into accepting terms of an attacking military that they might otherwise find repugnant, and so makes for a fitting example containing the characteristics of a terrorist act.

These examples of violence against inanimate objects serve not to support the inclusion of ecotage within the category of terrorism, but instead to suggest how the definition might be justifiably broadened to include certain kinds of indirect threats to persons as among the primary or secondary targets of terrorist acts. Destruction of a basic human need like shelter or sources of potable water amounts to an indirect physical attack upon persons (insofar as it places persons at serious risk of illness or death by deprivation), and so approaches the wrongness of a direct attack upon those same persons. Palpable threats against a population's water or energy supply—when such an attack would have severely deleterious effects upon the health and welfare of that population—can produce the requisite fear and intimidation characteristic of terrorism. The destruction of whole cities or other significant sites during wartime further damages the culture and identity of a targeted population well beyond any casualties that might accompany such an attack, as the loss of artifacts and records that provide crucial connections with a people's history can have a similarly devastating effect upon the welfare of a population, and threats of such destruction can serve as a similarly illegitimate form of intimidation if significantly palpable. Hence, one might postulate a category of attack or threat against inanimate objects but not (at least directly) against persons that seems deserving of the name *terrorism*.

Such considerations suggest that the conventional limits set upon the definition of terrorism (as requiring acts or threats of violence against civilians) need not necessarily serve as the principled guardrail preventing the slide down the slippery slope, but that any expansion of the definition of terrorism to include inanimate objects (and not persons) as among the targets of terrorist acts must be carefully circumscribed so as not to trivialize the morally relevant distinction between persons and mere objects. One clear case for expansion of the definition involves the nature of the secondary threat implied by the initial act of violence. If an attack against a well-chosen inanimate object threatens further violence against persons (as in "shock and awe" airstrikes designed to pressure civilians to agitate for quick surrender), then that act ought to count as terrorism. After all, the unique offense of terrorism lies not in the primary target of

attack, but in the secondary targets who are threatened (and therefore illegitimately intimidated toward specified ends) with future attacks. If significant attacks against inanimate objects can so terrorize a population with fear for their personal safety, then they are structurally identical with attacks in which the primary targets are persons. On the other end of the spectrum, many acts can use fear in order to coerce a population for political ends (e.g., fear of economic insecurity or cultural decline) without that fear being constitutive of terrorism.

One might further expand the definition of terrorism to allow in violence against inanimate objects insofar as—even though they neither target persons directly in the initial attack nor threaten to do so in the future—they indirectly threaten the survival of persons or groups through threats or attacks against critical infrastructure or objects of extraordinary cultural importance. Destruction of property that merely threatens the further destruction of property (as, for example, by the ELF), where no people need to fear for their personal safety and no cultural artifact of major significance to a people is threatened with obliteration, must be regarded as a categorically distinct act. Conflating it with genuine terrorism unfairly associates those who observe a crucial moral distinction with those who do not.

Dave Foreman (a cofounder of Earth First! and author of a field guide to ecotage) has elucidated several principles of what might tendentiously be termed the *ethics of ecotage* (a topic explored further below). It is, he stresses, never directed at living things, but only "at inanimate machines and tools that are destroying life." In addition to this key constraint (which he calls the "first principle"), a further principled limit is issued: ecotage is not "mindless, erratic vandalism" but rather consists in a calculated targeting of specific objects that are ecologically destructive. Without this second limit, acts of ecotage would be "counterproductive as well as unethical" since sabotage only works if the tools belong to the "real culprit" and because "senseless vandalism leads to loss of popular sympathy."[8] Whatever else can be said against acts of ecotage, they cannot (so long as this principle is observed) justifiably be condemned as the equivalent of the willful killing (or threatened killing) of persons characteristic of genuine terrorism.

CIVIL DISOBEDIENCE AND ECOTAGE

To dissociate ecotage from terrorism is not to defend the actions of the ELF, nor is it to suggest that the group's tactics may sometimes serve as legitimate forms of protest or vehicles for change. The intentional destruction of property constitutes a violation of rights (though not an act of terrorism), regardless of whether committed from simple malice or a well-meaning commitment to ecological sustainability. Insofar as ecotage entails the destruction of property, therefore, it must be regarded as *prima facie* objectionable. The defense of ecotage has thus far considered only its relative seriousness, in comparison with acts that target (and thereby terrorize) persons, and has found the association of ecotage with terrorism to rest upon a mistaken conception of the specific offense that terrorism entails. A more ambitious defense (and one that the remainder of this paper shall attempt) would hold not only that ecotage must be categorically distinguished from terrorism, but also that its use might, in some cases, be justified.

Ecotage, as conceptually distinct from and less serious than terrorism, occupies an intermediate ethical space along a continuum of political tactics between terrorism (which is never justified) and civil disobedience (which may be in some cases unjustified, but is elsewhere defensible). Less serious acts of resistance (and so situated between civil disobedience and ecotage) include illegal but largely symbolic acts of vandalism (e.g., billboard modification through "subvertising") or trespass (e.g., squatting in trees slated for extraction), as these primarily aim for social change through the mobilization of public support, while ecotage instead aims primarily at the profitability of acts taken to be ecologically destructive. In comparison with civil disobedience, ecotage is plainly a more serious and objectionable tactic to employ, given its negative and galvanizing effect upon public opinion, its heightened tendencies toward disorder and lower fidelity for law, and the dangers of both its abuse and unintended consequences. For this reason, the latter could never be defensible in cases where the former was also available. However, one might posit a circumscribed range of cases in which ecotage might be defensible as a political tactic, provided that it is appropriately limited by ethical considerations. One might further speculate that, if circumstances ever justify the resort to ecotage, then its application may, like civil disobedience, become a moral duty grounded in the obligation to remedy injustice.

John Rawls, for example, finds a positive duty to commit acts of civil disobedience in certain well-defined cases, grounded in the natural duty "to assist in the establishment of just arrangements when they do not exist."[9] Like ecotage, civil disobedience also involves a *prima facie* objectionable political tactic (creating civil unrest through targeted lawbreaking), but has gained broad acceptance as a legitimate vehicle of social change in serious cases of injustice in which lesser means of social change have been exhausted. To be sure, civil disobedience and ecotage share some common features but also differ in some important respects, and so the case for ecotage must begin with a consideration of the established case for civil disobedience. Insofar as the two tactics are relevantly similar, the justification for ecotage may rest upon similar ethical foundations as those for civil disobedience. Insofar as they are dissimilar, however, ecotage must either identify a unique justification for its application, or else remain (as popularly construed) a lesser offense than terrorism but a moral transgression nonetheless, however noble the goals of the perpetrator might otherwise be.

Terrorism is likewise an objectionable tactic for reasons discussed above, but its use in certain circumstances has nonetheless been defended by philosophers[10] (although mistakenly so), with the primary objection to such arguments arising from their consequentialist justifications. Generally, defenders of all three tactics rely upon arguments from necessity, which suppose that all lesser avenues of recourse have already been exhausted, and that no preferable alternatives remain for avoiding an outcome that is significantly worse than the tactics employed to avoid it. Sanctioning evil means in the service of putatively defensible ends invokes a deservedly notorious history of means/ends rationalization, and any such claim must be met with a critical skepticism. The burden of proof ought to be placed upon the defender of ecotage (or civil disobedience, or terrorism) to demonstrate not only that all lesser means have already been exhausted, but also that the potentially avoided bad consequences (discounted by the tactic's probability of success) compare favorably with the certain bad consequences that result from the use of the tactic itself. Such a test is beset with difficulties, not least of which is the uncertainty surrounding such predictions about future outcomes. Nonetheless, we might posit that, in principle, some otherwise objectionable tactics may be justified by the seriousness of the consequences to be avoided. Supposing otherwise disqualifies many historically vindicated extralegal means of dissent and resistance, and opens the door to forms of oppression that some of these tactics might otherwise discourage.

Of the three, only terrorism ought to be categorically prohibited as a legitimate tactic, regardless of the gravity of the outcome to be avoided. Although Walzer flirts with the notion that "supreme emergency" (e.g., the imminent destruction of an entire political community) may justify violation of the noncombatant immunity principle, he aptly rejects those arguments that seek to justify terrorism by necessity: "Those who make them, I think, have lost their grip on the historical past; they suffer from a malign forgetfulness, erasing all moral distinctions along with the men and women who painfully worked them out."[11] Besides the historical argument that many of the worst atrocities in human history have relied upon similar claims, Walzer notes a crucial moral difference between terrorism and other tactics. Terrorism "breaks across moral limits beyond which no further limitation seems possible," and as such can never successfully appeal to the sympathies of a larger community. By explicitly rejecting all moral limits on action, and seeking power solely through the spread of fear and intimidation, terrorism appeals to force alone and not to justice (even if based in valid complaints of injustice), and so is bound to be self-defeating as a form of grievance. Even in cases of brutal oppression and exploitation, a minimal reciprocity between parties must remain a prerequisite: one cannot recognize the validity of any claim of injustice that is premised upon a willingness to abandon all pretense of justice.

Civil disobedience, however, is another matter. In his "Letter from Birmingham Jail," Martin Luther King, Jr. defends civil disobedience through a version of the argument from necessity, claiming that "the city's white power structure left the Negro community with little alternative."[12] Recognizing the *prima facie* case against causing social unrest, King sets two

crucial limits upon the application of the targeted lawbreaking of civil disobedience that provide useful contrast with ecotage: first, that it must demonstrate fidelity to law while calling attention to a particular injustice (hence the willingness of protestors to accept legal punishment), and second, that it is premised upon the priority of good faith negotiation, in that efforts at negotiation should first be made, and that the targeted disobedience has as its goal the return to negotiations. He writes,

> Nonviolent direct action seeks to create such a crisis and foster such tension that a community which has constantly refused to negotiate is forced to confront the issue. It seeks to dramatize the issue so that it can no longer be ignored.

Those engaged in civil disobedience, that is, may resort to an otherwise objectionable tactic (i.e., targeted lawbreaking) only in cases of serious injustice and after sincere efforts at social change through conventional legal and political channels fail (the South, he writes, has "been bogged down in a tragic effort to live in monologue rather than dialogue"). Indeed, nonviolent direct action is itself situated between normal politics (the preferred tactic, *ceteris paribus*) and the "frightening racial nightmare" of Black Nationalism, to which King's movement is offered as the preferable alternative.

The primary tension in King's advocacy of civil disobedience as a tactic for the civil rights struggle is instructive for evaluating its structural similarities and disparities in comparison with ecotage. King emphasizes that "the means we use must be as pure as the ends we seek" and that "it is wrong to use immoral means to attain moral ends," but nonetheless ends up sanctioning targeted lawbreaking on grounds that "it is just as wrong, or perhaps even more so, to use moral means to preserve immoral ends." The problem, in other words, lies in weighing two distinct moral offenses, and endorsing one if a necessary condition for avoiding the other. This claim is based on a familiar judgment about the obligations of citizenship: persons have a duty to follow just laws, but to oppose unjust ones. Lawbreaking is not *always* wrong, and may be permitted (given appropriate constraints) when disobedience aims to remedy injustice *and* when it stands a reasonable chance of successfully doing so. Insofar as following unjust laws (for example, the Jim Crow segregationist statutes of the kind that King opposed) perpetuates injustice, person are not only negatively excused from following those laws, but also positively obligated to violate them (in a public way, and accepting the legal consequences that follow).

Since the established case for civil disobedience rests largely upon its consequences (where the remedy to serious injustice outweighs the otherwise objectionable lawbreaking), and since Walzer's rejection of the arguments for terrorism depends upon similar considerations (where, by contrast, terrorism is assumed to be ineffective in advancing its putative aims), one must consider ecotage as political strategy in any defense of the tactic. Rawls, for example, suggests that civil disobedience may only be "wide or prudent" in cases where it is reasonably likely to be effective in its desired aim, and not when it "serves to provoke the harsh retaliation of the majority."[13] In either a society without an adequate sense of justice (so that the appeals of civilly disobedient acts fall upon deaf ears) or one without a reasonably responsive democratic government (so that a remedy to injustice is unavailable through an appeal to the sympathies of a larger political community), civil disobedience (because wrong *prima facie*) is not recommended (as a matter of "practical considerations" rather than principle for Rawls). He further cautions that a limited public capacity for considering the grievances of protestors entails an "upper limit" on the quantity of effective civilly disobedient campaigns at any given time, reserving justification only for the most serious cases of injustice at a given time.

Whereas the nonviolent approach of civil disobedience makes for an effective appeal to society's sense of justice, the violent approach of terrorism fails. Presumably, the distinction between tactics is separate from that between causes that they may aim to advance, so the lack of public sympathy for causes linked to terrorist acts owes to the outright rejection of ethical limits in their indiscriminate targeting of innocent persons, and not to the associated causes themselves. In effectively declaring war upon a community (as terrorism does), the opportunities for sympathy from and reciprocity with that community are negated, and the appeal rests entirely upon fear rather than justice. Civil disobedience, by contrast, appeals not to fear but to the public moral outrage at a particular injustice. Though ecotage (like terrorism) endorses violence, it does

so (unlike terrorism) within circumscribed ethical limits. Can it, then, appeal to the sense of justice of a political community (and so mobilize democratic pressure for change), or does it (as Walzer suggests of terrorism) appeal to force alone, and not to justice? Does a defense of ecotage depend upon its effectiveness as political strategy, depending in turn upon its ability to sympathetically appeal to large numbers of people?

Ecotage as strategy for popular political mobilization may be effective in either of two ways. Like civil disobedience, it may be designed to appeal directly to the sense of justice of a larger political community, which may in turn pressure lawmakers to remedy some serious injustice. Though defenders of the tactic deny that such acts are designed to influence public opinion (insisting instead that they merely aim to make ecological destruction more expensive), many such acts contain elements of political theater that seem explicitly designed to appeal to a wider audience. Their effectiveness in this regard, however, is another matter. Though a small number of eco-radicals may be stirred to action by ELF acts of ecotage, these are unlikely by themselves to make for successful political strategy, as potential allies among mainstream environmentalists may be repelled by the lawlessness of ecotage (viewing ELF action as bombastic and counterproductive, even if they are sympathetic to ELF goals), and those not already sympathetic to the green agenda are unlikely to be persuaded to sign onto it by what are certain to be perceived as nothing short of criminal acts (as they have been legally rendered by majoritarian political institutions).

Media coverage of successful attacks against organizations believed by more moderate environmentalists to be major offenders (timber companies, Hummer dealerships) draws public attention to such causes (publicity that is facilitated by the ELF claiming responsibility for such acts), though this publicity can only effectively mobilize a wider population if it endorses the group's goals *and* is not repulsed by its tactics. Whether such publicity outweighs the inevitable backlash against the mainstream environmental movement by members of the public outraged by ELF actions is another question, but as a political strategy this comprises one possible (though dubious) avenue of efficacy.

The other strategy relies upon this general public outrage against the audacity of ELF actions, but uses this off-putting radicalism to the advantage of mainstream environmental organizations, which appear more reasonable as a result of ELF actions. King's positioning of the SCLC as a more moderate alternative to the Nation of Islam offers a parallel from the civil rights movement for such a "good cop, bad cop" strategy. Working in concert with more moderate groups (regardless of whether or not they do so with the knowledge or approval of more centrist groups), those on the ideological extremes can have the effect of moving the median in the direction of those extremes (providing a power-balancing disincentive against the noncooperation of ecological offenders during negotiations), and political history is replete with successful campaigns to manipulate the center in exactly such a manner.

In his defense of ecotage, Foreman appears to acknowledge such strategic considerations: "The ELF does not engage in more traditional tactics simply because they have been proven not to work, especially on their own."[14] Here, tactics closer to the mainstream are not rejected out of principle, nor because they are demonstrably ineffective, but because they don't work "on their own," suggesting at least some conscious effort to employ this strategy even while denying that ecotage aims to influence either general public opinion or the willingness of opposition forces to bargain with more mainstream environmental groups. Either of these two strategies for appealing to a wider public, of course, may work in tandem with the explicitly acknowledged ELF strategy of raising the costs of doing ecologically destructive business, though the first appears often to be counterproductive and the second entails a morally relevant difference from the established case for civil disobedience, and suggests a further objection insofar as (to be explored in more detail below) it violates the obligation to engage in good faith negotiations before resorting to *prima facie* objectionable extralegal tactics, using the latter only in order to return to the former.

At this point, several dissimilarities between nonviolent civil disobedience and ecotage suggest that the two tactics may be too disanalogous to rest upon the same moral foundations. Both employ direct action through targeted defiance of laws, practices, or institutions taken to be unjust, and see these actions as both necessary given the failure of good faith negotiations and

potentially effective in educating the public and mobilizing political support for social change. Civil disobedience, however, is conducted in the light of day by protestors who are willing to bear legal responsibility for their actions (indeed, this is seen as essential for reopening closed negotiations), while ecotage is typically committed under the cover of darkness, figuratively if not literally, as individual activists aim to avoid detection while groups like the ELF claim responsibility. Since accepting responsibility for one's defiant acts is assumed to be an essential condition of demonstrating fidelity to the system of laws (which is itself assumed to be a necessary condition for effective political strategy), ecotage represents a more significant departure from normal politics than does civil disobedience. The anonymity of the saboteur may likewise work against the publicity strategy of civil disobedience, which relies for its sympathy-generating power upon media coverage of nonviolent protestors being badly treated by police, or otherwise by putting a human face upon an injustice. As such, the defense of ecotage may not be able to rest upon an extension of the established case for civil disobedience. Whether this difference amounts to one in kind or merely in degree remains a central question.

IS THERE AN ETHICS OF ECOTAGE?

The aim of civil disobedience, as Rawls notes, is a rhetorical one that operates through the persuasion and mobilization of a political community; one intends "to address the sense of justice of the majority and to serve fair notice that in one's sincere and considered opinion the conditions of free cooperation are being violated."[15] As King and Rawls both maintain, civil disobedience does not accomplish social change by itself, but instead forces deliberation or thrusts a previously ignored issue onto the public agenda. Chances of successful change depend upon the consonance between the sense of justice of protestors and of the larger community; appealing to a larger community that did not share the protestor's moral outrage would accomplish little beyond short-term disruption. In this sense, civil disobedience serves as a publicity check against injustice, and hence "helps to maintain and strengthen just institutions."[16]

Ecotage does not appear to share this causal process, even if drawing public attention to ecologically destructive practices is occasionally an ancillary effect. The intended primary audience of ELF actions, unlike the direct action of environmental groups like Greenpeace that engage in political theater, is not the mass public but rather the polluter or developer that is responsible for some ongoing act of ecological destruction. The sabotage is not retaliation for some past offense, but an effort to make certain present and future acts more expensive, and hence to discourage them. Saboteurs do not aim to intimidate through force or threats of violence against persons, but rather (according to ELF literature, at least) seek change through the manipulation of the economic incentives surrounding ecologically destructive activities. Whether or not the mass public is sympathetic to ecotage as a tactic affects its efficacy as a political strategy, but its express aims lie not in mobilizing the mass public so much as manipulating private balance sheets. Because ecotage is not primarily a rhetorical act, it cannot serve the same watchdog role as is provided through civil disobedience. Likewise, the public's sense of justice cannot serve as a check upon ecotage as it does with civil disobedience (chastening protestors with silence when their complaints stray too far from public sympathies), since moral dissonance between protestors and the mass public is largely irrelevant to the success of the former but is fatal to the latter.

Because civil disobedience is designed to appeal to the public's sense of justice, Rawls specifies that civil disobedience must be committed in public, which means that "it is engaged in openly with fair notice; it is not covert or secretive." This publicity requirement is a central justification for the emphasis upon nonviolence, since the act is a form of address, and acts which injure others or "any interference with the civil liberties of others tends to obscure the civilly disobedient quality of one's act."[17] The public nature of civil disobedience also ensures that protests remain parts of ongoing democratic deliberation about justice, which can thereby be checked by standards of justice latent in public culture. Ecotage, by contrast, need not be concerned with these publicity requirements, since it neither appeals primarily to a larger sense of justice nor depends upon one for its success. The facts that persons engaged in ecotage seek to

avoid legal responsibility for their acts and that ecotage may entail violence against property (a serious offense, but a categorically different one from violence against persons) are largely explained by these structural differences. While civil disobedience attempts to persuade, and so must avoid acts which alienate its intended audience, ecotage instead aims at the balance sheet of what its perpetrators take to be an offender (or, in some cases, to physically stop ongoing acts of ecological destruction), and intentionally draw the ire of their audience.

Supposing that ecotage be treated as a more serious *prima facie* offense than civil disobedience—and thus that the circumstances in which the former may be justified be more restrictive than those for the latter—is a version of the "sliding scale" argument in *jus in bello*.[18] Rawls invokes something like it in his discussion of the "militant action and obstruction" (which, like ecotage, he treats as more objectionable than civil disobedience, even if he does allow for its possible justification) against which he seeks to distinguish civil disobedience:

The militant, for example, is much more deeply opposed to the existing political system. He does not accept it as one which is nearly just or reasonably so; he believes either that it departs widely from its professed principles or that it pursues a mistaken conception of justice altogether. While his action is conscientious in its own terms, he does not appeal to the sense of justice of the majority (or those having effective political power); since he thinks that their sense of justice is erroneous, or else without effect.[19]

The militant, he goes on to note, does not take legal responsibility for his act, and so disavows the fidelity to law taken to be essential for civil disobedience. Although he suggests that "sometimes if the appeal fails in its purpose, forceful resistance may later be entertained" and that "in certain circumstances militant action and other kinds of resistance are surely justified,"[20] Rawls dissociates his defense of civil disobedience from these more objectionable forms of resistance, which he sets aside without further ethical examination.

Ecotage is neither civil disobedience, with its demonstrated fidelity to law and targeted legal anomaly in an otherwise just world, nor militant uprising, with its wholesale rejection of the mores of the community. Indeed, despite the expressed sympathy for Luddites found throughout

Foreman's work and in its inspiration, Edward Abbey's *The Monkey Wrench Gang,* neither describes monkey wrenchers as violent anarchists bent on bringing down the industrial order. Foreman, for example, insists that ecotage is "not revolutionary" and is "not major industrial sabotage"—its aims and acts are narrowly confined to specific offenses, and it does not aim "to overthrow any social, political, or economic system."[21] Whereas the militant that Rawls describes disavows any commitment to public order or the rule of law, the practitioner of ecotage that Foreman proposes observes a set of strict ethical limits upon allowable action, and targets their actions specifically to a narrow range of offensive practices rather than to an entire political or legal system. As such, ecotage would seem to occupy a space closer to civil disobedience than to militant action, given its relative restraint and commitment to principled limits on action.

As is the case with civil disobedience theory, several of the limits attached to ecotage serve both ethical and strategic considerations. Following the requirement of good faith negotiation prior to direct action in order to make lawbreaking a last resort (prior to more revolutionary change, that is), Foreman urges that ecotage not be used while nonviolent direct action is taking place, or during negotiations. Not only might ecotage bring negative publicity to a particular environmental battle, but it also violates the trust that is essential to good faith negotiation. Here, Foreman's own endorsement of the use of ecotage as a strategic device to manipulate the political center and encourage relevant policy makers to negotiate with the mainstream groups that appear more reasonable as a consequence of ELF radicalism can be seen as a violation of the good faith that is necessary for any effective negotiations, however effective that may be as political strategy. Ethical considerations require that it be reserved for cases in which less objectionable tactics have already failed (and negotiations are no longer ongoing), and not merely that it not be used concurrently with them. Given Foreman's occasional emphasis upon strategy rather than principle (as noted above), this additional restriction becomes critical. Ecotage should never be used before both legal and nonviolent extralegal tactics have been exhausted not only for the practical reason that such tactics undermine ongoing negotiations and alienate political constituencies rather than cultivate them as potential forces of change, but also

because a more objectionable tactic can never be ethically justified if a lesser one will do.

The emphasis within civil disobedience theory upon nonviolence likewise serves both ethical and strategic purposes, and so is instructive for promoting the persuasive efficacy of ecotage, which also risks alienating persons who are otherwise sympathetic to its aims but repulsed by its placing persons at risk. Though ecotage cannot renounce violence against inanimate objects, a central ethical constraint upon its use must be a principle of discrimination that guards against exposing persons to risk of harm. The evolution of the Earth First! tactic of tree spiking illustrates how such a principle may be operationalized in practice. Early acts of tree spiking involved driving metal or ceramic (which elude metal detectors) spikes into the trunks of trees slated for harvest; a practice which injured several loggers when their chainsaws hit the spikes, bringing immense negative publicity (and the first "eco-terrorism" laws)[22] upon the group and the practice for its apparent indifference to human welfare. One faction of Earth First! (led by Judi Bari) disavowed the practice entirely, while another (led by Foreman) urged that spikes be driven high enough so that only sawmill blades and not chainsaws are threatened by them, suggesting further that spiking be appropriate only for "large timber sales where the trees are destined for a corporate, rather than a small, family-oriented mill," as the former have protective shields that prevent injury to mill workers when sawmill blades are shattered by spikes, and since the latter "are seldom a major threat to wilderness."[23] While this concern should have been exercised at the outset, the changing practices nonetheless reflect one manner of insuring against morally repugnant and strategically self-defeating actions. As an additional safeguard, the broader publicity requirement in civil disobedience might be applied in a more limited way to ecotage by requiring not that ecoteurs themselves act in the open (as in civil disobedience) but rather that their actions be transparent to those who might otherwise be harmed by them. Where an action might place a person at risk of injury, those risks must be sufficiently publicized in order that they may readily be avoided.[24] While marking all and only those trees which have been spiked may undermine the efficacy of the practice (as timber operations could simply harvest all unmarked trees), creative modifications of the practice (for example, marking all mature trees in some stand in an ecologically and aesthetically nondamaging but obvious way whether or not spiked) may be able to adequately protect persons (thereby maintaining adherence to principle and avoiding bad publicity) while maintaining the tactic's deterrent value.

Is Ecotage Ever Justified?

Under what circumstances might a resort to ecotage be warranted? If its use is ever to be justified, a necessary condition must be that all lesser tactics have been exhausted, and that nothing less than ecotage might avert a serious wrong. Rawls aptly limits justified civil disobedience to "the special case of a nearly just society" as opposed to cases of more pervasive injustice or in societies which are not well ordered, since only in the former might an injustice be remedied through the rhetorical force of direct action as an appeal to the sense of justice of a political community. Similarly, one might posit that ecotage (or "other kinds of dissent or resistance")—insofar as it is less likely to appeal to the sympathies of a larger community than is civil disobedience, and is therefore unlikely to be effective in mobilizing popular support for some cause where civil disobedience has already failed—is appropriate only in societies where serious injustices are more broadly tolerated, where political processes are unresponsive to public opinion, or where rhetorical appeals are otherwise unlikely to produce positive effects. Consider, for example, the following cases in which activists turn to ecotage as a tactic of resistance:

Case 1. A "cut and run" logging operation is illegally harvesting rare and valuable old growth timber from a protected area on public lands. State officials, although in full knowledge of these activities, refuse to take adequate steps to halt them or to prosecute the offenders, in part because of an institutionalized sympathy with the timber industry and an ideological hostility to the environmental protection laws that now prohibit the state from selling this timber. Opponents of this illegal logging have attempted to compel the state to enforce its own laws through lawsuits, and to protect the forests directly through nonviolent action (blocking roads, encouraging boycotts of illegal wood products), but to no avail. Finally,

opponents begin driving metal spikes into the "protected" trees—which destroy sawmill blades if the trees are illegally harvested but do not harm the trees themselves—in an effort to dissuade these operations by increasing their costs.

Case 2. By law, large parcels of "untrammeled" public lands (i.e., those without roads or other signs of human habitation) are eligible for inclusion within a protected national wilderness system. Inventories of suitable land have been controversial, because wilderness designations (which must be approved by the legislature) permanently protect parcels of land from extractive or other ecologically damaging uses. The legislature has for some time refused to designate some suitable lands as wilderness, and so they remain unprotected. In order to permanently prevent these lands from being added to the wilderness system, anti-environmental "property rights" groups are building illegal roads across them. The relevant state officials ignore these acts, since they share an interest in opening these lands for development, and hence in the budget-enhancing sales of extraction permits from them. Private citizens have attempted to halt these illegal road-building projects nonviolently, but to no avail. In order to halt one such operation, opponents sabotage a group of bulldozers and road graders by draining their oil and pouring sugar in their gas tanks.

Case 3. Due to a loophole in automobile fuel efficiency standards, vehicles weighing over three tons were left exempt from regulations designed to reduce gasoline consumption and its deleterious ecological consequences. Though originally an exemption intended only for a few heavy work trucks, the increasing popularity of large SUVs for regular transportation led several manufacturers to intentionally design vehicles heavy enough to gain this exemption (necessary given their fuel inefficiency) and one company ("Bummer") to specialize in such large and ecologically destructive vehicles. Various groups urge legislators to close this loophole (which undermines the aims of the regulations), but to no avail, and public relations campaigns by environmental groups against the purchase of such vehicles (including a protestor chaining herself to one in order to draw attention to their harmful effects) are similarly unsuccessful. Given an unwillingness of policy makers to amend existing regulations in order to bring such vehicles under fuel efficiency standards, and in order to counter a highly effective marketing campaign for the SUVs, a small group of activists sets fire to a Bummer dealership, vandalizing and spray painting "I [heart] pollution" on several of the vehicles.

The first two of these cases have several instructive features in common, which can instructively be contrasted with the third case. To simplify, they both involve acts that are both illegal and (arguably) unjust. The more difficult third case (representative of a category of grievance which is far more vulnerable to abuse) targets an act (selling or driving large and fuel-inefficient SUVs) that is legal but arguably unjust (or at least highly damaging), but fails to meet the necessary conditions for a justified resort to ecotage (and shall be discussed as such further below). In all three cases, the state is complicit in the acts in question, and so standard legal avenues of appeal are unlikely to be effective. Given that the democratic responsiveness of political institutions is assumed to be a prerequisite for the use of rhetorical tactics like civil disobedience, and since the institutions are in these three cases unresponsive to political and legal pressure, one might surmise that further publicity of the offenses in question will fail to move the relevant actors toward remedial action. Finally, all three cases involve failed attempts at both legal and less offensive extralegal oppositional tactics, and in the first two cases (though not the third) the resort to ecotage is taken only as a last resort and in cases of clear emergency, where further delay would likely lead to long-term and irreversible damage.

The above cases suggest a set of necessary conditions for the application of ecotage as a tactic of political resistance: (1) some act is being undertaken which is contrary to both law and justice; (2) state officials charged with enforcing relevant laws are unwilling or unable to do so; (3) serious damage is imminent and, once complete, will be durable and irreversible; (4) legal means were attempted and proved unsuccessful; and (5) appeals to the sense of justice of the community have either already failed or would be frustrated by the unresponsive policy making or enforcement processes. They suggest also (especially in conditions 1 and 3, above) why the third case presents neither an adequately serious, nor unique, nor immanent threat to justify the acts described (which are equally unlikely to deter the manufacture and purchase of such vehicles as well as the passage of relevant regulatory legislation). Following the civil disobedience literature, one might further specify that damage be narrowly targeted to the offensive inanimate object in question, that the economic damage inflicted be proportional to the offense in question, and that any sabotage must inflict the least damage necessary in order to avoid the bad outcome. Under no circumstances (whether intentional or as the result of inadequate care) should persons be physically harmed or subjected to undue risk, either directly or indirectly.

Taken together, do the above constitute sufficient conditions for justified ecotage? Ruled out would be cases that are not narrowly tailored to an identifiable offense, such as case 3's protest of the state and auto industry's indifference to fuel economy, or the burning of a timber company office as a general protest against the industry's unsustainable logging practices. Likewise excluded would be ecotage against acts which may be environmentally destructive but which are not obviously unjust, such as the arson of luxury homes in sprawling subdivisions or the vandalism of property carrying the logo of a particularly anti-environmental corporation. Targeting research facilities that develop genetically modified crops would likewise be prohibited, on the grounds that technologies in development do not yet pose an imminent threat, and so cannot justify the more aggressive and immediate response of ecotage. Taken together, that is, the above conditions may constitute both necessary and sufficient conditions for a resort to ecotage, at least if any circumstances warrant such acts.

CONCLUSION

Supposing that ecotage may be justified in at least a narrow range of cases, ethical limits similar to those from *jus in bello* constrain both the acts themselves and the circumstances in which they may be undertaken. Several limits have been suggested above. Four final remarks underscore the need to recognize principled restraints on the application of any *prima facie* objectionable political tactics, including ecotage.

First, ecotage must be understood as an act that must be reserved for extraordinary circumstances and then narrowly targeted to the exigencies of specific cases. It is not, as defended here, militant resistance or insurrectionist in nature. Foreman comes perilously close to undermining his own case for ecotage when he describes it as a kind of self-defense, urging that "it is aimed at keeping industrial civilization out of natural areas and causing industry's retreat from areas that should be wild" and that "it is defensive in that it is used to prevent destructive development in wild places and in seminatural areas next to cities."[25] While the image of an environmental militia in defense of the earth may stir the passions of potential followers, it also risks the blurring of the above ethical limits suggested for acts of ecotage. If ecotage is to be sufficiently disciplined to observe these limits, seeking to alter economic incentives that are presently unjustly skewed toward ecological destruction but not to inflict gratuitous damage, then the rhetoric of defensive warfare is unhelpful. Rhetoric such as this may motivate the already converted, but risks alienating potential allies and encouraging the transgression of the necessary moral limits set upon acts of ecotage.

Second, the risks associated with ecotage as political strategy are immense, and must therefore be kept in mind throughout this analysis. It remains unclear that ELF actions have thus far had any positive effects on public opinion, nor have they advanced the agenda of mainstream environmental groups (moderate alternatives to ELF radicalism) in any obvious ways. Though they've inflicted in excess of $100 million in damage (primarily through arson), these costs have been borne primarily by insurance companies rather than agents of environmental destruction, giving rise to justified skepticism that ELF actions have been effective in any of their possible avenues of social or political change. On the other hand, the lawlessness of ecotage risks alienating mainstream public opinion for the very reason that Walzer identifies as the failure of terrorism and both King and Rawls identify as the strength of civil disobedience: it fails to make its case in a straightforward and public way, and it fails to accord adequate respect to the system of law and justice toward which it directs its action. This downside risk is a serious one, especially in light of the lack of a corresponding upside to ecotage, and activists must remain mindful of this potential for a backlash of public opinion against the environmental movement if they sincerely desire to bring about the requisite changes to achieve a more sustainable society.

Third, and related to the risk of a backlash of opinion, ecotage presents the risk of violating its own principles, either by inadvertently causing harm to persons or in appearing to sanction violence such that the strategy could be hijacked by less principled cohorts. Historically, clandestine groups that employ limited violence have experienced difficulty in maintaining their principled opposition to the expansion of that violence, and have as a consequence crossed the lines separating the defensible from the criminal. In that ecotage eschews the publicity condition requisite for civil disobedience, it forgoes the check against wielding the tactic without adequate grievance in serious injustice that is provided by the process of public deliberation of which civil disobedience remains a component. It therefore risks violation of many of the ethical limits elucidated above: refraining from harming persons, targeting only extraordinary offenders in clear cases of injustice where serious damage is imminent and potentially irreversible, narrowly tailoring its attacks to particularly destructive equipment, and resorting to ecotage only when all lesser means have been exhausted. One might minimize this risk by requiring that acts of ecotage be preceded by careful deliberative processes designed to replicate the functions of the failed democratic institutions whose authority is being challenged through such extralegal acts, but the prospects of effective deliberation in clandestine groups like the ELF are, at best, limited. Even if justifiable cases for ecotage may be articulated in theory, one must worry about the effect of its principled limits in practice.

Finally, claims of injustice surrounding acts that are ecologically destructive must be met with the proper critical scrutiny, and the burden of proof must be placed on those seeking remedial action through ecotage, but such claims ought not to be dismissed out of hand (as, for example, through the misleading moniker *eco-terrorism*). Present threats to the integrity of the biosphere are multifarious and pervasive, and the radical environmental movement was born of a frustration with the slow pace of remedial change accomplished through mainstream politics. It must be remembered that, as King notes in his famous letter, "law and order exist for the purpose of establishing justice, and that when they fail to do this they become dangerously structured dams that block the flow of social progress."[26] Likewise, as Rawls notes, a preference for order and stability cannot rule out efforts to rectify injustice categorically, for "if justified civil disobedience seems to threaten civic concord, the responsibility falls not upon those who protest but upon those whose abuse of authority and power justifies such opposition."[27] One may have an obligation to first pursue social change within the confines of mainstream politics and good faith negotiation, and then through civil disobedience, but ruling out ecotage categorically would, like foreswearing nonviolent direct action, be in some cases excluding a defensible avenue of social change.

NOTES

1. See, for example, Eric Lichtblau, "FBI Scrutinizes Antiwar Rallies," *New York Times,* online edition, November 23, 2003, http://www.nytimes .com. The story documents the monitoring of antiwar demonstrators as part of the FBI's counterterrorism efforts.

2. Earth Liberation Front, "Frequently Asked Questions about the Earth Liberation Front (ELF)," North American ELF Press Office, 2001, http://www .earthliberationfront .com, 27.

3. Ibid., 31.

4. Noam Chomsky, "Terror and Just Response," in *Terrorism and International Justice,* ed. James Sterba (New York: Oxford University Press, 2003), 69.

5. Michael Walzer, *Just and Unjust Wars* (New York: Basic Books, 1977), 197–206.

6. *U.S. Code,* sec. 2332b, title 18.

7. *U.S. Code,* sec. 844i, title 18.

8. Dave Foreman, "Strategic Monkeywrenching," in *Ecodefense: A Field Guide to Monkeywrenching,* 3rd ed., ed. Dave Foreman and Bill Haywood (Chico, Calif.: Abbzug Press, 1993), 9.

9. John Rawls, *A Theory of Justice* (Cambridge, Mass.: Belknap, 1971), 334.

10. See, for example, Jean-Paul Sartre's preface to Franz Fanon's *The Wretched of the Earth,* trans. Constance Farrington (New York: Grove, 1986), 7–31, in which Sartre defends FLN (National Liberation Front, or Front de Libération Nationale) terrorism in Algeria through the argument from necessity. For a critical reply, see Walzer, *Just and Unjust Wars,* 204–6.

11. Walzer, *Just and Unjust Wars,* 204.

12. Martin Luther King Jr., "Letter from Birmingham Jail," in Martin Luther King Jr., *Why We Can't Wait* (New York: Harper & Row, 1964), 77–99.

13. Rawls, *A Theory of Justice,* 376.

14. Earth Liberation Front, "Frequently Asked Questions," 20.

15. Rawls, *A Theory of Justice,* 382–83.

16. Ibid., 383.

17. Ibid., 366.

18. See, for example, Walzer, *Just and Unjust Wars,* 229–32.

19. Rawls, *A Theory of Justice,* 367.

20. Ibid., 368.

21. Foreman and Haywood, *Ecodefense,* 10.

22. Anti-spiking legislation was added as a rider to the Anti-Drug Abuse Act of 1988 in a subsection entitled "Hazardous or Injurious Devices on Federal Lands" that prohibits "tree spiking devices including spikes, nails, or other objects hammered, driven, fastened, or otherwise placed into or on any timber" (*U.S. Code,* sec. 1864, title 18).

23. Foreman and Haywood, *Ecodefense,* 19.

24. Foreman (in *Ecodefense*) urges that "anyone spiking trees has a moral obligation to notify the 'proper authorities' that a particular area contains spiked trees and that it would be hazardous to cut those trees" (31), and that the goal is to raise the costs of timber sales and thus to provide a "long term deterrent" against further incursions into federally managed wilderness. To this publicity requirement, an additional marker on each spiked tree would provide an additional safeguard against injury.

25. Dave Foreman, *Confessions of an Eco-Warrior* (New York: Harmony Books, 1991), 118.

26. King, "Letter from Birmingham Jail," 88.

27. Rawls, *A Theory of Justice,* 390–91.

6

MEDIA COVERAGE OF TERRORISM

If only there were evil people somewhere insidiously committing evil deeds and it were necessary only to separate them from the rest of us and destroy them. But the line dividing good and evil cuts through the heart of every human being, and who is willing to destroy a piece of his own heart?

—Alexander I. Solzhenitsyn

The relationship between journalists and terrorists is both basic and complex. To paraphrase Carlos Marighella, who wrote the manual for urban guerrillas, "The media are important instruments of propaganda for the simple reason that they find terrorist actions newsworthy" (Weimann & Winn, 1994, p. 112). Yet as instruments of propaganda, the media may be used by both guerrillas and governments. The attacks on 9/11 were obviously extremely newsworthy, but the public was concerned about the ways in which the media might promote terrorist propaganda. Instead, an examination of the mainstream U.S. news reporting in the weeks following 9/11 shows that the American news media degenerated into an irresponsible organ of patriotic propaganda. The media not only used loaded language to promote a "war on terrorism" but they also remained silent on uncomfortable issues and marginalized dissenting opinions (Eisman, 2003). Open debate of past U.S. actions was absent from media discussions.

Interaction between the media and terrorists intensified in the latter part of the 20th century because of the increase in available information and around-the-clock news coverage. CNN with its global reach, 24-hour news cycle, and foreign affairs agenda came to encapsulate the idea of a media-driven foreign policy, sometimes known as the "CNN effect" (Robinson, 2005). With news being presented in multimedia packages and delivered in innovative and interactive ways, revolutionaries with political agendas have many more avenues for promoting their ideologies. At the same time, state-sponsored terrorism has a broader audience for mass propaganda campaigns and manipulation of news.

Although government influence on the media is evident, Internet technology makes it possible for disenfranchised individuals both to have access to information and to disseminate it. The Net has brought about a democratization of the media. Some would argue that anyone with a Web site is capable of being a journalist online (Kees, 1998). In his study of Islamist Web sites, Maguire (2005) identified four clusters: religious modernists, Saudi opposition, pro-Saudi traditionalists, and Jihad enthusiasts. The last cluster, which is focused on Jihad, contains a variety of viewpoints and strategies. Differences in ideology and allegiances generate a great deal of controversy.

There are those who question the credibility of the Jihad Web sites, suggesting that the Mujahiddin on the Internet are more virtual than real. Still others think that the sites are used by Western intelligence agencies to accomplish nefarious ends (Maguire, 2005, p. 123). Rather than being a clear mirror of Islamic sentiment and scholarship, the Internet often distorts Islamic ideas. The sites may be prisms created by individual, sectarian Muslim technophiles with distorted or disturbed notions, who are the Web masters.

Anderson (2003) notes that new media technologies have transformed the nature of risk in contemporary society. The Internet has come to act as a key vehicle for the rapid circulation of rumors and hoaxes as well as legitimate stories. It significantly contributes to growing anxieties about future terrorist attacks.

MEDIA, LAW, AND TERRORISM

Freedom of speech is guaranteed by the First Amendment to the U.S. Constitution. Its central meaning, according to President James Madison, was that the people had the power of censorship over the government, and not the government over the people. He considered this principle to be fundamental to the U.S. form of government (Findlaw, 1998). Even with this protection in place, there have been many attempts to regulate malicious writings. One of the first was the Sedition Act of 1798, which prohibited utterances that excited the hatred of the people against the government.

Media law historically has been divided into two areas: telecommunications and print. The growth of the Internet and digital media has begun to blur the boundaries between the segments, and the bases for the distinctions in law between the two areas are no longer clear (Legal Information Institute, 2001).

Several recent laws address the interaction between media and terrorism. The Antiterrorism and Effective Death Penalty Act of 1996 includes a provision to regulate media cooperation with insurgents (Cole, 1996). Journalists have been concerned that, broadly interpreted, the 1996 law would prohibit them from developing valid stories about terrorist groups (Hudson, 2000). The antiterrorism legislation of 2001, the USA PATRIOT Act, which was reauthorized in 2006, limits journalists' abilities to interact with terrorist groups even further (U. S. Dept. of Justice, 2006).

Opposition to government through speech alone has been subject to punishment throughout much of U.S. history, but laws criminalizing speech have also been struck down regularly by higher courts as inconsistent with the First Amendment (FindLaw, 1998). Some defenders of First Amendment liberties insist that terrorism exists because, in a larger sense, justice does not exist. According to those in opposition to authority, the present corrupt legal system protects the guilty and persecutes the innocent. The ideology of a terrorist group identifies the "enemies" of the group, giving rise to the idea that certain people or things are somehow legitimate targets (Drake, 1998). If they perceive the government as illegal, citizens may believe they have the constitutional right to join a militia group, become a reclusive anarchist, or join violent demonstrations to get political power (Hinckley, 1996).

A free press is essential to the democratic process, but increasingly the idea of the United States as an "open society" has been called a myth. Snow and Taylor (2006) point to several myths about the media and government in the United States. One myth, as they see it, is the supposed adversarial relationship between government and the media. This is a myth that is convenient for both sides and is sustained for their mutual benefit.

Another common myth is that overt censorship in news organizations does not exist. It does, and has historical precedent. Censorship is the result of both individual self-censorship and media complicity in government efforts to mislead the public through disseminating domestic propaganda (Snow & Taylor, 2006, p. 407). The U.S. government relies on a form of censorship known as "censorship at source"; in other words, those unnamed official sources of the news whom we often see referenced in our newspapers and magazines. This type of censorship keeps both journalists and the public in the dark.

Two converging trends—further consolidation of the media and a less open and democratic government—limit access to information today. In the global media environment today, the best journalist is increasingly the diligent journalist. He or she understands the symbiotic relationship between official channels of information sources and the news story product. Ultimately, the real challenge in the global struggle for hearts and minds is that, in the process of selling democracy, the United States does not sell out (Snow & Taylor, 2006).

Other countries with democratic forms of government have different histories. Benjamin Netanyahu, the former prime minister of Israel, asserted in 1995, "There is apparently a moment of truth in the life of many modern democracies when it is clear the unlimited defense of civil liberties has gone too far and impedes the protection of life and liberty, and governments decide to adopt active measures against the forces that menace their societies" (p. 32). The "moment of truth," as Netanyahu terms it, involves the decision to limit the democratic process. In Peru, for example, the threat of the Shining Path terrorist group generated drastic limits to the democratic process in the late 1980s. Along with increased police powers came increased corruption, and a great deal of brutality was authorized by the state (Palmer, 1994).

Throughout the world, direct state-imposed censorship is a common response to terrorism. In France, the *Bastille syndrome* is the term used to describe various presidents' intensive interference in broadcasting (Weimann & Winn, 1994). Creating a generalized fearfulness among the public gives state leaders greater freedom of action. Terrorism has been used repeatedly to advance tyrannical agendas, justify exceptional legislation, encroach on individual rights, increase internal surveillance, enlarge the role of military forces, and put pressure on journalists to cooperate with agents of the state (Herman & O'Sullivan, 1989). A fear of terrorism has contributed to the vulnerability of democracies to exercise repressive tendencies (Weimann & Winn, 1994). A real threat of subversion is posed not only by guerrillas but also by the reaction of the forces of authority. A common reaction involves censorship and control of public information.

IRRESPONSIBLE REPORTING

In covering terrorism, the media are dammed if they do and damned if they do not exercise self-restraint (Nacos, 1994). The public's need to be informed has to be balanced by journalists' responsibility to prevent unnecessary harm. Three issues are at stake when media sources provide information about terrorism: interference, cooperation, and commercialism.

Interfering in State Operations Against Terrorism

Journalists have become targets of terrorist activity and are repeatedly threatened for expressing opinions contrary to terrorist goals. Throughout Spain, for example, ETA (*Euskadi ta Askatasuna,* or Basque Fatherland and Liberty) terrorists describe journalists and the media who do not share their radical nationalist ideology as Basque traitors or Spanish invaders. According to ETA pronouncements, the media are the mouthpiece for a strategy to instigate war in Basque country, an area that lies along the border between Spain and France. Some 100 journalists have been placed under police protection in response to mail bombs and attacks against two of the largest newspapers in the Basque region. Still other journalists were exiled (Mather, 2000). In the United States, NBC newscaster Tom Brokaw and other media-related targets were the intended victims of anthrax sent by mail by terrorists in 2001. In 2002, *Wall Street Journal* investigative reporter, Daniel Pearl, was ritually decapitated in Pakistan, and the horrific image of his severed head was widely published in the press and on the Internet (Levy, 2003).

Many U.S. journalists have been held hostage, assassinated, or threatened by homegrown and transnational terrorists at home and abroad. Journalists may be targeted because of their views or what they have reported. It is just as likely that their notoriety makes reporters valuable regardless of their opinions.

How reporters and photographers should act in tense terrorist situations is only one part of the equation for measuring journalistic responsibility. Another is how news managers decide under enormous pressure what should be aired live, what should be aired later, and what should never appear before the public. According to many in law enforcement, the public does not need to see tactical police activity live (Shepard, 2000). Although this may make sense from the standpoint of counterterrorism efforts, from a First Amendment standpoint it provides opportunities for brutal and destructive tactics to be obfuscated. Terrorist attacks can be re-created to fit particular political agendas unless they are recorded for the public by journalists and others on the scene who represent outside interests. In contrast, the BBC faced a scandal in Britain over its publication of the evidence from Dr. David Kelly, a noted arms expert, that Parliamentary reports of eminent threat from Iraq had been "sexed up" to mislead the public and create a climate favorable for intervention. Although the misleading reports came from Parliament, the BBC was eventually blamed for the suicide of Dr. Kelly and for its mishandling of the information (Schlesinger, 2006, p. 299).

Many questions have been raised about the impact of the media on terrorism. The sheer volume of information provided makes a difference with regard to the outcome of terrorist events. When the group Black September took hostages at the Munich Olympics in 1972, the media became involved in the minute details. Because media coverage of the Olympics was already in place, the attack became the center of attention for the entire world. The coverage of the kidnapping of Israeli Olympic athletes increased worldwide support and sympathy for Israel. It also created the image of hooded, enigmatic, and angry Arab terrorists armed with machine guns who killed 11 hostages in cold blood. However, the coverage did not explore the complexities of the conflict nor did it ever explain the incompetence and misdirection of the authorities in Munich (Morrison, 2000). The documentary, *One Day in September* (Columbia Tri Star, 1999, 97 min.), explores the ineffectiveness of the government response to this attack.

Other aspects of the form and presentation of the news may affect terrorism in unknown ways (Barnhurst, 1991). Journalists amplify, arbitrate, and create their own rhetoric about terrorist acts. According to Picard (1991), reporters can choose from four different traditions of reporting to relate terrorist events. In the *information* tradition, reports are expected to be factual and reliably documented. News about terrorism is notably poorly corroborated, although it may appear to be in the information tradition. In the more *sensationalist* tradition, coverage includes emotions, alarm, threat, anger, and fear. Tabloids have an extremely large audience for sensationalized coverage not only in the United States but also globally, and the tabloid style is sometimes found in mainstream daily newspaper reporting about terrorism. When the tradition is toward *feature stories,* the focus is on individuals as heroes, villains, victims, and perpetrators. Feature stories provoke readers by focusing on an actual person with whom to relate in emotional ways, using methods similar to the tabloid style, but they are taken more seriously. Features are expected to be the product of reliable reporting. In the *didactic* tradition, the report is intended as an explanation, and the goal is purported to be educating the public. Despite the stated goal, documentaries about terrorists and terrorism reveal a particular perspective, support news industry agendas, and pander to sponsors' interests. Explanations carry a slant and a viewpoint that reflect the people and organizations making them, though these individuals and groups may consider themselves to be neutral. Each of these four traditions is useful in different ways and times to both journalists and terrorists.

The impact of media accounts also varies depending on the audience receiving the reports, the types of events being reported, and other events that may preempt public attention. Complex factors must be considered in assessing the media's responsibilities in reporting terrorist events. Whatever the complexity of the issue, though, critics have noted that the news media are even more responsible than the government when they allow false governmental claims to stand without challenge (Elliott, 2004).

News organizations have sets of standards and policies in place on how to react to a variety of conditions in reporting the news. Few of these organizations, however, were prepared to deal with the questions and issues raised by a case such as that of the Unabomber in 1995. Theodore Kaczynski was a disenchanted mathematics professor turned anarchist who espoused an "earth first" ideology. By sending mail bombs to researchers and others in academia, he attacked the representatives of modernity and of biotechnology in particular, for which he is now serving an unconditional life sentence. The Unabomber built explosives in a remote, ramshackle cabin where he lived in isolation in Montana. His terrorist pursuits spanned 17 years, killed 3 people, and maimed 29 others. The FBI called the case UNABOM after the first targets, *UN*iversity researchers and *A*irline executives (Walton, 1997). Kaczynski was the author of lengthy diatribes against the course of development and the federal government. He threatened to continue bombings unless his major treatise was published. The decision by *The Washington Post* and the *New York Times* to publish the Unabomber's 35,000-word manifesto against technology is one instance of media cooperation that has had long-term troubling implications for media managers everywhere. The decision was debated heatedly and widely (Harper, 1995). Critics insist that publication of the manifesto set a precedent that encourages terrorists to use the mass media to promote their political views. Since then, the Unabomber has become an icon on the Internet, and his manifesto is available in its totality on several Web sites (Walton, 1997).

Cooperating With Terrorists or With Government Control

News stories are symbolic expressions that create but also are created by culture. The ideal of media objectivity versus the reality of subjective bias provides a good example of a basic conflict in U.S. culture. According to Solomon (1999), there is an Orwellian logic behind calling bombings by Third World countries "terrorism," whereas bombings by the United States are righteous "strikes against terror." A content analysis of U. S. newspaper articles describing violence in Iraq in 2003 revealed that words implying destruction and devious intent were typically used in reference to violent actions associated with Iraq and opponents of the United States, whereas more benign words were used in reference to the United States and its allies (Dunn, Moore, & Nosek, 2005). The authors conclude that word usage guides perceptions of violence as terrorism or patriotism, thereby affecting people's attitude toward and memory of violent events.

Herman and O'Sullivan (1989) point out that media accounts in the United States seldom cover the precipitating events from which subsequent terrorist events have sprung. Instead, terrorism is commonly reported as an isolated event, out of context, making the perpetrators seem unprovoked and inexplicably evil. Nevertheless, most of the concern about media cooperation has to do with journalists' support for terrorist interests, whereas the cooperation of the media with government interests frequently goes unnoticed.

A study of 258 reports of 127 incidents of political violence showed that the media quoted primary sources less than 6% of the time. That proportion is far below what would normally be considered good practice (Picard & Adams, 1991). Indications are that journalists rely on government sources, particularly the FBI, for most of the information that is reported about terrorists in the United States. Therefore, what the public knows about terrorists is largely filtered through a process of government control of information. Although the First Amendment prohibits censorship, it makes no reference to restricting information by ensuring that journalists voluntarily rely on only one official source of information.

Wilkinson (1997) asserts that it is intrinsic to the very activity of terrorization that some form of media, however crude, is used as an instrument to disseminate the messages of threat and intimidation. The theory that the media are, in part, a cause of terrorism is based on the assumption that, by attacking a Western democracy, terrorists will receive benefits from the media through coverage of the incident. The three primary benefits that terrorists may expect are publicity to spread their message, opportunities to provide a context and interpretation for their actions, and a level of legitimacy that would otherwise be unobtainable (Becker, 1996).

Targets of terror do not lose their usefulness to terrorists even when violent incidents result in negative media coverage, public outcries against brutality, and widespread sympathy for victims. A nation enraged by terrorism does not inhibit and may even encourage governmental responses that may actually serve terrorist aims (Nacos, 1994). Yet it is often difficult to see the gain obtained through media spotlights on terrorist events. As one example, U.S. public opinion data show conclusively that the bombing of the Murrah Federal Building in Oklahoma City did not provoke personal apprehension and fear and therefore failed as an act of terrorism. It changed neither the public's assessment of danger nor their reported behavior (Lewis, 2000).

It would be simplistic and naïve, however, to presume that media impact may be measured by the response to one event. Media images may influence subjects at a deeper level. In Tel Aviv, Slone (2000) found that media portrayals of terrorism, political violence, and threats to national security provoked anxiety in individual viewers. In an environment in which bombings are frequent occurrences, Slone questioned the veracity of studies claiming that the influence of the mass media is negligible and benign. There is no simple index of negative or positive impact that can determine how the media and terrorism are related.

In the search for a simple explanation, the idea that media are the contagion of terrorism has been widely heralded. According to the theory of contagion, terrorism is cultivated and spread by media coverage. The fear of an epidemic of violence has been used repeatedly to justify efforts to alter media coverage, even though there is no significant evidence that media act as a contagious element (Picard, 1991). Because terrorism is a "creature" of the media, according to widespread public belief, the media are expected to be aware of their operative role in the terror syndrome and to cooperate with law enforcement (Onder, 1999). Media cooperation with law enforcement in support of government is more likely than media cooperation with terrorist aims. Journalists have more to gain from upholding the status quo than from attacking it.

In the United States, the media are responsible for vast and intractable errors because of their highly skewed perspective about the Middle East and the Southern Hemisphere. A preeminent belief in Israelis as victims and a pattern of preference for news about Muslim terrorists accompany a general disposition of the press to downplay terrorist events occurring in the predominantly Spanish-speaking continent of South America. The media perspective in the United States obscures the complete picture that readers deserve (CAMERA Media Report, 1995; "Media Coverage Related to Terrorism," 1999; Weimann & Winn, 1994).

A Knight-Ridder poll in January 2003 found that 44% of respondents thought that most or all of the hijackers on 9/11 were Iraqi; in fact, none were. A *New York Times*/CBS poll in February 2003 found that 72% of those asked thought that it was very, or somewhat, likely that Saddam Hussein played a direct role in the 9/11 attacks. In August 2003 a *Washington Post* poll found that the number of people who believed this untrue statement stayed steady at 70% (Elliott, 2004, p. 34). These are good examples of the way government biases are reflected in public misinformation.

An analysis of the coverage of the run-up to the Iraq war in five major newspapers from the United States, United Kingdom, Pakistan, and India suggests that, in addition to the practices of journalists, deeper influences were at work. The war frame and overall military strategy dominated the U.S. and UK newspapers, but with a crucial difference: the U.S. papers reflected broad public support, whereas the UK papers reflected divided opinion. On the other hand there was more coverage of the Iraqi viewpoint and of civilian deaths in the Pakistani and Indian newspapers (Ravi, 2005).

Selling Terrorism: Commercial and Political Interests in Media Reports

The mass media are large, profit-seeking corporations, owned and controlled by wealthy people, heavily dependent on advertising for revenue, and interlocked with other members of the corporate system. The media focus on nonstate terrorism, with themes often based on a threat to democracy. State terrorism, when it is reported, is rarely that committed by the United States or its allies. Emphasis on the specific, dramatic, terrorist event diverts public attention away from *wholesale* terror that is compatible with corporate, state, political, and propaganda interests. The basic rule has been that, if foreign violence clashes with capitalism, it may be designated as "terrorist"; if not, the word is not applied (Herman & O'Sullivan, 1989).

A survey of journalists conducted in association with the *Columbia Journalism Review* in 1999 found that newsworthy stories are purposely avoided and good stories all too frequently are not pursued because of commercial and competitive pressures (Pew Research Center, 1999). At the same time, the global media have been accused of "overkill." For instance, it is widely agreed that in 1996, TV news and the weekend news analysis programs overplayed the Olympic park bombing in Atlanta and the crash of TWA Flight 800. They were accused of pandering to the public's supposed need for instant villains by overhyping the unproved terrorism angle (Douglas, 1996).

News about terrorism may be manufactured in several ways. One way is to inflate the menace on the basis of modest, not very threatening, but real actions. Another is the false transfer of responsibility for a terrorist act to a convenient scapegoat. The private sector also manufactures terrorism, sometimes in collusion with agents of the state, to incriminate organizers, resisters, activists, and political enemies (Herman & O'Sullivan, 1989). Although news stories of terrorist events are seldom outright fabrications, they may be altered by the inclusion of selected elements and assumptions, with the support of both commercial and government interests. Journalists are being asked to achieve an equilibrium between market orientation and a mission to bolster public confidence (Rosenfeld, 1996). Achieving this balance has nothing to do with either validity of the information or impartial reporting of events.

MAKING MARTYRS: TERRORISTS AND THE DEATH PENALTY

The execution of Oklahoma City bomber Timothy McVeigh in 2001 raised many profound conflicts about terrorists that reflect the impact of culture on the media. Jessica Stern, who served on the National Security Council, has argued that when it comes to terrorism, national security concerns about the effectiveness of the death penalty should be paramount. According to Stern (2001), executions play right into the hands of the country's adversaries, turning criminals into martyrs, inviting retaliatory strikes, and enhancing public relations and fundraising for national enemies. Moreover, dead terrorists don't talk, whereas live terrorists can become an intelligence asset because they are sources of much-needed information.

McVeigh was 29 years old when he was captured in 1995, very shortly after the bombing of the federal building in Oklahoma City in which 168 people were killed. He was convicted in 1997 of what was then considered the single worst terrorist act in U.S. history. Even though his biography describes an unremarkable, lonely life marked by frustration and an obsession with guns, the former Army corporal became one of the best known and least understood media figures of the 1990s (CNN, 1998; Pastore, 1997). His death may actually have served the cause of antigovernment, right-wing militias. His execution may have made him an inspiration to a future generation of terrorists.

A comparison of the American public's reaction to the execution of McVeigh with the reaction in Peru when the leader of the Shining Path, Abimael Guzmán, was captured in 1992 is a remarkable illustration of cultural influences on the media. Guzmán's career in terror spanned more than 10 years in Peru. The terrorist era destabilized Peru, causing both social and economic crises (Barnhurst, 1991). The Shining Path is not typical of modern terrorist organizations because it eschewed media attention. The group used violent tactics as the most potent tool with which to communicate with the public.

On the other hand, Peruvian antiterrorist forces were ambivalent about media attention. From the standpoint of generating propaganda and manipulating public opinion, journalists appeared useful to the government, but their reporting of police brutality and the corruption of counterterrorist forces made journalists a threat. Opinion polls in several Latin American countries indicate that the news media are held in high public regard, outstripping all other national institutions, including the Roman Catholic Church (Bilello, 1998). The status of journalists made them a formidable interest group with which Peruvian authorities needed to cooperate and over which they wanted control.

When he took office in 1990, President Fujimori used the press to promote his political agenda, but prevented it from covering areas of potential scandal in the name of national security against the threat of terror. Because the threat was real, public opinion generally was influenced to favor strict measures of control. The counterterrorist squad was given a new name to

PHOTO 6.1   May, 1995: TIME Cover of Timothy McVeigh.

attract the public's attention. The celebrated officer in charge had a strong presence in both print and television news. Media reports were dependent on government sources or hearsay, for the most part, because the terrorists distrusted journalists and the misuse of information and so did not provide information to the media. Throughout his years in hiding, personal reports from Guzmán were limited to two videos and some writings that surfaced during his life underground. Most of the details about the leaders of the Shining Path still have not come to light because of the strong code of secrecy that protected the group (Mahan, 1997).

The details that were made public were disseminated by government news authorities. From the picture that emerged in the press, Guzmán was an unlikely terrorist. A former university

PHOTO 6.2   A photo of the Alfred P. Murrah Federal Building shows the scope of the destruction caused by the blast, which killed 168 people and injured hundreds more.

professor, he was said to be both weak and unyielding. His capture was a special event, planned and staged for the media. In the video of his first statement, Guzmán, who was seriously myopic, was not wearing his eyeglasses, and he appeared befuddled and goofy. Later, in custody, Guzmán was dressed in a special uniform designed expressly for press appearances by notorious terrorists. The huge black-and-white stripes of his outfit, a technique of theatrical costuming, were designed to make him appear guilty and powerless.

In his first appearance in custody, Guzmán was shown in a large, cage-like structure. The cameras were set up a good distance from him, as they might be when filming a dangerous animal. The microphone was installed inside the cage. In the video, which was shown on major news outlets throughout the world, Guzmán appeared to be ranting and raging because he was yelling at the cameras, not realizing the microphone was nearby. The image is dramatic and at the same time laughable. Through staging, the man who had been considered powerful and even immortal throughout Peru became instantly foolish and impotent.

In the media rush following his capture, the coverage glorified the skills and cunning of the agents of antiterrorism. At the same time, it exposed the weaknesses of the enemy. The public found out that Guzman, 55 years of age, had been tracked by his use of medications for his psoriasis and tendency toward upper respiratory illnesses. The agents found medicine bottles in the trash that led them to his last hideout. He was captured after more than 15 years of clandestine life because of his known ailments. In short order, Guzmán went from being a threat to being a joke in journalists' reports about him (BBC, 1999; "Dr. Abimael Guzmán's [Chairman Gonzalo] 'Speech From a Cage,'" 2000).

Some of the final media images of Guzmán are of the stronghold set up to hold him and the barren island where he will spend the remainder of his days. Guzmán is completely closed off from the rest of the world but lives just out in the harbor from the capital in Lima, mostly forgotten. He will die in ignominy as far as most Peruvians are concerned. The government has little reason to fear that he will be viewed as a martyr or incite more violence.

Photo 6.3   Abimael Guzmán, the leader of Peru's *Sendero Luminoso* (Shining Path), shortly after his capture in September 1992. His "speech from the cage" was manipulated by the Peruvian government and witnessed by more than 200 international journalists.

COMPETING CONCERNS

There are at least three competing interests when it comes to media coverage of terrorism (Perl, 1997). For one, the media want to be the first with the story. They want to make the story as timely and dramatic as possible, yet to be thought of as professional and accurate. Reporters want to protect their ability to operate as securely and freely as possible. They want to protect readers' rights to know while at the same time playing a constructive role in solving specific terrorist situations if this can be done without excessive personal or professional costs. Gilboa (2005) has shown that, when journalists become involved in international conflict resolution, difficult professional, practical, and ethical questions are raised for negotiators and policymakers as well as for the media.

The second competing concern involves government leaders who want the media to advance their agenda and not that of the terrorists. If possible, government officials prefer that the media not cover terrorists. If they do, government agencies want the media to present terrorists as criminals. When journalists receive information about terrorists, those in the government want first access to it. They would like to diffuse the public reaction of anxiety and encourage the media to keep the public reasonably calm. Airing emotional appeals from relatives of victims of terrorism builds public pressure on governments to make concessions and is not useful to government officials. Counterterrorism specialists in the government also do not want the media to reveal antiterrorism strategies. They want to control terrorists' access to information. Government officials look to the media to boost their image, and in extreme cases they may seek cooperation of the media to disseminate some disinformation that they believe will neutralize a terrorist threat (Perl, 1997).

The third competing perspective is that of terrorists who basically need publicity. Certainly most terrorists seek a favorable understanding of their mission, and they would like media coverage that causes damage to their enemies. Terrorists want the press to give legitimacy to what is often portrayed as inexplicable violence. Additionally terrorist groups would like the media to give legitimacy to those nongovernmental organizations and study centers that publish positive messages about the terrorists that are contrary to official government propaganda (Perl, 1997).

These three interest groups—journalists, government authorities, and terrorists—are competing for the attention and acceptance of the public. In the context of U.S. society, fear that the media will promote the cause of terrorism or its methods may be overshadowed by concern for freedom of the press and the erosion of constitutional rights. Responsible media coverage is essential. Two elements are necessary for the temperate, considered reporting of terrorism: audiences who prefer reasoned discourse on the news to "infotainment" and "terrorvision" and a professional culture of journalists who have sensitivity to the impact of reporting (Weimann & Winn, 1994). Regulation of the media, by either internal or external authority, will not provide these elements nor will limiting the democratic process. The relationship between the media and terrorism is much too complex; it is controlled by the culture, not regulations from any single source.

HIGHLIGHTS OF REPRINTED ARTICLES

Ian R. McDonald and Regina G. Lawrence (2004). Filling the 24 × 7 news hole: Television news coverage following September 11. *American Behavioral Scientist, 48*(3), 327–340.

McDonald and Lawrence studied television news coverage following September 11 to determine whether television networks used the additional time and freedom from the constraints of commercials to develop more sustained treatments of the subject at hand. In addition, they wanted to find out if having the additional time led to the development of a more meaningful political and historical context in the media presentations. Finally, McDonald and Lawrence suggest that television reporters covered the attacks of September 11 more like a crime story than a political story. Their study provides an in-depth look at broadcasts from ABC, NBC, and CNN over the three days from September 11 to September 14, 2001. Their investigation provides insight into an actual event and the real-life coverage that followed.

Terry Anderson (1993). Terrorism and censorship: The media in chains. *Journal of International Affairs, 47*(1), 127–136.

Terry Anderson is a well-known journalist who was taken hostage in Lebanon in 1985. He provides a valuable perspective on conflicts of interest among terrorists, the authorities, and the media. From his experience, Anderson raises many disturbing questions about national security and journalistic responsibility to victims. He concludes that there can be no one standard media response to terrorism. Instead, the questions about responsibility for the lives of hostages and the risks involved with reporting terror that journalists encounter in their work can be

PHOTO 6.4   Terry Anderson raises his arms in triumph at a press conference after being released by
Lebanese terrorists who had held him hostage for almost seven years.

answered only individually, in response to each situation. Anderson's article shows how one
reporter has struggled with balancing the public's right to know with the culpability and obligation for those involved that journalists must carry.

EXPLORING MEDIA AND TERRORISM FURTHER

- To see the source of much of the information that is used by the media, go to the FBI Web page,
  which provides numerous links to the official U.S. government versions of terrorist events.
- The Web sites of all the global news series—CNN, Reuters, ABC, NBC, CBS, BBC, and others—
  maintain archives of information about terrorism, which makes it possible to compare viewpoints
  and check facts about a specific group or event.
- The Pew Research Center for the People and the Press is a good source of research and policy
  suggestions for the media with regard to terrorism. How is media self-regulation possible?
- For the complete record of the trial of Unabomber Theodore Kaczynski, see the Time/CNN site.
  Does the press have a responsibility to make public whatever information they receive? Do you
  support limiting the freedom of the press to protect citizens? What limits are appropriate?
- The CNN effect was most directly observable during the aftermath of the attack on 9/11. Explore
  other sources about the CNN effect. According to McDonald and Lawrence in the first article, how
  were the media influenced during that period?
- Instead of the actual news coverage that was presented 24 × 7 following the crisis of 9/11, what
  changes in coverage do McDonald and Lawrence believe would have served the U.S. public better?
- According to Anderson in the second article, when do terrorists see their acts as successful? How
  can this perception of success be eliminated?
- Anderson describes a balance for the media between responsibility or self-restraint and reporting
  events even when lives are at stake. What is this balance? What examples have been seen in the
  media lately?

VIDEO NOTES

How terrorism was actually reported in one extreme example is documented by the film *One Day in September* (Columbia TriStar, 1999, 91 min.), which details the kidnapping of Israeli athletes at the Munich Olympics in 1972.

❖

Filling the 24 × 7 News Hole

Television News Coverage Following September 11

Ian R. McDonald and Regina G. Lawrence

In the days following the September 11, 2001, terrorist attacks, all the major television networks devoted their broadcasts to continuous news coverage without commercial interruption. This article analyzes the prime-time broadcasts from ABC, NBC, and CNN over the 3 days from September 12 to 14, 2001. First, the authors ask whether the networks used the additional time to develop longer reports and more sustained treatment of news subjects. Second, the authors consider whether the news coverage provided a meaningful political and historical context for the attacks both in terms of explaining global terrorism and characterizing its geopolitical and military consequences. These observations provide the context for a third theme, that television covered the attacks of 9/11 more like a crime story than a political story. After reviewing the data supporting these conclusions, the authors speculate about the effects of such coverage on public understandings of the events of September 11.

In the days following the September 11, 2001, terrorist attacks, all the major television networks devoted their broadcasts to continuous news coverage without commercial interruption. This wall-to-wall news coverage has since been praised by journalists and by some media critics for signaling a positive turn in media performance. For example, Leonard Downie, Jr., a reporter and editor with four decades of journalistic experience and the author of *The News About the News: American Journalism in Peril,* was asked by an interviewer, "When do you think the American people were served the best by the news business?" Downie responded,

> Well, we certainly have seen it since September 11th, beginning on September 11th, shows— shows how the media can perform at its very best.

The network news shows covered the events of September 11th and—and the impact of them over the next several days continuously, without interruption by commercials, without interruption by entertainment programs. . . . I think we saw the news media at its best immediately after September 11th. (Booknotes .org, 2002)

This study examines some of the content of these broadcasts, with three research themes in mind. First, we ask whether the networks used the additional time and freedom from the constraints of commercial breaks to develop longer reports and more sustained treatment of the news subject at hand. Second, we consider whether that additional time led to greater thematic emphasis in the selection and treatment of news topics. More specifically, did the news coverage provide a

SOURCE: From "Filling the 24 × 7 News Hole," in *American Behavioral Scientist, 48,* by Ian R. McDonald and Regina G. Lawrence © 2004, p. 327. Reprinted with permission from Sage Publications, Inc.

AUTHORS' NOTE: The authors thank Bartholomew Sparrow for his helpful comments on an earlier draft of this work.

meaningful political and historical context for the attack both in terms of explaining global terrorism and characterizing its geopolitical and military consequences? The data presented here suggest that despite the greatly expanded news hole and the unprecedented nature of the events, the content and format of television news following September 11 actually differed little from television news during more normal times. These observations provide the context for a third theme, that television covered the attacks of September 11 more like a crime story than a political story. After reviewing the data supporting these conclusions, we speculate about the effects of such coverage on public understandings of the events of September 11.

PUTTING SEPTEMBER 11 NEWS IN CONTEXT

In considering the content and editorial choices made during the days following September 11, we must be mindful of the extraordinary circumstances the network news organizations faced. First, the story of the attacks needed several days to unfold, as the magnitude of the damage was assessed, the looming possibility of more attacks subsided, and important revelations about the role of Osama bin Laden and al-Qaida came to light. In the days immediately following the attacks, the networks devoted significant airtime to episodes that ultimately yielded very little important news, such as the pursuit of three alleged witnesses at Copley Square in Boston on September 12. The role of al-Qaida and global Islamic terrorism became clear early but not instantly. The risk of a premature focus on Islamic terrorism—a leap made and then widely criticized in the aftermath of the 1996 Oklahoma City bombing (see Goodman, 1995)—was an important constraint in the first 24 to 36 hours following the September 11 attack. Given these uncertainties at the time, it may seem unfair to criticize certain news decisions with the clarity of 20–20 hindsight. Nevertheless, we contend that television news could have done more to illuminate the political and historical backdrop of September 11 or at least of terrorism in general, especially given the enormous news hole to be filled. We find that the networks relied heavily on

an ad hoc interview format and that they relied extensively on a handful of experts and political figures at the expense of stories that offered a broader context. Moreover, this pattern persisted as the week progressed. As we show in the following, it is not that the news lacked any analysis of what had just occurred. Indeed, many of the minutes taken by anchors, reporters, and interviewees were filled with commentary and analysis. What was lacking was broader context presented through prepared news reports drawing on a wide range of expert commentators.

A second caveat is that in the weeks following the attack, news coverage unquestionably shifted away from the attack itself toward the American military response in Afghanistan and other topics. This shift may have provided a global perspective on the attacks to a degree not seen, as we report in the following, in the immediate aftermath of September 11. The aftermath, however, was probably the time of maximum public attention to news about terrorism, and so any increase in TV's coverage of the global politics of terrorism during subsequent months may have been offset by a decline in viewership.

Finally, the important emotional gratifications the American people received from TV after September 11 cannot be overlooked. In the context of national crisis, political elites spoke and journalists echoed a reassuring language of core American values, American unity, and American strength (Domke, 2004), and that is presumably a language that much of the public wanted to hear. Television acted as a source of emotional release and reassurance at least as much as information for shell-shocked Americans, and this recognition might have dictated much of the news content and style. Indeed, the networks exhibited a self-conscious recognition of the profound cultural reaction to the events of September 11 and television's role in shaping and directing this reaction. Considering the unprecedented nature and scale of American losses, television quite defensibly responded to the emotional gratifications sought by the public as well as to the public need for information. Our examination of the networks' early September 11 coverage suggests, however, that emotional content outweighed information in a way that did not necessarily serve the public's long-term interests and that calls into question the praise that some have offered for post–September 11 TV.

For all of these reasons, the news broadcasts analyzed here offer only an imperfect case study of news decisions made during more normal times. Our study asks, however, how different from "normal" television news really was in the days following September 11, and from that perspective, post–September 11 news offers an excellent case study of the norms and constraints guiding the construction of news overall. Before proceeding to our analysis, therefore, we briefly discuss what was unique about the post–September 11 environment.

Most important, the networks' decision to forego their normal program scheduling and to run no advertising released them from what is generally considered a powerful constraint on TV news content, specifically, time. Similarly, any pressures normally felt to please or at least not to offend advertisers were less pressing. Media companies lost significant advertising revenues in the aftermath of September 11, as they had during the 1992 Gulf War. For example, News Corporation, owner of the Fox News channel, reportedly lost $100 million in the first week after the September 11 attacks (Kirkpatrick, 2003). This is not to suggest that the networks were suddenly freed from any and all financial considerations as they undoubtedly still looked ahead to how their coverage of the attacks might affect their future ratings and even shape their reputations for the foreseeable future. But at a moment when many elites and reporters were openly speculating that 20,000 people may have died in an unprecedented attack, it seems logical to assume that commercial considerations carried at least somewhat less weight than usual.

Indeed, the extreme gravity of the situation presumably urged journalists to put their best foot forward, foregoing some of the news reporting habits, such as the "game framing" of politics, widely criticized by scholars and media critics (Fallows, 1997; Patterson, 1994). As Jamieson and Waldman (2003) observed of post–September 11 news, "In ordinary times, the press adopts a distanced stance to those it covers. However, in times of crisis reporters abandon irony [and] cynicism to see the world through a patriotic...lens" (pp. 130–131). Meanwhile, in the context of intense drama and uncertainty stemming from the September 11 attacks, news organizations were probably aware that their viewership was about to dramatically (if temporarily) increase, just as it has after other major events, such as the

1991 Iraqi invasion of Kuwait (Ansolabehere, Behr, & Iyengar, 1993).

These broadcasts therefore offer a rare and valuable natural experiment in which the time constraint and advertiser pressures on television news were significantly relaxed while the professional incentives to produce the best possible reporting were presumably high. If the networks actually covered the attacks of September 11 in much the same way they cover other daily news events, this suggests that lack of airtime is not the constraint it is often claimed to be and that key norms of the television news business—the very norms that define "high quality news" among television news workers—create more uniformity than substance in television news. Such findings would also suggest that ironically, television formats developed largely with economic constraints in mind are maintained even when those constraints are relaxed.

METHOD

To study the networks' post–September 11 coverage, we accessed archives of broadcasts maintained by Television Archive.[1] We analyzed the prime-time broadcasts from ABC, NBC, and CNN over the 3 days from September 12 to 14, 2001, from 7 pm to 11 pm EDT, reviewing a total of 36 hours of programming. We chose to look at prime-time broadcasts not only because they presumably had the greatest viewership but because our initial review of the broadcasts quickly revealed that the networks avoided thematic news in other time slots that were reserved exclusively for breaking news and recaps. Prime-time broadcasts were conspicuously more reflective and analytical, and if any pattern of thematic treatment of the attacks was provided during these days, we presume that prime time is where it will be found.

The unit of analysis for coding the broadcasts was the individual reports, features, and interludes that we call news *segments*. A single news segment comprised a single report or discussion with a particular topical emphasis and format (or occasionally, several contiguous reports or discussions that were directly linked by subject matter). Transitions between news segments were invariably marked by the presence of a news anchor who would offer summary remarks for one story leading into an introduction to the next one. On occasion, a news segment would feature an anchor exclusively, depending on the subject matter. The 36 hours of coverage provided 502 individual national news segments (three half-hour breaks to local news were eliminated from the sample).

Each news segment was coded for the following three variables: topic, format, and episodic versus thematic framing. In addition, 12 topics were identified, including the category "headline" to capture brief recaps on a series of recent events. The following three formats were identified: (a) prepared reports, in which a reporter described an event or issue in narrative form, either live or taped; (b) live interviews with newsmakers, content experts, or story principals; and (c) newsroom analysis, where a journalist from within the studio analyzed and/or prognosticated. The framing of news segments was coded as either episodic or thematic. Following Iyengar's (1991) definition, episodic news segments focused on discrete events, did not place those events in larger context, lacked any discussion of historical sequence or causes, and did not consider larger, more general consequences of the events. All four of these criteria had to be met for a story to be coded as episodic. News segments that introduced any one of the three latter elements into the discussion were considered to be at minimum partially thematic. Therefore, the thematic news data reported in the following include these partially thematic news segments, which provides a generous test of the thematic content of post–September 11 news. In addition, interviews with content experts and newsmakers were in most cases coded as thematic insofar as these interviews included some amount of generalizing or prognostication. A random subsample of news segments was then coded by a second coder unfamiliar with the hypotheses of the research, yielding agreement on 98% of a 46-story subsample for each of these three variables.

FINDINGS

The first conclusion to be drawn from the data is that news segments in post–September 11 news were somewhat longer than those aired during normal prime-time news broadcasts, but given the absence of the normal time constraints, most were not dramatically longer. The average length of all news segments in our sample was 5.3 minutes, significantly more than the average evening news report, which lasts approximately 1 minute, 20 seconds (Comstock & Scharrer, 1999). This statistic is to some degree a methodological artifact, however, because when a network occasionally covered the same topic over two or more contiguous news segments, we combined these and treated them as one segment. In fact, relatively few segments were significantly longer than average. We found that 54 segments or contiguous segments (10.7%) lasted 10 minutes or longer (these were equally distributed among the three networks). The modal segment length was approximately 3 minutes, indicating that a small number of relatively long segments drove up the average. As Figure 1 shows, the bulk of news segments clustered at between 0 and 4 minutes in duration.

The second conclusion to be drawn is that TV news did not treat the attacks primarily as a political or policy story. Table 1 groups the 12 topics identified in the news segments into subgroups of political and nonpolitical stories. It shows that 36% of the news segments focused on political topics such as analysis of domestic security policy or U.S. military response options. It is noteworthy that Osama bin Laden and al-Qaida were the focus of only 13, or 2.5%, of all news segments broadcast during this time; seven of these stories aired on September 14 but constituted only 5% of news segments aired that day. Coverage of the attack scenes themselves, both live and recorded, combined with recaps or descriptions of the details of the attacks were the single most prominent topics.

The small number of stories focusing on al-Qaida reveals that militant Islamic fundamentalism received little exposure during the days immediately following the attacks. That finding is perhaps unsurprising given the small amount that was initially known about the attack's instigators. What is more noteworthy is that in general, the stories we classified as political did not often consider any political antecedents of the attacks or their political implications, such as the implications of a military response. Many of these stories were classified as political because they simply featured the immediate reaction to the attacks by a political actor, primarily the president.

A third conclusion to be drawn from these data is that the bulk of TV news coverage of the September 11 attacks was not even partially thematic in nature. Table 2 shows the overall percentage of episodic versus thematic coverage based on minutes of coverage. The data indicate that the majority of the networks' coverage—62%

of the minutes of airtime—took the form of purely episodic news reports. This proportion is not dramatically different than that found by Iyengar's (1991) study of television news coverage of foreign terrorism in the late 1980s, in which "74 percent of all news stories on terrorism consisted of live reports of some specific terrorist act, group, victim, or event, while 26 percent consisted of reports that discussed terrorism as a general political problem" (p. 27). And again, it should be noted that our methods may give more benefit of the doubt to thematic coverage. We coded items as thematic that included thematic material but were not fully thematic, whereas in Iyengar's study, stories were only coded as thematic "if the thematic frame predominated" (p. 19).

The analysis also reveals that virtually half of the news segments coded as thematic were live interviews. Separating these from reports and newsroom analysis reveals that only 15% of total broadcast time was taken by prepared reports that included thematic content. Figure 2 illustrates this point further. The lengthiest thematic segments tended to be interviews rather than prepared reports or newsroom analysis. Significantly, the majority of these interviews were with elected officials, members of the Bush administration, and former government officials; these three categories combined comprised 48% of all interviewees and

59% of interviewees in thematic segments. Senators and members of Congress alone made up 33% of all thematic segment interviewees, with several appearing more than once in these few days (Senator Joseph Biden of Delaware, ranking member of the Foreign Relations Committee, appeared seven times, and Senator John McCain of Arizona appeared four times). Therefore, the bulk of thematic content was provided not by independent professional experts in national security and terrorism (17% of all thematic segment interviewees) but by elected officials.

This analysis of interviews and reports reveals one of the few significant differences in the three networks' coverage. All three networks broadcast purely episodic news—either prepared reports, newsroom analysis, or interviews, such as with eyewitnesses—about 70% of the time. ABC's thematic coverage however was much less reliant on the interview format and made significantly greater use of prepared reports; by comparison, CNN's thematic news segments were predominantly live interviews. But the overall pattern is clear. Episodic news dominated the post–September 11 coverage, and essentially half of the coverage that was classified as thematic took the form of interviews with politicians or, more rarely, with content experts.

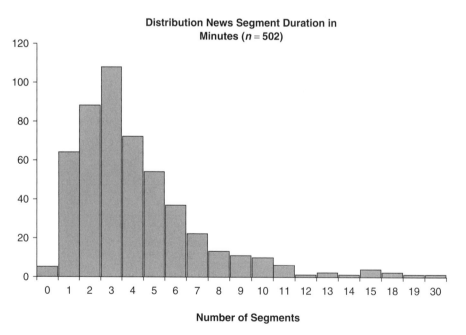

Distribution News Segment Duration in Minutes ($n = 502$)

Number of Segments

Figure 1   News Segment Duration

TABLE 1   News Segments by Topic and Network (Percentage)

Topic	ABC	CNN	NBC	Total
Coverage of attack scenes or Manhattan	28.5	18.8	21.9	23.5
Events of 9/11[a]	9.8	11.7	9.0	10.2
Domestic citizen response	9.3	11.0	6.5	9.0
Investigation	9.3	9.7	7.7	9.0
Disruptions within United States (including air travel/financial markets)	6.2	1.9	7.7	5.4
Economic impact	2.6	0.0	0.6	1.2
All nonpolitical	**65.7**	**53.1**	**53.4**	**58.3**
Domestic political response	10.4	16.9	14.2	13.5
Domestic security and U.S. intelligence	11.4	9.1	5.8	9.0
Possible military response	2.6	7.8	7.1	5.6
Overseas response and background	3.1	4.5	7.1	4.8
bin Laden/al-Qaida	3.1	0.6	3.9	2.6
Harassment of Arabs and others	0.5	0.0	1.9	1.0
All political	**31.1**	**39.9**	**40.0**	**36.5**
Headlines	3.2	7.0	6.6	5.2
Total	100.0	100.0	100.0	100.0
	$N = 193$	$N = 154$	$N = 155$	$N = 502$

a. Events of 9/11 category includes recaps and descriptions of the attacks.

TABLE 2   Percentage of Broadcast by Episodic/Thematic, Network, and Format

Network	Episodic			Thematic		
	Report	Interview	Analysis	Report	Interview	Analysis
ABC	64.7	3.3	0.8	22.9	8.2	0.0
CNN	58.9	14.6	0.0	1.9	18.5	6.1
NBC	63.6	6.5	0.0	11.9	14.9	3.1
Grand total	62.4	8.1	0.3	12.3	13.8	3.1

QUALITATIVE ASSESSMENT OF THE COVERAGE

Perhaps the most noteworthy aspects of television's coverage of September 11 in the days after the attack are qualitative aspects. Viewing these many hours of coverage, it is difficult to escape the conclusion that the networks relied almost exclusively on a conventional breaking-news format. This modality is marked by a look and feel developed by the advent of 24-hour cable news services, noteworthy in the following respects:

- repetition of key stories and themes;
- reliance on unscripted, extemporaneous commentary from newsmakers, content experts, and journalists;
- a preference for live coverage and focus on breaking stories that "stands watch" for the viewer, even after new developments subside.

Moreover, viewing these broadcasts leaves the distinct impression that TV covered the September 11 attacks in much the same way that TV typically covers daily crime stories. As Gilliam and Iyengar (1999) observed, local TV crime stories typically follow a "crime script" in which

- a crime is announced and described in some detail;
- visuals center on live action footage, accompanied by eyewitness testimony;
- the storyline focuses on the reaction of witnesses, family members, and neighbors and

on potential or known perpetrators and law enforcement efforts to apprehend them.

Relying on a familiar set of actors (victims, loved ones, criminals, and police) set against a backdrop of violence and tragedy, the crime script elevates the dramatic tension and personal dimension of crime while suggesting the promise of a satisfying closure (i.e., apprehension and punishment of the criminal).

The September 11 attacks created a national news story far greater in scope than the coverage of any single local crime. Nevertheless, we were struck by the similarities between daily TV crime coverage and the structure of much September 11 coverage. The repetition of reports about the attack itself, the predominance of live coverage and live eyewitness interviews, the search for and identification of the perpetrators, and the visibility of authority figures seeking to bring closure to the story all resemble significant elements of the crime script.

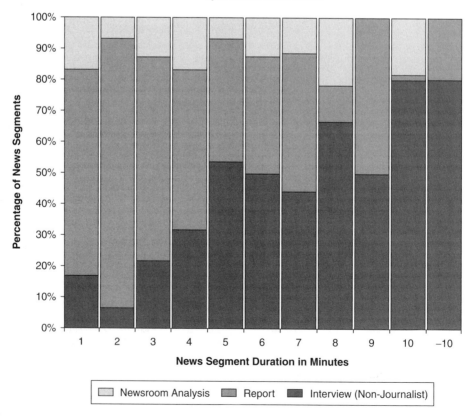

Percentage of News Segments With Some Thematic Content by Duration and Format

FIGURE 2   Duration of Thematic News Segments

DISCUSSION

Given the unique circumstances of post–September 11 news, how decisively did television news coverage really break away from established news construction habits? Overall, despite the praise bestowed by some observers on post–September 11 TV, the data presented here do not suggest a significant increase in the average length of news segments or in the thematic content of prepared news reports in particular. Neither did these segments depart dramatically in terms of style and depth from typical network news. Consequently, we question whether the sheer availability of additional broadcast time—even in moments of supreme gravity—necessarily leads to the practice of longer stories with greater depth.

In fact, these data suggest that patterns of news construction noted by scholars across a variety of news contexts were just as evident in post–September11 news. In particular, TV coverage of September 11 demonstrates news organizations' ongoing need to "routinize the unexpected" (Tuchman, 1980). Tuchman (1980) observed that journalists must "transform the idiosyncratic occurrences of the everyday world into raw materials that can be subjected to routine processing and dissemination" (p. 58). Similarly, Cook (1998) observed that a "consensus on routines of news-making...exists across news organizations in order to crank out a predictable regular product" (p. 167). The standard news categories used by news organizations when Tuchman conducted her research did not yet include breaking news, but her larger point is borne out that news organizations essentially decide what kind of story an event is and cover it accordingly. Essentially, the kind of story an event such as September 11 is, converted into today, almost inevitably looks like any other story as covered by cable news. Today, the consensus on routines that Cook (1996) observed reflects contemporary "production values" associated with the style and feel of 24-hour cable news.

Thus, despite the unprecedented nature of the events of September 11 and in keeping with their need to convert an unpredictable world into a predictable product, the major networks rather quickly converted those events into an unfolding news drama with the predictable characteristics of breaking news. Despite some differences in the amount of time they allotted to interviews versus newsroom analysis, the three networks analyzed here packaged their coverage quite similarly. And despite the enormity, gravity, and novelty of the attacks, news coverage of them very quickly came to resemble news coverage of virtually any other breaking news story.

In part, this breaking-news format reflects the networks' ongoing economic considerations. These approaches to high-volume news broadcasts satisfy two demands placed on 24-hour news channels. First, they accommodate an audience that consumes news on demand for short intervals (Kerbel, 1994). Extensive, in-depth coverage is presumably not the product sought by an audience that quickly tunes in and out. Second, repetitious and extemporaneous news is more scalable in terms of cost. In large volumes, this kind of news is cheaper and more easily produced than scripted, extensively researched background reporting. But applying the breaking news format to the unprecedented crisis of the September 11 attacks also reflects norms prevalent in the TV industry today. Such coverage, we contend, is not only economically predetermined but also reflects some shared sense among TV news workers that this is the right way to cover big stories.

Our reading of these broadcasts suggests that the networks also borrowed heavily from the established way of covering crime on TV. Consequently, TV covered the attacks of September 11 more like a crime story than a political story. This distinction is not fully captured in the quantitative data presented here, although the analysis of news segment topics does clearly show that political topics were outweighed by other topics, especially the emphasis on live coverage of the attack scenes, the simple recounting of event details, and the investigation of the attacks. As Gilliam and Iyengar (1999) explained, the crime script underlying countless local television news stories focuses on the details of a particular crime rather than on the social or political context of crime. Similarly, viewers of 24-hour commercial-free news in the aftermath of September 11 could have learned a great deal more about the details of the "crime" than about the social and political context of terrorism. This distinction strikes us as important given the essentially political nature of terrorism; political objectives are by most definitions what sets terrorism apart from mass murder. Undoubtedly and understandably, the networks were drawn to the dramatic visual images associated with the destruction of the World Trade Center and to the poignant images of human suffering, hope, and courage in the days that followed. But that is essentially the point. September 11 provided a plethora of the very same kinds of images that draw television coverage of violent crime on a daily basis.

Gilliam and Iyengar (1999) theorized that the crime script is significant because it shapes public understandings and expectations regarding crime and crime control. In particular, they found audiences tend to fill in elements of the well-known script, such as the presence (and the racial identity) of a perpetrator, even when that information is not actually provided in a news story. The present content analysis of TV coverage of September 11 cannot test directly the theory that public response to September 11 was shaped by this crime script reporting. But if we are correct that that reporting resembled typical crime coverage, that raises a crucial question: Did the style and substance of television coverage reinforce any predisposition on the part of the public to think about September 11 as a closed-ended crime story instead of a protracted political conflict?

The crime script impels the viewer to look for closure: The story ends and the script is fulfilled when the perpetrator is caught. It is noteworthy that the bulk of the interviews we coded as thematic, which comprised the majority of all thematic coverage in the days following September 11, focused not on the subject of terrorism per se—its history, its political and religious roots, its current structure worldwide—but on identifying particular agents of terror and discussing how they should be identified and "punished." Much of the discourse focused on the simple questions of who was to blame (whether it be individuals such as Osama bin Laden, organizations such as al-Qaida, or countries such as Iraq) and how quickly the United States should retaliate (in other words, how much proof of blame would be required before the United States would strike). As in most crime reporting, larger questions were rarely asked: Why do certain groups resort to such unthinkable violence? Do the terrorists have a meaningful base of political support? What policy choices might address the problem? Just as crime script coverage leaves the public unable to think critically and holistically about the problem of crime (Iyengar, 1991), so

too might this crime script coverage of the attacks of September 11 have primed Americans to look for easy answers and quick resolution of the terrorism problem.

CONCLUSION

The findings suggest further avenues of research using these broadcast data. Perhaps most obviously, later periods in TV coverage of September 11 and coverage of related topics should be compared with these early broadcasts to determine if TV news became more political or thematic as the story unfolded. There may be little reason to suspect, however, that the news became more substantive as the normal constraints of prime-time news resumed.

If additional research bears out the findings suggested here, the political implications of the way TV covered September 11 may be significant. Routinized, packaged television news may put citizens at an emotional and intellectual remove from real-world events. As Hart (1999) suggested, television can produce paradoxical feelings of intense personal involvement with isolation from the world and can produce a sense of "exhaustion" even as it replaces real involvement. It "encourages [a] sort of standing back" by making political events "a display, a curiosity, something to be seen but not engaged" (Hart, 1999, p. 85). For example, footage of the second plane crashing into the World Trade Center and the twin towers collapsing in flames was replayed repeatedly; airtime that could have been devoted to producing new insight into the attacks was instead devoted to burning these images into the public mind. One possible effect of this repetitive focus on reliving the events of that day may have been ironically to deaden our collective experience of September 11.

One final consideration about coverage during this period, unique to such an extraordinary crisis, is the degree to which viewers were willing to consume significant amounts of news for long periods. If ratings not only increased but viewers tuned in for longer periods and paid closer attention than usual to TV, this may suggest a greater public propensity to consume in-depth, thematic news than is normally assumed by television reporters and producers. Indeed, much of the coverage analyzed here seemed to be premised on an assumption that viewers would not be tuning in for long—hence the continued short segments only occasionally interspersed with more lengthy segments. If another crisis similar to the September 11 attacks were to emerge, would the networks, who often organize news broadcasts for an audience that darts in and out, adapt to this different pattern of viewership? During such an extraordinary crisis, the willingness and ability of news organizations to depart from these ingrained habits of ordinary news delivery could have a very direct and permanent effect on public attitudes and perspective as the crisis recedes.

NOTE

1. Television Archive, PO Box 29244, San Francisco, CA 94129-0244; phone 415-561-6767; http://www.televisionarchive.org/html/index.html; archived news programming is at http://tvarchive1.archive.org/ and http://tvarchive2.archive.org.

REFERENCES

Ansolabehere, S., Behr, R., & Iyengar, S. (1993). *The media game.* New York: Macmillan.

Booknotes.org. (2002). *The news about the news: American journalism in peril* (Transcript of interview with Leonard Downie, Jr., Brian Lamb host). Retrieved March 1, 2004, from http://www.booknotes.org/Transcript/?ProgramID=1670

Comstock, G., & Scharrer, E. (1999). *Television: What's on, who's watching, and what it means.* San Diego, CA: Academic Press.

Cook, T. E. (1996). Political values and production values. *Political Communication, 13,* 469–481.

Cook, T. E. (1998). *Governing with the news.* Chicago: University of Chicago Press.

Domke, D. (with Hutcheson, J., Billeaudeaux, A., & Garland, P.). (2004). U.S. national identity, political elites, and a patriotic press following September 11. *Political Communication, 21,* 27–51.

Fallows, J. (1997). *Breaking the news.* New York: Vintage.

Gilliam, F., & Iyengar, S. (1999). *Prime suspects: The corrosive influence of local television news on the viewing public.* Retrieved March 1, 2004, from http://pcl.stanford.edu/common/docs/research/gilliam/1999/primesuspects.pdf

Goodman, W. (1995, April 28). Although unrestrained in a crisis, television is a tie that binds. *The New York Times,* p. A27.

Hart, R. (1999). *Seducing America.* Thousand Oaks, CA: Sage.

Iyengar, S. (1991). *Is anyone responsible?* Chicago: University of Chicago Press.

Jamieson, K. H., & Waldman, P. (2003). *The press effect.* Oxford, UK: Oxford University Press.

Kerbel, M. R. (1994). *Edited for television: CNN, ABC, and the 1992 presidential campaign.* Boulder, CO: Westview.

Kirkpatrick, D. D. (2003, February 10). News industry plans for war and worries about lost ads. *The New York Times,* p. C1.

Patterson, T. (1994). *Out of order.* New York: Vintage.

Tuchman, G. (1980). *Making news.* New York: Free Press.

❖

Terrorism and Censorship

The Media in Chains

Terry Anderson

When Israel invaded south Lebanon on 6 June 1982, I had been covering southern Africa out of Johannesburg for nearly a year and was eager to get out. Southern Africa was quiet and I was restless. Lebanon was a war—the world's biggest story—and I was a journalist. The Middle East was the natural place to go.

Lebanon was exciting. The country fascinated me with its religious diversity, its endless complications, its small feuds and larger wars. The Maronites, the Sunnis, the Shi'a, the Druze, the Palestinians—each had splintered factions and shifting goals. There was incredible violence at a scale and intensity I had never seen before in my six years as a foreign correspondent. But there were also the stubborn, brave, independent people who somehow survived the brutality.

By 1982, Western reporters had become accustomed to wandering freely around Lebanon—subject to the occasional verbal abuse or roughing up—but accepted by even the most radical of factions as journalists, independent of and apart from the U.S. and British governments. A year later, however, the atmosphere had begun to change.

Beginning with the victory of Ayatollah Khomeini in Iran, Iranian money poured into Lebanon to influencé the Shi`a, a Muslim sect disaffected with their native leadership. Religious conflicts intensified, and Washington's shifted position on Lebanon inspired a more personal hatred for the United States in particular, and the West in general. In Beirut, more and more bearded men—young Shi'a—appeared on the streets, carrying signs echoing Iran's revolutionary fervor and anti-Western propaganda.

Journalists' encounters with such bitter gunmen became a little harder to escape without injury.

In December 1983, a group of Iranian-inspired Shi'a launched an attempt to destabilize Kuwait with attacks on the U.S. and French embassies, power stations and other installations. Despite the destruction, the attempt failed miserably. Hundreds of Shi'a were rounded up, and 17 were charged. Some were given long prison terms and others were handed death sentences. As it took place far off in the Gulf, the event was soon forgotten—at least by the West. There was no immediate connection with events in Lebanon, no hint that the repercussions would involve half a dozen countries and leave Westerners, including me, in chains for months or years.

By the time I was kidnapped in March 1985, the U.S. embassy and the Marine barracks had been bombed; Malcolm Kerr, the president of the American University, Beirut had been murdered; and a handful of Westerners had been taken hostage. Beirut had turned into a kind of perpetual chaos.

The U.S. embassy had been quietly warning Americans to leave Beirut—a warning that most news people just ignored, although a few took the advice or moved to East Beirut, which was considered a much safer place. I stayed, determined to cover the story. On 16 March 1985, I was kidnapped.

SOURCE: Terry Anderson, "Terrorism and Censorship: The Media in Chains," *Journal of International Affairs* 47, 1 (1993): 127–136. Reprinted with permission.

The Islamic Jihad claimed responsibility and demanded the release of the Da'wa 17, the 17 jailed in Kuwait. Thus began my almost seven years in captivity—seven years during which I witnessed firsthand the tenuous and powerful relationship between terrorism and the press.

THE MEDIA-TERRORISM RELATIONSHIP

There can be no denying it: The media are part of the deadly game of terrorism. Indeed, the game can scarcely be played without them. In my experience, publicity has been at once a primary goal and a weapon of those who use terror against innocent people to advance political causes or to simply cause chaos. And they are quite good at the public relations game—which is why their attacks, kidnappings and murder are usually so spectacularly vicious.

In my opinion, the very reporting of a political kidnapping, an assassination or a deadly bombing is a first victory for the terrorist. Without the world's attention, these acts of viciousness are pointless. Furthermore, unless the terrorist can attach his political message to the headlines he has caused, he has failed. When newspapers run long analyses about the Islamic Jihad, its hatred of Israel and the West and its reliance on fundamentalist interpretations of Islam, "Islamic Jihad" becomes a legitimate force—something politicians and civilians alike must take seriously.

No matter that the analyses may be uniformly condemnatory, and that the reader has automatically and completely rejected the organization's premises. The acts that have won terrorists this public notice—whether kidnapping or bombing or murder—are seen by terrorists as successful. They have forced the world to take notice of them, indicating their sense of self-importance.

THE ROLE OF THE MEDIA

Everyone uses the media; journalists are accustomed to being used by presidents, kings, parliaments, entertainers, political activists or ordinary citizens trying to attract the world's attention—that's a major part of the media's role. The media carry messages to anyone from anyone with the knowledge, skill or importance to make use of them. It may be propaganda or it may be truth, but either way, the media carry powerful influence.

I was raised in journalism by old-fashioned editors who ingrained in me a fundamental belief in objectivity. According to my teachers, journalists were meant to present the facts and the facts only, and the audience—armed with seemingly unbiased material—was appointed to analyze and draw conclusions. The journalistic ideal means by allowing the public access to the widest possible range of information, they will be able to judge that which rings true and seems useful, and then utilize it to develop informed opinions and make wise decisions. The ideal is tested constantly in this age of mass marketing, public relations and so-called spin doctors who attempt to distribute information with a specific goal in mind.

But there are facts and there is truth. During my years in captivity, I had plenty of time to reassess the journalist's role in covering news. Objectivity and neutrality are vital, but they do not necessarily entail putting aside a personal desire to see the violence that we cover come to an end.

TERRORIST MANIPULATION OF THE MEDIA

I am not the first to question the precarious relationship between media and terrorism. A wide-ranging debate about the subject was initiated after the 1979 seizure of the U.S. embassy and the taking of American hostages in Iran in 1979. The Teheran hostage crisis dominated network television coverage of Iran—indeed, the percentage of stories about that country escalated from about one percent in the early 1970s to over 30 percent by 1980.[1]

A half decade later, one event in particular made clear the symbiotic relationship between the media and terrorism, setting off a second flurry of analysis: the hijacking of TWA Flight 847 to Beirut. Here, the media—television in particular—became the primary conduit between the terrorists and the governments.[2]

During the hijacking, the captors set up televised interviews with the hostages and held the first televised hostage news conference. Early on, the event turned into a shameful circus with one television network buying the rights to the story from the Shi'a Amal militia, and thereafter taking over the Summerland Hotel where the hostages were trotted out to meet the press. The amount of money involved is unknown except to those who paid and received it, but rumors suggested it was in the tens to hundreds of thousands of dollars, cash. Regrettably, the fact that one American, Navy diver Robert Stethem, had already been murdered by the hijackers and dozens of lives were in the balance became only a reason for more hype—not for caution and prudence. This was a big story; it was especially a television story and the media were not about to turn off their cameras.[3]

In my situation, the Islamic Jihad did not wage a similar all-out public relations campaign. For months on end, they offered the media so little information that we hostages were deemed forgotten, and friends, relatives and colleagues felt compelled to wage their own campaign for publicity. But when the Islamic Jihad did use tactics to manipulate the media, they were generally successful.

The players on both sides of this long game displayed their understanding of the media in many ways. The Reagan administration first tried to cut the press out of the game. They insisted that there would be no "deals with terrorists," while pursuing the favorite tactic of diplomats—secret negotiations.[4] When the so-called arms-for-hostages deal blew up in their faces, they tried to use the press, through purported unofficial leaks in a campaign to "devalue" the terrorists.

When that failed as well, they sent signals to Iran, which sponsors and funds Hizballah, that they were willing, even eager to discuss the matter.[5] Iran returned the signals frequently. Yet it was in comments to independent newspapers, or by government-controlled newspapers in Iran, that the idea of a swap of hostages for Lebanese prisoners held by Israel was first publicly suggested.[6] The kidnappers blatantly used the press to push their agenda, finally signalling their willingness to talk, and even to publicize their disagreements with Iranian sponsors.

Similar manipulation of the media was shown by captors of American officials at the U.S. embassy in Iran five years earlier. Hostage-takers aired their demands through staged demonstrations scheduled to coincide with nightly newscasts and ABC's "America Held Hostage" program, now known as "Nightline."[7] Many terrorist organizations have press offices, complete with spokesmen, press releases and audiovisual material.

In our case, photographs and videos were released along with demands as if our faces—mine in particular—were some sort of instantaneous press pass. No media outlet could deny their audience, and especially not a hostage's relatives, a glimpse of the Americans held in Lebanon. It was a natural way to grab the world's attention.

Still, the videos—a clear manipulation of the media by our captors—were also our only connection to our families, and for that reason alone, allowed us a bit of hope. At least the world would know we were alive. It was by no means an easy thing to do. When one day one of my keepers told me to make a videotape, I thought long and hard about whether I should refuse. I reflected on my Marine Corps training about how to behave as a prisoner, and struggled with the notion of aiding and comforting the enemy.

But in the end, I decided nobody would believe any of it; nobody would really think these were my opinions, and it was likely to be the only way I could reassure my family that I was alive and well. So I read their propaganda—rationalizations of their actions, attacks on President Reagan, vague but ominous threats couched in harsh language—and by so doing, I played a part in the media game.

There were times, however, when the media game—especially the release of videos—backfired on our captors. Terrorists pay enormous attention to the news reports about the things they do. In 1986, when Father Martin Jenco was released, he carried with him a videotape made by fellow hostage David Jacobsen. In the tape, Jacobsen sent his condolences to the "wife and children" of William Buckley, who had died some time before in prison.[8] Jacobsen did not know that Buckley was not married.

An over-enthusiastic journalist used that discrepancy to construct a theory that there was a so-called secret message on that tape. Worse, his television network prominently speculated on the theory. We were allowed by our captors to watch the first few television news reports of our companion's release. I remember seeing a yellow banner across the television screen in one report, emblazoned "Secret Message?" The question mark, I guess, was meant to justify use of the story.

Our captors also saw the story. They were very paranoid people, and believed it. They were extremely angry. We suffered, losing the few privileges we had—books, pen, paper—and were dumped in a vile and filthy underground prison for the next six months. We were lucky one or more of us were not killed.

The Question of Censorship

How do we balance the public's right to know—so vital to our society—and the duty of the press to reveal, with the knowledge that publicity seems so often to serve the purposes of terrorists? Because terrorists want and need publicity, should we therefore not give it to them? Should there be censorship, imposed or voluntary, about such news reports?

Persistent analyses of how the media should and should not respond to terrorism will continue as long as such activities take place, and we may never come up with satisfactory answers. I believe—like all journalists I know—that the press must fulfill its duty to expose and present information objectively, thereby serving the public good. Censorship by government officials would be a grievous mistake, and so-called general guidelines are too often vague or unsuited to particular events to be useful in these kinds of situations.

However, when lives are at stake, journalistic self-restraint may be necessary. In some cases, it will be imperative that information be reported even if the result is loss of life. In others, a journalist will have to choose whether to release, delay or withhold information. In each case, the individual journalist must ask him or herself: Should I report this if it jeopardizes a human life?

When the arms-for-hostages deal was revealed in the press, I was due to be the next hostage released. New clothes to wear home had been bought for me. But the news reports blew the whole deal out of the water. It was five years before I would finally be free. Nonetheless, I agree with the decision my colleagues in the press made to make the negotiations public. The very highest officials in the land, even the president, were engaged in talks that directly contradicted their public statements, indeed broke both U.S. law and violated the Constitution. That was more important than my fate, or that of the others still held.

Such is not often the case. There are times, I have learned, when information should be withheld. In early 1983, when I was reporting on the Middle East out of Beirut, I became aware through impeccable sources that the Palestine Liberation Organization was negotiating with the kidnappers of David Dodge, another president of the American University, Beirut who had been snatched in 1982. The PLO believed it had some hope of winning Dodge's freedom, and at the very least had confirmed he was alive and well—something no one had been able to do in the six months since his abduction.

Though I had second thoughts about the wisdom of reporting the negotiations, I allowed my boss to talk me into filing the story. It got "good play"—headlines in many papers in the United States. My sources, who had not realized how much they were telling me, were furious, and fearful that reports would kill the negotiations. As it happens, they did not: Dodge was eventually released. Still, I knew I had made a mistake. The story served no purpose and advanced no ideal, except maybe my career. If I had wanted Dodge's family to know I had learned he was alive and well, I could have told them privately. As it was, my report could very well have blown the secret talks away, as publicity later did to the arms-for-hostages deal. It could have cost the elderly Dodge more years in filthy prisons.

That realization had a strong effect on me. When I later had occasion to learn information about people who had been kidnapped, I was very, very careful how I used it, and often did not.

There is no simple formula. My experience as both journalist and hostage has provided me with a personal look at terrorists' manipulation of the media and the impact of the media's coverage of such events. The reply seems obvious: Don't give the terrorists what they want. Don't give them publicity. Don't report on their demands, or even—for the most adamant of media critics—on their actions. If they cannot expect publicity, they will go away.

As with the most obvious answers, this one is both philosophically mistaken and practically impossible. We are, after all, a democracy. That means at least theoretically—and I believe in practice to a greater extent than cynics would have us believe—that the public decides important issues by electing its representatives and changing them when they do poorly. They cannot do so intelligently without a free press, for any controls on the press become rapidly political ones, and in my opinion, will be used by those in power to keep themselves there.

But even if the theory behind full reporting of terrorist acts is sound, what about the practice? Surely the media behave irresponsibly often in the single-minded pursuit of headlines or air time.

We are a nation that has learned to be very suspicious of our leaders, and in particular any attempt by them to overtly control the information to which we have access. A bomb in a public place, or even the kidnapping of a prominent person, are not events that can be easily hidden or ignored. Trying to do so simply gives rise to rumors and false reports—always exaggerating the extent of the incident, and therefore giving the terrorist something he likes even more than publicity—the spreading of fear. I have found that the best antidote to fear is information, even if the information is bad.

Furthermore, the media are not a single entity that can be cautioned, leaned on or controlled. It is difficult to get a group of journalists to agree on something as simple as a basic code of ethics. It is unrealistic to expect any widespread voluntary restraint in matters that involve such attention-grabbing events as terrorist attacks.

Another factor that mitigates against control is that the public does not want it. Despite disparagement of the media for its so-called sensationalism, people seem to want blood-and-guts reports in their daily newsfare. A news organization that does not supply this kind of variety will not last long.

Conclusion

The philosophical justification for full reporting on terrorist acts does not give journalists a free hand. In each case they must weigh the theoretical or philosophical value of what they do with the fact that individual human lives are at stake. What they report can have a direct impact on the victims, as terrorists pay enormous attention to the news reports about the things they do.

I tell my colleagues: In each and every report you do where a human life is at risk, you must see in your mind that person's face. You must understand that what you report might well kill the person, and accept the responsibility for that. That doesn't mean you will abandon or even tone down your report. In some cases, one person's life, or even the lives of several people, cannot outweigh the necessity to publish the story.

When a government pleads with journalists to withhold stories about terrorists or terrorist incidents because of national security, or danger to negotiations involving hostages, should the journalist bow to those entreaties? Should the well-being of the hostages override all other considerations, as far as journalists are concerned? Or are there other things that are more important? I believe that each of these questions that so many journalists encounter in their work can only be answered individually, and as each case occurs. They should be, and I believe for the most part are, answered with intelligence and responsibility, and a full and careful regard for the lives that may be at stake. But general "guidelines" too often do not fit all cases. Certainly, we should not allow, or implicitly approve censorship by government officials, who will try to impose censorship in any case. Public approval of their acts simply encourages an even heavier hand.

Notes

1. James F. Larson, "Television and U.S. Foreign Policy: The Case of the Iran Hostage Crisis," Journal of Communication 36 (1986) p. 116.

2. Patrick O'Heffernan, "TWA Flight 847: Terrorism that Worked (Almost) . . . ," in Patrick O'Heffernan, Mass Media and American Foreign Policy: Insider Perspectives on Global Journalism and the Foreign Policy Process (Norwood, NJ: Ablex, 1991).

3. For more specific analyses of TWA incident, see Robert G. Picard, Media Portrayals of Terrorism: Functions and Meaning of News Coverage (Ames, IA: Iowa State University Press, 1993).

4. Los Angeles Times, 28 July 1986.

5. "Bush Seems to Appeal to Iran on Hostage Issue," Washington Post, 21 January 1989.

6. The Washington Post, 30 April 1990.

7. Picard, p. 53.

8. William Buckley was a CIA bureau chief stationed in Beirut. He was kidnapped, tortured and killed by the Islamic Jihad.

7

Women Terrorists

Compared with the wholesale violence of capital and government, political acts of violence are but a drop in the ocean. That so few resist is the strongest proof how terrible must be the conflict between their souls and unbearable social iniquities.

—Emma Goldman

Consistently far fewer women than men are involved as terrorists. Some female terrorists have created immense climates of fear, however. Women have carried on long-term, low-level conflict at a deadly rate in disparate countries at different times. In a few terrorist conflicts, the highest levels of leadership have included female cadres, and rarely some terrorist ideology has dealt explicitly with gender-related issues. Study of these exceptional women can reveal much about the society and culture against which they revolt.

Those who have studied women's participation as terrorists have noted that female activity is widening ideologically, logistically, and regionally because of contextual pressures. There are several reasons for this increase. For one, economic and social devastation provides the impetus for women to become terrorists. A mutually reinforcing process drives terrorists to recruit women at the same time that women's motivations to join these groups increase. During times of war and conflict, deprivation and necessity may become more important than traditional restraints on women's participation in public life. In some societies, controls over women lose strength as a result of conflict, which calls for more overt political participation on their part. Operational imperatives may make female members highly effective actors for their organizations. The usefulness of female operatives may induce terrorist leaders to consider innovation as a way of gaining strategic advantage against their adversaries (Cunningham, 2003). The Chechen separatist movement presents an illustration of the contextual pressures leading to expanded roles for women in terrorism.

The Black Widows of Chechnya

On October 23, 2002, a group of heavily armed men accompanied by 19 women wearing traditional Muslim headscarves and bombs strapped to their waists seized about 800 hostages in a Moscow theater. Taking over the theater, the Chechen separatists created their own highly emotional drama (Nivat, 2005). The Russian media dubbed the 19 women, "the Black Widows," the name by which female members of Chechen terrorist groups are still known.

Fifty-six hours after the takeover began, Russian special operations forces ended the siege by using a gaseous sedative to incapacitate everyone in the theater. The terrorists' dead bodies were shown on worldwide television. Questions linger over why Russian forces executed all of the Chechens on the spot, even though the gas had already rendered them unconscious (Weir, 2003). Although 130 hostages died from the gas, only 3 died directly from the terrorist actions (Speckhard et al., 2005).

A second dramatic incident involving Chechen terrorists occurred on September 1, 2004, the Day of Knowledge, a Russian national day of celebration for the first day of school for first graders. While children gathered with their proud parents, a large truck pulled up to the entrance of Beslan School No. 1. Heavily armed men and two women quickly entered and surrounded the building and herded more than 1,200 people, including children, parents and teachers, into the school gym. There was no food or water. The end of the standoff began with an explosion 52 hours into the siege. Survivors believe the explosion was accidental, but it set off a gun battle that lasted for ten hours. Russian investigators report that 330 hostages and 32 terrorists died (CBS News, 2005).

These dramatic incidents were just 2 of the 28 acts of suicide terrorism carried out by Chechen terrorists from June 2000 to 2005. The highest frequency of attacks occurred in 2003 and 2004 (Speckhard & Ahkmedova, 2006). Female suicide bombers have been reported as participants in many of these high-profile Chechen operations, which have taken place at a rock concert, in a car outside a hotel, in a subway car during rush hour, and, in the most deadly attack, on two commercial planes flying from Moscow to the south. The two suicide bombers who were responsible for the attacks on the airplanes bought their tickets for as little as $40 each (Nivat, 2005).

The Kremlin alleges that the "Black Widows" were imported into Chechnya by other terrorist groups, who now control the Chechen rebel movement (Weir, 2003). However, a study of 38 female suicide terrorists in Chechnya, based on interviews with their relatives and friends, found no evidence of foreign influence. All of the women bombers joined the rebel movement willingly (Speckhard & Ahkmedova, 2006), seeking out terror groups or deepening their involvement with them in response to deeply traumatic personal experiences involving the death or near death by torture of a close family member. All had witnessed widespread trauma. Revenge is a strong motivation in Chechen society, and the desire to avenge the death of a loved one is important for both men and women. Choosing to die on one's own terms can also be extremely compelling for those who are fleeing Russian special agents. Death in a terrorist incident is a much less terrible and more heroic end than what they would face if caught.

The influx of females into terrorist groups in Chechnya is the result not of foreign influence but of the villages that have been wrecked and the lives that have been shattered by years of cruel Russian domination. The war with Russia has been both vicious and of long duration. Under Russian occupation, many human rights violations have been clearly documented. Local control is nonexistent. Both the president and the prime minister of the republic were put into power by the Kremlin after corrupt elections (Parfitt, 2006). Frequent abductions are but one reflection of the climate of fear in Chechnya. On August 30, 2006, 2,736 Chechens were registered as missing according to Human Rights Watch (MosNews, 2006b). This compares with 1,700 who were reported missing in Chechnya in 2004 (Hrw.org, 2005). These figures may actually be grossly underestimated because families are afraid to report the disappearance of a family member for fear of drawing more attention from Russian police. Others believe that Russian-backed politicians have underreported disappearances to serve their own best interests (MosNews, 2006b).

The horror of the war with Chechnya has tainted all of Russian society. In 2006, two notorious assassinations of highly respected Russian authors were traced directly to the Chechen conflict. Anna Politkovskaya, a renowned Russian journalist, was shot dead and her body left in the elevator of her Moscow apartment block (*The Economist*, 2006). Her direct reports from the war-torn republic brought her international respect; these articles were collected in her book, *The Dirty War*. Another famous Russian author and former official of the KGB, Alexander Litvinenko, was poisoned by radiation in London in a slow and agonizingly painful death. He denounced the war in Chechnya as a crime and called for compensation to the Chechens (BBC, 2006). At the time of his death, he was looking into corruption within the Russian intelligence service and was investigating the murder of Anna Politkovskaya. He was best known for his book, *Blowing up Russia: Terror From Within.* Not surprisingly, the deaths of both of these critics of the Kremlin have been attributed to the brutal Russian regime.

From the Russian perspective, the brutal war against Chechens provides an object lesson to any other groups who seek independence and to leave the Russian Federation. The war provides an opportunity for the Russian government to consolidate its power and to suppress the Russian media, and it presents the occasion for many officials' personal enrichment (Blank, 2004).

The demands of the Chechen terrorists are clear: to force the withdrawal of all Russian military and security forces from Chechnya, to end armed conflict there, and to gain national independence (Speckhard & Ahkmedova, 2006). The indiscriminate use of the Russian army's raw force has thus far failed either to reduce the number of Chechen separatist fighters or to break their will (Torbakov, 2004). Instead, it has led them to undertake desperate and innovative terrorist actions. From the start of their terrorism campaign, Chechens have made much greater use of women terrorists than any other Islamic-related terror groups, and they have done so with no reservations nor need for *fatwas* to support their decision (Speckhard & Ahkmedova, 2006). That does not mean that the Chechen separatists have challenged traditional roles for women. Men are the dominant force in Chechen terror groups. Women who do not become suicide bombers play subservient roles, such as cooks and nurses. In the hierarchy, men are the planners and decision makers and the women take orders.

FEMALES AS TERRORISTS

Today's female terrorists take roles similar to those held by women in revolutionary organizations from earlier times. Knight (1979) points out that, in the 1905 Revolution in Russia, women showed a dogmatic devotion to violence and a strong tendency toward extremism: "Several became fanatics, seeing terror and their own heroic self-sacrifice as an end in itself. The ultimate test of their commitment and devotion to the revolution was their willingness to die" (p. 149).

At the beginning of the 21st century, women continue to be willing to die for their revolutionary ideals. The role of women in the LTTE (Tamil Tigers) separatists in Sri Lanka exemplifies their significance for terrorism. Human rights abuses by state-supported military authorities, including disappearances, murders, rapes, and torture, have been well documented in Sri Lanka. As in Russia, women have become involved in violence in response to crimes of domination and repression perpetrated by their national government.

In Sri Lanka, female warriors are among the deadliest weapons in the LTTE's arsenal. As suicide bombers, they have taken thousands of lives, left countless others injured, and cost millions of dollars in damage to property. It has been estimated that women make up fully half of the rebels and that they are also highly represented among the deadly Black Tigers, who are trained as suicide bombers. A female LTTE Black Tiger killed herself and Indian Prime Minister Rajiv Gandhi in 1991 ("Emergency Rule in Sri Lanka," 2002; Schweitzer, 2000).

Women began to be recruited as cadres in the LTTE when more fighters were needed and the number of available male youth decreased. The young women were organized into female guerrilla units operating side by side with men until 1986. In 1987, the first training camp for women was opened, and an independent unit for women was established. Female terrorists are motivated by everyday experiences of violence, displacement, hunger, and lack of opportunity. Those who cannot afford to marry abroad and have no prospects within Sri Lanka are likely to join. Female LTTE cadres cut their hair, carry guns, act as troop leaders, talk about women's liberation, and work closely with male cadres (Brun, 2005).

Despite the gender-liberating discourse, gender relations within the LTTE remain patriarchal. The terrorist group is commonly equated with a family, and the leader of the organization is known as "elder brother." The LTTE has created a highly localized and patriarchal understanding of womanhood despite the presence of female cadres (Brun, 2005).

For several decades, female suicide bombers have been part of the Palestinians' arsenal of terror (Scripps Howard, 2002). Fatah is reported to promote female terrorists as role models. The first female suicide terrorist for Fatah, Wafa Idris, blew herself up in downtown Jerusalem in January 2002. Since then, parades, concerts, summer camps, as well as university courses have been developed in her honor (IsraelNationalNews Staff, 2005). According to the Israel Insider Web site, a female master bombmaker recruited by Hamas was arrested by Israeli security forces in the West Bank town of Tulkarem in 2005 where she had been sent to teach terrorists how to prepare bombs. Encouraging women to accept an active role in the fighting against Israel is not a new direction, but rather reinforces an existing tendency to glorify the image of the Palestinian woman fighter, a mythical woman patriot ready to die for her homeland (Marcus, 2002).

Muslim women are found in many theaters of terrorist operation. Attacks by women in Iraq, Egypt, and Uzbekistan—women unrelated by culture and national identities—are said to reflect a crisis in Muslim society. Women have begun to challenge their perceived enemies, and formerly male-only terrorist groups have reevaluated their exclusion of women (Ali, 2005), particularly after the High Islamic Council in Saudi Arabia issued a *fatwa,* or edict, that decreed that women should join men as suicide martyrs for Islam (Hoffman, 2002). Recently, al-Qaeda also began very publicly reaching out to women on the Internet. *Al-Khansaa* is a Web magazine ostensibly written by women and specifically targeting women by offering tips to female terrorists (Jacinto, 2004). According to the *Washington Times,* these tips include the following: "A female militant must be content with what is strictly necessary, sending televisions and air conditioning to be burned. She should offer her own money for the cause and know how to shoot and how to carry munitions on her shoulder" (Phillips, 2005, p. 1).

Women also have been well-publicized members of several Western terrorist organizations (Radu & Tismaneanu, 1990). The Zapatistas (EZLN) in the southern Mexican state of Chiapas are a revolutionary group in which more than one-third of the members are women. The EZLN decided from its inception that, to be truly revolutionary, it would have to include women in formulating its policies. Women's Revolutionary Laws were hotly debated, but eventually became a decree within the movement. Analysts now agree that their influence has reshaped Mexican politics and challenged the nation's prevailing gender stereotypes (Clayton, 1997; Rojas, 1994).

Counterterrorism experts emphasize that female terrorists are not a recent phenomenon and that religion is usually not a factor in their recruitment or activity. However, it may require a dramatic psychological shift in the mindset of security forces for them to view women and men equally as potential adversaries (Kassman, 2004).

ROLES AND ACTIVITIES FOR FEMALE TERRORISTS

Through the ages, women have performed many, significantly different kinds of activities as participants in revolutionary groups, but their leadership roles have been limited (Vetter & Perlstein, 1991). Women play four different roles in today's guerrilla groups: sympathizers, spies, warriors, and dominant forces.

Sympathizers

At one end of the activity spectrum, women serve as camp followers in rebel groups. They cook, sew, and do other household chores for the revolution and also may be available for sex. They are involved in the struggle through their relationships with male terrorists. For example, in the early 1800s, as Simón Bolívar waged a revolution for independence from Spain through what is now Venezuela, Colombia, Peru, and Bolivia, his troops were followed by dozens of *Juanas Cholas.* These women managed to survive by serving the needs of the insurgents (Cherpak, 1978).

At the same level of involvement are female sympathizers who provide access to resources and enable the rebels to carry on a clandestine life in the midst of warfare. Supportive women provide food and hiding places. These women might be called on only once or at irregular intervals to give shelter, donations, weapons, or time and effort to the rebel cause. Their participation in the terrorists' campaign is less direct, and of necessity they are not usually identified publicly with the group. The roles of these female sympathizers nevertheless are crucial to the success of terrorist attempts to disrupt the social order.

Hate groups in the United States, as an example, may have many female members (Blee, 2002). There is little evidence, however, that women's traditional roles have changed within these right-wing extremist groups. There were no reports of female commanders or strategists among racist or Christian Identity terrorist groups in the United States at the end of the 20th century (Potok, 1999).

Spies

Further along the spectrum of involvement, women have served as decoys, messengers, intelligence gatherers, and spies. Women's work and women's status may be exploited for the cause; baby carriages and women who are actually or pretending to be pregnant prove useful for hiding weapons of war. Women working in banks may be helpful to insurgents, as are other women with respectable positions who can provide financial and strategic support essential for the rebels. These women may be above suspicion by virtue of their traditional roles in their societies. Without the assistance of mothers and sisters, wives, aunts, daughters, and female friends, the success of an uprising is not likely. In most groups, female rebels maintain their traditional sex roles while working for the army. They do not expect to have a political impact in the upcoming society they are helping forge. Like the camp followers, these female revolutionaries have no political agenda for themselves as women after the revolution achieves its goal. They expect to return to their previous sex roles as mothers and wives.

Warriors

At the next level of involvement are women who act as warriors, using weapons and incendiary devices. They fight in battles on an equal level with men, but they are not leaders. They seldom have any say in the policies or plans they are carrying out. When the revolution is over, there is no explicit scheme to change their status in society. For example, Tatiana Leontiev, a lady-in-waiting to the Russian tsar in the late 1800s, planned to shoot him with a revolver concealed in a bouquet of flowers. She was arrested during the assassination attempt. Her wealthy family passed her off as insane, and she was banished to a hotel in Switzerland; however, she eventually served a long prison sentence for shooting a businessman journeying through Switzerland because she believed he was the Russian minister of the interior traveling incognito. She was no more than 20 years old at the time (Vetter & Perlstein, 1991).

In Bolivia, Tamara Burke became well known because of her connections to Che Guevara and the revolution in which he lost his life. Known as Camarada Tania, she established and controlled urban guerrilla warfare in her country during the 1960s. Because of her brave and forceful reputation, the Symbionese Liberation Army in California used the *nom de guerre* of Tania for heiress Patricia Hearst after they kidnapped her and she joined their cause in 1974. As a prototype of a female warrior, Camarada Tania was the perfect propaganda image (Radu & Tismaneanu, 1990).

Dominant Forces

At the extreme end of the spectrum are women who are dominant forces within terrorist groups. A few women provide ideology, leadership, motivation, and strategy for their groups. When women are included in the commando group at the center of a terrorist organization, they may inspire greater fear than do men because their actions are so far outside the boundaries of traditional behavior expected from women.

PHOTO 7.1   Fighters for Abdullah Ocalan's PKK (Kurdistan Workers' Party) gather around a portrait of Zilan, a "kamikaze" who died in a suicide attack.

When the revolution is over, these commanders envision a society in which the role of women will be changed drastically. Instead of returning to their lives at home, they plan to be running the country and carrying on the international struggle. In the United States, Bernardine Dohrn was an example of a dominant force in the Weather Underground of the 1970s. Hers was a prominent voice in the ideology of the New Left movement that hoped to redefine the nature of society to eliminate the dominance of White males. She is known to have asserted, "The best thing that we can be doing for ourselves, as well as for the. . . revolutionary black liberation struggle is to build a f—ing white revolutionary movement" (Jacobs, 1997, from the book cover).

TWO EXCEPTIONAL TERRORIST GROUPS

Women played a dominant role in the RAF (Rote Armee Fraktion, or Red Army Faction) in Germany in the 1970s and 1980s (Huffman, 1999) and in the SL (*Sendero Luminoso*, or Shining Path) in Peru in the 1980s and early 1990s (Poole & Rénique, 1992). In these groups, women were as important as men from many standpoints.

Terrorist organizations in which women establish control are exceptional because of the ways the early leaders develop ideology for the group. Two exemplary female terrorists, Ulrike Meinhof of the RAF and Augusta La Torre Guzmán of the SL, were instrumental in developing similar revolutionary ideologies in two very disparate countries in different historical settings. Both had similar deaths as well, dying at an early age in reported suicides under suspicious circumstances; neither saw the end of the movements they began. Yet their lives were not irrelevant. They demonstrated the circumstances in which women could become the most nefarious terrorists of all (Demaris, 1977; McClintock, 1986).

The RAF in Germany

By the late 1960s, the RAF had become famous for its systematic bombings of department stores. Leftists allied with Palestinians, RAF members were trained in tactics of guerrilla warfare, which they directed primarily toward "imperialists" at U.S. installations in Germany and German sites connected with the military-industrial complex. The RAF was responsible for drastic changes in German life, including a new level of security force to combat insurgencies and a huge new prison complex for holding terrorists and conducting trials. The RAF's campaign of terror also increased levels of suspicion and repression throughout German society (Becker, 1977; Horchem, 1986; Rojahn, 1998).

The *Sendero Luminoso* in Peru

In Peru, the SL's first known guerrilla action took place in 1980. The SL managed to hold the country in fear by launching unpredictable violent attacks until its leaders finally came to light after a score of high-profile arrests in the early 1990s. Like the RAF, the members of the SL were leftists. Their goal was to redistribute Peru's wealth equitably. In the end, the SL was responsible for the economic and social devastation of one state in Peru and for wreaking havoc with the way of life of the entire nation (DeGregori, 1994; Palmer, 1994; Tarazona-Sevillano, 1990).

TWO FEMALE TERRORISTS

Ulrike Meinhof

Ulrike Meinhof's parents died young, leaving Ulrike and her sister in the care of a devoted socialist who had been their mother's friend. After marrying the publisher of a left-wing student newspaper, Meinhof joined the radical student movement and ultimately became the celebrity of the RAF. From the late 1950s on, she was well known and outspoken, maintained a high profile, and asserted her opinions on questions of women's rights. In the 1970s, Meinhof became armed and militant. She was named an outlaw when she joined with Gudrun Ensslin and Andreas Baader to rob banks and bomb buildings. The three joined Horst Mahler in Berlin and made plans for continued violence against the government they saw as fascist. They were known to the press as the Baader-Meinhof gang and later as the first generation of the RAF.

Meinhof was seized by authorities in 1972 and held in isolation for four years. She and other RAF leaders took part in high-profile hunger strikes backed by leftist lawyers who openly supported their ideals. It took three years to bring her and other prominent RAF leaders to trial. After helping Andreas Baader escape prison, she was sentenced to an additional eight years in custody. Meinhof faced the possibility of an even longer prison sentence when all the charges against her would be decided. When she died, Meinhof was mourned by thousands of supporters and was eulogized as one of the most significant women in German politics at her gravesite on May 15, 1976 (Becker, 1977; Demaris, 1977; Huffman, 1999; Vague, 1994). She was alleged to have committed suicide, but she left no farewell note, even though she wrote daily at her typewriter until her death. Three subsequent suspicious suicides by RAF leaders in prison were called murders by their followers.

Augusta La Torre Guzmán

Augusta La Torre was born in the remote foothills of the Andes mountains in a small town known for its resistance to the central government in Lima, Peru. Her father was a politician. She met her future husband, Abimael Guzmán, when he came to her house to plot liberal political strategy with her father and his cronies. La Torre was 18 years old and her husband 27 when they married. Many have credited La Torre for the dramatic origins of the SL.

PHOTO 7.2   Ulrike Meinhof, German journalist and member of the RAF (Red Army Faction).

Abimael Guzmán was considered an intellectual, but was not much of a speaker. La Torre was the spark who set his ideas on fire. She was intensely concerned about the plight of the downtrodden in Peruvian society, especially the indigenous peoples living in the Andes altiplano region. She was widely recognized as an organizer and a strategist for Guzmán. When he went to China, she went along. They both studied revolutionary tactics.

La Torre's ideas were behind the formation of the original central committee of the SL. She attracted female scholars and professionals into the movement. After her prominence in the founding of the SL, however, little was heard of La Torre. She went into hiding with Guzmán in 1978; after that, the stories about her were few and were mostly rumors.

It is believed that La Torre died in 1988. In 1991, the police made public a video about her death. No one appeared in the video except Guzmán, who directed the camera to film a woman's body wrapped in a red flag bearing the communist symbol of a hammer and sickle. In a distant and confused voice, he delivered the formal SL version of La Torre's death. She "annihilated herself." The police doubted the story, and journalists raised serious questions about whether her death was suicide or murder. Her corpse was never found (Kirk, 1993; McClintock, 1986; Palmer, 1994).

IDEOLOGY AND FEMALE TERRORISTS

The terrorist groups in which women serve as dominant forces are set apart by their ideologies from other groups in which women remain in the roles of supporters and sympathizers. Female terrorists' worldviews about the causes of their acts of violence are often utopian. It is likely that the goal for prominent female terrorists involves creating a new society, not restoring a traditional way of life. Demoralization and a sense of hopelessness with the existing system were the psychological root of both the German RAF and the Peruvian SL movements (Andreas, 1985; Becker, 1977). These female terrorists saw themselves as being advanced and intellectually superior. Their ideologies were spawned by academics and philosophers, particularly by critical sociological theories. The university was their fostering mother, although many of the members were not students. They saw violence as the only tool for political change. For the members of the RAF and the SL, there was only one course of action to be followed, and that was armed struggle (Becker, 1977; DeGregori, 1994).

Intellectuals in both Germany and Peru fueled the flames of resentment into guerrilla war. They took popular liberal rhetoric and pushed it to extremes. They thought of themselves as the beacons of world revolution and the vanguards of global communism. They sneered at other intellectuals whose weapons were no more than pens. For the members of the RAF and the SL, everyday life was war. The propaganda of the deed attracted militant women who were frustrated by conventional society. They planned to revise the entire global order (Aust, 1987; Grant, 1994; Herzog, 1993). This profile contrasts with the findings of Gonzales-Perez (2006) that women are more likely to be actively engaged at the highest levels in groups with domestic or nationalistic goals and that those guerrilla organizations that reject women or relegate them to subservient support roles are more likely to focus on international agendas and external enemies.

Clearly, terrorist groups in which a significant number of the members of the high command are female are likely to be guided by an ideology developed with consideration for women. The ideology of female-dominated terrorists groups varies considerably from group to group and time to time; however, one consistent belief is the empowerment of women, along with a redefinition of the functions of women in the division of labor. The inclusion of women in multiple roles in the earliest stages of development sets these groups apart from others in which women's roles are subordinate.

Some researchers have pointed out that, rather than revising the traditional female gender roles of caregiving and nurturing, terrorist women have played these same roles with greater fervor but in a different direction (Andreas, 1990; O'Connell, 1993). Rather than being liberated from traditional sex roles, female terrorists replace the restrictions of marriage with extreme attachment to a leader or cause. Instead of the responsibilities of motherhood, they are burdened with passionate concern for society at large. Female terrorists may be even more fanatic than males. In negating conventional roles, they turn their traditional roles against themselves (Neuburger & Valentini, 1996).

HIGHLIGHTS OF REPRINTED ARTICLES

Brigitte L. Nacos (2005). The portrayal of female terrorists in the media: Similar framing patterns in the news coverage of women in politics and in terrorism. *Studies in Conflict and Terrorism, 28,* 435–451.

The public image of terrorists is constructed from many sources, but the media are the principal basis on which individuals develop their beliefs and knowledge about terrorism or freedom fighters. In this article Nacos analyzes the patterns in news reporting about female terrorists and the significance of these patterns for public policy. She finds that both women terrorists and female politicians are described most often as interlopers in an utterly male domain.

This article presents the most frequent frames of reference related to the media image of female terrorists. In one common scenario, female terrorists are portrayed as "tough as males," as women who want to be men. In another version, female terrorists are the product of women's liberation and feminist ideas. Another common focus for the media coverage of female terrorists is on family issues and the women's early experiences. News reports explore these terrorists' relationships because they are thought to be attracted to the cause for love of a man. But the most common frame of reference is that of physical appearance. How women terrorists look is much more important to the media portrayal than their ideas or even their actions.

Kathleen M. Blee (2005). Women and organized racial terrorism in the United States, *Studies in Conflict and Terrorism, 28,* 421–423.

Blee's analysis of women's participation in organized racial terrorism in the United States provides insight into two important issues: the history of organized violence against racial minorities from the context of women's participation and connections between terrorist strategic directions and tactical choices and the involvement of women. Beginning with the post–Civil War period when White supremacists in the United States first emerged and continuing through the present, Blee examines the involvement of women in racial terrorism. She shows that women are capable of participating in the most deadly kinds of terrorist activities on behalf of supremacist ideology, but there has been a great deal of variability in their involvement. Although women's participation in organized racial violence has been increasing, it is not a simple, temporal relationship. There have been variations in groups, contexts, and roles for females as terrorists. Because of social changes in the United States and racial terrorist group dynamics, women's participation may not continue to increase.

EXPLORING WOMEN AS TERRORISTS FURTHER

- Background on the "Women Behind the Masks" among the Zapatistas (EZLN) in Mexico can be obtained in Spanish at the EZLN Web site and in other links such as "Zapatistas in Cyberspace." This material gives you access to numerous viewpoints about their movement. Which Zapatista policies were initiated by women?
- More information about the German Red Army Fraction (RAF), Baader-Meinhof, and the Shining Path (SL) Committee to Support the Revolution in Peru is available on Web sites maintained by their supporters. How are women depicted in these reports?
- Today three groups deserve investigation because of the position of women within them: the Tamil Tigers (LTTE) of Sri Lanka, the Free Aceh of Indonesia (GAM), and the Chechen separatists. They receive attention because of their large numbers of women terrorist members and the need for timely information about their ideology and leadership. Numerous Internet sites and sources exist for them.
- In her article about the portrayal of female terrorists, Nacos does not consider the effect of the journalist's gender. Develop a content analysis of news reports about terrorism written by female journalists compared to the same number of articles about terrorism written by males. Use the print media so that the articles are the ideas of the journalist, not a script written for him or her. Try to balance the types of reports so that there is an equal representation of several types of publications for both males and females. Your first finding will likely be the difficulty of finding news reports of terrorism written by women. What impact does a journalist's gender have on the accuracy of the reports? What other patterns emerge?
- Nacos has compared framing patterns in the media for female politicians and female terrorists. Can you think of other identifiable groups of high-profile women who might be placed in similar frames? What other frames of reference are likely for women who are portrayed as powerful?
- The article about women in organized racial terrorism by Blee provides a look at hate-inspired violence from after the Civil War until 2005. What is the present role of women in organized hate crimes in the United States? A good place to find an answer to this question is the Southern Poverty Law Center. You will find links to other sources on their Web site.

- Blee's article concerns hate crime in the United States. What has been reported about women's participation in organized hate crime in other countries? What has been the role of women in perpetrating genocide and other racially motivated attacks? Reports about women as victims of genocide are available, but are there reports about women's role in supporting or actively participating in international organized racial terrorism?

VIDEO NOTES

The film, *The Dancer Upstairs* (Twentieth Century Fox, 2002, 113 min.) presents a dramatized depiction of the SL. The frame of reference for the women of *Sendero* in this movie is through the eyes of men.

The Legend of Rita (Kino Video, 2001, 101 min.) depicts a young woman terrorist from a German perspective. There is a sense of pathos about the legendary Rita who, the viewer is led to suppose, was connected to the Red Army Faction.

❖

The Portrayal of Female Terrorists in the Media

Similar Framing Patterns in the News Coverage of Women in Politics and in Terrorism

Brigitte L. Nacos

Although women have been among the leaders and followers of terrorist organizations throughout the history of modern terrorism, the mass media typically depict women terrorists as interlopers in an utterly male domain. A comparison of the framing patterns in the news about women in politics and the entrenched stereotypes in the coverage of female terrorists demonstrates similarities in the depiction of these legitimate (women in politics) and illegitimate political actors (women in terrorism). Just like the managers of election campaigns are cognizant of the electorate's stereotypical gender perceptions, terrorist organizations know about and exploit cultural gender clichés that are reinforced by the media. The argument here is that the implementation of anti- and counterterrorist policies must not be influenced by the mass-mediated images of female terrorists because they do not reflect reality.

"Her nails manicured and hair pulled back from her face, the Palestinian woman asks that she be called by an Arabic name for a faint star—Suha." Following this opening sentence, the next paragraph revealed that Suha, a future suicide bomber for the Al Aqsa Martyrs Brigade, "is barely 5 feet tall, fair-skinned and pretty, with a quick smile and handshake." The up-front sketch of a beautiful young woman, determined to become a human bomb in order to kill others, was contrasted with the description of her bodyguard as "grim-looking."[1] Whether intended or not, the reader of this article, published in April 2002 in one of the leading U.S. newspapers, was left with the paradox of a pretty girl as suicide terrorist and a tough-looking male as presumably content to live. Three months earlier, an American news magazine published an article that linked terrorism to male hormones. The authors wrote, "Testosterone has always had a lot to do with terrorism, even among secular bombers and kidnappers like Italy's Red Brigade and Germany's Baader-Meinhof gang."[2] Here the reader was explicitly told that terrorism is the domain of men. The implicit message was inescapable as well: females do not fit the terrorist profile.

Contrary to the gender stereotypes in the earlier citations and contrary to conventional wisdom, women terrorists are neither misfits nor rare. Throughout the history of modern terrorism, females have been among the leaders and chief ideologues (i.e., in the American Weather Underground, in Italy's Red Brigade, and Germany's Red Army Faction) and followers in terrorist groups. And today, according to Christopher Harmon, "more than 30 percent of international terrorists are women, and females are central to membership rosters and operational roles in nearly all insurgencies."[3] Other estimates range from 20 percent to 30 percent for many domestic and international terrorist groups. Typically, left-wing organizations have far more female members than conservative ones. Yet, whenever women commit acts of terror, most people react with an extra level of shock and horror.

There is no evidence that male and female terrorists are fundamentally different in terms of their recruitment, motivation, ideological fervor, and brutality—just as there is no evidence that male and female politicians have fundamentally different motivations for seeking political office and abilities in different policy areas. Yet, the media's treatment of female terrorists is consistent with the patterns of societal gender stereotypes in *general* and of gender biases in the news coverage of female politicians in particular. In other words, gender stereotypes are found in the news about nonviolent and violent political actors.

Research has demonstrated that mass-mediated societal gender stereotypes affect the behavior of female politicians and the campaign tactics of their advisers.[4] Similarly, there is also evidence that gender clichés influence the tactical considerations and decisions of terrorist groups and the behavior of female terrorists. Therefore, the intelligence community, law enforcement, and others involved in the implementation of anti- and counterterrorism would benefit from understanding and highlighting the gap between the stereotypical female terrorist and the reality of gender roles in terrorist organizations.

The research presented here is based on a content analysis of U.S. and non-American English language print and broadcast news and, to a lesser extent, on an examination of the relevant literature in the field.[5] As an aside, this material also allowed a comparison between American and European reporting. Although European women have won elective and appointed offices in far larger numbers than their American counterparts and increasingly served in the highest-ranking government and party posts (i.e., British Prime Minister Margaret Thatcher), male and female media sources and commentators in Europe are just as likely as their American counterparts to see female terrorists through the prism of gender stereotypes.

OF NEWS FRAMES AND STEREOTYPES

Whether print or television, the media tend to report the news along explanatory frames that cue the reader, listener, and viewer to put events, issues, and political actors into contextual frameworks of reference.[6] Framing can and does affect the news in many ways, for example, in the choice of topics, sources, language, and photographs. According to Entman, "a frame operates to select and highlight some features of reality and obscure others in a way that tells a consistent story about problems, their causes, moral implications, and remedies."[7] Accordingly, reporters, editors, producers, and others in the news media make constant decisions as to what and whom to present in the news and how. Some framing patterns seem especially important with respect to terrorism news because they have strong effects on the perceptions and reaction of news receivers. Iyengar, for example, found that in the United States TV-network coverage of terrorism is overwhelmingly episodic or narrowly focused on who did what, where and how, rather than thematic or contextual that would explore why terrorism occurs. His research demonstrated furthermore that narrowly focused coverage influenced audiences to hold individual perpetrators responsible, whereas thematic reporting was more likely to assign responsibility to societal conditions and the policies that cause them. By highlighting and dwelling on the fact that a woman perpetrated a horrific act of terrorism, the media frame such news inevitably in episodic terms and affect news consumers' attribution of responsibility: When exposed to episodic framing of terrorism, people are more inclined to support tougher punitive measures against individual terrorists; when watching thematically framed terrorism news recipients tend to be more in favor of policies designed to alleviate the root causes of terror.[8]

A generation ago, Gans concluded that in the United States "the news reflects the white male social order. . . ."[9] Although contemporary newsrooms are more diverse than 25 years ago, entrenched prejudices and stereotypical perceptions have not disappeared. As one newsman observed more recently, "Newsrooms are not hermetically sealed against the prejudices that play perniciously just beneath the surface of American life."[10] The result is that the media continue to use different framing patterns in the news about women and men. Research revealed, for example, that "journalists commonly work with gendered 'frames' to simplify, prioritize, and structure the narrative flow of events when covering women and men in public life."[11] Norris found evidence for the prevalence of sex stereotypes, such as the female compassionate nature and the male natural aggressiveness, that affect people to expect men and women to behave differently. As a result, "Women in politics are commonly seen as compassionate, practical, honest, and hardworking, while men are seen as ruthless, ambitious, and tough leaders."[12] Moreover, by perpetuating these sorts of stereotypes, the news magnifies the notion that the softness of female politicians qualifies them for dealing capably with social problems and policies, such as education and welfare, but not with national security and foreign relations—areas best left to tough males. Although preferring "stereotypes of women politicians as weak, indecisive, and emotional," the news sometimes reflects the opposite image of the mean and tough female politician, the "bitch," who does not fit the conventional profile of the soft woman. Or female politicians are portrayed as "outsiders," the exception, not the norm.[13] Indeed, women are "most newsworthy when they are doing something 'unladylike.' "[14] Researchers found furthermore that the media report far more on the physical appearances (their figure, their hair style, their make-up, their attire, their overall look) and the personal traits of female candidates and office holders, whereas male politicians receive more issue-oriented coverage.[15] Female politicians are far more often defined by their family status than male politicians and typically identified as the wives of a multimillionaire husband, the daughters of a well-known politician, the unmarried challengers of male incumbents, the mothers of several children, and so on.[16] Finally, even after reporting the initial news that a woman has accomplished another "first," the media tend to forever identify these females as trailblazers (i.e., Geraldine Ferraro, the first female nominee for vice-president of a major political party; Madeline Albright, the first female secretary of state).

When we cannot understand women in roles that cultural norms and prejudices perceive as inherently male (i.e., women as political leaders, women as violent political actors), there is a tendency to resort to stereotypical explanations (i.e., her good looks opened doors; her family affected her path; she is tough like a man, not a real woman).

WOMEN TERRORISTS AND THE MEDIA

In the early 1980s, Crenshaw noted that there was "considerable speculation about the prominent position of women in terrorist groups" and that it would be "interesting to find out if female participation in violence will have an effect on general social roles or on the stereotyping of women."[17] To what extent the roles and images of women in social, political, and professional settings have been affected by female terrorist leaders and perhaps of male terrorists' acceptance of women in leadership roles is difficult to assess—if there have been such effects at all. But a survey of the limited literature on female terrorists reveals that a number of explanations have been advanced to understand what kind of woman becomes a terrorist and why. Although some of these explications reflect reality, others are rooted in conventional gender stereotypes. More importantly, an analysis of pertinent material in the news media demonstrates that the similar framing modes are found in the news about female politicians and female terrorists. The following reporting patterns, images, and stereotypes are most obvious in the way the media portray female terrorists.

The Physical Appearance Frame

In 1995, a year after Idoia Lopez Riano of the Basque separatist organization ETA was arrested and charged with 23 assassinations, Anne McElvoy reported in the *Times* of London that the female terrorist, known as The Tigress, "has the looks of a Mediterranean film star" and "is one of the few women who manages to look good even in a police shot."[18] The Tigress was furthermore described as "wearing hefty eye make-up, fuchsia lipstick and dangling earrings that tinkle as she tosses her hair of black curls."[19] When reading these kinds of descriptions of female terrorists, nobody could be less surprised than women in public life, especially politicians, because they know about the media's interest in the way they look and dress. U.S. Senator Barbara Mikulski of Maryland, for example, has noted that the Baltimore press always described her as "short and round," when she first ran for a seat in the upper chamber of the U.S. Congress. By emphasizing her physical characteristics the news perpetuated the idea that this candidate did not fit the profile of a United States senator—a tall, trim gentleman.[20] Other female politicians learned, too, that the press paid a great deal of attention to their appearance and that this reporting reflected the predominant cultural sentiments. Thus, after Blanche Lincoln was elected to the U.S. Senate in 1998, she remarked that "it doesn't matter what I say about an issue. If I have a run in my panty hose, that's all anybody will talk about."[21] In other words, when it comes to women, their appearance is deemed more important than their ideas, policies, and positions. This coverage pattern differs from the way the news reports about male politicians.

Just as the media find the physical appearance of women in politics especially newsworthy, the news dwells on the looks, the ready smiles, or the carefully chosen apparel of female terrorists that seem in sharp contrast to the image of a tough terrorist. Thus, a newspaper article about the first female Palestinian suicide bomber Wafra Idris began with the sentence, "She was an attractive, auburn haired graduate who had a loving family and likes to wear sleeveless dresses and make-up."[22] In another report Idris was described as a woman with "long, dark hair tied back with a black-and-white keffiyeh."[23] A report about the wave of "Palestinian women strapping explosives to their bodies and becoming martyrs" on the website of the Christian Broadcasting Network was headlined "Lipstick Martyrs: A New Breed of Palestinian Terrorists."[24] An article in the *New York Times* that emphasized the similarities between a Palestinian suicide bomber and her Israeli victim, both girls in their teens, began with the following words: "The suicide bomber and her victim look strikingly similar. Two high school seniors in jeans with flowing black hair . . ."[25] A would-be suicide bomber who got cold feet and ended up in an Israeli prison was described in one news account as a "petite, dark 25-year old with an engaging smile and an infectious giggle" and as a woman who "was well-suited to her job arranging flowers for weddings in her village near Jenin in the West Bank."[26] This attention to the appearance of female terrorists in the news is not a recent trend. More than 30 years ago, Leila Khaled of the Popular Front for the Liberation of Palestine was described as a trim and dark-eyed beauty with sex appeal. Even three decades after Khaled's involvement in terrorism, reporters dwelled on the attention she received as the first female hijacker because of her "beauty," her "pin-up" looks, and her "delicate Audrey Hepburn face."[27] One interviewer told Leila Khaled three decades after her career as hijacker ended, "You were the glamour girl of international terrorism. You were the hijack queen."[28] And well after Khaled had retired from active terrorist duty, "a Norwegian newspaper made jokes about her 'bombs' (Norwegian slang for breasts). . . ."[29]

Not only "The Tigress" Lopez Riano but other especially brutal women members of ETA have frequently been described as beautiful by reporters themselves and by the sources they cited. Thus, according to one story, a Spanish man who had met her years ago, described Lierni Armendariz, an ETA leader, as "flirtatious, pretty and the furthest away from someone you would think of as a terrorist."[30] As one European reporter put it, "Female terrorists, from Palestinian Leila Khaled to German Ulrike Meinhof, have long fascinated the popular imagination with their frequent combination of feminine charms and ability to kill in cold blood."[31] After her indictment as co-conspirator in a bombing plot in Boston and the revelation that she moved in White supremacy circles, the news media described the accused young woman as "bright-eyed" and so "attractive" that she "caught the eyes of many men, including World Church founder Matt Hale."[32]

If one takes the news at face value, female terrorists are almost always good-looking, trim, and pleasant. Aside from one reference to the nickname "Fatty" of a leading woman in the Basque separatist organization ETA, there were simply no descriptions of less than pretty women terrorists. Although this focus helps to dramatize the contrast between these women and their violent occupations, readers, listeners, and viewers do not always appreciate such emphasis. As a reader of the *Los Angeles Times* wrote in a letter-to-the-editor, "Your article affectionately describes this particular day's suicide bomber with 'doe-brown eyes and softly curled hair.' . . . How desensitized are we readers expected to become to these continuing satanic acts, this one committed by a woman?"[33] But such protests have not diminished the media's attention to female terrorists' physical attributes.

To be sure, at times news stories do mention details about the physical characteristics of male terrorists—most of the time in order to explain a particular facet of their actions or of police investigations. When a report on a male terrorist's prison breakout says that he is very slim, this information may explain how he could escape through a small window. Information about a male terrorist's hair color is most likely discussed in the context of color change on the part of a fugitive or captured perpetrator.

The Family Connection Frame

Even though women in politics are no longer the exception in the United States and in comparable liberal democracies, the news media tend to define female politicians based on their family status. When Christine Todd Whitman, who had long been active in New Jersey politics, ran for governor in her state, an article in a leading newspaper characterized her as "the preppy wife of a multimillionaire investment banker." Along the same lines, a female columnist described U.S. Senator Kay Bailey Hutchison as a "typical Republican housewife."[34] In view of this kind of media focus, it is hardly surprising that the news pays a great deal of attention to the family backgrounds of female terrorists. When women terrorists are especially pretty, reporters wonder why they are not married or engaged. The young Leila Khaled preempted such questions when she declared that she was engaged to the revolution. This statement was often cited in reports about the "glamorous" Palestinian terrorist.[35] In the case of the unmarried ETA terrorist Idoia Lopez Riano, the media linked the fact that this beauty was single to her "mythical sexual prowess"[36] and her alleged habit of "picking up police officers, normally ETA targets, in bars and having one-night stands with them."[37]

But just as common are reporters' references to and explorations of female terrorists' family backgrounds that might explain, or not explain, their violent deeds. One instructive example is the catchy sound bite "Black Widows" that the news media coined and repeated over and over again, when reporting on female Chechen terrorists. By invoking the image of the widow, clad from head to toe in black, the news perpetuated the image of the vengeance-seeking widow who becomes a terrorist because her husband was killed by Russian troops—a woman with a strong personal rather than political motive. To be sure, some of these women lost their husbands and others reacted to the violent death or disappearance of their sons, brothers, or fathers. But by lumping them together as "Black Widows" with personal grievances, the media ignored that some, perhaps many, of these women were not at all motivated by personal but political grievances.

What the news revealed about Wafra Idris, the female Palestinian suicide bomber who started a wave of similar attacks in January 2002, was based on interviews with her parents, siblings, cousins, other relatives, and her ex-husband. But an allegedly grief-stricken husband seemed more compelling in a human-interest story than one who had divorced the female "martyr." As one correspondent reported, "Ahmed Zaki is a very proud husband indeed—he is the husband of the first female Palestinian suicide bomber, Wafa Idris." By not reporting up front that he had divorced Wafa Idris against her wish because she could not bear him children and had married another woman, the reporter presented Zaki as the person who knew why Wafa became a suicide bomber: She was "a nationalist," he said. The article mentioned eventually in passing that the couple had separated six months ago but that the husband (as he was called in the headline) still loved her.[38]

Even in scholarly writings the family background of female terrorists tends to get far more attention than that of male members of the same organizations. With respect to the Red Army Faction in Germany, for example, references to the parents of Ulrike Meinhof, one of the group's co-founders, have been far more common than similar information about Andreas Baader, also a co-founder. When writing about another leading RAF member, Gudrun Ensslin, experts rarely failed to mention that her father was a Lutheran minister.[39]

Terrorist for the Sake of Love

Related to the previous category is the popular image of the women terrorist for the sake of love—not for deeply held political reasons. Although seemingly without a parallel in the cliché of female politicians, one can actually construe even a "politician for the sake of love" frame in admittedly extraordinary cases: When a woman is appointed to serve out the term of her deceased husband, the widow tends to enjoy—at least initially—a great deal of sympathy in her home district or state—and even beyond. In such situations, political opponents tend to temper their behavior. Although not explicitly stated, there is the notion that a loving wife continues her husband's work after years of supporting him. This, in turn, tempers the behavior of political opponents. But the stereotype of the female terrorist following her lover or husband or perhaps her father, brother, or cousin into terrorist groups and activities transcends by far the special circumstances of some female politicians. The "politician for the sake of love" frame differs also from the stereotype of the women who resort to political violence in the wake of personal tragedies or disappointments. Although the idea of terrorism for the sake of love or because of lost love "diminishes women's credibility and influence both within and outside organizations,"[40] as Karla Cunningham has suggested, it has been a common theme emphasized by experts in the field, by reporters, and even by female members of extremist groups. Supporting the notion that females are drawn to terrorism by the men they love, Robin Morgan has argued that most women do not want to admit to that connection. According to Morgan, "These women would have died—as some did—rather than admit that they had acted as they did for male approval and love."[41] Surveying a host of female terrorists and their relationships with male colleagues as well as the many affairs enjoyed by "Carlos the Jackal" and other male terrorists, Morgan concluded that women in terrorist organizations, whether followers or leaders, are involved in a "rebellion for love's sake [that] is classic feminine—not feminist—behavior."[42] Morgan told an interviewer that female terrorists are "almost always lured into it by a father, a brother or most commonly by a lover."[43] In her view "Carlos, the Jackal" is the perfect example of a pied piper attracting females as a free man, fugitive, and prisoner. As Morgan described it, "In 1994, after a worldwide manhunt and numerous escapades, the notorious 'Carlos, the Jackal' was caught and sentenced to prison for life, following several already incarcerated members of his 'harem,' his many female lovers (some of whom were aware of his exploits—and each other—and some of whom weren't)."[44] Just as telling was the fact that Carlos's attraction

did not wane behind bars: In 2002 he announced his engagement to and plan to marry his French attorney Isabella Coutant, a high society figure, who characterized their love according to news accounts as a "meeting of hearts and of minds."[45]

The "love connection" has been a frequent theme in the media's coverage of gender terrorism. To explain the large number of female members of the German Red Army Faction in the 1970s, the news cited male criminologists who said that "a few male terrorists and extremist lawyers in West Germany have had the fanatical devotion of female gang members" and that women join because they "admire someone in the terrorist movement."[46] Female members in White supremacy organizations, such as the Ku Klux Klan, also spread the word that most of them joined because of their husbands or boyfriends. According to one long-time female KKK member, a woman who uses the pseudonym Klaliff, "My introduction into the White Pride Movement (WP Movement) was in college where I fell in love with another college student, a man who had been an activist in the WP Movement." She reveals that many women got involved because they had a boyfriend in the Movement. "I cannot speak for all women in the WP Movement," she wrote, "but I see the men in the WP Movement as manly men with strong ideals and courage."[47] The writer notes furthermore that she married her husband because of "his [WP] beliefs."[48] In the recent case of a young woman in Boston, accused of participating in a White supremacy bomb plot, the media reported that it was her romantic involvement with a former prison inmate that pushed her into a federal conspiracy."[49] Although true in many instances, but not many others, the media's emphasis on the love connection has produced the cliché of the female "demon lover" a la Morgan.

The flip-side of the coin is the girl or woman who acts because of a lost love. When a 20-year-old Palestinian student was recruited as a suicide bomber, she was reportedly "out to avenge the death of her fiancé, a member of a terrorist group." She was said to believe that the young man had been killed by the Israeli military even though the Israelis reported that he had blown himself up in an accident.[50] When reporting on one of ETA's leaders, Maria Soledad Iparaguirre, the news media rarely failed to mention that she allegedly became a brutal terrorist after her boyfriend was shot by the police in the early 1980s.[51]

It has been the exception, not the rule, for the media to scrutinize this conventional image. The writer of one such exceptional article stated,

> There remains a misleading, but popular Patty Hearst image of female terrorists. The idea of women only killing, maiming and bombing when duped by a boyfriend or partner is an alluring one. It allows us to believe that the sexes are different, and to fall in behind all the cosy [*sic*] discriminations which flow from such a fallacy. Women are not simply brainwashed molls desperate to please hardened criminal lovers. On an individual level, this may hold true for some, but it is insulting to suggest women are so easily led that they will commit murder simply for a partner's approval.[52]

In sum, then, the mass media reinforce the stereotype of the female terrorist for the sake of love. In reality, when it comes to the recruitment of terrorists, both males and females are typically inspired and enlisted by relatives, friends, and acquaintances. In her study of Italy's Red Brigade, della Porta found, for example, that "in as many as 88 percent of the cases in which the nature of the tie with the recruiter is known, she or he is not a stranger; in 44 percent, she or he is a personal friend, and in 20 percent, she or he is a relative."[53] There were no gender differences with respect to recruits and recruiters. Because "the presence of strong affective ties is . . . a powerful explanation of individual motivation [to join a terrorist organization],"[54] it can be assumed that some male terrorists, just as their female counterparts, were recruited by their lovers as well. But the news is silent on this angle. It may well be that far fewer men are recruited by women than the other way around. But even when it comes to Muslim extremists this is not out of the question. The author has seen websites with text that tells "sisters" why they should encourage their husband to join *jihad*.

The Women's Lib/Equality Frame

In the past, far more than today, many female politicians tried to perform balancing acts in order to cultivate a positive, mass-mediated image of the capable candidate or office holder and, at the same time, avoid the negative stereotype of the overly aggressive feminist. Seemingly not at all concerned about their public image,

female terrorists have been often described as women's lib extremists. Although this was very common in the past, the contemporary news still explains the motives of female terrorists as the expression of gender equality or the struggle to achieve gender equality quite frequently. During the 1970s, when it became clear that women played starring roles in leftist terrorist groups in the United States, Europe, Latin America, and Japan, media sources often explained this phenomenon as a manifestation of women's liberation. Thus, *Newsweek* quoted an expert on the prevention of crime who had said tongue in cheek, "You might say that women terrorists have passed the Equal Rights Amendment and now play a variety of prominent roles."[55] Mentioning in particular the role of females in the Weather Underground and the Symbionese Liberation Army, the article's authors concluded:

> Inevitably, some scholarly analysts claim to see a connection between the recent flowering of the feminist movement and the dramatic upsurge in violent crimes attributed to women since the 1960s. First, the civil rights movement drew women students into the vortex of direct social action; later, anti-war protests baptized them in the harsher politics of confrontation. Before the decade was out, the logic of liberation brought women into the Weather Underground and other terrorist organizations.[56]

Similarly, criminologist Freda Adler explained female terrorist activity in an interview with the *New York Times* as "deviant expression of feminism."[57] According to the *Times*, Dr. Adler said that the publicity surrounding terrorism gives female terrorists "a platform to say, 'I am liberated from past stereotypes, I am accepted in the ultimate masculine roles.'"[58] Earlier, in her book *Sisters in Crime*, Adler wrote, "Despite their broad political pronouncements, what the new revolutionaries [such as the Weather Underground] wanted was not simply urban social gains, but sexual equality."[59] Pointing in particular to the female terrorists of the Symbionese Liberation Army, she added:

> That such women turned so drastically toward a new and highly volatile identity caused a good portion of the nation to ask incredulously, "How could women do this sort of thing?" Perhaps the question itself was the very point of the episode. The fires which consumed the ramshackle Los Angeles house

where the small band staged its last shoot-out also burned away a large part of the prevailing American illusion about women.[60]

In Europe, experts provided similar explanations for the large number of female members in terrorist organizations, such as the Red Brigades in Italy and the Red Army Faction in West Germany. According to one news account in 1977, "Italian and German sociologists and news commentators, all of them men, have suggested over the last few weeks that the significant female membership in radical and terrorist groups was an unwelcome consequence of the women's liberation movement."[61] Male sociologists and commentators in Europe were not the only ones to blame women's lib. Sharing this view, a female German politician told the media, "These women demonstratively negate everything that is part of the established feminine character."[62] A male professor in Munich wondered whether these female terrorists "see violence in society as the prerogative of males and ask, 'Why shouldn't we participate?' "[63] *Newsweek* quoted the former neighbor of German terrorist Susanne Albrecht who complained, "She sang Communist songs all night and never cleaned the stairs."[64] Given the prevalence of such attitudes, one West German criminologist told a reporter, "Maybe we are paying the price a little bit for having such a male-dominated society."[65]

In the early 1990s, an American reviewer of British journalist Eileen MacDonald's book *Shoot the Women First* wrote,

> There is no question that most of these women— particularly the younger generation—identify with feminism and with a larger struggle against political oppression. One young Basque woman says, "Men are used to being seen as strong and macho and women are expected to follow them. . . . But in revolutionary groups, the basic understanding is that we are equal."[66]

More recently there were many media accounts that explained female terrorists in traditionally male-dominated countries and regions as expressions of gender equality. In early 2002, following the first lethal bombing inside Israel proper by a female suicide attacker, some observers seemed not terribly surprised because, as the media reported, "Palestinian women have been the most liberated [compared to other Arab societies] in spite of the fact that Palestinian society remains male-dominated."[67] For Abdel

Hamuda, the editor of an Egyptian weekly, the first female suicide bombing was a monumental event in that it "shattered a glass ceiling" and "elevated the value of Arab women and, in one moment, and with enviable courage, put an end to the unending debate about equality between men and women."[68] His colleague Mufid Fawzie wrote in the Egyptian daily *Al Aalam al Youm,* "She bore in her belly the fetus of rare heroism, and gave birth by blowing herself up. What are the women of velvet chatting in the parlors next to the act of Wafa Idris?"[69] Although declaring that her purpose was not to "morally justify" female suicide bombers, the writer of a paper, available on the Internet, wrote nevertheless:

> As an American woman, I rejoice at the implementation of the female suicide bomber for the same reason Muslim women rejoiced. It is the purest form of enactment and dissention against Islamic fundamentalism. Moreover, the female suicide bomber empowers Muslim women to no longer accept their inferior status. But while western societies hail the trend of gender equality in Muslim society, the use of the female suicide bomber as a way to achieve gender equality is not comprehended nor accepted.[70]

In a lengthy commentary in the *Chicago Tribune,* a terrorism expert noted that by "attacking the Israelis, these female suicide bombers are fighting for more than just national liberation; they are fighting for gender liberation."[71] She pointed out that the funeral held for Wafa Idris, the first Palestinian woman to carry out a successful suicide mission, "looked like a feminist rally, with hundreds of women paying her homage. Female students all over the West Bank and Gaza City say they want to be next in line for a bombing mission." But in the end the female commentator rejected suicide bombing as a means to advance the women's rights movement and recommended "peaceful resistance and civil disobedience" as appropriate strategy, not human rights violations.

The Tough-as-Males/ Tougher-Than-Men Frame

When female politicians rise to the very top, they are often described as particularly tough females. Thus, British Prime Minister Thatcher was frequently called "the Iron Lady." Similarly, there is the mass-mediated notion of the female terrorist who, in order to prove that she belongs, tends to be more fanatical, more cruel, more deadly. More than 25 years ago, a female German politician said in an interview about female terrorists in West Germany and Italy, "Women, unfortunately, can be particularly fanatical."[72] At least some former terrorists seem to agree. Matias Antolin, the author of a of a book about female members of the Basque ETA organizations, told a correspondent, "Once in an active service unit they tend to be more cold-blooded and more lethal than the men because they have to prove their worth."[73] Reports about the violent take-over of a Moscow theater by heavily armed Chechen men and women emphasized that the females were "the most determined and aggressive of the hostage takers" and that they were especially "cruel and threatening and eager to die. . . ."[74]

Another image creeps into the tough-as-male frame—that "of the terrorist as lesbian, because everyone knows no 'real woman' would hijack planes or cripple middle-age men by shooting them in the kneecaps."[75] But apart from the lesbian label, the idea that terrorists are not "real women" tends to be expressed especially in the context of the mother who chooses political violence over her own children. Such was the case of the Red Army Faction's Ulrike Meinhof and Gudrun Ensslin who reportedly "put contacts with their children completely out of their minds, presumably because they interfered with their soldierly poses, Ensslin from the beginning and Meinhof from Christmas 1973."[76] It speaks to the prevalent double standard with respect to gender roles that similar issues have not been raised in the media or the scholarly literature with respect to male terrorists who happen to be fathers.

The Bored, Naïve, Out-of-Touch-With-Reality Frame

This last stereotype seems the only one without obvious parallels in the mass-mediated depiction of women politicians. With respect to female terrorists the notion of the naïve, bored, non-political, out-of-touch-with-reality woman who turns to terrorism, too, is perpetuated in the media—mostly by news sources, sometimes by reporters themselves. In the late 1970s a female criminologist said in an interview:

> Sometimes a woman turns to terrorism out of simple boredom. It sounds strange, I know, but boredom is one of the pathetic rights and

privileges of the middle-class woman. What does a middle-class woman do who doesn't happen to be interested in a career or college? What does she do in 1978?[77]

Around the same time, a male professor in West Germany said that women who become terrorists have "deficiencies in their socialization process."[78] Probably because most of the females in the Baader-Meinhof group were former students, this professor described West Germany's females in general as "unpolitical" and his own female students as "sort of educated housewives."[79]

More than 20 years later, after interviewing two young women who had been recruited by a male cousin to plant incendiary devices in a store in Bahrain, the interviewer wrote a story that was headlined, "From Boredom to Bombs: Two Female Terrorists." The report described the women as non-political and clueless about the motives of the young man who had recruited them. Pondering what he called a "naïve response," the male interviewer wrote, "I concluded halfway through the interview, there is no crusade here to spread the word of Islam, or to overthrow the regime then! I had the strong suspicion that many arson attacks are copycat attacks by bored kids."[80] Not surprisingly, there are no comparable news accounts of male terrorists whose motivation is said to be boredom.

IMPLICATIONS OF THE "FEMININE PARADOX" FOR ANTI- AND COUNTERTERRORISM

Gender stereotypes persist in the mass-mediated portrayal of women whether they are involved in legitimate political activities (campaigning for and filling public offices) or in political roles that are widely perceived to be illegitimate (joining terrorist groups and carrying out terrorist acts). But whereas the stereotypical framing patterns of female politicians weakened somewhat in the last two decades or so, the entrenched gender clichés have proved far more enduring in the mass-mediated portrayal of women terrorists. Women in politics have come a long way. Today, many people can imagine a female U.S. president some time in the future. Strangely, however, although women figure prominently into the history of terrorism, the female terrorist continues to be perceived as an exception to the rule. In a welcome departure from the common coverage patterns the writer of an article in *USA Today* asked readers to close their eyes "and imagine a woman—perhaps of slight build, perhaps a young mother—piloting American Airlines Flight 11 into the World Trade Center."[81] Although deeming the scenario difficult to imagine, the writer concluded that "it can happen, and we need to think about the possibilities."[82]

Even in the recent past, realistic assessments of female terrorists and the threats they pose were rare in the media. Instead, the news has continued to frame these stories along the lines of traditional stereotypes that portray the female terrorist as a paradox. Because these clichés tend to cue readers, viewers, and listeners to resort to deeply ingrained gender stereotypes in order to process and make sense of the news, they are likely to affect the opinions and attitudes of the general public and people charged with fighting terrorism as well. As a result, women are thought to have a far better chance than their male comrades to carry out terrorist attacks without being suspected and intercepted. According to one expert,

> Women are able to use their gender to avoid detection on several fronts: first, their "non-threatening" nature may prevent in-depth scrutiny at the most basic level as they are simply not considered important enough to warrant investigation; second, sensitivities regarding more thorough searches, particularly of women's bodies, may hamper stricter scrutiny, and third, a woman's ability to get pregnant and the attendant changes to her body facilitate concealment of weapons and bombs using maternity clothing as well as further impeding inspection because of impropriety issues.[83]

Terrorists have been aware of these tactical advantages for a long time. With respect to the Red Army Faction, Harmon wrote,

> German male terrorist "Bommi" Bauman of the late Second of June Movement has observed that "Women can get closer to the target. If a man in a high position, perhaps knowing that he may be a target for terrorists, is approached by a woman, he may think, she is a prostitute. Women can go straight to the target's doorstep; sometimes they do it in pairs, two women, saying they are lost. If two men approached him, he would be suspicious."[84]

What Bauman described was precisely the script for several of the kidnappings and assassinations conducted by West German terrorists in which women exploited the fact that they were not as suspicious as men—although it was well known that females were well represented in these groups. Terrorists elsewhere followed this blueprint as well. Before Dhanu, a female member of the Black Tigers, assassinated Rajiv Gandhi, she had "garlanded him, bowed at his feet, and then detonated a bomb that killed them both. . . ."[85] Playing the role of a female admirer of Gandhi she did not have any problem getting close to him. It is telling that one of the members of a two-person back-up team was a young woman as well. The Kurdish Workers Party, too, decided to use female members for suicide attacks because of their tactical advantages. More recently, a wave of attacks against Russian targets by female Chechen suicide bombers succeeded because these women were able "to move more freely than Chechen men, who are routinely harassed by Russia's police and security services."[86]

Groups that have shied away from recruiting female terrorists in the past manage to surprise their targets when they make changes in this respect. In early 2004, after Hamas claimed responsibility for dispatching the first female suicide bomber to kill Israelis, the group's spiritual leader Sheik Ahmed Yassin cited "purely tactical reasons," when asked why his organization had decided on selecting a woman, saying, "It could be that a man would not be able to reach the target, and that's why they had to use a woman."[87] For the same reason, Al-Qaeda and similar groups are likely to recruit women to carry out terror attacks. Indeed, in early 2003, American law enforcement officials learned that bin Laden's organization planned to enlist women to infuse an element of surprise into the terror war against the United States.[88] In early 2004 European intelligence services monitored a conversation between Al-Qaeda terrorists in which the ringleader revealed that a female operative was discovered but that there were other female recruits.[89]

Security officials in some societies came to understand over time that female terrorists were just as likely as their male comrades to commit deadly acts of terrorism. When West Germany was faced with a wave of terror by the Red Army Faction and its successor groups, the country's antiterrorism units were allegedly ordered by their superiors to "shoot the women first."[90] In responding to the increased attacks by Chechen females, Russian authorities expanded their security checks to women in traditional Muslim attire. One wonders, therefore, whether the gender advantage of female terrorists will disappear altogether. For this to happen, it is not enough for top officials to understand that the female paradox in terrorism is a myth—rather, the men and women who implement anti- and counterterrorist policies day-in and day-out must have this understanding as well and must act accordingly.

Unfortunately, even in societies that have experienced repeated attacks by women terrorists, there remains a tendency to view and treat males and females differently. Israel is a perfect example here. After the country was hit repeatedly by female suicide bombers, Israeli security personnel still made a gender distinction as demonstrated in January 2004: when a 22-year-old Palestinian woman, pretending to be crippled, told Israelis at a Gaza checkpoint that she had metal plates in her leg that would sound the alarm, they allowed her to wait for a woman to search her in a special area. Moments later, the woman blew herself up and killed four Israelis. Lamenting the cynical exploitation of his soldiers' consideration for the dignity of women, the officer in charge said:

> We're doing our best to be humanitarian, to consider the problems associated with searching women. She said she had a medical problem, that's why the soldiers let her in, to check her in private because she is a woman. That's very cruel, cynical use of the humanitarian considerations of our soldiers.[91]

CONCLUSION: GENDER STEREOTYPES AND COUNTERTERRORISM

In conclusion, then, there is no doubt that gender clichés persist in the mass-mediated portrayal of women whether they are involved in legitimate political activities or in political roles widely perceived to be illegitimate. But whereas the stereotypical framing patterns of female politicians weakened somewhat in the last several decades, the entrenched gender frames have proved more enduring in the mass-mediated portrayal of women terrorists. Because these kinds of news frames reflect and reinforce deep-seated societal attitudes, terrorist groups are able to take advantage of their target societies' gender prejudices. Therefore, the lesson is that gender reality must inform the measures designed to prevent and respond to terrorism and, perhaps more important, the implementation of anti- and counterterrorist policies. Otherwise terror groups will increasingly exploit the tactical advantages of female terrorists in target societies that deem women far less suspect and dangerous than men.

NOTES

1. Greg Zoroya, "Her decision to be a suicide bomber." *USA TODAY,* 22 April 2002, p, A1. Retrieved from the ProQuest archive on 1 November 2003.

2. Christopher Dickey and Gretel C. Kovach, "Married to Jihad." *Newsweek,* 14 January 2002, p. 48.

3. Christopher C. Harmon, *Terrorism Today* (London: Frank Cash, 2000), p. 212.

4. Kim Fridkin Kahn, *The Political Consequences of Being a Woman: How Stereotypes Influence the Conduct and Consequences of Political Campaigns* (New York: Columbia University Press, 1996).

5. I used "female terrorist," "woman (as) terrorist," "women (as) terrorist," and "female suicide bomber" to retrieve articles and transcripts from the LexisNexis and ProQuest archives for all available dates.

6. See, Pippa Norris, ed., *Women, Media, and Politics* (New York: Oxford University Press, 1997).

7. Robert M. Entman, "Reporting Environmental Policy Debate: The Real Media Biases." *Harvard International Journal of Press/Politics,* 1(3), pp. 77, 78.

8. Shanto Iyengar. *Is Anyone Responsible?* (Chicago: University of Chicago Press, 1991), pp. 26–45.

9. Herbert J. Gans, *Deciding What's News* (New York: Vintage Books, 1980), p. 61.

10. David K. Shipper, "Blacks in the Newsroom." *Columbia Journalism Review* (May, June 1998), p. 28.

11. Norris, *Women, Media, and Politics,* p. 6.

12. Ibid., p. 7.

13. Maria Braden, *Women Politicians and the Media* (Lexington: University of Kentucky Press, 1996), especially chapter 1.

14. Braden, *Women Politicians and the Media,* p. 4.

15. Braden, *Women Politicians and the Media;* James Devitt, "Framing Gender and the Campaign Trail: Women's Executive Leadership and the Press" (Washington, DC: Women's Leadership Fund: 1999).

16. For examples see Braden, *Women Politicians and the Media;* and Devitt, "Framing Gender and the Campaign Trail."

17. Martha Crenshaw, "Introduction: Reflection on the Effects of Terrorism," in *Terrorism, Legitimacy and Power: The Consequences of Political Violence,*

edited by Martha Crenshaw (Middletown, CT: Wesleyan University Press, 1983), p. 24.

18. Anne McElvoy, "The Trapping of a Tigress." *Times of London,* 9 September 1995.

19. Ibid.

20. Braden, *Women Politicians and the Media,* pp. 5, 6.

21. Cited in Sean Aday and James Devitt, "Style over Substance: Newspaper Coverage of Female Candidates." The Second in the White House Project Education Fund Series: Framing Gender on the Campaign Trail, 2000, p. 5.

22. Christopher Walter, "Twisted by anger, she turned to terror." *The Times of London,* 31 January 2002.

23. National Public Radio's program "All Things Considered," 7 February 2002.

24. CBN.com, retrieved 4 November 2003.

25. Joel Greenberg, "2 Girls, Divided by War, Joined in Carnage." *New York Times,* 5 April 2002, p. A1.

26. Media organizations in Europe and in North America reported frequently on the Chechen "black widows," especially after a large group of heavily armed Chechen women and men seized a Moscow theater with hundreds of Russians inside in October 2002.

27. Katharine Viner, "Palestinian liberation fighter Leila Khaled." *The Guardian,* 26 January 2001.

28. Philip Baum interviewed Khaled for *Aviation Security International.* See (http://www.avsec.com/editorial/leilakhaled.htm).

29. Viner, "Palestinian liberation fighter Leila Khaled."

30. Antonella Lazzeri, "They're deadly, they are ruthless, they're women." *The Sun* (UK), 4 August 2002.

31. Sinikka Tarvainen, "The life of female terrorists: guns, reluctant sex, and longing." Deutsche Presse Agentur, 2 November 1997, BC Cycle.

32. Thanassis Cambanis, "Witness tells of accused pair's ties." *Boston Globe,* 17 July 2002, p. B4. The full name of Hale's white supremacist hate organization is World Church of the Creator.

33. The letter-to-the-editor appeared in the *Los Angeles Times* on 2 February 2002, p. M4 in response to an article headlined "Palestinian bomber stood out from the rest," published on 31 January 2002.

34. Braden, *Women Politicians and the Media,* pp. 150, 162.

35. See, for example, Bernard Weintraub, "Woman Hijacker Feels 'Engaged to the Revolution.'" *New York Times,* 9 September 1970, p. 19.

36. McElvoy, "The Trapping of a Tigress."

37. Giles Tremlett, "ETA brings women fighters to the fore." *The Guardian* (London), 27 August 2002, p. 13.

38. Alex Williams, "Exclusive: Suicide Bomber's Husband on Why He Is Proud of Her Military Act." *The Mirror,* 1 February 2002, p. 15.

39. See, for example, Thomas G. Otte, "Red Army Faction: The Baader-Meinhof Gang." In *Encyclopedia of World Terrorism, Volume 3, edited by* Martha Crenshaw and John Pimlott (Armonk, NY: M.E. Sharpe, 1997), pp. 552–556.

40. Karla J. Cunningham, "Cross-National Trends in Female Terrorism." *Studies in Conflict & Terrorism,* 26(3) (May–June 2003), p. 163.

41. Robin Morgan, *The Demon Lover: The Roots of Terrorism* (New York: Washington Square Press, 2001), p. 204.

42. Ibid., p. 208.

43. Judy Mann, "Terrorism and the Cult of Manly Men." *Washington Post,* 19 December 2001, p. C10.

44. Morgan, *The Demon Lover,* p. xv.

45. Ibid.

46. Michael Getler, "Women play growing role in slayings by West German terrorist groups." *Washington Post,* 6 August 1977.

47. Klaliff, "Women in the White Pride Movement." Available at (http://women.stormfront.org/writings/women.htm), retrieved 20 October 2003.

48. Ibid.

49. Thanassis Cambanis, "Witness tells of accused pair's ties." *Boston Globe,* 17 July 2002, p. B4.

50. James Bennett, "Rash of new suicide bombers exhibit no patterns or ties." *New York Times,* 21 June 2002, p. A1. Arien Ahmed did not go through with the suicide mission and ended up in an Israeli jail.

51. See, for example, Tremlett, "ETA brings women fighters to the fore."

52. Linda Watson-Brown, "Gender warriors." *The Scotsman,* 26 September 2000, p. 4.

53. Donatella della Porta, "Left-Wing Terrorism in Italy," in *Terrorism in Context,* edited by Martha Crenshaw (University Park: Pennsylvania State University Press, 1995), p. 141.

54. Ibid.

55. Kenneth L. Woodward and Phyllis Malamud, "Now, the violent woman." *Newsweek,* 6 October 1975, p. 29.

56. Ibid.

57. Judy Klemesrud, "A Criminologist's View of Women Terrorists." *New York Times,* 9 January 1979, p. A24.

58. Ibid.

59. Freda Adler, *Sisters in Crime* (New York: Waveland Press, 1975), p. 20.

60. Ibid., pp. 21, 22.

61. Paul Hofmann, "Women active among radicals in Western Europe." *New York Times,* 14 August 1977, p. 7.

62. Hanna-Renate Laurien, a conservative, was quoted by Kim Wilkinson, "The Hit Women." *Newsweek,* 15 August 1977, p. 30.

63. Getler, "Women playing growing role in slayings."

64. Ibid.

65. Ibid.

66. Susan Jacoby, "Terrorism is Women's Work Too." *Washington Post,* 2 October 1992, p. C8.

67. Libby Copeland, "Female Suicide Bombers: The New Factor in Mideast's Deadly Equation." *Washington Post,* 27 April 2002, p. C1.

68. James Bennett, "Arab Press Glorifies bomber as Heroine." *New York Times,* 11 February 2002, p. 8.

69. Ibid.

70. Laura Ann Trombley, "Female Suicide Bomber: The Newest Trend in Terrorism." Available at (http://www.nyu.edu/classes/keefer/joe/tromb1.html).

71. Stephanie Shemin, "Wrongheadedness of female suicide bombers." *Chicago Tribune,* 18 June 2002, p. 23.

72. Hofman, "Women active among radicals."

73. Tremlett, "ETA brings women fighters to the fore."

74. Peter Goodspeed, "Cruel 'black widows' eager to die." *National Post* (Canada), 30 October 2002, p. 3.

75. Jacoby, "Terrorism is women's work too."

76. Peter H. Merkl, "West German Left-Wing Terrorism," in *Terrorism in Context,* edited by Martha Crenshaw (University Park: Pennsylvania State University Press, 1995), pp. 161–210.

77. Klemesrud, "A criminologist's view of women terrorists."

78. Getler, "Women playing growing role in slayings."

79. Ibid.

80. Adel Darwish, "From Boredom to Bombs—Two Female Terrorists." *WIN Magazine,* April 1999.

81. Patricia Pearson, "Hard to imagine female bad guy? Think again." *USA TODAY,* 30 January 2002, p. 13A.

82. Ibid.

83. Cunningham, "Cross-national trends in female terrorism," pp. 171, 172.

84. Harmon, pp. 219, 220.

85. Cunningham, "Cross-national trends in female terrorism," p. 180.

86. Steven Lee Myers, "Female Suicide Bombers Unnerve Russians." *New York Times,* 7 August 2003, p. 1.

87. Hamas's first female suicide bomber was Reem al-Reyashi, a 22-year-old mother of two small children. Yassin was quoted in Greg Myre, "Gaza Mother, 22, Kills Four Israeli Soldiers." *New York Times,* 15 January 2004, p. A3.

88. Available at (http://stacks.msnbc.com/news/888153.asp).

89. Elaine Sciolino, "Terror Suspect in Italy Linked to More Plots." *New York Times,* 11 June 2004, p. A3.

90. Shoot the Women First was therefore chosen as the title of a book exploring the phenomenon of female terrorists. See Eileen MacDonald, *Shoot the Women First* (New York: Random House, 1992).

91. Brigadier-General Gadi Shamni, the Gaza divisional commander, was quoted in Chris McGreal, "Human-bomb mother kills for Israelis at Gaza checkpoint." *The Guardian,* 15 January 2004, p. 17.

❖

Women and Organized Racial Terrorism in the United States

Kathleen M. Blee

Racial terrorism—violence perpetrated by organized groups against racial minorities in pursuit of white and Aryan supremacist agendas—has played a significant role in U.S. society and politics. Women have been important actors in much of this violence. This article examines women's involvement in racial terrorism from the immediate post-Civil War period to the present. Although organized racial violence by women has increased over time, this trend may not continue. The strategic directions and tactical choices of Aryan and white supremacist groups are likely to alter the extent and nature of women's involvement in racial terrorism in the future.

In April 2003, 28-year-old Holly Dartez of Longville, Louisiana was sentenced to a year and a day in prison and fined $1,000 for her part in a Ku Klux Klan (KKK) cross burning the previous year. Ms. Dartez, whom the U.S. Attorney's Office characterized as secretary to the local Klan chapter, pled guilty to conspiracy for driving four other KKK members to the residence of three African-American men, recent migrants from Mississippi, where a cross was erected and set ablaze. Among the Klan members convicted in this episode was her husband Robert, described as a leader of the local Klan, who received a 21-month sentence and a $3,000 fine. Despite these arrests and convictions, the African-American men targeted in the attack clearly received the message intended by the Klan's action. All abandoned their desire to move their families to Longville and returned to Mississippi.[1]

That same year, 23-year-old Tristain Frye was arrested for her part in an attack and murder of a homeless man in Tacoma, Washington. The attack was carried out by Ms. Frye and three men, among them her boyfriend David Pillatos, with whose child she was pregnant, and Kurtis Monschke, the 19-year-old reputed leader of the local neo-Nazi Volksfront. The four, all known racist skinheads, had set out to assault a Black drug dealer, but instead attacked Randy Townsend, a 42-year-old man suffering from paranoid schizophrenia. Frye's involvement in the attack was apparently motivated by her desire to earn a pair of red shoelaces, a symbol of her participation in violence against a minority person. Although Frye reportedly made the initial contact with Townsend and admitted to kicking him in the head, hard, three or four times, her agreement to testify against Monschke and the prosecutors' conclusion that she had not been dedicated to White supremacy—despite the Nazi and racist tattoos on her back—were sufficient to get her charges reduced to 2nd degree murder.[2]

A year earlier, Christine Greenwood, 28, of Anaheim, California and her boyfriend John McCabe, already imprisoned for a separate offense, were charged with possessing bombmaking materials, including 50 gallons of gasoline and battery-operated clocks that could be used as timers. Greenwood was described as the co-founder of "Women for Aryan Unity," a group to integrate women into White supremacism, and a member of the militant racist skinhead gang "Blood and Honor." She pled guilty to this charge as well as an enhancement charge of promoting a criminal gang and received a short sentence and probation. She has not been visible in racist activities since her arrest, but both groups with which she was associated continue, with elaborate websites claiming chapters and affiliates across the globe.[3]

The women in these three vignettes were arrested for very different kinds of racist violence. Holly Dartez was involved with a Ku Klux Klan group in a cross-burning, an act whose violence was symbolic rather than physically injurious. Tristain Frye took part in the murder of a homeless man—an act of brutal physical violence—with a racist skinhead group, but the victim was White. Christine Greenwood—with her White supremacist group affiliations and bombmaking equipment—seemed intent on racial mayhem, although her target was unclear. As these cases suggest, women in the United States today participate in acts of racial-directed violence whose nature, targets, and social organization vary considerably.

This article explores women's involvement in racial violence associated with the major organized White supremacist groups in the United States: the Ku Klux Klan, White power skinheads, and neo-Nazis.[4] Such violence is best understood as *racial terrorism*. As commonly specified in the scholarly literature and by federal counterterrorist agencies, terrorism requires three components: acts or threats of violence, the communication of fear to an audience beyond the immediate victim, and political, economic, or religious aims by the perpetrator(s) (Cunningham 2003, 188; Hoffman 1998, 15; also Crenshaw 1988), each of which is characteristic of White supremacist racial violence. Racial terrorism, then, is considered here as *terrorism undertaken by members of an organized White supremacist or pro-Aryan group against racial minorities to advance racial agendas.*

Considering the violence of organized racist groups as a form of racial terrorism brings together scholarships on terrorism and organized racism that have largely developed in parallel tracks. With few exceptions (e.g., Blazak 2001; Cunningham 2003), research on terrorism has paid relatively little attention to the growing tendency of White supremacism in the United States to adopt the organizational structures, agendas, and tactics more commonly associated with terrorist groups in other places. Similarly, studies of U.S. organized racism have rarely portrayed racist groups as perpetrating racial

terrorism, although at least some of their actions clearly fall under the U.S. State Department's definition of terrorism as "premeditated, politically motivated violence perpetrated against noncombatant targets by subnational groups or clandestine agents, usually intended to influence an audience."[5]

To analyze the nature and extent of women's involvement in U.S. racial terrorism, it is useful to consider two dimensions of terrorism. The first is the nature of the intended ultimate target; what organized racist groups consider their enemy. Some acts of racial terrorism are "intended to coerce or to intimidate"[6] governments; others are directed toward non-state actors such as members of minority groups. The second dimension is how violence is organized. Some acts of racial terrorism are strategic, focused on a clear target and directed by the group's agenda. Others are what the author terms "narrative," meant to build solidarity among racist activists and communicate a message of racial empowerment and racial vulnerability but instigated outside of a larger strategic plan (Blee 2005; Cooper 2001; Perry 2002). This article explores women's roles in racial terrorism from the immediate post-Civil War era to the present along these two dimensions. It concludes with a proposition about the relationships among women's participation, definitions of the enemy, and the organization of terroristic violence in the U.S. White supremacist movement.

PERCEPTIONS OF THE ENEMY

Organized White supremacism has a long history in the United States, appearing episodically in response to perceptions of gains by racial, ethnic, or religious minorities or political or ideological opportunities (Chalmers 1981). White supremacism is always organized around a defined enemy. African Americans have been the most common enemy of organized racists over time, but other enemies have been invoked on occasion. The massive Ku Klux Klan of the 1920s, for example, targeted Catholics, Jews, labor radicals, Mormons, and others, in addition to African

Americans. Today's small and politically marginal KKK, neo-Nazi, and White supremacist groups express little hostility toward Catholics, Mormons, or labor radicals, focusing their anger instead on Jews, Asian Americans, gay men and lesbians, and feminists, in addition to African Americans and other persons of color.[7]

Each wave of organized White supremacism has been accompanied by terrorist acts against its enemies, although the nature of such violence has varied considerably over time and across groups. The KKK of the 1920s, for example, amplified its periodic and vicious physical attacks on African Americans, Catholics, Jews, and others with frequent terrifying displays of its economic and political strength, including rallies and parades, boycotts of Jewish merchants, and electoral campaigns (Blee 1991; Chalmers 1981). Today, a few White supremacist groups, particularly some KKK chapters and Aryan-rights groups such as the National Association for the Advancement of White People (NAAWP), a former political outlet for racist media star David Duke, follow the lead of the 1920s Klan in seeking public legitimacy for agendas of White rights, but most openly advocate or engage in physical violence against enemy groups. The form of such racial terrorism ranges from street-level assaults against racial minority groups to efforts to promote a cataclysmic race war.

Women's involvement in racial terrorism is strongly associated with how organized White supremacists define the nature of their enemies. Although variation in the racist movement, even within a single historical period, makes it impossible to make broad generalizations that hold for every racist group, there have been changes since the Civil War in how racist groups define their enemies. Particularly important for understanding women's involvement is the changing focus on members of racial/ethnic groups versus institutions of the state as the primary enemy of organized racist groups. The following sections focus on definitions of the enemy in three major periods of racial terrorism: the immediate postbellum period, the first decades of the twentieth century, and the present.

Postbellum Racial Terrorism

Most White supremacist groups in the immediate postbellum period directed their violence at racial minority groups, but the ultimate target of their actions was the state apparatus imposed on the defeated southern states during the Reconstruction era. The quintessential White supremacist organization of this time—the Ku Klux Klan—emerged in the rural south in the aftermath of the Civil War, inflicting horrific violence on newly emancipated African Americans and their White, especially northern, allies. Organized as loose gangs of White marauders, the first Klan may have had a chaotic organizational structure, but its goals and efforts were focused and clear—to dismantle the Reconstructionist state and restore one based on White supremacism. Women played no direct role in this Klan. Indeed, its moblike exercise of racial terrorism on behalf of traditional southern prerogatives of White and masculine authority left no opening for the participation of White women except as symbols for White men of their now-lost privileges and lessened ability to protect "their" women against feared retaliation by former slaves (Blee 1991).

Racial Terrorism in the Early Twentieth Century

The first wave of the KKK collapsed in the late nineteenth century, but its legacy of mob-directed racialized violence continued into the first decades of the twentieth century through extra-legal lynchings and racially biased use of capital punishment to execute African Americans.[8] The re-emergence of the Klan in the late 1910s (a Klan that flourished through the 1920s) substituted political organization for mob rule, enlisting millions of White, native-born Protestants in a crusade of racism, xenophobia, anti-Catholicism, and anti-Semitism that included contestation of electoral office in some states. The violence of this second Klan also took a new form, mixing traditional forms of racial terrorism with efforts to instill fear through its size and political clout and create financial devastation among those it deemed its enemies (Blee 1991).

The targets of lynchings, racially biased capital punishment, and the 1920s Klan were mostly members of racial, ethnic, and religious minority groups; they also constituted its primary enemies. The racial terror of lynching and racially biased capital punishment both depended on state support, either overtly or covertly. Similarly, for the second Klan, located primarily in the north, east, and western regions rather than the south, the state was not an enemy; instead, it was a vehicle through which White supremacists could enact their agendas. Rather than attack the state, in this period, organized racism was explicitly xenophobic and nationalist, embracing the state through an agenda they characterized, in the Klan's term, as "100% American."

Women were active in all aspects of racial terrorism in the early twentieth century, including lynchings and the public celebrations that often accompanied, and added enormously to the terror of, these events. It is difficult to assess the precise role of women in such forms of violence because the historical record is mute about how often a woman tied the noose around a lynched person's neck or struck the match to burn an African-American corpse, or a living person. Yet, it is clear that women were integrally and fully involved in these events. Photographic records of lynchings, often the only means by which these were recorded, show large numbers of women, often with their children, gathered around lynched bodies, partaking in the spectacle with a fervor and brutality that shocks contemporary observers (Allen 2000). The inclusion of women and children helped make such racial murders possible, even respectable, in many areas of the country.

Women also were active in the second KKK, adding more than half a million members to its ranks in female-led chapters, the Women of the Ku Klux Klan. They participated actively and avidly in the terrorist actions of this Klan which, unlike Klans that preceded and followed it, practiced racial terror largely through mechanisms of exclusion and expulsion. Women Klansmembers were instrumental, even leaders, in the effort to rid communities of Jews, Catholic, African Americans, and immigrants through tactics such as financial boycotts of Jewish merchants, campaigns to get Catholic schoolteachers fired from their jobs, and attacks on the property and sometimes the bodies of African Americans and immigrants (Blee 1991).

Part of the explanation for women's increased involvement in racial politics and terror in the early decades of the twentieth century lies in changing gender roles and possibilities in this time. The granting to women of the right to vote in all elections in 1920 made women attractive recruits for the second Klan as it sought to increase its size, financial base, and electoral strength. At the same time, women's increasing involvement in other forms of public life, including prohibition politics, the paid labor force, and civic improvement societies, made women more likely to join racist groups. But women's participation was also the result of tactics of racial organization and violence that were more compatible with the lives of (White) women than had been the case in previous decades. Women could, and did, contribute to the Klan's strategy of creating economic devastation, for example, by spreading vicious rumors about Catholic schoolteachers or Jewish merchants without stepping far from their roles as mothers and consumers. Such factors also made women's participation in mob-directed racial terrorism like lynching more likely. The rigid patriarchal ideas that precluded White southern women's entrance into the first Klan had crumbled significantly by the 1920s, making more acceptable the notion that women could act in the public sphere. Moreover, racial lynchings and other forms of mob-directed racial terrorism often were enacted as large-scale community events in which women could join without straying from their primary roles as mothers and wives, for example, by bringing their children to what Tolnay and Beck (1995) termed the "festival of violence " of lynching (also Allen 2000; Patterson 1998).

Racial Terrorism Today

In the later decades of the twentieth century, the nationalist allegiances of many White supremacist groups began to crumble. Much of this shift can be traced to the widespread adoption of new forms of anti-Semitic ideology, especially the idea that the federal government[9] had been compromised by its allegiance to the goals of global Jewish elites. This understanding, commonly summarized in the belief that the United States is a "Zionist Occupation Government (ZOG)," shifted the central axis of organized White supremacism. Additional pressures toward global pan-Aryanism diminished the allegiance of U.S. White supremacism to nationalist agendas and, increasingly, Jews became the focus of its vitriol, with African Americans and other persons of color regarded as the lackeys or puppets of Jewish masters. With this ideological shift—codified in the precepts of the widely embraced doctrines of "Christian Identity," a vicious racist theology that identifies Jews as the anti-Christ—the U.S. government itself became a target of White supremacist violence. The bombing of the Oklahoma City federal building, assaults on federal land management agencies in the West, and a series of aborted efforts to attack other government installations were the outcome of this shift toward the U.S. state as an enemy of White supremacism.

Identifying the state as a primary enemy has had complex effects on the participation of women in organized White supremacism and racial terrorism. Some racist groups have made considerable effort to recruit women in recent years (Blee 2002; Cunningham 2003), especially those, like some chapters of the KKK, that want to develop a durable and intergenerational racist movement. These groups see women as key because of their centrality in family life and their (perceived) lesser likelihood to become police informants. Some neo-Nazi and Christian Identity groups are also recruiting women heavily, but generally to create a more benign image for White supremacism (Blee 2002).

Following the influx of women into racist groups, there has been an apparent rise in the participation of women in racist terrorism, as suggested by the vignettes at the beginning of this article. However, the number of women involved appears to be relatively low, despite their increasing numbers in racist groups. Firm statistics on the gender composition of perpetrators of racially motivated violence are not available (see, e.g., FBI, 2000), but reports compiled by the Southern Poverty Law Center in Montgomery, Alabama (SPLC 2004),[10] the most highly regarded non-official source of such data, indicate that the clear majority of perpetrators are still male. In particular, the SPLC reports indicate that, relative to men, women have low levels of involvement in racial terrorism targeted at state institutions, with somewhat greater involvement in violence directed at racial minority groups.

What can be concluded from this brief history? Although any generalization needs to be treated with caution, given the heterogeneity of organized White supremacism, the historical data examined suggest that in the United States *women are more likely to be involved in organized racial terrorism that is directed at racial/ethnic minorities than racial terrorism directed against the state.*

THE ORGANIZATION OF RACIAL TERROR

White supremacism has taken a variety of organizational forms in the United States, each typically associated with a particular form of violence. Much organized White supremacism is highly structured and hierarchical, with clear (if often violated) lines of authority, like the second and subsequent Ku Klux Klans. However, some White supremacist groups are very loosely organized with highly transient memberships and little hierarchy, such as contemporary racist skinheads, which operate like gangs bound together by ideology rather than territory. The following sections consider how the form of racist organization is associated with the level and nature of women's involvement in racial terrorism, although particular racist groups may be involved in different forms of violence. What is proposed is an analytic abstraction meant to highlight specific aspects of racial terrorism rather than a firm typology of racial violence and racist groups.

Structured, Hierarchical Organization

White supremacism is an ideology that puts tremendous value on ideas of hierarchy. Indeed, the very premise of modern-day Western racism is the idea that human society is naturally divided into racial categories that can be ranked by their moral, political, cultural, and social worthiness (Frederickson 2003; Winant 2002). This ideology is mirrored in how racist groups are typically constituted, with strong demarcations between leaders and followers, a high valuation on acceptance of internal authority, and firm boundaries against participation by those of inferior categories, including not only those from enemy groups, but also, at many times, White Aryan women. This form of organization is characteristic of racist groups like the second and subsequent Ku Klux Klans, World War II–era Nazi groups, and some racial terrorist groups in the late twentieth century.

In recent years, a number of those involved in the racist movement have embraced a new structure known as "leaderless resistance," a concept developed in response to racist groups' desires to shield themselves from authorities. The principle of leaderless resistance is simple: the activities of racist activists are coordinated by their allegiance to a set of common principles rather than by communication among racist groups. In practice, leaderless resistance requires that racist activists develop very small cells in which plans are developed and enacted, with little or no communication between cells that would allow the police to trace a chain of racist groups.

Strategic racial terrorism is generally, although not always, associated with structured, hierarchical groups, including those that follow the model of leaderless resistance. This is violence that is planned, focused on precise targets, and calculated to have predictable consequences. Typically, such violence is developed in a small leadership group and disseminated to members for activation, or, in the case of leaderless resistance, created and executed by a small, tightly knit group. Strategic racial terrorism is exemplified by efforts to foment race war or to terrorize racial minority communities by burning crosses, scrawling swastikas on buildings, or assaulting racial minority persons. It also includes attacks on government agencies or efforts to precipitate cataclysmic economic collapse and social chaos, thereby hastening the demise of the Jewish-dominated government. One example in which a number of women were implicated was a paramilitary survivalist, Christian Identity–oriented group known as the Covenant, Sword, and Arm of the Lord (CSA). Insisting that Jews were training African Americans to take over the nation's cities, CSA members initiated a series of strategic terrorist activities, including firebombing a synagogue and a church and attempting to bomb the pipeline that supplied the city of Chicago with natural gas. When the FBI raided the CSA compound in 1985, they found supplies for further terrorism: weapons, bombs, an anti-tank rocket, and quantities of cyanide apparently intended for the water supply of an undisclosed city.

One woman from a highly structured racist group talked of her involvement in terms that succinctly summarize strategic racial terrorism. In an interview conducted for a study of women in contemporary racist activism (Blee 2002), she told me that she felt it was necessary to:

> prepare yourself for war constantly—don't speak if you can't defend yourself in every way. Prepare by knowing—first of all, then work on guns and ammo, food and water supply, first aid kits,

medication, clothing, blankets, try to become self-sufficient and [move] away from the city, if possible. Don't get caught into the "debit" or "marc" cards, etc—[that is, in the] new world order.

This woman, as well as Christine Greenwood whose efforts on behalf of the Women for Aryan Unity included making bombs, are examples of women who participate in strategic racial terrorism. But men are far more likely than women to be arrested for direct involvement in such acts. The strict principles of social hierarchy embraced by most tightly organized racist groups tend to exclude women from leadership, even from inclusion, and thus from a role in executing violence (also see Neidhardt 1992; Neuburger and Valentini 1998; Talbot 2000). Women's involvement in strategic racial terrorism is generally indirect, like Holly Daretz's role as a driver for the Klansmen arrested for the Louisiana cross-burning. This indirect involvement in strategic racist terrorism takes three forms: serving as legitimation, promoting group cohesion, and providing abeyance support. Women are used to *legitimate* strategic racial terrorism by creating an air of normalcy that belies the violence of organized racism (Blee 2002; Dobie 1997), a tactic increasingly common among terrorist groups across the globe (Cunningham, 2003). In the United States, this legitimation role can be seen in efforts like those of the Women's Frontier/Sisterhood, female affiliates of the violent World Church of the Creator (WCOTC), whose Web publications stress benign topics like motherhood that serve to blunt the violent activities of its members, including Erica Chase and Leo Felton, arrested for attempting to detonate bombs to incite a "racial holy war" (Ferber 2004, 7; Rogers and Litt 2004; also Bakersfield *Californian* 24 July 2004). Women also function to *promote group cohesion* in organized racism—making possible its agendas of strategic terrorism—by working to create solidarity within existing racist groups and recruit new members (Blee 2002). An example of this cohesive function is the effort of Women for Aryan Unity's campaign "White Charities—by Whites for Whites"[11] to provide support to imprisoned White racists. This campaign, one of a number in which racist women are involved, target those they term "prisoners of war" through pen pal programs, prison visitation, and aid to the families of POWs as well as by reintegrating former prisoners into the racist movement. And, finally, women create *abeyance support* (Taylor 1989) by standing in for male racist leaders when they die or are in prison. One example is that of Katja Lane, whose husband David was arrested for murder and other crimes during his involvement in the underground Aryan supremacy group, Silent Brotherhood. During David's imprisonment, Katja has risen to prominence in the racist movement for her work in maintaining movement publications and a prison outreach program for White supremacist prisoners (Dobratz & Shanks-Meile 2004; Gardell 2003).

Loose Organization

White supremacist groups that operate with loose, ganglike forms of organization typically exhibit high levels of violence. Indeed, such groups often eschew tighter forms of organization in the effort to avoid detection and arrest for their violent actions.[12] Klansmen who terrorized African Americans and their allies in the immediate postbellum period operated in this way, as do racist skinheads whose thinly linked groups operated under names like "Confederate Hammerskins" or "Blood and Honor."

Loosely organized White supremacist groups often practice what can be termed *narrative* instead of, or in addition to, strategic racial terrorism. Narrative racial terrorism is at least somewhat spontaneous, in which victims are chosen impulsively and without clear purpose, and whose consequences are rarely calculated by the perpetrators in advance. Practices of narrative racial terrorism include street assaults on African Americans, gay men or lesbians, or Jews, like the description of the actions of one racist woman who would provoke her husband to go with her to "find a homosexual or someone and beat them up" (ABC News.com 2004a) or the acts of brutality inflicted on African Americans by the night riders of the first Klan. It also includes acts of violence that seem inexplicable, like the murder of the White homeless man by Tristain Frye and her fellow skinheads, or those that seem attributable to the immaturity or psychological pathologies of their perpetrators, such as violence and savagery against fellow White supremacists or self-inflicted violence (Blee 2002; Christensen 1994; Hamm 1994).

What distinguishes narrative from strategic racial terrorism is not the character of the acts of violence, but its incorporation into a larger set of plans and tactics. Strategic racial terrorism is intensely focused on disabling, undermining, or exterminating those considered to be the enemies of White supremacism. Narrative racial terrorism is less clearly focused on specific enemies; it targets enemies for violence, but that violence also has an internal purpose: to strengthen, sometime even to create, organized White supremacism, to attract new members, to instill a sense of collective identity among existing members and bind them closer to each other, and to instill the passion and commitment that will sustain their efforts into the future.

Women are directly involved in narrative racial terrorism, although in lesser number than are male racists (Christensen 1994; Dobie 1997; but see Blazak 2004). Yet, there is evidence that women's role in narrative racial terrorism may be increasing, as racists skinheads and similar groups attract larger number of women who see themselves as empowered through the enactment of physical violence (Blee 2002). A description of narrative racial terrorism was related by a racist activist, in response to the present author's question about whether she had been involved in physical fights:

> Yes. [With] about 20–25 women, six men. Some of who were nonwhites, i.e., gangbangers— people who don't like people like me so they start trouble with me—and others were White trash traitors who had either screwed me over, started trouble because they don't believe in my ways or caused trouble in the movement. Some were hurting, physically, friends of mine, so I involved myself in it.

It is unclear whether women's increasing participation in groups that practice narrative racial terrorism is due to pull or push factors. It is likely that both are operating. Women may be attracted to groups that practice narrative violence are less likely than those engaged in strategic violence to have the rigid ideological and organizational structures that have excluded women from power and decision making in the U.S. White supremacist movement since its inception. Indeed, there have been at least fledgling attempts to organize all-women racist skinhead groups under the joint banner of "White power/women power" (Blee 2002), efforts that would be unimaginable in other parts of the White supremacist movement. But it is also the case that groups that practice narrative racial terrorism, like White-power skinheads, can be surprisingly receptive to the inclusion of women because their boundaries are loosely guarded, relatively permeable, and often fairly undefined. For example, it can be more difficult to ascertain who is a member of a group that is bound together by the practice of violence and often-fragile and superficial connections between people than a group that has a more clearly defined agenda, strategy, and sense of what constitutes membership. There are instances in which White-power skinheads have later become active in anti-racist skinhead groups that fight racist skinheads, often with a great deal of violence. Such ideological switching is an indication that commitment to violence may outweigh commitment to racist ideas, a phenomenon rarely found among those who practice strategic racial terrorism.

What can be concluded about the relationship between gender and the organization of racial terror? Again, the diversity within organized racism means that any generalization can only be provisional, but the evidence presented here suggests that *women participate in strategic racial terrorism to a lesser extent than they do in narrative racial terrorism, and women participate in strategic racial terrorism largely through indirect means, whereas women participate in narrative racial terrorism more directly.*

CONCLUSION

Thus far, the relationships of gender to definitions of the enemy and to the organization of racial terror have been considered separately. The brief case studies of White supremacist groups can also be used to think about the three-way relationships among gender, enemies, and violence, as presented in Table 1.

The case in which the state is perceived as the main enemy and violence is narrative in nature (cell A) is rare in the history of modern U.S. White supremacism. The first Ku Klux Klan is the paradigmatic example, and in this Klan women had no direct involvement either as members or as participants in Klan violence. For the first KKK, women's exclusion is explicable by the specific historical and sociopolitical situation of the Reconstruction-era South and by this Klan's

intense emphasis on White men as the protector of vulnerable White women. Whether women would always be excluded from this type of racial terrorism is unclear because there are no major subsequent racist movements that have this set of characteristics. Indeed, this form of racial terrorism is unlikely to recur in the foreseeable future in the United States as it is associated with situations of profound political uncertainty and fluctuations in the organization of the state, as in the Reconstruction era. With the consolidation of federal state power, racial terrorism directed at the state is much more likely to be strategic in nature, both because the enemy is more clearly defined and because the state has the power to monitor and suppress its opponents.

The case in which racial minorities are the primary enemy group and violence is expressed in a narrative form (cell B) is exemplified today by racist skinheads. In these groups, women generally participate substantially less than do men, but women's role appears to be increasing in recent years. A similar situation exists when the state is the enemy, but violence is strategic in nature (cell C). This is the case with many racial terrorist groups today, especially those that target the state as a agent of Jewish domination. For these groups too, women tend to participate at considerably lower rates than men, but their participation has increased in recent years and is likely to continue to increase. Both require very public and assertive actions—the street-level violence of skinheads or bombing campaigns of ZOG-focused groups—that contradict traditional ideas about women's passivity and subservience. Further, participation in these forms of racist terrorism challenges the traditional male leadership and public image of such groups. Yet, it is likely that the barriers to women's participation in these forms of racist terrorism will decline over time. Gender ideologies are crumbling in racist groups as elsewhere in U.S. society (Blee 2002). Moreover, media attention to recent instances of women in gender-traditional societies who are involved in terrorism against the state, in such places as Chechnya, Israel, Germany, and Sri Lanka (ABC News 2004b; Cunningham 2003), as well as women's involvement in domestic terrorism against the U.S. government by groups such as the Weather Underground and Black Panther Party (Brown 1994; Zwerman 1994) have provided models for the incorporation of women into these forms

TABLE 1   Gender, Enemies, and Violence

| | Definitions of the Enemy | |
Type of Violence	State	Racial Minorities
Narrative	A (no women)	B (some women, increasing)
Strategic	C (some women, increasing)	D (many women, steady)

of organized racial terror. These factors are likely to result in an increase in women's activity in narrative forms of terror against racial minorities and strategic forms of terror against the state.

The case in which racial minorities are the enemy and violence is expressed in a strategic form (cell D) is different. This is characteristic of groups like the 1920s Klan or some Klans and other White supremacist groups today. In these, women's participation is often high—although always lower than men's—as this organization of racial terror provides structural openings for women to participate without challenging existing ideas about gender hierarchies. Women in these groups often work to facilitate and promote violence behind the scenes or in less directly confrontational ways. They recruit and cultivate new racist group members and steer them toward ideas of strategic violence, spray-paint swastikas on houses and cars of new immigrants to convince them to move, and burn crosses in the yards of interracial couples. Each of these forms of racial terrorism can be undertaken from within the perimeters of the group's existing gender hierarchies, resulting in a level of women's participation that is higher than other forms of racial terrorism, although unlikely to increase further in the future.

This brief history of women's role in organized U.S. racial terrorism suggests that women are fully capable of participating in the most deadly kinds of terrorist activities on behalf of agendas of White or Aryan supremacy. But it also points to the variability of women's involvement in racial terrorism. Although women's participation in racist terrorism has increased over time in the United States, it is not the case that there is a simple temporal pattern to women's involvement in such violence. Rather, the conditions under which women are likely to become involved in racist terrorism reflect not only broader societal changes in the acceptability of

women's involvement in politics and in violence, but also the strategic directions and tactical choices of organized White supremacist groups.

NOTES

1. *State-Times Morning Advocate*, Baton Rouge, Louisiana, 19 April 2003; accessed 31 July 2004 at (www.lexis-nexis.com/universe).

2. Heidi Beirich and Mark Potok, "Two Faces of Volksfront," available at (www.splcenter.org/intel/intelreport/article.jsp?aid=475@printable=1); "'To Do the Right Thing.' A Guilty Plea," *News Tribune* (Tacoma, Washington), 26 February 2004.

3. "Domestic Terrorism Ties?" NBC 4, 18 November 2002, available at (www.nbc4.tv/prnt/1793308/detail.html); "ADL Assists in OC White Supremacists Arrest," *The Jewish Journal of Greater Los Angeles*, available at (www.jewishjournal.com/home/print.php?id=9642); "Out of the Kitchen: Has the Women's Rights Movement Come to the Extreme Right?" ABC News, 12 December 2003, available at (http://abcnews.go.com/sections/us/DailyNews/extreme_women021212.html).

4. This excludes individual acts of racial violence, such as hate crimes.

5. Title 22 of the United States Code, Section 2656f(d), available at (http://www.state.gov/s/ct/rls/pgtrpt/2003/31880.htm/October 21, 2004).

6. From DoD definition of terrorism, cited in Cunningham (2003, 188, n. 4).

7. The idea that racist movements express sentiments of anger needs to be used with caution. For a discussion of the theoretical and political implications of understanding emotions such as anger as expressions of individual sentiment versus group-level emotions, see Blee (2003, 2004); also della Porta (1992).

8. The exact number of lynchings is difficult to determine, both because of the extralegal, secret nature of most lynchings and because of the overlap of lynchings with legal forms of execution of African Americans such as misapplications of the death penalty, what George C. Wright (1990) terms "legal lynchings" (also Tolnay and Beck 1995).

9. Some groups, especially those who regard local and county government as less likely to be under the control of ZOG, support devolving government power to these levels. Some of these complexities are explored by Levitas (2002).

10. Analysis not reported, but available from the author.

11. 4 September 2004 accessed at (http://www.faughaballagh.com/charity.htm).

12. In this sense, there is a continuum from the loose organization of groups like racist skinheads to the very ephemeral racist groups that operate with little or no lasting organization such as lynch mobs, but this article considers only groups with some level of organization.

REFERENCES

ABC News. 2004a. "Out of the kitchen: Has the women's rights movement come to the extreme right?" Accessed from ABCNEWS.com, 5 August 2004.

ABC News. 2004b. "Black Widows: Hell hath no fury like Chechnya's ruthless widows of war," accessed from ABCNEWS.com, 4 September 2004.

Allen, James. 2000. *Without Sanctuary: Lynching Photography in America.* Santa Fe, NM: Twin Palms.

Bakersfield Californian. 2004. "Making fascist statements over frappuccinos," 24 July.

Blazak, Randy. 2001. "White boys to terrorist men: Target recruitment of Nazi skinheads," *American Behavioral Scientist,* 44(6) (February), pp. 982–1000.

Blazak, Randy. 2004. "'Getting it': The role of women in male desistence from hate groups," in *Home-Grown Hate: Gender and Organized Racism,* edited by Abby L. Ferber. New York: Routledge, pp. 161–179.

Blee, Kathleen. 1991. *Women of the Klan: Racism and Gender in the 1920s.* Berkeley: University of California Press.

Blee, Kathleen. 2002. *Inside Organized Racism: Women in the Hate Movement.* Berkeley: University of California Press.

Blee, Kathleen. 2003, 2004. "Positioning hate," *Journal of Hate Studies,* 3(1), pp. 95–106.

Blee, Kathleen. 2005. "Racial violence in the United States," *Ethnic and Racial Studies* 28(4) (July), pp. 599–619.

Brown, Elaine. 1994. *A Taste of Power: A Black Woman's Story.* New York: Anchor/Doubleday.

Chalmers, David M. 1981. *Hooded Americanism: The History of the Ku Klux Klan.* Durham, NC: Duke University Press.

Christensen, Loren. 1994. *Skinhead Street Gangs.* Boulder: Paladin Press.

Cooper, H. 2001. "Terrorism: The problem of definition revisited," *American Behavioral Scientist,* 45, pp. 881–893.

Crenshaw, Martha. 1988. "Theories of terrorism: Instrumental and organizational approaches," in *Inside Terrorist Organizations,* edited by David C. Rapoport. New York: Columbia University Press, pp. 13–31.

Cunningham, Karla J. 2003. "Cross-regional trends in female terrorism," *Studies in Conflict and Terrorism,* 26(3) (May–June), pp. 171–195.

Della Porta, Donatella. 1992. "Introduction: On individual motivations in underground political organizations," in *International Social Movement Research,* Vol. 4, *Social Movements and Violence: Participation in Underground Organizations,* edited by Donatella Della Porta. London: JAI Press, pp. 3–28.

Dobie, Kathy. 1997. "Skingirl Mothers: From Thelma and Louise to Ozzie and Harriet," in *The Politics of Motherhood: Activist Voices from Left to Right,* edited by Alexis Jetter, Annelise Orleck, and Diana Taylor. Hanover, NH: University Press of New England, pp. 257–267.

Dobratz, Betty A. and Stephanie L. Shanks-Meile. 2004. "The white separatist movement: Worldviews on gender, feminism, nature, and change," in *Home-Grown Hate: Gender and Organized Racism,* edited by Abby L. Ferber. New York: Routledge, pp. 113–142.

Federal Bureau of Investigation (FBI). 2002. Hate Crime Statistics. Available at (http://www.fbi.gov/ ucr/hatecrime2002.pdf).

Ferber, Abby L. 2004. "Introduction." in *Home-Grown Hate: Gender and Organized Racism,* edited by Abby L. Ferber. New York: Routledge, pp. 1–18.

Fredrickson, George M. 2003. *Racism: A Short History.* Princeton, NJ: Princeton University Press.

Gardell, Mattias. 2003. *Gods of the Blood: The Pagan Revival and White Separtism.* Durham, NC: Duke University Press.

Hamm, Mark S. 1994. *American Skinheads: The Criminology and Control of Hate Crimes.* Westport, CT: Praeger.

Hoffman, Bruce. 1998. *Inside Terrorism.* New York: Columbia University Press.

Levitas, Daniel. 2002. *The Terrorist Next Door: The Militia Movement and the Radical Right.* New York: Thomas Dunne Books/St. Martin's Press.

Neidhardt, Friedhelm. 1992. "Left-wing and right-wing terrorist groups: A comparison for the German case," in *International Social Movement Research,* Vol. 4: *Social Movements and Violence: Participation in Underground Organizations,* edited by Donatella della Porta. London: JAI Press, pp. 215–235.

Neuburger, Luisella de Cataldo, and Tiziana Valentini. 1998. *Women and Terrorism.* New York: St. Martin's Press.

Patterson, Orlando. 1998. *Rituals of Blood: Consequences of Slavery in Two American Centuries.* Washington, DC: Calvados Counterpoints.

Perry, Barbara. 2002. "Defending the color line: Racially and ethnically motivated hate crime," *American Behavioral Scientist,* 46(1), 72–92.

Rogers, Joann, and Jacquelyn S. Litt. 2004. "Normalizing racism: A case study of motherhood in White supremacy," in *Home-Grown Hate: Gender and Organized Racism,* edited by Abby L. Ferber. New York: Routledge, pp. 97–112.

Southern Poverty Law Center (SPLC). 2004. On-line copies of the SPLC *Intelligence Report* and other publications, accessed 5 September 2004 from (www.splcenter.org).

Talbot, Rhiannon. 2000. "Myths in the representation of women terrorists," *Beire-Ireland: A Journal of Irish Studies,* 35(3), pp. 165–186.

Taylor, Verta. 1989. "Social movement continuity: The women's movement in abeyance," *American Sociological Review,* 54, pp. 761–75.

Tolnay, Stewart E., & E. M. Beck. 1995. *A Festival of Violence: An Analysis of Southern Lynchings, 1882–1930.* Urbana: University of Illinois Press.

Winant, Howard. 2002. *The World Is a Ghetto.* New York: Basic Books.

Wright, George C. 1990. *Racial Violence in Kentucky, 1865–1940: Lynchings, Mob Rule, and "Legal Lynchings."* Baton Rouge: Louisiana State University Press.

Zwerman, Gilda. 1994. "Mothering on the lam: Politics, gender fantasies and maternal thinking in women associated with armed, clandestine organizations in the United States," *Feminist Review,* 47, pp. 33–56.

8

Technology and Terrorism

Violence does, in truth, recoil upon the violent, and the schemer falls into the pit which he digs for another.

—Sir Arthur Conan Doyle

Traditional terrorist tactics, including assassinations, hijackings, kidnappings, and bombings, are still the first choice of most terrorists. The September 11, 2001, attacks on the World Trade Center and the Pentagon demonstrated that these standard tactics can be used to inflict horrifying devastation. However, the availability of advanced technology and its ability to increase the harm caused by terrorists escalate the threat posed by contemporary terrorism. This chapter discusses two types of terrorist tactics that rely on advanced technology: CBRNE attacks and the use of the Internet to spread propaganda and destroy vital infrastructures.

CBRNE is the term used to describe chemical, biological, radiological, nuclear, and explosive weapons. Some of these weapons have always been available: for example, when the ancient Romans contaminated their enemies' drinking water with dead horses, it was a form of biological assault. Chemical warfare, especially in the form of mustard gas, was well known to soldiers fighting in the foxholes and tunnels during World War I. However, although the threat is not new, advances in technology have made it more likely that the world will one day experience a CBRNE attack of greater magnitude than ever before.

The use of the Internet to spread propaganda, raise funds, incite violence, and plan attacks has been studied extensively (see, e.g., Colarik, 2006; Laqueur, 1997; Verton, 2003). A decentralized network of communications, which is the hallmark of the contemporary Internet, was initially created in the 1970s by the U.S. Department of Defense out of fear of a nuclear attack launched by the Soviet Union (Weimann, 2006b). Now, ironically, modern terrorists, who are perhaps the single greatest threat to the security of the United States, are making increasing use of the Internet to further their cause. The threat posed by digital terrorism, which includes both information warfare and cyberterrorism, has dramatically increased in recent years. Using the Internet to successfully attack critical infrastructure, such as water, power, and communication systems, increases the lethality of the weapons available to today's terrorists.

As noted by David Rapoport in the first reading to accompany Chapter 2, technology does not cause terrorism: the Zealots-Sicarii, the Assassins, and the Thugs used whatever primitive technology available to them. It can be no surprise then that modern terrorists continue to employ extant technologies to achieve their goals.

Today's terrorist can choose from a potent array of weapons capable of destroying large portions of our planet, causing hundreds of thousands and even millions of deaths and injuries. The use of these weapons by terrorists could incite global panic and paralyze governments' attempts to respond to the ensuing crisis. Worst-case scenarios paint horrific images of the potential destruction of the environment and all the flora and fauna on earth.

For more than a century, terrorists have fantasized about weapons that could obliterate large portions of the earth. Karl Heinzen, the mid-19th-century German radical philosopher who thought prizes should be given for inventing new poisons and explosives (Laqueur, 1977), fantasized about weapons like "rockets, poison gases, and land mines, that one day would destroy whole cities with 100,000 inhabitants" (Laqueur, 1999, p. 13). Imagining doomsday has long been a favorite preoccupation of science fiction writers. The mad scientists, bent on destroying the world, were well known in the late 19th and early 20th centuries to readers of H.G. Wells and other authors of the science fiction genre.

The difference between now and then is that today the raw materials for producing and dispersing CBRNE, manipulating the Internet, and engaging in digital terrorism are more readily available. The decline in the 1990s of left-wing terrorist groups, which flourished in the 1970s and 1980s, was accompanied by a rise in right-wing groups. Where left-wing terrorists focused primarily on economic and political causes, many of today's right-wing terrorists, like those accused of the 9/11 attacks, are driven by religious zealotry (Laqueur, 1999). Thus, technological advances come at a time when right-wing fanatical terrorism is growing.

The destructive consequences of just one terrorist staging a CBRNE or Internet attack are extraordinarily high. Although some terrorists are deterred by the horrific consequences of such attacks, others want to maximize fatalities by using technologically sophisticated weaponry. Rogue governments may be afraid to use such weapons against more powerful enemies for fear of retaliation, but they may nevertheless be willing, either for profit or to further their political agendas, to supply terrorists with the raw materials to produce the weapons.

CBRNE

A variety of terms have been used to describe massively destructive weapons, and the terminology changes as new incidents occur. The terminology has evolved from WMD (weapons of mass destruction) to NBC (nuclear, biological, and chemical weapons) to CBW (chemical and biological weapons), to CBRN (chemical, biological, radiological, and nuclear weapons), and now to CBRNE (chemical, biological, radiological, nuclear, and explosive weapons; Ballard & Mullendore, 2003). One can only wonder what new term will be developed next to describe the horrifying future array of devices of devastation.

Chemical Weapons

Chemical agents can be gases or liquids. They include poisons, such as arsenic, Prussic acid, and strychnine. Choking agents, like chlorine and phosgene, can cause fluid to accumulate in the lungs and may lead to respiratory failure. Blistering agents, such as mustard gas, can also affect the lungs, as well as harming the eyes, respiratory system, and skin. Nerve gases, such as sarin and tabun, attack the body's muscles and nervous systems (Laqueur, 1999).

In the 1870s, Irish nationals, referred to as the Fenians, were apparently the first group to try to use poison gas against their enemies; they hoped to spray it on the House of Commons in London (Laqueur, 1999, p. 242). Chemical gas attacks by the Germans in World War I killed thousands of Allied soldiers; the British and French retaliated, killing thousands of Germans. Chemical weapons subsequently were banned by international agreements, but that did not stop Adolf Hitler from using nerve gases against Jews in concentration camps. They were used more recently by Iraq in the war against Iran in the mid-1980s, by Libya against Chad in 1987, and by Saddam Hussein of Iraq against the Kurds in 1988 (Falkenrath, Newman, & Thayer, 2000).

Many chemical agents are used for legitimate medical, insecticide, and cleaning purposes and thus are readily available and often relatively cheap to purchase. In addition to the relative ease of their acquisition, the nerve gases manufactured today are more toxic than those of earlier eras.

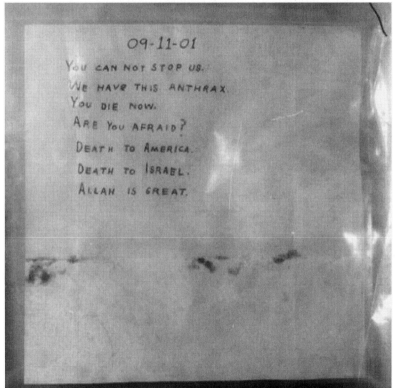

PHOTOS **8.1 and 8.2**   The FBI released these images of the envelope and the threatening letter containing anthrax that were sent to U.S. Senator Thomas Daschle (D-South Dakota).

Biological Weapons

A dead human body can be turned into a biological weapon. In the 14th century, the Tartars are believed to have catapulted plague-infected corpses over the walls of their enemies' castles, initiating the Great Plague, also called the "Black Death," that eventually devastated much of Europe. Scientists confirmed that Japan used biological weapons against China and the Soviet Union during the early years of World War II (Falkenrath et al., 2000, p. 91).

In addition to spreading plagues, biological weapons can be used to spread smallpox, typhus, tuberculosis, Legionnaires' disease, Ebola virus, and other infectious diseases. Biological weapons are relatively easy to produce and hide. By contaminating food and water, a small amount can wreak havoc.

The danger of bioterrorism became apparent for the first time to many people in the United States a few weeks after the 9/11 attacks when letters containing anthrax were sent through the U.S. mail: 5 people died from anthrax exposure and another 18 were known to be infected. More than a thousand people were tested for contact with anthrax, and about 30,000 people were given antibiotics to prevent infection.

Hundreds of other people reported exposure to substances that they feared were anthrax; most were false alarms. Health care professionals complained that the supply of antibiotics to counter anthrax was inadequate, and the Bush administration announced that it would buy antibiotics to treat up to 12 million people.

The ensuing investigation of the anthrax letters found no clear links to the September 11 attacks, and many officials speculated that homegrown bioterrorists were responsible. Subsequently, President Bush sent to Congress a proposed budget for fiscal year 2003 that sought an additional $11 billion over two years to protect the nation against biological terrorism; this amount quadrupled what was spent before the September 11 attacks to counter bioterrorism. Money also was earmarked for improving the nation's public health system and for pumping up budgets of federal agencies involved in biodefense. Funding was also provided to expand the national stockpile of vaccines and antibiotics, build anticontamination laboratories, research new drugs, and improve coordination among local, state, and federal emergency preparedness teams. The first reading that accompanies this chapter discusses the progress, or lack thereof, of many of these initiatives.

Views differ on the likelihood of bioweapons proliferation. Vogel (2006) has examined the development of the Soviet Union's biological weapons programs and the subsequent threat of bioweapons proliferation. She argues that, with the fall of the Soviet Union and the adoption of U.S. nonproliferation assistance programs, more innovative studies are required to determine whether the knowledge possessed by former Soviet scientists might affect nonproliferation and counterterrorism policies in the future.

Radiological Weapons

A change in the nucleus of an unstable atom can result in the release of excess energy in the form of radiation. A radiological attack can kill and injure an untold number of people and animals and contaminate a large geographic area, perhaps for years or even centuries (Ballard & Mullendore, 2003). Terrorists can launch a radiological assault in two ways: attacking a nuclear facility or using a radiological device (Nuclear Threat Initiative, 2006).

When Abu Zubaydah, supposedly a high-level member of al-Qaeda, was captured in Pakistan in 2002, he told authorities about possible nuclear and radiological attacks. Many did not believe his claims until Jose Padilla was arrested later that year at Chicago's O'Hare International Airport for "plotting to use a radiological bomb somewhere in the United States. The 'dirty bomber,' as he was labeled by the media, was now the person who the skeptics needed to believe that the threat was real" (Kushner, 2003, p. 1).

A "dirty bomb" uses common explosives, such as TNT, to spread radioactive material, but does not result in a nuclear explosion. Radioactive devices can come in many forms, including those that facilitate the transport of radioactive particles by air currents (Nuclear Threat Initiative, 2006).

Nuclear waste, from electric power generated at commercial nuclear plants and fissile materials at defense facilities, may take centuries to decay, posing major problems of waste disposal. The nation's spent nuclear fuel and radioactive waste are currently stored in more than 120 sites around the country (U.S. Department of Energy, 2007). In 1982, Congress passed the Nuclear Waste Policy Act designed to establish a national policy on the disposal of nuclear waste and

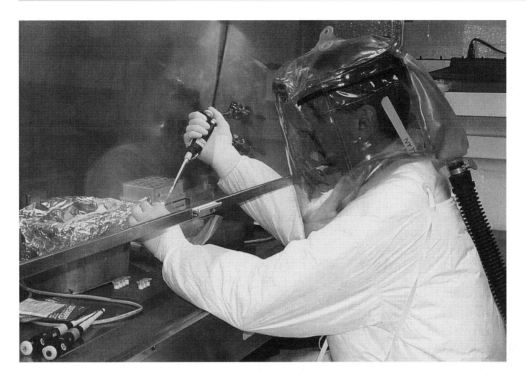

PHOTO 8.3   Under a hood, Dr. David Norwood processes samples that may contain a significant aerosol
and respiratory hazard. Norwood and fellow employees at the U.S. Army Medical Research
Institute of Infectious Diseases received as many as 700 samples in one day during the Fall
2001 anthrax mail crises.

subsequently approved the development of a long-term underground geologic repository on
federal land at Yucca Mountain, in a remote area of Nevada. The current plans call for construction to start in 2009, with materials beginning to be received in 2017 (U.S. Department of
Energy, 2007).

The Yucca Mountain project has received a great deal of negative attention over the years, in
part from those who feared a terrorist attack while the spent nuclear fuel and radioactive wastes
were being transported to the new facility. Ballard and Mullendore (2003, p. 772) describe the
scope of the transportation problem in noting the following:

> Local communities in more than 40 different states will be faced with an average of 3 to 6 shipments
> per day that are leaving the current storage facilities and traveling on the interstate highways,
> railways, and waterways of America toward Nevada and the Yucca facility. . . . [T]his level of activity
> will transpire every day, 365 days a year, and for at least 24 years. . . . The risk of a terrorist attack on
> nuclear waste shipments could be easily dismissed as someone else's problem if it were not for the
> fact that these cargos will be in such easily identifiable vehicles and traveling set routes with such a
> frequency and duration that any potential saboteur or terrorist adversary would have no problem
> planning an attack against these materials.

Although the Department of Energy is still hoping to move forward with its timetable for
Yucca Mountain, with the victory of Democrats in the 2006 Congressional elections, the future
of the project is uncertain. The new Senate majority leader, Harry Reid of Nevada, has long
opposed the project; in his new position of power, he has promised to prevent any pro-Yucca
legislation, including funding, from being passed (Werner, 2006).

Nuclear Weapons

The world has witnessed two nuclear attacks: In 1945, the United States detonated nuclear bombs on the Japanese cities of Hiroshima and Nagasaki. The bombings brought a quick end to World War II, but at an awful cost to innocent Japanese civilians.

The ability to manufacture nuclear weapons depends on the availability of high-quality uranium and plutonium. These materials are frequently in transit from one nuclear reactor site to another, making them vulnerable to theft. Domestic pressures and international political differences make it difficult for the key nuclear states of Russia, China, France, India, and the United States to agree on methods of stopping the growth of nuclear weaponry (Barletta, 2001).

Pakistan has tested a nuclear device, and North Korea, Iran, and Iraq have developed or tried to develop nuclear capacity. When North Korea detonated a nuclear bomb in October 2006, all doubts were erased about the seriousness of the challenge facing Japan, South Korea, and ultimately the United States and its allies.

The United Nations Security Council imposed sanctions on Iran's nuclear program at the end of 2006. In response, Iranian President Mahmoud Ahmadinejad asserted that the UN resolution designed to deprive his regime of nuclear materials was "invalid." He opined that his country "is wise and will stick to its nuclear work and is ready to defend it completely" ("Ahmadinejad Says Iran's Nuclear Plans Are Still On," 2007).

Explosive Devices

Explosives are categorized as low or high depending on their rates of decomposition. Low explosives decompose rapidly, but do not usually explode on their own. High explosives decompose slowly and can explode on their own. High explosives can be divided further into primary explosives, like nitroglycerine, and secondary explosives, like TNT and dynamite. When Timothy McVeigh used a homemade truck bomb to blow up the Murrah Federal Building in Oklahoma City, he vividly demonstrated the harm that could be done by large-scale explosive devices.

The information necessary to construct explosive devices is readily available on the Internet. Such Web sites as "The Explosives and Weapons Forum" (http://www.roguesci.org/theforum) maintain bulletin boards that allow people to discuss their experiences with explosives and to assist others in their attempts to build better explosive devices.

How Real Is the Threat?

There have been many more hoaxes, pranks, and unconfirmed allegations reported than actual uses of CBRNE weapons. Most of the confirmed attacks have been made with simple "household" agents, which are unlikely to cause massive casualties. In addition, many CBRNE incidents have been criminally rather than politically motivated (Pate, Ackerman, & McCloud, 2001).

The Center for Nonproliferation Studies at the Monterey Institute of International Studies reported that the vast majority of CBRNE incidents were either failed attempts to acquire weapons of mass destruction, hoaxes, or pranks. Relatively few incidents resulted in death or serious injury (Monterey Institute for International Studies, 2001).

There are also many unconfirmed allegations of CBRNE attacks. For example, the United States has accused the Soviet Union of using toxic weapons against the Hmong tribesmen in Laos and against civilians and Khmer Rouge forces in Cambodia in the 1970s. South Africa was accused of using anthrax in the Rhodesian civil war of 1978–1980 and of releasing a deadly strain of malaria in Angola in the 1980s. Fidel Castro repeatedly has accused the United States of conducting biological attacks against Cuban crops (Falkenrath et al., 2000). In January 2000, a Russian general accused Chechen rebels of giving toxic wine and fruit to Russian soldiers in Chechnya (Pate et al., 2001).

In a report issued before the 9/11 attacks, the Henry L. Stimson Center, a nonprofit public policy research organizations, maintained that the United States was poorly prepared to react to a significant attack using CBRNE weapons (Smithson & Levy, 2000). The Stimson Center's study criticized the federal government for inadequately financing the disease surveillance and hospital systems that would likely be overwhelmed in a large-scale attack. According to the study, the government has funded training of emergency response teams of dubious value (Smithson & Levy, 2000). For example, more than $134.7 million was spent to prepare and train National Guard teams to help in the event of a germ or chemical terrorist attack, but the study found that the teams probably would not arrive in time to provide significant help to local populations because the germs and chemicals spread so quickly.

The Stimson Center study recommended that the United States stop funding emergency preparedness training programs and abolish the National Guard units responsible for responding to CBRNE attacks. Instead, it urged that funding be directed to outfit hospitals and fire stations with decontamination capabilities and to increase research and training. Further, the study criticized the lack of coordination of federal efforts, which resulted in the creation of about 90 terrorism training preparedness courses with different missions, resources, and requirements.

THE INTERNET AND TERRORISM

Terrorists have always cultivated technology to further their goals, and the use of computer networks to this end is no exception to the historical pattern. Cyberspace is appealing to extremists for numerous reasons, including its easy access and relative lack of regulations, its ability to reach a large audience, its anonymity, and its inexpensiveness.

According to Weimann (2006b), a search of terrorists' presence on the Internet in 2006 revealed that more than 4,800 Web sites were maintained by terrorists or their supporters; this figure compares to a relative handful of terrorist sites only a decade ago. These sites may contain bulletin boards, chat rooms, publications, and videos. They may be official or unofficial Web sites of terrorist organizations, and they come in many languages and formats.

The Internet is used as a propaganda tool, of course, but that is just the tip of the iceberg (Weimann, 2006b). Terrorists also use it to contact colleagues, tap new sources of financial support, and plan attacks. They use the Internet to conduct debates and settle disputes. It also provides an abundance of detailed instruction for anyone interested in making bombs, rockets, flamethrowers, and dozens of other lethal weapons and poisons.

The Sri Lankan Tamils' use of the Internet is a good example. Tamils living outside of Sri Lanka established a Web presence more than 10 years ago, posting to Usenet groups and launching several Web sites (Enteen, 2006). The goal of most of these Web sites is to advocate for national recognition for the Tamil people. The Tamil terrorist organization, the Liberation Tigers of Tamil Eelam, has likewise been a leader in the use of the Internet to get out its message and promote its long-range goals.

Digital Terrorism

The Internet has another, even more sinister potential: digital terrorism. Comprised of both information warfare and cyberterrorism, digital terrorism presents frightening possibilities for crippling vital economic, social, governmental, and other infrastructure.

Taylor, Caeti, Loper, Fritsch, and Liederbach (2006, p. 21) define six components of information warfare:

1. psychological operations: using information to influence the mental state of the adversary

2. electronic warfare: denying accurate information to an adversary

3. military deception: misleading foes about military capabilities or plans

4. physical destruction: destroying information systems

5. security measures: protecting information systems from enemy infiltration

6. information attacks: corrupting existing information without harming the physical structure where the information is located

A simpler definition is that "information warfare is any sort of strike or protective measure against an information system, whatever the means. Implanting a virus into a military computer is an information warfare tactic. On the other end of the spectrum, blowing up a cellular phone tower could also be considered information warfare" (Taylor et al., 2006, p. 21).

Cyberterrorism is the second component of digital terrorism. It is defined as a "premeditated, politically or ideologically motivated attack or threat of attack against information, computer systems, computer programs, and data that can result in violence against civilian targets" (Taylor et al., 2006, p. 23). A prolonged loss of water or power or serious disruption to the national economy, for example, could be socially destabilizing and deadly.

Whether a particular event should be categorized as information warfare or cyberterrorism may be difficult to determine, but taken together they demonstrate the threat posed by digital terrorism. For a legal and historical analysis of extremists' use of computer networks, see Levin (2002).

Theoretically, it would take but one talented terrorist to devastate a country's infrastructure and generate panic and death. Military bases, hospitals, airports, banks, power plants, and other critical components of daily life depend on computers. Boilers could be programmed to explode, national security data could be altered, air traffic control systems could be sabotaged, food and water sources could be poisoned through changes in computer-driven controls—the possibilities are limited only by terrorists' skill and imagination.

How Real Is the Threat?

The Internet continues to evolve, as does its exploitation by terrorists. After the 9/11 assaults, Osama bin Laden issued a statement saying that "hundreds of young men had pledged to him that they were ready to die and that thousands of Muslim scientists were with him and who use their knowledge in chemistry, biology, and ranging from computers to electronics [*sic*] against the infidels" (Colarik, 2006, pp. 34–35).

Although the threat is real, thus far there have been no significant cyberattacks by terrorists on U.S. government information systems, transportation systems, power grids, nuclear power plants, or other key infrastructure components (Weimann, 2006a, p. 164). Cyberattacks are common, but they have been primarily conducted by nonterrorist hackers. A report issued by the IBM Global Security Analysis Lab in 2002 found that 90 percent of hackers were amateurs with limited skills, 9 percent had more skills, and only 1 percent were highly skilled (Weimann, 2006a, p. 165). D. Thomas (as cited in Weimann, 2006a) interviewed hundreds of hackers and reached the same conclusion: few hackers have the skills needed to launch a serious cyberattack. Thus, as with CBRNE attacks, the likelihood of a major digital terrorism attack is unknown.

AUM SHINRIKYO: A TERRORIST CULT

Only one large-scale attack with WMD by nonstate terrorists has been confirmed. The March 20, 1995, chemical weapons attack on Tokyo's subways by the Aum Shinrikyo apocalyptic and millenarian cult was said to herald a new age of "catastrophic" terrorism (Smithson & Levy, 2000, p. xi).

Aum Shinrikyo was controlled by the messianic and highly eccentric Shoko Asahara. A large and wealthy cult, the members of which included several scientists, Aum Shinrikyo experimented with both chemical and biological weapons. It was able to obtain many of its raw materials from Russia and the United States.

Aum Shinrikyo was "a terrorist nightmare—a cult flush with money and technical skills led by a con-man guru with an apocalyptic vision, an obsession with chemical and biological weaponry, and no qualms about killings" (Smithson & Levy, 2000, p. xii). The group nevertheless could not overcome the technical and scientific difficulties in WMD production and dissemination, and the death toll from the attack fell far short of Aum Shinrikyo's intent. Put another way, the attacks "were less deadly than some single-person shooting sprees, and required considerably more effort to prepare and carry out" (Falkenrath et al., 2000, p. 23).

Shoko Asahara: A Chaotic Leader

Shoko Asahara's background seems bizarre for a terrorist leader (see, e.g., Cameron, 1999; Falkenrath et al., 2000; Laqueur, 1999; Mullins 1997; Walsh, 1995). Born Chizuo Matsumoto in 1955 on Kyushu, one of Japan's major islands, he was blind in one eye and partly blind in the other. At the age of 5, he was sent to a special school for the blind, where his partial sight gave him a big advantage over the other students. He quickly turned this advantage into a position of power. With partial vision, Matsumoto helped his classmates, but in return he bullied and intimidated them into doing his bidding. After graduating from the school in 1977, Matsumoto moved to Tokyo. When he was refused entry into Tokyo University, he started studying acupuncture and herbal medicine. He married, and he and his wife opened a small shop selling traditional Chinese herbs and health tonics. The business went bankrupt after Matsumoto was arrested and fined for selling fake cures.

In 1984, Matsumoto opened a yoga school, began to gather disciples, and founded Aum Shinrikyo. Two years later, as his following grew, Matsumoto traveled to India, where he claimed to have become enlightened while alone in the Himalayan mountains. On returning to Japan, he changed his name to the "holy" Shoko Asahara. *Aum* in Sanskrit symbolizes the "powers of destruction and creation in the universe," and *shinrikyo* means the "teaching of the supreme truth" (Reader, 2000, p. 15). As the name suggests, its leader's mission was to teach his followers the truth about the universe.

As a religion, Aum was "a hodgepodge of ascetic disciplines and New Age occultism, focused on supposed threats from the U.S., which [Asahara] portrayed as a [conspiracy] of Freemasons and Jews bent on destroying Japan. The conspiracy's weapons: sex and junk food" (Walsh, 1995). Asahara was demanding of his followers; for example, they were supposed to kiss his feet before addressing him.

From Bizarre to Dangerous

Aum was approved as a religious group under Japan's Religious Corporations Law, which meant that it had tax benefits, the right to own property, and protection from government interference. It soon grew into a large organization with thousands of members. It also became rich with the money demanded from members: the group's assets were estimated to be between $300 million and $1 billion (Senate Permanent Subcommittee, 1996). Aum owned many companies worldwide, including "a computer firm, a chain of restaurants and a fitness club in Japan; a Taiwanese import/export company; and a tea plantation in Sri Lanka" (Cameron, 1999, p. 284). It also had extensive land holdings in Japan and elsewhere. Many of Asahara's followers were well educated, and several were doctors, engineers, and computer experts.

Why was Aum able to attract so many followers? One observer offers this explanation: "The time was ripe for gurus. Japan's galloping economic miracle in the 1970s and '80s also spawned a boom in new religions offering spiritual refuge to Japanese alienated by materialism. Asahara's messianic self-image expanded to help fill this void" (Walsh, 1995). Aum targeted people who were alienated from society, including lonely and emotionally needy people (Cameron, 1999, p. 284).

Asahara discouraged dissent and promoted his own unchallenged authority. To ensure obedience, he used brainwashing techniques, including sleep deprivation, poor diet, electric shock

PHOTO 8.4   Shoko Asahara, the leader of the doomsday cult, Aum Shinrikyo, which spread sarin gas in the Tokyo subway system in 1995.

treatments, and physical isolation. The cult also manufactured its own LSD and may have sold it to others (Sayle, 1996). Leaving the cult was not easy. Members were frightened, and some apparently were murdered for trying to escape. Outsiders who criticized the cult, including a lawyer, his wife, and their baby, were also murdered. That lawyer had been planning to sue Aum on behalf of some of the cult members' parents (Kaplan & Marshall, 1996).

Aum continued to grow and expanded to Russia. Asahara once preached to a crowd of 15,000 in a Moscow sports stadium (Walsh, 1995). At its height, the cult was estimated to have 50,000 followers, of whom 10,000 were in Japan and up to 30,000 were in Russia (Cameron, 1999, p. 284).

In 1989, Asahara formed the Shinrito ("Supreme Truth") political party in an effort to expand Aum's base of support. In 1990, the party ran 25 candidates in the election for Japan's Lower House Diet. All of them lost. Legal problems mounted when hundreds of the group's followers were accused of falsifying their legal residence so they could vote in Ashara's district (Reader, 2000).

Stunned and humiliated by the defeat at the polls, Asahara became further alienated from the rest of Japanese society. His ambition switched from simply controlling Japan to destroying it (Cameron, 1999, p. 280). It is roughly around this time that Asahara became obsessed with the idea of the coming of Armageddon (Senate Permanent Subcommittee, 1996). He decided to fulfill this prophecy himself.

Aum apparently tried and failed several times to develop and disseminate biological weapons. The cult experimented with anthrax, Q fever, and botulinum, as well as trying to collect samples of the Ebola virus. In 1990, cult members drove around the area outside the Japanese parliament spraying a botulinum toxic aerosol. The Japanese Crown Prince's wedding in 1993 was targeted for biological attack, but the group's toxin was not ready in time; later that year, cult members again drove around the city spraying the toxin. In 1993, they tried to spray anthrax spores from the rooftop of their Tokyo headquarters (Cameron, 1999). None of these events caused any deaths (Kaplan & Marshall, 1996).

Aum had more success with developing chemical agents. The cult tested sarin gas on sheep at its farm in Australia (Cameron, 1999). Yet, the group again encountered numerous technical difficulties. For example, it had problems building electrolysis tanks and reactor vessels, and their Russian-made helicopters, which were to have been used to spray and disperse the gas, crashed (Cameron, 1999). In 1994, they nevertheless produced enough sarin gas to attack three judges who were presiding over a land fraud suit against the cult. The attack killed 4 and injured 150 people (Falkenrath et al., 2000, p. 20).

Not until 1995, however, did the Tokyo Metropolitan Police begin to seriously investigate Aum's role in these assaults. Under Japan's laws, religious organizations generally are exempt from official investigation. Its status as a recognized religion enabled Aum to keep its plans secret. Now, with the police investigating, Asahara felt pressured to quickly launch Armageddon, and he hatched a flimsy plan to release sarin gas in the Tokyo subway. The group did not wait to secure sufficiently pure sarin or to devise an effective dissemination strategy, dooming its plan for Armageddon.

The Attack

On the morning of March 20, 1995, five members of Aum Shinrikyo boarded subway trains at five different stations around Tokyo. Each member carried two sealed plastic pouches of sarin nerve gas and a sharpened umbrella. As the trains neared the center of the city, the terrorists put the plastic pouches on the floor and punctured them with the umbrellas. They then fled the subways as the liquids leaked quickly out of the bags. The effects were almost instantaneous: passengers began to sweat, their noses ran, they coughed and wheezed, some vomited, and others had seizure-like symptoms.

Twelve people died and more than 5,000 were injured (Senate Permanent Subcommittee, 1996). It could have been much worse. Had a more sophisticated approach been used, thousands could have been killed.

The Aftermath

After the attack, the police focused immediately on Aum Shinrikyo and raided the cult's facilities. They seized large stockpiles of chemicals, including ingredients for nerve gases, such as sarin, VX, tabun, soman, and hydrogen cyanide (Cameron, 1999). On May 16, 1995, Asahara was arrested and charged with masterminding the subway attacks, as well as with 16 other crimes, including murders, attempted murders, manufacture of illegal drugs, and production of WMD. Japan's so-called trial of the century began.

Asahara pled not guilty to most of the charges. He began his trial by firing his lawyer, and he refused to cooperate with any of his court-appointed attorneys. Often pictured wearing pajamas and reported to be sleeping or mumbling to himself during the court proceedings, the bushy-bearded Asahara used his trial to reinforce his eccentric reputation.

Japan's court system is complex, and it was not until February 2004 that he was sentenced to death. Several appeals ensued, but in September 2006, the Japanese Supreme Court rejected his final appeal, setting the stage for his eventual execution, provided the defense team does not apply for a retrial or an emergency appeal. It is unknown at this time when or if Asahara will be executed for his crimes.

After the attack, many members of Aum Shinrikyo tried to distance themselves from Asahara. The cult was reorganized, and its name was changed to Aleph, a name that symbolizes renewal. The cult apparently has renounced the belief that it is acceptable to commit murder to achieve its goals, but many Japanese still believe that Asahara controls the group.

HIGHLIGHTS OF REPRINTED ARTICLES

The first article selected to accompany this chapter extends the above discussion about Aum Shinrikyo by applying the lessons learned from the sarin gas attack on the Tokyo subway to the United States. The second article examines the likelihood of a nuclear attack and how the probabilities of nuclear occurrences are calculated.

Randal Beaton et al. (2005). The sarin gas attacks on the Tokyo subway—10 years later/lessons learned. *Traumatology, 11*(2), 103–119.

This article examines lessons to be learned from the sarin gas attacks on the Tokyo subway system. The authors analyze the psychological barriers to interagency communications under disaster conditions. Using the 9/11 attacks as a point of comparison, the article examines the continuing problems of communication and coordination between Emergency Medical System (EMS) personnel at the attack site and area hospitals that received the injured victims.

In both Tokyo and the 9/11 attacks, many victims went on their own to the nearest treatment facility. This self-transport makes it difficult to determine which walk-in victims need the most help, hindering the allocation of resources during a disaster. Most hospitals in the United States lack enough beds, personnel, equipment, and isolation units to deal with a large-scale terrorist attack. Problems are also caused by the "worried well"; that is, people who fear they have been contaminated but have not been.

Micah Zenko (2006). Intelligence estimates of nuclear terrorism. *The Annals of the American Academy of Political and Social Science, 607*, 87–102.

The second article selected to accompany this chapter discusses the process for arriving at the official estimates of the likelihood of nuclear terrorism. The research is based on declassified Central Intelligence Agency (CIA) National Intelligence Estimates (NIEs), as well as on unclassified CIA analyses, information on intelligence estimates leaked to the media, reports of government agencies and commissions, and comments by senior governmental officials. The reader is struck with the political, as opposed to purely scientific, nature of these estimates.

EXPLORING TECHNOLOGY AND TERRORISTS FURTHER

- Examine the Web site of the Center for Nonproliferation Studies at the Monterey Institute (http://cns.miis.edu/index.htm). What do their reports indicate about the possibility of CBRNE attacks?

- The Carnegie Endowment for International Peace's Non-Proliferation Project (http://www.carnegieendowment.org/npp/) posts news and analysis on a variety of problems associated with CBRNE attacks. Its Web site posts critiques of the Bush administration's policies as well as threats and capabilities of nations around the globe.
- Examine the United Nations Web site on weapons of mass destruction. Topics include treaties and conventions on unconventional weapons, as well as transcripts from the latest symposiums on terrorism and disarmament. The Web address is http://disarmament.un.org/wmd/.
- The Henry L. Stimson Center (http://www.stimson.org/home.cfm), a nonprofit, nonpartisan organization, posts online publications such as "Iraq: Hard Choices, Real Consequences," "Can the United States Contain Iran?" and "Next Steps on North Korea: Options Beyond Sanctions."
- Learn more about the underground geologic repository at the Yucca Mountain site from http://www.ocrwm.doe.gov/ym_repository/index.shtml.
- The first reprint for this chapter, by Beaton et al., discusses the TopOff2 exercise of May 2003. Describe the exercise and the conclusions drawn from it.
- According to Beaton et al., what types of problems can arise from victims transporting themselves to nearby medical centers? Who are the "worried well" and what types of problems do they pose?
- Beaton et al. describe the Strategic National Stockpile (SNS). What is the SNS and what types of problems might hinder an effective emergency response to a terrorist attack of this sort?
- Discuss the four major conclusions drawn by Zenko, the author of the second article reprinted in this chapter.
- Explain Zenko's analysis of the NIEs of Iraq's weapons of mass destruction program. How did these estimates influence U.S. behavior?
- According to Zenko, what is known about al-Qaeda's attempts to obtain nuclear materials?

VIDEO NOTES

Although weapons of mass destruction may seem like something from a movie plot, modern films contain few good studies of the threat of biological and chemical weapons. A celebrated drama about a global nuclear crisis spawned by terrorists is *Crimson Tide* (Hollywood Pictures, 1995, 115 min.).

❖

The Sarin Gas Attacks on the Tokyo Subway—10 Years Later/Lessons Learned

Randal Beaton, Andy Stergachis, Mark Oberle,
Elizabeth Bridges,[1] Marcus Nemuth,[2] and Tamlyn Thomas[3, 4]

This paper considers "lessons learned" from the March 20, 1995, covert terrorist attack on the Tokyo, Japan, subway system employing a neurotoxic agent. The following lessons from this disaster are reviewed in light of prevailing practice and policy in the U.S. in 2005: timely communication of vital information; operational logistics including triage, surge capacity and decontamination; secondary contamination of emergency responders and hospital personnel; assessment and treatment of the "worried well"; secondary traumatization of rescue workers; and behavioral health preparedness measures and treatment for disaster victims. In some respects little progress has been made, for instance, in developing new, evidence-based therapies for disaster victims with posttraumatic stress disorder. On the other hand, some recently developed and implemented initiatives, such as the Strategic National Stockpile (SNS), represent enhancements to U.S. preparedness compared to that which existed during the 1995 terrorist attacks on the Tokyo, Japan, subway system.

This paper focuses on some of the lessons learned from the sarin gas attack on the Tokyo, Japan subway a decade ago. In that attack, on the morning of March 20, 1995, members of a "doomsday" cult released sarin gas, a neurotoxic agent, in the Tokyo subway system, killing twelve people and causing more than five thousand people to seek medical care. The aim of this paper is to revisit the many lessons of the sarin gas attacks on the Tokyo subway system (especially the "psychosocial lessons") and to compare and contrast present-day preparedness for a similar disaster and the ensuing psychosocial sequelae in the United States—10 years later. Lessons learned from the Tokyo subway sarin gas attacks were based not only on articles by Taneda (2005) and Kawana, et al. (2005) but also on a review of the published works of Okumura et al. (1998a, 1998b,

1998c), Matsui, Ohbu & Yamashina (1996) and Ohbu et al. (1997) among others.

COMMUNICATION OF VITAL INFORMATION

Although more than six years had elapsed since the sarin gas attacks on the Tokyo subway system, pre-hospital communication at the Pentagon terrorist disaster site on 9/11/2001 was suboptimal. According to the Arlington County after-action report prepared by Titan Systems, "Almost all aspects of communications continue to be problematic, from initial notification to tactical operation: In the first few hours following the attack on the Pentagon, foot messengers at times proved to be the most reliable means of communication." This report also noted that "communications and coordination were deficient between Emergency Medical System (EMS) control at the incident site and area hospitals receiving injured victims" (Department of Justice, 2002)

Since 9/11 there has been a concerted effort, including federal funding in the U.S., to provide emergency and rescue organizations with interoperable radios and communication protocols (FEMA, 2003). In King County, Washington (U.S.) the police, the State Department of Health, the county, the state, the Emergency Operation Centers (EOC's) and all local hospitals use a common communication device with preset channels (Mariotti, Personal Communication, 2004).

Still, very little is known to date about the psychosocial barriers or impediments to interagency communication under disaster conditions. As recently as the second Top Officials (TopOff 2) exercise in May of 2003, interagency communication at all levels appeared to be problematic. In addition to infrastructure problems, communication was adversely affected by power differentials between local, state and federal authorities and a "cultural clash" between agencies. TopOff 2 was the largest and most comprehensive multi-agency terrorism exercise ever held in the U.S. It brought together top government officials from more than 100 federal, state and local agencies as well as the Canadian government to test the domestic response to mock terrorist attack(s) employing weapons of mass destruction. In the Illinois venue sixty-four hospitals responded to a simulated outbreak initiated by a bioterrorist attack. The TopOff 2 after-action report noted that " . . . the lack of a robust and efficient emergency communications infrastructure was apparent." Most importantly, communication problems were the primary cause of flawed public policy decision making (DHS, 2003), as was the case in the original TopOff exercise in 2000 and in the case of the anthrax attacks in Florida in 2001.

In the event of a covert attack employing an imperceptible chemical or biologic agent, early communication and identification of the causative agent may well be crucial in initiating timely treatment designed to protect emergency workers and to initiate risk communication messages. While a chemical assay and confirmation of the sarin as the neurotoxic agent used in the Tokyo subway attack was not available until several hours after the attack (Taneda, 2005), there are now emerging technologies that may allow practically instantaneous point-of-service analysis of a chemical or bio-agent. The latter might include detection of a pathogen even before victims show signs or symptoms; e.g., BioWatch program (The White House, 2004). Thus, some recent advances in point-of-service technology under development in the U.S. might improve initial communication and timely diagnosis of victims of a covert bioterrorist or chemical attack. This would, in turn, guide initial treatment, prophylaxis, and improve the safety of rescue workers and hospital personnel alike.

A recently published series of articles on developing risk communication messages for terrorist events employing so-called Weapons of Mass Destruction (WMD) has the potential to improve the effectiveness of early post-event information for the general public. Based on findings from a series of focus groups with diverse community representation, Centers for Disease Control and Prevention (CDC) researchers learned how U.S. citizens and U.S. EMS personnel were likely to view a threat of or an actual WMD event, what kind of information they need to be able to respond appropriately and what communication channels they will likely rely upon (Vanderford, 2004; Becker, 2004, Wray & Jupka, 2004, Glik, Harrison, Davoudi & Riopelle, 2004). Timely and accurate risk communication could reduce unwarranted fear in the general populace and perhaps reduce, to some extent, demands on the health care system stemming from psychosocial factors, e.g., the "worried well" victims seeking treatment. Improved risk communication in the immediate aftermath of a terrorist attack employing a biological, chemical or radiologic agent could also improve the efficiency and safety of any ensuing emergency medical service response.

OPERATIONAL LOGISTICS

As with many, if not most, disasters, victims self-transported to nearby treatment facilities. For many victims of the Tokyo sarin gas attacks this was St. Luke's Medical Center (Taneda, 2005). Similarly on September 11, 2001, at the Pentagon disaster site some surviving victims drove themselves or walked to nearby treatment facilities (DoJ, 2002). The problems arising from this self-transfer phenomenon are serious and complex. Without a pre-hospital triage system, such as Simple Triage and Rapid Transport (START), seriously injured victims who need immediate care might not get the timely and appropriate treatment (Hafen, Karren, & Mistrovich, 1992). Furthermore, the pre-hospital Incident Command System cannot accurately evaluate walk-in victim needs and appropriately meter the allocation of pre-hospital and area hospital resources (DoJ, 2002).

While there is ample evidence that disaster victims self-refer and self-transport to the nearest hospital, usually within minutes of a disaster, current Joint Committee on Accreditation of Healthcare Organizations (JCAHO) standards for emergency management hospital plans do not explicitly identify the problem of self-referral or self-transport (www.jcaho.org). Current JCAHO emergency management hospital standards also do not include plans for responding to surge capacity; that is, the influx of a massive number of disaster casualties and the need to treat them in a short period of time. The reality is that the casualty flow to nearby hospitals begins within minutes of a disaster with most casualties arriving at nearby hospitals on their own, in non-emergency vehicles within an hour and a half of the disaster impact (Auf der Heide, 1996). This is one of the operational lessons from the sarin gas attacks on the Tokyo subway system that we have yet to heed (Taneda, 2005).

Even if all available pre-hospital and hospital resources are allocated appropriately, surge capacity remains a problem for most EMS, Emergency Department and trauma hospital systems in the U.S. (AHRQ, 2004). Most hospitals in the U.S. lack adequate beds, equipment, isolation facilities and staff to respond to a large-scale terrorist attack. The Health Resources and Services Administration (HRSA) has set a critical surge capacity benchmark for all U.S. states, but converting from a current capacity system to a surge capacity system within a matter of hours still remains a daunting task in the U.S. (HRSA, 2004).

One federal program that predated 9/11 and which was developed to address at least one component of the problem of surge capacity is the Strategic National Stockpile (SNS). The SNS is a national repository of antibiotics, chemical antidotes, antitoxins and medical supplies needed in the event of a large scale mass casualty disaster or a bioterrorist event. It is managed, jointly by the Department of Homeland Security and the Department of Health and Human Services and is designed to augment state and local resources during a large-scale disaster or bioterrorism (Esbitt, 2003; Havlak, Gorman & Adams, 2002). The SNS is designed to supplement and resupply state and local efforts in the event of an emergency anywhere and at anytime within the U.S. or its territories, within 12 hours of approval of a request. The SNS maintains caches of medications and chemical antidotes that could be accessed in the event of a chemical or biodisaster regarding the latter, many hazardous materials teams and medic personnel in the U.S. have been trained in the pre-hospital administration of nerve gas antidotes such as pralidoxime chloride (2 PAM or 2 PAM chloride). In fact, the patient care protocols of Pierce County Washington recently authorized emergency medical technicians to administer the Mark I nerve agent antidote for the first time (Medical Program Director— Pierce County, 2005). A combination of pralidoxime chloride (2-PAM or 2-PAM Chloride) and atropine may be administered for nerve gas poisoning. The availability of drugs in the field is crucial, since the optimal time window for administration of nerve gas antidote is brief—in the case of a significant exposure to certain neurotoxic agents the time window for the administration of the antidote is only seconds to minutes (Holstege, Kirk & Sidell, 1997). The SNS represents an advance in our U.S. preparedness circa 2005 since nerve gas antidotes stocks were insufficient in the aftermath of the Tokyo sarin gas attack and no plan or system was in place to augment their stores (Okamura, Suzuki, Fukuda et al., 1998).

Unfortunately the 12-hour response time for SNS is inadequate for a nerve agent exposure, where treatment must be accomplished quickly in order to save as many lives as possible. As a result, the CDC established the CHEMPACK program for the "forward" placement of sustainable repositories of nerve agent antidotes in numerous locations throughout the U.S., so that they can be immediately accessible for the treatment of affected persons. Presently a pilot program, the CDC maintain ownership of the CHEMPACK stockpile (CDC, 2004), but in conjunction with state and local officials, locate the antidotes in numerous strategically placed containers under controlled and monitored storage conditions for use in the event of an emergency involving nerve and other chemical agents.

We also need to consider surge capacity for mental health needs to provide care for victims, co-victims and communities following a terrorist attack with massive numbers of casualties (Hall, Norwood & Fullerton, 2002). Current JCAHO emergency management plans for U.S. hospitals do not include any mention of "worried well" nor other disaster mental health issues (www.jcaho.org). Just as medical care providers may be overwhelmed by a mass casualty incident, likewise the social work staff of medical centers may be overwhelmed. Communities need to have plans in place to recruit those trained in mental health support from a wide range of fields—crisis intervention call lines, clergy, chaplains, counselors, clinics, etc.

Secondary Contamination of Emergency Responders and Hospital Personnel

Certainly EMS and hospital staffs in the U.S. are much more aware now of the potential for a terrorist attack in their communities employing nerve gas and other chemical agents. This awareness probably stems more from the events of 9/11 and anthrax attacks on the East Coast in this country in 2001 than from lessons learned from the Tokyo subway sarin gas attacks. Most urban fire departments and hospital personnel in the U.S. have, by now, been offered at least some awareness-level training and many now possess response teams with some Weapons of Mass Destruction (WMD) operational capabilities (Beaton & Johnson, 2002). Many U.S. public health workers and health providers have participated in WMD training and mass casualty drills, which have been documented to enhance knowledge and/or their perceived competency to respond to a WMD event in their communities (Beaton & Johnson, 2002; Beaton & Oberle et al., 2003; Beaton et al., 2004). An enhanced awareness of the signs and symptoms of a large-scale chemical attack could greatly limit, or even entirely prevent, secondary contamination of

EMS and hospital staff, for instance, which was prevalent in the Tokyo sarin gas attacks (Taneda, 2005). Secondary transmission of sarin gas can occur since clothing and other belongings release sarin vapor for about 30 minutes after contact with sarin, leading to exposure of other people (i.e., secondary contamination). People may not be aware that they were exposed to sarin gas and other neurotoxic agents because they are odorless and colorless.

Another legacy of the Tokyo subway sarin gas attacks has been an increased appreciation of the importance of pre-hospital and hospital decontamination facilities (Jagninas & Erdman, 2004). Only limited decontamination of the Tokyo subway sarin gas attack victims was performed (Okamura, 1998). Pre-hospital or hospital decontamination could conceivably have reduced these victims' symptoms arising from sarin gas exposures via absorption and inhalation routes as well as many, if not most, cases of secondary contamination of hospital personnel. A related psychosocial assumption is that primary victims of a chemical attack with few or mild symptoms that quickly resolve might be less likely to have lasting and/or severe psychosocial sequelae (DeWolfe, 2003).

Partnered with the decontamination, hospital and EMS directives in the U.S. regarding Personal Protective Equipment in response to identified or unidentified hazardous materials exposure could further reduce the likelihood of secondary contamination of First Responders and hospital personnel (OSHA, 2004 29CFR1910.120[g]). Some staff at receiving hospitals in Tokyo in the aftermath of the sarin gas attacks were not even wearing latex gloves or gauze masks, let alone hazardous material suits with respiratory protection which is the current U.S. standard to respond to a potential nerve gas agent. Of course, the Tokyo EMS and hospital personnel did not know what they were dealing with for several hours following the sarin gas attacks.

The "Worried Well"

One of the most challenging problems associated with a terrorist event are "worried well" who seek treatment out of fear or concern even though they have not been exposed to the chemical agent or pathogen (Bartholomew & Wessely, 2002). Following the terrorist attack on the Tokyo subway system "worried well" patients outnumbered patients with an exposure by a ratio of > 4:1. This response pattern is problematic since these "worried well" victims may consume scarce resources and may block access of critically-ill disaster victims who have experienced an actual exposure (Evans, Crutcher, Shadel, et al., 2002). These "worried well" patients, sometimes referred to as victims of "mass hysteria," represent a problem for the disaster response, but they also should be considered patients who are "not well" and who, at the very least, need an initial medical evaluation, understanding, guidance and a plan (Stein et al., 2004; Pastel, 2004).

Obviously, some kind of definitive test or pathognomic sign of exposure would be helpful in making a differential diagnosis but, lacking that, and complicating matters further, certain signs and symptoms of chemical and bio-exposure may overlap with cognitive and behavioral signs and symptoms of stress and anxiety (Beaton & Murphy, 2002). Therefore, it might be prudent to triage and hold presumably "worried well" patients for observation since more definite signs/symptoms of an actual exposure might emerge after some delay. Even if they have no direct exposure "worried well" victims would benefit from reassurance, some relevant information such as a fact sheet with guidance, a follow-up protocol, and available community resources. However, methodological sound research on such interventions for the "worried well" is still lacking (North & Pfefferbaum, 2002). At a pre-hospital WMD incident site such a triage protocol for "worried well" patients might also be possible (Copass, personal communication, 2001). However, given the large footprint of most disaster event sites and the perception by the public that definitive care is given at hospitals, medical centers must continue to expect and prepare for large numbers of self-referred victims with vague or mild complaints.

In a larger community context, timely and accurate risk communication might have reduced the number of worried well seeking medical treatment in the aftermath of a mass casualty event such as those seeking treatment in Tokyo two days or more following the attack. Effective risk communication might also have reduced the number of "white powder incidents" in the U.S. and calmed fears worldwide in the aftermath of

the anthrax "attacks" on the Eastern seaboard of the U.S. in the fall of 2001 (ABC news, 2001). In these "attacks" anthrax powder was mailed in envelopes to several media and congressional authorities via the U.S. Postal system. As a result, a small number of individuals developed cutaneous or pulmonary anthrax and a large number of those potentially exposed received prophylactic antibiotics. For several months there were hundreds of reports of suspicious "white powder/ possibly anthrax" that were investigated. Virtually all of these "white powder" substances after December of 2001 (or west of the Mississippi) tested negative for anthrax. A distinct improvement from past practice, current response plans in many U.S. communities incorporate formation of a Joint Information Center (JIC). JICs utilize local expertise and leadership to provide a single unified "voice" regarding important health risk communication information of the event, utilizing local media to distribute information broadly.

LACK OF MENTAL HEALTH PREPAREDNESS FOR RESCUE WORKERS

Even though most samples of rescue and recovery workers show emotional resilience during and in the aftermath of disasters (Norris, Friedman, Watson, et al., 2002) at least some emergency responders such as firefighters do evidence secondary traumatic stress symptomatology (Beaton, Murphy, Johnson, Pike & Corneil, 1999). In certain cases their secondary traumatic stress reactions are transitory (Beaton, Murphy, Johnson & Nemuth, 2004), but some manifest chronic post traumatic stress disorder in the aftermath of disasters (McFarlane, 1989). Obviously any intervention that could prevent the onset and progression of post traumatic stress disorder in emergency workers would be well received. Critical incident stress debriefing (CISD) has been proffered as potentially therapeutic (Mitchell & Everly, 2001). There is and continues to be, however, an ongoing controversy regarding the clinical efficacy of CISD as a stand-alone intervention, or even within the context of a critical incident stress management program (CISM; McNally, Bryant & Ehlers, 2003). In fact, an NIH Consensus Conference Report on Mass Violence in 2002 noted the absence of methodologically sound data

TABLE 1   Psychological First Aid

What You Can Do On-Site

Taking care of yourself will help you to stay focused on hazards at the site and to maintain the constant vigilance you need for your own safety. Often responders do not recognize the need to take care of themselves and to monitor their own emotional and physical health—especially when recovery efforts stretch into several weeks. The following guidelines contain simple methods for helping yourself. Read them while you are at the site and again after you return home.

- Pace yourself. Rescue and recovery efforts at the site may continue for days or weeks.
- Take frequent rest breaks. Rescue and recovery operations take place in extremely dangerous work environments. Mental fatigue over long shifts can place emergency workers at greatly increased risk for injury.
- Watch out for each other. Co-workers may be intently focused on a particular task and may not notice a hazard nearby or behind.
- Be conscious of those around you. Responders who are exhausted, feeling stressed, or even temporarily distracted may place themselves and others at risk.
- Maintain as normal a schedule as possible: *regular eating and sleeping are crucial.* Adhere to the team schedule and rotation.
- Make sure that you drink plenty of fluids such as water and juices.
- Try to eat a variety of foods and increase your intake of complex carbohydrates (for example, breads and muffins made with whole grains, granola bars).
- Whenever possible, take breaks away from the work area. Eat and drink in the cleanest area available.
- Recognize and accept what you cannot change—the chain of command, organizational structure, waiting, equipment failures, etc.
- Talk to people when *YOU* feel like it. You decide when you want to discuss your experience. Talking about an event may be reliving it. Choose your own comfort level.
- If your employer provides you with formal mental health support, use it!
- Give yourself permission to feel rotten: You are in a difficult situation.
- Recurring thoughts, dreams, or flashbacks are normal—do not try to fight them. They will decrease over time.
- Communicate with your loved ones at home as frequently as possible.

SOURCE: Excerpted from NIOSH fact sheet "Traumatic Incident Stress: Information for Emergency Response Workers."

---

showing that debriefing actually deterred the onset or progression of PTSD and did not recommend its use for either rescue workers or for primary victims (NIMH, 2002). This same NIH Consensus Conference suggested that the term "debriefing" should no longer be used to describe this technique and also pointed to research evidence that it might actually cause psychological harm in some trauma victims. Likewise, "Psychological First Aid" for disaster workers (See Table 1) has been promulgated as potentially helpful (NIOSH, 2001) but this "intervention" has not been studied rigorously either.

BEHAVIORAL HEALTH PREPAREDNESS AND TREATMENT FOR DISASTER VICTIMS

One arena in which we have made very little progress in our mass casualty planning has been that of behavioral or mental health preparedness. This has been on the "back burner" and not integrated into most U.S. or state disaster plans. In fact, as recently as 2003, a systematic review of 31 U.S. state and territory plans concluded the state mental health disaster plans were "both variable and incomplete" and that "virtually all of the reviewed state (mental health) plans lacked key elements" (HHS, 2003). On a more positive note, this recent document observed that state mental health plans in process were now paying closer attention to terrorism and terrorist events (HHS, 2003). Most of the barriers to mental health disaster preparedness are well known and long standing. In addition to the persisting stigma of mental problems/disorders, many of the limitations and barriers to disaster mental health planning are noted in Table 2.

Best practice "early intervention" guidelines to assist disaster victims in the immediate aftermath of a disaster have been identified and represent a range of options including efforts to reduce immediate danger, provide safety, foster resilience and provide social support, all in an effort to reduce long-term psychological disorders and to treat acute psychiatric reactions (Ritchie et al., 2004). We also have a better appreciation of the short-term and longer-term impacts of disasters in general, and of terrorist-induced disasters in particular, on the emotional and behavioral health of primary victims and co-victims in surrounding communities (Shariat, et al., 1999; Okumura, et al., 1998a; DeWolfe, 2000; North, et al., 1999; Pfefferbaum, 2000; Schuster, et al., 2001; Schlenger et al., 2002). We also recognize that certain vulnerable populations, such as children, may have special psychological needs following a terrorist disaster (Pfefferbaum, et al., 1999; Pfefferbaum et al., 2002). (See Table 3 for a listing of other vulnerable populations based on disaster research and findings with combat veterans.)

One compelling lesson from the sarin gas attacks on the Tokyo subway is that some victims of terrorist events continue to have post trauma symptoms even with treatment. For many victims post trauma symptoms persist for years following the event (Kawana et al., 2005). However, while we may now more clearly recognize the short-term and long-term impact of a terrorist event on primary and secondary victims, we still do not have conclusive evidence that early interventions are effective. Furthermore, the available evidence suggests that the standard early and long-term interventions for trauma victims (Cognitive Behavioral Treatment (CBT), Eye Movement Desensitization and Reprocessing (EMDR) and Stress Management) are not helpful for all survivors. Dropout rates from studies of CBT in trauma samples are about 20% (Ballenger et al., 2000). Even in samples of PTSD patients who complete CBT, more than half may still meet the DSM-IV Criteria for PTSD at the post treatment assessment (Resick et al., 2002; Tarrier et al, 1999). Furthermore, even if PTSD symptoms are partially ameliorated, not all PTSD patients receiving CBT rate their post-treatment functioning as "good" (Marks et al., 1998).

Another lesson of the sarin gas attacks on the Tokyo subway system, also supported by other empirical findings and theoretical perspectives, is that trauma victims may manifest their symptoms cognitively, socially, behaviorally, emotionally, as well as physically (Van der Kolk, 1988; Van der Kolk, 1994; Krystal, et al., 1989). The assessment of post trauma symptomatology reported by Kawana, et al. (2005) purposely included physical symptoms in an effort to detect and measure "masked PTSD" in sarin gas

TABLE 2   Barriers to Disaster Mental Health Planning

- Lack of human and financial resources to do the work
- Little political will to focus on disaster mental health over many years, once a disaster passes
- Mental health being overlooked in favor of safety and security concerns
- The lack of collaboration and consistency among federal departments and agencies including SAMHSA/CMHS, the Department of Justice, the Centers for Disease Control and Prevention, and the Health Resources and Services Administration and corresponding state departments and agencies receiving disaster and terrorism funding
- The lack of well-defined, "proven" and easily implemented programs in disaster mental health that can be adopted widely

SOURCE: From HHS, 2003.

TABLE 3   Vulnerable Populations to Post-Disaster and Combat Distress

- Pre-existing mental illness (Yehuda, 2002)
- Prior mental illness (McFarlane, 1989)
- Females (more short-term distress in U.S. sample post 9/11) and more long-term post-trauma symptoms in Japanese sarin gas attack victims (Kawana, et al., 2005; Silver, 2002)
- Those with intense and/or prolonged trauma exposures (Goldberg, et al., 1990)
- Hispanic and other immigrant populations, including refugees (Galea, et al., 2002)
- Weak or deteriorating psychosocial resources (Norris, et al., 2002)
- Pre-existing chronic medical illness (Bromet et al., 1998)

attack survivors. Too, there may be some conceptual overlap between "masked PTSD" and "multiple unexplained physical symptoms" not infrequently observed in the aftermath of chemical, biological and/or radiological incidents (Pastel, 2004). A chronic bioneuroendocrine dysfunction has been hypothesized that may, in part, account for these physical symptoms in trauma survivors (Yehuda, et al., 1991)

CONCLUSIONS AND FUTURE DIRECTIONS

Compared to the 1995 Tokyo subway sarin gas disaster, there are no doubt both an increased awareness and improved, although still imperfect, communication and logistical capabilities to respond to a similar mass casualty event in the U.S. in 2005. However, most U.S. hospitals have yet to adopt realistic policies to triage and decontaminate and treat large numbers of victims of such a chemical attack who may self-transfer to the nearest available health care facility. There are also no current U.S. hospital standards nor widely adopted health care protocols to respond to the needs of the "worried well," co-victims of a covert or overt chemical or biological attack. The basis for effective health risk communication in the immediate aftermath of a WMD terrorist event has improved, at least in theory. Yet we still have a paucity of evidence-based treatments designed to ameliorate the distress of victims of a terrorist attack employing chemical weapons or to prevent the onset and progression of post traumatic stress disorders and other adverse psychological outcomes in rescue workers and in hospital personnel. In most U.S. hospitals, states and jurisdictions there is still no mental health response component

integrated into existing all-hazards disaster plans (HHS, 2003).

Use of psychotropic medications to ameliorate symptoms and sequelae of Acute Stress Disorder (ASD) and PTSD is a promising new area of treatment. Much has been learned from managing military combat-related PTSD, resulting in new approaches (Morgan, Krystal & Southwick, 2003). Propranolol, a beta-blocker, has benefited acutely traumatized burn victims (Pittman, et al., 2002), and stimulated further research. An important recent finding is the significant reduction in hyper-vigilance, flashbacks, intrusive memories, nightmares and insomnia in post-trauma patients given Prazosin, and alpha-1 antagonist (Raskind, et al., 2003). A "morning after" pill designed to mitigate psychic damage from acute trauma may not be too far off.

Chronic PTSD now has a range of FDA approved medication treatments including SSRI antidepressants (Sertraline, Fluoxetine, Paroxetine) and combination therapies with low dose mood stabilizers (Asnis et al., 2004) and/or low dose atypical antipsychotics (Stanovic, James & Vandevere, 2001). Carefully employed psychotropic medication combined with behaviorally oriented goal-directed therapy has the potential to offer disaster trauma victims better outcomes.

In terms of future directions, we still have not applied many of the psychosocial lessons learned from the sarin gas attack on the Tokyo subway system a decade ago. There may be special features of a deliberate, man-made covert terrorist attack, such as "uncertainty" that are particularly distressing and anxiety provoking and increase the risk of long-term mental health sequelae (Stein, et al, 2004). We are challenged to develop new interventions and to modify current standard trauma interventions to better treat victims of "the next" sarin gas attack.

NOTES

1.   Randal Beaton, PhD, EMT, Andy Stergachis, PhD, RPh, Mark Oberle, MD, MPH, and Elizabeth Bridges, RN, PhD are affiliated with the University of Washington. Correspondence should be addressed to: Randal D. Beaton, PhD, EMT, Research Professor, University of Washington, Department of Psychosocial & Community Health, Box 3257263, Seattle, WA 98195-7263/(206) 543-8551/e-mail: randyb@u.washington.edu

2.   Marcus Nemuth, MD is affiliated with the Veterans Affairs Administration of Puget Sound.

3.   Tamlyn Thomas, STAT RN is affiliated with the University of Washington Medical Center.

4.   Acknowledgements: This article was made possible by grant number 1 T01HP01412–01–00 from the Health Resources and Service Administration, DHHS, Public Health Training Center Program and was also supported, in part, by a cooperative agreement from the Center for Disease Control and Prevention (CDC) through the Association of Schools of Public Health (ASPH), Grant Number U36/CCU300430–21. The contents of this article are solely the responsibility of the author and do not necessarily represent the official views of CDC or ASPH.

REFERENCES

ABC News.com. (2001). The Terror of the Times: Bioterror Fever Grips the World Available at http://abcnews.go.com/International/story?id=80475&page=1 accessed 12/30/04.

AHRQ. (2004). Publication No. 04-P008. Optimizing surge capacity: Hospital Assessment and Planning. Bioterrorism and Health System Preparedness, Issue Brief No. 3. Available at http://www.ahrq.gov/news/ulp/btbriefs/btbrief3.htm accessed 12/30/04.

Asnis, G.M., et al. (2004). SSRI's versus non-SSRI's in post-traumatic stress disorder: An update with recommendations. Drugs, 64(4), 383–404.

Auf der Heide, E. (1996). Disaster planning Part II: Disaster problems, issues and challenges identified in the research literature. Emergency Medicine Clinics of North America, 14 (2), 453–480.

Ballenger, J.C., Davidson, J.R., Lecrubier, Y., Nutt, D.J., Foa, E.B., Kessler, R.C., McFarland, A.C., & Shalev, A.Y. (2000). Consensus statement on posttraumatic stress disorder from the International Consensus group on Depression and Anxiety. Journal of Clinical Psychiatry, 5, 60–66.

Bartholomew, R.E., & Wessely, S. (2002). Protean nature of mass sociogenic illness: From possessed nuns to chemical and biological terrorism fears. British Journal of Psychiatry, 180, 300–306.

Beaton, R., & Johnson, C. (2002). Evaluation of domestic preparedness training for first responders. Prehospital and Disaster Medicine, 17, 119–125.

Beaton, R., & Murphy, S. (2002). Psychosocial responses to biological and chemical terrorist threats and events: Implications for the workplace. Journal of the American Association of Occupational Health Nurses, 50 (4), 182–189.

Beaton, R., Murphy, S., Johnson, C., Pike, K., & Corneil, W. (1999). Coping responses and posttraumatic stress symptomatology in urban fire service personnel. Journal of Traumatic Stress, 12, 293–308.

Beaton, R., Murphy, S., Johnson, C., & Nemuth, M., (2004). Secondary traumatic stress response in firefighters in the aftermath of 9/11/2001. Traumatology, 10, 7–16.

Beaton, R., Oberle, M., Wicklund, J., Stevermer, A., & Owens, D. (2003). Evaluation of the Washington State National Pharmaceutical Stockpile Dispensing Exercise Part I—Patient Volunteer Findings. Journal of Public Health Management and Practice, 9, 368–376.

Beaton, R., Oberle, M., Wicklund, J., Stevermer, A., & Owens, D. (2004). Evaluation of the Washington State National Pharmaceutical Stockpile Dispensing Exercise Part II—Dispensary Site Worker Findings. Journal of Public Health Management and Practice, 10, 77–85.

Becker, S. M. (2004). Emergency communication and information issues in terrorist events involving radioactive materials. Biosecurity and Bioterrorism: Biodefense Strategy, Practice, and Science, 2 (3), 195–207.

Centers for Disease Control and Prevention (CDC). (2004). Continuation Guidance—Budget Year Five Attachment J–CHEMPACK Public Health Preparedness and Response for Bioterrorism available at http://www.bt.cdc.gov/planning/continuationguidance/pdf/chempack-attachj.pdf, accessed 01/04/05.

Copass. (2002). Personal communication from director of Harborview Medical Center Trauma Unit.

Department of Homeland Security (DHS). (2003). Top Officials (TopOff) Exercise Series: TopOff 2. After Action Summary Report for Public Release. Available at http://www.dhs.gov/interweb/assetlibrary/Initial_NRP_100903.pdf, accessed 12/30/04.

Department of Justice (DoJ). (2002). Arlington County After-action Report on the September 11 Terrorist Attack on the Pentagon. Prepared by Titan Systems Corporation. Contract Number G310F0084K, order number 2001F_341.

DeWolfe, D. (2003). *Population Exposure Model in U.S. Department of Health and Human Services.* Mental Health All-Hazards Disaster Planning Guidance, Available at http://www.mentalhealth .org/publications/allpubs/SMA03–3829/, accessed 12/30/04.

Esbitt, D. (2003). The strategic national stockpile: Roles and responsibilities of health care professionals for receiving stockpile assets. *Disaster Management Response, 1,* 68–70.

Evans, R.G., Crutcher, J.M., Shadel, B., Clements, B., Bronze, M.S. (2002). Terrorism from a public health perspective. *The American Journal of the Medical Sciences, 323* (6), 291–298.

Federal Emergency Management Agency (FEMA). (2003). *Preparedness-Emergency Operations Center and Interoperable Communications Grants.* Available at http://www.fema.gov/ preparedness/eoc_grants.shtm, accessed on 12/30/04.

Glik, D., Harrison, K., Davoudi, M., & Riopelle, D. (2004). Public perceptions and risk communications for Botulism. *Biosecurity and Bioterrorism: Biodefense Strategy, Practice, and Science, 2* (3), 216–223.

Hafen, B., Karren, K., & Mistrovich, J. (1992). *Prehospital Emergency Care.* Brady Prentice Hall: NJ, 798–801.

Hall, M., Norwood, A.E., & Fullerton, C.S. (2002). Preparing for bioterrorism at the state level: Report of an informal survey. *American Journal of Orthopsychiatry, 72*(4), 486–491.

Havlak, R., Gorman, S.E., & Adams, S.A. (2002). Challenges associated with creating a pharmaceutical stockpile to respond to a terrorist event. *Clinical Microbiological Infection, 8,* 529–533.

Health and Human Services (HHS). (2003). *Mental Health All Hazards Disaster Planning Guidance.* Available at http://media.shs.net/ken/pdf/ SMA03–3829/All-HazGuide.pdf, accessed 01/04/05

Health Resources and Services Administration (HRSA). (2004). *Focus on Bioterrorism.* HRSA requirements available at www.hrsa.gov, accessed 12/30/04.

Holstege, C., Kirk, M., & Sidell, F. (1997). Chemical Warfare: nerve agent poisoning. *Critical Care Clinicians, 13*(4), 923–942.

Jagninas, L., & Erdman, D. (2004). CBRNE—Chemical Decontamination. *E-medicine,* Available at http://www.emedicine.com/emerg/ topic893.htm, accessed on 12/3004.

Joint Committee on Accreditation of Healthcare Organizations (JCAHO) available at www.jcaho.org, accessed 12/30/04.

Kawana, N., Ishimatsu, S., Matsui, Y., Tamki, S., & Kanda, K. (2005). The chronic posttraumatic stress symptoms in victims of Tokyo subway sarin gas attack. *Traumatology, the International Journal, 11*(2).

Krystal, J.H., Kosten, T.R., Southwick, S., Mason, J.W., Perry, B.D., & Giller, E.L. (1989). Neurobiological aspects of PTSD: Review of clinical and preclinical studies. *Behavior Therapy, 20,* 177–198.

Marks, I., Lovell, K., Noshirvani, H., Livanou, M., Thrasher, S. (1998). Treatment of posttraumatic stress disorder by exposure and/or cognitive restructuring a controlled study. *Archives of General Psychiatry, 55,* 317–325.

Mariotti, D. (2004) Emergency Preparedness Liaison Harborview Medical Center, Personal Communication.

Matsui, Y., Ohbu, S., & Yamashina A. (1996 July). Hospital deployment in mass sarin poisoning incident of the Tokyo subway system—an experience at St. Luke's International Hospital, Tokyo. *Japan Hospital, 15,* 67–71.

McFarlane, A.C. (1989). The aetiology of post-traumatic morbidity: Predisposing, precipitating and perpetuating factors. *British Journal of Psychiatry, 154,* 221–228.

McNally, R., Bryant, R., & Ehlers, A. (2003). Does early psychological intervention promote recovery from post traumatic stress? Psychological Science in the Public Interest, 4, 45–79.

Medical Program Director—Pierce County. (2005). Pierce County Emergency Medical Services Patient Care Protocol. Department of Emergency Management, Revised January 2005.

Mitchell, J.T., & Everly, G.S., Jr. (2001). *Critical Incident Stress Debriefing: An operations manual for CISD, defusing and other group crisis intervention services* (3rd ed.). Ellicott City, MD: Chevron.

Morgan, C.A., Krystal, J.H., & Southwick, S.M. (2003). Toward early pharmacological posttraumatic stress intervention. *Biological Psychiatry, 53*(9), 834–843.

National Institute of Mental Health (NIMH) Mass Violence: Mental Health and Mass Violence: Evidence-Based Early Psychological Intervention for Victims/Survivors of Mass Violence. Available at http://www.nimh.nih.gov/ healthinformation/massviolence_intervention .cfm, accessed 12/30/04.

National Institute for Occupational Safety and Health (NIOSH). (2001). Psychological First Aid Website available at http://www.cdc.gov/ niosh/unp-trinstrs.html, accessed 12/30/04.

National Mental Health Information Center (NMHIC). (2000). Field Manual for Mental Health and Human Service Workers in Major Disasters. Available at http://www.mentalhealth .org/publications/allpubs/ADM90–537/default .asp, accessed 12/30/04.

Norris, F.H., Friedman, M.J., Watson, P.J., Byrne, C.M., Diaz, E., de Kaniasty, K. (2002). 60,000 disaster victims speak: Part I. An empirical review of the empirical literature, 1981–2001. *Psychiatry, 65,* 207–239.

North, C.S., Nixon, S.J., Shariat, S., Mallonee, S., McMillen, J.C., Sptiznagel, E.L., & Smith, E.M. (1999). Psychiatric disorders among survivors of the Oklahoma City bombing. *Journal of the American Medical Association, 282*(8), 755–762.

North, C., & Pfefferbaum, B. (2002). Research on the mental health effects of terrorism. *Journal of the American Medical Association, 288,* 633–636.

Ohbu, S., Yamashina, A., Takasu, N., Yamaguchi, T., Murai, T., Nakano, K., Matsui, Y., Mikami, R., Sakurai, K., & Hinohara, S. (1997). Sarin poisoning on Tokyo subway. *Southern Medical Journal, 90*(6), 587–598.

Occupational Safety and Health Administration (OSHA). (2004). Technical Manual. Personal Protective Equipment, Available at http://www.osha.gov/dts/osta/otm/otm_viii/otm_viii_1.html, accessed on 12/30/04.

Okamura, T., Suzuki, K., Fukuda, A., Kohama, A., Takasu, N., Ishimatsu, S., & Hinohara, S. (1998a). The Tokyo subway sarin attack: Disaster management, Part 1: Community emergency responses. *Academic Emergency Medicine, 5*(6), 613–617.

Okumura, T., Suzuki, K., Fukuda, A., Kohama, A., Takasu, N., Ishimatsu, S., & Hinohara, S. (1998b). The Tokyo subway sarin attack: Disaster management, Part 2: Hospital response. *Academic Emergency Medicine, 5*(6), 618–624.

Okumura, T., Suzuki, K., Fukuda, A., Kohama, A., Takasu, N., Ishimatsu, S., & Hinohara, S. (1998c). The Tokyo subway sarin attack: Disaster management, Part 3: National and international responses. *Academic Emergency Medicine, 5*(6), 624–627.

Pastel, R.H. (2004). Psychological effects of 'weapons of mass disruption.' *Psychiatric Annals, 34*(9), 679–686.

Pfefferbaum, B. (1999). Mental health services for children in the first two years after the 1995 Oklahoma City terrorist bombing. *Psychiatric Services, 50*(7), 956–958.

Pfefferbaum, B., North, C.S, Flynn, B.W., et al. (2002). Disaster mental health services following the 1995 Oklahoma City bombing: Modifying approaches to address terrorism. *International Journal of Neuropsychiatric Medicine, 7*(8), 575–579.

Pitman, R.K., Sanders, K.M., Zusman, R.M., et al. (2002). Pilot study of secondary prevention of posttraumatic stress disorder with Propranolol. *Biological Psychiatry, 51,* 189–142.

Raskind, Murray A., et al. (2003). Reduction of nightmares and other PTSD symptoms in combat veterans by Prazosin: A placebo-controlled study. *American Journal of Psychiatry, 160,* 371–373.

Resick, P.A., Nishith, P., Weaver, T.L., Astin, M.C., & Feuer, C.A. (2002). A comparison of cognitive-processing therapy with prolonged exposure and a waiting condition for the treatment of chronic posttraumatic stress disorder in female rape victims. *Journal of Consulting and Clinical Psychology, 70,* 867–879.

Ritchie, E.C., Friedman, M., Watson, P., Ursano, R., Wessely, S., & Flynn, B. (2004). Mass violence and early mental health intervention: A proposed application of best practice guidelines to chemical, biological, and radiological attacks. *Military Medicine, 169*(8), 575–578.

Schlenger, W.E., Caddell, J.M., Ebert, L., Jordan, B.K., Rourke, K.M., Wilson, D., Thalji, L., Dennis, J.M., Fairbank, J.A., & Kulka, R.A. (2002). Psychological reactions to terrorist attacks: Findings from the National Study of Americans' reactions to September 11. *Journal of the American Medical Association, 288,* 581–588.

Schuster, M.A., Stein, B.D., Jaycox, L.H., Collins, R.L., Marshall, G.N., Elliott, M.N., Zhou, A.J., Kanouse, D.E., Morrison, J.L., & Berry, S.H. (2001). A national survey of stress reactions after the September 11, 2001 terrorist attacks. *New England Journal of Medicine, 345*(20), 1507–1512.

Shariat, S., Mallonee, S., Kruger, E., Farmer, K., & North, C. (1999). A prospective study of long-term health outcomes among Oklahoma City bombing survivors. *Journal of Oklahoma State Medical Association, 92*(1), 178–186.

Stanovic, J.K., James, K.A., & Vandevere, C.A. (2001). The effectiveness of risperdone on acute stress symptoms in adult burn patients: A preliminary retrospective pilot study. *Journal of Burn Care Rehabilitation, 22*(3), 210–213.

Stein, B.D., Taneilian, T.L., Eisenman, D.P., Keyser, D.J., Burnam, M.A., & Pincus, H.A. (2004). Emotional and behavioral consequences of bioterrorism: Planning a public health response. *The Milbank Quarterly, 82,* 1–32.

Taneda, K. (2005). The sarin nerve gas attack on the Tokyo subway system: Hospital response to mass casualties. *Traumatology, the International Journal, 11*(2).

Tarrier, N., Pilgrim, H., Sommerfield, C., Faragher, B., Reynolds, M., Graham, E., & Barrowclough, C. (1999). A randomized trial of cognitive therapy and imagined exposure in the treatment of chronic posttraumatic stress disorder. *Journal of Consulting and Clinical Psychology, 67,* 13–18.

Vanderford, M.L. (2004). Breaking new ground in WMD risk communication: The pre-event message development project *Biosecurity and Bioterrorism: Biodefense Strategy, Practice, and Science 2,*(3), 193–194.

Van der Kolk, B.A. (1988). The trauma spectrum: The interaction of biological and social events in the genesis of the trauma response. *Journal of Traumatic Stress, 1,* 273–290.

Van der Kolk, B.A. (1994) The body keeps the score: Memory and the evolving psychobiology of PTSD. *Harvard Review of Psychiatry, 1,* 253–265.

White House. (2004). Watch Program available at http://www.whitehoU.S.e.gov/bioshield/bioshield2.html, accessed 12/30/04.

Wray, R., & Jupka, K. (2004). What does the public want to know in the event of a terrorist attack using Plague? *Biosecurity and Bioterrorism: Biodefense Strategy, Practice, and Science, 2* (3), 208–215.

Yehuda, R., Giller, E.L., Southwick, S.M., Lowy, M.T., & Mason, J.W. (1991). Hypothalamic-pituitary-adrenal dysfunction in posttraumatic stress disorder. *Biological Psychiatry, 30,* 1031–1048.

Intelligence Estimates of Nuclear Terrorism

Micah Zenko

Nuclear terrorism is not a post-9/11 or even post–cold war phenomenon. In fact, this review of declassified intelligence estimates spanning the past five decades reveals that the prospect of a clandestine nuclear attack on the United States—be it from the Soviet Union, China, or al-Qaeda—has been a regular concern for U.S. officials since the advent of nuclear weapons. Although the estimates themselves have been a mixed bag of quiet successes and failures, this article's key findings suggest that the threat of nuclear terrorism is very real and that the U.S. government remains ill prepared to counter that treat.

This article represents the first comprehensive analysis of publicly available intelligence assessments regarding the threat of nuclear terrorism to the United States. It draws primarily on declassified Central Intelligence Agency (CIA) National Intelligence Estimates (NIEs) but also on unclassified CIA analyses, intelligence estimates leaked to the media, the findings of relevant government agencies and commissions, and statements made by senior intelligence and political officials. Since nuclear terrorism lies at the nexus of three arenas that the U.S. government treats with supreme secrecy—intelligence, nuclear weapons, and terrorism—this discussion will necessarily remain unfinished until all of the relevant information is declassified. Nevertheless, given the past, present, and future threat posed by nuclear terrorism, it is essential to understand the collective judgments of the U.S. Intelligence Community (IC) on the subject—not only during the past five years, but over the past fifty.

I proceed in five sections. I begin with a discussion of the purpose, production, and inherent limitations of community-wide intelligence estimates. Turning to the evidence, I first review intelligence estimates on the possibility of Soviet or Chinese clandestine nuclear attacks on the United States, the first manifestation of nuclear terrorism during the 1950s and 1960s. Next, I explore the era of modern international terrorism that emerged in the late 1960s, along with concerns about U.S. civilian nuclear safeguards and unsecured American nuclear storage depots abroad. I then address the breakup of the Soviet Union, including the subsequent insecurity of its nuclear arsenal and the arrival of the international jihadist groups with nuclear ambitions, most notably al-Qaeda. Finally, I analyze the key themes that stand out upon examining more than a half-century of declassified intelligence estimates of the nuclear terror threat. A careful review of the available evidence reveals four key findings: (1) nuclear weapons or materials can be stolen or diverted with relative ease; (2) terrorist groups are obsessed with obtaining a nuclear weapon; (3) a bomb could be smuggled into America without detection; and (4) the U.S. government has been, and remains, insufficiently prepared to counter these threats.

WHAT ARE INTELLIGENCE ESTIMATES?

Intelligence estimates are analytical products developed by the IC to establish both the state of knowledge of an important issue and clear gaps in understanding.[1] Government agencies, businesses, and large organizations produce versions of intelligence estimates to better comprehend their operating environments and to develop long-range action plans. Because competitors and adversaries continuously hide their true intentions through denial and deception, intelligence estimates naturally suffer from a lack of information. In the U.S. government, the crown jewel of intelligence estimates is the NIE. According to the CIA,

> A National Intelligence Estimate (NIE) is the most authoritative written judgment concerning a national security issue prepared by the Director of Central Intelligence. Unlike "current intelligence" products, which describe the present, most NIEs forecast future developments and many address their implications for the United States. NIEs cover a wide range of issues—from military to technological to economic to political trends. NIEs are addressed to the highest level of policymakers—up to and including the President. They are often drafted in response to a specific request from a policymaker. Estimates are designed not just to provide information but to help policymakers think through issues.[2]

The process of writing an NIE begins either when the director of national intelligence (DNI) chooses to produce one, or when the executive branch, the Joint Chiefs of Staff, or, more rarely, Congress, requests one. Once the request is approved, Terms of Reference are drafted to outline "issues and key questions to be covered in the Estimate."[3] Next, a national intelligence officer in the National Intelligence Council (NIC), or an outside expert, drafts the Estimate based on all of the available information on the subject. The author then distributes it for approval to the fifteen intelligence agencies that comprise the wider IC, which are allowed to include dissenting opinions in footnotes on key issues of disagreement. The NIE is then forwarded to the National Intelligence Board—a group chaired by the DNI and composed of senior IC officials—for its prompt approval. Finally, the NIE is disseminated as a classified document to policymakers under the signature of the DNI.[4]

The NIE arrived with infamy onto the national scene after an October 2002 Estimate, "Iraq's Continuing Programs for Weapons of Mass Destruction," concluded that Iraq had chemical and biological weapons and would have a nuclear weapon within eight years' time.

Charles Duelfer, director of the CIA's Iraq Survey Group, later acknowledged that in estimating Saddam Hussein's weapons of mass destruction (WMD) programs, "we were almost all wrong."[5] According to the various bodies that investigated the October 2002 NIE, the ninety-three page estimate of Iraq's WMD capabilities suffered from an assortment of intelligence tradecraft errors. The Senate Select Committee on Intelligence found it was compiled hurriedly and approved in twenty days, whereas the IC ideally prefers three months. The CIA's after-action assessment noted that "[the NIE] was the product of three separate drafters, each responsible for independent sections, drawing from a mixed bag of analytic product." The Commission on the Intelligence Capabilities of the United States regarding Weapons of Mass Destruction listed as "a central flaw of the NIE" that it took "defensible assumptions (of Saddam Hussein's prior behavior) and swathed them in the mystique of intelligence, providing secret information that seemed to support them but was in fact nearly worthless, if not misleading."[6] A key difference between this flawed NIE and those presented below is that the Iraq Estimate was an action-forcing document written to influence a congressional vote to approve the Iraq war, while most NIEs are stand-alone products that inform the ongoing process of national security policy making.

1950s AND 1960s: THE CLANDESTINE PROBLEM

The United States lost its short-lived nuclear monopoly when, on August 29, 1949, the Soviet Union conducted its first successful atomic test at Semipalatinsk, Kazakhstan.[7] In its first NIE after the Soviet test, the CIA warned that "the continental U.S. will be for the first time liable to devastating attack."[8] Before the advent of the first Soviet intercontinental ballistic missiles (ICBMs) in 1957 and nuclear-armed submarines in 1960, bombers were judged to be Moscow's most likely means of nuclear attack on the United States. Nevertheless, a November 1950 NIE warned that "the Soviet Union has the capability for clandestine atomic explosions in ports and in selected inland areas."[9]

In 1951, the CIA updated that estimate and produced its first complete analysis of the issue with an NIE titled "Soviet Capabilities for Clandestine Attack against the U.S. with Weapons of Mass Destruction and the Vulnerability of the U.S. to Such Attack."[10] This fascinating document demonstrates that, within two years of Soviet acquisition, the CIA had mapped out many of the pathways that a state—or nonstate—actor could use to discretely deliver a bomb into the United States to this day. This NIE found that the Soviet Union, from the least to greatest probability, could

- "Smuggle an atomic bomb through customs as a commercial shipment."
- Conduct a "clandestine attack with civilian aircraft of a type used by U.S. or foreign transoceanic airlines."
- "(Utilize) a merchant ship for delivering an atomic weapon into a key U.S. harbor."
- "[Smuggle] . . . an atomic bomb, especially if disassembled, from a Soviet port into an isolated section of the U.S."

This final method was deemed the most likely means of a Soviet clandestine atomic attack on the United States. "The USSR," the NIE concluded, "will have no scruples about employing any weapon or tactic which promises success in terms of over-all Soviet objectives." Given this assessment, one would hope that the U.S. government would have been sufficiently alarmed to act on such an analysis. Unfortunately, the Estimate included a troubling assessment as relevant today as it was fifty-five years ago:

> No coordinated over-all plan has yet been complete for the detection and prevention of the smuggling of atomic weapons into the U.S. at secluded points. Until such a plan is complete and put into effective operation, the U.S. will remain vulnerable to this threat.

Throughout the 1950s, the CIA periodically updated its estimate of the clandestine threat to reflect how such an attack corresponded with the Soviet Union's growing strategic capabilities for striking the United States. One such NIE, written in 1955, explores the possibility of "Clandestine Introduction of Nuclear Weapons under Diplomatic Immunity."[11] This Estimate noted that weapons ranging "from one kiloton to one megaton in yield . . . could be designed to break down into components weighing from a few pounds up to 25 pounds in the case of

small-yield weapons and up to approximately 200 pounds in the case of large yield weapons." By using the shield of diplomatic immunity, it was envisioned that Moscow could place nuclear weapons at Soviet diplomatic establishments, such as at its Washington embassy, or in its United Nations delegation offices in New York City. According to the Estimate, "In this way [the Soviet Union] could virtually ensure successful attack on two major targets without using a large number of personnel and without incurring the risks involved in transporting nuclear weapons to areas which do not enjoy diplomatic immunity." The NIE ultimately estimated that "the chances are now slightly better than even that the USSR would not undertake" an attack using diplomatic immunity. In an interesting dissenting footnote, the assistant director of the FBI contended—and the director of naval intelligence concurred—that "it is impossible to predict whether the USSR would or would not attempt to utilize the diplomatic pouch to clandestinely introduce nuclear weapons into the U.S."[12] Given that, to this day, there are no limitations to the size of a diplomatic pouch, there was no technical constraint precluding the FBI's concerns.[13]

The Cuban Missile Crisis in 1962 rekindled interest in protecting the United States from a clandestine nuclear attack. In the collective cold war memory, the crisis is remembered as an "eyeball to eyeball" confrontation between Khrushchev and Kennedy in which the Soviets blinked first.[14] This triumphalist attitude, however, should have been tempered by the fact that, despite persistent intelligence collection on Cuba and Soviet freight shipping to the island, Moscow succeeded in covertly dispatching approximately 130 nuclear warheads—with an explosive power of more than fifty megatons—ninety miles from the U.S coastline.[15] An NIE approved six months prior to the Soviet shipment concluded erroneously that it was "unlikely that the [Soviet] Bloc will provide Cuba with strategic weapon systems."[16] After Moscow and Washington negotiated an end to the crisis, 98 tactical nuclear warheads remained in Cuba, unbeknownst to the United States.[17] Fidel Castro requested that the warheads stay on the island to deter an American invasion, but Moscow refused, and on Christmas Day, the remaining Soviet nuclear arsenal was removed from Cuba.[18]

After the Cuban Missile Crisis, President John F. Kennedy became concerned that nuclear weapons or other WMD could be smuggled into the United States.[19] The CIA thus reexamined the threat of clandestine nuclear attacks, and a March 1963 NIE reconfirmed that such an attempt would be easy. "Nuclear weapons yielding up to 300 [kilotons]," the NIE stated, "could be brought into the United States by a variety of means such as by ground or air transport across land borders or at points along U.S. seacoasts."[20] Even in the ballistic missile age, clandestine attacks retained the comparative advantage of "extreme accuracy or the desire to deny warning time." But, given the "growing number and dispersal of U.S. delivery vehicles," and subsequent "limited advantages of this course of action," it was ultimately deemed unlikely that the Soviets would introduce nuclear weapons clandestinely."

In January 1968, the Joint Chiefs of Staff requested that the 1963 NIE be updated to reflect the proliferation of nuclear weapons capabilities, and more specifically the threat from China, which tested its first bomb in October 1964.[21] From its allies, this NIE confidently concluded that "we can foresee no changes in the world situation so radical as to motivate the UK, France, or any of the other potential nuclear powers to attempt to clandestinely introduce nuclear weapons into the U.S." From China, however, the Estimate noted that, "because the Chinese have no other means of attacking the U.S. with nuclear weapons, they might consider a clandestine emplacement effort with the object of deterring the U.S. from attack on Communist China." Beijing was believed to have faced greater difficulties in smuggling a bomb than Moscow. First, "Chinese weapons are probably fairly large and would probably require more detailed assembly and check out after being brought in than would Soviet designs"; and second, "There are no Chinese Communist diplomatic establishments in the U.S. Canada, or Mexico. The absence of such bases precludes the use of diplomatic pouches for the clandestine introduction of nuclear weapons or their components." Although Beijing could have overcome these disadvantages, it was deemed unlikely they would do so because a detonated smuggled bomb would not deter the U.S. from launching a devastating nuclear attack on China.[22]

These early NIEs make clear that a clandestine nuclear attack from Russia or China was alarmingly achievable and a constant possibility. The CIA, however, never considered such an attack by either country to be likely, and to date no available evidence shows that Moscow or Beijing ever considered such an attack during the cold war. The NIEs envisioned that a smuggled bomb would be detonated only after either state decided to commence a general war with the United States and only as a subsidiary component of an all-out attack. None of the declassified NIEs ever concluded that an all-out war with China or the Soviet Union was likely in the foreseeable future during the time period in which they were published.

Interestingly, although the CIA quickly dismissed the clandestine threat from Great Britain or France, no NIEs mention how—or even if—the U.S. government could attribute the source of the fissile material used in a bomb through forensic attribution if no state claimed responsibility. A 1970 NIE even found it "conceivable that the Chinese Communists might seek to introduce into the U.S. a nuclear device with the intention of detonating it under certain circumstances . . . in hope that it would lead U.S. authorities to conclude that the action had been perpetrated by the Soviets" or, alternatively, "introduce into the U.S. a nuclear device so constructed as to appear to be of Soviet origin, and intended not to be detonated but to be discovered by U.S. authorities."[23]

MODERN TERRORISM

International terrorism was only a distant concern to the U.S. national security community prior to the late 1960s. Reflecting on his time in the Pentagon, former secretary of defense Robert McNamara later noted, "I don't think we used the term terrorist."[24] Influenced by the tactics of the Vietcong in the Vietnam War, government documents termed acts of terrorism as conducted by "insurgents," "guerrillas," "extremists," or "dissident groups." In March 1967, the JASONs—a group of some forty scientists who conducted secret research projects for the Pentagon—studied the likely consequences of the American use of tactical nuclear weapons (TNWs) in Vietnam.[25] Under the leadership of physicist Freeman Dyson, the JASON study found that the U.S. military would see few battlefield advantages from using TNWs because the Vietcong moved in small groups under the cover of the jungle and could quickly rebuild damaged transportation routes. Crossing the nuclear threshold in Southeast Asia, however, could lead the Soviets or Chinese to provide the Vietcong TNWs—in the form of atomic demolition devices, nuclear mortars, or recoilless rifles—which would have had devastating effects on the Saigon airport, densely populated U.S. bases, and Army and Air Force logistics facilities. Furthermore, if the Vietcong attacks succeeded, "insurgent groups everywhere in the world would take note and would try by all available means to acquire TNWs by themselves. . . . It is therefore of tremendous long-range importance to avoid setting a precedent for the use of TNW by guerilla forces."[26]

International terrorism in its modern connotation exploded onto the world stage when the Palestinian Liberation Organization conducted a series of airline hijackings, embassy attacks, and the massacre of eleven Israeli athletes at the 1972 Munich Olympics. In the wake of Munich, the CIA's Directorate of Intelligence created its first analytical team to systematically collect data on significant terrorist events and terror groups, and published the results in Weekly Situation Reports.[27] It was not until April 1976 that the CIA produced its first comprehensive analysis of international terrorism, "International and Transnational Terrorism: Diagnosis and Prognosis."[28] The study concluded that "there has been a marked and enduring upsurge in *transnational terrorism* since 1967." The emergent phenomenon was characterized by five factors: (1) "a substantial increase in the number of terrorist groups," (2) "a trend toward greater international contact and cooperation among terrorist groups," (3) "a trend toward bolder and more dramatic actions," (4) "the general popularity of American targets," and (5) "significant regional differences in the intensity and nature of such violence." Exacerbating these factors was "the diffusion of terrorist-adaptable technological know-how," which led the CIA to estimate that

> the prospect of nuclear-armed terrorists can, in fact, no longer be dismissed. But because of the major problems that would be involved in the acquisition, storage, transport, and employment of a nuclear device, a more likely scenario—at least in the short term—would be a terrorist seizure of a nuclear weapons storage facility or a nuclear power plant to exploit the publicity and the bargaining power in the attendant threat of radiological pollution.[29]

Since the late 1960s, officials in the Atomic Energy Commission (AEC) had been scrutinizing the relative insecurity of nuclear reactor facilities in the United States. In 1965, six bombs' worth of highly enriched uranium (HEU) from the Nuclear Materials and Equipment Corporation in Apollo, Pennsylvania, were found to have gone missing.[30] In 1966, twenty low-enriched uranium (LEU) fuel canisters were stolen—and later recovered—from the Bradwell Nuclear Power Station in Essex, England.[31] Spurred by these incidences of nuclear loss or theft, the AEC directed seven outside nuclear industry experts, lawyers, and accountants to study the issue of U.S. nuclear safeguards. In March 1967, the panel recommended that the AEC require nuclear power operators to improve and upgrade existing safeguards—specifically, physical protection, accounting, and oversight—to prevent the diversion of nuclear material.[32] The panel also warned, for the first time in a U.S. government publication, that "safeguards programs should also be designed in recognition of the problem of the terrorist or criminal groups clandestinely acquiring nuclear weapons or materials useful therein."[33]

Though the AEC succeeded in implementing some of the panel's recommendations, a "perfect storm"—a combination of more lethal terrorist attacks, nuclear terror hoaxes, and a constellation of dedicated physicists and academics warning about the relative ease of stealing fissile material and making a crude nuclear device—led the U.S. government to further study the issue.[34] In 1974, the AEC directed five independent experts to evaluate the safeguards in place in America's civilian nuclear facilities.[35] Led by technology consultant David Rosenbaum, the *Special Safeguards Study* warned that the U.S. system was "entirely out of proportion to the danger to the public" because of the contemporary nature of terrorism:

> Terrorists groups have increased their professional skills, intelligence networks, finances, and levels of armaments throughout the world. International terrorist organizations, particularly those of the Arabs, probably have the ability to infiltrate highly trained teams of 10 to 15 men into this country without detection. . . . Because of the widespread dissemination of instructions for processing special nuclear materials and for making simple nuclear weapons, acquisition of special nuclear material remains the only substantial problem facing groups which desire to have such weapons.[36]

Senator Abraham Ribicoff, causing an uproar over the issue, leaked a draft copy of the *Special Safeguards Study* to the press. According to the AEC, "due to the amount of public attention being given to the safeguards area and the resulting flood of information in the media, and the increase of terrorism," the federal agency subsequently revised its rules, adopting most of the recommendations that emanated from the *Study*.[37]

During the 1970s, the U.S. government also became worried about the security of its nuclear weapons arsenal, which was deployed in twenty-seven countries and territories during the cold war.[38] Spurred by the gang-bombing of the Fifth Army Corps Headquarters in Frankfurt, Germany, in 1972, and the assassination of the CIA station chief in Athens, Greece, in 1975, concern arose about the potential nuclear terror threat from Western European terrorist groups. Terrorist groups and nuclear-peace activists surveyed some of the more than one hundred isolated depots where U.S nuclear weapons were maintained and published detailed handbooks of the warhead transportation and safeguards procedures.[39]

In 1978, a leaked CIA estimate identified the more than six thousand warheads stored in NATO nuclear depots in Western Europe as "the most vulnerable and therefore most likely targets for future terrorist activity."[40] One year earlier, the Pentagon's Studies, Analysis and Gaming Agency conducted a week-long hypothetical exercise with thirty-five members of the national security community to consider how they would react if terrorists obtained a bomb and used it to blackmail the United States.[41] Although the exercise results were never declassified, participants reported that the seized weapon ended up in the hands of an unpredictable third-world leader.[42]

A December 1975 CIA report, "Managing Nuclear Proliferation: The Politics of Limited Choice," echoed the concerns of the Pentagon exercise.

> If a terrorist group does acquire nuclear explosives, it can rely upon unconventional delivery methods which would be inappropriate for any but the most desperate or irrational state. Any form of transport—airplane, boat, truck, or train—could conceivably be employed. Unlike a state, terrorists with a mobile base of operations need not be concerned with the threat of counter-attack, hence they are not subject to the deterrence of defense systems that constrains states.[43]

On a positive note, the study observed that there were "sufficient systemic constraints against nuclearly-armed [*sic*] terrorists that non-state actors seem more likely to be an aberration than a characteristic of nuclear proliferation." Among these constraints: a nuclear terrorist group would have to be "well-established and well-financed," the bomb might be too large for nonmissile or nonplane delivery, and the group would be "the most sensitive to adverse public reactions."[44]

LOOSE NUKES AND THE JIHADIST TERROR THREAT

When the Soviet Union disbanded on December 25, 1991, the IC was deeply troubled about the Red Army's command and control of its nuclear arsenal.[45] The Soviet arsenal, consisting of more than thirty thousand nuclear warheads, was dispersed throughout eleven time zones in Russia, in all fifteen former Soviet republics, as well as in East Germany, Hungary, Poland, Bulgaria, and Czechoslovakia.[46] A June 1991 NIE, titled "Implications of Alternative Soviet Futures," warned that the worst-case scenario would be a fragmentation of the Soviet Union in which Moscow lost any effective central control over its former republics. According to the NIE,

> This scenario is potentially the most dangerous for the West because of the chaos and unpredictability of events. Although the USSR would disappear as a cohesive military power, the prospects of nuclear and other weapons of mass destruction falling into the hands of some republics, mutinous troops, or radical groups would pose a new set of risks. . . . There would also be a greater chance for nuclear materials and expertise finding their way to foreign states seeking to develop nuclear weapons.[47]

Another NIE on the topic, written three months later, warned of the potential threats from fragmentation in more stark terms: "The disappearance of reliable central control over nuclear weapons in some republics, as well as uncertainty over their disposition, would increase the prospect of nuclear weapons falling into terrorist hands."[48]

As far as is known, the dissolution of the Soviet Union did not lead to the worst-case scenario—loose nukes in the hands of terrorists. But the loss of a nuclear warhead or fissile material from the 221 nuclear facilities in the former Soviet Union remained, in the words of FBI Director Louis Freeh, "the greatest long-term threat to the security of the United States."[49] In late 1994, the DCI's Joint Atomic Energy Intelligence Committee (JAEIC, pronounced "Jake")—an interagency group that meets bimonthly to discuss items related to nuclear intelligence—conducted a comprehensive examination that came to the chilling conclusion that "none of these facilities in Russia or other newly independent states had adequate safeguards or security measures by international standards for weapons-useable materials."[50] Although there are no known instances in which nuclear material leaked from Russia into terrorist hands, the CIA's National Intelligence Council later concluded that "weapons-grade and weapons-usable nuclear materials have been stolen from some Russian institutes. We assess that undetected smuggling has occurred." Although the report goes on to say that "we do not know the extent or magnitude of such thefts," it then lists four specific instances of smuggling between 1992 and 1999.[51]

Despite the U.S. Cooperative Threat Reduction program, which has advanced the goal of dismantling and securing the former Soviet nuclear arsenal since 1991, a September 1996 leaked CIA report demonstrated how persistent and challenging the problem of protecting Russia's nuclear weapons remained. The top secret report, "Prospects for Unsanctioned Use of Russian Nuclear Weapons," warned that "the Russian nuclear command and control system is being subjected to stresses it was not designed to withstand as a result of wrenching social change, economic hardship, and malaise within the armed forces." The report further noted that Russia's twenty-thousand-plus tactical nuclear weapons "appear to be the weapons most at risk"—a daunting assertion considering that some of these could have been carried by one person, weighing as little as sixty-five pounds.[52] Finally, the report shattered the false sense of security that Russia's weapons would ultimately be protected from unauthorized use by permissive action links, stating that "all technical [security] measures can be circumvented—probably within weeks or days depending on the weapons involved."[53]

Along with the threat of loose nuclear material, the decline of the Soviet Union assisted in creating the second significant modern nuclear terror threat. In February 1989, Moscow withdrew the last Red Army soldiers from Afghanistan, in effect conceding victory to the Islamic mujahideen. The Arab and Afghan jihadis, under the leadership of Osama Bin Laden and others, renamed their successful resistance organization al-Qaeda. As early as 1993, U.S. intelligence officials learned of Bin Laden's efforts to acquire nuclear materials or warheads from former Soviet republics.[54] These attempts failed as al-Qaeda brokers were conned into buying low-grade reactor fuel and radioactive waste.[55] In 1993, Jamal al-Fadl, a senior al-Qaeda operative, purchased a three-foot cylinder of weapons-grade uranium for $1.5 million from a former Sudanese military officer.[56] According to Michael Scheuer, former chief of the Bin Laden Unit in the CIA's Counterterrorism Center (CTC), by mid- to late 1996, the "Bin Laden unit acquired detailed information about the careful, professional manner in which al-Qaeda was seeking to acquire nuclear weapons . . . there could be no doubt after this date that al-Qaeda was in deadly earnest in seeking nuclear weapons."[57]

In 1993, the Pentagon's Office on Special Operations and Low Intensity Conflict convened a panel of forty-one retired intelligence analysts and counterterrorist experts to brainstorm about the evolution of international terrorism. Their still-classified report, *Terror 2000: The Future Face of Terrorism*, was a departure from other government-sponsored studies that catalogued the post–cold war terrorist groups and warned of their capabilities and intentions. The *Terror 2000* report predicted that terrorists would use chemical or biological agents on a major subway system; conduct multiple, simultaneous attacks to strain government response capabilities; strike a major financial center in the United States; and hijack civilian airliners to strike American landmarks. The report noted that "horrified civilians will get to watch every step in a terrorist plot. CNN and other networks will certainly air the footage."[58] This prescient report also concluded that

> easy access to biological, chemical and nuclear technologies will bring many new players to the game of mass destruction. They may not even be limited to states and traditional terrorist groups. Organized crime, fanatical single-issue groups and even individuals all will be able to acquire weapons once limited to regional and world powers. . . . [A WMD attack on the U.S.] is

increasingly probable, perhaps within the next five years.[59]

The *Terror 2000* report was reprinted and circulated within the Pentagon, Justice Department, and Federal Emergency Management Agency. A sanitized version was also prepared in book form for public consumption. The federal government, however, never released the report in declassified form because of concerns that it would inspire terrorists, that the scenarios were too far-fetched, and, in the words of report's manager, that it was "a little too scary for the times."[60]

September 11, 2001, demonstrated that the United States was both a host to, and victim of, attacks that former DCI George Tenet aptly described as "professionally conceived and executed."[61] Two facets of 9/11 caused the IC to reevaluate the threat of nuclear terrorism. First, the use of conventional means—civilian airliners—led the December 2001 NIE to conclude that "the Intelligence Community judges that U.S. territory is more likely to be attacked with WMD using nonmissile means—most likely from terrorists—than by missiles, primarily because nonmissile delivery means are less costly, easier to acquire, and more reliable and accurate."[62] It had been the opinion of the IC for decades that the political prestige and deterrence strength of missiles made them the weapon of choice for WMD attacks on the United States.[63]

Second, the avalanche of media and government investigations into 9/11, and documents recovered from al-Qaeda safe houses in Afghanistan, revealed that Osama bin Laden meant it when he declared in 1998 that obtaining a weapon of mass destruction was "a religious duty." A biannual CIA report to Congress on the "Acquisition of Technology Relating to Weapons of Mass Destruction and Advanced Conventional Munitions" said of the documents, "We have uncovered rudimentary diagrams of nuclear weapons inside a suspected al Qa'ida safehouse in Kabul. These diagrams, while crude, describe essential components—uranium and high explosives—common to nuclear weapons."[64] The fall of the Taliban also revealed that Bin Laden had met with scientists from the Pakistani nuclear weapons program on several occasions before 9/11, leading the CIA's Weapons Intelligence, Nonproliferation, and Arms Control unit to determine that al-Qaeda "probably had access to nuclear expertise

and facilities and that there was a real possibility of the group developing a crude nuclear device."[65] The Commission on the Intelligence Capabilities of the United States regarding Weapons of Mass Destruction later revealed that "[intelligence] analysts were largely unaware of the extent of al-Qa'ida's weapons of mass destruction research and development."[66]

In the past few years, the IC has focused on the threat of nuclear terrorism to an unprecedented extent. The NIC's 2020 Project report, *Mapping the Global Future*, aptly summarizes the IC's current consensus opinion on the subject:

> With advances in the design of simplified nuclear weapons, terrorists will continue to seek to acquire fissile material in order to construct a nuclear weapon. Concurrently, they can be expected to continue to purchase or steal a weapon, particularly in Russia or Pakistan. Given the possibility that terrorists could acquire nuclear weapons, the use of such weapons by extremists before 2020 cannot be ruled out.[67]

CONCLUSION

American intelligence estimates about the development of nuclear weapons by other states and their intentions for their use have been a mixed bag of quiet successes and notable failures. Knowing the capabilities and intentions of nonstate groups interested in obtaining nuclear weapons is undoubtedly a much more difficult proposition. Nevertheless, in reviewing the history of known intelligence estimates of the threat of nuclear terrorism, several important themes emerge: the proliferation of interest among nonstate actors in obtaining a bomb, the acknowledged ease with which terrorists could assemble a crude nuclear device, the ease with which any malicious actor could smuggle it into the United States, and the continued surprise of the U.S. government that this threat has persisted over a half century. The intelligence estimates presented above demonstrate beyond any doubt that the United States has been sufficiently warned about the very real possibility of a nuclear terror attack. If a terrorists' bomb were detonated on American soil tomorrow, given the sustained strategic warning that the IC has provided to policy makers, it would be a "bolt from the blue" only to the indifferent, but not the unaware.

NOTES

1. Scholars interested in further studying National Intelligence Estimates (NIEs) can visit the CIA's "Electronic Reading Room" Web site: http://www.foia.cia.gov/nic_collection.asp. There are more than one thousand declassified NIEs posted, searchable by title, geographic area, and function.

2. CIA, "Declassified on the Soviet Union and International Communism," http://www.foia.cia.gov/soviet_estimates.asp.

3. Senate Select Committee on Intelligence, *Report on the U.S. Intelligence Community's Prewar Intelligence Assessments on Iraq,* July 7, 2004, pp. 9–11, http://www.gpoaccess.gov/serialset/creports/iraq.html.

4. Ibid.

5. Testimony before the Senate Armed Services Committee, October 6, 2004.

6. Senate Select Committee on Intelligence, *Report on the U.S. Intelligence Community's Prewar Intelligence Assessments on Iraq,* 11; Richard Kerr, Thomas Wolfe, Rebecca Donegan, and Aris Pappas, "Intelligence and Analysis on Iraq: Issues for the Intelligence Community," *Studies in Intelligence* 49, no. 3 (2005): 47–54; and Commission on the Intelligence Capabilities of the United States regarding Weapons of Mass Destruction (WMD Commission), March 31, 2005, p. 10, http://www.wmd.gov/report/.

7. Highlighting the inherent difficulty of uncovering the nuclear intentions and capabilities of other states, *three weeks* after the first Soviet test, on September 20, 1949, the CIA issued Intelligence Memorandum no. 225, "Estimate of Status of Atomic Warfare in the USSR," which stated, "The current estimate of the Joint Nuclear Energy Intelligence Committee is that the earliest possible date by which the USSR might be expected to produce an atomic bomb is mid-1950 and that the most probable date is mid-1953."

8. CIA, ORE 91–49, "Estimate of the Effects of the Soviet Possession of the Atomic Bomb upon the Security of the United States and upon the Probabilities of Direct Soviet Military Action," April 6, 1950, p. 7.

9. CIA, NIE-3, "Soviet Capabilities and Intentions," November 15, 1950, p. 4.

10. CIA, NIE-31, "Soviet Capabilities for Clandestine Attack against the U.S. with Weapons of Mass Destruction and the Vulnerability of the U.S. to Such Attack," September 4, 1951.

11. CIA, SNIE 11–9–55, June 28, 1955.

12. Ibid., 2.

13. Customs agents were reportedly trained to search the luggage of some Soviet citizens traveling to the United States, but this would not have included diplomatic pouches. See "Customs Hunting Atom Smugglers," *New York Times,* February 16, 1954, p. 2.

14. The quote is attributed to the secretary of state, Dean Rusk, who stated, "We are eyeball to eyeball, and I think the other fellow just blinked." McGeorge Bundy, *Danger and Survival: Choices about the Bomb in the First Fifty Years* (New York: Random House, 1988), 405.

15. Graham Allison and Philip Zelikow, *Essence of Decision: Explaining the Cuban Missile Crisis,* 2nd ed. (New York: Longman, 1999), 204–5, 348.

16. CIA, NIE 85–62, "The Situation and Prospects in Cuba," March 12, 1962.

17. Anatoli I. Gribkov and William Y. Smith, *Operation Anadyr: U.S. and Soviet Generals Recount the Cuban Missile Crisis* (Chicago: Edition Q, Inc., 1994), 172.

18. Aleksandr Fursenko and Timothy Naftali, *One Hell of a Gamble: Khrushchev, Castro and Kennedy, 1958–1964* (New York: Norton, 1997), 315.

19. Timothy Naftali, *Blind Spot: The Secret History of American Counterterrorism* (New York: Basic Books, 2005), 17.

20. CIA, NIE 11–7–1963, "The Clandestine Introduction of Weapons of Mass Destruction into the U.S.," p. 4.

21. Joint Chiefs of Staff (JCS) Memorandum to Secretary of Defense Robert McNamara, "Clandestine Introduction of Nuclear Weapons to the United States," January 2, 1968, JCSM-3–68.

22. CIA, NIE 4–68, "The Clandestine Introduction of Weapons of Mass Destruction into the US," June 13, 1968.

23. CIE, NIE 4–70, "The Clandestine Introduction of Weapons of Mass Destruction into the US," July 7, 1970, pp. 4–5.

24. Naftali, *Blind Spot,* 18.

25. Freeman Dyson, Robert Gomer, S. Courtenay Wright, and Stephen Weinberg, *Tactical Nuclear Weapons in Southeast Asia* (Washington, DC: Institute for Defense Analyses, March 1967).

26. Ibid., 46.

27. These reports were not actually published weekly. See Naftali, *Blind Spot,* 55.

28. CIA, author David L. Milbank, Research Study, "International and Transnational Terrorism: Diagnosis and Prognosis," April 1976.

29. Ibid., 4–5.

30. J. Samuel Walker, *Containing the Atom: Nuclear Regulation in a Changing Environment, 1963–1971* (Berkeley: University of California Press, 1992), 227.

31. Office of Technology Assessment (OTA), Nuclear Proliferation and Safeguards: Appendix Volume II, Part One, June 1977, pp. 28, 39.

32. Walker, *Containing the Atom,* 229.

33. "Report to the Atomic Energy Commission by the Ad Hoc Advisory Panel on Safeguarding Special Nuclear Material," March 10, 1967. Reprinted in U.S. Senate, Committee on Government

Operations, *Peaceful Nuclear Exports and Weapons Proliferation: A Compendium,* April 29, 1975, p. 567.

34. Matthew Bunn, "The History of U.S. Nuclear Security: What Factors Have Driven Improvement Efforts?" (unpublished manuscript, n.d.).

35. J. Scott Walker, "Regulating against Nuclear Terrorism: The Domestic Safeguards Issue, 19701979," *Technology and Culture* 42 (January 2001): 118.

36. David Rosenbaum, John N. Googin, Robert M. Jefferson, Daniel J. Kleitman, and William C. Sullivan, *Special Safeguards Study,* April 1974. Reprinted in U.S. Senate, *Peaceful Nuclear Exports and Weapons Proliferation,* 467.

37. Walker, "Regulating against Nuclear Terrorism," 120.

38. Robert S. Norris, William M. Arkin, and William Burr, "Where They Were," *Bulletin of the Atomic Scientists* 55, no. 6 (1999): 26–35.

39. Frank Greve, "Warhead Depots: A Weak Link in NATO's Security," *Philadelphia Inquirer,* March 13, 1983, p. F2.

40. Hans M. Kristensen, *U.S. Nuclear Weapons in Europe: A Review of Post-Cold War Policy, Force Levels, and War Planning* (Washington, DC: Natural Resources Defense Council, February 2005), 24; and Greve, "Warhead Depots," F2.

41. Richard Burt, "Pentagon Games Simulates a Nuclear Blackmail Case," *New York Times,* November 15, 1977, p. 10.

42. Ibid., 10.

43. CIA, Directorate of Intelligence, Office of Political Research, "Managing Nuclear Proliferation: The Politics of Limited Choice," December 1975, p. 29, http://www.gwu.edu/?nsarchiv/NSAEBB/NSAEBB155/prolif-15.pdf.

44. Ibid., 30–31.

45. Robert M. Gates, *From the Shadows: The Ultimate Insider's Story of Five Presidents and How They Won the Cold War* (New York: Touchstone, 1996), 528.

46. Robert Norris and Hans Kristensen, "Global Nuclear Stockpiles, 1945–2002," *Bulletin of the Atomic Scientists* 58, no. 6 (2002): 103–4; and Robert Norris and William Arkin, "Estimated Russian Stockpile," *Bulletin of the Atomic Scientists* 51, no. 5 (1995): 62–63.

47. CIA, NIE—11–18–1991, "Implications of Alternative Soviet Futures," June 1, 1991, p. 10.

48. CIA, SNIE—11–18.2–9, "The Republics of the Former USSR: The Outlook for the Next Year," September 1, 1991, p. 16.

49. General Accounting Office (GAO), *Nuclear Safety: Concerns with Nuclear Facilities and Other Sources of Radiation in the Former Soviet Union,* November 1995, p. 1; and Testimony before the Senate Committee on Governmental Affairs, "International Organized Crime and Its Impact on the U.S." May 25, 1994.

50. Matthew Bunn, "Cooperation to Secure Nuclear Stockpiles: A Case of Constrained Innovation," *Innovations: Technology, Governance, Globalization* 1 (1): 121, 136, fn. 5; and John Deutch, Testimony before the Senate Committee on Government Affairs, "Global Proliferation of Weapons of Mass Destruction, Part II," March 20, 1996. For information on the Joint Atomic Energy Intelligence Committee (JAEIC), see Jeffrey T. Richelson, "Verification: The Ways and Means," *Bulletin of the Atomic Scientists* 54, no. 6 (1998): 53–54.

51. CIA, National Intelligence Council, "Annual Report to Congress on the Safety and Security of Russian Nuclear Facilities and Military Forces," February 2002, pp. 2–3, http://www.dni.gov/nic/special_ russiannucfac.html.

52. Nikolai Sokov, "'Suitcase Nukes': Permanently Lost Luggage" (Monterey, CA: Center for Nonproliferation Studies, Monterey Institute of International Studies, February 13, 2004).

53. Bill Gertz, "Russian Renegades Pose Nuke Danger," *Washington Times,* October 22, 1996, p. A1.

54. Douglas Waller, "Inside the Hunt for Osama," *Time,* December 21, 1998, p. 32.

55. Ibid., 32.

56. National Commission on Terrorist Attacks upon the United States, *The 9/11 Commission Report* (New York: Norton, 2004), 60.

57. Anonymous, "How *Not* to Catch a Terrorist," *Atlantic Monthly,* December 2004, p. 50.

58. Joby Warrick and Joe Stephens, "Before Attack, U.S. Expected Different Hit," *Washington Post,* October 2, 2001, p. A1.

59. Robin Wright, "Prophetic 'Terror 2000' Mapped Evolving Threat," *Los Angeles Times,* August 9, 1998, p. A1.

60. Warrick and Stephens, "Before Attack, U.S. Expected Different Hit," p. A1.

61. George J. Tenet, "Unclassified Version of Director of Central Intelligence George J. Tenet's Testimony before the Joint Inquiry into Terrorist Attacks against the United States," June 18, 2002, http://www.cia.gov/cia/public_affairs/speeches/2002/dci_testimony_06182002.html.

62. CIA, NIE, "Foreign Missile Developments and the Ballistic Missile Threat through 2015," December 2001.

63. One month after 9/11, a CIA agent, code-named DRAGONFIRE, reported that terrorists had obtained a ten-kiloton nuclear weapon from Russia and planned to smuggle it into New York City. After weeks of investigating, intelligence officials determined DRAGONFIRE's information was false. See Massimo Calabresi and Romesh Ratnesar, "Can We Stop the Next Attack?" *Time,* March 11, 2002, p. 24.

64. CIA, *Unclassified Report to Congress on the Acquisition of Technology Relating to Weapons of Mass Destruction and Advanced Conventional Munitions, 1*

January through 30 June 2001, published January 30, 2002.

65. The WINPAC report was produced on November 23, 2001. As quoted in WMD Commission, pp. 271, 277, fn. 66.

66. WMD Commission, p. 273.

67. National Intelligence Council, *Mapping the Global Future,* Report of the National Intelligence Council's 2020 Project, December 2004, p. 95, http://www.dni.gov/nic/NIC_globaltrend2020.html.

9

COUNTERTERRORISM

The greatest dangers to liberty lurk in insidious encroachment by men of zeal—well-meaning but without understanding.

—Louis D. Brandeis

The attacks of September 11, 2001, seared the consciousness of the United States, provoking calls for military retaliation abroad and new antiterrorism laws at home. The ensuing military operations to wrest Osama bin Laden away from his hosts, the Taliban government of Afghanistan, failed to capture either bin Laden or Mullah Omar, the head of the Taliban. Although the Taliban regime and al-Qaeda troops were forced to flee Afghanistan and an ostensibly pro-U.S. government was installed, the Taliban recently appear to be making a resurgence in some areas of the country. The apparent failure of the coercive diplomacy used in Afghanistan has been attributed to several factors, especially the Taliban's Pushtunwali code of honor and their brand of ultra-extremism, both of which have made them seemingly impervious to U.S. intervention (Tarzi, 2005).

The war against Iraq is still ongoing as this book goes to print. Although weapons of mass destruction, whose alleged presence in Iraq prompted the war, were never found, the U.S. military presence in the country may continue to grow. As of January 10, 2007, more than 3,000 U.S. military personnel have died since the beginning of the Iraq War in March 2003. Our allies have also suffered casualties, although on a lesser scale: 128 British, 33 Italians, 18 soldiers each from the Ukraine and Poland, 13 Bulgarians, 11 Spaniards, and fewer for the other allies of Denmark, El Salvador, Slovakia, Latvia, Estonia, The Netherlands, Thailand, Australia, Hungary, Kazakhstan, and Romania (*Guardian Unlimited*, 2007). It is difficult to obtain accurate estimates on how many Iraqi citizens have been killed, but a survey by an American and Iraqi team of public health researchers found that more than 600,000 Iraqi deaths have been caused by the invasion (Burnham, Doocy, Dzeng, Lafta, & Roberts, 2006). President George Bush proposed in January 2007 to send additional troops and increase the war budget (Hunt, 2007, p. 1).

Although the link between al-Qaeda and Saddam Hussein's regime was likely weak before the U.S. invasion, one thing is clear: The war in Iraq is serving as a battlefield and a rallying cry for terrorists who have direct and indirect connections to al-Qaeda. Nesser (2006) analyzed Jihadism in Western Europe after the invasion and occupation of Iraq and found a significant "spillover effect" from the war. Terrorist groups that share al-Qaeda's philosophy that "Muslims are under a worldwide military attack from the United States, Israel, and their allies" have sent an untold number of recruits to Iraq (Nesser, 2006, p. 324); the Iraq War has also inspired terrorism in other areas around the globe.

More than ever before, a government's counterterrorism policy is seen as an integral part of its foreign affairs strategy. New alliances and shifting priorities will likely characterize counter-terrorism foreign policy for years to come.

Domestic counterterrorism policies in the United States and elsewhere have likewise been subject to change in the post–September 11 world. Demonstrating a renewed focus on terrorism, on October 8, 2001, President George W. Bush created the Department of Homeland Security, which was first headed by Tom Ridge, former governor of Pennsylvania. The department's mission is to develop a national strategy for detecting, protecting, and responding to terrorist assaults. Among the priorities identified by the new office are airport security, emergency response teams, border security, and biodefense. Anyone who has flown on a commercial airline in the past few years has been exposed to the most visible component of the Department of Homeland Security: TSA (Transportation Security Administration) officers at security checkpoints.

A proliferation of state networks of surveillance, created to enhance domestic security, have increased the power of governments all over the world (Shields, 2006). To succeed in the long run, domestic counterterrorism strategies in the United States and in other democratic societies must preserve cherished principles of liberty and equality, and government officials must resist the temptation to diminish the freedoms on which democracies are based.

This chapter discusses counterterrorism policy from two interrelated perspectives: foreign and domestic affairs.

COUNTERTERRORISM AND FOREIGN POLICY

Before September 11, 2001, citizens of the United States and its holdings, both at home and abroad, were increasingly targets of terrorism, but the United States itself was far from the most targeted nation in the world. Colombia suffered the most terrorist incidents in 2000, many of which involved bombings of a multinational oil pipeline that was a symbol to many people of the oppressiveness of the United States. India was second in 2000 and had already been the target of the airline attack that caused the greatest number of deaths before September 11— the 1985 bombing of an Air India jet off the coast of Ireland that killed all 329 people aboard. The U.S. Department of State blamed Sikh and Kashmiri terrorists for that attack.

Since September 12, 2001, North America has witnessed the fewest number of terrorist fatal-ities and injuries of any region on the globe, with the Middle East/Persian Gulf region experi-encing the most (see Table 9.1).

Before 2001, roughly one-third of all terrorist attacks worldwide had been aimed at U.S. citizens or property outside the country, and the proportion was higher in the 1990s than in the 1980s (Pillar, 2001). The pattern is continuing in the first decade of the 21st century. In addi-tion, attacks against citizens of countries that support the United States or that cater to tourists from the United States and their allies show no sign of easing.

A Global Perspective on Transnational Terrorism

Varying explanations have been offered as to why the United States and its interests are so attractive to transnational terrorists. Most of the explanations center on the changes wrought in international politics by the collapse of the Soviet Union and the end of the Cold War. The emergence of the United States as the world's only remaining economic and military super-power has fueled resentment in many areas around the globe. In addition, the opportunities for terrorism against the United States are magnified by the open nature of our society; our long, virtually undefended borders; the enormous number of international visitors to our land; and the many visible signs of our presence around the world.

Many observers believe that poverty and injustice contribute to terrorism, and they argue that counterterrorism activities should include attempts to improve living conditions in less pros-perous countries (Schweitzer, 1998). Although a long-term strategy to provide disadvantaged

TABLE 9.1   Terrorist Incidents by Region, September 12, 2001–January 11, 2007

	Incidents	Injuries	Fatalities
Africa	198	1,290	935
East & Central Asia	59	67	53
Eastern Europe	804	3,521	1,340
Latin America & the Caribbean	1,133	1,907	1,073
Middle East/Persian Gulf	9,975	35,648	19,741
North America	65	54	9
South Asia	3,954	13,162	5,594
Southeast Asia & Oceania	1,058	3,403	1,157
Western Europe	1,517	1,277	285
Total	18,763	60,329	30,187

SOURCE: MIPT Terrorism Knowledge Base. TKB incidents by region (9/12/01–1/11/2007). Retrieved January 11, 2007, from http://www.tkb.org

people with employment and other opportunities for a better life might deter some potential terrorists, it would be ineffective in discouraging the most fanatic. A "core of incorrigibles," including but not limited to al-Qaeda, seems determined to wreak violence against the United States and its allies.

Chapter 3 discussed the conceptual clash postulated by Barber (1992, 1995) between "Jihad" and "McWorld." Barber predicts that religious extremism and global capitalism are on a collision course that inevitably will lead to violent confrontation. Following the September 11 attacks, as many Americans struggled to understand how such horrific events could have happened, Barber's argument gained renewed attention.

According to Barber, the forces of "McWorld"—which include the international marketing of American pop culture, fast food, and violent videogames, among other elements—are deeply offensive to the religious value systems of many Muslims and Arabs. In an interview shortly after September 11, 2001, Barber said that the aggressive marketing of American products had left many people in other nations with a distorted image of the United States. He observed, "We don't even export the best of our *own* culture, as defined by serious music, by jazz, by poetry, by our extraordinary literature, our playwrights—we export the worst, the most childish, the most base, the most trivial of our culture. And we call that American" (Rosenfeld, 2001, ¶ 20 of print article).

Barber argues that consumerist capitalism and religious fundamentalism are both threats to the development of global democracy. The only way to avoid an unprecedented explosion of violence is to promote democracy around the world: "If we export capitalism without democracy, we breed anarchy and terrorism" (Rosenfeld, 2001, ¶ 16). Few genuine democracies exist in those portions of Africa and Asia believed to be the wellspring of much of the terrorism directed against the United States today; many are ruled by kings, military dictators, or clerics.

Samuel Huntington is another author whose mid-1990s book has been quoted frequently since September 11. In *The Clash of Civilization and the Remaking of the World Order,* Huntington (1996) identifies eight civilizations: Sinic (China, Vietnam, Korea), Japanese, Hindu-Indian, Islamic, Orthodox-Russian, Western, Latin American, and African. He predicts that conflicts in the 21st century will not be between nations but between distinct civilizations that have different cultures and religions. This clash of civilizations will dominate global politics and define the battle lines of the future. Huntington predicts that the greatest conflicts will be between the predominantly Christian nations of the West and Muslim nations in Africa and Asia.

In an interview after September 11, 2001, Huntington said the current war against terrorism did not meet his definition of clashing civilizations because the governments of many Muslim and Arab nations were cooperating with the United States in fighting terrorism. Huntington expressed concern, however, that the West's counterterrorism strikes, including the war against the Taliban, might enrage citizens of Muslim and Arab nations, making them more likely to attempt to overthrow the pro-U.S. governments in the region. Huntington said, "I fear that while September 11 united the West, the response to September 11th will unite the Muslim world" (Healy, 2001). Pakistan may be particularly vulnerable to violent revolution because of its high concentration of ethnic Pashtuns, who are the same ethnicity as the Taliban (Rashid, 2001). Pakistan's nuclear arsenal in the possession of extremists is a frightening scenario.

Huntington's thesis has been criticized for being too simplistic and ignoring the numerous currents and countercurrents that define any religion or culture. The late Edward W. Said (2001) argued that civilizations are much more complex and varied than Huntington admits:

> The personification of enormous entities called "the West" and "Islam" is recklessly affirmed, as if hugely complicated matters like identity and culture existed in a cartoon-like world where Popeye and Bluto bash each other mercilessly, with one always more virtuous pugilist getting the upper hand over his adversary. (p. 1, ¶ 3)

Said further faulted the clash of civilization concept for not recognizing "that the major contest in most modern cultures concerns the definition or interpretation of each culture. . . . [A] great deal of demagogy and downright ignorance is involved in presuming to speak for a whole religion or civilization" (p. 1, ¶ 3). Instead of seeing verification of a clash of cultures in the September 11 attacks, Said argued that we should look at the attacks as a "carefully planned and horrendous, pathologically motivated suicide attack and mass slaughter by a small group of deranged militants" (p. 1, ¶ 5).

The United Nations' Response to Terrorism

No international criminal code, international police force capable of combating terrorism, or international court with jurisdiction over all acts of terrorism exists. Governments around the globe nevertheless engage in collaborative counterterrorism activities, primarily by passing laws against terrorism and entering into cooperative agreements with one another. Many examples of cooperation among nations were seen in the aftermath of the September 11 attacks.

The membership of the United Nations (UN), which was founded in 1945 following World War II by 51 "peace loving" nations, has grown to 192 member states. The UN's mission is to maintain international peace and security, promote human rights, and help member states resolve political, cultural, and economic problems. In fulfillment of that mission, member states have signed many global treaties, regional conventions, and bilateral agreements. The UN Charter governs the use of force between states, and several conventions and treaties outline the obligations of the member states. Thirteen major multinational conventions detail states' responsibilities for combating terrorism. Among these are several conventions against offenses committed aboard aircraft and against diplomats and senior government officials, against unlawful taking of nuclear materials and plastic explosives, against taking of hostages, and against ships or fixed offshore platforms on the continental shelf. The UN General Assembly and the Security Council also pass resolutions aimed at specific states. For example, in 2000, the Security Council called on Afghanistan's Taliban to close its terrorist training camps, stop providing sanctuary to international terrorists, and cooperate with international efforts to bring indicted terrorists to justice (UN Resolution 1333, December 19, 2000).

Shortly after 9/11, the UN Security Council adopted Resolution 1376, which required member states to adopt strict regulations against terrorism and created a Counter-Terrorism Committee. In a subsequent study of Resolution 1376, researchers found that compliance was "spotty" and "even where the international community has reached a resolute commitment, implementation will not necessarily follow" (Stiles & Thayne, 2006, p. 167).

In 2006, the UN "opened a new phase in their counter-terrorism efforts by agreeing on a global strategy to counter terrorism. . . . This is the first time that all Member States have agreed to a common strategic approach to fight terrorism, not only sending a clear message that terrorism is unacceptable in all its forms and manifestations but also resolving to take practical steps individually and collectively to prevent and combat it" (United Nations General Assembly, 2006). The strategy calls for a high level of cooperation among members, as well as measures to address conditions conducive to the spread of terrorism, and is reprinted in Appendix B.

The UN has been criticized as being ineffective against terrorism. Member states have in the past argued about who are the aggressors and who are the victims. Many nations object when more powerful members of the UN try to impose their views of what constitutes terrorism. For example, Israel repeatedly has asserted that a state that supports terrorism is guilty of an armed attack on the state that is victimized. However, the UN Security Council has condemned many of the counterterrorism operations conducted by Israel or condemnation has been avoided only by a veto by the United States (Travalio, 2000).

International Cooperation and the Use of Military Forces

Nonstate-sponsored terrorism committed against the citizens or holdings of a state generally is not a violation of international law, but rather a violation of the domestic criminal laws of the victim state or the state where the terrorist act occurred. *State-sponsored terrorism* is a violation of international law that invokes the victimized state's right of self-defense (Sharp, 2000, p. 37). Disputes exist about the degree of culpability necessary to label a state a sponsor of terrorism. The UN Charter gives victim states the right to respond with military force in the event of an "armed attack," but does not define that term. A weak government that cannot prevent terrorists from using its country for training or recruiting, or as a base from which to launch attacks, is not considered guilty of an armed attack on another state (Travalio, 2000, p. 152). On the other hand, there is "a raging debate among international lawyers" over whether a state that provides active support for international terrorists is engaged in an armed attack. Clearly, the United States and its allies considered the Taliban's support of al-Qaeda as an armed attack justifying military intervention.

The United States was not alone in its military response to September 11. The day after the attack, the 19 members of NATO agreed to invoke NATO's mutual defense clause, which considers an attack on one member an attack on all, as long as the United States supplied evidence of the involvement of bin Laden and al-Qaeda. On October 2, 2001, NATO announced that the United States had provided the necessary "clear and compelling proof." NATO nations granted the United States open access to their airfields and seaports and agreed to enhance intelligence cooperation relating to terrorist threats. Putting a stamp of approval on America's decision to attack Afghanistan, NATO also agreed to send its military troops into combat as necessary. NATO has grown to 26 member countries as the European Union has expanded, and it is currently involved in providing training, equipment, and other noncombat forms of assistance in Iraq.

Other nations, including many predominantly Muslim and Arab nations such as Pakistan, Saudi Arabia, and Egypt, also offered to cooperate in the hunt for those behind the September 11 attacks. Governments around the world, including those in Africa, the Middle East, and Asia, are threatened by extremism. A large American military presence, some fear, could provoke a popular uprising capable of toppling the governments that assist the United States. With these concerns in mind, the United States sought nonmilitary support from some countries, including use of airspace and sharing of intelligence information. Uzbekistan, a primarily Muslim nation that borders Afghanistan, allowed the United States to station forces there to launch search-and-rescue missions. An offer of cooperation even came from Sudan, although it was not accepted. Just three years earlier, the United States had launched a cruise missile attack in the Sudanese capital, Khartoum, based on a belief that a suspected chemical weapons factory was implicated in the bombings of the U.S. embassies in Kenya and Tanzania.

The United States also received considerable international cooperation in seizing terrorists' assets. President Bush issued an expanded list of organizations and suspected associates of terrorists, and he authorized the Treasury Department to halt transactions with any banks that refused to freeze terrorists' assets. Nations were asked to seize the assets of many groups and individuals believed to be associated with global terrorism.

After September 11, the Bush administration announced that its war on terrorism would extend far beyond Afghanistan and bin Laden. Cautioning that the war would be protracted, the president portrayed the war in Afghanistan as only the first stage of a multistage effort. And as was soon made evident in Iraq, the United States has demonstrated a willingness to invade and occupy other countries.

Many unintended and unwanted consequences resulted from the occupation of Iraq. For example, the practice of torture, although widely condemned in the past by most nations, is now considered by some as a necessary component of a successful counterterrorism strategy. Because "torture has been recognized as a most profound violation of human dignity," it appears that the "U.S. executive branch has been attempting to reduce the scope of what is meant by torture and degrading treatment, as well as to define a category of detainees who can be subjected to coercive methods of interrogation" (Foot, 2006, pp. 132–133).

Images of the torture and sadistic treatment of prisoners in Abu Ghraib, a U.S.-run prison in Iraq, horrified much of the world. In the U.S. detention facility at Guantanamo Bay in Cuba, prisoners from around the world have been housed for prolonged periods without access to lawyers, without formal charges, and with few human rights. Gordon (2006) argues that "[e]xcessive force, civil disability and the loss of internationally guaranteed rights, and indefinite detention are central means by which the wars on both terror and crime (civilian mass imprisonment) are executed" (p. 42). Gordon (2006) further observes that the photographs from Abu Ghraib "most closely resemble the photographs taken of lynchings in the U.S. between the 1880s and the 1930s; resemble them not only in their images of White women and men smiling and grinning at the mutilated bodies of Black women and men hanging from trees and posts, but also in the extent to which they were openly distributed and sold as keepsakes of an afternoon well-spent" (p. 44).

Yet, the United States is not alone in using questionable methods toward its prisoners. Governments around the globe have done likewise throughout history and many continue to do so (see Chapter 2).

The risks and burdens of America's and other nations' foreign policy are not fully known, but history suggests that retaliation begets retaliation.

The High Cost of Retaliation

Many terrorist experts and policymakers endorse the concept that a strong offense is the best defense, but some warn that the United States is partially responsible for the heightened terrorist threat the world faces. According to the Pentagon's Defense Science Board (1997), "historical data show a strong correlation between U.S. involvement in international situations and an increase in terrorist attacks against the United States" (p. 15). Eland (1998) further examines the correlations noted by the Defense Science Board and concludes that American military intervention in foreign countries inevitably led terrorists to retaliate against the United States. It is not American pop culture, depravity, or materialism that provokes terrorism, Eland argues; instead, it is America's exercise of its military might overseas.

Eland suggests that the number of attacks against the United States could be reduced if it used military restraint in other countries. Tracing retaliatory terrorist incidents since 1915, Eland (1998) observes that

> the interventionist foreign policy currently pursued by the United States is an aberration in its history. Adopting a policy of military restraint would return the United States to the traditional foreign policy it pursued for the first century and a half of its existence before the Cold War distorted it. (p. 7)

Proposals to return to a less interventionist foreign policy are controversial, and many observers believe that, in the long run, aggressive responses to terrorism will reduce future

PHOTO 9.1   Ali Shalah, who said he was tortured by U.S. guards at Abu Ghraib prison in Iraq, delivers a speech at an antiwar conference in Kuala Lumpur, Malaysia, in 2007.

attacks against the United States. Others argue, as does the author of the first reprint for this chapter, that aggressive tactics produce a blowback effect that intensifies terrorism.

Because there is no agreement on the root causes of terrorism, it is difficult to agree on the proper scope of foreign counterterrorism policy. Domestic counterterrorism policy is similarly contentious.

DOMESTIC COUNTERTERRORISM

Counterterrorism activities within a nation's own borders operate in the context of each nation's laws and policies, history, politics, and culture. In democratic societies, "the rule of law is guaranteed by the legitimacy legal norms enjoy from whom such norms apply, on one hand, and by the threat of enforcement from specialized agents of control, on the other" (Deflem,

2006, p. 240). But how vigorously can a democratic country fight terrorism and remain a democracy? How can democracies play by their own rules when terrorists obey no rules? Which of our civil liberties should we be willing to give up, and what kind of proof do we need that sacrificing personal freedom is an effective antidote to terrorism?

Should the U.S. follow Israel in using barriers to keep out terrorists (and nonterrorists) from its borders? For example, because of the extreme impact of terrorism in Jerusalem, where Arabs and Jews live in small, separate neighborhoods, Israel counterterrorism authorities have felt justified in building concrete barriers (Savitch & Garb, 2006). Envisioning the United States encircled in fences or concrete walls is troubling for many, although some would like to see a barrier built at the border with Mexico.

The United Kingdom has long been plagued by the IRA terrorist campaign. The Northern Ireland Act suspended many civil liberties and allowed British military personnel to search the homes, seize the property, and imprison suspected terrorists without a warrant; roughly a quarter of a million such searches were conducted (Martin, 2006). When two IRA bombs exploded in London's financial district in 1993 and 1994, the government began installing a "ring of steel"—a network of closed-circuit television cameras. Since then, the British use of surveillance cameras has burgeoned: an estimated 2.5 million cameras exist throughout the city (Rosen, 2001, p. 304).

In the 1990s, the Algerian government established special emergency courts to prosecute suspected terrorists. Before the fighting ended in 1999 with the government's offer of amnesty, nearly 10,000 people were sentenced to death or imprisoned for terrorist activities (Martin, 2006). In Italy the terrorists of the Red Brigade, which terrorized the country during the 1970s and 1980s, were granted amnesty. Should the United States do likewise and offer amnesty to terrorists?

There are, of course, no easy answers. Balancing civil liberty with homeland protection is especially complex and dynamic in governments claiming to abide by democratic processes.

The discussion to follow centers on four aspects of U.S. domestic counterterrorism policy:

1. Laws: provisions of and controversies around recent antiterrorism legislation, including the USA PATRIOT Act (2001) passed in response to September 11 and reauthorized in 2006

2. Detentions and military tribunals: rights and treatment of enemy combatants and noncitizens

3. Law enforcement: sharing information on terrorists to "connect the dots"

4. Historical examples: three infamous and overreaching counterterrorism operations from U.S. history that may shed light on current antiterrorism activities

Legislating Against Terrorism

Many nations treat terrorism as a criminal act, not a political one. Outlawing terrorism implies faith in the legal system, and antiterrorism legislation in democratic countries generally incorporates constitutional rights and judicial review (White, 1998). Critics of the U.S. government's counterterrorism policy have long argued that lawmakers overrate terrorist threats to achieve their political goals, with the result that civil liberties are sacrificed without an increase in public safety. Similar criticisms have been leveled against the two U.S. antiterrorism laws discussed below: the Antiterrorist Act of 1996 and the USA PATRIOT Act of 2001 (reauthorized in 2006).

Antiterrorism Act of 1996

The Antiterrorism and Effective Death Penalty Act of 1996 was the culmination and merger of disparate legislative efforts, some of them stretching back more than a decade. The bombings of the World Trade Center in 1993 and of the Alfred P. Murrah Federal Building in Oklahoma City in 1995 supplied the impetus for the 1996 law, although other issues such as habeas corpus and immigration aided passage of the bill. Most of the criticism against the legislation focused on its domestic law enforcement provisions, not those relating to foreign policy (Pillar, 2001).

The 1996 law made some terrorist acts federal crimes punishable by death, thereby avoiding statute of limitation restrictions that apply to nondeath penalty crimes. It established a formal list of Foreign Terrorist Organizations (FTOs) to be designated by the Secretary of State. Blocking FTO financing was an integral part of the bill, and it froze those groups' assets. Penalties of up to 10 years in prison were established for anyone supplying material support or resources to an FTO. The law also prohibited the provision of support for humanitarian purposes, such as funding to schools and hospitals affiliated with FTOs.

In addition, the law revived a previous practice of denying visas to foreigners based merely on their membership in terrorist groups; no proof that the individual furthered the illegal activities of the group was necessary. Further, the bill authorized deportation of anyone who was associated with a terrorist group at the time of otherwise legal entry into the United States.

Before implementation of the law, the FBI had been prohibited from opening or expanding a criminal investigation if the basis for the investigation was an activity protected by the First Amendment, such as speech or assembly. The prohibition was repealed. The law permitted private citizens who were victimized by terrorism to file suit for damages against state sponsors in U.S. courts. This provision created an exception to the doctrine of sovereign immunity that normally protects states from being sued. In addition and not directly related to terrorism, the 1996 act placed a one-year statute of limitations on habeas corpus petitions, which allow federal courts to review cases of inmates who claim that state courts violated their constitutional rights.

Critics argue that the 1996 antiterrorist legislation was "one of the worst assaults on the Constitution in decades" (Dempsey & Cole, 1999, p. 2). The charges leveled against the act include the following:

- The bill added to the chaos surrounding a capital punishment system already fraught with error. Further, many foreign nations oppose the death penalty and might be unwilling to cooperate with U.S. efforts to apprehend terrorists on foreign soil if doing so might lead to their execution. Members of the European Union, for example, refuse to extradite fugitives to the United States without an assurance that the death penalty will not be sought (Pillar, 2001, p. 85).
- Following the terrorist money trail is extremely difficult and unlikely to achieve results. Most of the financial transactions of terrorists take place outside the United States, and many also take place outside formal banking systems. Terrorists use multiple false names that obscure their ties with one another. Informal money-by-wire arrangements are common, as are the physical movements of currency from the hands of one terrorist to another. Offshore banking businesses make it easier to conceal financial transactions, and the complex organizational links among overlapping groups make it unlikely that terrorists' "lifeblood" can be controlled sufficiently through U.S. legislation.
- Making crimes of activities protected by the First Amendment, including support for peaceful humanitarian and political activities of groups labeled as terrorist, resurrects the concept of guilt by association.
- The law denies deportees basic due process rights, especially the right to confront their accusers.
- The law's limits on the "Great Writ" of habeas corpus are unrelated to terrorism and serve the political agenda of conservatives without increasing public safety.

Supporters of the bill acknowledged that some of the criticisms might be valid, but they argued that tough measures were needed to protect the public. As discussed below, somewhat similar criticisms were leveled against the USA PATRIOT Act, passed in the aftermath of the September 11 attacks and reauthorized in 2006 in very similar form.

The USA PATRIOT Act

Shortly after the September 11 attacks, President Bush asked Congress to enact another counterterrorism package. Unlike the 1996 law, which was the product of a full year of legislative debate, the act to "Provide Appropriate Tools Required to Intercept and Obstruct Terrorism" (the USA PATRIOT Act) sailed quickly through Congress, passing the House of Representatives by a vote of 356 to 66 and the Senate by 98 to 1. The sole dissenting senator, Russell D. Feingold (D-Wisc.), said that the bill's search and seizure provisions were unconstitutional, as was punishing people for vague associations with possible terrorist organizations. Nevertheless, the lopsided vote was a clear indication of the support of Congress for domestic counterterrorism operations. President Bush signed the USA PATRIOT Act into law on October 26, 2001, less than six weeks after 9/11.

The Act is best known for authorizing indeterminate periods of imprisonment, without due process protections, for foreigners suspected of terrorism, as well as for permitting new forms of surveillance on U.S. citizens (Paye, 2006). Although many laws that potentially violate privacy rights were enacted long before 2001, the PATRIOT Act has become a lightning rod for criticism.

The Act significantly expanded law enforcement's investigative powers under the Foreign Intelligence Surveillance Act of 1978 (FISA), which had been enacted in response to the inappropriate use of wiretaps by the administration of President Richard Nixon. The FISA was intended to serve as a "firewall between foreign and domestic intelligence gathering" (Jaeger, Bertot, & McClure, 2003, p. 297). By separating the two types of electronic surveillance, the FISA was designed to preserve Fourth Amendment protections for U.S. citizens in criminal cases while allowing much lower standards of proof for obtaining court orders from the Foreign Intelligence Surveillance Court (FISC) for surveillance of foreign nationals. Initially designed as a judicial check on executive power, the secret FISC procedures appear to have become a rubber stamp for the executive branch: from 1979 to 1999, the FISC granted all of the 11,883 FISA warrants requested during that period by the Attorney General's Office (Jaeger et al., 2003, p. 297).

The PATRIOT Act expanded the scope of FISA investigations, requiring only that foreign intelligence activities be a *significant* purpose (as opposed to the *sole* purpose) of an investigation. This change removed a major component of the "firewall" distinction between foreign and domestic surveillance. Further, the records that could be collected were no longer limited to specific, narrow categories; instead, law enforcement authorities could examine "any tangible thing," such as books, records, papers, and other documents. The PATRIOT Act also prohibited subjects from disclosing that they had received a FISA order.

The major provisions of the 2001 Act included the following:

- *Roving wiretaps.* Law enforcement officials could obtain a wiretap warrant from FISC for a wiretap on any telephone used by a suspected terrorist. Previously, separate authorization had been needed for each phone used by the suspect.
- *"Sneak-and-peek."* These provisions allowed federal investigators to secretly enter and search private domains, such as electronic records, homes, and offices, while the occupant is elsewhere. During the surreptitious search, the agents can take photographs, examine the hard drives of computers and install programs that track keystrokes, examine records and other physical property, and then leave without informing the subject of the inquiry about their presence. The standard of proof for "sneak-and-peek" is lower than the Fourth Amendment requirement of probable cause, and there is no requirement for specificity in regard to the items searched. Instead, the secret surveillance requires only that the person may be engaged in criminal activity.
- *National search warrants.* Search warrants could be used nationwide.
- *Detention.* Immigrants suspected of involvement in terrorism could be held for up to seven days for questioning, a substantial increase from the previous limit of two days. After a week, they must be charged with a crime or released, although under certain conditions their detentions could be extended by six-month periods.
- *Wiretaps and purpose of investigation.* Previously, to obtain a wiretap from FISA, obtaining foreign intelligence had to be the only purpose of the investigation. Under the new law, as noted above, authorities could apply for a wiretap in cases where obtaining foreign intelligence is a significant purpose of the investigation but not the sole purpose. Critics argue that these vague standards encourage federal officials to go on "fishing expeditions" to find some evidence of any type of violation.
- *Criminal penalties raised.* The law increased sentences for terrorist acts, harboring terrorists, and financing terrorism.

- *Bioterrorism.* The law made it a crime to possess substances that could be used as biological or chemical weapons for any reason other than a "peaceful" purpose.
- *Monitoring computers.* Computers are likened to telephones, and officials were given the power to subpoena e-mail communications of suspected terrorists.
- *Intelligence sharing.* The bill sought to expand the role of local law enforcement officials by authorizing them to share information, including grand jury testimony, with national security officials.
- *Money laundering.* The Treasury Department was given greater authority to force foreign banks to determine the sources of large bank accounts. U.S. financial transactions with foreign banks that refused to release information on depositors to U.S. investigators could be cut off, even if the foreign bank was following its nation's bank secrecy laws.
- *Shell banks.* The law prohibited dealing with offshore shell banks, which are not regulated by the banking industry.
- *Sunset provisions.* The expanded powers of wiretaps for telephones and computers were set to expire in four years.

Like the 1996 legislation, the 2001 legislation has been both praised and criticized. In testimony before the U.S. Judiciary Committee on October 3, 2001, several witnesses commented on the strengths and weaknesses of the proposed bill. Douglas W. Kmiec, dean of the Law School of the Catholic University of America in Washington, D.C., expressed his support for the bill by noting

> that our founder's conception of freedom was not a freedom to do anything or associate for any purpose, but to do those things which do not harm others and which, it was hoped, would advance the common good. Freedom separated from this truth is not freedom at all, but license. Congress can no longer afford, if it ever could, to confuse freedom and license—because doing so licenses terrorism, not freedom. (Kmiec, 2001, p.1)

Speaking against the bill, another law professor, David Cole, said that the bill was an overreaction based on fear, that it sacrificed the bedrock principles of political freedom and equal treatment, and that it traded the liberty of vulnerable immigrants for the safety of the rest of society. Cole (2001) concluded that the

> overbreadth of the bill reflects the overreaction that we have often indulged in when threatened. The expansive authorities that the Administration bill grants, moreover, are not likely to make us safer. To the contrary, by penalizing even wholly lawful, nonviolent, and associational activity, we are likely to drive such activity underground, to encourage extremists, and to make the communities that will inevitably be targeted by such broad-brush measures disinclined to cooperate with law enforcement. As Justice Louis Brandeis wrote nearly 75 years ago, the Framers of our Constitution knew "that fear breeds repression; that repression breeds hate; and that hate menaces stable government." . . . In other words, freedom and security need not necessarily be traded off against one another, maintaining our freedom is itself critical to maintaining our security. (p. 8)

The PATRIOT Act was scheduled to expire at the end of 2005, and Congress twice temporarily extended the provisions of the bill. On March 9, 2006—a day before most of the controversial provisions were set to expire—President Bush signed the reauthorization bill, but not before a great deal of debate and a threatened Senate filibuster led by Senator Feingold. Ultimately, a limited compromise was reached, and the bill was passed by only two votes more than needed under the rules requiring a two-thirds majority.

Most of the 2001 law was reauthorized, including the key components of the more controversial provisions, such as "roving wiretaps" and "sneak-and-peak" laws ("After Close Call," 2006, p. 7). Three changes were designed to ameliorate civil libertarian complaints. One altered the so-called library clause by exempting libraries, functioning in their traditional capacity, from receiving national security letters, which are subpoenas for financial and electronic records. However, libraries that operate as Internet service providers remain potential subjects of demands for electronic surveillance. Second, the reauthorized legislation requires law enforcement officials to specifically describe the records they are seeking. Third, recipients of the letters were given the right to challenge the subpoenas in court (Weiss, 2006).

It is unclear how many requests for business records have been made. The Justice Department said in 2005 that only slightly more than 200 such requests had been made, whereas the *Washington Post* reported later that same year that the FBI had issued more than 30,000 demands a year for records (ACLU, 2006). Although most of the provisions of the reauthorization of the original Act were made permanent, the provisions allowing "roving" wiretaps and requiring the production of business records under the Foreign Intelligence Surveillance Act are set to expire in four years.

The 2001 law was passed as an emergency response to the terrorist attacks of 9/11. With the 2006 reauthorization, "the exception becomes the rule. . . . the temporary becomes permanent" (Paye, 2006, p. 2).

Controversial Detentions and Military Tribunals

Detentions

In the hours following the 9/11 attacks, federal law enforcement agents began what may end up to be the most extensive criminal investigation in U.S. history. Focusing on non-U.S. citizens, particularly immigrants and visitors from Arab and Muslim nations, federal investigators ultimately detained more than 1,000 foreigners. A small number of those imprisoned were held as material witnesses to the September 11 assaults, and the rest were held on immigration violations (e.g., expired visas) and criminal charges, such as traffic violations and misdemeanors unrelated to terrorism. Had it not been for September 11, most of the criminal charges and immigration violations would have been ignored or resolved easily.

In New York City and nearby New Jersey, the dragnet was especially all encompassing. Many South Asian and Middle Eastern Muslim men endured lengthy detention, without charges or lawyers, prompting some observers to claim racism. According to an anthropologist who speaks Urdu and helped the detainees and their families, these arrests were "part of a package of policies—surveillance of Muslim neighbourhoods and mosques, random questioning of Muslim men by the FBI, shutting down of popular Muslim charities and freezing their assets, vilification of Muslims in the media—that may be characterized as 'structured anti-Muslim racism'" (Mathur, 2006, pp. 32–33).

Government officials justified the detentions as a necessary response to an extraordinary situation, and they noted that federal agents were merely enforcing existing laws. For instance, Mindy Tucker, a spokeswoman for the Justice Department, said that

> Sept. 11 has forced the entire government to change the way we do business . . . Our No. 1 priority right now is to prevent any further terrorist attacks. Part of that entails identifying those who may have connections to terrorism who are here in America and making sure they're not in a position to carry out any further terrorism. (as quoted in Wilgoren, 2001, p. 1)

Shortly after the attack, the Bush administration announced that it had rewritten the detention rules so as to allow the indefinite detention of immigrants suspected of crimes during a national emergency. Human rights groups have repeatedly criticized indefinite detention practices in other countries, and they quickly objected to President Bush's administrative order. Legal scholars noted, however, that the indefinite detention of immigrants is consistent with Supreme Court rulings. For example, in 1999, the Supreme Court ruled that immigrants singled out for deportation because they associated with a terrorist organization had no right to challenge their deportation on First Amendment grounds (*Reno v. American-Arab Anti-Discrimination Committee*, 1999). The Court based its holding on the 1996 antiterrorism legislation and the argument that aliens do not enjoy the constitutional rights granted to U.S. citizens. Critics of the Supreme Court's decision noted that "the Court put immigrants on notice that if they engage in political activity of which the government disapproves, they are vulnerable to selective retaliatory enforcement of immigration laws" (Dempsey & Cole, 1999, p. 3).

In opposition to the Supreme Court's ruling and the Bush administration's policy, human rights advocates argue that noncitizens should be afforded the basic legal protections of the U.S. Constitution. They argue that the Founding Fathers intended to protect the natural rights of all human beings, regardless of their citizenship. Among these are the rights to be formally charged, confront accusers, present evidence, and require rigorous standards of proof.

Few, it any, of those arrested are believed to have known any of the suspected hijackers. The U.S. attorney general, however, opined that the roundup had prevented more terrorism, and the Justice Department announced that it would try to interview about 5,000 Arab and Muslim men living in the United States on temporary visas. Immigration attorneys and Arab-American community leaders expressed concern that those who cooperated with government authorities might be detained and deported. Some law enforcement officials spoke out against the interviews as a form of racial profiling. For example, the acting police chief of Portland, Oregon, Andrew Kirkland, refused to assist federal authorities on the grounds that Oregon law prohibits local police from questioning immigrants who are not suspected of a crime (Butterfield, 2001).

Military Tribunals

On November 15, 2001, President Bush signed an executive order allowing foreigners suspected of international terrorism to be tried in special military tribunals. Military tribunals are formed under the power of the executive branch of government and are independent of the judicial branch. The prosecutors and judge-commissioners are military officers, responsible to the president. The procedures are also different than in the judicial branch. Defendants can have lawyers, but not necessarily those of their choosing. Hearsay evidence, typically barred from civilian trials, is permitted, and the proceedings can be held in secret to protect classified information. Sentences, including death, can be imposed with a two-thirds vote of the presiding military officers. No juries are allowed, and decisions of the military tribunals cannot be reviewed by the federal judiciary (Wilke, 2005).

Critics quickly complained that President Bush had seized dictatorial power and betrayed basic American values. The administration responded that the tribunals were necessary in a time of war and that they would proceed more quickly than judicial trials while preventing the disclosure of classified national security information.

Subsequent rules drafted by the administration afforded more due process protections for defendants than originally announced. Under the new rules, imposing the death penalty would require a unanimous verdict, although only a two-thirds vote of the panel of military officials would be needed for a guilty verdict. Proof beyond a reasonable doubt would be required, but hearsay evidence would be allowed. Defendants would have military lawyers appointed to their cases, or they could hire their own lawyers.

President Bush's counsel at the time, Alberto R. Gonzales, who later became the Attorney General, defended the plan for military tribunals by noting that

> it specifically directs that all trials before military commissions will be "full and fair." . . . The American military justice system is the finest in the world, with longstanding traditions of forbidding command influence on proceedings, of providing zealous advocacy by competent defense counsel, and of procedural fairness. . . . The suggestion that these commissions will afford only sham justice like that dispensed in dictatorial nations is an insult to our military justice system. (2001, ¶ 6)

However, nationally syndicated columnist William Safire (2001) described these military tribunals as "kangaroo courts":

Photo 9.2   U.S. Army military police escort a detainee to his cell in Camp X-Ray at the U.S. Naval Base at Guantanamo Bay, Cuba. Detainees are suspected members of Afghanistan's Taliban and al-Qaeda.

Military attorneys are silently seething because they know that to be untrue. The U.C.M.J. [United Code of Military Justice] demands a public trial, proof beyond reasonable doubt, and accused's voice in the selection of juries and right to choose counsel, unanimity in death sentencing and above all appellate review by civilians confirmed by the Senate. Not one of those fundamental rights can be found in Bush's military order setting up kangaroo courts for people he designates before "trial" to be terrorists. Bush's fiat turns back the clock on all advanced in military justice, through three wars, in the past half-century. (p. A17)

The idea of military tribunals was also criticized outside the United States. When the United States moved captured Taliban soldiers and al-Qaeda members from Afghanistan to Guantanamo Bay, Cuba, for further investigation and prosecution, many U.S. allies protested U.S. plans for trying them in military tribunals. Further, as noted in the second article in this chapter, most of the detainees at Guantanamo Bay were not given an opportunity to have a hearing even before a military tribunal (Wilke, 2005).

Nevertheless, historical precedent exists for using military tribunals during wartime. Major John Andre, a British spy whose capture during the Revolutionary War exposed Benedict Arnold's plan to surrender West Point to the British in exchange for money and a military commission, was tried by a group of 14 military officers in 1780 and hanged after his conviction. During the Civil War, President Abraham Lincoln ordered hearings before military tribunals for Confederate agents suspected of sabotaging railroads. In 1942, six months after the attack on Pearl Harbor, the Supreme Court upheld the use of military tribunals for eight spies who had landed submarines on beaches in Florida and Long Island; six of the eight were executed.

Law Enforcement Information Sharing

In the child's game "connect-the-dots," an image is revealed by drawing lines in the correct sequence between the numbered dots. Since the 9/11 terrorist attacks against the United States, connect-the-dots has become a metaphor for linking data elements to uncover terrorist plots.

Automated information sharing among police agencies is widely viewed as an important component of the nation's counterterrorism policy.

From the many postmortem analyses conducted after 9/11, one of the more prevalent conclusions was that law enforcement agencies should have detected and then pursued suspicious patterns in existing databases. For example, the former chairman of the U.S. Senate Intelligence Committee, Bob Graham, D-Florida (ret.), asked "why these dots weren't seen and connected" (CNN, 2005). Likewise, the U.S. Congress Joint Inquiry into the Intelligence Community Activities Before and After the Terrorist Attacks of September 11, 2001 referred repeatedly to the failure to connect the dots (Taipale, 2003, p. 3). And the FBI Director, Robert Muller, said that there were "red flags out there or dots that should have been connected" (Lewis, 2002). As noted by Reynolds et al. (2006),

> Two months before Mohammed Atta, the alleged ringleader of the terrorist group, launched the attacks on the World Trade Center, he had been stopped in Delray Beach, Florida for speeding. The officer was unaware that a warrant for Atta's arrest had previously been issued in Broward County after Atta failed to appear in court for driving without a license. If information from nearby counties had been available on the Delray Beach's patrol-car computer, Atta might have been sitting in a jail cell on September 11 instead of in an American Airlines' cockpit. (p. 3)

In response to the 9/11 attacks, the Markle Foundation, a New York-based private philanthropy, created the Task Force on National Security in the Information Age. In its subsequent reports, the Task Force has stressed the importance of rejecting the Cold War approach to information sharing, with its "need-to-know" mentality, and replacing it with automated information sharing. Rejecting the widely held notion that federal and state authorities were alone responsible for domestic security, the Task Force noted that local law enforcement was vital to national security. Concerned about privacy and civil rights, it urged the creation of a decentralized network, whereby individual agencies would retain control of their data. The Task Force rejected the traditional data warehousing approach, which forces agencies to surrender control of their data to a central computer system (Markle Foundation, 2002, 2003).

The Markle Foundation's recommendations were echoed by the 2004 report of the National Commission on Terrorist Attacks Upon the United States (also known as the 9–11 Commission). The federal government incorporated the recommendations of both blue-ribbon panels into the National Intelligence Reform and Terrorism Prevention Act of 2004. Specifically, Section 1016 of this Act calls for an automated information sharing approach to national security based on the connection of existing systems through a decentralized, rather than a central warehouse, architecture.

Yet, as of early 2007, relatively few of the nearly 18,000 local law enforcement agencies in the United States participate in information sharing. At Congressional hearings in October 19, 2005, Zoe Baird, the president of the Markle Foundation, noted her disappointment at the slow pace of change in the information sharing environment (Baird, 2005). Baird likewise commented that "very little progress" has been made in sharing intelligence (i.e., collated data) with state and local officials (p. 6). Stating that "the federal government has not yet realized the value of information identified by state and local entities," she said that doing so was a "critical component of national security" and represented a "gap" that must be filled (pp. 5–6).

The 9–11 Commission, now a private organization named the 9/11 Public Discourse Project, has expressed similar disappointment. In its mid-2005 status report, it noted that there has been "minimal progress" in changing the culture of law enforcement information sharing (9/11 Public Discourse Project, 2005, p. 5). And yet, local law enforcement is increasingly expected to develop an intelligence capacity.

Integration Projects

No exhaustive list of data sharing projects exists, although Scott (2004) recently identified more than 200 automated criminal-justice information sharing programs that were mentioned in the scholarly, trade, and professional literature. When he contacted many of these programs, however, Scott found that few were currently operative; many had never been implemented. Often, the only written material about the projects was found on the Web sites of commercial vendors. The potential for exaggerated claims emanating from the for-profit sector makes it important that specific information sharing case studies appear in the scholarly literature.

The Bureau of Justice Assistance (BJA) Center for Program Evaluation lists several data sharing projects across the country on its Web site (http://www.ojp.usdoj.gov/BJA/evaluation/psi_isii/index.htm). Relatively little scholarly research has emanated from these projects, and the majority of publications focus on implementation and usability issues. BJA attributes the lack of information to the "newness of work in this area" (see, e.g., Chen et al., 2003; Lin, Jen-Hwa Hu, & Chen 2004; Schroeder, 2001).

The main findings from the usability studies are that police need and want information sharing. One such data sharing initiative began in the late 1990s in San Diego County, California. ARJIS, which stands for Automated Regional Justice Information System, connects 38 regional law enforcement agencies. Using for comparison a similar sized agency that did not participate in information sharing, Zaworski (2005) conducted a usability survey and found that information sharing contributed positively to the San Diego officers' perceptions of their productivity and ability to clear cases. Information sharing also enhanced officers' perceptions of their safety. Of the officers in the comparison group, only 50% reported receiving information from other law enforcement agencies, in contrast to 100% of the survey respondents from San Diego. Less than 5% of the comparison group reported being happy with the information received from other law enforcement agencies; 56% of the San Diego officers were satisfied. Officers in both groups noted that information is very important to street cops (85% in the control group and 94% in the San Diego user group; Zaworski, 2005). The San Diego data underscore the importance of electronic information sharing; its implementation remains a critical need for most law enforcement officers in the nation.

Three Infamous Cases From the U.S. History of Counterterrorism

Domestic counterterrorism activities that appear to many people at the time to be justified by the seriousness of the threat may in hindsight be seen as harmful and unnecessary. History has demonstrated that fear and inflamed passions can lead to overzealous enforcement and scapegoating of innocent people. Three examples from the 20th century are presented below: the Palmer Raids, the internment of Japanese Americans, and the House Un-American Activities Committee and McCarthyism.

The Palmer Raids

One infamous example of overreaction occurred shortly after World War I, when America was struggling with rampant inflation, high unemployment, labor strikes, and race riots. A climate of fear and repression centered on the growing Communist Party. The "Red Scare" intensified when A. Mitchell Palmer, President Woodrow Wilson's attorney general, claimed that communism was "eating its way into the homes of the American workman" (Palmer, 1920, ¶ 3). Palmer recruited J. Edgar Hoover as his special assistant; together, they used the Espionage Act of 1917 (H.R. 291, 1917) and an amendment to it, the Sedition Act of 1918, to launch a campaign against radicals and left-wing organizations.

A series of bombings began in the late spring of 1919, and on June 2, bombs went off in eight cities, including Washington, DC, in which Palmer's home was partially destroyed. It was never determined who set the bombs, but the communists were quickly blamed for them. Palmer claimed that the communists were trying to take over the government. In an essay titled "The Case Against the Reds," Palmer (1920, ¶3) charged that "tongues of revolutionary heat were licking the altars of the churches, leaping into the belfry of the school bell, crawling into the sacred corners of American homes, seeking to replace marriage vows with libertine laws, burning up the foundations of society."

In response, Attorney General Palmer ordered the Justice Department to conduct raids of radical and leftist organizations around the country. On January 2, 1920, 500 FBI agents

PHOTO 9.3   Japanese American internees line up for the noon meal at the Manzanar War Relocation Authority (WRA) Camp in California in 1943. This photo is part of a series of photographs of the Manzanar internment camp taken by the renowned photographer Ansel Adams.

arrested union leaders, scientists, former antiwar protesters, and others suspected of supporting leftist causes. Federal officials, acting without judicial warrants, broke into offices of labor unions and other targeted groups, rummaging through and destroying political and personal documents. Within a few months, more than 5,000 people were taken into custody; after lengthy detentions, most were released without charges being filed. Among those arrested was Emma Goldman, a well-known feminist and anarchist author. She, along with 249 other aliens, was deported and put on a ship bound for the Soviet Union.

Attitudes about the actions of Attorney General Palmer changed when the communist takeover failed to materialize, and he was denounced for violating the arrestees' civil liberties. Some critics claimed that Palmer had devised the "Red Scare" to help him become the Democratic presidential candidate in 1920. Ultimately, Palmer was convicted of misappropriating government funds, and charges against the remaining prisoners were dropped. For more on the Palmer Raids, see Feuerlicht (1971), Hoyt (1969), Labor Research Association (1948), and McCormick (1997).

Japanese Internment

America's internment of people of Japanese heritage is another infamous example of overzealous counterterrorism at the expense of cherished American values. World War II was already devastating Europe when Japanese forces attacked the U.S. naval base at Pearl Harbor on December 7, 1941, stunning the nation and pushing it into the war. Anti-Asian prejudice was already strong in the United States, and the attack of Pearl Harbor cast even greater suspicion on people of Japanese ancestry.

Although he had no direct evidence that the Japanese intended to invade the United States, on February 19, 1942, President Franklin D. Roosevelt signed into law Executive Order No. 9066, authorizing the Secretary of War to define military areas from which "any or all persons may be excluded as deemed necessary or desirable." Fearing an attack on the West Coast, the government created military areas in California, Washington, Oregon, and parts of Arizona, from which all persons of Japanese ancestry were banned. It created the War Relocation Authority, and the army forcibly moved more than 110,000 people of Japanese descent, most of whom were American citizens, to one of 10 internment camps set up in California, Idaho, Utah, Arizona, Wyoming, Colorado, and Arkansas. The internment camps were euphemistically called "relocation centers."

The camps were overcrowded and the housing was primitive, with no plumbing or cooking facilities (War Relocation Authority, 1943). Coal for fires was scarce, food was rationed, and internees faced many cold nights with just a blanket. Several young Japanese Americans refused to be drafted into the military from the camps, arguing that they were willing to fight for the United States, but not until their families were released; they were prosecuted and imprisoned. In addition to being forced to live in squalid conditions, the internees lost their property, businesses, and livelihoods.

In 1944, President Roosevelt rescinded the order, and the last internment camp was closed at the end of 1945. Four decades later, the government recognized the harm caused by its overzealous counterterrorism efforts, and the Civil Liberties Act of 1988, signed by President Ronald Reagan, "acknowledged the fundamental injustice of the evacuation, relocation, and internment of United States citizens and permanent resident aliens of Japanese ancestry during World War II" (Civil Liberties Act, 1988). Each of the approximately 60,000 surviving internees received payments of $20,000, and the U.S. government issued a formal apology. For more on the Japanese internments, see Harth (2001), Houston and Houston (1983), Myer (1971), and Robinson (2001).

More Red Scares: HUAC and McCarthyism

Guilt by association was the driving force behind the House Un-American Activities Committee (HUAC), which began operations in 1938. Looking to rout out radicals and communists, especially those from Hollywood and members of labor unions, HUAC made vague and sweeping accusations against individuals and asked witnesses to "name names." The hearings seemed designed to get people to renounce their past, rather than to establish criminal guilt: HUAC already knew most of the names that it demanded from the witnesses. Many witnesses refused to name names, and their careers and reputations were ruined. One group of writers and directors, known as the Hollywood Ten, was sent to prison for not cooperating with the HUAC.

With a reputation built on making unsubstantiated accusations that the government had been infiltrated by communists, Senator Joseph McCarthy became chairman of the Senate Permanent Investigations Subcommittee in 1953, a position from which he exercised great power. Through widely publicized television hearings, using unidentified informers, and making outlandish accusations, McCarthy ruined the careers of many people, with little or no evidence. His methods eventually came under attack by the press and his colleagues, and in 1954 the U.S. Senate voted to condemn him for misconduct. McCarthy is remembered today by many as a demagogue and witch-hunter; others treat his legacy more generously, crediting him with bringing the serious threat of communism to the attention of America. For more on the Red Scare, see Fried (1991), Herman (2000), McCarthy (1985), and Schrecker (1994).

HIGHLIGHTS OF REPRINTED ARTICLES

The two articles selected to accompany this chapter reflect two dimensions of the counterterrorism policy of the United States. The first discusses the possible ramifications of the Iraq War, and the second examines issues surrounding the detention and court processing of enemy combatants.

Peter Bergen and Alec Reynolds (2005). Blowback revisited. *Foreign Affairs, 84*(6), 2–6.

The war waged by Islamist militants against the Soviet Union in Afghanistan in the 1980s ultimately led to the growth of the current global Jihad. A second, and even more serious, blowback can be anticipated when the Iraq War ends. The authors call on the administration of President Bush to prepare for the end of the Iraq War, which is "breeding a new generation of terrorists."

Christiane Wilke (2005). War v. justice: Terrorism cases, enemy combatants, and political justice in U.S. courts. *Politics and Society, 33*(4), 637–669.

Zacarias Moussaoui, John Walker Lindh, Richard Reid, José Padilla, Yaser Hamdi—these are a few of the infamous terrorists whose cases have become familiar to the public in the recent annals of counterterrorism in the United States. Extraordinary rendition, Guantanamo Bay, enemy combatants, military tribunals—these terms have entered our lexicon forcefully over the past several years. In this reading, Wilke not only discusses these cases and explains the terminology but she also develops a two-stage model of political justice.

EXPLORING COUNTERTERRORISM FURTHER

- The U.S. Office of the Coordinator for Counterterrorism (http://www.state.gov/s/ct) is the agency within the Department of State officially responsible for developing, coordinating, and implementing American counterterrorism policy.
- The Web site of the International Policy Institute for Counterterrorism (http://www.ict.org.il), a private research organization, includes information on UN resolutions, international treaties, and international and national laws against terrorism.
- The Congressional Research Services (CRS; http://www.cnie.org/NLE/CRS) publishes a variety of reports on counterterrorism policy. Type in "terrorism" in the "report title" part of the search box to find many fascinating articles.
- The international response to U.S. counterterrorism policy in the aftermath of September 11, 2001, is of great concern to human rights organizations. Amnesty International (http://www.amnesty-usa.org) recently issued a report titled "Shut Down Guantanamo!"
- According to Bergen and Reynolds, authors of the first reprint for this chapter, what was the blowback from the war against the Soviet Union in Afghanistan?
- Why do Bergen and Reynolds think that the blowback from the Iraq War will be even worse than what followed the war in Afghanistan?
- Find out more about Sheikh Omar Abdel Rahman, the so-called blind sheikh.
- Christiane Wilke, the author of the second reprint for this chapter, proposes a two-stage model of political justice. Explain her model.
- According to Wilke, what are the key characteristics of military tribunals, and how are they different from regular criminal court proceedings?

VIDEO NOTES

The threat from the military in response to terrorism may be overplayed in *Siege* (20th Century Fox, 1998, 120 min.), but the film provides some sobering images about fighting violence with violence.

One noted exploration of the role of U.S. policy in the blowback of transnational terrorism is titled *CIA: America's Secret Warriors* (Discovery Channel, 1997, 2 vols., 50 min. each).

The movie *Munich* (Universal, 2005, 2 hr. 44 min.) dramatizes the secret Israeli squad assigned to track down and assassinate the 11 Palestinians believed to have planned the 1972 massacre of 11 Israeli athletes in Munich.

The *Road to Guantanamo* (Sony Pictures, 2006, 95 min.) is an award-winning docudrama based on the true story of three British Muslims who were captured in Afghanistan and detained by U.S. forces. The controversial film is a stark and brutal indictment of U.S. policy regarding the Guantanamo Bay prison.

❖

Blowback Revisited

Peter Bergen and Alec Reynolds

The article argues that the insurgents of the U.S.-led war in Iraq will become global terrorists after the war has ended. Foreign volunteers fighting U.S. troops in Iraq will lead a global jihad when the war ends. The U.S. President George W. Bush administration has devoted little time to preparing for the long-term consequences of the Iraq War. U.S. policymakers must deal with the jihadists in Iraq by limiting the numbers entering the fight. The U.S. should bring more internal security to Iraq by securing the borders. The article suggests that foreign governments silence calls to jihad. Also, the U.S. intelligence community should work on creating a database that can identify and track terrorists.

TODAY'S INSURGENTS IN IRAQ ARE TOMORROW'S TERRORISTS

When the United States started sending guns and money to the Afghan mujahideen in the 1980s, it had a clearly defined Cold War purpose: helping expel the Soviet army, which had invaded Afghanistan in 1979. And so it made sense that once the Afghan jihad forced a Soviet withdrawal a decade later, Washington would lose interest in the rebels. For the international mujahideen drawn to the Afghan conflict, however, the fight was just beginning. They opened new fronts in the name of global jihad and became the spearhead of Islamist terrorism. The seriousness of the blowback became clear to the United States with the 1993 bombing of the World Trade Center: all of the attack's participants either had served in Afghanistan or were linked to a Brooklyn-based fund-raising organ for the Afghan jihad that was later revealed to be al Qaeda's de facto U.S. headquarters. The blowback, evident in other countries as well, continued to increase in intensity throughout the rest of the decade, culminating on September 11, 2001.

The current war in Iraq will generate a ferocious blowback of its own, which—as a recent classified CIA assessment predicts—could be longer and more powerful than that from Afghanistan. Foreign volunteers fighting U.S. troops in Iraq today will find new targets around the world after the war ends. Yet the Bush administration, consumed with managing countless crises in Iraq, has devoted little time to preparing for such long-term consequences. Lieutenant General James Conway, the director of operations on the Joint Staff, admitted as much when he said in June that blowback "is a concern, but there's not much we can do about it at this point in time." Judging from the experience of Afghanistan, such thinking is both mistaken and dangerously complacent.

COMING HOME TO ROOST

The foreign volunteers in Afghanistan saw the Soviet defeat as a victory for Islam against a superpower that had invaded a Muslim country. Estimates of the number of foreign fighters who fought in Afghanistan begin in the low thousands; some spent years in combat, while others came only for what amounted to a jihad vacation. The jihadists gained legitimacy and prestige from their triumph both within the militant community and among ordinary Muslims, as well as the confidence to carry their jihad to other countries where they believed Muslims required assistance. When veterans of the guerrilla campaign returned home with their experience, ideology, and weapons, they destabilized once-tranquil countries and inflamed already unstable ones.

Algeria had seen relatively little terrorism for decades, but returning mujahideen founded the Armed Islamic Group (known by its French initials, GIA). GIA murdered thousands of Algerian civilians during the 1990s as it attempted to depose the government and replace it with an Islamist regime, a goal inspired by the mujahideen's success in Afghanistan. The GIA campaign of violence became especially pronounced after the Algerian army mounted a coup in 1992 to preempt an election that Islamists were poised to win.

In Egypt, after the assassination of Egyptian President Anwar Sadat in 1981 prompted a government crackdown, hundreds of extremists left the country to train and fight in Afghanistan. Those militants came back from the war against the Soviets to lead a terror campaign that killed more than a thousand people between 1990 and 1997. Closely tied to these militants was the Egyptian cleric Sheikh Omar Abdel Rahman, "the Blind Sheikh," whose preaching, according to the 9/11 Commission, had inspired Sadat's assassins. Abdel Rahman's career demonstrates the internationalization of Islamist extremism after Afghanistan. The cleric visited Pakistan to lend his support to the Afghan jihad and encouraged two of his sons to fight in the war. He also provided spiritual direction for the Egyptian terrorist organization Jamaat al-Islamiyya and supported its renewed attacks on the Egyptian government in the 1990s. He arrived in the United States in 1990—at the time, the country was regarded as a sympathetic environment for Islamist militants—where he began to encourage attacks on New York City landmarks. Convicted in 1995 in connection with the 1993 bombing of the World Trade Center, Abdel Rahman is serving a life sentence in the United States. But his influence has continued to be felt: a 1997 attack at an archaeological site near the Egyptian city of Luxor that left 58 tourists dead and almost crippled Egypt's vital tourism industry was an effort by Jamaat al-Islamiyya to force his release.

The best-known alumnus of the Afghan jihad is Osama bin Laden, under whose leadership the "Afghan Arabs" prosecuted their war beyond the Middle East into the United States, Africa, Europe, and Southeast Asia. After the Soviet defeat, bin Laden established a presence in Sudan to build up his fledgling al Qaeda organization. Around the same time, Saddam Hussein invaded Kuwait and hundreds of thousands of U.S. troops arrived in Saudi Arabia. The U.S. military presence in "the land of the two holy places" became al Qaeda's core grievance, and the United States became bin Laden's primary target. Al Qaeda bombed two U.S. embassies in Africa in 1998, nearly sank the U.S.S. Cole in Yemen in 2000, and attacked the World Trade Center and the Pentagon in 2001. Bin Laden expanded his reach into Southeast Asia with the assistance of other terrorists who had fought in Afghanistan, such as Riduan Isamuddin, known as Hambali, who is the central link between al Qaeda and the Indonesian terror group Jemaah Islamiyah, and Ali Gufron, known as Mukhlas, a leading planner of the 2002 Bali bombing that killed more than 200 people.

ON-THE-JOB TRAINING

The Afghan experience was important for the foreign "holy warriors" for several reasons. First, they gained battlefield experience. Second, they rubbed shoulders with like-minded militants from around the Muslim world, creating a truly global network. Third, as the Soviet war wound down, they established a myriad of new jihadist organizations, from al Qaeda to the Algerian GIA to the Filipino group Abu Sayyaf.

However, despite their grandiose rhetoric, the few thousand foreigners who fought in Afghanistan had only a negligible impact on the outcome of that war. Bin Laden's Afghan Arabs began fighting the Soviet army only in 1986, six years after the Soviet invasion. It was the Afghans, drawing on the wealth of their American and Saudi sponsors, who defeated the Soviet Union. By contrast, foreign volunteers are key players in Iraq, far more potent than the Afghan Arabs ever were.

Several factors could make blowback from the Iraq war even more dangerous than the fallout from Afghanistan. Foreign fighters started to arrive in Iraq even before Saddam's regime fell. They have conducted most of the suicide bombings—including some that have delivered strategic successes such as the withdrawal of the UN and most international aid organizations—and the

Jordanian Abu Musab al-Zarqawi, another alumnus of the Afghan war, is perhaps the most effective insurgent commander in the field. Fighters in Iraq are more battle hardened than the Afghan Arabs, who fought demoralized Soviet army conscripts. They are testing themselves against arguably the best army in history, acquiring skills in their battles against coalition forces that will be far more useful for future terrorist operations than those their counterparts learned during the 1980s. Mastering how to make improvised explosive devices or how to conduct suicide operations is more relevant to urban terrorism than the conventional guerrilla tactics used against the Red Army. U.S. military commanders say that techniques perfected in Iraq have been adopted by militants in Afghanistan.

Finally, foreign involvement in the Iraqi conflict will likely lead some Iraqi nationals to become international terrorists. The Afghans were glad to have Arab money but were culturally, religiously, and psychologically removed from the Afghan Arabs; they neither joined al Qaeda nor identified with the Arabs' radical theology. Iraqis, however, are closer culturally to the foreigners fighting in Iraq, and many will volunteer to continue other jihads even after U.S. troops depart.

IN BAGHDAD AND IN BOSTON

President George W. Bush and others have suggested that it is better for the United States to fight the terrorists in Baghdad than in Boston. It is a comforting notion, but it is wrong on two counts. First, it posits a finite number of terrorists who can be lured to one place and killed. But the Iraq war has expanded the terrorists' ranks: the year 2003 saw the highest incidence of significant terrorist attacks in two decades, and then, in 2004, astonishingly, that number tripled. (Secretary of Defense Donald Rumsfeld famously complained in October 2003 that "we lack metrics to know if we are winning or losing the global war on terror." An exponentially rising number of terrorist attacks is one metric that seems relevant.) Second, the Bush administration has not addressed the question of what the foreign fighters will do when the war in Iraq ends. It would be naive to expect them to return to civilian life in their home countries. More likely, they will become the new shock troops of the international jihadist movement.

For these reasons, U.S. allies in Europe and the Middle East, as well as the United States itself, are vulnerable to blowback. Disturbingly, some European governments are already seeing some of their citizens and resident aliens answer the call to fight in Iraq. In February, the *Los Angeles Times* reported that U.S. troops in Iraq had detained three French militants—and that police in Paris had arrested ten associates who were planning to join them. In June, authorities in Spain arrested 16 men, mostly Moroccans, on charges of recruiting suicide bombers for Iraq. In September, prosecutors in the United States indicted a Dutch resident, Iraqi-born Wesam al-Delaema, for conspiring to bomb U.S. convoys in Fallujah. These incidents presage danger not only for European countries but also for the United States, since European nationals benefit from the Visa Waiver Program, which affords them relatively easy access to the United States.

But it is Saudi Arabia that will bear the brunt of the blowback. Several studies attest to the significant role Saudi nationals have played in the conflict. Of the 154 Arab fighters killed in Iraq between September 2004 and March 2005, 61 percent were from Saudi Arabia. Another report concluded that of the 235 suicide bombers named on Web sites since mid-2004 as having perpetrated attacks in Iraq, more than 50 percent were Saudi nationals. Today, the Saudi government is exporting its jihadist problem instead of dealing with it, just as the Egyptians did during the Afghan war.

A SWITCH IN TIME

American success in Iraq would deny today's jihadists the symbolic victory that they seek. But with that outcome so uncertain, U.S. policymakers must focus on dealing with the jihadists in Iraq now—by limiting the numbers entering the fight and breaking the mechanism that would otherwise generate blowback after the war.

The foreign jihadists in Iraq need to be separated from the local insurgents through the political process. Success in that mission will require Iraq's Sunni Arabs to remain consistently engaged in the political process. Shiite and Kurdish leaders will have to back down from their efforts to create semiautonomous states in the north and the south. But the prospects for these developments appear dim at the moment, and reaching a durable agreement may increasingly be beyond U.S. influence.

To raise the odds of success, the United States must deliver more security to central Iraq. This means securing Iraq's borders, especially with Syria, to block the flow of foreign fighters into the country. The repeated U.S. military operations in western Iraq since May have shown that at present there are insufficient forces to disrupt insurgent supply lines running along the Euphrates River to the Syrian border. Accomplishing this objective would require either more U.S. troops or a much larger force of well-trained Iraqi troops. For the moment, neither of those options seems viable, and so additional U.S. soldiers should be rotated out of Iraq's cities and into the western deserts and border towns, transitioning the control of certain urban areas to the Iraqi military and police.

Foreign governments must also silence calls to jihad and deny radicals sanctuary once this war ends. After the Soviet defeat, jihadists too often found refuge in places as varied as Brooklyn and Khartoum, where radical clerics offered religious justifications for continuing jihad. To date, some governments have not taken the necessary steps to clamp down on the new generation of jihadists. Although the Saudis largely silenced their radical clerics following the terrorist attacks in Riyadh in May 2003, 26 clerics were still permitted late in 2004 to call for jihad against U.S. troops in Iraq. The United States must press the Saudi government to end these appeals and restrict its nationals from entering Iraq. In the long run, measures against radical preaching are in Riyadh's best interest, too, since the blowback from Iraq is likely to be as painful for Saudi Arabia as the blowback from Afghanistan was for Egypt and Algeria during the 1990s.

Finally, the U.S. intelligence community, in conjunction with foreign intelligence services, should work on creating a database that identifies and tracks foreign fighters, their known associates, and their spiritual mentors. If such a database had been created during the Afghan war, the United States would have been far better prepared for al Qaeda's subsequent terror campaign.

President Jimmy Carter's national security adviser, Zbigniew Brzezinski, once asked of the Soviet defeat in Afghanistan: "What is most important to the history of the world? The Taliban or the collapse of the Soviet empire? Some stirred-up Muslims or the liberation of Central Europe and the end of the Cold War?" Today, the Bush administration is implicitly arguing a similar point: that the establishment of a democratic Iraqi state is a project of overriding importance for the United States and the world, which in due course will eclipse memories of the insurgency. But such a viewpoint minimizes the fact that the war in Iraq is already breeding a new generation of terrorists. The lesson of the decade of terror that followed the Afghan war was that underestimating the importance of blowback has severe consequences. Repeating the mistake in regard to Iraq could lead to even deadlier outcomes.

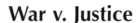

War v. Justice

Terrorism Cases, Enemy Combatants, and Political Justice in U.S. Courts

Christiane Wilke

What mechanisms led to the intractable legal situation of "enemy combatants" detained by the U.S. government in Guantánamo Bay and elsewhere? And what does the role of the judiciary in the enemy combatants cases suggest about politically contentious court cases in general? This article develops a two-stage theory of political justice that is based on the U.S. post-9/11 terrorism cases. It demonstrates mechanisms by which politically contentious cases turn into political justice. Political justice in these cases is mainly the result of violations of the separation of powers that are legitimized by portraying the defendants/detainees as enemies beyond the law.

This nation's enemies may not enlist America's courts to divert efforts and attention from the military offensive abroad to the legal defensive at home.

—Former U.S. Attorney General John Ashcroft

I. INTRODUCTION

After the attacks of September 11, 2001, the United States government vowed "to fight back, to summon all our strength and all our resources and devote ourselves to better ways to identify, disrupt, and dismantle terrorist networks."[1] Under the heading of the "war on terrorism," the U.S. government conducted military campaigns in Afghanistan and elsewhere. U.S. personnel engaged in "targeted assassinations" of presumed terrorists. A significant number of persons were detained by U.S. personnel in various places on the suspicion of having committed terrorist acts or being members or supporters of terrorist organizations. These persons were quickly labeled "unlawful enemy combatants." Their number is unknown, and their fates were diverse: very few of them were tried and convicted in U.S. federal courts. The majority of the detainees were kept incommunicado in places like Guantánamo Bay (Cuba) or Bagram Air Base (Afghanistan)—or in the United States, if they were U.S. citizens. Reports about mistreatment and torture in these detention facilities surfaced soon but caused little public outrage in the United States.[2] Other persons were detained—or abducted—by U.S. personnel abroad, and then handed on to other states known to mistreat or torture prisoners. This practice was called "extraordinary rendition."[3] A number of the detainees held in Guantánamo and elsewhere have been released, often in response to diplomatic pressures

SOURCE: From "War v. Justice: Terrorism Cases, Enemy Combatants, and Political Justice in U.S. Courts," in *Politics & Society* (*33*) 4 by Christiane Wilke © 2005. Reprinted with permission from Sage Publications, Inc.

AUTHOR'S NOTE: Previous versions of this article were presented at the conference on the United States and Global Human Rights at the Rothermere American Institute of the University of Oxford in November 2004, at Carleton University in December 2004, and at the Jacob Landynski Memorial Conference on Constitutionalism and Social Justice at the Graduate Faculty of the New School for Social Research in February 2005. The author thanks those who provided comments and suggestions at various stages, especially David Plotke, Andrew Arato, Michael Goodhart, Amy Bartholomew, and Nehal Bhuta.

rather than legal requirements. The fates of the detainees suspected of being or becoming terrorists differed, but the wide majority of them were subject to a unique form of detention. These detentions were not based on the detainees' alleged past wrongdoing, but on assessments of their dangerousness as "enemy combatants" who might engage in terrorist acts when released. This detention rationale allows for a potentially indefinite detention.

This article examines U.S. court cases arising from the "war on terror" with two purposes: first, the article aims to offer an assessment of these cases in light of the debates about human rights and terrorism. Second, the U.S. post-9/11 cases provide an occasion for the development of a theory of political justice. However, the cases examined here concern only a subsection of the "enemy combatant" detainees. Most detainees have no access to lawyers or courts. The litigation examined here accordingly concerns comparatively privileged detainees but sheds light on the larger mechanisms by which the legal-political figure of the "enemy combatant" extinguishes public concern for the rights and well-being of the detainees. In fact, one central problem about the court cases is that the detainees are too often not viewed as persons with rights, but as enemies who lack the attributes of persons. The U.S. legal approach in the "war on terror" has, to a large degree, shifted from what criminal law theorists have called a "criminal law for citizens" to a "criminal law for enemies."[4] While the "criminal law for citizens" treats its addressees as law-abiding persons, the "criminal law for enemies" treats its subjects as "dangerous individuals" who cannot be convinced but only forced into submission to the law.[5] The U.S. approach to the "war on terror," however, ventures beyond the "criminal law for enemies" period by placing the "enemy combatants" beyond the law: criminal law becomes a moot point where detention is solely based on a person's alleged dangerousness. In this process, the "enemy combatants" are stripped not only of rights but also of their legal personality that is the basis for having rights. Insofar as the detainees are accorded procedural rights by the courts, these rights are understood in relation to the separation of powers within government—which branch may decide what and how—and not as a matter of the detainees' human or civil rights. This approach stands in a marked contrast to the decision of the British House of Lords on the similar subject of indefinite detentions of non-U.K. citizens who cannot be deported.[6] This decision was largely based on international human rights treaties and their domestic incorporation.

What can these terrorism-related cases teach us about political justice? These cases demonstrate one prominent mechanism whereby court cases that are politically contentious turn from "normal" justice—as imperfect as it might be—into instances of political justice. I am proposing a two-stage model of political justice. First, there are—always—some court cases that are politically contentious: they differ from standard cases in that significant political hopes and arguments are attached to their outcome. These politically contentious cases can, but need not, develop two dimensions that transform them into instances of problematic political justice. First, the judicial process in these cases might violate the norms of the separation of powers, usually through executive intrusions into the judicial process. And second, the public vilification of one party to the trial heightens the stakes and shapes the outcome of the case. The portrayal of one party as an "enemy"—regardless of whether this exact term is used—is significant insofar as it implies the suggestion that "enemies" are not to be treated like "friends" or, as Jakobs wants to call them, "citizens."[7] To be sure, war—and enmity in war—are not lawless. But in some legal and political imaginaries, lawless and ruthless enemies have to be fought without the constraints of the law. These enemies are placed beyond the law. Their treatment becomes a matter of ethics and policy; thus it is not lawless. Still, the treatment of these enemies is dictated by policy concerns, and not by their rights as persons. They are accordingly beyond the law: they are governed by the law without being constituted by the law as persons with rights. This article will argue that both dimensions of problematic political justice occurred in the post-9/11 terrorism trials.

Examining the two dimensions of political justice—violations of the separation of powers rules and the vilification of one party—separately, I will argue that the courts were more assertive in rejecting the executive branch's reinterpretations of the separation of powers than they were in questioning the assessments of the detainees' and defendants' status as enemies beyond the law. The courts' eagerness to dispute executive assertions of unchecked authority over detainees coincides with the courts' institutional self-interest in reserving a role for the judiciary in the determination of the fate of enemy combatants and presumed terrorists.

Three groups of court cases that arose as part of the "war on terrorism" form the basis for this article. In the first group of cases, there are the criminal trials for terrorism or siding with the enemy: the cases of John Walker Lindh, Zacarias Moussaoui, and Richard Reid. Second, there are cases in which the U.S. government detains U.S. citizens as "enemy combatants" within the United States: the cases of José Padilla and Yaser Hamdi. Third, there are cases of "enemy combatants" who are not U.S. citizens, and who were detained outside the U.S. In June 2004, the U.S. Supreme Court ruled on aspects of the cases of Padillia and Hamdi as well as on the third group of cases: detainees held in Guantánamo Bay, a place where the United States has jurisdiction but no complete sovereignty. The analysis will ask how the cases unfolded, which arguments were used by the parties, and how the courts reacted to these arguments. I first introduce the cases and the main issues they raised. In a next step, I develop my theory of political trials and utilize it for explaining the deficits in the proceedings as well as the arguments used by the courts in the analyzed cases.

II. THE CASES

2.1. The Criminal Cases

Zacarias Moussaoui, a French citizen, was arrested on August 17, 2001, on immigration charges. He had aroused the suspicion of teachers at his flight school when he only wanted to learn how to fly but not how to start or land a plane. He is the only defendant in a U.S. criminal case who is suspected of having been part of the conspiracy that led to the 9/11 attacks. It is alleged that he would have been the "twentieth hijacker" on the plane that crashed in Pennsylvania. On December 11, 2001, the government announced that Moussaoui would be tried in a federal court, not in one of the military tribunals that had been established by executive order a month earlier.[8] Even though Moussaoui's case was left in the civilian court system, the specter of a military tribunal resurfaced later when the trial moved into impasses.

The pretrial proceedings were marked by a high degree of antagonism between Moussaoui—who insisted on acting without a lawyer—and the prosecution.[9] Moussaoui proudly admits to being an Al Qaeda member and views the court and his lawyers as part of a government conspiracy to have him executed.[10] His court filings and speeches were saturated with slurs to the point that his sanity was in doubt.[11] Moussaoui's insistence that the trial was a mockery was reinforced by the government's intransigent stance on defendants' rights in relation to security concerns.[12] The main point of contention was Moussaoui's request to interview witnesses who are being held incommunicado as enemy combatants in Guantánamo Bay and elsewhere. As a result of these disputes, the proceedings were widely perceived as a "circus," and Moussaoui was blamed for this undignified process. Soon critics began wondering whether a military tribunal would not have been more appropriate: there Moussaoui would not get an audience for his political views, and he would not get the access to the witnesses he requested. Moussaoui's latest guilty plea of April 2005 contains detailed statements about his connections to Al Qaeda and Osama bin Laden.[13] If the plea is eventually accepted despite the doubts about Moussaoui's mental health, this means that this terrorism case does not have to be argued out in court. Thus the law, the access to evidence, and the interrogation methods remain legally largely uncontested.

John Walker Lindh was captured in Afghanistan after the Taliban prisoner uprising in Mazar-i-Sharif in late November 2001. While he was awaiting medical attention, he told a CNN journalist and military interrogators that he enjoyed his experience in Afghanistan and identified with jihad. Already at the time of Lindh's interrogation and incommunicado detention in Afghanistan, the U.S. public discussed his apparent treason.[14] It was widely thought that by joining the Taliban, he had become an enemy of the United States and thereby morally—or even legally—forfeited his U.S. citizenship.[15] Lindh's case accustomed the public to the idea that enemies of the United States might carry a U.S. passport that they don't "deserve": the enemy status was made more important than the citizenship status, paving the way for the later treatment of José Padilla and Yaser Hamdi that only few people objected to.

John Lindh claims that he was interrogated while being held under inhumane conditions and being denied proper medical treatment and access to a lawyer.[16] U.S. authorities denied any mistreatment and maintained that Lindh did not need or could not get a lawyer because he was held as a wartime captive, not as a criminal suspect.[17] The interrogations were aimed at gathering vital intelligence about the enemy and were legally part of the battlefield actions, so the Miranda rights did not have to be read. Yet the criminal case against Lindh rested on statements from these interrogations.

During the trial, the government tried to connect Lindh to the death of CIA officer Michael Spann during the prisoners' uprising in Mazar-i-Sharif. The connection between the "hero" Spann and the "traitor" Lindh galvanized public support for the legally weak case against Lindh.[18] Treason could not legally be proved, but administration officials suggested that when Lindh was interviewed shortly before the uprising and remained silent, he had chosen sides by failing to warn his fellow countrymen of the imminent uprising that would bring about the death of Michael Spann.[19] Given the uncertainties of a jury trial in an atmosphere in which many potential jurors saw him as a radical enemy and wanted to strip him of his citizenship, Lindh entered a plea arrangement. On July 12, 2002, he pleaded guilty to two minor charges and was sentenced to twenty years in prison. The government did not need to argue out the case and did not have to disprove the allegations of mistreatment.

Richard Reid, a U.K. citizen, tried to ignite his explosives-filled sneakers on an American Airlines flight from Paris to Miami on December 22, 2001. He was subdued by passengers and crew members. Although then–Attorney General John Ashcroft repeatedly announced that Reid was charged as an Al Qaeda–trained terrorist,[20] the indictment was not based on any Al Qaeda link. Reid decided to plead guilty, and was sentenced to life in prison. In his guilty plea, he rejected the authority of U.S. law and confirmed the Justice Department's designation as a public enemy: Reid stated that he used a destructive device in an act of war.[21] The judge rejected Reid's self-proclaimed warrior status, saying that he did not consider Reid an enemy combatant but a terrorist. Calling Reid a soldier, the judge reasoned, would give him too much of a standing.[22] Both sides grasped the political importance of distinguishing between criminals (who supposedly accept the authority of domestic law) and warriors (who reject the enemy's domestic law but are possibly subject to international legal norms). Reid squarely attacked the authority of the U.S. law in order to pose as a captive warrior who is illegitimately subjected to the enemy's law. The judge, in turn, defended the authority of the court and—in contrast to the government's stance in the *Padilla* and *Hamdi* cases—rejected the rhetoric of war and enemy. The stress on the absence of war and the depiction of Reid as a criminal was meant to enhance the legitimacy of the court decision as an impartial judgment rather than a case of wartime victor's justice. This is the only politically contentious U.S. terrorism case examined here that did not turn into a case of political justice.

2.2. U.S. Citizens as Enemy Combatants

José Padilla, a U.S. citizen, was arrested at Chicago O'Hare Airport on May 8, 2002. He was first detained as a material witness in a "dirty bomb" plot until, a month later, the government suddenly changed the rationale for his detention: speaking from Moscow, John Ashcroft ordered José Padilla's detention as an "enemy combatant," adding that the arrest "disrupted an unfolding terrorist plot to attack the United States."[23] The government soon acknowledged that the alleged plot had not advanced beyond the initial planning stages.[24] Padilla was suddenly detained as an enemy combatant and not as a criminal suspect because the government could not construct a criminal case against him. Therefore, the detention rationale was based not on what he had done but on what he might do if released. In addition, his "intelligence value" should justify his continued detention:

> Our interest really in this case is not law enforcement, it is not punishment because he was a terrorist or working with the terrorists. Our interest at the moment is to try and find out everything he knows so that hopefully we can stop other terrorist acts.[25]

Within days of the detention, an administration advisor on terrorism trials and two former government anti-terrorism lawyers took to the op-ed pages to justify the detention. Administration advisor Ruth Wedgwood assures that habeas corpus review would still be available.[26] Victoria Toensing, who established the terrorism unit in the Justice Department under President Ronald Reagan, states less soothingly that the criminal justice system is not the proper place for fighting enemies, and that keeping Padilla there would be a threat to national security.[27] Douglas Kmiec, former counsel to George Bush Sr. and Reagan, reminds the readers that the country is at war. This, he continues, is key to understanding and approving the military detention of Yaser Hamdi and José Padilla.[28]

What were the intended legal consequences of designating Padilla an "enemy"? The government's position was that, being an enemy combatant, Padilla has no right to meet his lawyer, Donna Newman, or to challenge his status as an enemy combatant. Even habeas corpus review should be unavailable because Padilla is not held as a criminal suspect but as an enemy: a habeas petition would "interject this court into the president's conduct of ongoing hostilities."[29] This assertion is based on the logically prior and irrefutable designation of Padilla as a public enemy. Indeed, the government's position is that this designation is virtually a "decision" in the Schmittian sense: not reducible to a subsumption of a case under a general rule, and beyond the possibility of independent rational review.[30] This decision moves Padilla into an exceptional status beyond the normal law: legal recourse should not be available to him because he was not accused of breaking the law, but of being a threat to the law who needs to be kept beyond the law. If Padilla's case were still in the area of criminal law, it would be in the field of Jakobs's "criminal law for enemies": there, "punishment serves as a prevention of future crimes, not as a retribution for past ones."[31] But the case is not a case of "criminal law for enemies" because there are no significant references to criminal conduct. All we are told is that Padilla is dangerous. Therefore, he is placed in a legal situation in which he ceases to exist as a person with rights.

The courts were partially at unease when they were asked to certify their own abdication of authority in this case. The U.S. District Court agreed that the government possesses the authority to detain Padilla under the given circumstances, but the U.S. Court of Appeals reversed the decision. In the U.S. Supreme Court decision of June 28, 2004, the material question of whether the government has the authority to detain Padilla was not resolved because the Supreme Court held that the habeas petition was filed in the wrong jurisdiction. The Court did, however, address the question of possible government justifications for detaining Padilla indirectly in its related decision in the case of Yaser Hamdi.[32]

Yaser Esam Hamdi was arrested in Afghanistan in late November 2001 during the Mazar-i-Sharif prison uprising, and subsequently brought to the Guantánamo Bay detention center. In early April 2002, U.S. authorities found out that Hamdi, who was born in Louisiana, holds U.S. citizenship. He was still considered an enemy combatant, but the newly discovered facts about his citizenship led to his transfer to a military prison in the continental United States: like Padilla and Lind, he is both a citizen and an enemy. Unlike Lindh, however, Hamdi did not enjoy the benefits of criminal procedure. On May 10, 2002, Hamdi's court-appointed lawyer, Frank Dunham, filed a writ of habeas corpus. A district judge initially allowed Dunham to meet his client in private.[33] The government appealed this ruling to a panel of the Fourth Circuit Court, which remanded the case to the district court because the latter did not properly "consider what effect petitioner's unmonitored access to counsel might have on the government's ongoing gathering of intelligence."[34]

The publicized factual basis for Hamdi's enemy combatant status was thin: the prosecution only produced a declaration of six pages written by Michael Mobbs, a special advisor to Defense Department Undersecretary Douglas Feith, which is based on third-party information. In the document, Mobbs admits that "some information provided by the sources remains uncorroborated and may be part of an effort to mislead or confuse U.S. officials."[35] These doubts notwithstanding, the appellate court unanimously held that "asking the executive to provide more detailed factual assertions would be to wade further into the conduct of war then [sic] we consider appropriate" and rejected the lawyer's petition.[36] The court accepted a thinly substantiated "enemy combatant" designation by the government on the grounds that in wartime, the courts' deference to the executive authority gains in importance and "the Constitution does not specifically contemplate any role for courts in the conduct of war, or in foreign policy generally."[37] The designation of Yaser Hamdi as a dangerous public enemy thus leads an appellate court to assume that the detention of a U.S. citizen on U.S. territory is a matter of "foreign policy." Is such a conclusion possible because in this political logic, enemies—even those who are nominally citizens—become foreigners? In any case, the "enemy" designation makes the difference between the treatment that Hamdi was accorded and the treatment that a criminal suspect in the United States is normally accorded.

In the Supreme Court, the *Hamdi* case raised separation of powers issues more directly than the *Padilla* case because if a habeas petition was allowed at all, it was filed in the correct jurisdiction. The two central questions both concerned the scope of presidential and judicial powers: first, is there a constitutional or congressional authorization for the executive to detain an American citizen under the conditions and circumstances in which Hamdi was detained? And, second, which procedure is someone who is detained under these powers entitled to in order to challenge the factual or legal basis for their detention? The Supreme Court plurality of three justices argued that Congress's resolution authorizing the president to use "necessary and appropriate force" to counter the attacks of 9/11 was sufficient as an authorization of the detention of enemy combatants defined as persons who are "part of or supporting forces hostile to the United States or coalition partners." Hamdi is, however, entitled to a "fair opportunity" to rebut the facts on which his detention is based in front of a "neutral decisionmaker."[38]

This balancing act did not command widespread agreement. Justice Clarence Thomas argues that this compromise is an unjustified intrusion into executive power, while Justice Antonin Scalia proposes that Hamdi is entitled to a full criminal trial as long as Congress does not suspend habeas corpus. The case was primarily framed and argued as a dispute about the separation of powers rules—and not, for example, about Hamdi's human rights. The most extreme attempt by the U.S. government to assert unchecked authority over detainees, however, was the establishment of detention centers in Guantánamo Bay and other places outside the U.S. sovereign territory in the hope to enter a jurisdictional void.

2.3. The Guantánamo Bay Detainees

The U.S. detainees in Guantánamo Bay were arrested over the course of the U.S. military action in Afghanistan. The first detention facilities opened in January 2002, and the area has been redesigned for long-term detention. Up to 600 detainees were held there at the same time; the numbers are gradually declining.[39] The Guantánamo detainees were not meant to have access to the U.S. judicial system because of their personal status (as enemy combatants) and the place of their detention: they are not U.S. citizens and, moreover, are presumed unlawful enemy combatants; and the United States has jurisdiction but no full sovereignty in Guantánamo Bay. This has previously been interpreted to preclude the jurisdiction of U.S. federal courts—at least as far as non-U.S. citizens are concerned. In fact, the location was chosen for the detention facility precisely because of this unique legal status. While the "war on terror" provides one rationale for creating exceptions from the rule of law for an indeterminate period of time, the status of Guantánamo Bay legitimizes a spatial exception from the rights normally accorded to detainees under U.S. control.[40] However, since the "war on terrorism" provides for a potentially indefinite temporal exception, the war-induced state of exception is becoming permanent—though confined to Guantánamo Bay and other marginal "permanent spaces of exception."[41]

Habeas corpus petitions brought on behalf of Guantánamo detainees were initially rejected by courts in California and the District of Columbia.[42] Although courts have thought that the detainees "have some form of rights under international law,"[43] they did not review the petitions. "Some form of rights" was simply not sufficient for noncitizen enemy combatants detained by the United States outside U.S. sovereign territory. According to the government, the detainees should eventually be tried in military tribunals. The tribunals would offer a minimum of process, but their decisions cannot be appealed to any U.S., foreign, or international court. The complaint of the detainees was, however, that they had not even been accorded a military tribunals procedure to determine the legality of their detentions after 2-1/2 years in Guantánamo Bay.[44] About 150 detainees were released over time, but the releases are due as much to diplomatic pressure from their home countries as to executive determinations that they did not pose a threat anymore.[45]

The Supreme Court had to decide whether federal courts have jurisdiction to review habeas petitions brought on behalf of Guantánamo detainees, or whether the personal status of the detainees or of their place of detention precludes jurisdiction. The majority argued that the decision widely thought to be a precedent, *Johnson v. Eisentrager* (1950), does not apply.[46] First, the detainees are not clearly enemy combatants or enemy aliens because they are not nationals of countries with which the United States is formally at war.[47] Thus, they do not fit the classic definition of "enemy alien."[48] Second, they dispute having been engaged in illicit warfare against the U.S. And finally, they have not been accorded a judicial or other procedure to determine the veracity of their claims, or have even been formally charged with any wrongdoing.[49] In addition, the Court argues that the case at hand posed the danger of creating an "unconstitutional gap" in the authority of federal courts with regard to jurisdiction over habeas claims: no single court clearly has statutory jurisdiction, but the detainees have a constitutional right to have their petitions heard.[50] The Court fills the gap by resorting to "constitutional fundamentals," arguing that a legal vacuum depriving persons in U.S. custody of access to the U.S. court system cannot be tolerated, and by construing the habeas statute to confer federal courts jurisdiction over the petitions brought from the Guantánamo detainees.[51] The Court did not, however, detail the procedures due to the detainees trying to challenge their status. The Supreme Court thus enlarged the scope of judicial power against the explicit claims of the executive that wanted to keep Guantánamo Bay beyond the reach of civilian courts—without, however, providing immediate juridical benefits to the detainees. In order to comply with the Supreme Court decision, the military created "Combatant Status Review Tribunals" (CSRT). Detainees have to argue their cases for themselves and cannot see the complete evidence against them. One-third of the detainees have declined to attend their hearings; their cases were decided in absentia. The CSRTs have found that all except for thirty-three detainees were held properly as unlawful enemy combatants.[52] This miniscule chance of release on the basis of a procedure in which the detainees have little chance to effectively rebut the evidence against them suggests that while the government might have been unsuccessful at devising military commissions to try and convict or acquit enemy combatants, there is less judicial resistance to the detentions of

prisoners as "enemy combatants" without charges for an indeterminate period of time.

What lessons can be drawn from these cases? How are they different from other court cases? First, the criminal cases against John Walker Lindh, Richard Reid, and Zacarias Moussaoui were very public, and were publicly connected to political agendas. The courts were portrayed as arms of the government engaged in the war on terror. The introduction of the war logic in the criminal cases led to a low tolerance for acquittals: once a case is promoted as part of the war on terror, the government cannot afford to lose it. In this logic, the courts represent a potential obstacle to a deserved prison sentence for a proven terrorist rather than a forum for testing the evidence.[53] If a case may not be lost because it is part of a war, the government takes further steps to challenge the authority of the court: In the Moussaoui case, for example, the government repeatedly raised the specter of transferring Moussaoui to a military tribunal where procedures are shorter, defendants' rights are fewer, and judges as well as prosecutors are under military command. The case against Richard Reid was so clear-cut that not even the war rhetoric by government officials and the defendant could damage the trial. And in the case of John Walker Lindh, accusations of torture and misinterpreted evidence linger long after he decided to plead guilty to lesser charges. The government portrayed all three trials as part of the war on terrorism and emphasized the alleged or admitted links between the defendants and Al Qaeda.

The enemy combatant cases, in contrast, started in relative political silence. In these cases, the executive branch did not want to use the courts as part of an all-embracing strategy in the war on terror. Instead, the courts were portrayed as obstacles in this war. By connecting these detentions to the "war on terror," the government tried to convince the courts that they could not "second-guess" executive determinations and military decisions because courts have no role in fighting a war. The Supreme Court decisions established some limits to executive power over the detainees. Still, the limited role of the courts in the enemy combatant cases suggests that the government has succeeded in carving out a space of exception for its designated enemies.

Second, the judicial component of the war on terror has shifted its emphasis away from the criminal trials of the initial post-9/11 period and toward the legal figure of executive detention of unlawful enemy combatants. Thus, criminal law, whether "criminal law for citizens" or "criminal law for enemies," has declined in importance for U.S. counterterrorism policy. The executive detention policies pose as preventive measures. They are not designed to adjudicate responsibility for past wrongdoing, or even for the preparation stages of future acts of terrorism. Instead, the "unlawful enemy combatants" are held for as long as they are deemed dangerous.

Third, in the criminal cases and the challenges to executive detentions, the government and—to a limited degree—the courts agreed that the defendants and detainees are not merely criminals. But they could not agree on the legal and political significance of the enemy status. The government was especially vocal in the introduction of the "war" and "enemy" terminology into the courtrooms. The purpose of this terminology is to suggest that the persons concerned should not enjoy the standard procedural rights. At the extreme, the designated enemies become "non-persons" who have no rights or legal personality to be reckoned with.[54] Only the discursive force of the enemy designation can explain how, for example, the detention of U.S. citizen Yaser Hamdi on U.S. territory becomes a matter of U.S. foreign policy.

These groups of cases—the criminal cases as well as the enemy combatant cases—were unusual in their political dimension, in the frequent usage of "war" and "enemy" language, and in their implications for the separation of powers. The political stakes of the cases call for a closer analysis. In the next section I will argue that the cases surveyed above suggest a powerful mechanism by which politically contentious cases develop into cases of political justice.

III. THE CONCEPT OF POLITICAL JUSTICE

Which types of trials are political trials? I argue for a two-step model. First, any open court system will confront a number of cases that are politically contentious because they raise politically salient issues. Some of these politically contentious cases reach stage two as they develop two problematic dimensions: first, the careful separation of roles between the executive and the judiciary might collapse if the executive values winning the case higher than judicial independence; and, second, in many politically contentious cases, one party is declared a "public enemy" with the understanding that this person does not deserve full rights in court. At the extreme, the "public enemy" is treated as a "non-person" (Jakobs). Thus, the question is no longer which rights enemies should enjoy, but whether enemies are persons capable of having rights at all.

These two dimensions of political justice signal the problems that are often referred to by the term "political justice." Benjamin Constant, for example, complains about the changes in the judicial system caused by Napoleon's wars, such as the improper influence of the military, for whom opposition is "disorder . . . the courts councils of war, the judges soldiers under orders, the accused enemies and the trials battles";[55] the addition of "representatives of the government" to local courts; and the introduction of special military courts.[56] Constant objects to military courts because they see defendants as enemies, and protests the decline of judicial independence that arises from the militarization and executive domination of the judicial system. These are the primary reasons why, according to Constant, political trials are objectionable.

Before further explaining the two prevalent dimensions of political justice, I want to distinguish my use of the term from three frequent usages in order to avoid misunderstandings. These accounts differ most importantly in their understanding of what the "political" in "political justice" refers to. Political trials are often defined (1) by the bias or unwitting partiality of the judiciary in certain cases, (2) in reference to a specified "political" area of law and state activity that the trials touch upon, or (3) by the presence of a political adversary in court whose actions are being incriminated.

1. *The political bias model* maintains that political justice is defined by the way a judicial decision is arrived at. In the radical version of this model, judges consciously decide cases in accordance with their own political views.[57] More subtle and sociologically founded accounts stress that judges are often recruited from a particular social background, and that this background and the training they receive make them systematically more receptive to certain claims

than to others. The political bias model has two important problems. First, it cannot delimit the area of political justice. If political trials were different because their decisions manifest explicit or implicit judicial bias, which trials would not be political trials? At the extreme, the political bias theory only states the obvious: that the judiciary is never insulated from the political and social context. Though valuable as a corrective to a purely legalistic understanding, this model cannot point to a theory of political justice. Second, the political bias model tends to be a rationalization for lost trials rather than an analytical model. Friedrich Wolff, an East German lawyer with the rare distinction of first defending scores of political defendants in the GDR and then defending the former East German head of state Erich Honecker in court, accordingly states in his book, titled *Lost Trials 1953–1998: My Defenses in Political Cases,* "All cases that I thought were political trials were seen as unpolitical trials by the prosecution and the judges. . . . My political trials are thus political trials according to my interpretation."[58] If only lost trials are political trials, cases will be "political" according to one party and "unpolitical" according to the other party; and the model has little analytical value.

2. *The political core model* identifies political trials according to the area of law and state activity they touch upon. It presumes that there is a "core" of state activity that is "political" and thus the object of "political" trials.[59] This center of state activity is "immediately concerned with the conflicts about the type of political system,"[60] with the "protection of the state, the political order, its institutions and representatives, its symbols, and the political process of forming opinions and majorities."[61] Political justice according to the "political core" model takes place when the judiciary "takes on the task of defending the existing power structures in an unmediated way and thereby becomes a part of the conflict about the political order."[62] This concept also raises serious problems. First, the "political core" model views intense political conflict as a challenge to the "core" of the polity. A concept of politics that centers on the preservation of the state makes it harder to carve out a space for political arguments that are not perceived as threats, and thus not liable to be criminalized. The nongovernmental party to a conflict is easily criminalized or

vilified because conflict is viewed as a threat to the state, and not just to a particular policy. In this model, the "political core" of state activity is vigorously protected, even with means that include the partial breakdown of the separation of powers and the vilification of the perceived challenger to the state. Thus, the "political core" model tends to condone the instances of political justice that it can identify. Second, the approach not only adopts the perspective (though not always the point of view) of the prosecuting party but also tends to accept the existence of the two problematic dimensions of political justice as necessary for warding off challenges against the state. If a conflict is portrayed as a threat to the state, the challenger turns into an enemy of the state, and the standard procedural safeguards are thus more easily cast aside. Critics of political trials who adopt this model therefore often feel the need to point out that the challengers on trial were in fact no credible or imminent threat to the state.[63] Finally, the "political core" model operates with a too narrow and state-centered concept of politics. Politically contentious cases need not challenge the political system, and they need not arise under laws designed to protect the state. Instead, political conflicts can concern important principles that do not challenge the political system. For example, cases like *Brown v. Board of Education* (1954) or *Roe v. Wade* (1973) concerned fundamental political issues, but not the continued existence of the political system. So why should they not be viewed as potentially political cases? It is obvious that a concept of politics that centers on the preservation of the state is too narrowly concerned with some areas of law, at the risk of neglecting other fields in which different political views are adjudicated. The "political core" model is thus problematic because it views political conflicts as challenges to the present political order in a way that gives too much deference to the evaluation of the executive.

3. *The political conflict model* maintains that political justice describes trials in which political adversaries use the court in order to have their claims legitimized, and to change the distribution of political power.[64] Political justice according to this model is "a political conflict argued out with legal means."[65] The political conflict model presumes that the other party in court is a political adversary and that the presence of this

political adversary transforms the trial into a "political" one. Some political trials follow this pattern, but others don't. In many political cases, the characters involved in the courtroom drama are secondary because the dominant political aspect of the case is an issue, and not a person. Moreover, the courtroom adversary might not be a competitor for social or political power at all. Some defendants might have committed crimes for political reasons but are not part of a sizable and coherent political group that the state might take the trouble to delegitimize through legal proceedings; such is the case with terrorists like Timothy McVeigh and the current slate of Al Qaeda suspects. In these cases, the government does not want to criminalize a political party through judicial action but wants public approval for the chosen strategy in dealing with a perceived threat. The issue is certainly political, but the persons in court are not political adversaries.

In sum, the three alternative definitions of political justice are not sufficient because they implicitly take sides with either the state party (political core model) or challengers who lost a case (the political bias model), or they narrow down the number of potential political cases in accordance with a too narrow concept of politics. In contrast to these three definitions, I propose a two-stage model: some trials are politically contentious because they deal with politically salient issues. Some of these trials, in turn, become instances of political justice because they violate the separation of powers rules or vilify one party to the case. This definition does not place restrictions on the area of law under which the cases arise, and it does not suppose that a case under the sedition laws is any more "political" than a case about equal opportunity in education. This definition also does not adopt an evaluation of actions as "political" or "unpolitical" by either party. And, finally, this definition allows us to tell which trials are political trials regardless of which party has "won" and irrespective of whether the claims of the prosecution, of the defense, or of certain political groups have been upheld.

In this model, political trials occur when at least one of two dimensions is present: the violations of the separation of powers norms, and the construction of one party to the case as a public enemy. However, this model is primarily based

on the U.S. post-9/11 cases. What are the limitations that arise from these sources? First, the interlocking mechanisms of vilification and abridgment of the separation of powers might be specific to terrorism cases—although this need not be the case. Thus, it is possible to imagine other political-legal mechanisms that steer trials away from the normal mode of interaction between the judiciary, the political branches, and the public. Second, the U.S. cases arise in a context in which a stated adherence to the rule of law, separation of powers, and nonvilification of defendants is the norm. Political justice appears as an exception to that norm—an exception that is triggered predominantly by the convergence of executive interference and vilification of the defendants or detainees. This model of political justice thus presupposes that the administration of justice normally operates in a different mode, and that political justice is the exception that needs a political legitimization. Where show trials are the norm, this model of political justice has only limited analytical purchase.

I will now introduce the idea of politically contentious cases and the two problematic dimensions of political trials, explain the dynamics arising from them, and examine the U.S. post-9/11 trials in light of this model of political justice.

3.1. Politically Contentious Cases

Some cases raise politically salient issues. But how can we know which issues are salient at any given time and place? I propose that a case is politically contentious if one party credibly claims that the issues at stake are of central importance to the political life of the jurisdiction in which the case arises. This criterion does not rely on a consensus about whether any given case is "political." It might falsely identify some trials as "politically contentious" on the basis of fraudulent claims about the political dimensions of a case. Still, since "politically contentious" is not a reproach but an analytical category, it is better to scrutinize more cases for the potential presence of the two troubling dimensions of political justice than to ignore some politically contentious cases altogether.

Why are the U.S. post-9/11 terrorism cases politically contentious? The government and the defense lawyers raised fundamental questions and suggested answers to the courts. The government portrayed the cases as part of the "war against terrorism." It asked the courts to confirm the incommunicado detention of citizens and foreigners as enemy combatants, and publicly questioned whether the courts were up to the task of defending the country against terrorists. More importantly, the government asked the courts to confirm their version of the political reality—an open-ended war on a transnational terrorist network—against alternative interpretations. The lawyers for the detainees and defendants stressed related questions: is the president authorized to declare persons enemy combatants in a war undeclared by Congress and without review by the courts? How does the law change when there is a war? Who can properly recognize "enemies," and how? Can information obtained from interrogations "on the battlefield" without the presence of a lawyer be used in court?

The courts' early answers to these questions often confirmed the administration's outlook on the situation. The Supreme Court justices, though disagreeing on the legal evaluations of the cases, repeatedly stressed the fundamental political questions involved: the minority in *Rasul v. Bush,* for example, accuses the majority of "an irresponsible overturning of settled law in a matter of extreme importance to our forces currently in the field."[66] In making this change, the minority in *Rumsfeld v. Padilla* agrees, with the majority that the case is politically important. Yet the majority disagrees with the minority's account of the nature of the political stakes.

> At stake in this case is nothing less than the essence of a free society. Even more important than the method of selecting the people's rulers and their successors is the character of the constraints imposed on the Executive by the Rule of Law. Unconstrained executive detention for the purpose of investigating and preventing subversive activity is the hallmark of the Star Chamber. Access to counsel for the purpose of protecting the citizen from official mistakes and mistreatment is the hallmark of due process.[67]

The plurality opinion in *Hamdi v. Rumsfeld* starts its attempt to strike a compromise between the interests involved by noting that "at this difficult time in our Nation's history, we are called upon to consider the legality of the government's detention of a United States citizen on United States soil."[68] The courts and the Supreme Court justices were keenly aware of the political importance of these cases. Their disagreements mainly stem from diverging evaluations of the rights and interests at stake, not from a refusal to recognize the political significance of their decisions. The political salience of cases raises the stakes, but it does not turn them into instances of political justice. Still, these politically contentious cases have the potential of turning into political justice. In the post-9/11 world, the primary mechanism by which politically contentious cases became instances of political justice was the convergence of vilification and executive interference.

3.2. Political Justice I: Overstepping the Boundaries of the Separation of Powers

The separation of powers imposes limits on the executive interference in the ongoing judicial business. The institutional aspects of a court case can affect the balance of powers between the three branches of government: which branch may decide what, and in which procedure? In political trials, the most common violation of the rules establishing the separation of powers is the executive interference in judicial proceedings. The interference can be so extreme that the executive virtually delivers the "script" of the trial in which the prosecution and the judges are merely acting in their assigned roles.[69] But not only totalitarian and authoritarian regimes are liable to violating separation of powers rules in cases that are dear to the government. The problem regularly appears—though to a lesser degree—in constitutional democracies. In order to see why governments are tempted to overstep the boundaries of the separation of powers, and why they nonetheless usually refrain from it, it is necessary to consider the role that the separation of powers plays with regard to judicial decisions.

Courts legitimize and authorize actions of the other, "political," branches. They can fulfill this task because they operate according to preestablished rules and maintain their independence from the executive and the legislative. The courts' independence and the legality of the proceedings thus give the court decisions their public legitimacy.[70] And because the courts are relatively well insulated against the claims of political power, they can also decide against the current power holders. The legal and political ramifications of a politically contentious case can be "almost as uncertain as the outcome of an election campaign."[71] In order to reduce this uncertainty, those in positions of political power sometimes try to take shortcuts when they insist that they cannot afford to lose the case. The only way to secure a favorable outcome, of course, is by disregarding some of the boundaries set by the separation of powers. The price to be paid for this transgression will be a lower political surplus value of the court decision. Court decisions that seemed predetermined will not legitimize government action or convince people to change their views on an issue.[72]

Governments face the dilemma of either being sure to win a case or being certain that the decision with an uncertain outcome will command public legitimacy. Constitutions order governments to choose the second alternative, but governments sometimes find seemingly compelling reasons for why they cannot lose a certain case even at the price of violating ordinary separation of powers rules. In these cases, it is justified to speak of political justice. In the post-9/11 cases specifically, the violation of the separation of powers was linked to a prior vilification of the defendants or petitioners. The asserted dangerousness of a defendant or detainee is one of the most convincing arguments to this effect. Indeed, the potential damage that could be inflicted by someone who was let free because of lack of evidence or because he was "only planning" to commit terrorist acts would be immense. And in times of public fear of further terrorist attacks, even a minimal risk of another attack committed by one of the designated "enemy combatants" can suffice to legitimize the detention policy in the eyes of a wary public. Ruth Wedgwood, an advisor to the government, states that traditionally, the criminal justice system is based on the assumption that cases might be lost and criminals might wrongly be released. It might happen that a rapist goes free and assaults more women. Yet the calculus is different, Wedgwood implores the readers, if you are dealing with persons who might kill 100,000 people if they are not detained.[73]

Such risk assessments, whether exaggerated or not, seem to introduce the "preventive strike" doctrine into criminal and administrative law. How would you know that a defendant would be "going to do something to cause 100,000 casualties," and how justified could these beliefs be if judge and jury dismiss the evidence? From this perspective, counterterrorism becomes an epistemological problem. In the end, concurrence with presidential threat assessments might be rooted in the simple fear of incurring a small risk of a large-scale attack by questioning executive authority.

In the U.S. post-9/11 terrorism cases, the government undermined the separation of powers rules mainly by two interlocking strategies. First, the administration consistently argued that courts should play no role in the conduct of warfare and hence not challenge executive determinations in the context of the "war on terrorism." And, second, the establishment of military tribunals, or the threat thereof, squarely challenged the jurisdiction of civilian courts. In addition, there were restrictions on the defense—justified with regard to security concerns—in the criminal cases, and lack of access to lawyers in the enemy combatant cases. These restrictions also serve to either hinder the defense or prevent court cases altogether, but they will not be discussed here. Instead I will concentrate on the direct challenges to the courts' authority.

First, the government argued that the courts are not entitled to review government determinations of who is an enemy combatant and which witnesses in Pentagon custody can be interviewed. In the case of José Padilla, judges were warned not to second-guess the military's enemy combatant determination. Doing this, the prosecution argued, would interfere with the constitutional prerogatives of the commander in chief.[74] Even a writ of habeas corpus would "interject this court into the president's conduct of ongoing hostilities."[75] This strategy could only succeed because the government could convince the courts that the detentions and the interrogations in Afghanistan, South Carolina, and Guantánamo are part of an ongoing war, so that any procedural hurdles or judicial review would move the battlefield into the courtroom.[76] The enemy appears not as a person, but as a danger to be contained.

In *Hamdi v. Rumsfeld*, the separation of powers perspective shaped the justices' responses to the question of whether there was a congressional authorization for the detention. To be legal, the detention of Hamdi needed to be part of the military campaign that was authorized by Congress, as the plurality holds. The opinions by Justice David Souter (concurring in part and dissenting in part) and Justice Scalia (dissenting) argue that the presumed authorization is too vague to allow such grave deprivations of liberty like the potentially indefinite detention of citizens as enemy combatants.[77] Both opinions explicitly argue that finding an authorization in a vague congressional resolution would give the executive powers that jeopardize the separation of powers—in relation to both Congress and the judiciary.

The separation of powers perspective controls not only the issue of an alleged authorization of the detention but also the decision on what procedure Hamdi is entitled to in order to challenge his status. The more procedural rights Hamdi is accorded, the less will the government's determination be taken at face value, and the more will the government have to give public and substantiated reasons for his continued detention. According to the view of the administration, any judicial inquiry into the enemy combatant designations would be a challenge to executive authority. Yet any measure of procedure accorded to Hamdi could strengthen the legitimacy of the detention by subjecting it to added independent scrutiny. To be sure, judicial inquiries into the grounds of the detention could also reveal that the detention was unjustified.

In the Guantánamo case (*Rasul v. Bush*), the justices again stress the implication of the decision for the separation of powers. While the majority rules on very narrow grounds by comparing the facts in the case with the facts in the alleged precedent of *Eisentrager*, the concurring opinion by Justice Anthony Kennedy explicitly stresses the separation of powers aspect. Granting that *Eisentrager* "indicates that there is a realm of political authority over military affairs where the judicial power may not enter," he stresses, "a necessary corollary of *Eisentrager* is that there are circumstances in which the courts maintain the power and the responsibility to protect persons from unlawful detention even where military affairs are implicated."[78] The dissenters also view the scope of executive power as the primary issue at stake, but they disagree with the majority on how the interest of the executive in its own unchallenged power should be balanced against the interest of the detainees in challenging their status: "The Commander in Chief and his subordinates had every reason to expect that the internment of combatants at Guantanamo Bay would not have the consequence of bringing the cumbersome machinery of our domestic courts into military affairs."[79] In sum, the Guantánamo Supreme Court decision clearly justified the expansion of judicial authority against the strongly voiced claims of the executive by the need to safeguard detainees against potentially

illegal detention—against a dissenting opinion that finds greater virtue in heightened deference to the executive in wartime.

Second, in the terrorism trials the civilian courts were reminded that military tribunals constitute another available option in the "war on terrorism." The government asked the courts to play their part by allowing the incapacitation of enemy combatants through continued detention and without concrete charges by privileging the military over the juridical logic.[80] Courts were expected to justify the government's treatment of enemy combatants and terrorism suspects and to satisfy the public's wish for the legitimacy of legality. Courts were hailed as long as they fulfilled these expectations. When John Walker Lindh pleaded guilty, a government attorney interpreted this as a victory for the American people, adding that the case shows that the criminal justice system is suitable for combating terrorism.[81] On the other hand, when the prosecution and the judge had diverging assessments about the conditions needed for a fair trial, the idea of military tribunals reemerged. Suddenly, what is at stake in the Moussaoui case is whether the courts can still be an option in the war on terror.[82] The cases were pictured as challenges to the courts, and the courts might fail.

Normally the government cannot remove cases from civilian courts unless it wishes to drop the indictment. In the post-9/11 cases, however, the government has carved out a novel legal space where the cases can be transferred to military tribunals. These tribunals emanate from a presidential order issued on November 13, 2001. As of July 2005, only 4 of about 560 detainees have formally been charged. Moreover, the legality of the entire procedure is in doubt.[83] Still, the option of switching to military tribunals was consistently part of the discussions in the cases. "Given the danger to the safety of the United States and the nature of international terrorism," declares the executive order, "it is not practicable to apply in military commissions under this order the principles of law and the rules of evidence generally recognized in the trial of criminal cases in the United States district courts."[84] Military tribunals differ from federal courts not only in the procedures and laws that are applied. Military tribunals are established under the auspices of the executive power and are not independent courts. Both the prosecutors and the commissioners in military tribunals are military officers and "are ultimately answerable to the Secretary of Defense and the President."[85] Moreover, the rules according to which the detainees might be tried are also devised by the executive branch. The tribunals' decisions are beyond judicial review, as the Military Tribunals Order states: persons convicted by a military tribunal "shall not be privileged to seek any remedy" in any court of the United States, any foreign court, or any international tribunal.[86] Once a case is in the military tribunals system, it will never again be subject to normal independent judicial review.

Decisions issued by these military tribunals would not carry the legitimacy that the federal court decisions still have in spite of executive incursions into the proceedings. This might be a reason why the government in practice preferred federal criminal courts to military tribunals. Yet, since the tribunals are established while the federal courts are working, the prosecution can at least threaten to move the case to a "safer" venue in case the courts do not accept the government claims. The criminal trials were influenced by the background threat of a "streamlined" procedure in military tribunals for cases which civilian courts could not handle. The detainees who lodged habeas petitions, however, complained that they had not even had the benefit of a military tribunal procedure. Given the legal dispute on the military commissions, it is not likely that these commissions will be used to a significant degree. For the Guantánamo detainees, the most likely path to being released is a determination by an "administrative review board" that they do not pose a threat anymore—that they ceased to be enemies, irrespective of whether they have committed war crimes.

In sum, the post-9/11 terrorism cases were explicitly viewed through the lens of the separation of powers. The executive wanted the war powers expanded to include detentions of enemy combatants at home and abroad. Based on assessments of the risks of letting terrorism suspects go free, some federal courts initially acquiesced to the stipulations of the executive. The Supreme Court, however, strongly asserts that courts have to play a role in these policy areas: "[I]t does not infringe on the core role of the military for the courts to exercise their own time-honored and constitutionally mandated roles of reviewing and resolving claims like those presented here."[87] Yet it took the courts more than two years to develop a consistent and independent position on these urgent matters, and the actual improvement of the legal status of the designated enemy combatants is still limited as the litigation over the scope and depth of the procedure accorded to the detainees is ongoing.[88]

3.3. Political Justice II: Constructing Public Enemies

The second problematic dimension of political justice is the construction of one party as a public enemy. At a minimum, the allusions to "war" and "enemies" suggest the plausibility of relaxed standards. At the extreme, the enemy designation denies the other's legal and moral personality. Public vilification can therefore legitimize infringements on defendants' rights and violations of the separation of powers rules. In a constitutional democracy, the sustained exercise of political justice in violation of procedural standards and the separation of powers needs a legitimization.[89] The construction of a "clear and present danger" posed by a dangerous enemy is a frequent rationale for such a slighting of the rule of law standards. The "enemy" in these cases is not the traditional belligerent who shares notions of the laws and customs of war with the adversary. Rather, the enemy figure used in the "enemy combatant" designations is at the intersection of a tradition in Western thought about the laws of war that excludes certain enemies from the law, and a concept of the enemy proposed by Carl Schmitt.

Within the codified international law of armed conflict as well as within political thought on war, we find at least two different ideas of the enemy. Some enemies are defined and recognized by the law, and other enemies are recognized by the law only insofar as they are placed beyond it. Articles 4 and 5 of the Third Geneva Convention, for example, define those participants in war who are entitled to the protected prisoner of war status when they are captured. They can be tried for war crimes, and their enemy status is legally bounded and regulated. Those who fall outside the definition of these articles, in contrast, are enemies beyond the specific scope of the convention. This bifurcation of the enemy status in the Geneva Conventions—which is often assumed to be no longer operative—is a reflection of a much older distinction in Western thought about international norms: for many thinkers, these norms primarily apply to what they call Christian or civilized states; and the rules for fighting Christian enemies and fighting those who are outside the scope of these norms are very different. For example, the 1912 edition of Lassa Oppenheim's seminal international law treatise states that international law is the "body of customary and conventional rules which are considered legally binding by civilized States in their intercourse with each other."[90] The scope of the application of these rules is determined by the "facts of the present international life."[91] There are states—Oppenheim lists "Persia, Siam, China, Morocco, Abyssinia, and the like"—where "civilization has not yet reached that condition which is necessary to enable their governments and their population in every respect to understand and carry out the command and rules of International Law."[92] Reciprocity demands that the rules of international law can only be applied in relation to actors who can equally be expected to observe them: "[I]t is discretion, and not International Law, according to which the members of the Family of Nations deal with such states as still remain outside that family."[93] Outside of the "family of nations" there is no law, but only ethics and policy. This distinction is based on the assumption that some actors do not merely violate international law, but they don't recognize it even in its violation. Because international law needs to rely on reciprocity, it cannot be applied in relation to those who cannot be expected to apply it. The others' presumed lawlessness thus turns into a justification for placing them beyond the law. The reciprocity-based idea of international law has, as far as basic norms on the treatment of persons are concerned, largely been superseded by the universalizing logic of human rights. These rights are thought to be universal regardless of express consent. If the treatment of detainees was based on the human rights framework, the reciprocity-based argument would therefore have no purchase. The relatively wide acceptance of the reciprocity-based argument about the Geneva Conventions in the "war on terror" indicates, however, that the older limited and reciprocity-based view of the law of war has not completely lost its traction. The "discretion" in the treatment of enemies beyond the law allowed by the reciprocity concept of international obligation is filled with other, related notions of the enemy.

In the post-9/11 cases, the enemy beyond the law resembles the Schmittian enemy:[94] the enemy is not a competitor for political power but "existentially something different and alien." He "intends to negate his opponent's way of life and therefore must be repulsed or fought in order to preserve one's own form of existence."[95] This is an extreme characterization of an ideal-type enemy from which the U.S. government has borrowed in this and other occasions. Enemies can be created and shaped in political discourse. The terrorist, for example, "could be made to take on all characteristics that the accusing party decided upon."[96] The image of the terrorist enemy draws on real-world events but interprets them to suit preconceptions about the moral character of the specific enemy: rational and callous, ruthless, or irrational and fanatic. There is a long history of Western societies imagining different groups of Muslims and Arabs as existential enemies.[97] Carl Schmitt himself uses such an example to illustrate the apparent plausibility of his enemy model that does not allow for compromise: "Never in the thousand-year struggle between Christians and Moslems did it occur to a Christian to surrender rather than defend Europe."[98] If the conflict is pictured as existential, there are no independent third parties or legal rules common to both adversaries. The sovereign "decides" on the "enemy." In this stark view of the "enemy," neither law nor independent judgment nor the idea of a justiciable offense has a place. This stark portrayal of the "existential enemy" helps to identify the elements from which the Bush administration's rhetoric borrowed.

At first, the administration tried to argue that the Guantánamo detainees (and those detained in undisclosed locations abroad as well as some of the detainees in the continental U.S.) are prisoners of war—traditional belligerents bound by the common laws of war. But the administration backtracked from this designation insofar as it would have implied according the detainees the protections of the Geneva Conventions. The administration thus created a novel legal category that resonated with the war language without imposing legal obligations on the government. The categories of "illegal combatant," "enemy combatant," and "unlawful enemy combatant" are poorly defined.[99] They have the effect of placing the designated enemy outside the law and beyond justice. According to President George W. Bush, Padilla is "a bad guy" who is "where he needs to be, detained."[100]

The "enemy combatant" cases highlight another crucial element of the designation of persons as "enemies" as distinct from criminals. Criminals are judged on what they could be shown to have done. "Enemies," in contrast, are judged by their stipulated hostile commitment that constitutes them as an abstract threat. For dealing with enemies, prevention rather than punishment is the rule. The introduction of the "preventive strike" doctrine into criminal and administrative law is based on the logically prior designation of the detainees as dangerous and unpredictable public enemies by the president.

Where there are enemies, war is not far behind.[101] The almost unanimous description of the situation as a war, even after major fighting in Afghanistan ended and before the war in Iraq started, is noteworthy.[102] The state of war intensifies the political friend/enemy distinction, legitimizes heightened executive power, and paves the way for the detention of enemies during wartime. Given the description of the task of the war, there is no foreseeable end to the regime of exceptionalism. The war language implies that the courtroom case was not the United States versus Zacarias Moussaoui, but the United States versus the Enemy. Far from affirming the value of adversarial proceedings, the war language of the administration suggests a strict friend/foe distinction. And how could a court rule against the United States in such a context? Can a court even be "independent" in adjudicating between the U.S. and an enemy? It is the state, according to Carl Schmitt, which decides on who is an enemy; and conflicts among enemies "can neither be decided by a previously determined general norm nor by the judgment of a disinterested and therefore neutral third party."[103] The U.S. government is not following a purely Schmittian line. Yet by portraying the defendants or petitioners as enemies against whom the U.S. needs to be defended, the government suggests that they are beyond the law, and that any legal process they are accorded is a matter of policy or grace, but not of rights: "This nation's enemies may not enlist America's courts to divert efforts and attention from the military offensive abroad to the legal defensive at home," as Attorney General John Ashcroft put it.[104] Thus, if enemies are not criminals but are a danger beyond guilt and innocence, and civilian courts might interfere with the conduct of warfare, the prospect of military tribunals or prolonged detention without access to the judicial system seems acceptable.

With the exception of Justice Thomas in his dissent in *Hamdi v. Rumsfeld,* none of the Supreme Court justices subscribe to the view that enemy combatant designations cannot be subject to review. But are the other justices convinced that Hamdi, Padilla, and the Guantánamo detainees are not really the enemies they were portrayed as? The decisions suggest that the Supreme Court justices have no doubt that at least some of the detainees might warrant a designation as public enemies. Yet in their view, judicial procedures are capable of finding the enemies among the detainees. "Indefinite detention without trial or other proceeding," argues Justice Kennedy, concurring in the Guantánamo decision, "allows friends and foes alike to remain in detention."[105] He does not object to "foes" being in detention, but trusts in the ability of judicial procedures to tell friends from foes. This reasoning applies to the Guantánamo detainees, who are not U.S. citizens. In the case of U.S. citizen Yaser Hamdi, however, both Justice Souter and Justice Scalia dispute that an enemy combatant status distinct from the status of a criminal is necessary or legal. In reviewing the presumed congressional authorization for the enemy combatants designations, Justice Souter argues,

> There is no reason to think Congress might have perceived any need to augment Executive power to deal with dangerous citizens within the United States, given the well-stocked statutory arsenal of defined criminal offenses covering the gamut of actions that a citizen sympathetic to terrorists might commit.[106]

Justice Scalia, pointing to previous wars in U.S. history, argues that "where the Government accuses a citizen of waging war against it, our constitutional tradition has been to prosecute him in federal court for treason or some other crime" as long as habeas corpus is not suspended by Congress.[107] The idea that there could be a status of an enemy that is distinct from that of a criminal by being outside the categories of criminal guilt and innocence raised more objections when it was applied to U.S. citizens than when it was applied to other persons. Still, the plurality opinion holds that "there is no bar to this Nation's holding one of its own citizens as an enemy combatant."[108] Eventually, we are led to believe, the enemy status trumps the citizenship status.

The Court opposed the government's infringements of separation of powers rules more than it opposed the idea that some of the persons involved in the cases are public enemies. However, by requiring some procedure to review the enemy combatant designations, the Supreme Court changed the nature of these designations: they are no longer decisions beyond review and appeal based on few or no publicized facts—quasi-Schmittian sovereign decisions. Instead, the designation of someone as an enemy combatant under the Supreme Court guidelines would get closer to a rational administrative decision for which reasons have to be given, and which might be tested in court according to preexisting general standards. The enemy status is almost converted from a Schmittian "political" decision into a "liberal" legal determination; it is hedged within the confines of the law. Still, the Supreme Court leaves the purpose of this enemy designation—the enemy, once properly designated, is beyond the law—intact.

The Supreme Court uses similar arguments for answering the question of whether there is an ongoing war that might be complicated by adding legal requirements for executive actions. The question was answered in the affirmative: "Active combat operations against Taliban fighters apparently are ongoing in Afghanistan."[109] Yet the existence of a war does not mandate the silence of the courts, as both the plurality and a dissenting opinion point out: "We have long since made clear that a state of war is not a blank check for the President when it comes to the rights of the Nation's citizens."[110] Justice Scalia argues explicitly that the Constitution is no stranger to the state of war:

> Whatever the general merits of the view that war silences law or modulates its voice, that view has no place in the interpretation and application of a Constitution designed precisely to confront war and, in a manner that accords with democratic principles, to accommodate it.[111]

War does not appear as an extralegal event unforeseen by an old Constitution, but it is hedged within the constitutional rules and precedents. Thus both the public vilification of detainees with their designation as "enemy combatants" and the description of the political context as a "war on terrorism" are curtailed but largely accepted by the Supreme Court. Yet the Court undermines the traction of the "enemy" and "war" language by nevertheless requiring some form of judicial proceedings for the

detainees. Had the government's claims about the "enemies" found less acceptance, the Court might have accorded the detainees more robust procedural rights. Now an enemy combatant who is a U.S. citizen is merely entitled to "notice of the factual basis for his classification, and a fair opportunity to rebut the government's factual assertions before a neutral decisionmaker." In the proceeding, hearsay evidence can be admitted, and "the Constitution would not be offended by a presumption in favor of the government's evidence, so long as that presumption remained a rebuttable one and fair opportunity for rebuttal were provided."[112] If the current implementation of this standard is approved by the judiciary, Guantánamo Bay and other places will remain a "permanent space of exception" (Agamben). These spaces are not outside of the law—the applicable legal regulations are too dense to allow such a claim. Rather, the situation is peculiar in that the detainees are in a place of rightlessness in a context that is not lawless. The law, however, fails to recognize them as full persons that become subjects, and not mere objects, of the law.

In sum, the language of enemies and war helped to suggest that the detainees and defendants in the post-9/11 cases do not have the same rights as other persons would have. Enemies are not guilty of specific acts, but they are abstractly dangerous. According to the administration's views, the status of an "enemy" is not subject to review. This view was largely upheld by the lower courts but was only partially shared by the Supreme Court. Although the Supreme Court accepted the suggestion that there are enemy combatants who are not criminals and yet need to be detained, the Court subjects the decision about the enemy combatant status to a limited form of judicial process.

IV. CONCLUDING EVALUATIONS

The post-9/11 terrorism trials in the U.S. inevitably stirred emotions and prompted discussions about the responsibility for the attacks, the status of Al Qaeda and the Taliban, and the reasonable scope of civil liberties. The cases that found their way to the courts were bound to be politically contentious. It was not inevitable, however, that the administration would turn most of these cases into political justice by interfering with judicial proceedings, portraying the defendants as enemies beyond the law, and literally trying to enlist the courts in the war against terrorism. This executive-dominated political justice even jeopardized the "image-creating capacity" (Kirchheimer) of the trials. Over time, the importance of the strict criminal justice framework in the "war on terror" declined. The administration went beyond even the "criminal law for enemies" and used means of executive detention entirely unconnected to any reproach of past wrongdoing. As of July 2005, only 4 out of more than 560 detainees at Guantánamo Bay have been charged with any crimes.[113] This shift from criminal law to detention is based not only on practical but also on ideological considerations: during the 2004 presidential election campaign, Vice President Dick Cheney warned that a Democratic administration would pose a danger to national security because it would fall back into the pre-9/11 mindset of assuming that terrorist attacks are criminal acts, and that there is no war.[114]

The post-9/11 trials demonstrate the attractions and dangers of highly politicized cases in times of public fear. The omnipresent language of enemies and war was clearly meant to legitimize the abrogation of defendants' rights and limits on courts' autonomy. In the cases concerning the detention of enemy combatants, the war talk was effectively used for introducing the "preventive strike" doctrine into criminal law—or for going beyond criminal law altogether. Accordingly, the problems with political trials are not limited to issues that can be neatly described as "human rights" or "rule of law issues." The violation of the separation of powers rules is predicated upon a political designation of persons as enemies beyond the law. This designation diminishes or denies the detainees' legal personality. In order to reverse the legal surface of the situation exemplified by Guantánamo Bay, these underlying vilifications need to be addressed. Only when the detainees are publicly imagined as persons whose pain, fear, hopes, and rights have to be taken into account by others will they be able to gain standing as full legal and moral persons. Yet only little information about the detainees and their experiences is available. A letter written by Moazzam Begg, a UK citizen detained by U.S. and Pakistani authorities on January 31, 2002, and since held as Bagram Air Base and then Guantánamo Bay, sheds a bit more light on the experiences of persons who, for example, had not seen daylight or fresh food for a year, and who

had been subjected to psychological and physical mistreatment. Any statements he made, writes Begg, "were signed and initialed under duress":

> The said interviews were conducted in an environment of generated fear, resonant with terrifying screams of fellow detainees facing similar methods. In this atmosphere of severe antipathy toward detainees was the compounded use of racially and religiously prejudiced taunts. This culminated, in my opinion, with the deaths of two fellow detainees, at the hands of U.S. military personnel, to which I myself was partially witness.[115]

In spite of this treatment and his almost complete isolation, Begg continues, "I have maintained a compliant and amicable manner with my captors, and a cooperative attitude."[116] Moazzam Begg and three other UK citizens were released from Guantánamo Bay in January 2005.[117] After a brief questioning by the British police, they were released without charges.[118] Their release was not obtained on the level of law alone: being citizens of a key U.S. ally in the war on terror, they had a government that could (and finally did) press for their release. From the point of view of the UK public, the four were primarily citizens, and maybe secondarily criminal suspects. They were not released from Guantánamo Bay for being nonenemies, or human beings, but for being citizens of a close ally. For the purpose of achieving their release, their humanity was mediated through their citizenship.

What are the potential and limit of litigation in these cases? U.S. courts have taken different positions on the rights of detainees and the scope of executive power to detain or try them. There is no clear tendency to raise the evidential and procedural thresholds for detention in favor of the detainees. The most recent decisions in the case of Salih Ahmed Hamdan demonstrate that the detainees should not pin their hopes on the judiciary: while a district court found the "military commissions" for trying Guantánamo detainees in violation of standing law,[119] an appeals court reversed this decision,[120] allowing the commissions with curtailed procedure to continue. Courts seem indeed more vigorous at rejecting one dimension of political justice (the violation of the separation of powers rules) than the other dimension (the vilification of the defendants and detainees). When courts counter unreasonable claims of authority from the executive, their action coincides with their institutional self-interest in having a role in an of the detainees and defendants, it seems, will not primarily be achieved in the courts.

NOTES

1. Former U.S. Attorney General John Ashcroft, statement before the Senate Judiciary Committee, quoted from "U.S. Detention of Aliens in Aftermath of September 11 Attacks," *American Journal of International Law* 96, no. 2 (2002): 473.

2. See Joseph Lelyveld, "Interrogating Ourselves," *New York Times Magazine,* June 12, 2005.

3. See, for example, Scott Shane, "Detainee's Suit Gains Support from Jet's Log," *New York Times,* March 29, 2005, on the case of Maher Arar, a Canadian "rendered" by U.S. authorities to Syria.

4. See Günther Jakobs, "Bürgerstrafrecht und Feindstrafrecht," *Höchstricherliche Rechtsprechung Strafrecht* (2004): 88–95.

5. Ibid.

6. *Lords of Appeal, Judgment in the Cause A and Others v. Secretary of State for the Home Department,* and *X and Another v. Secretary of State for the Home Department, 2004 UKHL 56. Decision of December 16, 2004.*

7. Jakobs, "Bürgerstrafrecht und Feindstrafrecht," 88. Jakobs treats "enemies" and "citizens" as opposites. Thereby he alludes to the more common opposites associated with these terms: "enemies" are opposed to "friends," and "citizens" to "foreigners." The conclusion that "citizens" are "friends" and "enemies" are "foreigners" (or "foreigners" are "enemies") is not suggested by Jakobs. Still, Jakobs' odd opposition calls for a closer examination of the connection between citizenship and the enemy status. This issue also appeared directly in the U.S. cases. See, for example, George Fletcher, "Citizenship and Personhood in the Jurisprudence of War," *Journal of International Criminal Justice* 2, no. 4 (2004): 953–66.

8. On the criteria for the military tribunals, see Presidential Military Tribunals Order, November 13, 2001, available at http://www.whitehouse.gov/news/releases/2001/11/print/20011113–27.html (accessed July 19, 2005). Senator Joseph Lieberman (D-CT) immediately suggested trying Moussaoui in one of these tribunals; see Don van Natta with Benjamin Weiser, "Compromise Settles Debate over Tribunal," *New York Times,* December 12, 2001; and Robert Jackson, "Pentagon Argues Case for Military Tribunals System," *Los Angeles Times,* December 13, 2001.

9. See Philip Shenon, "Terror Suspect Says He Wants U.S. Destroyed," *New York Times,* April 23, 2002.

10. See Neil Lewis, "Defendant in Sept. 11 Plot Accuses Judge of Trickery," *New York Times,* June 26, 2002.

11. See Philip Shenon, "Terror Suspect Says He Wants U.S. Destroyed," *New York Times,* April 23, 2002; and Brooke Masters, "Defiance Could Delay Terror Trial: Moussaoui Refuses to Meet Psychiatrist," *Washington Post,* May 16, 2002.

12. See Philip Shenon, "Lawyers Seek Information behind Theory on Hijacking," *New York Times,* April 25, 2003; and "Crime and Justice," editorial, *Washington Post,* March 27, 2003.

13. See Richard Serrano, "Moussaoui Pleads Guilty to Terror Plot," *Los Angeles Times,* April 23, 2005.

14. There was consensus that Lindh had voluntarily chosen to be an enemy. Some criticized the president's military tribunals order for not including citizens: "[O]ne's status of fighting for the enemy, not one's status as a noncitizen," should be decisive, according to law professor David Cole; see Brooke Masters and Edward Walsh, "U.S. Taliban Fighter to Have His Rights, Rumsfeld Says," *Washington Post,* December 5, 2001; also see Edward Epstein, "Boxer Says Marin Taliban Should Face Court-Martial," *San Francisco Chronicle,* December 19, 2001.

15. See, for example, Jim Wooten, "Trials Would Give Enemies an Advantage," *Atlanta Journal—Atlanta Constitution,* December 16, 2001.

16. For a defense statement, see Richard Serrano, "Lindh Team Offers List of Abuses," *Los Angeles Times,* March 23, 2002. The descriptions seemed rather unlikely at the time, but seem much more plausible now after similar forms of abuse have been reported from Iraq and other detention centers in Afghanistan.

17. See Edward Epstein, "Prosecutors Belittle Lindh's Brutality Claim," *San Francisco Chronicle,* July 2, 2002.

18. Legal commentators frequently remarked that the charges were weak and changing, so the prosecution had to rely on the symbolic meaning of Lindh's actions and statements in addition to the scattered evidence; see Leon Friedman, "It Won't Be Easy to Convict John Walker," *New York Times,* December 29, 2001; and Naftali Bendavid, "Analysts See Trouble Spots in Legal Case against Lindh," *Chicago Tribune,* February 10, 2002.

19. David Pace, "Lindh Torture Claims Disputed; Government Fights Bid to Exclude His Statements from Trial," *Houston Chronicle,* July 3, 2002.

20. Wayne Washington, "Suspect in Bomb Attempt Indicted," *Boston Globe,* January 17, 2002.

21. Shelley Murphy, "Defiant Reid Pleads Guilty," *Boston Globe,* October 5, 2002.

22. Pam Belluck, "Unrepentant Shoe Bomber Sentenced to Life," *New York Times,* January 31, 2003.

23. Dan Eggen and Susan Schmidt, "'Dirty Bomb' Plot Uncovered, U.S. Says," *Washington Post,* June 11, 2002.

24. Patrick Tyler, "A Message in An Arrest," *New York Times,* June 11, 2002.

25. News briefing by Secretary of Defense Donald Rumsfeld. Quoted from U.S. Supreme Court, *Rumsfeld v. Padilla,* No. 03–1027. Decision of June 28, 2004. Justice John Paul Stevens, dissenting, 11.

26. Ruth Wedgwood, "The Enemy Within," *Wall Street Journal,* June 14, 2002.

27. Victoria Toensing, "Citizenship Doesn't Matter," *USA Today,* June 14, 2002.

28. Douglas Kmiec, "This Is War, and Military Justice Is Appropriate," *Los Angeles Times,* June 14, 2002.

29. *Padilla v. Rumsfeld,* No. 4445, Motion to Dismiss Amended Writ of Habeas Corpus in the U.S. District Court for the Southern District of New York, June 26, 2002, 7.

30. See Carl Schmitt, *The Concept of the Political,* trans. George Schwab (1932; reprint, Chicago: University of Chicago Press, 1996), 27.

31. Jakobs, "Bürgerstrafrecht und Feindstrafrecht," 92.

32. *Hamdi v. Rumsfeld,* Decision of June 28, 2004, No. 03–6696.

33. Brooke Masters, "Access to Lawyers Ordered for Detainee," *Washington Post,* May 30, 2002.

34. U.S. 4th Circuit Court of Appeals, *Hamdi v. Rumsfeld,* No. 02–6895. Decision of July 12, 2002. Also see Philip Shenon, "Appeals Court Keeps American Detainee and His Lawyer Apart," *New York Times,* July 13, 2002.

35. Michael Mobbs, "Declaration," August 27, 2002, 2.

36. U.S. 4th Circuit Court of Appeals, *Hamdi v. Rumsfeld,* No. 02–7338. Decision of January 8, 2003, p. 37.

37. Ibid., 38.

38. *Hamdi v. Rumsfeld,* Justice Sandra Day O'Connor, plurality opinion, at 9, 10.

39. See Tim Golden, "After Terror, a Secret Rewriting of Military Law," *New York Times,* October 24, 2004.

40. The creation of spatial exceptions in areas of de facto control is not new; see the Supreme Court decision in *Johnson v. Eisentrager,* 339 U.S. 763 (1950).

41. Giorgio Agamben, *Means without Ends: Notes on Politics* (Minneapolis: University of Minnesota Press, 2000), 44.

42. On the decisions of the trial courts and the appeals courts, see "Ability of Detainees in Cuba to Obtain Federal Habeas Corpus Review," *American Journal of International Law* 96, no. 2, 481–82; Neely Tucker, "Judge Denies Detainees in Cuba Access to U.S. Courts," *Washington Post,* August 1, 2002; Henry Weinstein, "Suit on Behalf of Prisoners Blocked," *Los Angeles Times,* November 19, 2002; and Neil Lewis, "Bush Administration Wins Court Victory on Guantánamo Detentions," *New York Times,* March 12, 2003.

43. U.S. District Court for the District of Columbia, *Rasul v. Bush,* No. 02–299. Decision of July 31, 2002, 30.

44. The recent District Court decision invalidating the Military Commission process for different reasons does not increase the likelihood that the "enemy combatants" will be charged with any war crimes: it seems easier for the government to continue the detention under the enemy combatant rationale than to comply with the demanded changes in the Military Commission procedure. See U.S. District Court for the District of Columbia, *Hamdan v. Rumsfeld,* No. 04–1519. Decision of November 8, 2004.

45. See Tim Golden, "Tough Justice: Administration Officials Split over Stalled Military Tribunals," *New York Times,* October 25, 2004; and Neil Lewis, "Guantánamo Prisoners Getting Their Day, but Hardly in Court," *New York Times,* November 8, 2004.

46. *Rasul v. Bush,* No. 03–334. Decision of June 28, 2004.

47. The petitioners in the *Rasul et al.* and *Odah et al.* cases that were joined by the Supreme Court were Kuwaitis and Australians. The Court did not indicate whether this reasoning would apply to citizens of Afghanistan as well. However, since citizenship is only one of many criteria, it may be assumed that the decision also applies to Afghan citizens.

48. Also see Fletcher, "Citizenship and Personhood," 963.

49. *Rasul v. Bush,* Justice Stevens, majority opinion, 7–8.

50. Ibid., 9.

51. Ibid., 16–17.

52. See Neil Lewis, "Ruling Lets U.S. Restart Trials at Guantánamo," *New York Times,* July 16, 2005.

53. The initial hard line of the prosecution in terrorism-related cases seems to have relaxed after more than two years. Recently, prosecutors in a Detroit case against a suspected "sleeper cell" asked the judge for a reversal of a conviction and a retrial after discovering misconduct by the prosecutor in the original case. Evidence contrary to the prosecution's theory had been ignored, and the court, the jury, and the defense had been misled about evidence. The first prosecutor is being investigated for misconduct. See Danny Hakim, "Judge Reverses Conviction in Detroit 'Terrorism' Case," *New York Times,* September 3, 2004.

54. See Günther Jakobs, "Das Selbstverständnis der Strafrechtswissenschaft vor den Herausforderungen der Gegenwart," in *Die Deutsche Strafrechtswissenschaft vor der Jahrtausendwende,* ed. Albin Eser, Winfried Hassemer, and Björn Burkhardt (Munich: C. H. Beck, 2000), 53.

55. Benjamin Constant, "The Spirit of Conquest and Usurpation and Their Relation to European Civilization," in *Benjamin Constant: Political Writings,* ed. Biancamaria Fontana (Cambridge: Cambridge University Press, 1988), 61.

56. Editorial footnote in Constant, "The Spirit of Conquest," 61.

57. This is Ernst Fraenkel's definition of political justice as distinct from his analysis of class justice; see Ernst Fraenkel, *Zur Soziologie der Klassenjustiz* (1931; reprint, Darmstadt, Germany: Wissenschaftliche Buchgesellschaft, 1968), 26.

58. Friedrich Wolff, *Verlorene Prozesse 1953–1998: Meine Verteidigungen in politischen Verfahren,* 2nd ed. (Baden-Baden, Germany: Nomos Verlag, 1999), 7.

59. This model has often been used in analyses of German postwar political trials. See, for example, Alexander von Brünneck, *Politische Justiz gegen Kommunisten in der Bundesrepublik Deutschland 1949–1968* (Frankfurt am Main: Suhrkamp, 1978), where the political core model is part of a more elaborate theory; Dieter Sterzel, "Funktionen der politischen Justiz," in *Politische Justiz,* ed. Axel Görlitz (Baden-Baden, Germany: Nomos, 1996); and Herwig Roggemann, *Systemunrecht und Strafrecht* (Berlin: Berlin-Verlag, 1993).

60. Von Brünneck, *Politische Justiz,* 12.

61. Roggemann, *Systemunrecht und Strafrecht,* 17.

62. Sterzel, "Funktionen der politischen Justiz," 116.

63. See, for example, von Brünneck, *Politische Justiz.*

64. See Otto Kirchheimer, *Political Justice: The Use of Legal Procedure for Political Ends* (Princeton, N.J.: Princeton University Press, 1961); and Alexander von Brünneck, *Politische Justiz.*

65. Von Brünneck, *Politische Justiz,* 335.

66. *Rasul v. Bush,* Justice Scalia, dissenting opinion, 1.

67. *Rumsfeld v. Padilla,* Justice Stevens, dissenting opinion, 11.

68. *Hamdi v. Rumsfeld,* Justice O'Connor, plurality opinion, 1.

69. For an analysis of two trials belonging to this species, see Clemens Vollnhals, *Der Fall Havemann: Ein Lehrstück politischer Justiz,* 2nd ed. (Berlin: Ch. Links Verlag, 2000).

70. See von Brünneck, *Politische Justiz,* 365.

71. Kirchheimer, *Political Justice,* 117.

72. See von Brünneck, *Politische Justiz,* 13.

73. Karen Branch-Brioso, "Quality of Evidence Colors How U.S. Handles Suspects," *St. Louis Post-Dispatch,* June 16, 2002.

74. Tom Jackman and Dan Eggen, "'Combatants Lack Rights, U.S. Argues," *Washington Post,* June 20, 2002.

75. *Padilla v. Rumsfeld,* No. 4445, Motion to Dismiss Amended Petition for Habeas Corpus in the U.S. District Court for the Southern Circuit of New York, June 26, 2002, 1.

76. An appellate court judge suggested that this would be the immediate consequence of a further inquiry into the circumstances of Yaser Hamdi's arrest, quoted from Tom Jackman, "Judges Wary of Interference in Hamdi Case," *Washington Post,* October 29, 2002.

77. *Hamdi v. Rumsfeld,* Justice Souter, concurring in part and dissenting in part, 3; and Justice Scalia, dissenting, 22.

78. *Rasul v. Bush,* Justice Kennedy, concurring, 3.

79. *Rasul v. Bush,* Justice Scalia, dissenting, 19.

80. Katharine Q. Seelye, "War on Terror Makes for Odd Twists in Justice System," *New York Times,* June 23, 2002.

81. Richard Serrano, "Lindh Pleads Guilty, Agrees to Aid Inquiry," *Los Angeles Times,* July 16, 2002.

82. Jerry Markon, "Much Rides on Terror Case," *Washington Post,* February 19, 2003.

83. Tim Golden, "After Terror, a Secret Rewriting of Military Law," *New York Times,* October 24, 2004.

84. Military Tribunals Order, November 13, 2001.

85. Harold Hongju Koh, "The Case against Military Commissions," *American Journal of International Law* 96, no. 2 (2002): 339.

86. Military Tribunals Order, November 13, 2001, sec. 4(b).

87. *Hamdi v. Rumsfeld,* Justice O'Connor, plurality opinion, 28.

88. See Neil Lewis, "Ruling Lets U.S. Restart Trials at Guantánamo," *New York Times,* July 16, 2005.

89. Von Brünneck, *Politische Justiz,* 336.

90. Lassa Oppenheim, *International Law,* vol. 1, 2nd ed. (New York: Longmans, Green, 1912), 3.

91. Ibid., 30.

92. Ibid., 33.

93. Ibid., 34–35.

94. Schmitt makes a rather large point of the distinction between foe and enemy. Following common contemporary usage, I am collapsing his not altogether clear distinctions into different models of "enemies," not "foes."

95. Schmitt, *The Concept of the Political,* 27.

96. Lon Troyer, "Counterterrorism: Sovereignty, Law, Sovereignty," *Critical Asian Studies* 35, no. 2 (2003): 260.

97. See Gil Anidjar, *The Jew, the Arab: A History of the Enemy* (Stanford, Calif.: Stanford University Press, 2003).

98. Schmitt, *The Concept of the Political,* 29.

99. The term "unlawful combatant" seems lifted from the Supreme Court decision in *Ex Parte Quirin,* 317 U.S. 1 (1942), while the "enemy combatant" terminology is strikingly similar to the "enemy alien" language in *Johnson v. Eisentrager,* 339 U.S. 763 (1950).

100. Stephen Hedges, "U.S. Flouts Legal Rights, Lawyer Says," *Chicago Tribune,* June 12, 2002.

101. War is not strictly required for the existence of enemies, but in the 9/11 cases, the administration constantly emphasized the existence of a war even when courts could not see it.

102. See Troyer, "Counterterrorism," 269.

103. Schmitt, *The Concept of the Political,* 27.

104. Lyle Denniston, "Court Gives No Rights to Detained: Military's Prisoners Can't Appeal," *Boston Globe,* March 12, 2003. Ashcroft is, whether intentionally or not, paraphrasing the Eisentrager decision: It would be difficult to devise more effective fettering of a field commander than to allow the very enemies he is ordered to reduce to submission to call him to account in his own civil courts and divert his efforts and attention from the military offensive abroad to the legal defensive at home. (*Johnson v. Eisentrager,* 339 U.S. 763 [1950], at 779)

105. *Rasul v. Bush,* Justice Kennedy, concurring, 4.

106. *Hamdi v. Rumsfeld,* Justice Souter, concurring in part and dissenting in part, 9–10.

107. *Hamdi v. Rumsfeld,* Justice Scalia, dissenting, 1.

108. *Hamdi v. Rumsfeld,* Justice O'Connor, plurality opinion, 11.

109. Ibid., 13.

110. Ibid., 29.

111. *Hamdi v. Rumsfeld,* Justice Scalia, dissenting, 27.

112. *Hamdi v. Rumsfeld,* Justice O'Connor, plurality opinion, 26–27.

113. See Neil Lewis, "Detainee Trials to Resume Soon," *New York Times,* July 19, 2005.

114. "Edwards Demands Action on Remark," *New York Times,* September 9, 2004.

115. Moazzam Begg, letter, July 12, 2004, http:// image.guardian.co.uk/sys-files/Guardian/ documents/ 2004/10/01/guan_letters.pdf (accessed July 19, 2005).

116. Ibid.

117. See Associated Press, "Last Four Britons Let Go from Guantánamo," January 25, 2005.

118. See Associated Press, "British Police Release Former Gitmo Inmates," January 26, 2005.

119. U.S. District Court for the District of Columbia, *Hamdan v. Rumsfeld,* No. 041519. Decision of November 8, 2004.

120. U.S. Court of Appeals for the District of Columbia Circuit, *Hamdan v. Rumsfeld,* No. 04–5393. Decision of July 15, 2005.

APPENDIX A

Locations of Worldwide Terrorist Activity (Maps 1–8)

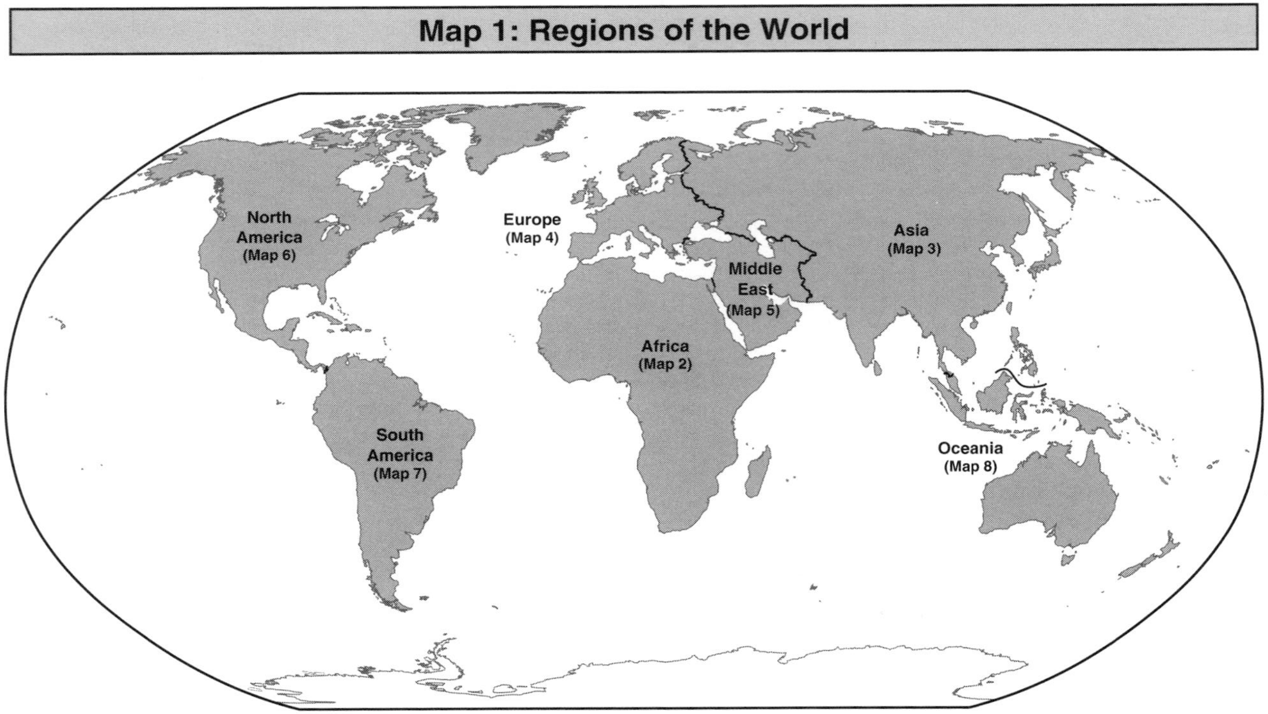

Map 1: Regions of the World

Asia (Map 3)

Oceania (Map 8)

Middle East (Map 5)

Africa (Map 2)

Europe (Map 4)

South America (Map 7)

North America (Map 6)

MAP 1   Regions of the World

Map 2: Africa

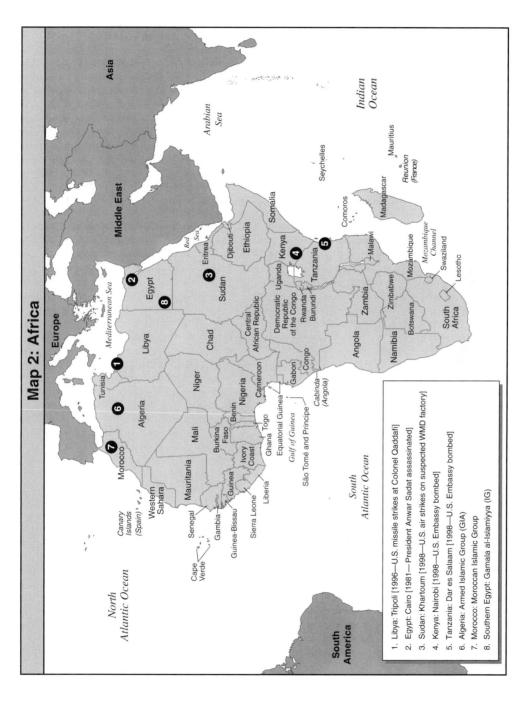

1. Libya: Tripoli [1996—U.S. missile strikes at Colonel Qaddafi]
2. Egypt: Cairo [1981— President Anwar Sadat assassinated]
3. Sudan: Khartoum [1998—U.S. air strikes on suspected WMD factory]
4. Kenya: Nairobi [1998—U.S. Embassy bombed]
5. Tanzania: Dar es Salaam [1998—U.S. Embassy bombed]
6. Algeria: Armed Islamic Group (GIA)
7. Morocco: Moroccan Islamic Group
8. Southern Egypt: Gamala al-Islamiyya (IG)

MAP 2   Africa

367

Map 3: Asia

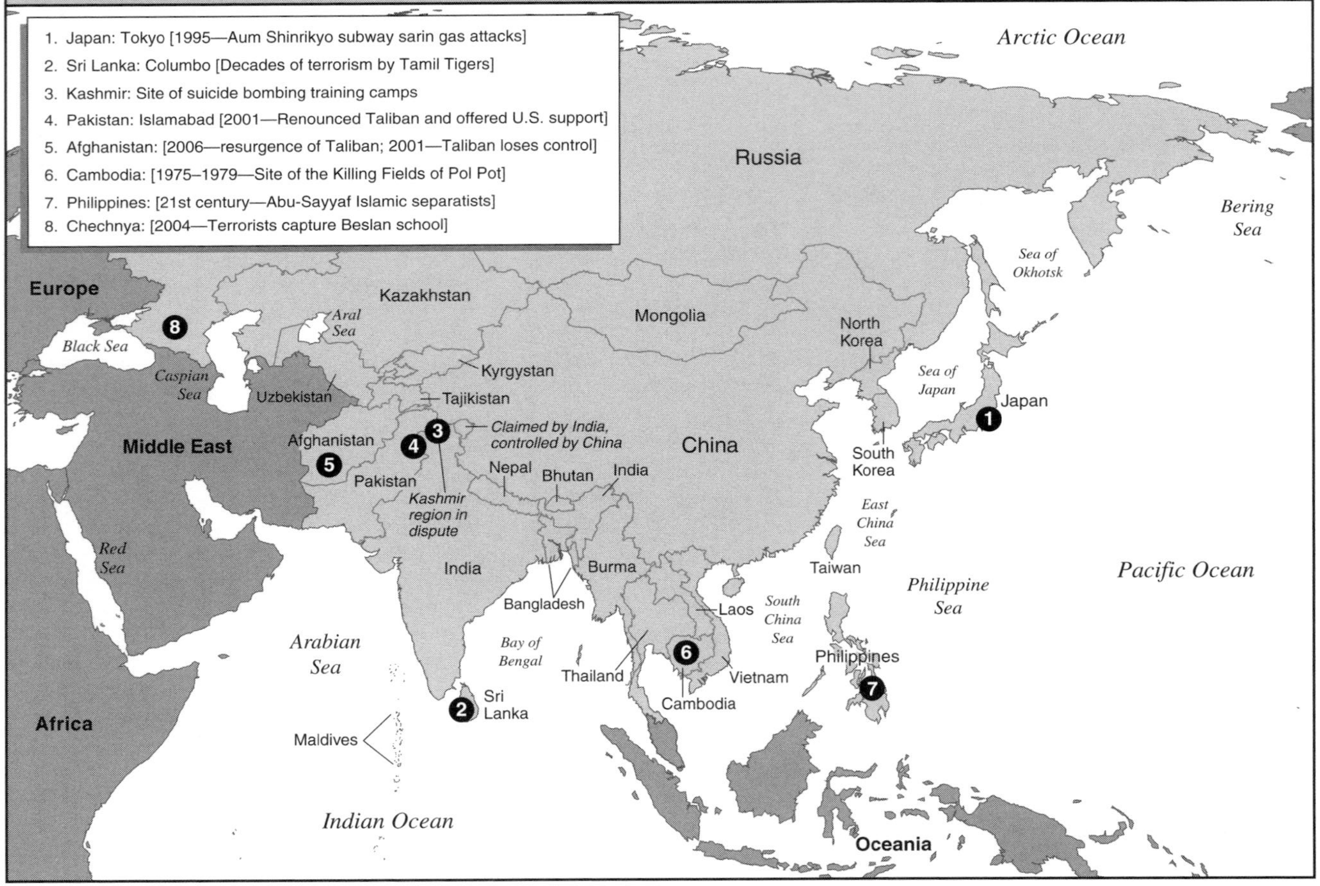

1. Japan: Tokyo [1995—Aum Shinrikyo subway sarin gas attacks]
2. Sri Lanka: Columbo [Decades of terrorism by Tamil Tigers]
3. Kashmir: Site of suicide bombing training camps
4. Pakistan: Islamabad [2001—Renounced Taliban and offered U.S. support]
5. Afghanistan: [2006—resurgence of Taliban; 2001—Taliban loses control]
6. Cambodia: [1975–1979—Site of the Killing Fields of Pol Pot]
7. Philippines: [21st century—Abu-Sayyaf Islamic separatists]
8. Chechnya: [2004—Terrorists capture Beslan school]

Arctic Ocean

Bering Sea

Pacific Ocean

Russia

Sea of Okhotsk

Sea of Japan

Japan ❶

North Korea

South Korea

East China Sea

Philippine Sea

Philippines ❼

Oceania

Mongolia

China

Taiwan

South China Sea

Laos

Vietnam

Burma

Thailand

Cambodia ❻

Kyrgystan

Tajikistan

Claimed by India, controlled by China

India

Nepal

Bhutan

Bangladesh

Bay of Bengal

Kazakhstan

❸

❹

Kashmir region in dispute

India

Sri Lanka ❷

Afghanistan

Pakistan

❺

Uzbekistan

Aral Sea

Arabian Sea

Maldives

Indian Ocean

Europe

❽

Middle East

Black Sea

Caspian Sea

Red Sea

Africa

MAP 3   Asia

368

Map 4: Europe

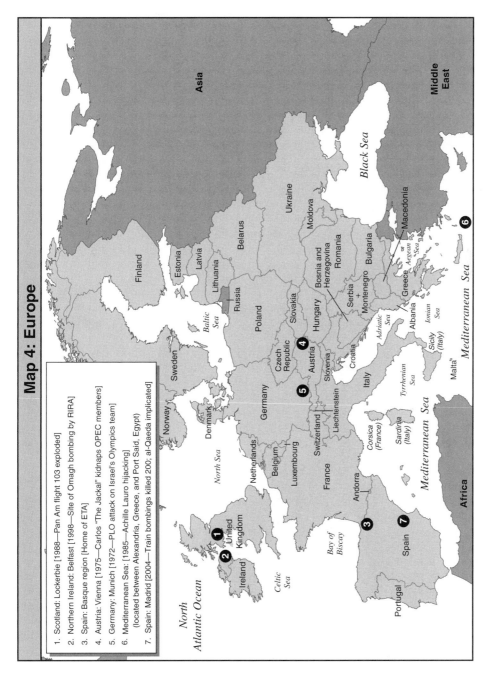

1. Scotland: Lockerbie [1988—Pan Am flight 103 exploded]
2. Northern Ireland: Belfast [1998—Site of Omagh bombing by RIRA]
3. Spain: Basque region [Home of ETA]
4. Austria: Vienna [1975—Carlos "The Jackal" kidnaps OPEC members]
5. Germany: Munich [1972—PLO attack on Israel's Olympics team]
6. Mediterranean Sea: [1985—Achille Lauro hijacking]
   (located between Alexandria, Greece, and Port Said, Egypt)
7. Spain: Madrid [2004—Train bombings killed 200; al-Qaeda implicated]

Europe

Map 4

369

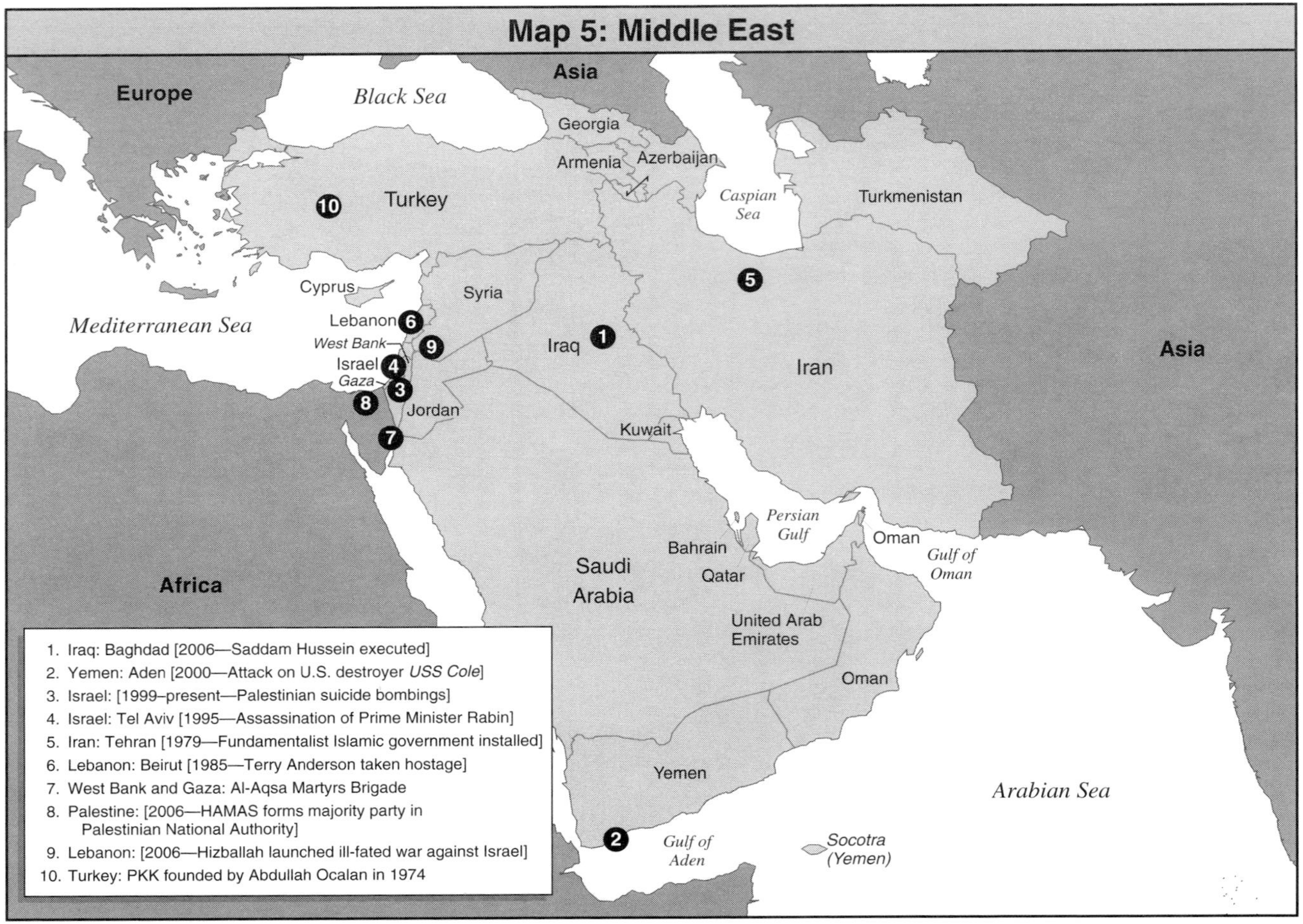

Map 5: Middle East

Europe

Asia

Black Sea

Turkey

Georgia
Armenia
Azerbaijan

Caspian Sea

Turkmenistan

Cyprus

Mediterranean Sea

Syria

⑤

Iran

Asia

Lebanon ⑥
West Bank ⑨
Israel ④ ③
Gaza ⑧ Jordan

⑩

① Iraq

Kuwait

Persian Gulf

Bahrain
Qatar

United Arab Emirates

Oman

Gulf of Oman

Africa

Saudi Arabia

Yemen

Gulf of Aden

②

Oman

Arabian Sea

Socotra (Yemen)

1. Iraq: Baghdad [2006—Saddam Hussein executed]
2. Yemen: Aden [2000—Attack on U.S. destroyer *USS Cole*]
3. Israel: [1999–present—Palestinian suicide bombings]
4. Israel: Tel Aviv [1995—Assassination of Prime Minister Rabin]
5. Iran: Tehran [1979—Fundamentalist Islamic government installed]
6. Lebanon: Beirut [1985—Terry Anderson taken hostage]
7. West Bank and Gaza: Al-Aqsa Martyrs Brigade
8. Palestine: [2006—HAMAS forms majority party in Palestinian National Authority]
9. Lebanon: [2006—Hizballah launched ill-fated war against Israel]
10. Turkey: PKK founded by Abdullah Ocalan in 1974

MAP 5   Middle East

370

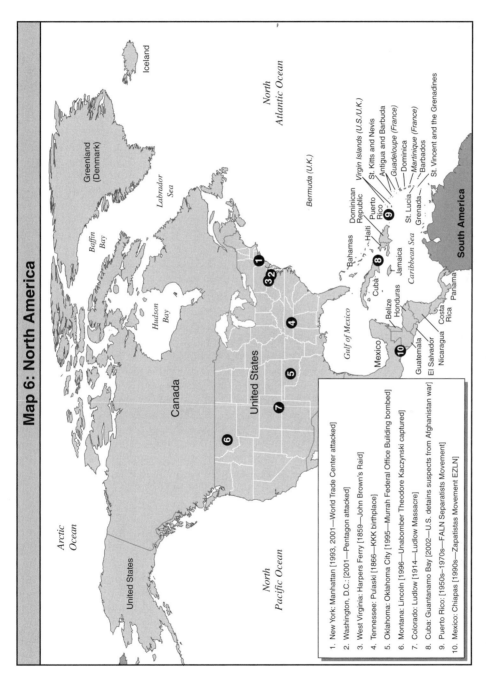

Map 6: North America

Arctic
Ocean

United States

North
Pacific
Ocean

Canada

United States

Baffin
Bay

Hudson
Bay

Greenland
(Denmark)

Iceland

Labrador
Sea

North
Atlantic Ocean

Bermuda (U.K.)

Gulf of Mexico

Bahamas

Cuba

Mexico

Belize
Honduras
Guatemala
El Salvador
Nicaragua
Costa
Rica
Panama

Jamaica

Haiti

Dominican
Republic

Puerto
Rico

Caribbean Sea

Virgin Islands (U.S./U.K.)
St. Kitts and Nevis
Antigua and Barbuda
Guadeloupe (France)
Dominica
Martinique (France)
Barbados
St. Lucia
Grenada
St. Vincent and the Grenadines

South America

1. New York: Manhattan [1993, 2001—World Trade Center attacked]
2. Washington, D.C.: [2001—Pentagon attacked]
3. West Virginia: Harpers Ferry [1859—John Brown's Raid]
4. Tennessee: Pulaski [1866—KKK birthplace]
5. Oklahoma: Oklahoma City [1995—Murrah Federal Office Building bombed]
6. Montana: Lincoln [1996—Unabomber Theodore Kaczynski captured]
7. Colorado: Ludlow [1914—Ludlow Massacre]
8. Cuba: Guantanamo Bay [2002—U.S. detains suspects from Afghanistan war]
9. Puerto Rico: [1950s–1970s—FALN Separatists Movement]
10. Mexico: Chiapas [1990s—Zapatistas Movement EZLN]

MAP 6   North America

371

Map 7: South America

North Pacific Ocean

North Atlantic Ocean

North America

Caribbean Sea

Galapagos Islands (Ecuador)

Trinidad and Tobago
Guyana
Suriname
French Guiana

Venezuela

Colombia

Ecuador

Peru

Brazil

Bolivia

Paraguay

Chile

Argentina

Uruguay

South Pacific Ocean

South Atlantic Ocean

Africa

Falkland Islands (U.K.)

1. Colombia: Bogota [Numerous bombings and assassinations by FARC]
2. Peru: Lima [1996—Tupac Amaru Revolutionary Movement (MRTA) hostage-taking at Japanese Ambassador's residence]
3. Bolivia: [1967—Che Guevara executed]
4. Chile: [1970–1973—President Nixon ordered CIA to overthrow President Salvador Allende]
5. Colombia: National Liberation Army (ELN)
6. Peru: Shining Path formed in the 1960s as Maoist group.

MAP 7   South America

372

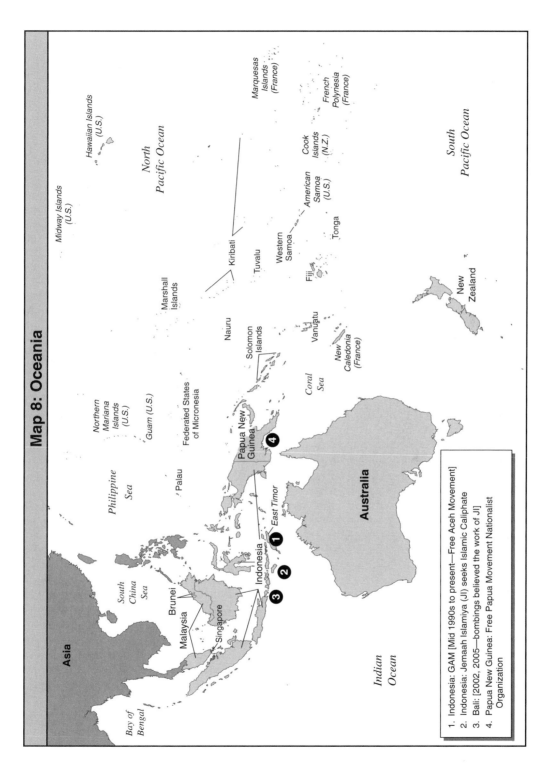

Map 8: Oceania

1. Indonesia: GAM [Mid 1990s to present—Free Aceh Movement]
2. Indonesia: Jemaah Islamiya (JI) seeks Islamic Caliphate
3. Bali: [2002, 2005—bombings believed the work of JI]
4. Papua New Guinea: Free Papua Movement Nationalist Organization

Map 8   Oceania

373

APPENDIX B

UNITED NATIONS GENERAL ASSEMBLY ADOPTS GLOBAL COUNTER-TERRORISM STRATEGY

The United Nations Global Counter-Terrorism Strategy was adopted by Member States on 8 September 2006. The strategy—in the form of a Resolution and an annexed Plan of Action—is a unique global instrument that will enhance national, regional and international efforts to counter terrorism. This is the first time that all Member States have agreed to a common strategic approach to fight terrorism, not only sending a clear message that terrorism is unacceptable in all its forms and manifestation but also resolving to take practical steps individually and collectively to prevent and combat it. Those practical steps include a wide array of measures ranging from strengthening state capacity to counter terrorist threats to better coordinating United Nations system's counter-terrorism activities. The adoption of the strategy fulfils the commitment made by world leaders at the 2005 September Summit and builds on many of the elements proposed by the Secretary-General in his 2 May 2006 report, entitled Uniting against Terrorism: Recommendations for a Global Counter-Terrorism Strategy.

Following is the full text of the Resolution and the Plan of Action:

Resolution Plan of Action

I. Measures to address the conditions conducive to the spread of terrorism

II. Measures to prevent and combat terrorism

III. Measures to build States' capacity to prevent and combat terrorism and to strengthen the role of the United Nations system in this regard

IV. Measures to ensure respect for human rights for all and the rule of law as the fundamental basis of the fight against terrorism

Resolution: The United Nations Global Counter-Terrorism Strategy

The General Assembly,

Guided by the purposes and principles of the Charter of the United Nations and *reaffirming* its role under the Charter, including on questions related to international peace and security,

Reiterating its strong condemnation of terrorism in all its forms and manifestations, committed by whomever, wherever and for whatever purposes, as it constitutes one of the most serious threats to international peace and security,

Reaffirming the Declaration on Measures to Eliminate International Terrorism, contained in the annex to General Assembly resolution 49/60 of 9 December 1994, the Declaration to

Supplement the 1994 Declaration on Measures to Eliminate International Terrorism, contained in the annex to General Assembly resolution 51/210 of 17 December 1996, and the 2005 World Summit Outcome, in particular its section on terrorism,

Recalling all General Assembly resolutions on measures to eliminate international terrorism, including resolution 46/51 of 9 December 1991, and Security Council resolutions on threats to international peace and security caused by terrorist acts, as well as relevant resolutions of the General Assembly on the protection of human rights and fundamental freedoms while countering terrorism,

Recalling also that at the 2005 World Summit Outcome world leaders rededicated themselves to support all efforts to uphold the sovereign equality of all States, respect their territorial integrity and political independence, to refrain in our international relations from the threat or use of force in any manner inconsistent with the purposes and principles of the United Nations, to uphold resolution of disputes by peaceful means and in conformity with the principles of justice and international law, the right to self-determination of peoples which remain under colonial domination or foreign occupation, non-interference in the internal affairs of States, respect for human rights and fundamental freedoms, respect for the equal rights of all without distinction as to race, sex, language or religion, international cooperation in solving international problems of an economic, social, cultural or humanitarian character and the fulfillment in good faith of the obligations assumed in accordance with the Charter,

Recalling further the mandate contained in the 2005 World Summit Outcome that the General Assembly should develop without delay the elements identified by the Secretary-General for a counter-terrorism strategy, with a view to adopting and implementing a strategy to promote comprehensive, coordinated and consistent responses, at the national, regional and international levels, to counter terrorism, which also takes into account the conditions conducive to the spread of terrorism,

Reaffirming that acts, methods and practices of terrorism in all its forms and manifestations are activities aimed at the destruction of human rights, fundamental freedoms and democracy, threatening territorial integrity, security of States and destabilizing legitimately constituted Governments, and that the international community should take the necessary steps to enhance cooperation to prevent and combat terrorism,

Reaffirming also that terrorism cannot and should not be associated with any religion, nationality, civilization or ethnic group,

Reaffirming further Member States' determination to make every effort to reach an agreement on and conclude a comprehensive convention on international terrorism, including by resolving the outstanding issues related to the legal definition and scope of the acts covered by the convention, so that it can serve as an effective instrument to counter terrorism,

Continuing to acknowledge that the question of convening a high level conference under the auspices of the United Nations to formulate an international response to terrorism in all its forms and manifestations could be considered,

Recognizing that development, peace and security, and human rights are interlinked and mutually reinforcing,

Bearing in mind the need to address the conditions conducive to the spread of terrorism,

Affirming Member States' determination to continue to do all they can to resolve conflict, end foreign occupation, confront oppression, eradicate poverty, promote sustained economic growth, sustainable development, global prosperity, good governance, human rights for all and rule of law, improve intercultural understanding and ensure respect for all religions, religious values, beliefs or cultures,

1. Expresses its appreciation for the report "Uniting against terrorism: recommendations for a global counter-terrorism strategy" (doc. A/60/825), submitted by the Secretary-General to the General Assembly;

2. Adopts the present resolution and its annex as the United Nations Global Counter-Terrorism Strategy ("the Strategy");

3. Decides, without prejudice to the continuation of the discussion at its relevant committees of all their agenda items related to terrorism and counter-terrorism, to undertake the following steps for the effective follow-up of the Strategy:

   a. To launch the Strategy at a high-level segment of its sixty-first session; To examine in two years progress made in implementation of the Strategy, and to consider updating it to respond to changes, recognizing that many of the measures contained in the Strategy can be achieved immediately, some will require sustained work through the coming few years, and some should be treated as long term objectives;
   b. To invite the Secretary-General to contribute to the future deliberations of the General Assembly on the review of the implementation and updating of the Strategy;
   c. To encourage Member States, the United Nations and other appropriate international, regional and sub-regional organizations to support the implementation of the Strategy, including through mobilizing resources and expertise;
   d. To further encourage non-governmental organizations and civil society to engage, as appropriate, on how to enhance efforts to implement the Strategy.

4. Decides to inscribe in the provisional agenda of its sixty-second session an item entitled "The United Nations Global Counter-Terrorism Strategy."

ANNEX

Plan of Action

We, the States Members of the United Nations, resolve:

1. To consistently, unequivocally and strongly condemn terrorism in all its forms and manifestations, committed by whomever, wherever and for whatever purposes, as it constitutes one of the most serious threats to international peace and security.

2. To take urgent action to prevent and combat terrorism in all its forms and manifestations and, in particular:

   a. To consider becoming parties without delay to the existing international conventions and protocols against terrorism, and implementing them, and to make every effort to reach an agreement on and conclude a comprehensive convention on international terrorism;
   b. To implement all General Assembly resolutions on measures to eliminate international terrorism, and relevant General Assembly resolutions on the protection of human rights and fundamental freedoms while countering terrorism;
   c. To implement all Security Council resolutions related to international terrorism and to cooperate fully with the counter-terrorism subsidiary bodies of the Security Council in the fulfillment of their tasks, recognizing that many States continue to require assistance in implementing these resolutions.

3. To recognize that international cooperation and any measures that we undertake to prevent and combat terrorism must comply with our obligations under international law, including the Charter of the United Nations and relevant international conventions and protocols, in particular human rights law, refugee law and international humanitarian law.

I. Measures to Address the Conditions Conducive to the Spread of Terrorism

We resolve to undertake the following measures aimed at addressing the conditions conducive to the spread of terrorism, including but not limited to prolonged unresolved conflicts, dehumanization of victims of terrorism in all its forms and manifestations, lack of rule of law and violations of human rights, ethnic, national and religious discrimination, political exclusion, socio-economic marginalization, and lack of good governance, while recognizing that none of these conditions can excuse or justify acts of terrorism:

1. To continue to strengthen and make best possible use of the capacities of the United Nations in areas such as conflict prevention, negotiation, mediation, conciliation, judicial settlement, rule of law, peacekeeping and peacebuilding, in order to contribute to the successful prevention and peaceful resolution of prolonged unresolved conflicts. We recognize that the peaceful resolution of such conflicts would contribute to strengthening the global fight against terrorism.

2. To continue to arrange under the auspices of the United Nations initiatives and programmes to promote dialogue, tolerance and understanding among civilizations, cultures, peoples and religions, and to promote mutual respect for and prevent the defamation of religions, religious values, beliefs and cultures. In this regard, we welcome the launching by the Secretary-General of the initiative on the Alliance of Civilizations. We also welcome similar initiatives that have been taken in other parts of the world.

3. To promote a culture of peace, justice and human development, ethnic, national and religious tolerance, and respect for all religions, religious values, beliefs or cultures by establishing and encouraging, as appropriate, education and public awareness programmes involving all sectors of society. In this regard, we encourage the United Nations Educational, Scientific and Cultural Organization to play a key role, including through inter-faith and intra-faith dialogue and dialogue among civilizations.

4. To continue to work to adopt such measures as may be necessary and appropriate and in accordance with our obligations under international law to prohibit by law incitement to commit a terrorist act or acts and prevent such conduct.

5. To reiterate our determination to ensure the timely and full realization of the development goals and objectives agreed at the major United Nations conferences and summits, including the Millennium Development Goals. We reaffirm our commitment to eradicate poverty and promote sustained economic growth, sustainable development and global prosperity for all.

6. To pursue and reinforce development and social inclusion agendas at every level as goals in themselves, recognizing that success in this area, especially on youth unemployment, could reduce marginalization and the subsequent sense of victimization that propels extremism and the recruitment of terrorists.

7. To encourage the United Nations system as a whole to scale up the cooperation and assistance it is already conducting in the fields of rule of law, human rights and good governance, to support sustained economic and social development.

8. To consider putting in place, on a voluntary basis, national systems of assistance that would promote the needs of victims of terrorism and their families and facilitate the normalization of their lives. In this regard, we encourage States to request the relevant United Nations

entities to help them to develop such national systems. We will also strive to promote international solidarity in support of victims and foster the involvement of civil society in a global campaign against terrorism and for its condemnation. This could include exploring at the General Assembly the possibility of developing practical mechanisms for assistance to victims.

II. Measures to Prevent and Combat Terrorism

We resolve to undertake the following measures to prevent and combat terrorism, in particular by denying terrorists access to the means to carry out their attacks, to their targets and to the desired impact of their attacks:

1. To refrain from organizing, instigating, facilitating, participating in, financing, encouraging or tolerating terrorist activities and to take appropriate practical measures to ensure that our respective territories are not used for terrorist installations or training camps, or for the preparation or organization of terrorist acts intended to be committed against other States or their citizens.

2. To cooperate fully in the fight against terrorism, in accordance with our obligations under international law, in order to find, deny safe haven and bring to justice, on the basis of the principle of extradite or prosecute, any person who supports, facilitates, participates or attempts to participate in the financing, planning, preparation or perpetration of terrorist acts or provides safe havens.

3. To ensure the apprehension and prosecution or extradition of perpetrators of terrorist acts, in accordance with the relevant provisions of national and international law, in particular human rights law, refugee law and international humanitarian law. We will endeavour to conclude and implement to that effect mutual judicial assistance and extradition agreements, and to strengthen cooperation between law enforcement agencies.

4. To intensify cooperation, as appropriate, in exchanging timely and accurate information concerning the prevention and combating of terrorism.

5. To strengthen coordination and cooperation among States in combating crimes that might be connected with terrorism, including drug trafficking in all its aspects, illicit arms trade, in particular of small arms and light weapons, including man-portable air defence systems, money laundering and smuggling of nuclear, chemical, biological, radiological and other potentially deadly materials.

6. To consider becoming parties without delay to the United Nations Convention against Transnational Organized Crime and to the three protocols supplementing it, and implementing them.

7. To take appropriate measures, before granting asylum, for the purpose of ensuring that the asylum seeker has not engaged in terrorist activities and, after granting asylum, for the purpose of ensuring that the refugee status is not used in a manner contrary to the provisions set out in paragraph 1 of this section.

8. To encourage relevant regional and sub-regional organizations to create or strengthen counter-terrorism mechanisms or centres. Should they require cooperation and assistance to this end, we encourage the United Nations Counter-Terrorism Committee and its Executive Directorate and, where consistent with their existing mandates, the United Nations Office of Drugs and Crime and the International Criminal Police Organization, to facilitate its provision.

9. To acknowledge that the question of creating an international centre to fight terrorism could be considered, as part of the international efforts to enhance the fight against terrorism.

10. To encourage States to implement the comprehensive international standards embodied in the Financial Action Task Force's Forty Recommendations on Money Laundering and

Nine Special Recommendations on Terrorist Financing, recognizing that States may require assistance in implementing them.

11. To invite the United Nations system to develop, together with Member States, a single comprehensive database on biological incidents, ensuring that it is complementary to the International Criminal Police Organization's contemplated Biocrimes Database. We also encourage the Secretary-General to update the roster of experts and laboratories, as well as the technical guidelines and procedures, available to him for the timely and efficient investigation of alleged use. In addition, we note the importance of the proposal of the Secretary-General to bring together, within the framework of the United Nations, the major biotechnology stakeholders, including industry, scientific community, civil society and governments, into a common programme aimed at ensuring that biotechnology's advances are not used for terrorist or other criminal purposes but for the public good, with due respect to the basic international norms on intellectual property rights.

12. To work with the United Nations, with due regard to confidentiality, respecting human rights and in compliance with other obligations under international law, to explore ways and means to:

    a. coordinate efforts at the international and regional level to counter terrorism in all its forms and manifestations on the Internet, and;

    b. use the Internet as a tool for countering the spread of terrorism, while recognizing that States may require assistance in this regard.

13. To stepup national efforts and bilateral, sub-regional, regional and international co-operation, as appropriate, to improve border and customs controls, in order to prevent and detect the movement of terrorists and to prevent and detect the illicit traffic in, inter alia, small arms and light weapons, conventional ammunition and explosives, nuclear, chemical, biological or radiological weapons and materials, while recognizing that States may require assistance to that effect.

14. To encourage the United Nations Counter-Terrorism Committee and its Executive Directorate to continue to work with States, at their request, to facilitate the adoption of legislation and administrative measures to implement the terrorist travel-related obligations, and to identify best practices in this area, drawing whenever possible on those developed by technical international organizations such as the International Civil Aviation Organization, the World Customs Organization and the International Criminal Police Organization.

15. To encourage the Committee established pursuant to Security Council resolution 1267 (1999) to continue to work to strengthen the effectiveness of the travel ban under the United Nations sanctions regime against Al-Qaida and the Taliban and associated individuals and entities, as well as to ensure, as a matter of priority, that fair and transparent procedures exist for placing individuals and entities on its lists, for removing them and for granting humanitarian exceptions. In this regard, we encourage States to share information, including by widely distributing the International Criminal Police Organization-United Nations Special Notices concerning people subject to this sanctions regime.

16. To step up efforts and co-operation at every level, as appropriate, to improve the security on manufacturing and issuing identity and travel documents and to prevent and detect their alteration or fraudulent use, while recognizing that States may require assistance in doing so. In this regard, we invite the International Criminal Police Organization to enhance its database on stolen and lost travel documents, and we will endeavour to make full use of this tool as appropriate, in particular by sharing relevant information.

17. To invite the United Nations to improve co-ordination in planning a response to a terrorist attack using nuclear, chemical, biological or radiological weapons or materials, in particular by reviewing and improving the effectiveness of the existing inter-agency co-ordination

mechanisms for assistance delivery, relief operations and victim support, so that all States can receive adequate assistance. In this regard, we invite the General Assembly and the Security Council to develop guidelines for the necessary co-operation and assistance in the event of a terrorist attack using weapons of mass destruction.

18. To step up all efforts to improve the security and protection of particularly vulnerable targets such as infrastructure and public places, as well as the response to terrorist attacks and other disasters, in particular in the area of civil protection, while recognizing that States may require assistance to that effect.

III. Measures to Build States' Capacity to Prevent and Combat Terrorism and to Strengthen the Role of the United Nations System in This Regard

We recognize that capacity-building in all States is a core element of the global counter-terrorism effort, and resolve to undertake the following measures to develop State capacity to prevent and combat terrorism and enhance coordination and coherence within the United Nations system in promoting international cooperation in countering terrorism:

1. To encourage Member States to consider making voluntary contributions to United Nations counter-terrorism cooperation and technical assistance projects, and to explore additional sources of funding in this regard. We also encourage the United Nations to consider reaching out to the private sector for contributions to capacity-building programmes, in particular in the areas of port, maritime and civil aviation security.

2. To take advantage of the framework provided by relevant international, regional and sub-regional organizations to share best practices in counter-terrorism capacity-building, and to facilitate their contributions to the international community's efforts in this area.

3. To consider establishing appropriate mechanisms to rationalize States' reporting requirements in the field of counter-terrorism and eliminate duplication of reporting requests, taking into account and respecting the different mandates of the General Assembly, the Security Council and its subsidiary bodies that deal with counter terrorism.

4. To encourage measures, including regular informal meetings, to enhance, as appropriate, more frequent exchanges of information on cooperation and technical assistance among Member States, United Nations bodies dealing with counter terrorism, relevant specialized agencies, relevant international, regional and sub-regional organizations, and the donor community, to develop States' capacities to implement relevant United Nations resolutions.

5. To welcome the intention of the Secretary-General to institutionalize, within existing resources, the United Nations Counter-Terrorism Implementation Task Force within the Secretariat, in order to ensure overall co-ordination and coherence in the United Nations system's counter-terrorism efforts.

6. To encourage the United Nations Counter-Terrorism Committee and its Executive Directorate to continue to improve the coherence and efficiency of technical assistance delivery in the field of counter-terrorism, in particular by strengthening its dialogue with States and relevant international, regional and sub-regional organizations and working closely, including by sharing information, with all bilateral and multilateral technical assistance providers.

7. To encourage the United Nations Office on Drugs and Crime, including its Terrorism Prevention Branch, to enhance, in close consultation with the United Nations Counter-Terrorism Committee and its Executive Directorate, its provision of technical assistance to States, upon request, to facilitate the implementation of the international conventions and protocols related to the prevention and suppression of terrorism and relevant United Nations resolutions.

8. To encourage the International Monetary Fund, the World Bank, the United Nations Office on Drugs and Crime and the International Criminal Police Organization to enhance cooperation with States to help them to comply fully with international norms and obligations to combat money-laundering and financing of terrorism.

9. To encourage the International Atomic Energy Agency and the Organization for the Prohibition of Chemical Weapons to continue their efforts, within their respective mandates, in helping States to build capacity to prevent terrorists from accessing nuclear, chemical or radio-logical materials, to ensure security at related facilities, and to respond effectively in the event of an attack using such materials.

10. To encourage the World Health Organization to step up its technical assistance to help States improve their public health systems to prevent and prepare for biological attacks by ter-rorists.

11. To continue to work within the United Nations system to support the reform and mod-ernization of border management systems, facilities and institutions, at the national, regional and international level.

12. To encourage the International Maritime Organization, the World Customs Organization and the International Civil Aviation Organization to strengthen their co-opera-tion, work with States to identify any national shortfalls in areas of transport security and pro-vide assistance upon request to address them.

13. To encourage the United Nations to work with Member States and relevant interna-tional, regional and sub-regional organizations to identify and share best practices to prevent terrorist attacks on particularly vulnerable targets. We invite the International Criminal Police Organization to work with the Secretary-General so that he can submit proposals to this effect. We also recognize the importance of developing public-private partnerships in this area.

IV. Measures to Ensure Respect for Human Rights for All and
the Rule of Law as the Fundamental Basis of the Fight Against Terrorism

We resolve to undertake the following measures, reaffirming that the promotion and protec-tion of human rights for all and the rule of law is essential to all components of the Strategy, recognizing that effective counter-terrorism measures and the protection of human rights are not conflicting goals, but complementary and mutually reinforcing, and stressing the need to promote and protect the rights of victims of terrorism:

1. To reaffirm that General Assembly resolution 60/158 of 16 December 2005 provides the fundamental framework for the "Protection of human rights and fundamental freedoms while countering terrorism."

2. To reaffirm that States must ensure that any measures taken to combat terrorism comply with their obligations under international law, in particular human rights law, refugee law and international humanitarian law.

3. To consider becoming parties without delay to the core international instruments on human rights law, refugee law and international humanitarian law, and implementing them, as well as to consider accepting the competence of international and relevant regional human rights monitoring bodies.

4. To make every effort to develop and maintain an effective and rule of law-based national criminal justice system that can ensure, in accordance with our obligations under international law, that any person who participates in the financing, planning, preparation or perpetration of terrorist acts or in support of terrorist acts is brought to justice, on the basis of the principle to extradite or prosecute, with due respect for human rights and fundamental freedoms, and that

such terrorist acts are established as serious criminal offences in domestic laws and regulations. We recognize that States may require assistance in developing and maintaining such effective and rule of law-based criminal justice system, and we encourage them to resort to the technical assistance delivered, inter alia, by the United Nations Office on Drugs and Crime.

5. To reaffirm the United Nations system's important role in strengthening the international legal architecture by promoting the rule of law, respect for human rights, and effective criminal justice systems, which constitute the fundamental basis of our common fight against terrorism.

6. To support the Human Rights Council, and to contribute, as it takes shape, to its work on the question of the promotion and protection of human rights for all in the fight against terrorism.

7. To support the strengthening of the operational capacity of the Office of the United Nations High Commissioner for Human Rights, with a particular emphasis on increasing field operations and presences. The Office should continue to play a lead role in examining the question of protecting human rights while countering terrorism, by making general recommendations on States' human rights obligations and providing them with assistance and advice, in particular in the area of raising awareness of international human rights law among national law-enforcement agencies, at States' request.

8. To support the role of the Special Rapporteur on the promotion and protection of human rights and fundamental freedoms while countering terrorism. The Special Rapporteur should continue to support States' efforts and offer concrete advice by corresponding with Governments, making country visits, liaising with the United Nations and regional organizations, and reporting on these issues.

APPENDIX C

Video Notes

CHAPTER 1 VIDEO NOTES

The film *Paradise Now* (Warner Brothers, 2005, 91 min.) is recommended as a most insightful and unvarnished look at the motivations of terrorism.

CHAPTER 2 VIDEO NOTES

Many historical films about regional and class conflicts might be useful for envisioning the present global situation. For example, the history of the Irish Republican Army is portrayed in *Michael Collins* (Warner Bros., 1996, 132 min.).

Another classic video is *Battle of Algiers* (Criterion Collection, 1966, 125 min.). With the French Foreign Legion using the tactic of torture and the Algerians using home-made bombs, this gripping film presents an unbiased account of one of the bloodiest revolutions in modern history.

CHAPTER 3 VIDEO NOTES

Background about international terrorism is explained often in documentaries about the Central Intelligence Agency. One noted exploration of the U.S. role in the "blowback" of transnational terrorism is titled *C.I.A.: America's Secret Warriors* (Discovery Channel, 1997, 2 vols., 50 min. each).

With a focus on big money, the movie *Syriana* (Warner Brothers, 2005, 128 min.) covers the deadly web of corruption and deceit stretching from Houston, to Washington and on to the Middle East, which ensnares industrialists, princes, spies, politicos, oilfield laborers, and terrorists.

CHAPTER 4 VIDEO NOTES

A documentary produced by a former CIA agent titled *The Cult of the Suicide Bomber* (Disinformation, 2005, 96 min.) clearly untangles the history, background, and nations behind suicide bombing.

A fascinating drama about conventional terrorism unfolds in the film *Four Days in September* (Miramax, 1998, 110 min.). The film relates both the political and the personal issues that arise when an ambassador is kidnapped by terrorists.

The television series, *Sleeper Cell*, which began airing on the Showtime Channel in 2006, is an intriguing look at a group of Jihadists who come from various parts of the world to Los Angeles to plot acts of destruction. The threat may be exaggerated in the series, but there are enough accurate details in the programs to make them interesting.

The award winning film, *God Grew Tired of Us* is scheduled for release in 2007 by New Market Films (89 min.). This true story of child soldiers in Sudan was originally released by Lost Boys Productions and also by National Geographic films.

CHAPTER 5 VIDEO NOTES

Many excellent movies have portrayed KKK-inspired attacks and assassinations. *Mississippi Burning* (Orion, 1988, 128 min.) is a film dramatization of a case that has been well researched in many other sources.

An insightful documentary, *Theodore J. Kaczynski: The Unabomber* (Biography: A&E, 1996, 50 min.), provides a developmental look at the life of this terrorist; a good deal of the information came from his family. Several fine documentaries available from the History Channel and A&E Television are relevant and illustrate many aspects of terrorism.

CHAPTER 6 VIDEO NOTES

How terrorism was actually reported in one extreme example is documented by the film *One Day in September* (Columbia TriStar, 1999, 91 min.), which details the kidnapping of Israeli athletes at the Munich Olympics in 1972.

CHAPTER 7 VIDEO NOTES

A dramatized version of *Sendero Luminoso* may be found in the film *The Dancer Upstairs* (Twentieth Century Fox, 2002, 113 min.). The frame of reference for the women of *Sendero* in this movie is through the eyes of men.

The Legend of Rita (Kino Video, 2001, 101 min.) depicts a young woman terrorist from a German perspective. There is a sense of pathos about the legendary Rita who, the viewer is led to suppose, was connected to the Red Army Faction.

CHAPTER 8 VIDEO NOTES

Although weapons of mass destruction may seem like something from a movie plot, modern films contain few good studies of the threat of biological and chemical weapons. A celebrated drama about a global nuclear crisis spawned by terrorists is *Crimson Tide* (Hollywood Pictures, 1995, 115 min.).

CHAPTER 9 VIDEO NOTES

The threat from the military in response to terrorism may be overplayed in the *Siege* (20th Century Fox, 1998, 120 min.), but the film provides some sobering images about fighting violence with violence.

One noted exploration of the role of U.S. policy in the "blowback" of transnational terrorism is titled *CIA: America's Secret Warriors* (Discovery Channel, 1997, 2 vols., 50 min.).

The movie *Munich* (Universal, 2005, 2 hours, 44 min.) dramatizes the secret Israeli squad assigned to track down and assassinate the 11 Palestinians believed to have planned the 1972 massacre of 11 Israeli athletes in Munich.

The Road to Guantanamo (Sony Pictures, 2006, 95 min.) is an award-winning docudrama based on the true story of three British muslims who were captured in Afghanistan and detained by U.S. forces. The controversial film is a stark and brutal indictment of U.S. policy regarding the Guantanamo Bay prison.

PHOTO CREDITS

Introduction

Photo 01.1 FEMA Report, http://www.fema.gov/pdf/library/fema403_ch1.pdf page 7

Chapter 1

Photo 1.1 © ANTOINE GYORI/CORBIS SYGMA

Chapter 2

Photo 2.1 Getty Images

Photo 2.2 Painting by Jean-Pierre Louis Laurent Houel (1735-1813), entitled Prise de la Bastille ("The storm of the Bastille").

Chapter 3

Photo 3.1 Time & Life Pictures/Getty Images

Photo 3.2 Photo provided courtesy of the Federal Bureau of Investigation.

Photo 3.3 Getty Images

Chapter 4

Photo 4.1 © Bettmann/CORBIS

Photo 4.2 © Reuters/CORBIS

Photo 4.3 AFP/Getty Images

Chapter 5

Photo 5.1 Photo provided courtesy of the Library of Congress.

Photo 5.2 Denver Public Library, Western History Collection, Denver News, X-21542

Photo 5.3 Photo courtesy of the Federal Bureau of Investigation.

Chapter 6

Photo 6.1 Time & Life Pictures/Getty Images

Photo 6.2 Federal Emergency Management Agency (FEMA)

Photo 6.3 AFP/Getty Images

Photo 6.4 © David Turnley/CORBIS

Chapter 7

Photo 7.1 © WAYMAN RICHARD/CORBIS SYGMA

Photo 7.2 Permission granted by Werner Meinhof's granddaughter, Bettina Röhl.

Chapter 8

Photo 8.1 Photo courtesy of the Federal Bureau of Investigation.

Photo 8.2 Photo courtesy of the Federal Bureau of Investigation.

Photo 8.3 U.S. Army Medical Research Institute of Infectious Diseases

Photo 8.4 AFP/Getty Images

Chapter 9

Photo 9.1 AFP/Getty Images

Photo 9.2 Photo courtesy of the U.S. Navy.

Photo 9.3 Photo courtesy of the Library of Congress, Prints & Photographs Division, Ansel Adams, photographer.

REFERENCES

Abanes, R. (1996). *American militias: Rebellion, racism and religion*. Downers Grove, IL: InterVarsity Press.

ABC News. (2001, January 30). ELF making good on threat. Retrieved June 6, 2002, from http://www.abcnews.go.com/sections/us/DailyNews

Accountability Board Report, Dar Es Salaam. (1998). Bombings of the US embassy in Dar es Salaam, Tanzania—Discussion and findings. *The Terrorism Research Center*. Retrieved June 17, 2002, from http://www.terrorism.com/state

Accountability Board Report, Nairobi. (1998). Bombings of the US embassy in Nairobi, Kenya— Discussion and findings. *The Terrorism Research Center*. Retrieved June 17, 2002, from http://www .terrorism.com/state/

After close call, Patriot Act renewed. (2006). *Information Management Journal, 40*(3), 7.

Ahmadinejad says Iran's nuclear plans are still on. (2007, January 3). *Taipei Times*. Retrieved on January 3, 2007, from http://www.taipeitimes.com/News/world/archives/2007/01/03/2003343204

Ahmed, E. (1998). *Terrorism: Theirs and ours*. Paper presented at the University of Colorado, Boulder, October 12, 1998. Retrieved September 7, 2006, from http://www.sangam.org/ANALYSIS/Ahmad.htm

Albrecht, K. (2001). World-wide women. *The Futurist*. Retrieved June 10, 2002, from http://www.wfs .org/esalbrecht.htm

ALFront (2006). ARM logo. Retrieved December 27, 2006 from http://www.animalliberationfront.com

Ali, F. (2005). Muslim female fighters: An emerging trend. *Terrorism Monitor, 3*(21). Retrieved March 29, 2006, from http://jamestown.org/terrorism/digArchive.phpnews/article.php?articleid=236982

American Civil Liberties Union. (2006, October 27). *Citing improvements to law, ACLU withdraws Section 215 case but vows to fight individual orders*. Retrieved on January 14, 2007, from http://www.aclu.org/safefree/patriot/27211prs20061027.html

American Psychological Association. (1998). *Hate crimes today: An age-old foe in modern dress*. Retrieved June 6, 2002, from http://www.apa.org/releases/hate.html

Anderson, A. (2003). Risk, terrorism and the Internet. *Transaction, 16*(2), 24–33.

Anderson, J. L. (1998). *Che Guevara: A revolutionary life*. New York: Grove Press.

Anderson, S., & Sloan, S. (1995). *Historical dictionary of terrorism*. Metuchen, NJ: Scarecrow Press.

Anderson, T. (1993). Terrorism and censorship: The media in chains. *Journal of International Affairs, 47*(1), 127–136.

Andreas, C. (1985). *When women rebel: The rise of popular feminism in Peru*. Westport, CT: Lawrence Hill.

Andreas, C. (1990). Women at war. *NACLA Report on the Americans, 24*(4), 20–27.

Anti-Defamation League. (1999). *The Farrakhan library*. Retrieved June 6, 2002, from http://www.adl.org

Antiterrorism and Effective Death Penalty Act 1996, Pub. L. No. 104–132, 110 Stat. 1214 (1996).

Antiterrorism and Effective Death Penalty Act, Pub. L. No. 104–132 (2001).

Appel, K. (1997). Interview with Subcomandante Insurgente Marcos, January 1997. *Café Rebelion*. Retrieved September 25, 2006, from http://www.caferebelion.com/interviews.html

Arnold, R. (1997). *Ecoterror*. Bellevue, WA: Free Enterprise Press.

Atran, S. (2004, June 3). Soft power and the psychology of suicide bombing. *Terrorism Monitor, 2*(11) Retrieved March 29, 2006 from http://www.jamestown.org/terrorism/news/article.php?search=1&articleid=2368050

Aust, S. (1987). *The Baader-Meinhof group: The inside story of a phenomenon* (Anthea Bell, Trans.). London: Bodley Head.

Baard, J. (2004). Aquinas's account of anger applied to the ALF. In Steven Best & Anthony Nocella II (Eds.), *Terrorists or freedom fighters?* New York: Lantern Books.

Baird, Z. (2005, October 19). *Statement of Zoe Baird, President, Markle Foundation.* Washington, DC: House Permanent Select Committee on Intelligence, U.S. House of Representatives. October 19.

Ballard, J. D., & Mullendore, K. (2003). Weapons of mass victimization, radioactive waste shipments, and environmental laws: Policy making and first responders. *American Behavioral Scientist, 46*(6), 766–781.

Bandura, A. (1973). *Aggression: A social learning analysis.* New York: Prentice Hall.

Bandura, A. (1998). Mechanisms of moral disengagement. In Walter Reich (Ed.), *Origins of terrorism: Psychologies, ideologies, theologies, states of mind.* Washington DC: Woodrow Wilson Center Press.

Barber, B. R. (1992). Jihad vs. McWorld. *Atlantic Monthly, 269*(3), 53–65.

Barber, B. R. (1995). *Jihad vs. McWorld.* New York: Times Books.

Barletta, M. (2001). *WMD threats 2001: Critical choices for the Bush administration* (Monterey Proliferation Strategy Group Occasional Paper #6). Monterey, CA: Monterey Institute of International Studies, Center for Nonproliferation Strategies.

Barnard, Jeff. (2006). Two plead guilty in 1998 Vail ski resort fire. *Santa Fe New Mexican,* December 15. Retrieved December 27, 2006, from http://www.freenewmexican.com/nbews/53743.html

Barnhurst, K. G. (1991). Contemporary terrorism in Peru: Sendero Luminoso and the media. *Journal of Communication, 41*(4), 75–89.

BBC News. (1999, July 15). *Peru's Shining Path—Who are they?* Retrieved June 7, 2002, from http://news.bbc.co.uk/hi/english/world/americas/newsid_395000/395370.stm

BBC News. (2006, November 24). Obituary: Alexander Litvinenko. Retrieved January 3, 2007, from http://news.bbc.co.uk/go/pr/fr/-/2/hi/uk_news/6163502.stm

Beah, I. (2007, January 14). The making and unmaking of a child soldier. *The New York Times.* Retrieved January 15, 2007, from http://www.nytimes.com/2007/01/14soldier.t.html

Beam, L. (1992, February). Leaderless resistance. *The Seditionist.* Retrieved June 10, 2002, from http://www.louisbeam.com/leaderless.htm

Beaton, R., Stergachis, A., Oberle, M., Bridges, E., Nemuth, M., & Thomas, T. (2005). The sarin gas attacks on the Tokyo subway—10 years later/lessons learned. *Traumatology, 11*(2), 103–119.

Becker, J. (1977). *Hitler's children: The story of the Baader-Meinhof terrorist gang.* Philadelphia: Lippincott.

Becker, J. B. (1996). *The news media, terrorism, and democracy: The symbiotic relationship between freedom of the press and acts of terror.* Retrieved June 7, 2002, from http://eob.org/eob-tr2.htm

Bell, S. (2006). Carlos the Jackal sues French captors over "illegal" Sudan arrest. *The Scotsman,* June 29, 2006. Retrieved on January 5, 2007, from http://www.thescotsman.scotsman.com/index.cfm?id= 946802006

Bellamy, P. (2000). *Carlos the Jackal: Trail of terror.* Retrieved June 4, 2002, from http://www.crimelibrary.com/terrorists_spies/terrorists/jackal/1.html

Bilello, S. (1998, October 7). Popularity of Latin American press outstrips other institutions. *Freedom Forum.* Retrieved June 17, 2002, from http://www.freedomforum.org/templates/

Blank, S. (2004). Cynicism personified: Moscow and Riyadh's collaboration against Chechnya. In *Unmasking terror* (pp. 113–117). Washington, DC: Jamestown Foundation.

Blanning, T. C. W. (1998). *The French Revolution: Class war or culture clash?* New York: St. Martin's Press.

Blazak, R. (2001). White boys to terrorist men. *American Behavioral Scientist, 44*(6), 982–1000.

Blee, K. (2002). *Inside organized racism: Women in the hate movement.* Berkeley: University of California Press.

Blee, K. (2005). Women and organized racial terrorism in the United States. *Studies in Conflict and Terrorism, 28,* 421–423.

Bloom, M. (2005). *Dying to kill.* New York: Columbia University Press.

Blythe, W. (2000, June 8). The guru of white hate. *Rolling Stone, 99.*

Bodansky, Y. (1999). *Bin Laden: The man who declared war on America.* Rocklin, CA: Prima.

Bratkowski, S. (2005). Killing and terror: The cultural tradition. *American Behavioral Scientist, 48*(6), 764–782.

Brun, C. (2005). Women in the local/global fields of war and displacement in Sri Lanka. *Gender, Technology and Development, 9*(1), 57–80.

Burghardt, T. (1995). Leaderless resistance and the Oklahoma City bombing. *Bay Area Coalition for Our Reproductive Rights.* Retrieved June 10, 2002, from http://www.nwcitizen.us/publicgood/reports/leadless.htm

Burnham, G., Doocy, S., Dzeng, E., Lafta, R., & Roberts, L. (2006). *The human cost of the war in Iraq: Mortality study, 2002–2006.* Retrieved January 11, 2007, from http://i.a.cnn.net/cnn/2006/images/10/11/human.cost.of.war.pdf

Bush Telegraph. (1997, December 17). *Mission and project support.* Retrieved June 17, 2002, http://www
.mapsupport.com/thedatabase/bushtel/Default.htm

Butterfield, Fox. (2001, November 22). Police are split on questioning Mideast men. *The New York Times.*
Retrieved June 19, 2002, from http://www.nytimes.com/2001/11/22/national/

Camejo, P. (1972). *Guevara's guerilla strategy.* New York: Pathfinder Press.

CAMERA Media Report (The Committee for Accuracy in Middle East Reporting in America). (1995).
Media bury Israeli dead, 6(1). Retrieved June 17, 2002, from http://world.std.com/~camera/docs/
cmr61/bury61.html

Cameron, G. (1999). Multi-track microproliferation: Lessons from Aum Shinrikyo and Al Qaida. *Studies
in Conflict and Terrorism, 22,* 277–309.

Carr, C. (2002). *The lessons of terror.* New York: Random House.

Carter, J. (2006). *Palestine: Peace, not apartheid.* New York: Simon & Schuster.

Caryl, C. (2007, January 22). Iraq: The next Jihadists. *Newsweek,* 24–34.

Castaneda, J. G. (1997). *Companero: The life and death of Che Guevara.* New York: Knopf.

CBS News. (2005, January 21). *New video of Beslan school terror.* Retrieved November 26, 2005, from
http://www.cbsnews.com/stories/2005/

Chandra, B. (1989). *India's struggle for independence.* Columbia, MO: South Asia Books.

Charan, B. (2000). *Bhagwati Charan (1907/8–1930).* Retrieved June 3, 2002, from www.webwallas.com/
characbhagwati.htm

Che Guevara Information Archive. (2001). Retrieved June 4, 2002, from http://www.geocities.com/
Hollywood/8702/che.html

Chen, H., Schroeder, J., Hauck, R.V., Ridgeway, I., Atabulkish, H., Gupta H., et al. (2003). COPLINK
connect: Information and knowledge management for law enforcement. *Decisions Support Systems,
34*(3), 271–285.

Cherokee Nation. (n.d.). *A brief history of the Trail of Tears.* Retrieved June 25, 2002, from http://www
.cherokee.org/home.aspx?section=culture&culture=culinfo&cat=R20KZVC/B7c=&ID=aZ38KzfgbsI=

Cherpak, E. (1978). The participation of women in the independence movement in Gran Colombia. In
A. Lavrin (Ed.), *Latin American women: Historical perspectives.* Westport, CT: Greenwood.

Chowder, K. (2000). The father of American terrorism. *American Heritage, 51*(1), 68.

Cilluffo, F., & Tomarchio, J. T. (1998). Responding to new terrorist threats. *Orbis, 42–43,* 439–452.

Civil Liberties Act of 1988, 50 App. U.S.C.A § 1989 (1988).

Clancy, C. (2001, September 21). Kidnapping businesspeople has become big business. *Business Journal.*
Retrieved June 10, 2002, from http://www.sanjose.bizjournals.com/sanjose/stories/2001/09/24/
smallb2.html

Clayton, L. (1997, March). Revolutionary Zapatista women in cultural perspective. *The Prism*
(University of North Carolina), 1–5.

CNN. (1998). Timothy McVeigh: Convicted Oklahoma City bomber. *CNN Newsmaker Profiles.* Retrieved
June 7, 2002, from http://www.cnn.com/resources/newsmakers/us/

CNN. (2005). *Senator: U.S. didn't connect "dots" before 9/11.* Retrieved on May 15, 2005, from http://
archives.cnn.com/2002/US/05/15/inv.fbi.terror/

Colarik, A. M. (2006). *Cyber terrorism.* London: Idea Group.

Cole, D. (1996). Terrorizing the Constitution. *The Nation.* Retrieved June 17, 2002, from http://www
.thenation.com

Cole, D. (2001). *On civil liberties and proposed anti-terrorism legislation.* Testimony before the Senate
Judiciary Committee. Washington, DC: Senate Judiciary Committee.

Cooper, H. H. A. (2001). Terrorism: The problem of definition revisited. *American Behavioral Scientist,
44*(6), 881–893.

Cornell, S. E. (2005). The interaction of narcotics and conflict. *Journal of Peace Research, 42*(6), 751–760.

Country Reports on Terrorism. (2005). Washington: U.S. Department of State. Retrieved November 11,
2006, from http://www.state.gov/s/ct/rls/crt

Crenshaw, M. (1995). Relating terrorism to historical contexts. In Martha Crenshaw (Ed.), *Terrorism in
context.* University Park: Pennsylvania State University.

Crenshaw, M. (1998a). The logic of terrorism: Terrorist behavior as a product of strategic choice. In
Walter Reich (Ed.), *Origins of terrorism: Psychologies, ideologies, theologies, states of mind.*
Washington DC: Woodrow Wilson Center Press.

Crenshaw, M. (1998b). Questions to be answered, research to be done, knowledge to be applied. In
Walter Reich (Ed.), *Origins of terrorism: Psychologies, ideologies, theologies, states of mind.*
Washington, DC: Woodrow Wilson Center Press.

Crenshaw, M. (2000). The psychology of terrorism: A agenda for the 21ˢᵗ century. *Political Psychology, 21*(2), 405–420.

Crenshaw, M., & Pimlott, J. (Eds.). (1997). *Encyclopedia of world terrorism.* Armonk, NY: M.E. Sharpe.

Cunningham, K. (2002). Cross-regional trends in female terrorism. *Studies in Conflict and Terrorism, 26,* 171–195.

Cunningham, K. (2003). Cross-regional trends in female terrorism. *Studies in Conflict and Terrorism, 25,* 171–195.

Dalrymple, T. (2005, November 3). The suicide bombers among us. *City-Journal.org.* Retrieved November 3, 2005, from http://www.frontpagemag.com/Articles/printable.asp?ID=20059

Daly, J. (2001, September 17). Suicide bombing: No warning, and no total solution. *Jane's Terrorism & Security Monitor,* 1–5. Retrieved June 17, 2002, from http://www.janes.com/security/international_security/news/jtsm/jtsm010917_1_n.shtml

Defense Science Board. (1997). *The Defense Science Board 1997 summer study task force on DOD responses to transnational threats* (Final Report, Vol. 1). Washington, DC: U.S. Department of Defense.

Deflem, M. (2006). Global rule of law or global rule of law enforcement? International police cooperation and counterterrorism. *Annals of the American Academy of Political and Social Science, 630,* 240–251.

DeGregori, C. (1994). The origins and logic of the Shining Path. In D. Palmer (Ed.), *Shining Path of Peru.* New York: St. Martin's Press.

Demaris, O. (1977). *Brothers in blood: The international terrorist network.* New York: Scribner.

Dempsey, J. X., & Cole, D. (1999). *Terrorism and the Constitution: Sacrificing civil liberties in the name of national security.* New York: First Amendment Foundation.

Derechos Human Rights. (1997, April 25). Peru: Possible extra-judicial executions of MRTA rebels. Retrieved June 10, 2002, from http://www.derechos.org/human-rights/actions/peru.html

Dietz, P. E. (1988). Dangerous information: Product tampering and poisoning. *Journal of Forensic Sciences, 33*(3), 1206–1217.

Dingley, J. (2001). The bombing of Omagh, 15 August 1998: The bombers, their tactics, strategy, and purpose behind the incident. *Studies in Conflict and Terrorism, 24,* 451–465.

Dobson, C. (1977). *The Carlos complex: A study in terror.* New York: Putnam.

DoCeuPinto, M. (1999). Some U.S. concerns regarding Islamist and Middle Eastern terrorism. *Terrorism and Political Violence, 11*(3), 72–96.

Doran, M. (2002). Somebody else's civil war. *Foreign Affairs, 81*(3), 22–42.

Douglas, S. (1996). Terror and bathos. *The Progressive, 60*(9), 40.

Dr. Abimael Guzmán's (Chairman Gonzalo) "Speech from a cage," September 24, 1992. (2000). *International Emergency Committee to Defend the Life of Dr. Abimael Guzmán-U.S.* Retrieved June 17, 2002, from http://www.csrp.org/speech.htm

Drake, C. J. M. (1998). The role of ideology in terrorists' target selection. *Terrorism and Political Violence, 10*(2), 53–85.

Drakos, K., & Gofas, A. (2006). The devil you know but are afraid to face: Underreporting bias and its distorting effects on the study of terrorism. *Journal of Conflict Resolution, 50*(5), 714–735.

Dunn, E., Moore, M., & Nosek, B. (2005). The war of the words: How linguistic differences in reporting shape perceptions of terrorism. *Analyses of Social Issues and Public Policy, 5*(1), 67–86.

The Economist. (2006, October 12). *Anna Politkovskaya, a Russian journalist, was shot dead on October 4, aged 48.* Retrieved January 3, 2007, from http://www.economist.com/obituary/displaystory.cfm?story_id=E1_RDNPPTG

Eisman, A. (2003). The media of manipulation: Patriotism and propaganda—mainstream news in the U. S. in the weeks following September 11. *Critical Quarterly, 45*(1–2), 55–72.

Eland, I. (1998). *Does U.S. intervention overseas breed terrorism? The historical record* (Foreign Policy Briefing No. 50). Washington, DC: Cato Institute.

Elliott, D. (2004). Terrorism, global journalism and the myth of the nation state. *Journal of Mass Media Ethics, 19*(1), 29–45.

Emergency rule in Sri Lanka. (2002, January 6). Retrieved June 17, 2002, from http://abcnews.go.com/sections/world/DailyNews/

Emerson, S., & Duffy, B. (1990). *The fall of Pan Am 103: Inside the Lockerbie investigation.* New York: Putnam.

Enders, W., & Sandler, T. (2000). Is transnational terrorism becoming more threatening? *Journal of Conflict Resolution, 44*(3), 307–322.

Engelberg, S. (2001, January 14). One man and a global web of violence [Electronic version]. Retrieved June 4, 2002, from *The New York Times on the Web*, www.library.cornell.edu/colldev/mideast/

Enteen, J. (2006). Spatial conception of URLs: Tamil Eelam networks on the world wide web. *New Media and Society, 8*(2), 229–249.

Eubank, W., & Weinberg, L. (2001). Terrorism and democracy: Perpetrators and victims. *Terrorism and Political Violence, 13*(1), 155–164.

Executive Order No. 9066, 3 C.F.R. 1092 (1942).

Falkenrath, R. A., Newman, R. D., & Thayer, B. A. (2000). *America's Achilles' heel: Nuclear, biological, and chemical terrorism and covert attack.* Cambridge, MA: MIT Press.

Fanon, F. (1962). *Black skin, white masks.* New York: Grove. (Original work published 1952)

Fanon, F. (1963). *The wretched of the earth.* New York: Grove. (Original work published 1959)

Farwell, B. (1991). *Armies of the Raj: From the mutiny to independence, 1858–1947.* New York: Norton.

FATF- GAFI. (2004, October 22). Nine special recommendations on terrorist financing. *Financial Action Task Force Standards.* Retrieved September 17, 2006, from http://www.fatf-gafi.org/document/9/0,2340,en_32250379_32236920_34032073_1_1_1_1,00.html

Federal Bureau of Investigation. (2006). *Terror 2000.* Retrieved June 19, 2006, from http://www.fbi.gov/publications/terror/terror2000_2001.htm.

Federation of American Scientists. (1998, August 8). National Liberation Army (ELN)—Colombia. *Intelligence Resource Program.* Retrieved June 10, 2002, from http://www.fas.org/irp/world/para/eln.htm

Ferrero, M. (2006). Martyrdom contracts. *Journal of Conflict Resolution, 50*(6), 855–877.

Feuerlicht, R. S. (1971). *America's reign of terror: World War I, the Red Scare, and the Palmer raids.* New York: Random House.

Fighel, Y. (2003, October 6). Palestinian Islamic Jihad and female suicide bombers. *Institute for Counter Terrorism.* Retrieved November 2, 2005, from http://www.ict.org.il/apage/5294.php

FindLaw. (1998). U. S. Constitution: First Amendment: Annotations. Retrieved June 7, 2002, from http://caselaw.lp.findlaw.com/data/constitution/amendment01/18.html

Follain, J. (2000). *Jackal: The complete story of the legendary terrorist, Carlos the Jackal.* New York: Arcade Publishing.

Foot, R. (2006). Torture: The struggle over a peremptory norm in a counter-terrorist era. *International Relations, 20*(20), 131–151.

Fraser, A. (1997). *Faith and treason: The story of the Gunpowder Plot.* Garden City, NY: Doubleday.

French, P. (1998). *India's journey to independence and division.* North Pomfret, VT: Trafalgar Square Books.

Fried, R. M. (1991). *Nightmare in red: The McCarthy era in perspective.* New York: Oxford University Press.

Fryer, J. (1999, January 14). Yemen: Arabia's Wild West. *BBC Online Network.* Retrieved June 10, 2002, from http://news.bbc.co.uk/hi/english/world/from_our_own_correspondent/newsid_253000/253004.stm

Ganor, B. (2006). Defining terrorism: Is one man's terrorist another man's freedom fighter? *The Institute for Counter Terrorism.* Retrieved September 1, 2006, from http://www.ict.org.il/Articles/define.htm

Gaouette, N. (1999, June 23). Muslim women in freedom fight. *The Christian Science Monitor.* Retrieved June 9, 2002, from http://www.csmonitor.com/atcsmonitor/specials/

Gibson, N. C. (1999). *Rethinking Fanon: The continuing dialogue.* Amherst, NY: Humanity Books.

Gilboa, E. (2005). Media-broker diplomacy: When journalists become mediators. *Critical Studies in Media Communication, 22*(2), 99–120.

Golden Ink. (n.d.). *About North Georgia: The Trail of Tears.* Retrieved June 25, 2002, from http://ngeorgia.com/history/nghisttt.html

Goldenberg, S. (2000, April 29). Israel lets in Achille Lauro hijacker turned peacemaker. *The Guardian* (Manchester, UK). Retrieved June 10, 2002, from http://www.guardian.co.uk/international/story/0,3604,215428,00.html

Gonzales, A. R. (2001, November 30). Martial justice, full and fair. *The New York Times.* Retrieved June 19, 2002, from http://usinfo.state.gov/topical/pol/terror/01120302.htm

Gonzales-Perez, M. (2006). Guerrillas in Latin America: Domestic and international roles. *Journal of Peace Research, 43*(3), 313–329.

Gordon, A. F. (2006). Abu Ghraib: Imprisonment and the war on terror. *Race and Class, 48*(1), 42–59.

Gordon, L. R. (1995). *Fanon and the crisis of European man: An essay on philosophy and the human sciences.* New York: Routledge.

Grant, M. (1994). *Critical intellectuals and the new media.* Unpublished doctoral dissertation, Cornell University, Ithaca, NY.

Greenberg, K. (1994). *Terrorism, the new menace.* New York: Millbrook Press.

Grigg, W. N. (1996). Hard left's "right-wing" kin. *New American, 12*(13). Retrieved June 10, 2002, from http://www.thenewamerican.com/tna/1996/v012n013/v012n013_right.htm

Guardian Unlimited. (2007). *U.S. military deaths in Iraq hit 3,017.* Retrieved on January 11, 2007, from http://www.guardian.co.uk

Guevara, C. (1961). *Guerrilla warfare.* New York: Monthly Review Press.

Guevara, C. (1967). *Man and socialism in Cuba.* Havana: Book Institute.

Guevara, C. (1968). *Reminiscences of the Cuban Revolutionary War.* New York: Monthly Review Press.

Guidelines. (2000, Spring). *Underground,* 25.

Gunaratna, R. (2000, October 20). Suicide terrorism: A global threat. *Jane's Intelligence Review.* Retrieved June 9, 2002, from http://www.janes.com/security/international_security/news/usscole/jir001020_1_n.shtml

Halberstam, M. (1988). Terrorism on the high seas: The Achille Lauro, piracy and the IMO Convention on Maritime *Safety. American Journal of International Law, 82*(2), 269–310.

Halperin, E. (1976). *Terrorism in Latin America.* Beverly Hills, CA: Sage.

Hamm, M. (1998). Terrorism, hate crime, and antigovernment violence. In Harvey Kushner (Ed.), *The future of terrorism.* Thousand Oaks, CA: Sage.

Handwerk, B. (2004, December 13). Female suicide bombers: Dying to kill., Retrieved November 2, 2005, from http://news.nationalgeographic.com/news/2004/12/1213_041213_tv_suicide_bombers.html

Hanrahan, G. (1985). *The terrorist classic: Manual of the urban guerrilla by Carlos Marighella.* Chapel Hill, NC: Documentary Publications.

Hansen, B. (2001, August 31). Children in crisis. *Congressional Quarterly Researcher, 11*(2), 657–680.

Harmon, C. (2000). *Terrorism today.* London: Frank Cass.

Harper, C. (1995). Did the Unabomber decision set a precedent? *American Journalism Review, 17*(9), 13–15.

Harris, R. (1970). *Death of a revolutionary: Che Guevara's last mission.* New York: Norton.

Harth, E. (2001). *Last witness: Reflections on the wartime internment of Japanese Americans.* New York: Palgrave.

Haynes, A. (1994). *The Gunpowder Plot: Faith in rebellion.* England: A. Sutton.

Healy, P. (2001, November 6). Harvard scholar's '96 book becomes the word on war. *Boston Globe.*

Hearst, P. (1982). *Every secret thing.* Garden City, NY: Doubleday.

Henck, N. (2002). *Broadening the struggle and winning the media war: "Marcos Mystique," "Guerrilla Chic" and Zapatista PR.* Montreal, Quebec: Kersplebedeb.

Herman, A. (2000). *Joseph McCarthy: Reexamining the life and legacy of America's most hated senator.* New York: Free Press.

Herman, E. S. (1982). *The real terror network: Terrorism in fact and propaganda.* Boston: South End Press.

Herman, E. S., & O'Sullivan, G. (1989). *The terrorism industry: The experts and institutions that shape our view of terror.* New York: Pantheon.

Herzog, K. (1993). *Finding their voice: Peruvian women's testimonies of war.* Valley Forge, PA: Trinity Press International.

Hinckley, T. (1996). *TWA 800 terrorist cover up? The media makes terrorism possible and profitable.* Retrieved June 7, 2002, from http://www.chuckbaldwinlive.com/twa2.html

Hinds, A. (2006, August 31). Mumbai bombings signal sustained rail terrorism trend. *Jane's Intelligence Review.* Retrieved September 14, 2006, from http://www.janes.com/security/law_enforcement/news/jir/jir060831_1_n.shtml

Hodges, D. C. (Ed.). (1977). *The legacy of Che Guevara: A documentary study.* London: Thames and Hudson.

Hoffman, B. (1997). The confluence of international and domestic trends in terrorism. *Terrorism and Political Violence, 9*(2), 1–15.

Hoffman, B. (1998). *Inside terrorism.* New York: Columbia University Press.

Hoffman, B. (1998a). The modern terrorist mindset: Tactics, targets and technologies. In *Inside terrorism.* New York: Columbia University Press.

Hoffman, B. (1998b, August 16). The new terrorist: Mute, unnamed, bloodthirsty. *Los Angeles Times.* Retrieved June 10, 2002, from http://www.rand.org/commentary/081698LAT.html

Hoffman, B. (1999). Terrorism trends and prospects. In Ian Lesser et al. (Eds.), *Countering the new terrorism.* Santa Monica, CA: RAND—Project Air Force.

Hoffman, B. (2001). Change and continuity in terrorism. *Studies in Conflict and Terrorism, 24,* 417–428.

Hoffman, B. (2006). *Inside terrorism.* (Rev. ed.). New York: Columbia University Press.

Hoffman, B., & McCormick, G. (2004). Terrorism, signaling, and suicide attack. *Studies in Conflict and Terrorism, 27*(4), 243–281.

Hoffman, L. (2001, October 4). How terrorists hide messages online. *Scripps Howard News Service.* Retrieved June 10, 2002, from www.s-t.com

Hoffman, L. (2002, February 6). *Women change the terrorist profile.* Washington, DC: Scripps Howard News Service.

Honest Reporting. (2005, June 20). *Three lessons from a woman terrorist.* Retrieved November 2, 2005, from http://www.honestreporting.com/articles/45884734/critiques/Three_Lessons_from_a_Woman_Terrorist.asp

Horan, D. (1998, June 7). Mohammad Abu Abbas stops running. *World News Inter Press Service.* Retrieved June 17, 2002, from www.oneworld.org/ips

Horchem, H. (1986). Terrorism in West Germany. *Conflict Studies, 186,* 1–21.

House Res. 291, 65th Cong., 40 Stat. 553–554 (1917).

Houston, J. W., & Houston, J. D. (1983). *Farewell to Manzanar: A true story of Japanese American experience during and after the World War II internment.* New York: Bantam Books.

Howard, R. D., & Sawyer, R. L. (2004*). Terrorism and counterterrorism: Understanding the new security environment, readings and interpretations.* New York: McGraw-Hill.

Hoyt, E. P. (1969). *The Palmer Raids, 1919–1920; An attempt to suppress dissent.* New York: Seabury Press.

Hrw.org. (2005, January 22). *Chechnya: Human rights defender abducted.* Retrieved January 3, 2007, from http://hrw.org/english/docs/2005/01/21/russia10055.htm

Huband, M. (1999). *Warriors of the prophet: The struggle for Islam.* Boulder, CO: Westview.

Hudson, D. (2000, March 8). Federal appeals panel finds anti-terrorism law unconstitutionally vague. *Freedom Forum.* Retrieved June 17, 2002, from http://www.freedomforum.org/templates/document.asp?documentID=11831

Huffman, R. (1999). *This is Baader-Meinhof.* Retrieved June 9, 2002, from http://www.baadermeinhof.com

Human Rights Watch. (1999). Children's rights—Human rights developments. *HRW World Report.* Retrieved June 17, 2002, from www.hrw.org/worldreport99/children/index.html

Human Rights Watch. (2006). Children's rights—Child soldiers. *HRW World Report.* Retrieved January 28, 2007, from http://hrw.org/campaigns/crp/index.htm

Hunt, J. (1998). *The French Revolution:* New York: Routledge.

Hunt, T. (2007, January 11). Bush admits errors in Iraq, commits 21,500 more troops. *Orlando Sentinel,* Volusia County Edition, p. A1.

Huntington, Samuel P. (1996). *The clash of civilizations and the remaking of the world order.* New York: Simon & Schuster.

ICT Institute for Counter Terrorism. Retrieved November 2, 2005, from http://www.ict.org.il/articles/articledet.cfm?articleid=499

Indian Removal Act of 1830, 4 Stat. 411 (1830).

Israel Insider. (2005, October 11). *Female bombmaker nabbed as security forces smash Hamas terror cells.* Retrieved November 3, 2005, from http://web.israelinsider.com/Articles/Diplomacy/7222.htm

Israeli Ministry of Foreign Affairs. (1995, December 6). Yigal and Haffai-Amir, and Dror Adani indictments. Communication by Ministry of Justice Spokesperson. Jerusalem. Retrieved June 17, 2002, from http://www.israel-mfa.gov.il/mfa/go.asp?MFAH01gn0

IsraelNationalNews Staff. (2005, July 18). *Abu Mazan's Fatah promotes female terrorists as role model—UNICEF funded girls camp named for suicide bomber.* Retrieved January 15, 2007, from http://www.militantislammonitor.org

Jacinto, L. (2004, September 23). Jihad's girl power. *ABC News International.* Retrieved November 2, 2005, from http://abcnews.go.com/sections/World/SciTech/

Jacobs, R. (1997). *The way the wind blew: A history of the Weather Underground.* London: Verso.

Jacquard, R. (2001, October 29). The guidebook of Jihad. *Time.* Retrieved June 17, 2002, from http://www.time.com/time/magazine/article/0,9171,1001077,00.html

Jaeger, P. T., Bertot, J. C., & McClure, C. R. (2003). The impact of the USA Patriot Act on collection and analysis of personal information under the Foreign Intelligence Surveillance Act. *Government Information Quarterly, 20,* 295–314.

Jamieson, A. (2000). Mafiosi and terrorists: Italian women in violent organizations. *SAIS Review, 20*(2), 51–64.

Jenkins, P. (1999). Fighting terrorism as if women mattered: Anti-abortion violence as unconstructed terrorism. In Jeff Ferrell & Neil Websdale (Eds.), *Making trouble: Cultural constructions of crime, deviance and control* (pp. 319–346). Hawthorne, NY: Aldine de Gruyter.

Jordan, J., & Horsburgh, N. (2005). Mapping Jihadist terrorism in Spain. *Studies in Conflict and Terrorism, 28,* 169–191.

Joshi, C. L. (2000, June 1). Ultimate sacrifice—Sri Lanka suicide bombers. *Far Eastern Economic Review,* 64. Retrieved June 17, 2002, from https://www.feer.com/cgi-bin/auth/wwwauth.pl?link=http://www.feer.com/articles/2000/0006_01/p64.html

Juergensmeyer, M. (2003). *Terror in the mind of God* (3rd ed.). Berkeley : University of California Press.

Kaplan, D. E., & Marshall, A. (1996). *The cult at the end of the world: The incredible story of Aum.* London: Arrow Books.

Kaplan, J. (1997). The American radical right's leaderless resistance. *Terrorism and Political Violence, 9*(3), 218.

Kassman, L. (2004, September 2). Women terrorists force changed thinking by security officials. *IWS— The Information Warfare Site.* Retrieved November 2, 2005, from www.iwar.org.uk/news-archive/2004/09–02.htm

Kean, T. A., & Hamilton, L. (Eds.). (2004). *9/11 Commission Report: Final Report of the National Commission on Terrorist Attacks upon the U.S.* Darby, PA: DIANE Publishing.

Kees, B. (1998, August 12). Net can renew democracy for disenfranchised, Godwin says. *Freedom Forum.* Retrieved June 17, 2002, from http://www.freedomforum.org/templates/document.asp?documentID=11300

Kellen, K. (1998). Ideology and rebellion: Terrorism in West Germany. In Walter Reich (Ed.). *Origins of terrorism: Psychologies, ideologies, theologies, states of mind.* Washington, DC: Woodrow Wilson Center Press.

Kelly, R. J. (1998). Armed prophets and extremists: Islamic fundamentalism. In H. Kushner (Ed.), *The future of terrorism.* Thousand Oaks, CA: Sage.

Kets de Vries, M. F. R. (2006). The spirit of despotism: Understanding the tyrant within. *Human Relations, 59*(2), 195–220.

Kirk, R. (1993). *Las mujeres de Sendero Luminoso.* Lima, Peru: Instituto Estudios Peruanos.

Kmiec, D. W. (2001, October 3). *On the constitutionality of various provisions of the proposed anti-terrorism act of 2001.* Testimony before the Senate Judiciary Committee. Washington, DC: Senate Judiciary Committee.

Knight, A. (1979). Female terrorists in the Russian Socialist Revolutionary Party. *Russian Review, 38,* 139–159.

Koch, J. (2000, December 9). *"Widows" of Aceh fight for freedom in a bitter land.* Retrieved June 9, 2002, from http://www.theage.com.au/news/2000/

Krakauer, J. (2004). *Under the banner of heaven.* New York: Anchor Books.

Kupfer, D. (2001, February/March). Luddism in the new millennium: An interview with Kirkpatrick Sale. *Earth First!, 21*(3). Retrieved June 25, 2002, from http://www.yeoldeconsciousnessshoppe.com/art42.html

Kushner, H. W. (2003). Introduction. *American Behavioral Scientist, 46*(6), 697–698.

Labor Research Association. (1948). *The Palmer Raids.* New York: International Publishers.

Laqueur, W. (1977). *Terrorism.* Boston: Little, Brown.

Laqueur, W. (1978). *The terrorist reader: A historical anthology.* Philadelphia: Temple University Press.

Laqueur, W. (1987). *The age of terrorism.* Boston: Little, Brown.

Laqueur, W. (1997). Terrorism via the Internet. *The Futurist, 31*(2), 624–626.

Laqueur, W. (1999). *The new terrorism: Fanaticism and the arms of mass destruction.* New York: Oxford University Press.

Laqueur, W. (2001). *A history of terrorism.* Somerset, NJ: Transaction Publishers.

Laqueur, W. (2004). *Voices of terror.* New York: Reed Press.

Lauber, M. (2004, October 21). Financing terror: An overview. *Terrorism Monitor, 2*(20). Retrieved March 29, 2006, from http://www.jamestown.org/terrorism/news/article.php?search=1&articleid=2368731

Lefebvre, G. (1962). *The French Revolution* (Elizabeth M. Evans, Trans.). New York: Columbia University Press.

Legal Information Institute. (2001). *Media law: An overview.* Retrieved June 7, 2002, from http://www.law.cornell.edu/topics/media.html

Lester, D., Yang, B., & Lindsay, M. (2004), Suicide bombers: Are psychological profiles possible? *Studies in Conflict and Terrorism, 27*(4) 283–295.

Levey, S. (2006, September 8). Prepared remarks by Stuart Levey, Department of the Treasury, Undersecretary for terrorism and financial intelligence, before the American Enterprise Institute for Public Policy Research. Retrieved September 17, 2006, from http://www.treasury.gov/press/releases/hp86.htm

Levin, B. (2002). Cyberhate: A legal and historical analysis of extremists' use of computer networks in America. *American Behavioral Scientist, 45*(6), 958–988.

Levy, B. H. (2003). *Who killed Daniel Pearl?* Hoboken, NJ: Melville House Press.

Lewis, C. W. (2000). The terror that failed: Public opinion in the aftermath of the bombing in Oklahoma City. *Public Administration Review, 60*(3), 201–210.

Lewis, N. A. (2002, May 29). F.B.I. chief admits 9/11 might have been detectable. *New York Times.*

Li, Q., & Schaub, D. (2004). Economic globalization and transnational terrorist incidents. *Journal of Conflict Resolution, 48*(2), 230–258.

Lin, C., Jen-Hwa Hu, P., & Chen, H. (2004). Technology implementation management in law enforcement: COPLINK systems usability and user acceptance evaluations. *Social Science Computer Review, 22*(1), 24–36.

Losen, M. (2004). Thomas Aquinas and the question of tyrannicide. In Walter Laquer (Ed.), *Voices of terror.* New York: Reed Press. (Original work published 1894)

Luthra, D. (2006, June 9). Discipline, death and martyrdom. *BBC News.* Retrieved June 9 2006, from http://newsvote.bbc.co.uk/mpapps/pagetools/print/news.bbc.co.uk/2/hi/south_asia/5051652.stm

Macey, D. (2002). *Frantz Fanon: A biography.* New York: St. Martin's Press.

Maguire, T. (2005) Islamist websites. *Global Media and Communication, 1*(1), 121–123.

Mahan, S. (1997, March). *Women of the Shining Path: A new model for terrorism in Peru.* Paper presented at the Academy of Criminal Justice Sciences, Louisville, KY.

Mannes, A. (2004, March 10). A life of terror. *National Review Online.* Retrieved January 22, 2007, from http://www.nationalreview.com/script/printpage.p?ref=/comment/mannes200403101409.asp

Marcus, I. (2002, March 12). Encouraging women terrorists. Special report #30 Palestinian Culture and Society. *Palestinian Media Watch,* Study #6. Retrieved November 2, 2005 from http://www.pmw.org.il/specrep-39.html

Marighella, C. (1985). *Manual of the urban guerrilla.* Chapel Hill, NC: Documentary Publications. (Original work published 1969)

Markle Foundation. (2002). *Protecting America's freedom in the information age.* New York: Markle Foundation, Task Force on National Security in the Information Age.

Markle Foundation. (2003). *Creating a trusted network for homeland security.* New York: Markle Foundation, Task Force on National Security in the Information Age.

Martin, G. (2006). *Understanding terrorism* (2nd ed.). Thousand Oaks, CA: Sage.

Mather, G. (2000, July 7). Basque separatists threaten safety of journalists, says reporters group. *Freedom Forum.* Retrieved June 17, 2002, from http://www.freedomforum.org/templates/

Mathur, S. (2006). Surviving the dragnet: "Special interest" detainees in the US after 9/11. *Race and Class, 47*(3), 31–46.

McCarthy, J. (1985). *The fight for America.* Random Lake, WI: Times Printing Co.

McClintock, C. (1986). *Sendero Luminoso guerrillas maoistas del Peru.* Lima, Peru: University of Lima, Faculty of Law and Political Sciences Research Publications.

McCormick, C. H. (1997). *Seeing reds: Federal surveillance of radicals in the Pittsburgh Mill District, 1917–1921.* Pittsburgh: University of Pittsburgh Press.

McDonald, I., & Rosenberg, R. (2004). Filling the 24 × 7 news hole. *American Behavioral Scientist, 48*(3), 327–340.

McGuckin, F. (Ed.). (1997). *Terrorism in the United States.* New York: H. W. Wilson.

McLaughlin, M. (1999, September 27). *U.S. liberals join right-wing attack on clemency for Puerto Rican nationalists.* Retrieved June 10, 2002, from http://www.wsws.org/articles/1999/sep1999/clem-s27.shtml

Media coverage related to terrorism. (1999, December 27). Retrieved June 7, 2002, from http://www.musalman.com/islamnews/ing-mediacoverageterrorism.html

Merari, A. (1998). The readiness to kill and die. In Walter Reich (Ed.), *Origins of terrorism: Psychologies, ideologies, theologies, states of mind.* Washington DC: Woodrow Wilson Center Press.

Miller, J. (1998, May 28). *An exclusive interview with Osama bin Laden: Talking with terror's banker.* Retrieved January 5, 2001, from http://www.abcnews.go.com/sections/world/dailynews/

Miller, J., & Miller, R. M. (2000). *Ecoterrorism and ecoextremism against agriculture.* Chicago: Miller Publications.

Miller, L. (2006) The terrorist mind: A psychological and political analysis. *International Journal of Offender Therapy and Comparative Criminology, 30*(2), 121–138.

Millett, M. (2000, December 13). Citizenship ruling to save Fujimori from Lima's wrath. *Sydney Morning Herald* (Sydney, Australia). Retrieved June 10, 2002, from http://old.smh.com.au/news

Millies, S. (1995, January 26). The Ludlow Massacre and the birth of company unions. *Workers World.* Retrieved June 26, 2002, from http://www.Hartford-hwp.com/archives/45b/030

Minuteman Project. (2006). MMP: Americans doing the job Congress won't do. Retrieved December 27, 2006, from http://www.minutemanproject.com

MIPT Terrorist Knowledge Base. (2006). *A comprehensive database of terrorist incidents and organizations.* Retrieved December 1, 2006, from http://www.tkb.org.

Monterey Institute for International Studies. (2001). *WMD database.* Monterey, CA: Monterey Institute of International Studies, Center for Nonproliferation Strategies. [Electronic version available by subscription.]

Morrison, M. (2000). *Munich massacre: The worst tragedy in modern Olympic history.* Retrieved June 7, 2002, from www.infoplease.com/spot/mm-munich.html

MosNews.com. (2006a, April 3). *Hundreds rally in Chechnya on World Disappeared Day.* Retrieved January 3, 2007, from http://www.mosnews.com/news/2006/08/30/groznyrally.shtml

MosNews.com. (2006b, December 27). *Chechnya's Pro-Moscow President says few abductions registered this year.* Retrieved January 3, 2007, from http://www.mosnews.com/news/2006/12/27/fewerabduct.shtml

Muhammad, E. (1999). My mission and objective. *The Supreme Wisdom, 2.* Retrieved June 25, 2002, from http://www.muhammadspeaks.com/Objective.html

Mullins, M. R. (1997). Aum Shinrikyo as an apocalyptic movement. In Thomas Robbins & Susan J. Palmer (Eds.), *Millennium, messiahs, and mayhem: Contemporary apocalyptic movements.* New York: Routledge.

Myer, D. S. (1971). *Uprooted Americans: The Japanese Americans and the War Relocation Authority during World War II.* Tucson: University of Arizona Press.

Nacos, B. L. (1994). *Terrorism and the media.* New York: Columbia University Press.

Nacos, B. L. (2005). The portrayal of female terrorists in the media: Similar framing patterns in the news coverage of women in politics and in terrorism. *Studies in Conflict and Terrorism, 28,* 435–451.

Najma's call to save children from terrorists. (2001, September 11. *The Hindu.* Retrieved June 10, 2002, from http://www.hinduonnet.com/thehindu/2001/09/11/stories/02110006.htm

National Commission on Terrorist Attacks Upon the United States. (2004). *The 9–11 Commission Report.* New York: Norton.

National Counterterrorism Center (NCTC). (2006). *NCTC fact sheet and observations related to 2005 terrorist incidents.* Retrieved December 1, 2006, from http://wits.nctc.gov/Methodology.do

National Security Archive. (2000). *Chile: 16,000 U.S. secret documents declassified* [Press release]. Washington, DC: National Security Archive.

Nesser, P. (2006). Jihadism in Western Europe after the invasion of Iraq: Tracing motivational influences from the Iraq war on jihadist terrorism in Western Europe. *Studies in Conflict and Terrorism, 29,* 323–342.

Netanyahu, B. (1995). *Fighting terrorism: How democracies can defeat domestic and international terrorists.* New York: Farrar, Straus & Giroux.

Neuburger, Luisella de Cataldo, & Valentini, Tiziana. (1996). *Women and terrorism* (Leo Michael Hughes, Trans.). New York: St. Martin's Press.

Nicholls, M. (1991). *Investigating the Gunpowder Plot.* New York: Manchester University Press.

9/11 Public Discourse Project. (2005, October 20). *Report on the status of 9/11 Commission recommendations.* Retrieved January 30, 2007, from http://www.9–11pdp.org/press/2005–11–14_report.pdf

Nivat, A. (2005). The black widows: Chechen women join the fight for independence—and Allah. *Studies in Conflict and Terrorism, 28,* 413–419.

Nuclear Threat Initiative. (2006). *Introduction to radiological terrorism.* Retrieved January 3, 2007, from http://www.nti.org/h_learnmore/radtutorial/chapter01_02.html

O'Connell, H. (Ed.). (1993). *Women and conflict.* Oxford, UK: Oxfam.

Oates, S. B. (1979). *Our fiery trial: Abraham Lincoln, John Brown, and the Civil War era.* Amherst: University of Massachusetts Press.

Onder, J. J. (1999). Media & law enforcement relations during hostage-taking terrorist incidences: A cooperative decision. *Responder Magazine, 6*(1), 26–33.

Overseas Security Advisory Council. (2001, January 24). *Daily global news.* Retrieved June 17, 2001, from http://www.ds-osac.org/globalnews/story

Palestinian women and children encouraged to become suicide bombers. (2001, August 5). *Israel News Agency.* Retrieved June 10, 2002, from http://www.israelnewsagency.com/suicide.html

Palmer, A. M. (1920). The case against the "Reds." *Forum, 63,* 173–185. Retrieved June 19, 2002, from http://chnm.gmu.edu/courses/hist409/palmer.html

Palmer, D. S. (Ed.). (1994). *Shining Path of Peru* (2nd ed.). New York: St. Martin's Press.

Pape, R. A. (2005) *Dying to win.* New York: Random House.

Parfitt, T. (2006, December 20). Fancy a no-frills break? *Guardian.* Retrieved January 3, 2007, from http://www.guardian.co.uk

Pastore, N. (1997, June 11). Execution would make Timothy McVeigh a martyr. *USA Today.* Retrieved June 17, 2002, from http:// www.cjpf.org/sentencing/mcveigh.html

Patchett, Ann. (2002). *Bel canto.* New York: Harper Perennial.

Pate, J., Ackerman, G., & McCloud, K. (2001). *2000 WMD terrorism chronology: Incidents involving subnational actors, and chemical, biological, radiological, or nuclear materials.* Monterey, CA: Monterey Institute of International Studies, Center for Nonproliferation Strategies.

Pattillo, L. (1998, April 24). *Shadowy threat of extremist hate groups quietly growing.* Retrieved June 10, 2002, from http://www.cnn.com/SPECIALS/views/y/9804/pattillo.unholywar/

Paye, J. -C. (2006). From the state of emergency to the permanent state of exception. *Telos, 136,* 154–167. Retrieved on January 30, 2007, from http://www.telospress.com/main/index .php?main_page=product_info&products_id=312

Paz, R. (2000, September). *Targeting terrorist financing in the Middle East.* Paper presented at the International Conference on Countering Terrorism through Enhanced International Cooperation, Mont Blanc, Italy. Retrieved June 4, 2002, from http://www.ict.org.il/index.php?sid=119&lang= en&act=page&id=5231&str=%22Targeting%20terrorist%20financing%20in%20the%20 Middle%20East%22

Perl, R. F. (1997, October 22). *Terrorism, the media, and the government: Perspectives, trends, and options for policymakers* (Congressional Research Service Issue Brief). Retrieved June 7, 2002, from http://www.au.af.mil/au/awc/awcgate/state/crs-terror-media.htm

Pew Research Center for the People & the Press. (1999). *Self censorship: How often and why.* Retrieved June 7, 2002, from http://people-press.org/reports/display.php3?ReportID=39

Phillips, J. (2005, January 17). Women's magazine offers tips to terrorists. *The Washington Times.* Retrieved November 2, 2005, from http://washingtontimes.com/world/20050117–122001– 8417r.htm

Picard, R. G. (1991). Journalists as targets and victims of terrorism. In Y. Alexander & R. G. Picard (Eds.), *In the camera's eye.* Washington, DC: Macmillan-Brassey's.

Picard, R., & Adams, P. (1991). Characterisations of acts and perpetrators of political violence in three elite U.S. daily newspapers. In A. O. Alali & K. K. Eke (Eds.), *Media coverage of terrorism.* Newbury Park, CA: Sage.

Pierce, W. (writing as Andrew MacDonald). (1996). *The Turner diaries* (2nd ed.). Hillsboro, WV: National Vanguard Books.

Pillar, P. R. (2001). *Terrorism and U.S. foreign policy.* Washington, DC: Brookings Institution.

Pitcavage, M. (2001). The militia movement from Ruby Ridge to Y2K. *American Behavioral Scientist, 44*(6), 957–981.

Poland, J. M. (1988). *Understanding terrorism: Groups, strategies, and responses.* Englewood Cliffs, NJ: Prentice Hall.

Poole, D., & Rénique, G. (1992). *Peru: Time of fear.* London: Latin America Bureau.

Post, J. (1998). Terrorist psycho-logic: Terrorist behavior as a product of psychological forces. In Walter Reich (Ed.), *Origins of terrorism: Psychologies, ideologies, theologies, states of mind.* Washington DC: Woodrow Wilson Center Press.

Potok, M. (1999, Summer). All in the family: Women in the movement. *Intelligence Report* (Southern Poverty Law Center), 12–22.

Praesidia Defence. (1996, September 6). *How Operation Sunrise failed—Lessons learned of the assassination of Rabin.* Retrieved June 10, 2002, from http://www.praesidia.de/Welcome/Press_and_ publications_on_terr/Assassination_of_Rabin_-_how_O/hauptteil_assassination_of_rabin_- _how_o.html

Pushkarna, V. (1998, April 19). *Terrorists' children.* Retrieved June 10, 2002, from http://www.the-week .com/98apr19

Radu, M., & Tismaneanu, V. (1990). *Latin American revolutionaries: Groups, goals, methods.* Washington, DC: Pergamon-Brassey's International Defense Publishers.

Ramakrishnan, P. (1994). *Gandhi and Indian independence.* Columbia, MO: South Asia Books.

Ranstorp, M. (2000). Religious terror. In Laura Egendorf (Ed.), *Terrorism: Opposing viewpoints.* San Diego: Greenhaven Press.

Rapoport, D.C. (1984). Fear and trembling: Terrorism in three religious traditions. *American Political Science Review, 78*(3), 658–677.

Rapoport, D. C. (2000). Democracy encourages terror. In Laura Egendorf (Ed.), *Terrorism: Opposing viewpoints.* San Diego: Greenhaven Press.

Rashid, A. (2001). *Taliban: Militant Islam, oil and fundamentalism in Central Asia.* New Haven, CT: Yale University Press.

Ravi, N. (2005). Looking beyond flawed journalism. *Harvard International Journal of Press/Politics, 10*(1), 45–62.

Reader, I. (2000). *Religious violence in contemporary Japan: The case of Aum Shinrikyo.* Honolulu: University of Hawaii Press.

Reeve, S. (1999). *The new jackals: Ramzi Yousef, Osama bin Laden and the future of terrorism.* Boston: Northeastern University Press.

Reich, W. (1998). Understanding terrorist behavior: The limits and opportunities of psychological inquiry. In Walter Reich (Ed.), *Origins of terrorism: Psychologies, ideologies, theologies, states of mind* (p. 261). Washington, DC: Woodrow Wilson Center Press.

Reno v. American-Arab Anti-Discrimination Committee, 117 F. 3d 97–1252 (9th Cir. 1999). U.S. Lexis 1514.

Reynolds, D. S. (2005). *John Brown, abolitionist: The man who killed slavery, sparked the Civil War, and seeded civil rights.* New York: Alfred A. Knopf.

Reynolds, K. M., Griset, P., & Scott, E., Jr. (2006). Law enforcement information sharing: A Florida case study. *American Journal of Criminal Justice, 3*(1), 1–17.

Reynolds, R. (1996, May 10). *Abu Abbas: From terrorist to peace activist.* Retrieved June 10, 2002, from http://www.cnn.com/WORLD/9605/10/abu.abbas/

Roberts, M. (2005). Tamil Tigers "martyrs": Regenerating divine potency? *Studies in Conflict and Terrorism, 28,* 495–514.

Robinson, G. (2001). *By order of the president: F.D.R. and the internment of Japanese Americans.* Cambridge, MA: Harvard University Press.

Robinson, P. (2005) The CNN effect revisited. *Critical Studies in Media Communication, 22*(4), 344–349.

Rojahn, C. (1998). Left-wing terrorism in Germany: The aftermath of ideological violence. *Conflict Studies, 313,* 1–21.

Rojas, R. (1994). *Chiapas, and the women?* Mexico, DF: Editiones La Correa Feminista, Centro de Investigation y Capacitacion de las Mujer. Mexico, DF.

Rosen, J. (2001, October 7). A cautionary tale for a new age of surveillance. *New York Times Magazine.* Retrieved http://www.nytimes.com/2001/10/07/magazine/07SURVEILLANCE.html

Rosenberg, T. (1991). *Children of Cain: Violence and the violent in Latin America.* New York: Penguin.

Rosenfeld, M. (2001, November 6). Global thinker. *The Washington Post,* p. C01. [Abbreviated versions of this article appear at http://www.nikeworkers.org/reebok/global_thinker and elsewhere]

Rosenfield, S. (1996). *Blood-red headlines feed terrorist propaganda* (IPI Report). Vienna: International Press Institute.

Ross, W. (2001, September 28). *Identical letters link terrorists on three hijacked flights September 11.* Washington, DC: U.S. Department of State, International Information Programs. Retrieved June 17, 2002, from http://usinfo.state.gov

Rubenstein, R. E. (1987). *Alchemists of revolution.* New York: Basic Books.

Sadler, A. E., & Winters, P. A. (1996). *Urban terrorism.* San Diego: Greenhaven Press.

Safire, W. (2001, November 26). Kangaroo courts. *New York Times,* p. A17.

Said, E. W. (2001, October 22). The clash of ignorance. *The Nation.* Retrieved June 19, 2002, from http://www.thenation.com/doc.mhtml?i=20011022&s=said

Sale, K. (1995). *Rebels against the future.* New York: Addison-Wesley.

Salij, J. (2005). The significance of "ineffective" methods of fighting terrorism. *American Behavioral Scientist, 48*(6), 700–709.

SANS Institute. (2001, October 4). Daily news report. *Dartmouth's Institute for Security Technology Studies.* Retrieved June 10, 2002, from http://www.incidents.org/ists

Savitch, H. V., & Garb, Y. (2006). Terror, barriers, and the changing topography of Jerusalem. *Journal of Planning, Education and Research, 26,* 152–173.

Sayle, M. (1996, April 1). Nerve gas and the four noble truths. *The New Yorker,* 56–71.

Schlesinger, P. (2006). Is there a crisis in British journalism? *Media, Culture and Society, 28*(2), 299–307.

Schmid, A., & Jongman, A. (Eds.). (1988). *Political terrorism: A new guide to actors, authors, concepts, data bases, theories, and literature.* New Brunswick, NJ: Transaction.

Schrecker, E. (1994). *The age of McCarthyism.* New York: St. Martin's Press.

Schroeder, J. (2001). *COPLINK: Database integration and access for a law enforcement intranet, final report.* Washington, DC: U.S. Department of Justice.

Schweitzer, G. E. (1998). *Super-terrorism, assassins, mobsters, and weapons of mass destruction.* New York: Plenum Trade.

Schweitzer, Y. (2000, April 21). *Suicide terrorism: Development & characteristics.* Institute for Counter Terrorism. Retrieved June 17, 2001, from http://www.ict.org.il/aarticles/c1847-i126.php

Scott, E. (2004). *Unpublished study of data-sharing programs identified in the literature.* Orlando: University of Central Florida.

Scripps, Howard. (2002, February 6). *Women suicide bombers since 1985.* Washington, DC: International Database.

Sedition Act of 1798. (1798). An act in addition to the Act, entitled An Act for the Punishment of Certain Crimes against the United States, 1 Stat. 112 1790.

Sedition Act of 1918, 40 Stat. 553–554 (1918).

Senate Permanent Subcommittee on Investigations of the Committee on Governmental Affairs. (1996). Staff statement, global proliferation of weapons of mass destruction: A case study of the Aum Shinrikyo. *Global proliferation of weapons of mass destruction, part I, hearings before the Permanent Subcommittee on Investigations of the Committee on Governmental Affairs, U.S. Senate, 104th Cong., 1st Sess.* Washington, DC: Government Printing Office.

Sharp, W. G., Sr. (2000). The use of armed force against terrorism: American hegemony or impotence? *Chicago Journal of International Law, 1*(1), 37–47.

Shepard, A. C. (2000). Safety first. *American Journalism Review, 22*(1), 22–28. Retrieved June 7, 2002, from http://www.ajr.org/Article.asp?id=518

Shepherd, N. (1997). *Kidnapping and extortion liability.* New York: Converium North America. Retrieved June 10, 2002, from http://www.zreclaim.com/closerLook/

Shields, P. (2006). Electronic networks, enhanced state surveillance and the ironies of control. *Journal of Creative Communications, 1*(1), 19–37.

Shuman, E. (2001, November 1). Trial of agent provocateur Raviv postponed, again. *Israel Insider.* Retrieved June 17, 2002, from http://www.israelinsider.com/channels/politics/articles/

Simonsen, C. E., & Spindlove, J. R. (2000). *Terrorism today: The past, the players, the future.* New York: Prentice Hall.

Slone, M. (2000). Responses to media coverage of terrorism. *Journal of Conflict Resolution, 44*(2), 508–522.

Smith, C. (1977). *Carlos: Portrait of a terrorist.* New York: Holt, Rinehart and Winston.

Smithson, A. E., & Levy, L. -A. (2000). *Ataxia: The chemical and biological terrorism threat and the U.S. response* (Report #35). Washington, DC: Henry L. Stimson Center.

Snow, N., & Taylor, P. (2006) The revival of the propaganda state. *The International Communications Gazette, 68*(5–6), 389–407.

Snow, R. . (1999). The *militia threat: Terrorists among* us: New York: Plenum.

Solomon, N. (1999). *The habits of highly deceptive media.* New York: Common Courage Press.

Southern Poverty Law Center. (2000a, Fall). Snarling at the white man. *Intelligence Report.* Retrieved June 25, 2002, from http://www.splcenter.org/intel/intelreport/article.jsp?aid=214 x

Southern Poverty Law Center. (2000b, Fall). The new romantics. *Intelligence Report.* Retrieved June 25, 2002, from http://www.splcenter.org/intel/intelreport/article.jsp?aid=236

Southern Poverty Law Center. (2006). Active U.S. hate groups in 2005. *Intelligence Project.* Retrieved December 27, 2006, from http://www.splcenter.org/intel/map/hate.jsp

Speckhard, A., & Ahkmedova, K. (2006). The making of a martyr: Chechen suicide terrorism. *Studies in Conflict and Terrorism, 29*(5), 429–492.

Speckhard, A., Tarabrina, N., Krasnov, V., & Mufel, N. (2005). Posttraumatic and acute stress responses in hostages held by suicide terrorists in the takeover of a Moscow theater. *Traumatology, 11*(1), 3–21.

Sprinzak, E. (1998). Extreme left terrorism in a democracy. In Walter Reich (Ed.). *Origins of terrorism: Psychologies, ideologies, theologies, states of mind.* Washington, DC: Woodrow Wilson Center Press.

Sprinzak, E. (2000, September/October). Rational fanatics. *Foreign Policy,* 66–73. Retrieved June 17, 2002, from www.foreignpolicy.com

Stafford, D. (1971). *From anarchist to reformist: A study of the political activities of Paul Brousse within the First International and the French Socialist Movement 1870–90.* Toronto: University of Toronto Press.

Stankiewicz, W. (2005). International terrorism at sea as a menace to the civilization of the 21st century. *American Behavioral Scientist, 48*(6), 683–699.

Staples, B. (2002, February 1). Enter Patty Hearst, and other ghosts from the 60's. *The New York Times.* Retrieved June 6, 2002, from http://www.crimelynx.com/patty60.html

Stern, J. (2001, February 28). Execute terrorists at our own risk. *New York Times.* Retrieved June 7, 2002, from http://bcsia.ksg.harvard.edu/publication.cfm?program=CORE&ctype=article&item_id=230

Stern, J. (2003). The ultimate organizations. In *Terror in the name of God: Why religious militants kill* (pp. 237–280). New York: HarperCollins.

Sterngold, J. (2002, January 18). New evidence paved way for arrests in a '75 killing. *The New York Times.* Retrieved June 6, 2002, from http://www.rickross.com/reference/symbionese/symbionese16.html

Stiles, K. W., & Thayne, A. (2006). Compliance with international law: International law on terrorism at the United Nations. *Cooperation and Conflict, 41*(2), 153–176.

Subcomandante Marcos, & Inacio Taibo II, P. (2006). *The uncomfortable dead.* New York: Akashic Books.

Subcomandante Marcos, & Ponce de Leon, J. (2002). *Our word is our weapon.* New York: Seven Stories Press.

Swango, A. (2006, May 8). A child soldier grows up. *NYC24,* New Media Workshop, Columbia University Graduate School of Journalism. Retrieved January 20, 2007, from http://www.nyc24.0rg/2006/newnewyorkers/childsoldier/index.html

Taipale, K. (2003, December). Data mining and domestic security: Connecting the dots to make sense of data. *Science and Technology Law Review, 2.*

Tan, A. (2000). Armed Muslim separatist rebellion in Southeast Asia: Persistence, prospects and implications. *Studies in Conflict and Terrorism, 23,* 267–288.

Tarazona-Sevillano, G., & Reuter, J. (1990). *Sendero Luminoso and the threat of narcoterrorism.* Washington Papers Series. New York: Praeger & Center for Strategic and International Studies.

Tarzi, S. M. (2005). Coercive diplomacy and an "irrational" regime: Understanding the American confrontation with the Taliban. *International Studies, 42*(1), 21–41.

Taylor, R. W., Caeti, T. J. D., Loper, K., Fritsch, E. J., & Liederbach, J. (2006). *Digital crime and digital terrorism.* Upper Saddle River, NJ: Pearson Education.

Terrorism Research Center. (2006). *Terrorist group profiles.* Retrieved November 6, 2006, from http://www.terrorism.com/modules.php?op=modload&name=TGroups&file=index

Terrorist Knowledge Base. (2006). MIPT (Memorial Institute for the Prevention of Terrorism). Retrieved December 8, 2006, from http://www.tkb.org

TerroristFinancing.com. (2006). Tactics & techniques. *The Counter Terrorist Financing Network.* Retrieved January 20, 2007, from http://www.terroristfinancing.com/index.php?op=kb&sec=tf_tech

Tilly, C. (2005). Terror as strategy and relational process. *International Journal of Comparative Sociology, 46*(1–2), 11–32.

Tooley, M. (1999, August 18). Clinton offers to free Puerto Rican terrorists. *Institute on Religion and Democracy. UM Action News.* Retrieved June 17, 2002, from http://hyperc.at.spry.com/umaction/archive/mtooley49.htm

Torbakov, I. (2004). Assessing the Moscow subway blast: Tragic accident or a lethal spillover from the war in Chechnya? In *Unmasking Terror* (pp. 110–112). Washington, DC: Jamestown Foundation.

Travalio, G. M. (2000). Terrorism, international law, and the use of military force. *Wisconsin International Law Journal, 18*(1), 145–191.

U.S. Congress. (1991, December 18). *Drug Enforcement Administration's alleged connection to the Pan Am flight 103 disaster.* Hearing before the Government Information Justice, and Agriculture Subcommittee of the Committee on Government Operations, House of Representatives, 101st Congress, 2nd Session. Washington, DC: Government Printing Office.

U.S. Department of Energy. (2007). *Yucca Mountain repository.* Retrieved January 3, 2007 from http://www.ocrwm.doe.gov/ym_repository/index.shtml.

U.S. Department of Justice. (2006). *Statement of President George W. Bush on Passage of the Bill to Reauthorize the USA Patriot Act.* Retrieved from http://www.lifeandliberty.gov/index.html

United Nations General Assembly adopts global counter-terrorism strategy. (2006). Retrieved on January 4, 2007, from http://www.un.org/terrorism/strategy-counter-terrorism.html

United Nations Resolution 1333, December 19, 2000.

United States Code Title 22, chapter 38&2656f.

United States Federal Regulations 28 CFR section 0.85.

USA PATRIOT Act of 2001. Uniting and Strengthening America by Providing Appropriate Tools Required to Intercept and Obstruct Terrorism Act, Pub. L. No. 107–56 (2001).

Vague, T. (1994). *Televisionaries: The Red Army Faction story.* San Francisco: AK Press.

Vanderheiden, S. (2005). Eco-terrorism or justified resistance? Radical environmentalism and the "War on Terror." *Politics & Society, 33*(3), 425–447.

Verton, D. (2003). *Black ice: The invisible threat of cyber-terrorism.* Emeryville, CA: McGraw-Hill/Osborne.

Vetter, H, J., & Perlstein, G. R. (1991). *Perspectives on terrorism.* Belmont, CA: Wadsworth.

Victoroff, J. (2005). The mind of the terrorist: A review and critique of psychological approaches. *Journal of Conflict Resolution, 49*(1), 3–42.

Vogel, Ka. (2006). Bioweapons proliferation: Where science studies and public policy collide. *Social Studies of Science, 36*(5), 659–690.

Wallace, R. (2001). *Lockerbie: The story and the lessons.* Westport, CT: Praeger.

Walsh, J. (1995, April 3). Shoko Asahara: The making of a messiah. *Time Magazine.*

Walton, A. (1997). *Unabomber became an icon on the 'Net.* Retrieved June 7, 2002, from www.cnn.com/SPECIALS/1997/unabomb/investigation/icon

War Relocation Authority. (1943). *Relocation of Japanese Americans.* Washington, DC: Author.

Wasserman, J. (2002, February 1). Ex-SLA members get $1M bail. *Associated Press.* Retrieved February 4, 2002, from http://www.story.news.yahoo.com/news

Weimann, G. (2006a). *Terror on the Internet.* Washington, DC: U.S. Institute of Peace.

Weimann, G. (2006b). Virtual disputes: The use of the Internet for terrorist debates. *Studies in Conflict and Terrorism, 29,* 623–639.

Weimann, G., & Winn, C. (1994). *The theater of terror: Mass media and international terrorism.* New York: Longman.

Weir, F. (2003, June 12). Chechen women join terror's ranks. *Christian Science Monitor.* Retrieved November 26, 2005, from http://www.csmonitor.com/2003/0612/p01s03-woeu.html

Weiss, Laurie B. (2006, April 1). Patriot Act reauthorized with few changes. *School Library Journal, 52*(4).

Werner, E. (2006, December 29). Lawmakers promise new fight against Yucca Mountain. *North Lake Tahoe Bonanza.* Retrieved on January 2, 2007, from http://www.tahoebonanza.com/article/200 ʼNevada/112290022

White F Secretary. (2001, September 24). *Executive Order on Terrorist Financing.* R http://www.whitehouse.gov/news/releases/2001/09/

White rth.

Whit nt extremism. *American Behavioral*

Wie Chicago: University of Chicago Press.

Wi h. In Martha Crenshaw (Ed.). ersity Press.

V ds sit in custody and ask, "Why?" *New*

nts, and political justice in U.S. courts.

t. *Terrorism and Political Violence,*

ostage-taking incidents. *Journal of Conflict*

May 15). *The Washington Post.* Retrieved June

los, the world's most wanted man. New York:

ion sharing technology (ARJIS): Examining its ugh the eyes of street level officers. Unpublished cument 210487.

ic Studies Institute (SSI). Army War College. te.army.mil/pubs/display.cfm?PubID=408

Zenko, M. (2006). Intelligence estimates of nuclear terrorism. *Annals of the American Academy of Political and Social Science, 607,* 87–102.

Zulaika, J., & Douglas, W. (2000). Variations on terrorism. In Laura Egendorf (Ed.), *Terrorism: Opposing viewpoints.* San Diego: Greenhaven Press.

Zwier, L. (1998). *War torn island.* Minneapolis: Lerner Publishing.

INDEX

ABOUT THE AUTHORS

Sue Mahan is an Associate Professor in the Criminal Justice Program at the University of Central Florida–Daytona Beach campus. She received a PhD in sociology from the University of Missouri–Columbia. She is the author of several other books, including *Unfit Mothers*; *Women, Crime and Criminal Justice* (with Ralph Weisheit); *Crack, Cocaine, Crime and Women*; and *Beyond the Mafia*, as well as journal articles and book chapters about crime and justice. As a member of Partners of the Americas, she has been involved in violence prevention projects in Colombia and Peru. Mahan has been awarded a Fulbright Group Grant to Mexico, a Kellogg Fellowship in International Development, and a Fulbright Distinguished Lectureship to Peru. This book is a result of her continuing interest in terrorism developed from her experiences in Peru.

Pamala L. Griset is an Associate Professor in the Department of Criminal Justice and Legal Studies at the University of Central Florida–Orlando campus. She received a PhD in criminal justice from the State University of New York at Albany. She was formerly employed as a probation officer, staff writer for the New York State Committee on Sentencing Guidelines, Executive Assistant to the New York State Director of Criminal Justice, and Deputy Commissioner of the New York State Division of Criminal Justice Services. Before turning her scholarly attention to the study of terrorism, she wrote a book and numerous articles on the theory and practice of determinate sentencing, monographs and book chapters on juvenile detention policy, and articles on law enforcement information sharing. Her fascination with the study of terrorism began in the late 1990s and has continued unabated.

ABOUT THE CONTRIBUTORS

Terry Anderson wrote a volume of poetry called *Den of Lions* during the seven years he was held hostage in Lebanon. His positions with the Associated Press included state editor, foreign desk editor, and chief Middle East correspondent. He received the Free Spirit Award from the Freedom Forum along with numerous awards for journalism and community service. He currently is a Scripps Visiting Professional at the E.W. Scripps School of Journalism at Ohio University.

Randal Beaton is a Research Professor in the Department of Health Services in the School of Public Health and Community Medicine at the University of Washington School of Nursing.

Peter Bergen is a Schwartz Senior Fellow at the New America Foundation and an Adjunct Professor at the School of Advanced International Studies at Johns Hopkins University. He is the author of *Holy War, Inc: Inside the Secret World of Osama bin Laden* (2001). Bergen is a print and television journalist who acts as a terrorism analyst for CNN.

Kathleen M. Blee is a Professor of Sociology at the University of Pittsburgh. She is the author of *Inside Organized Racism: Women in the Hate Movement* (2002), as well as numerous journal articles with a specialized interest in women and terrorism.

Elizabeth Bridges is a faculty member in Biobehavioral Nursing and Health Systems at the University of Washington.

H. H. A. Cooper is President of Nuevevidas International, Inc., a Texas consulting company specializing in safety and survival issues. He teaches at the University of Texas at Dallas and directed the national Advisory Committee Task Force on Disorders and Terrorism, 1974–1977. Cooper was also the Director of the Criminal Law Education and Research Center (CLEAR) and Deputy Director of the Center of Forensic Psychiatry of New York University. He is the author of many works dealing with manifestations of extraordinary violence.

Svante E. Cornell is the Research Director of the Central Asia-Caucasus Institute and the Silk Road Studies Program at Johns Hopkins University. He is the editor of the *Central Asia-Caucasus Analyst*, the Joint Center's biweekly publication, and the Joint Center's *Silk Road Papers* series of occasional papers. Cornell is also the author of *The Politicization of Islam in Azerbaijan* (2006).

Martha Crenshaw is a Professor of Government at Wesleyan University, Middletown Connecticut. Crenshaw is the Chair of the American Political Science Association's Task Force on Political Violence and Terrorism. She is the co-editor of the *Encyclopedia of Terrorism* (1997); the editor of *Terrorism in Context* (1995), and the author of *Terrorism and International Cooperation* (1989). Crenshaw has received both the Nevitt Sanford Award for Distinguished Scientific Contribution and the Jeanne Knutson Award for Service to the International Society of Political Psychology.

Bruce Hoffman is a Professor of Security Studies at Georgetown University's Edmund A. Walsh School of Foreign Service. He was formerly the Corporate Chair in Counterterrorism and Counterinsurgency at the Rand Corporation. Hoffman is a member of the Advisory Committee of the Terrorism and Counterterrorism Program, Human Rights Watch; a Senior Scholar at the Woodrow Wilson International Center; a Senior Fellow at the U.S. Military Academy; and a

Senior Fellow at the National Security Studies Center at Haifa University, Israel. He was the Founding Director of the Centre for the Study of Terrorism and Political Violence at the University of St. Andrews in Scotland. He is the editor-in-chief of the journal *Studies in Conflict and Terrorism* and author of *Inside Terrorism* (2006).

Nicola Horsburgh is a Research Fellow at the International Policy Institute at Kings College, University of London.

Javier Jordan is a Lecturer in the Department of Political Science, University of Granada, Spain. He was a Research Fellow at the Training and Doctrine Command of the Spanish Army and a NATO Research Fellow. He is currently editor-in-chief of JihadMonitor.org.

Manfred F. R. Kets de Vries is Professor of Leadership Development at INSEAD Global Leadership Center. He is the author and co-author or editor of more than 24 books and has published more than 250 scientific papers as chapters in books and as articles. His books and articles have been translated into 20 languages.

Regina G. Lawrence is the Chair of the Political Science Division and Director of the Northwest Communication Research Group at the Mark O. Hatfield School of Government at Portland State University. She was a Research Fellow at the Shorenstein Center on the Press, Politics, and Public Policy at the Kennedy School of Government at Harvard University.

Ian R. McDonald is a graduate student in political science at Duke University.

Brigitte L. Nacos is currently an Adjunct Professor of Political Science at Columbia University. She has published numerous articles on the news media and terrorism. She is the author of *Terrorism and the Media: From the Iran Hostage Crisis to the World Trade Center Bombing/From the Iran Hostage Crisis to the Oklahoma City Bombing* (1994, 1996) and *Mass-Mediated Terrorism: The Central Role of the Media in Terrorism and Counterterrorism* (2002).

Marcus Nemuth has collaborated on many book and journal articles. He is on the Clinical Faculty at the University of Washington School of Medicine and holds a position at the Veterans Health Administration, Puget Sound.

Mark Oberle is the Associate Dean and Professor of Epidemiology and Health Services at the University of Washington School of Public Health and Community Medicine.

David C. Rapoport is known as a historian of terrorism. He is Professor Emeritus of Political Science at UCLA and editor of the journal *Terrorism and Political Violence*. He is the author and editor of numerous books about assassination and terrorism, including *The Democratic Experience and Political Violence, Inside Terrorist Organizations, and Morality of Terrorism: Religious Origins and Ethnic Implications*.

Alec Reynolds is a Graduate Research Assistant at John Hopkins University's Advanced School of International Studies.

Andy Stergachis is a Professor of Epidemiology and Pharmacy at the University of Washington School of Public Health and Community Medicine.

Jessica Stern is a Lecturer in Public Policy at the John F. Kennedy School of Government at Harvard University. She is the author of *Terror in the Name of God: Why Religious Militants Kill* (2003) and *The Ultimate Terrorists* (2001), as well as numerous articles about proliferation of weapons of mass destruction. She served on President Clinton's National Security Council Staff in 1994–1995, and she was elected by *Time Magazine* in 2001 as one of the seven thinkers whose innovative ideas will change the world.

Tamlyn Thomas is the Emergency Management Coordinator of the Nursing Resource Team at the University of Washington Medical Center. Her work involves intensive care and resource nursing.

Steven Vanderheiden is an Assistant Professor of Political Science and Philosophy at the University of Minnesota Duluth. He has written articles on ecoterrorism and made presentations for the American Political Science Association and American Philosophical Association from 1998 to the present.

Jonathan R. White is the Director of the School of Criminal Justice and the Executive Director of the Homeland Defense Initiative at Grand Valley State University. He is also an Instructor at the FBI National Academy and the U.S. Department of State Counterterrorism Programs. He is the author of numerous books and articles about terrorism, including *Terrorism and Homeland Security* (2005) and *Defending the Homeland: Domestic Intelligence, Security and Law Enforcement* (2004).

Christiane Wilke is on the faculty of the Department of Law at Carleton University in Ottawa, Canada.

Micah Zenko is a Research Associate in the Belfer Center for Science and International Affairs at the John F. Kennedy School of Government at Harvard University. He was a Research Associate at the Brookings Institution and the Wisconsin Project on Nuclear Arms Control. Zenko was also a contributor to the Department of State's Kosovo History Project.